International Environmental Law

This book analyzes the law and policy for the management of global common resources. As competing demands on the global commons are increasing, the protection of the environment and the pursuit of growth give rise to all sorts of conflicts. The book analyzes issues in the protection of the global commons from fairness, effectiveness, and world order perspectives. The author examines whether current policy making and future trends point to a fair allocation of global common resources that will be effective in protecting the environment and in the pursuit of sustainable development. The author looks at the cost effectiveness of international environmental law and applies theories of national environmental law to international environmental problems. Chapters include analysis of areas such as marine pollution, air pollution, fisheries management, transboundary water resources, biodiversity, hazardous and radioactive waste management, state responsibility, and liability.

Elli Louka is the founder of Alphabetics Development & Investment (ADI), a company devoted to environment and development. Louka was a Senior Fellow at the Orville H. Schell Center for International Human Rights at Yale Law School and a Ford Foundation Fellow at New York University School of Law. Dr. Louka is currently the recipient of a Marie Curie Fellowship provided by the European Commission of the European Union. Other selected publications by Dr. Louka include *Conflicting Integration: The Environmental Law of the European Union* (2004), *Biodiversity and Human Rights* (2002), and *Overcoming National Barriers to International Waste Trade* (1994).

International Environmental Law

Fairness, Effectiveness, and World Order

Elli Louka

CAMBRIDGE
UNIVERSITY PRESS

CAMBRIDGE UNIVERSITY PRESS
Cambridge, New York, Melbourne, Madrid, Cape Town, Singapore, São Paulo

Cambridge University Press
32 Avenue of the Americas, New York, NY 10013-2473, USA

www.cambridge.org
Information on this title: www.cambridge.org/9780521868129

First published 2006

Printed in the United States of America

A catalog record for this publication is available from the British Library.

Library of Congress Cataloging in Publication Data

Louka, Elli.
International environmental law : fairness, effectiveness, and world order / Elli Louka.
    p.   cm.
Includes bibliographical references and index.
ISBN-13: 978-0-521-86812-9 (hardback)
ISBN-10: 0-521-86812-2 (hardback)
ISBN-13: 978-0-521-68759-1 (pbk.)
ISBN-10: 0-521-68759-4 (pbk.)
1. Environmental law, International.   2. Natural resources – Law and legislation.
3. Environmental protection.   I. Title.
K3585.L68   2006
344.04′6 – dc22   2006009174

ISBN-13   978-0-521-86812-9 hardback
ISBN-10   0-521-86812-2 hardback

ISBN-13   978-0-521-68759-1 paperback
ISBN-10   0-521-68759-4 paperback

Contents

Foreword

Law, as Dr. Elli Louka vividly demonstrates in this extraordinary book, is most usefully conceived as a process of clarifying and implementing the common interests of politically relevant actors. This conception is indispensable for understanding the development of international environmental law. The spread of industrialization, with its ever more intensive uses of the resources of the planet, followed by the evolution of a global civilization of science and technology and, in part as a consequence of those developments, the explosion of the population of the planet from 1.6 billion people in 1900 to 2.5 billion in 1950 and to more than 6 billion in 2000, have combined to put unprecedented and unrelenting stress on the ecological systems on which the life of our species depends. No other area of lawmaking and law-applying makes so clearly and vividly manifest the indispensable functions of all law: the maintenance of minimum order, the allocation and regulation of the use of scarce resources, and the conservation and allocation of the benefits and burdens of the world's resources in ways consistent with shared conceptions of equity.

Approaching this subject as if it could be studied as a body of static rules would be sterile. Instead, Dr. Louka presents a dynamic picture, in which the diverse actors in the international lawmaking process clarify key principles such as sovereignty over national resources, precautionary principles with respect to equitable cost-sharing of environmental externalities, principles of sustainable development, and common as well as differentiated responsibilities. Dr. Louka then shows how those principles are being applied in each of the major areas of international environmental law. Nor can general international law be excluded from such an examination, for the legal focus on the environment also has driven major changes in general international law, which has acknowledged the "tragedy of commons" and in response has authorized an increasing enclosure and nationalization of resources that for centuries had been part of the *res communis omnium*.

Using as a framework this dynamic process in which international environmental law is clarified, prescribed, and implemented, Dr. Louka reviews and synthesizes past trends and projections of probable future trends with respect to (1) the marine environment; (2) shared water resources; (3) fisheries resources; (4) the conservation of biodiversity; (5) air; (6) trade and environment; and (7) the disposal of hazardous and radioactive waste. Cutting across all of these trends and projection studies are the international efforts to establish and police reporting and information-sharing regimes, many now driven by the daunting challenge of prescribing for some measure of liability in circumstances in which acts with the potential for causing significant transnational damage are not prohibited by international law. One of the many strengths of Dr. Louka's book is that it presents in extraordinarily rich detail the entire spectrum of the modern process of international environmental law.

Much of the writing in contemporary international environmental law is passionately and uncritically advocative. Although Dr. Louka's book is plainly animated by a deep concern for the preservation of the environment of the planet and the realization that in the context of a global civilization of science and technology, it can be protected only by effective international efforts, the stance adopted is not uncritical and Dr. Louka never surrenders the scholarly role. Precisely because some of the areas that Louka treats are – good intentions notwithstanding – marked by missteps or – serious efforts notwithstanding – have registered no significant successes, Dr. Louka's book will be important for the practitioner in the vineyard of international environmental law no less than for the political leaders who are charged with its development.

Dr. Louka has produced a remarkable book that will be of great value to the profession.

W. Michael Reisman
Yale Law School
New Haven, Connecticut
December 2005

Abbreviations

AAUs/assigned amount units (of emissions)
ACCOBAMS/Agreement on the Conservation of Cetaceans of the Mediterranean and the Black Seas
ACP/African, Caribbean and Pacific (countries)
ACTO/Amazon Cooperation Treaty Organization
AIA/Advanced Informed Agreement (procedure)
APFIC/Asia Pacific Fishery Commission
ASCIs/Areas of Special Conservation Interest
ASCOBANS/Agreement on the Conservation of Small Cetaceans of the Baltic and North Seas
ASEAN/Association of South East Asian Nations
ATS/Antarctic Treaty System

BAT/best available technique
BATNEEC/best available technology not entailing excessive costs
BEP/best environmental practice

CAMPs/Coastal Areas Management Programmes
CBD/Convention on Biological Diversity
CBNRM/community-based natural resource management

CCAMLR/Convention for the Conservation of Antarctic Marine Living Resources
CCAS/Convention on the Conservation of Antarctic Seals
CCRF/Code of Conduct for Responsible Fisheries
CDM/Clean Development Mechanism
CDS/Catch Documentation Scheme
CECAF/Committee of the Eastern Central Atlantic Fisheries
CERCLA/Comprehensive Environmental Response, Compensation and Liability Act
CERs/certified emissions reductions
CFCs/chlorofluorocarbons
CGIAR/Consultative Group on International Agricultural Research
CIAT/International Center for Tropical Agriculture
CIFOR/Center for International Forestry Research
CIMMYT/Center for the Improvement of Maize and Wheat
CIP/International Potato Center
CITES/Convention on International Trade in Endangered Species of Wild Flora and Fauna
CLRTAP/Convention on Long-Range Transboundary Air Pollution
COP/Conference of the Parties

CRTD/Convention on Civil Liability for Damage Caused During Carriage of Dangerous Goods by Road, Rail and Inland Navigation Vessels

CSC/Convention on Supplementary Compensation for Nuclear Damage

CSD/Commission on Sustainable Development

CTE/Committee on Trade and Environment

DSB/Dispute Settlement Body

DWFS/distant water fishing states

EBRD/European Bank for Reconstruction and Development

EC/European Community

ECE/Economic Commission for Europe

ECJ/European Court of Justice

ECOSOC/Economic and Social Council of the United Nations

EEA/European Environment Agency

EEC/European Economic Community

EEZ/Exclusive Economic Zone

EIA/Environmental Impact Assessment

EMEP/Cooperative Programme for Monitoring and Evaluation of the Long-Range Transmission of Air Pollutants in Europe

EPA/Environmental Protection Agency

ERUs/Emission Reduction Units

ESCWA/Economic and Social Commission for Western Asia

ETS/European Treaties Series

EU/European Union

EUROBATS/Agreement on the Conservation of Bats in Europe

FAO/Food and Agriculture Organization

FFA/Forum Fisheries Agency

FFVs/foreign fishing vessels

FOC/flag of convenience

GAO/General Accounting Office

GATS/General Agreement on Trade in Services

GATT/General Agreement on Tariffs and Trade

GEF/Global Environment Facility

GESAMP/Joint Group of Experts on the Scientific Aspects of Marine Environmental Protection

GFCM/General Fisheries Council of the Mediterranean

GPA/Global Programme of Action

HELCOM/Helsinki Convention for the Protection of the Baltic Sea

IAEA/International Atomic Energy Agency

IARCs/International Agricultural Research Centers

IATP/Institute for Agriculture and Trade Policy

IATTC/Inter-American Tropical Tuna Commission

IBPGR/International Board for Plant Genetic Resources

IBRD/International Bank for Reconstruction and Development

ICARDA/International Center for Agricultural Research in Dry Areas

ICARM/Integrated Coastal and River Basin Management

ICCAT/International Convention for the Conservation of Atlantic Tunas

ICDM/Integrated Conservation and Development Management

ICJ/International Court of Justice

ICNAF/International Convention for the Northwest Atlantic Fisheries

ICPDR/International Commission for the Protection of the Danube River

ICPR/International Commission for the Protection of the Rhine

ICRAF/International Center for Research in Agroforestry

ICRISAT/International Crops Research Institute for the Semi-Arid Tropics

ICZM/Integrated Coastal Zone Management

IDPs/internally displaced persons
IFPRI/International Food Policy Research Institute
IITA/International Institute for Tropical Agriculture
ILC/International Law Commission
ILO/International Labor Organization
ILRI/International Livestock Research Institute
IMDG/International Maritime Dangerous Goods (Code)
IMF/International Monetary Fund
IMO/International Maritime Organization
INBO/International Network of Basin Organizations
IOFC/Indian Ocean Fishery Commission
IOTC/Indian Ocean Tuna Commission
IPCC/Intergovernmental Panel on Climate Change
IPF/Intergovernmental Panel on Forests
IPGRI/International Plant Genetic Resources Institute
IRBM/Integrated River Basin Management
IRBO/International River Basin Organizations
IRRI/International Rice Research Institute
ISA/International Seabed Authority
ISNAR/International Service for National Agricultural Research
ITLOS/International Tribunal for the Law of the Sea
ITP/individual tradable permit
ITQs/individual transferable quotas
ITTA/International Tropical Timber Agreement
ITTO/International Tropical Timber Organization
IUCN/International Union for the Conservation of Nature
IUU/illegal, unreported, and unregulated fishing
IWC/International Whaling Commission

IWIC/International Waste Identification Code
IWRM/Integrated Water Resources Management

LDC/London Dumping Convention
LLRWA/Low-Level Radioactive Waste Act
LULUCF/land-use, land-use change, and forest

MAP/Mediterranean Action Plan
MDBC/Murray-Darling Basin Commission
MPAs/Marine Protected Areas
MTAs/Material Transfer Agreements

NAFC/Northwest Atlantic Fisheries Convention
NAFO/Northwest Atlantic Fisheries Organization
NAFTA/North American Free Trade Agreement
NAMMCO/North Atlantic Marine Mammals Commission
NASCO/North Atlantic Salmon Conservation Organization
NATO/North Atlantic Treaty Organization
NEA/OECD/Nuclear Energy Agency of the Organization for Economic Co-operation and Development
NEAFC/North East Atlantic Fisheries Commission
NEPA/National Environmental Policy Act
NGOs/nongovernmental organizations
NIMBY/not in my backyard
NPAFC/North Pacific Anadromous Stocks Commission
NPFSC/North Pacific Fur Seals Commission
NWPA/Nuclear Waste Policy Act

OAS/Organization of American States
OAU/Organization of African Unity
ODA/Official Development Assistance
ODS/Ozone Depleting Substances

OECD/Organization for Economic Co-operation and Development
OPRC/Oil Pollution Preparedness, Response, and Co-operation
OSPAR/Convention for the Protection of the Marine Environment of the North East Atlantic

PCA/Permanent Court of Arbitration
PCIJ/Permanent Court of International Justice
PGR/Plant Genetic Resources
PIC/prior informed consent
POPs/persistent organic pollutants
PRTRs/pollutant release and transfer registers

RAC/Regional Activity Centre
RBAs/River Basin Authorities
RBMP/River Basin Management Plan
RBOs/River Basin Organizations
RCRA/Resource Conservation and Recovery Act
RFOs/Regional Fisheries Organizations

SAARC/South Asian Association for Regional Cooperation
SADC/Southern African Development Community
SARA/Superfund Amendment and Reauthorization Act
SBSTA/Subsidiary Body for Scientific and Technological Advice
SEAFO/South East Atlantic Fisheries Organization
SEA/Strategic Environmental Assessment
SOLAS/International Convention for the Safety of Life at Sea
SPFFA/South Pacific Forum Fisheries Agency
SPREP/South Pacific Regional Environment Program
SPS/Sanitary and Phytosanitary Measures

TACs/total allowable catches
TBNRM/transboundary natural resource management
TDPs/tradable discharge permits
TRIPs/Trade-Related Intellectual Property Rights
TURFs/Territorial Use Rights in Fishing
TVA/Tennessee Valley Authority

UNCED/United Nations Conference on the Environment and Development
UNCLOS/United Nations Convention on the Law of the Sea
UNCTAD/United Nations Conference on Trade and Development
UNDP/United Nations Development Program
UN/ECE/United Nations Economic Commission for Europe
UNESCAP/United Nations Economic and Social Commission for Asia and the Pacific
UNESCO/United Nations Educational, Scientific, and Cultural Organization
UNFF/United Nations Forum on Forests
UPOV/Union for the Protection of New Varieties of Plants

VMS/Vessel Monitoring System
VOCs/volatile organic compounds

WCPFC/Western and Central Pacific Fisheries Convention
WECAFC/Western Central Atlantic Fishery Commission
WFD/Water Framework Directive
WHO/World Health Organization
WIPO/World Intellectual Property Rights Organization
WSSD/World Summit on Sustainable Development
WTO/World Trade Organization

Introduction

This study examines the rules of international law governing the global commons. Because global common resources are shared among states, competition for the use of such resources and the sharing of externalities from resource use are bound to increase in the future. The book examines how the quest for a minimum order, fairness, and effectiveness has guided the development of international environmental law and policy making.

Chapter 1 provides an introduction to international law and international environmental law. It provides an overview of the actors of international lawmaking, the international lawmaking process, and the historical evolution of international environmental law. Concepts of international environmental law, such as sovereignty over national resources, the "polluter pays" principle, the precautionary principle, equitable cost-sharing of environmental externalities, sustainable development, and common but differentiated responsibilities are explored. The chapter examines human rights as the threshold principles of international environmental lawmaking. Issues of monitoring and enforcement in international law are also introduced.

Chapter 2 examines the foundations of international environmental law. The pursuit of minimum order, equity, and effectiveness in international law is analyzed and the interconnection among the foundations of international environmental law is explored. The chapter examines how issues of distributive equity often determine the effectiveness of international environmental lawmaking. Issues of cost-effectiveness as they influence the success of international environmental regimes are also examined. The enclosure of national common pool resources is introduced and analyzed. More specifically, it is examined how many national/local common pool resource systems could acquire differing forms of governance ranging from common property and state property to private property. The "Tragedy of Commons" rationale that precipitated the enclosure of common pool resources in national systems is driving the enclosure of global common resources. The gradual enclosure of global common resources – as it is taking place in fisheries, germplasm resources and related knowledge, freshwater resources, air, sea, waste management, and national biodiversity resources – is analyzed. Chapter 2 examines the interrelationship between the nature of different enclosures and the effectiveness of international environmental regimes. The inclusionary or exclusionary nature of enclosures as they affect perceptions of distributive equity is analyzed.

Chapter 3 examines the compliance and governance mechanisms of international environmental lawmaking such as environmental impact assessment, strategic environmental assessment, exchange of information, notification, consultation, the right to participation, and the right to information. The chapter examines whether such instruments have been effective in the pursuit of international environmental law objectives. The application of these instruments by international institutions and states is particularly emphasized. Reporting, monitoring, and compliance procedures as they are developing in different international environmental law regimes are scrutinized.

The seas are a common pool resource that has become an open-access resource in terms of pollution that states are putting into the seas. Chapter 4 examines the different regulatory efforts that states have engaged in so as to diminish the open-access character of the resource including the Law of the Sea Convention, the MARPOL Convention, various regional conventions, and safety regulations. The chapter concludes that – despite the efforts of states to enclose the global resources of the seas under national or international regulatory regimes – the seas have remained more or less an open-access resource in terms of pollution inputs.

Chapter 5 examines the problems associated with the management of shared water resources. Water resources are not global resources like the seas but often are shared among a number of states. As such, they are common pool resources that present the collective action problems encountered in other common pool resource systems. The chapter examines in detail the UN Watercourses Convention and its influence on the articulation of regional instruments on the allocation and protection of freshwater resources. Issues of equity in water allocation, efficiency, demand-led management, and water quality are examined as they have been elaborated in different regional fora, namely – Africa, Asia, Europe, the Middle East, and the American region. Integrated water management, as it incorporates issues of water quantity and quality at the river basin level, the establishment of Regional Basin Organizations (RBOs), and their role in equitable and sound water management are explored in depth.

Fisheries are a typical example of global common resources. Fisheries are by nature mobile resources, as they straddle sea areas under national jurisdiction and the high seas. The management of fisheries has been a highly contentious issue in international fora. Chapter 6 provides an overview of national regulatory systems for fisheries resources ranging from the typical command-and-control measures to privatization through Individual Transferable Quotas (ITQs). The enclosure of national fisheries resources has reverberated in international fora where states have been eager to enclose global fisheries resources. The enclosure movement with regard to fisheries resources has been mostly exclusionary because the establishment of Regional Fisheries Organizations, which increasingly assume rights beyond the Exclusive Economic Zone (EEZ) of states, is rarely accommodating to new entrants. There are even disputes among the states that are regime-insiders as they vie for the apportionment of fisheries resources. Chapter 6 examines the international instruments for the regulation of fisheries resources, including the 1995 Fisheries Agreement. Regional efforts for the enclosure of fisheries resources are examined for the purposes of revealing the degree of effectiveness of regional enclosure movements.

Most biodiversity resources, especially terrestrial biodiversity resources, are under a state's jurisdiction or are shared among a number of states in a region. Therefore, many biodiversity resources could not be characterized as the classic example of global common resources. The biodiversity loss that is witnessed today world-wide, however, has put biodiversity on the international agenda with a new sense of urgency. The international management of biodiversity is characterized by two trends. One trend has to do with the assertion of state sovereignty over germplasm resources situated in nature or in gene banks. The other trend has to do with the attempts of the international community to regulate national and local biodiversity protection systems so as to implement an international enclosure of national commons. As many states do not have adequate resources to protect and manage their biodiversity resources, such resources often become open-access resources and are degraded. National and transnational protected areas and regional and international gene banks are methods that have been used for the protection of biodiversity. The international system has attempted to regulate the national management of biodiversity through trade mechanisms, which prohibit or restrict the trade in endangered species, and through a number of conventions that address regional biodiversity issues or species-specific conservation issues. The effectiveness and equity of national and international mechanisms for the protection of biodiversity resources are examined in Chapter 7.

The Convention on Biological Diversity was the first convention to address biodiversity as a global common pool resource. The convention, in addition to dealing with issues of protection of biodiversity, addresses distributive issues with regard to the allocation of benefits from the exploitation of germplasm resources. Although "raw" germplasm resources have been, for all practical purposes, open-access resources, "worked" germplasm resources have been protected under various intellectual property rights systems, such as breeders' rights and biotechnology patent rights. The disparity in the treatment of germplasm resources has led developing countries to assert their jurisdiction over "raw" germplasm resources located within their territory and to demand fees from legal entities wishing to access such resources. It was believed that the market value of biodiversity, as it is used in pharmaceuticals and other biotechnology devices, would lead developed countries and companies to share the benefits from the commercialization of germplasm resources with developing countries. Chapter 7 analyzes the bilateral redistribution, transnational redistribution, and institutionalized redistribution of germplasm resources. The effectiveness of distributional mechanisms in terms of bringing wealth to developing countries and indigenous peoples and farmers is scrutinized.

Air quality is a global common pool resource as air pollution by some industries affects the quality of the air for the rest of users. The enclosure of global air resources has been inclusionary as countries quickly realized that control of air pollution by some states will not do much to improve air quality as long as other states continue to pollute. In the ozone and climate change regimes, developed countries have been willing to provide side-payments to developing countries for joining in for the outlawing of ozone-depleting substances and the reduction of greenhouse gases. Chapter 8 explores the regime for the protection of the ozone, the climate change regime, and transboundary air pollution regime. Issues of equity and effectiveness in the elaboration and possible future articulation of the regimes are further examined. Market-based instruments and their repercussions for the "privatization" of the air are addressed.

Chapter 9 examines international environmental issues as they intersect with trade issues. The case law of the World Trade Organization (WTO) is examined in the various cases in which free trade stumbles over regulatory measures that states have enacted for the protection of species or of human health. Chapter 9 analyzes the Trade-Related Intellectual Property Rights (TRIPs) system and its interaction with the world intellectual property rights system. The development of the TRIPs Agreement and its influence on intellectual property rights over pharmaceuticals and germplasm resources are analyzed. The issue of intellectual property rights over germplasm resources, concerns regarding the "enclosure of intellectual commons," and perceptions of fairness, as they have been articulated in related human rights instruments, are analyzed in depth.

Waste is not *prima facie* a global common resource. Generally, wastes are looked on as a negative resource in the sense that no value is assigned to them. Wastes are generally viewed as an externality produced by industries and households, and the question has been how to assign the costs associated with such an externality. The transfer of wastes from developed to developing countries with no infrastructure and lenient environmental laws brought the waste issue to the international arena and made imperative the development of a transnational system for the management of wastes. States have dealt with the waste issue as a forced enclosure issue. Generators are forced to own their wastes and, thus, bear the costs of the externalities produced by their wastes. Because wastes are perceived as a negative resource, unless ownership is forced, they could be found disposed of on common pool resources polluting the land, water, and air. The international instruments that regulate international waste shipments have imposed state self-sufficiency and safeguards on waste transfers based primarily on the prior notification and informed consent of the importing country before a waste transfer is realized. Chapter 10 examines the effectiveness and fairness of arrangements for the management and transfer of hazardous and radioactive wastes. The question that is examined is whether the forced enclosure of wastes, a so-called negative resource, has worked and whether the equity principles implied in the notion of self-sufficiency are the only principles that should guide the future international management of hazardous and radioactive wastes. National regulatory systems are examined, as it is the management and often mismanagement of wastes in national fora that has led to transnational waste shipments.

Chapter 11 explores the private liability regimes that have been developed to address issues of oil pollution, hazardous materials trade, nuclear energy, and liability for damage to the environment. The issue of state responsibility and associated case law are analyzed. The issue of international liability for acts not prohibited by international law (e.g., pollution that is not prohibited by international instruments), as it has been elaborated by the International Law Commission, is specifically scrutinized. A question addressed is whether state practice indicates liability of states for polluting activities originating within their territory or whether the principle that emerges is that of equitable sharing of costs of externalities caused by polluting activities.

Introduction to International Environmental Law

1. THE WORLD COMMUNITY AND INTERNATIONAL LAW

1.1. International Law

Modern international law has emerged from the ruins of two world wars. Before World War I, public international law regulated the conduct of war. During that period, states had the freedom to choose between war and peace. States had the right to pursue their goals by war. The distinction between just wars and unjust wars was not legally pertinent.[1]

The reorientation of international law came with the establishment of the League of Nations following World War I. The League condemned external aggression against the territorial integrity and political independence of League members.[2] Another important development during this period was the establishment of the Permanent Court of International Justice (PCIJ) and the International Labor Organization (ILO). However, these developments did not prevent the eruption of World War II.

In the aftermath of World War II, one of the most important developments was the establishment of the United Nations. The United Nations Charter outlawed war as a general means for the resolution of disputes among states.[3] After two world wars, states realized that some institutional framework must be established and some rules promulgated that would provide procedural and substantive safeguards to avert future wars. The United Nations was to serve primarily that purpose: preservation of peace among states.

International law is the law that states make to regulate matters among them: first and foremost, war and peace and, after the attainment of a minimum peace order, other matters including economic development, exchange rates, trade, the

---

[1] L. Oppenheim, International Law 177–78 (vol. 2, 7th ed., 1952). The issue of morality of war has preoccupied commentators, though. See Michael Walzer, Just and Unjust Wars: A Moral Argument with Historical Illustrations 3–13 (1977). See also Clarence Wilfred Jenks, Law, Freedom and Welfare 52 (1963).

[2] See also D.W. Bowett, The Law of International Institutions 15–16 (1963).

[3] See *infra* notes 13–15.

environment, and intellectual property rights. A number of organizations have been developed to deal with such matters, including the World Trade Organization (WTO) with regard to matters that affect trade and the United Nations Environment Program (UNEP) with regard to matters that affect the environment.

It would be wrong, however, to perceive international law as only the regulatory instrument of interstate relations. In order to prevent future egregious atrocities against human beings – prevailing especially during war – the international system developed a number of instruments that focus on the protection of the rights of the individual. These human rights instruments launched by the Universal Declaration of Human Rights present the order that the international system aspires to achieve. In addition to what could be called traditional human rights[4] (such as the right to life, the right to property, and the right to be free from discrimination), other rights have been proposed more or less persuasively. Such rights include the right to development,[5] the right to a decent environment,[6] and the right not to be forcibly displaced.[7]

Human rights articulate the demands for a maximum order of law. This order goes beyond the achievement of elementary peace and incorporates the aspiration for a better quality of life. Human rights shape the notion of human dignity, which gives direction for the future development of international law. The ultimate goal of the international law process is the protection of human dignity.[8]

1.2. States

1.2.1. Sovereignty

The United Nations Charter is based on the principle of sovereignty of states. According to the Charter, each state is sovereign and no state is to violate the

---

[4] The Universal Declaration of Human Rights, Dec. 10, 1948, reprinted in Basic Documents on Human Rights 106 (Ian Brownlie, ed., 1971).

International Covenant on Civil and Political Rights, G.A. res. 2200A (XXI), 21 U.N. GAOR Supp. (No. 16) at 52, UN Doc. A/6316 (1966), reprinted in 999 UNTS 171, entered into force Mar. 23, 1976.

International Covenant on Economic, Social and Cultural Rights, G.A. res. 2200A (XXI), 21 U.N.GAOR Supp. (No. 16) at 49, UN Doc. A/6316 (1966), reprinted in 993 UNTS 3, entered into force Jan. 3, 1976.

See also African Charter on Human and Peoples' Rights (Banjul Charter), June 27, 1981, reprinted in 21 ILM 58 (1982); Bangkok Declaration on Human Rights, April 2, 1993, A/CONF.157/ASRM/8.

[5] Initially controversial, this right is now more or less accepted as a legitimate right. For an articulation of the right in the Rio Declaration, see *infra* note 149.

[6] The right to live in a decent or a healthy environment has been the subject of debate, see, e.g., Dinah Shelton, Human Rights, Environmental Rights and the Right to Environment, 28 Stanford Journal of International Law 103 (1991). See also Günther Handl, Human Rights and Protection of the Environment: A Mildly "Revisionist" View, in Human Rights, Sustainable Development and the Environment 117 (Antonio Augusto Cancado Trindade, ed., 1992).

[7] Maria Stavropoulou, The Right not to Be Displaced, 9 American University Journal of International Law & Policy 689 (1994). For the right not to be displaced, see also *infra* note 290.

[8] See Myres S. McDougal & Harold D. Lasswell, The Identification and Appraisal of Diverse Systems of Public Order, 53 American Journal of International Law 1 (1959).

sovereignty of another state.[9] This principle of legal equality based on the sovereignty of states should not be confused with an assumption of equal power. In fact, the concept of sovereignty is fairly new in international affairs. Historically, sovereignty was not a given. Instead, states had to obtain the right to be called sovereign.[10] Sovereignty denotes the ability to self-govern, and many states today do not really possess that ability. In fact, some states are weaker than corporations and nongovernmental organizations (NGOs) in their capacity to run their own affairs.

As the reality of international politics indicates, certain states have more power, self-government, and control and, thus, yield more influence in the configuration of international relations than other states. The imbalance in the actual power of states is enshrined into the UN Charter. The Security Council of the United Nations, the body that makes decisions regarding war and peace, was formed by the victors of World War II.[11] The structure of power in the Security Council may be anachronistic but, nevertheless, reflects that even the constitutive organs of the international system could not have afforded to be oblivious of the importance of power in the making of international relations. Sometimes this power is authoritative. In other cases, it lacks legitimacy but, nevertheless, could still be effective in shaping the future of international order.[12]

The principle of sovereignty implies that states "shall refrain in their international relations from the threat or use of force against the territorial integrity or political independence of any state."[13] But, as explored later in this book, this principle contains its own antinomy in the UN Charter, as well as in the way that the Charter has been interpreted including the cases of use of force, self-defense,[14] or anticipatory self-defense.[15]

It is provided that the United Nations must not intervene "in matters which are essentially within the domestic jurisdiction of any state...."[16] The International Court of Justice, however, in the *Tunis-Morocco Nationality Decrees* case,[17] ruled that the scope of a state's domestic jurisdiction is relative and depends on the development of international law. The mere inclusion of a matter in the agenda of the General Assembly or the Security Council does not in itself constitute intervention within the meaning of article 2(7). The United Nations has engaged in activities considered

---

[9] Art. 2(1) & (4), United Nations Charter, June 26, 1945 available online at http://www.un.org/ aboutun/charter [hereinafter UN Charter].

[10] B. Buzan, National Security in the Post Cold War Third World, Paper presented at the Conference on National Security in Developing Countries, Jan. 26, 1994, Institute for Strategic Studies, University of Pretoria, South Africa.

[11] Art. 23, UN Charter, *supra* note 9. Permanent members of the Security Council are China, France, Russia, the United Kingdom, and the United States.

[12] W. Michael Reisman, Law from the Policy Perspective, reprinted in International Law Essays 1, 7 (Myres S. McDougal & W. Michael Reisman, eds., 1982).

[13] Art. 2(4), UN Charter, *supra* note 9.

[14] Art. 51, *id.*

[15] Myres S. Mc Dougal & Florentino P. Feliciano, Law and the Minimum World Public Order: The Legal Regulation of Coercion 231–41 (1961). See also Philip C. Jessup, A Modern Law of Nations 166–67 (1948); Oscar Schachter, The Rights of States to Use Armed Force, 82 Michigan Law Review 1620, 1633–35 (1984).

[16] Art. 2(7), UN Charter, *supra* note 9.

[17] Tunis-Morocco Nationality Decrees, Feb. 2, 1923, (1923) PCIJ, Ser.B, no.4, at 24.

traditionally to be the prerogative of a nation-state, for example, in cases of self-determination,[18] racial discrimination,[19] mass starvation,[20] and environmental regulation.

The unequal distribution of power is a constitutive element of international law from the creation of international regimes that formalize the division between haves and haves-not to the development of customary international law. The Nuclear Non-Proliferation Treaty is based on the presumption that it is legitimate for some countries to possess nuclear weapons, whereas for others it is not.[21] And customary international law often is based on the practice of states that happen to be able to shape international developments in an area. Space law has been developed by states with the technology to explore space.[22] The development of the Antarctic Treaty system is based on an alliance of states that were the first to be able to enunciate rights over the natural resources of Antarctica. The Antarctic Treaty regime could be characterized as a kind of trusteeship arrangement developed by the acquiescence of excluded states rather than by their willful consent.[23]

During the Cold War, the common reference to the United States and the Soviet Union as the world's superpowers, which mutually constrained each other, is well known. In today's world, a world in which one superpower has remained, the question for other states has been how to constrain that power. A potential contender – the European Union – has yet to acquire an independent voice and to amass military resources that would match its economic breakthroughs. There are regionally powerful states as well, such as India and China, which exert significant authority in regional circles and, as a consequence, in international circles.

1.2.2. Wealth

After the wars of decolonization were fought, new states became members of the international community. There was, therefore, the danger of a potential clash between the new states and those states that are, so to speak, the founders of most international law. New states generally have not adopted an outlook of international law that fundamentally undermines the traditional view of such law by Western states. The new states, however, came into international fora with a new set of interests and demands. Developing states have pursued the right to development, for instance, as a fundamental human right that is a precursor of other human rights.

---

[18] Legal Consequences for States of the Continued Presence of South Africa in Namibia (Advisory Opinion), June 21, 1971, (1971) ICJ Reports 16.

[19] E.S. Reddy, United Nations and Apartheid: Forty Years (1987).

[20] The United Nations and Somalia – 1992–1996, Blue Book Series, Vol. VIII (UN Publication Sales No. E.96.1.8).

[21] Treaty on the Non-Proliferation of Nuclear Weapons, July 1, 1968, reprinted in 729 UNTS 161. See also Edward L. Miles, Nuclear Nonproliferation, 1945 to 1995, in Environmental Regime Effectiveness: Confronting Theory with Evidence 273 (Edward L. Miles et al., eds., 2002).

[22] Malcolm N. Shaw, International Law 66 (1986).

[23] Some view the Antarctic Treaty regime as a sectoral *res communis*, a property that is held in trust by the few for the benefit of many, something like an international trusteeship system. However, there have been skirmishes in the development of the regime as some excluded countries have sought to be included as Antarctic Treaty Consultative Parties. Efforts to make the area a true *res communis* have been rejected by the Antarctic Treaty Consultative Parties. See Thomas M. Franck, Fairness in International Law and Institutions 402–04 (1997).

Developing states often espouse the view that environmental protection should not jeopardize their pursuit of wealth and development.

As new states came to the fore of the international arena, the economic gap between developed states and developing countries became a permanent feature of international relations. This division between developed states and developing states intensified the challenge against some rules of international law developed by the economically prosperous Western states. The division between developed and less developed states created demands for a new international economic order (NIEO) based on notions of sharing in wealth creation by all states. Ideas for the development of a new international economic order eventually faded. Demands for sharing prosperity, however, have not ceased to present themselves under different disguises in various international fora, including that of environmental lawmaking.

Distinctions between developed and developing states (the North-South division) are made in most international instruments and are prevalent in the international discourse. Most recent distinctions are those made between newly industrialized states (including mostly the southeast Asian states) and least-developed states (certain states in Africa). There is also the addition of states with economies in transition, states that came about after the breakup of the Soviet Union.

Because developing states do not have the same economic power as developed states,[24] they have formed the group G-77 (which now includes more than seventy-seven states) to confront the power of the elite with the power of numbers. This cluster of developing countries presenting a unified façade against developed states should not obfuscate the fact that there are divisions and disagreements among developing states as well. Sometimes developing states remain unified – under the umbrella of G-77 – both in appearances and in substance. Frequently, however, although appearances remain, the substance crumbles under the reality of different interests. An example in the environmental field involves the climate change negotiations. During these negotiations, small island-states fought for a strong normative treaty as a means to protect their islands from the real danger of flooding. By contrast, other developing states (including those perceived to be regional powers, such as China and India) pursued the usual path in international environment negotiations, reiterating their right to development and putting the blame on industrialized countries.[25]

The gap between developed and developing states continues to be wide. Although citizens of a minority of states are quite affluent, the citizens of the majority of states live under conditions of abject poverty. Citizens of the majority of states, for instance, have an income of less than $1 per day. Although some states have been able to break through the barrier between them and developed states, such is not the case for all states, especially certain states located in vulnerable regions including sub-Saharan Africa.

Despite the absence of a global war, states frequently engage regional conflicts that involve violations of human rights. Furthermore, even developed democratic states – which could be considered founders of human rights instruments – often engage in

---

[24] The GNP of a developing state may be less than the revenues of a multinational corporation.
[25] Daniel Bodansky, The United Nations Convention on Climate Change: A Commentary, 18 Yale Journal of International Law 451 (1993).

human rights violations.[26] States that are more powerful mingle in the affairs of –
and even invade – less powerful states under the real threat or the pretext of a threat
to their national security[27] or by simply pursuing the appropriation of other states'
resources.[28] Many states are ravaged by a number of diseases, including AIDS and
malaria. Under these global circumstances, the question that emerges is what the
role of international law is, and, more specifically, what the role of international
environmental law is. This is a question that Chapter 2 will attempt to answer.

1.2.3. Cooperation

States are not equal in their power and authority.[29] Whereas in decisions affecting
war and peace, the hegemonic power of some states is obvious, in the everyday affairs
of state interaction hegemonic tendencies tend to be subtler. Because war is not an
option for most societies under normal conditions, states have tried to cooperate
to achieve desirable outcomes. Even hegemonic states find it costly to affirm their
position constantly through the use of force. Often, therefore, they engage in some
sort of cooperative behavior with other states.

In game theory parlance, states find themselves captured in repeated games in
which the number of players is limited. Such players usually possess quite substantial
information about the past performance of other players. The international community is comprised of a small number of states; this community becomes even
smaller if one only counts states actively participating in most international matters.
States are avid collectors of information about the performance and general circumstances of other states, especially that of states that affect their interests. Thus, one
could conceive state interaction as one in which cooperation is the expected norm
rather than the exception.[30] The reluctance to use force, the absence of a centralized
enforcement authority, reciprocity, and cooperative patterns of behavior make the
international arena look like alternating from hierarchy to coarchy and vice versa.[31]

A result of cooperation is the establishment of networks or clubs among certain
states. The General Agreement on Tariffs and Trade (GATT) was, in effect, a trade
club among industrialized states. Various security regimes connect allies that happen
to possess similar ideological outlook and development orientation, for instance,
the North Atlantic Treaty Organization (NATO). Such organizations often lack
transparency, but the lack of open and transparent procedures is viewed as the key
to organizational effectiveness. This lack of transparency gives freedom to officials

---

[26] See U.S.: Abu Ghraib only the "Tip of the Iceberg," Human Rights Watch, Apr. 27, 2005. See also
David Scheffer, Beyond Occupation Law, in 97 American Journal of International Law 842 (2003) (on
the law of occupation and the potential liability of occupying states).

[27] See General Assembly Resolution 38/7, The Situation in Grenada, A/RES/38/7, Nov. 3, 1983. See
also Military and Paramilitary Activities in and Against Nicaragua (Nicaragua v. United States), (Merits),
June 27, 1986, (1986) ICJ Reports 14. See also John Yoo, International Law and the War in Iraq,
97 American Journal of International Law 563 (2003). But see Richard Falk, What Future for the UN
Charter System of War Prevention, 97 American Journal of International Law 590 (2003).

[28] Iraq's invasion of Kuwait was allegedly performed to take over Kuwait's oil resources. See also Security
Council Resolution 661, S/RES/661, Aug. 6, 1990.

[29] See Reisman, *supra* note 12.

[30] See, e.g., Robert Axelrod, The Evolution of Cooperation (1984).

[31] W. Michael Reisman, Sanctions and Enforcement, reprinted in International Law Essays 381, 405 (Myres
S. McDougal & W. Michael Reisman, eds., 1981).

involved in these organizations to put together package deals without being constantly scrutinized by the media and the public.[32]

The club model of international cooperation has been challenged by the excluded states. Developing countries have engaged in efforts to participate in the clubs of developed states so as to obtain advantages previously not available to them. India and China engaged in substantial lobbying to enter the World Trade Organization (WTO) club. Eastern European countries have engaged in efforts to participate in the NATO and the European Community (EC) clubs.

Environmental problems have, as a general rule, transboundary effects. Therefore, states realized early that cooperation, common rules, and standards are better than unilateral action. The outcome of cooperation in the environmental field can be seen in the number and quality of treaties and other instruments that have been put in place for the protection of environment. Not all these treaties are well monitored and enforced.[33] Nevertheless, treaties affirm the will of states to cooperate for the achievement of desirable outcomes. In the environmental field, developed states have been willing to compensate developing states for their participation in cooperative arrangements that are to have global beneficial environmental effects but that may, at the same time, slow the pace of growth.

1.3. International Organizations

The United Nations System

The Security Council

The Security Council of the United Nations is comprised of the victor states of World War II (France, the United Kingdom, the United States, Russia, and China)[34] as permanent members, and ten nonpermanent members selected by the General Assembly. The permanent members of the Security Council have the power to veto any decision of the Security Council,[35] reflecting the importance of authoritative power in the making of the international order.

The Security Council is the primary organ of the United Nations, which deals with matters of war and peace.[36] The Security Council is not generally involved in environmental matters. However, in exceptional cases, for instance, with regard to Iraq's invasion of Kuwait, it held Iraq liable for various damages inflicted on Kuwait including the damage to the environment.[37] The decisions of the Security Council are binding[38] and the powers of the Council are very extensive.[39]

---

[32] Robert O. Keohane & Joseph S. Nye, Jr., Between Centralization and Fragmentation: The Club Model of Multilateral Cooperation and Problems of Democratic Legitimacy 2, KSG Working Paper No. 01-004, John F. Kennedy School of Government, Harvard University, Feb. 2001 available online http://ssrn.com/abstract=262175 (Social Science Research Network).

[33] United States General Accounting Office (GAO), International Agreements Are Not Well Monitored (GAO-RCED-92–43, 1992).

[34] Art. 23, UN Charter, *supra* note 9.

[35] Art. 27(3), *id.*

[36] Arts. 39 & 41, *id.*

[37] Para. 16, Security Council Resolution 687, S/RES/687, April 3, 1991.

[38] See arts. 25 & 103, UN Charter, *supra* note 9.

[39] Art. 24. "In order to ensure prompt and effective action by the United Nations, its Members confer on the Security Council primary [not exclusive, though] responsibility for the maintenance of international peace and security . . . " *Id.*

The General Assembly

If the Security Council reflects some of the power elite of the world community, the General Assembly is the democratic institution comprised of all members of the United Nations.[40] In the General Assembly, each member state has one vote.[41] The General Assembly issues resolutions and recommendations that are not binding but are frequently influential in the shaping of international relations and, when adopted unanimously, could be considered sources of customary international law. The General Assembly can consider a variety of matters, such as economic, social, educational, cultural, health-related, or human rights–centered issues.

Given the broad scope of powers accorded to it, the General Assembly has been involved in various environmental issues. The General Assembly convened the 1972 UN Conference on the Human Environment (Stockholm Conference), the 1992 UN Conference on Environment and Development (UNCED, Rio Conference) and the 2002 World Summit on Sustainable Development (WSSD, Johannesburg Conference). All of these conferences are considered landmarks in the development of international environmental law.

The General Assembly has created two organs of the United Nations that have played an essential role in international environmental developments, namely, the United Nations Environment Program (UNEP) and the United Nations Development Program (UNDP). The Commission on Sustainable Development, a product of the UNCED Conference, functions under the auspices of the General Assembly. The General Assembly has taken bold steps in asking the International Court of Justice (ICJ) to give its opinion on the legality of nuclear weapons.[42]

International Court of Justice

The International Court of Justice (ICJ) or World Court is the principal judicial organ of the United Nations.[43] All member states of the UN become *ipso facto* parties to the Statute of the International Court of Justice.[44] Only a state party to the Court's Statute may be party to a contentious case.[45] The jurisdiction of the Court in contentious cases is based on the consent of states.

Consent may be given:

- *ad hoc* under article 36(1); States can submit a dispute to the Court by virtue of an agreement usually called *compromis*;
- by prior agreement in a treaty under article 36(1);
- by accepting the compulsory jurisdiction of the Court through a declaration under article 36(2).

Compulsory jurisdiction is conferred to the Court by a declaration of a concerned country.[46] Declarations are usually not retroactive and include reservations.

---

[40] Art. 9, *id.*

[41] There are have been claims, however, that votes should be weighted based on the population of each state. See Shaw, *supra* note 22, at 597.

[42] See *infra* note 224.

[43] Art. 92, UN Charter, *supra* note 9.

[44] Art. 93, *id.*

[45] Arts. 34 & 36(2), Statute of the International Court of Justice, June 26, 1945 available online at http://www.icj-cij.org.

[46] Art. 36(2)–(5), *id.*

Declarations may include the possibility of dispute settlement by other means and may provide that the ICJ does not have jurisdiction in matters falling under domestic jurisdiction ("self-judging" clause).[47] Several declarations exclude disputes arising under multilateral treaties unless all parties to the treaty affected by the decision are also parties to the case before the Court. A few declarations exclude disputes arising out of hostilities in which the declarant state is entangled or disputes that have to do with national security issues. An increasing number of states have included clauses in their declarations designed to avoid surprise lawsuits by states that accept the Court's jurisdiction and, immediately after that, bring a case against another state. Some states have excluded from the jurisdiction of the Court any dispute that was brought by a state less than twelve months after that state had accepted the jurisdiction of the Court. In order to further protect themselves, many states have reserved the right to modify or terminate a declaration peremptorily by means of notification to the Secretary General of the UN with effect from the moment of notification.[48]

A few treaties give the Court appellate jurisdiction. The 1944 Convention on International Civil Aviation, for example, provides for appeal to the Court of decisions of the Council of the International Civil Aviation Organization.[49]

The International Court of Justice is comprised of a body of fifteen independent judges elected, regardless of their nationality, although no two of these judges can be nationals of the same state.[50] Judges are persons of high moral character who possess qualifications for appointment in the highest judicial offices of their respective countries.[51] Members of the Court are elected by the Security Council and the General Assembly, each body voting separately.[52] Nominations are made by national groups in the Permanent Court of Arbitration.[53] An informal agreement among members of the United Nations generally governs the distribution of seats among the various regions of the world. Judges serve for nine years, with five judges rotating every three years.[54] Judges may be reelected and this is often the case. If a party in a case does not have a judge of its nationality sitting at the bench, it may designate an *ad hoc* such judge.[55] The Court generally has decided cases by full bench. It may, however, form chambers composed of three or more judges to deal with a particular case or a category of cases.[56] The ICJ has established a chamber devoted to environmental matters.

The principle of *stare decisis* does not apply to the decisions of the ICJ. As mentioned in article 59 of the Statute of the International Court of Justice: "The decision of the Court has no binding force except between the parties and in respect of that particular case." However, the Court frequently refers to its own decisions and to those of other tribunals.

---

[47] Shaw, *supra* note 22, at 530.
[48] *Id*. at 531.
[49] Art. 84, Convention on International Civil Aviation, Dec. 7, 1944, reprinted in 15 UNTS 295.
[50] Art. 3(1), Statute of the International Court of Justice, *supra* note 45.
[51] Art. 2, *id*.
[52] Arts. 4(1) & 8, *id*.
[53] Art. 4(1), *id*.
[54] Art. 13(1), *id*.
[55] Art. 31, *id*.
[56] Art. 29, *id*.

In addition to its function as a dispute settlement mechanism, the Court provides advisory opinions on any legal question at the request "of whatever body may be authorized by or in accordance with the Charter of the United Nations to make such request."[57] The General Assembly has the authority to ask the ICJ to give an advisory opinion on any legal matter.[58] Other organs of the UN and specialized agencies may request advisory opinions of the Court on "legal questions arising within the scope of their activities."[59] Based on this provision, the Court has been able to answer the General Assembly's request regarding the legality of nuclear weapons considering, *inter alia*, environmental matters.[60] The ICJ declared that it had no jurisdiction to give advisory opinion on the legality of nuclear weapons to the World Health Organization (WHO) because the legality of nuclear weapons did not arise within the scope of activities of WHO.[61]

Other Organizations

International institutions play multiple roles in the development of international environmental law. They provide the coordinating fora under which most environmental issues are discussed and decided. International organizations have some lawmaking function because they issue recommendations, resolutions, and other so-called soft law instruments that, although not binding on states, exert varying levels of influence on the development of international environmental law.[62]

UNEP has provided the forum for the discussion of many international treaties, such as the Basel Convention on the control of waste movements and the Biodiversity Convention. UNEP has taken a leadership role in the regional seas programs. The International Maritime Organization (IMO) has been instrumental in the production of the regulatory framework for the control of pollution from ships. The International Atomic Energy Agency (IAEA) has generated a number of guidelines on the protection of public health from nuclear materials, and also has been instrumental in the implementation of the Nuclear Non-Proliferation Treaty, generating rules for the disposal of radioactive waste. The World Meteorological Organization (WMO) has played a role in the climate change discussions. The World Health Organization (WHO) has been involved in a number of environmental issues including the control of pesticides and the trade in chemicals. The Food and Agriculture Organization (FAO) is primarily involved in fisheries, agricultural and forestry development and agrobiodiversity issues. The International Agricultural Research Centers (IARCs) have been involved in gene bank development. The World Trade Organization (WTO) is involved in trade matters, but its broad jurisdiction over trade regulation intersects often with environmental matters. The UN Economic and Social Council (ECOSOC) and the UNDP have been taking into consideration environmental concerns as they affect socioeconomic decisions. Various other permanent and *ad hoc*

---

[57] Art. 65(1), *id.*

[58] Art. 96(1), UN Charter, *supra* note 9.

[59] Art. 96(2), *id.*

[60] See *infra* note 224.

[61] *Id.*

[62] See, e.g., Kenneth W. Abbott & Duncan Snidal, Hard and Soft Law in International Governance, 54 International Organization 421 (2000).

institutions (e.g., various working groups, committees) have assisted in the growth of international environmental law.

Environmental considerations have had an impact on the agenda of many international organizations. Environmental considerations affect various areas of the economy including all sorts of development projects, agriculture and forestry. The World Bank (International Bank for Reconstruction and Development [IBRD]), for instance, in its pursuit of development (that may involve construction of dams, roads, or the development of protected areas) has found itself entangled in environmental and human rights matters. Similarly, the Global Environment Facility (GEF) finances many development projects in which environmental considerations are paramount.

Other organizations that have been involved in the development of international environmental law include the International Tropical Timber Organization (ITTO), which has been proactive in the sustainable management of tropical forests. Regional organizations – such as the European Bank for Reconstruction and Development (EBRD), the Organization for Economic Co-operation and Development (OECD), the Organization of African Union (OAU), the Organization of American States (OAS), the Association of South East Asian Nations (ASEAN), the Asian Development Bank and the South Asian Association for Regional Co-operation (SAARC) – have played an influential role in the development of international environment law.

Some institutions have monitoring character, such as the EMEP system (Cooperative Programme for Monitoring and Evaluation of the Long-range Transmission of Air Pollutants in Europe), which was developed under the UN/ECE regime regarding transboundary pollution in Europe. The Conference of the Parties (COP) – an institution provided for in most international environmental law treaties – has acquired increasing monitoring and enforcement powers in recent environmental conventions. State parties to a convention have to report to the COP of that convention on measures they have taken to implement that convention. Failure to report – depending on the will of other state parties – may trigger sanctions.[63] Some conventions establish dispute settlement mechanisms that may be optional or obligatory.[64] The ICJ is the primary judiciary organ, but other international tribunals have been established, such as the ITLOS (International Tribunal of the Law of the Sea) and the Appellate Body of the WTO.

A plethora of international institutions with overlapping capacities and responsibilities has generated demands to rationalize the international system and, more specifically, the international system for the protection of environment. Such rationalization may be needed depending on advantages/disadvantages of redundancy in the administration of international law. Given that some institutions are more competent or resilient than others allowing for some form of institutional competition by tolerating some redundancy in the international system may not be ill-advised. Completely streamlined institutional systems could be susceptible to failure in case of a challenge. Allowing for some jurisdictional overlap among

[63] See Chapter 3, Section 2.4.
[64] See Chapter 3, Section 3.

institutions that are not strictly identical yields more diversity and more flexibility in responses.[65]

One could claim, for instance, that the International Whaling Commission is a redundant organization and its responsibilities should fall under the CITES secretariat. A total bureaucratic streamlining would mandate to do away with the Commission and devote its resources to the CITES Secretariat. To many environmentalists, such an outcome would not be the most effective outcome for the protection of whales. It is questionable whether the CITES Secretariat would have the will to defend the ban on whale hunting as forcefully as the Whaling Commission has done.

Another example involves the jurisdictional overlap between the FAO and the Conference of the Parties (COP) of the Biodiversity Convention. The institutions have separate yet also overlapping jurisdiction, as the FAO is responsible for agrobiodiversity, whereas the COP is concerned with the general protection of biodiversity. In practice, the separation of jurisdictional reach has not worked well and there has been friction in the cooperation between the two institutions.[66] One could conclude, however, that the jurisdictional overlap has had some positive outcomes. The FAO has been able to broker a multilateral treaty on the dissemination of agricultural resources that is a first step in creating some predictability with regard to property rights over such resources. The Treaty on Plant Genetic Resources for Food and Agriculture is now contributing in the development of the equitable sharing of benefits derived from the manipulation of food and agricultural resources.[67]

1.4. Nongovernmental Actors

Environmental NGOs

There are roughly two broad categories of actors in the environmental movement: the mainstream environmentalists and the deep ecologists.

According to the official line of mainstream environmentalism, development has to be sought, but standards must be developed so that environmental deterioration is minimized for the benefit of public health and quality of life.

At the other end of the spectrum, deep ecologists have argued for a "protection of environment for the sake of environment" approach based on the belief that the "the interests of nature" override or, at least, are at the same footing as the interests

---

[65] See Bobbi Low et al., Redundancy and Diversity in Governing and Managing Common-Pool Resources, Paper Presented at the 8th Biennial Conference of the International Association for the Study of Common Property 7, Bloomington, Indiana, May 31–June 4, 2002. See generally Jonathan B. Bendor, Parallel Systems (1985); See also Herbert A. Simon, The Proverbs of Administration, 6 Public Administration Review 53 (1946), reprinted in Classics of Organization Theory (Jay M. Shafritz & J. Steven Ott, eds., 1992). For the role of administrative redundancy in fighting corruption and promoting accountability in developing countries, see Stephen B. Peterson, Another Path to Customs Reform: Mexico's Second Inspection, Discussion Paper No. 632, Harvard Institute for International Development, April 1998. The author argues that the system of double inspection in customs administration is designed to fight corruption by building overlapping layers of administration that would be pitted against each other.

[66] Chapter 7, Section 2.1.2.3.

[67] Chapter 7, Section 2.1.2.4.

of humans. According to these advocates, the current paradigm for development, one that is derived from the Judeo-Christian tradition, views human life as the center of all creation. According to deep ecologists, life must be reconsidered under an ecological-ethical perspective allowing for the creation of small communities[68] and survival through hunting, gathering, and gardening.[69] An offshoot of the deep-ecology approach is the animal rights movement, which has made its impact on international instruments, for instance, the instruments that prohibit whale hunting. Deep ecology is a result of the resentment against globalization – and what is implied by globalization, free markets. Some strands of deep ecology, it could be argued, have assumed the role of an alternative ideology to that supported by free markets.

The deep–ecology approach is based on different philosophical assumptions than those shared by the majority of people in the world today. As long as the assumptions differ, the chances for achieving a common ground are substantially reduced. Deep ecology stands against technological innovation and the model of industrialization as we experience it. It is tempting to point out, however, that pursuing "what is good for nature" will not be helpful in prescribing standards to manage and protect the environment. Only by attaching values – a human artifact – can the course of action be determined that is appropriate for the protection of the environment and human health.[70]

That the deep-ecology approach has been developed and has juxtaposed itself to the current model of development is not surprising. A quest of modern civilizations has been for a return to an unadulterated mythical past, one that probably never existed.[71] What is most striking is how deep ecology has affected some of the outputs of the mainstream environmental movement and international environmental law and policy. The influence of the deep-ecology approach on the mainstream environmental movement can be seen in the propagation of policies that favor strict preservation[72] and the establishment of exclusionary protected biodiversity areas through the forcible exclusion of people.[73] The effects of deep ecology can be seen on policies that ban animal hunting even when such hunting provides the sole source of income for certain indigenous societies.[74] A deep-ecology slant can be detected in the pursuit of self-sufficiency in the markets for the transfers of hazardous waste[75] and the articulation of policies that exhibit zero tolerance for pollution.[76]

---

[68] See, e.g., Fritz Schumacher, Small is Beautiful (1993).

[69] See, e.g., Lawrence E. Johnson, A Morally Deep World: An Essay on Moral Significance and Environmental Ethics (1993).

[70] For a critique of the deep–ecology approach, see Luc Ferry, Le Nouvel Ordre Ecologique (1995). See also James J. Kay, On the Nature of Ecological Integrity, in Ecological Integrity and the Management of Ecosystems 210 (Stephen Woodley et at., eds., 1990).

[71] Western civilization has been presented as corrupt, for instance, by the Romanticism movement that urged a return to nature.

[72] See, generally, Donald Show, Inside the Environmental Movement (1992).

[73] Chapter 7, Section 1.2.

[74] For instance, the campaign against trade in natural furs coming from certain species, without making clear distinctions between endangered and nonendangered species, has harmed indigenous groups that live in the Arctic regions and for which hunting is the only possible source of income.

[75] Chapter 10, Section 3.1.

[76] David Vogel & Timothy Kessler, How Compliance Happens and Doesn't Happen Domestically, in Engaging Countries: Strengthening Compliance with International Environmental Accords 19, 24 (Edith Brown Weiss & Harold K. Jacobson, eds., 1998).

The environmental movement had its birth in the developed world and has acted as an opposition to untrammeled development by emphasizing the importance of quality of life based on a clean environment. Environmental groups have lobbied governments in developed countries to adopt stringent regulations for the reduction of pollution and protection of natural resources. Although not always as successful as intended, these efforts have borne fruits and have improved the quality of life in many areas of the developed world.

Because many environmental problems have global dimensions, environmental groups have tried to spread their activities in the developing world. Environmental issues have received mixed response in the developing world. Sometimes governments support exclusionary protected areas for ecotourism or for achieving better control over ethnic minorities. But, in most cases, developing countries' governments balk at taking decisive action on other problems, such as marine pollution or the supply of clean drinking water.

The NGOs of developing countries have been overwhelmed by the more prosperous NGOs of developed countries. In fact, much of the funding for developing countries' NGOs comes from developed countries' foundations. Some economists have claimed that developed countries' NGOs have been able to set the agenda of the developing countries' NGOs and that, accordingly, such agendas have little to do with the problems that developing countries face.[77] Specific environmental problems prevalent in developing countries, such as dwindling supplies of drinkable water and malnutrition, are not adequately addressed.

Because of allegations of transposing developed world ideals to developing countries, many environmental organizations have changed their discourse and have proposed that the management of environmental problems has to be executed with the participation of local people. The participation of local communities, however, is not always applied in practice.

To be fair, environmental NGOs in developed countries are not always monolithic. Whereas for some members of these organizations, local participation is a simple switch in discourse to please new audiences, others view public participation as the means to change the substance of environmental policies. Community-oriented participation discourses, even if they do not end up in substantial public participation, are an important means of defining and legitimizing local interests. Community participation dialogues provide room for maneuverability to local groups who view the management of environmental problems as a way to address their economic and social needs.[78]

Environmental NGOs have challenged further the club model of interstate relations and have sought to become involved in intergovernmental fora. Environmental NGOs have had significant influence in the shaping of some environmental regimes. The evolution of the London Convention, the Whaling Convention, the Basel Convention, the CITES, and the World Heritage Convention has been influenced substantially by the actions of environmental NGOs.

---

[77] Jagdish Bhagwati, In Defense of Globalization 47 (2004).

[78] Sally Jeanrenaud, People Oriented Approaches in Global Conservation: Is the Leopard Changing its Spots? (International Institute for Environment and Development (IIED) & Institute for Development Studies (IDS), 2002).

In other cases, the impact of environmental groups has been weaker but, nevertheless, has remained influential. NGOs have attempted to infiltrate international organizations that are not *prima facie* confronted with environmental issues, such as the WTO, with less success. Interestingly, developing states, which are now entering these club-type organizations, are less prone to welcome NGOs than their developed countries' counterparts.[79]

Industry NGOs

Industry NGOs are not as visible as environmental NGOs, but they are not less powerful. Actually, in some fora, where expert advice is needed, industry could appear more credible because it has the resources to put together the expertise and, thus, provide an authoritative analysis of an environmental issue. It has been claimed, for instance, that industry NGOs are successful in the European Commission – the initiator of legislative proposals within the European Union.

Industry NGOs are generally perceived as reluctant to provide leadership for the abatement of environmental problems for which industries are responsible. Industry has attempted to delay or to curtail environmental action when such action is perceived as too costly. Industry has claimed frequently that scientific uncertainty is a valid reason for inaction. The standards that some industries apply for the protection of environment in developing countries often lag behind those adopted in developed countries.

Having said that, it would be wrong to classify all industries as culprits of environmental deterioration. Some industries have been innovators and are at the forefront of environmental engineering. Within an industry or a company are often dissenting voices that attempt to reorient discourse to corporate responsible solutions and to redefine the allegiance of corporations not strictly to shareholders but to a broader category of stakeholders that includes employees, the surrounding communities, and the general public. Industry has learned the hard way that environmentally irresponsible behavior is not only costly in terms of liability but also in terms of reputation.

Scientists

The role of science has been prominent in the development of international environmental law.[80] Scientists, however, rarely agree on the definition of an environmental problem or the prescriptions for its solution. Sometimes the disagreement is the result of the use of different data (for instance, in fisheries) or of the application of different models (climate change). Given the lack of scientific certainty, most decisions on environmental matters have to be made based on political considerations. However, scientific communities and informal networks among scientists[81] often frame the environmental discourse. UNEP, WMO, and national scientific institutions (such as the United States National Aeronautics and Space Administration [NASA]) have executed the research on ozone depletion. The Intergovernmental Panel on

---

79   See Keohane, *supra* note 32, at 6–8.

80   Peter M. Haas, Banning Chlorofluorocarbons: Epistemic Community Efforts to Protect Atmospheric Ozone, in Knowledge, Power, and International Policy Organization, 46(1) International Organization 201 (1992).

81   Abram Chayes & Antonia Handler Chayes, The New Sovereignty: Compliance with International Regulatory Agreements 171–72 (1995).

Climate Change (IPCC) was organized by UNEP and WMO to provide insights on the climate change debate.

The positions of scientists are used often by proponents or opponents of an environmental action to advance their own view. The climate change discourse has been influenced by the inability of scientists to reach consensus on whether climate change really exists and its possible repercussions. The lack of scientific consensus has provided some countries with justification to delay purposive action for the abatement of carbon dioxide emissions, the main culprit of climate change. By contrast, scientific consensus on the ozone hole over Antarctica precipitated decisive action to phase out ozone-depleting substances.

Environmental law could be conceived as a series of dialectic interactions between what are perceived as opposing trends: one devoted to development as usual and the other to the injection of ecodevelopment as "new" paradigm for development. The role of science in these series of dialectic interactions is the role of facilitator.

Indigenous Peoples

The Indigenous Peoples Forum is an informal network of indigenous groups that seeks to bring to prominence issues that affect indigenous peoples. The Indigenous Peoples Forum lacks a clear legal personality. However, it has been able, through a series of gradual steps, to establish itself as an influential international institutional network.

Indigenous peoples have asserted their fundamental human rights through the Draft Declaration on the Rights of Indigenous Peoples.[82] A number of ILO standards,[83] which are currently in force, are not considered sufficient to guarantee indigenous peoples rights. The interaction of indigenous peoples with environmental organizations has been ambivalent. Indigenous peoples have occasionally colluded with the environmental movement against corporations whose pollution adversely affects their traditional livelihoods. Other times, however, the indigenous people movement has collided with the environmental movement, especially, with regard to land-use rights. Environmental groups prefer state control over land, especially forested land. Environmentalists are not convinced that indigenous groups, if left to their own devices, would opt for environmentally sound solutions. Indigenous peoples prefer to exercise control over the land through property rights and, thus, to retain discretionary control over its use. The preference of environmental groups for state control perpetuates, as should be expected, a rift between the indigenous peoples' movement and the environmental movement.

2. INTERNATIONAL LAWMAKING PROCESS

International law develops as states get together to calibrate their interaction and formalize their relationships. States frequently enter into agreements with one another about matters of mutual concern. This way, states explicitly set the law that would

---

[82] Draft United Nations Declaration on the Rights of Indigenous Peoples, Aug. 26, 1994, reprinted in 34 ILM 541 (1995).

[83] Convention Concerning Indigenous and Tribal Peoples in Independent Countries, June 27, 1989, reprinted in 28 ILM 1382 (1989).

regulate their behavior. Other times, states engage in practice under the perception that such practice constitutes or should constitute law. If such practice is general and is exercised under the opinion that it constitutes law, it is considered general custom and, thus, a source of international law. Law could be derived from what are called general principles of law, judicial decisions, and the teachings of the "most highly qualified publicists."[84]

Article 38 of the Statute of the International Court of Justice is cited most often as the authoritative text on sources of law. According to that article:

> The Court, whose function is to decide in accordance with international law such disputes as are submitted to it, shall apply: 1.international conventions, whether general or particular, establishing rules expressly recognized by the contesting states; 2.international custom, as evidence of general practice accepted as law; 3.the general principles of law recognized by civilized nations; 4.subject to provisions of article 59, judicial decisions and the teachings of the most highly qualified publicists of the various nations as subsidiary for the determination of the rules of law.

2.1. Treaties

International agreements, called "treaties," "conventions," "covenants," and "charters," could be bilateral or multilateral. Usually, multilateral treaties signed by a number of states are deemed to have lawmaking effects, whereas bilateral treaties are viewed more or less the way contracts are viewed in domestic law (as having effect between the parties that signed them).[85] The process of multilateral treaty creation involves a number of states that wish to resolve an issue of international importance. These states usually request an international organization with authority on the subject matter (for instance, the World Health Organization, in matters of public health, the International Labor Organization on labor matters) to establish a working group to draft a treaty. This initiates a process of treaty negotiation and bargaining until a consensus is established. Usually, states attempt to reach consensus during treaty negotiations, which often results in the adoption of the lowest common denominator. Instances exist, however, in which states would adopt a convention without a consensus. Lack of a consensus in the adoption of a convention is likely to affect the lawmaking character of the convention. This is particularly the case if countries explicitly refuse to sign or ratify the convention.

The Vienna Convention on the Law of the Treaties[86] is the document used frequently to interpret the text of many international treaties. The Vienna Convention has codified some of the general principles that are enshrined in the law of the treaties such as *pacta sunt servanda*[87] and that treaties must not in principle have retroactive character.[88] The Vienna Convention demonstrates a preference for the peaceful settlement of disputes[89] and requires parties to perform their treaty

---

[84] See art. 38(d), Statute of the International Court of Justice, *supra* note 45.
[85] See J.G. Starke, An Introduction to International Law 78–81 (1963).
[86] Vienna Convention on the Law of the Treaties, May 23, 1969, reprinted in 8 ILM 679 (1969).
[87] Art. 26, *id.*
[88] Art. 28, *id.*
[89] See article 65 of the Vienna Convention, which refers to article 33 of the UN Charter, *id.*

obligations "in good faith."[90] The Vienna Convention provides for the establishment of a Conciliation Commission in case a disagreement arises during treaty performance,[91] but the decisions of the Conciliation Commission are not binding. The convention provides for the possibility of reference of a dispute to the ICJ or arbitration.[92]

States are free to make reservations to specific articles of a convention.[93] This creates in effect an *à la carte* convention system. Too many reservations on the text of a convention undermine the authoritative character of the convention. For this reason, certain treaties prohibit reservations.[94] Many environmental and human rights treaties do so. The prohibition of reservations enhances the consistency and uniformity of treaties but, at the same time, restricting the possibility of reservations implies less state participation in the treaty regime. If reservations are allowed, without any restriction, state participation is facilitated but the lawmaking attributes of a treaty are diluted.

After a convention is signed, it enters into a process of ratification. This means that states must ask their legislative organs (e.g., a parliament) to adopt the convention and to incorporate it into the domestic legal order. Unless a state ratifies a convention, the convention does not have binding effects on that state (provided that the rules included in the convention have not become a rule of customary law).

A convention specifies in one of its articles the number of states that are required for ratification. After this prespecified number of states ratify the convention, it is said that "the convention enters into force,"[95] that is, it has become binding law among the states that ratified it. The number of states required to ratify a convention varies depending on the reach of the convention. The Law of the Sea Convention (UNCLOS), which is considered the constitutive instrument of the law of the seas, required sixty ratifications.[96] Because of its wide reach, it took fourteen years for the UNCLOS to enter into force.[97] For some conventions, ratification by certain states is important because nonratification by these states would risk depriving these conventions of a convincing legal authority. For instance, the civil liability instruments for oil pollution attempt to ensure the participation of states where major carriers of oil reside. The climate change instruments attempt to ensure the participation of countries that are major emitters of carbon dioxide.

Many international environmental treaties are umbrella framework treaties – setting the parameters of international environmental action – followed by protocols defining the specific standards of state behavior. The model of a framework convention followed by specific protocols has been adopted as the regulatory archetype for a number of environmental problems, such as ozone depletion, acid rain, and climate change. The rationale behind the framework-protocol approach is for states to commit to engage, initially, in cooperative behavior to manage what seems to be

---

[90] For the element of good faith, see art. 26, Vienna Convention, *id.*
[91] See art. 66 and Annex to the Vienna Convention, *id.*
[92] Art. 66, *id.*
[93] Art. 2(d), *id.* See also art. 20, *id.*
[94] Art. 19, *id.*
[95] See art. 24, *id.*
[96] See Chapter 4, Section 3.1.
[97] *Id.*

an emerging environmental problem through a framework convention. As scientific evidence accumulates or the political will manifests to tackle the problem more decisively, further specific regulatory protocols can be adopted.

The framework/protocol legislative approach is not the only regulatory process for the management of environmental problems. In the case of marine pollution, specific conventions, such as the 1972 London Dumping Convention and the 1973 MARPOL Convention, preceded the 1982 UNCLOS. The UNCLOS is the framework convention that has established the basic rules that govern the oceans. The process of adopting a constitutional convention that attempts to address environmental and other issues presented in the exploitation and protection of a medium (for instance, seas, water, air) can be time-consuming, however. In the case of the UNCLOS, it took more than ten years to adopt a coherent text for the protection of the oceans.

2.2. Custom

The relevance of custom as a source of international law has been debated. Some scholars maintain that custom is an authoritative source of international law,[98] whereas others purport that custom is anachronistic and even hard to prove in an international environment rich in bilateral and multilateral agreements among states. According to article 38 of the Statute of the International Court of Justice, there are two elements that are needed for the establishment of international custom: general practice and *opinio juris (opinio juris sive necessitatis)*. General practice could be derived from a number of material acts, for instance, domestic law, newspaper reports, and government statements. *Opinio juris* requires that states behave in a certain way under the stated belief, which does not have to be a genuine belief, that their behavior is law or is becoming law.[99] The International Court of Justice has established that some degree of uniformity is required for custom to become law.[100] However, it is possible for custom to develop if a number of states follow consistently a practice that has had an impact on international relations because of the authoritative influence of these states. The role of maritime powers in the establishment of the law of the sea, and the role of the United States and the Soviet Union in the development of space law are indisputable.[101] Thus, even in the creation of international custom that, according to article 38, must be based on general practice, one can decipher the role of authoritative power in lawmaking. For the practice of a state to develop into custom, it is not necessary for that state to believe that its behavior constitutes law. What is necessary is that its behavior remains unchallenged by other states.[102] For a state not to be bound by customary international law it has to have objected consistently to the creation of such law (the doctrine of persistent objector).[103] Opposition

---

[98] Anthony D'Amato, The Concept of Custom in International Law (1971).

[99] Shaw, *supra* note 22, at 71–73.

[100] *Id.* at 64.

[101] *Id.* at 66–67.

[102] Michael Akehurst, Custom as a Source of International Law, 47 British Yearbook of International Law 1 (1974–75).

[103] Ian Brownlie, Principles of Public International Law 10 (1998).

expressed for the first time after a rule has been established firmly will not generally prevent a state from being bound.[104]

Eventually, one can never prove a rule of customary law in an absolute manner but only relatively. After all, the Statute of the International Court of Justice speaks of "general practice" – not universal practice. It has been maintained that the consent of half of the states of the world is sufficient or that the consent of third world states is necessary. Arguments also have been made about the existence of regional custom that is established among the states of a particular geographic region.[105]

Special custom prevails over general custom – *lex specialis derogat legi generali* – unless the general custom amounts to what has been called *jus cogens* or a peremptory norm of international law.[106] Examples of *jus cogens* include the prohibition of genocide and slave trade and the principle of diplomatic immunity. Treaties can provide evidence of customary international law – unratified treaties as well. This is so because treaties provide irrefutable evidence that some states believe that a certain practice is law. It is more difficult to try to assemble state practice found in disparate sources that could provide convincing proof of the combination of elements of state practice and *opinio juris*.

It is apparent from the development of customary international law that protest and consent play a vital part in the formulation of international law. The weight attached to protest and consent depends on the number and authoritative power of states that support them.

2.3. Principles of Law

Commentators are often at a loss about what to include under the rubric of general principles of law. Therefore, they resort to some of the incontrovertible elements of any legal system – such as that violation of an agreement involves an obligation of restitution and the principle of good faith or estoppel. The role of equity as a principle of international law has been contested.[107] Although international tribunals have used the principle of equity in a number of renowned cases regarding the delimitation of the continental shelf[108] or the allocation of water sources,[109] it has been argued that equity is an all-encompassing concept that introduces an unacceptable amount of uncertainty[110] in international law. Some commentators, by contrast, view equity as a normative principle of international law.[111]

---

[104] *Id.* at 10.

[105] Akehurst, *supra* note 102, at 29–31.

[106] Art. 53, Vienna Convention, *supra* note 86.

[107] For a comprehensive treatment of the concept of equity, see Thomas M. Franck, Fairness in International Law and Institutions 15–75 (1995).

[108] See, e.g., paras. 88–89, 91, 98, North Sea Continental Shelf Cases, Feb. 20, 1969, (1969) ICJ Reports 4.

[109] See, e.g., Meuse Case, *infra* note 221.

[110] Rosalyn Higgins, International Trade Law and the Avoidance, Containment and Resolution of Disputes, General Course in Public International Law, 230 Recueil des Cours 9, 292 (1991).

[111] Wolfgang Friedman, The Changing Structure of International Law 197 (1964).

2.4. Other Sources

Court Decisions

Decisions of the ICJ, arbitration tribunals, and national courts, although presented in article 38 as subsidiary sources of international law, are of importance in shaping expectations about the legitimacy and likelihood of success of different claims made under international law. States in their pleadings before courts often refer to prior decisions of international and domestic tribunals and the International Court of Justice itself, although not bound by the principle of *stare decisis*, frequently refers to its prior decisions.

Teachings of Scholars

The work of scholars is influential in further shaping the development of international law. This is especially the case with new evolving concepts of international environmental law, such as the polluter pays principle or the precautionary principle, which require further clarification for their successful application.

Soft Law Instruments

Other sources of law include decisions, recommendations, declarations, and resolutions of various institutions that have been established under international law. This is what has been called in some circles "soft law,"[112] which, in contrast to "hard law" (e.g., treaties, custom), does not have a binding character on state behavior. Despite its nonbinding character, soft law has the capability of creating expectations that shape the future direction of international law. It is not rare for a norm, articulated in a soft law instrument, to be incorporated into a treaty later and, thus, to become a state obligation. The transformation of soft law instruments into binding requirements is part of the norm creation in international law. Soft law instruments in conjunction with a set of international norms (such as treaties) solidify expectations and generate impetus for consistent future behavior of states and other international actors.

2.5. Content

After deciding on the type of instrument that would be most effective in addressing an environmental problem, policy makers must make a choice about the policies to be incorporated in that instrument. In domestic arenas, significant emphasis has been placed on regulatory approaches, called command-and-control regulations, that specify the standards and often the technologies that industry should adopt in order to be in compliance.

Economic instruments are relatively new regulatory instruments, the purpose of which is to provide incentives for industry to comply. Economic instruments can take the form of taxes or subsidies. A particular fuel, for instance, such as petroleum, could be taxed to discourage its use. Renewable technology could be subsidized to encourage its wide application. Overall economic instruments that could be used

---

[112] See Abbott, *supra* note 62.

to change industry and consumer behavior include taxes on polluting products such as fuels, fertilizers, pesticides, tax differentiation (between ecofriendly and polluting products), user charges (charges for using water or for mineral exploitation), and subsidies.

The problem with economic instruments is that political will needs to be invested in them to be adopted and then implemented. In order for taxes to influence a specific behavior, they often need to be set quite high; this could cause industry or consumer backlash. The fate of carbon tax within the European Union is well known.[113] Subsidies and other economic vehicles must be carefully calibrated; otherwise, they may spur wasteful investment. Other instruments such as tradable discharge permits[114] and transferable quotas[115] have been used in domestic arenas as more flexible methods to reduce pollution.

There is another problem with economic instruments and their application in the international arena. Economic instruments, such as tradable permits, tend to be complex instruments and demand a level of institutional maturity that has yet to be attained in many international institutions. Also, the more complex the instrument, the harder it would be to enforce it, given the fragmented enforcement possibilities available in the international system. And this is true not only for economic instruments but also for any other complex regulatory instrument. For instance, the MARPOL Treaty was initially based on effluent discharges and, as such, it was difficult to monitor and enforce. Since the treaty has switched from effluent discharges to technological standards, it has functioned better. This is because the adoption of new technology in a ship is easily monitored by a simple inspection, whereas what ships do in the high seas and the types or quantity of pollutants they discharge can be hardly monitored. Often, the effectiveness of international regimes has to do with the straightforward nature of standards they provide.[116]

Most international instruments that have been adopted follow the conventional command-and-control approach. With the exception of climate change and ozone protection instruments, which marginally flirt with incentive generation,[117] most of

---

[113] A carbon tax is a tax on energy sources that discharge carbon dioxide into the atmosphere. The European Union has been discussing the imposition of carbon taxes since the early 1990s, but carbon taxes have yet to be adopted. In the meantime, Sweden, the Netherlands, and Norway have introduced carbon taxes.

[114] Tradable discharge permits operate as follows: a country or a group of countries sets a cap for the emissions of a polluting substance. Then permits are issued to industries the aggregate number of which must not exceed the cap. Industries that produce less pollution than that allowed by their permits could sell their extra permits to other industries that exceed the amount of pollution allowed for in their permits. It is hoped that the emission trading that takes place would achieve environmental results with the least cost for the industry. On the issue of tradable discharge permits (TDPs) and trading of emissions, see Chapter 8.

[115] Individual Transferable Quotas (ITQ) work like TDPs. In this case, a country or a group of countries set a cap on the amount of a resource that is to be harvested (i.e., fisheries). This cap is usually called Total Allowable Catch (TAC). This TAC is distributed to fishers through permits that define how much each fisher is entitled to harvest from the oceans. Fishers who fish less than their assigned permits could trade their extra permits with fishers who wish to fish more. Regarding Individual Transferable Quotas (ITQs) in fisheries, see Chapter 6.

[116] Oran R. Young, The Politics of International Regime Formation: Managing Natural Resources and the Environment, in Foundations of Environmental Law and Policy 315 (Richard L. Revesz, ed., 1997).

[117] See Chapter 8, Sections 1 & 2.

international conventions still prescribe standards and, increasingly, procedures for the application of environmental law. Such procedures involve extensive reporting requirements and the provision of information and data that is sorely lacking in many domestic and international fora. The lack of credible data has undermined international lawmaking and crippled the ability of international institutions to monitor state behavior effectively.[118] Many problems in the implementation of international environmental law have to do with the lack of data that would function as a baseline for assessing future pollution reduction and resource exploitation.

3. PERSPECTIVES

3.1. Developed Countries

Environmental deterioration was put in front of Western audiences with the publication of *Silent Spring*,[119] a book that touted the adverse effects of pesticides, and primarily DDT, on ecosystems and human health. The book galvanized the environmental movement and launched a number of regulatory instruments in the United States with zero pollution as a goal.[120] Although European countries initially exhibited a less risk-adverse attitude than the United States,[121] they gradually developed equally complicated regulatory systems for environmental protection. The evolution of the European Community environmental legislation from an enumeration of environmental goals to the prescription of detailed procedures for standard application is documented.[122]

Although there have been ebbs and flows in the development of environmental regulations – ebbs usually associated with economic deflation and flows with economic prosperity – one can certainly detect an increase in the sophistication and in the number of international environmental standards. Because of the costs that such standards impose on industries, as industries have to revamp their technologies to become more environmentally friendly, it has been proposed that the command-and-control approach of environmental regulation must be supplemented with economic incentives. Various instruments have been proposed that would allow companies to choose not only the most effective way but also the most efficient way to meet environmental standards. Tradable emission allowances have been implemented in some developed countries as a way to reduce the costs of pollution prevention.[123] Property rights have been allocated to fishers in the hope of abating overfishing and the depletion of fish stocks.[124]

Compliance with and enforcement of environmental standards is not perfect. After all, some lack of compliance is endemic in all regulatory systems. Compliance with environmental regulations does not seem to be worse than compliance with other regulatory instruments to the point that some commentators even talk

[118] GAO, *supra* note 33.
[119] Rachel Louise Carson, Silent Spring (1962).
[120] See *supra* note 76.
[121] Elli Louka, Conflicting Integration: The Environmental Law of the European Union 67 (2004).
[122] *Id.*
[123] See Chapter 8, Section 2.2.3.
[124] See Chapter 6, Section 2.2.

of over-compliance with environmental regulations.[125] Compliance with environmental standards is evident in the better air quality in most cities of the developed
world,[126] the relatively cleaner beaches,[127] and the restitution of the ozone layer.[128]
Still, however, a lot remains to be accomplished in terms of restoring damaged
ecosystems.[129]

3.2. Developing Countries

During colonial times, environmental legislation in developing countries was generated by colonial governments and was resented by local people.

Colonial governments were the first to impose environmental management
accompanied with strict enforcement to protect natural areas that were previously
free access areas.[130] These areas were enclosed, called "nature reserves," and were
removed from consumptive use. The 1933 Convention Relative to the Preservation
of Fauna and Flora in their Natural State[131] was one of the first international conventions adopted for the protection of biodiversity. The convention presents many
similarities with the exclusionary conservation conventions adopted in later years.
According to the preamble of the convention, "the natural fauna and flora of certain
parts of the world, and in particular Africa, are in danger, in present conditions, of
extinction and permanent injury." According to the framers of the convention, such
preservation of natural resources can be achieved best by

(i)   the constitution of national parks, strict natural reserves, and other reserves within
      which the hunting, killing, or capturing of fauna, and the collection or destruction
      of flora shall be limited or prohibited,
(ii) the institution of regulation concerning the hunting, killing, and capturing of
      fauna outside such areas,
(iii) the regulation of the traffic in trophies,
(iv) the prohibition of certain methods of and weapons for the hunting, killing, and
      capturing of fauna.[132]

The convention went as far as to establish a list of Class A (strict protection) and
Class B (less strictly protected than Class A species) species whose hunting must be
prevented even by the "natives." According to article 8(1),

---

[125] Beyond Compliance: What Motivates Environmental Behavior?, Overcompliance with Environmental Regulations (Proceedings of a Workshop sponsored by the U.S. Environmental Protection Agency's
National Center for Environmental Economics and National Center for Environmental Research, Washington, DC, June 4, 2001).
[126] The UN/ECE CLRTAP in Europe is considered generally successful, see Chapter 8, Section 3.
[127] Many developed countries are investing in sewage infrastructure, see OSPAR and HELCOM regime,
Chapter 4, Sections 4.1 & 4.2.
[128] See Chapter 8, Section 1.
[129] See Chapter 7, Section 1.
[130] See, generally, Jack Westoby, Introduction to World Forestry (1989).
[131] Convention Relative to the Preservation of Fauna and Flora in their Natural State, Nov. 8, 1933. The
countries involved included the Union of South Africa, Belgium, the United Kingdom, Egypt, Spain,
France, Italy, Portugal, and the Anglo-Egyptian Sudan. (Because of lack of ratifications, the convention
did not enter into force.)
[132] Preamble, id.

Animals belonging to the species mentioned in Class B, whilst not requiring such
rigorous protection as those mentioned in Class A shall not be hunted, killed, or
captured, even by natives, except under special license granted by the competent
authorities.

Many governments that were established after the demise of colonialism adopted
similar exclusionary policies for protected areas. Exclusionary polices brought vast
land areas under state control and confirmed the authority of newly established
national governments over territories resided by people of diverse tribal and other
affiliations. Protected areas were pursued as a good source of foreign exchange –
income brought by tourism or safaris or donors willing to shoulder the cost of
land preservation. The exclusion of resident peoples from restricted nature reserve
areas was, and is still, such a constitutive element of preservation efforts that some
commentators have characterized it "coercive conservation."[133] Chapter 7 provides
more details on the phenomenon of coercive conservation and how it has affected
environmental policies.

Putting aside the pursuit of protected areas, however, most developing countries,
when they entered the international arena as independent sovereign states, were faced
with environmental problems that were of different nature than those experienced
by developed countries. Such problems included the spread of various infectious
diseases, unsafe drinking water, and a lack of adequate food supply and housing.
Some respected scientists have argued that the spread of malaria in some developing
countries justifies the use of DDT, a substance prohibited for use in many developing
and developed countries, underlying the different nature of problems and appropriate
solutions for different areas of the world.

Because of the urgent problems that many developing countries face, they have
been slow to adopt stringent environmental laws or have been reluctant, once they
adopt such laws, actually to enforce them. Lack of enforcement in developing countries is indicative of both the lack of capacity but also a certain lack of will, as
many developing countries are content to sacrifice more of their environmental
protection in the pursuit of their development goals. Developing countries often
have argued that developed countries were allowed to despoil their environment in
order to develop and that they, developing countries, should achieve some level of
development before they implement environmental measures. Developing countries
argue that, after some level of development and wealth is achieved, the pursuit of
environmental quality should follow, as it has happened in developed countries.

Given the different priorities of developing countries, it is not surprising that,
when developing countries understood that the North was attempting to impose,
through international lawmaking, its own environmental standards on them, they
were less than willing to comply. The different views of developing countries were
made evident during the Rio Conference and in the subsequent negotiations of
international regimes, such as the ozone regime and the climate change regime.
During these negotiations, developing countries asked in effect for compensation for
their participation in the functioning of international environmental laws that they

---

[133] Nancy Peluso, Coercive Conservation: the Politics of State Resource Control, 3 Global Environmental
Change – Human and Policy Dimensions 199 (1993).

deemed served primarily the interests and concerns of developed states. Financial compensation in exchange for environmental performance became the cornerstone of the ozone protection and climate change regimes.[134]

4. HISTORICAL EVOLUTION

4.1. Stockholm

In the late 1960s, as the environmental movement was emerging, the Swedish delegation asked the United Nations to convene a conference on the environment. The immense coordinating effort that such a conference required was put together by Canadian Maurice Strong, who was to become the first Executive Director of UNEP, the first UN institution devoted exclusively to the protection of the environment.

The Stockholm Conference produced the Stockholm Declaration on the Human Environment. Some believed that the declaration should begin with a sweeping articulation of every human being's right to a wholesome environment.[135] A rights approach, however, did not prevail. The declaration adopted an anthropocentric approach to the protection of the environment, as the full title of the declaration denotes: "Declaration of the United Nations Conference on the Human Environment."[136]

In the first article of the declaration, an explicit linkage is formulated between human rights and the conditions of living in an environment of quality. According to Principle 1:

> Man has a fundamental right to freedom, equality and adequate conditions of life *in an environment of a quality that permits a life of dignity* and well-being [emphasis added].

The declaration contains the seeds of provisions that were espoused by subsequent legislative instruments. For instance, Principle 2, which refers to the rights of "future generations," could be considered a distant predecessor of the intergenerational equity principle.[137] Principle 9 refers to the special environmental problems caused by underdevelopment, which "can best be remedied by accelerated development through the transfer of substantial quantities of financial and technological

---

[134] See Chapter 8, Sections 1 & 2.

[135] For a detailed analysis of the articles of the Stockholm Declaration and the negotiating history of the declaration, see Louis B. Sohn, The Stockholm Declaration on the Human Environment, 14 Harvard International Law Journal 423 (1973); See also Alexander Kiss, Ten Years after Stockholm: International Environmental Law, 77 Proceedings of the American Society of International Law 411 (1983); Jutta Brunée, The Stockholm Declaration and the Structure and Processes of International Law 67, in The Stockholm Declaration and the Law of the Marine Environment 67 (M.H. Nordquist et al., eds. 2003).

[136] Declaration of the United Nations Conference on the Human Environment, June 16, 1972, A/CONF.48/14 and Corr.1, reprinted in 11 ILM 1416 (1972). The Stockholm Conference was not the first environmental instrument to be adopted internationally. The 1968 African Convention on Conservation of Nature and Natural Resources (see Chapter 7, Section 4.2. and the 1971 Ramsar Treaty, see Chapter 7, Section 3.3, were some of the first conventions to establish stringent rules for the protection of biodiversity. The conventions regarding the prevention of pollution of the sea by oil were some of the first instruments for the regulation of pollution. See Chapter 11.

[137] See Edith Brown Weiss, In Fairness to Future Generations 24 (1989). Inter-generational equity requires each generation to "pass the planet on in no worse condition than it received it and to provide equitable access to its resources and benefits."

assistance . . . , " making, thus, indirect allusion to the right to development that is articulated later in the Rio Declaration. Principle 12 is an expression of the principle of additionality – the fact that *additional* financial assistance must be given to developing countries in order to enable these countries to protect the environment. The principle of additionality was discussed extensively during the climate change and ozone negotiations.

A well-known provision of the Stockholm Declaration is Principle 21. Principle 21 serves a double function. It asserts the sovereign right of states to exploit their natural resources, but it also provides for the

> responsibility [of states] to ensure that activities within their jurisdiction or control do not cause damage to the environment of other States or areas beyond the limits of national jurisdiction.

Principle 21 has launched a debate over the establishment of "international liability" of states for harmful activities that occur under their control but cause damage to the environment of other states.[138] The details of this debate are explored in Chapter 11.

The rest of the 1970s and the 1980s witnessed the accumulation of many environmental instruments. Some of these instruments have played an important role in defining environmental problems in a global or a regional setting. Some of these instruments include the 1972 London Dumping Convention, the Convention on the Trade in Endangered Species (CITES Convention), the UNEP Regional Seas Program, the MARPOL Convention with regard to pollution by ships, the Bonn Convention on the protection of migratory species, and the LRTAP Convention on transboundary air pollution. From a regulatory viewpoint, most of these treaties rarely provided clear standards for action that would bind states to certain outcomes. As these legislative instruments are maturing, their regulatory vise tightens and the inclusion of a command-and-control approach becomes clearer in most of the instruments and, especially, in the instruments that regulate pollution among developed countries.

A decade after the adoption of the Stockholm Declaration, the World Charter for Nature was adopted by the General Assembly.[139] The Charter was sponsored by thirty-four developing nations and was drafted by the International Union for the Conservation of Nature (IUCN) and independent experts. The Charter is divided into General Principles, Functions, and Implementation. The General Principles provide that nature must be respected and that the habitat and life forms must be safeguarded to ensure their survival. The Functions component of the Charter recommends controls on economic development and consideration for the long-term capacity of ecosystems to support human use. The Implementation component encourages countries to adopt domestic and international legislation, develop ecological education, set up funding and administrative arrangements, encourage public participation and planning, assess the impact of military activities on the environment, and establish administrative regulations. The Charter recommends the

---

[138] See Chapter 11, Section 6.
[139] General Assembly Resolution 37/7, World Charter for Nature, A/Res/37/7, Oct. 28, 1982, reprinted in 22 ILM 455 (1983).

application of the environmental impact assessment. Some developing countries opposed the inclusion of environmental impact assessment as they claimed that they were unable to conduct environmental impact assessments of the caliber of assessments performed by developed countries. Other countries objected to the provision of the Charter encouraging the use of best available technology. Some developing countries claimed that the provision makes developing countries, in effect, dependent on developed countries for technology transfers.

Another important development that paved the way to the Rio Summit was the publication of "Our Common Future" in 1987 by the World Commission.[140] The World Commission was created by a 1983 UN General Assembly Resolution and was assigned the task of looking at environmental and development issues and proposing better ways to address them. "Our Common Future" also called the "Brundtland Report" after the chairman of the World Commission (Gro Brundtland), provides a comprehensive overview of various global issues. Such issues include sustainable development, the international economy, the debt crisis, food security, species, ecosystems, industry, the urban challenge, peace and the arms race, climate change, and ozone depletion. A concept that reverberated long after the Brundtland report was completed is the concept of sustainable development, defined as development that satisfies the needs of present generations without jeopardizing the ability of future generations to meet their needs.[141]

In 1989, the UN General Assembly, noting the Brundtland Report, called for the UN Conference on Environment and Development.[142]

4.2. Rio

The UN Conference on Environment and Development (or Earth Summit) was held in Rio de Janeiro between June 3 and June 14, 1992, with the participation of an unprecedented number of NGOs. It produced a number of instruments that have shaped the development of international environmental law until today – the Rio Declaration on Environment and Development,[143] Agenda 21,[144] the Non-Binding Principles on the Sustainable Development of all Types of Forest,[145] the Treaty on Biological Diversity,[146] and the Treaty on Climate Change.[147]

---

[140] World Commission on Environment and Development, Our Common Future (Brundtland Report) (1987).

[141] Id. at 43.

[142] General Assembly Resolution 44/228, United Nations Conference on Environment and Development, A/RES/44/228, Dec. 22, 1989.

[143] Rio Declaration on Environment and Development, June 13, 1992, reprinted in 31 ILM 876 (1992).

[144] A voluminous document that provides the course of action for the management and prevention of many environmental problems. See Agenda 21, June 5, 1992 available online at http://www.un.org/esa/sustdev/documents/agenda21 (Division for Sustainable Development, United Nations Department of Economic & Social Affairs).

[145] Non-Legally Binding Authoritative Statement of Principles for a Global Consensus on the Management, Conservation and Sustainable Development of All Types of Forests, June 13, 1992, reprinted in 31 ILM 881 (1992).

[146] Convention on Biological Diversity, June 5, 1982, reprinted in 31 ILM 822 (1992).

[147] UN Framework Convention on Climate Change, May 9, 1992, reprinted in 31 ILM 849 (1992).

The negotiating history of the Rio Declaration[148] is interesting because it demonstrates the divergence of views between developed and developing countries about the purpose of environmental lawmaking. Some developed countries and NGOs wanted the Rio Summit to conclude with an "Earth Charter" that would concentrate strictly on environmental issues. Such a charter was immediately rejected by G-77 and China as an endorsement of environmental protection at the expense of development. Eventually, the title "Earth Charter " was dropped because the final version of the Rio Declaration failed to assume a purely environmental focus.

Principle 1 of the Rio Declaration reaffirms the anthropocentric character of international environmental law that was evident in the Stockholm Declaration. Principle 1 states that "[h]uman beings are at the centre of concerns for sustainable development." The anthropocentric character of the declaration was preserved because of the persistence of G-77 countries that argued that the Rio Conference was about people and their right to development. Western NGOs and governments, however, had preferred a more ecological and less anthropocentric orientation of the declaration. Developing countries influenced many of the provisions of the declaration including the articulation of a right to development,[149] the definition of sustainable development,[150] the focus on eradication of poverty[151] and on the special needs of developing countries.[152]

Another principle that acquired a more concrete articulation in later treaties[153] is the principle of common but differentiated responsibilities, which clarifies that all countries have responsibility to take measures to protect the environment but that, because "of the different contributions to global environmental degradation, States have common but differentiated responsibilities."[154]

Developed countries pushed for the inclusion of environmental provisions and provisions that promote transparency in decision making. The participation of citizens in the handling of environmental issues and the right to access to information especially with regard to hazardous activities are included in the declaration under the insistence of developed states.[155]

Furthermore, Principle 15 constitutes a careful articulation of the "precautionary approach" that "shall be widely applied by States according to their capabilities." According to the precautionary approach, as endorsed in the declaration:

> Where there are threats of serious or irreversible damage, lack of full scientific certainty shall not be used as a reason for postponing cost-effective measures to prevent environmental degradation.

---

[148] See David Wirth, The Rio Declaration on Environment and Development: Two Steps Forward and One Back or Vice Versa, 29 Georgia Law Review 599 (1995).

[149] Principle 3, Rio Declaration, *supra* note 143.

[150] Principle 4. "In order to achieve sustainable development, environmental protection shall constitute an integral part of the development process and cannot be considered in isolation from it." *Id.*

[151] Principle 5, *id.*

[152] Principle 6, *id.*

[153] See, e.g., Climate Change Treaty, Chapter 8.

[154] Principle 7, Rio Declaration, *supra* note 143. The initial articulation of the principle was more stringent placing essentially the blame on developed countries for the state of the world environmental degradation.

[155] Principle 10, *id.*

As analyzed later in this book, the precautionary principle has been quite controversial. There have been concerns that the precautionary principle can be used as a trade barrier[156] and could create a bias against new technologies and processes based on mere fear rather than scientific evidence.[157]

Another principle that was adopted in Rio under the pressure of developed countries is the "polluter pays principle."[158] It has been frequently said that polluters cause externalities (air emissions, water pollution) that are not borne by them exclusively but by the society as a whole. It has been claimed that if polluters are made to internalize (incorporate into the price of products and processes) the costs of pollution, pollution would subsequently be reduced. The final bearer of the costs of pollution, however, is the consumer, as industry passes on at least some of the cost of prevention of environmental degradation to the consumer. The question then is whether the consumer will be willing to internalize the costs of environmental degradation of products s/he uses. It is interesting to note that states have been reluctant to adhere to a strict polluter pays principle at the interstate level. After the Chernobyl disaster, none of the countries affected by the accident requested damages from the Soviet Union for the repercussions of the accident on its territory. Furthermore, some conventions are based on a solidarity rationale – in the sense that "victims" of pollution and "perpetrators" share in the cost of managing an environment problem – rather than on a strict polluter pays principle.[159]

Principle 7 is an enunciation of the requirement to apply environmental impact assessment "for proposed activities that are likely to have a significant adverse impact on the environment and are subject to a decision of a competent national authority." A treaty on Environmental Assessment had been adopted a year before the UNCED Conference under the auspices of the UN/ECE.[160]

Principle 19 articulates the duty of states to notify and consult with other states regarding activities that may have "a significant adverse transboundary environmental effect." The duty of notification and consultation has been included in many environmental instruments. Whether states do indeed notify and consult with their neighboring countries on activities that are likely to have damaging transboundary effects, however, probably depends on the interstate relationships in a region.[161]

Principle 2 is a rearticulation of Principle 21 of the Stockholm Declaration that reaffirms the sovereignty of states over their natural resources.[162] It is repeated in the principle that states have "the responsibility to ensure that activities within their jurisdiction and control do not cause damage to environment of other Sates or of areas beyond the limits of national jurisdiction."

---

[156] See *infra* Section 6.3.

[157] *Id.*

[158] Principle 16, Rio Declaration, *supra* note 143.

[159] See Convention on the Salinity of the Rhine, Chapter 5, Section 5.4.2.

[160] 1991 Convention on Environmental Impact Assessment, see Chapter 3, Section 1.

[161] In some cases, states simply present affected states with after-the-fact situations see, e.g., Chapter 5, note 313.

[162] Principle 2 provides for the "sovereign right [of states] to exploit their own resources pursuant to their own environmental and developmental policies." See Rio Declaration, *supra* note 143.

Principle 22 recognizes the role of indigenous peoples in environmental and developmental matters and encourages states to enable the effective participation of indigenous peoples in the pursuit of sustainable development.

Some commentators were disappointed by the outcome of the Rio Declaration, characterizing it as a step back from Stockholm.[163] The disappointment had to do with the fact that the declaration failed to deal with environmental concerns in a clear fashion and became infused, instead, with disparate provisions hard to hold together in a cohesive text. Others have appraised the declaration more positively[164] as an honest articulation of the needs and desires of a world comprised of countries with different levels of industrialization and wealth.

Agenda 21 is the multivoluminous voluntary agenda that was adopted by states at the Rio Conference. The agenda proposes the adoption of a number of national, regional, and global measures to address environmental problems and to promote sustainable development.

Agenda 21 covers a vast array of environmental issues including the protection of atmosphere and biodiversity; the protection of seas and oceans and integrated coastal zone management; the management of chemicals and hazardous and radioactive wastes; issues of poverty and population control; and the role of workers, trade unions, business and industry, farmers, and indigenous peoples in the promotion of sustainable development.[165]

Agenda a section on implementation. According to Agenda 21, the implementation of environmental legislation requires financial resources, technology transfers to developing countries, capacity building at the local and international levels, education, increase in public awareness and training, and international institutional development.[166]

Agenda 21 recommended the establishment of the Commission on Sustainable Development (CSD). The Commission on Sustainable Development was established as a functional commission of the ECOSOC. According to the General Assembly resolution, that established CSD, the role of the CSD is to monitor the progress of Agenda 21 by gathering information from various sources; reviewing the access to financial, technological, and other resources; and serving as a forum for the discussion of environmental and developmental issues.[167]

After the UNCED Conference, there were many legislative activities to update many of the 1970s and 1980s instruments, in accordance with the UNCED provisions, including the incorporation of the polluter pays principle and the precautionary principle, as well as more specific standards and regulations.

4.3. Johannesburg

The Johannesburg summit or World Summit on Sustainable Development (WSSD) was held in 2002, ten years after the Earth Summit. The WSSD was somewhat a

---

[163] See Wirth, *supra* note 148.
[164] David Freestone, The Road from Rio: International Environmental Law after the Earth Summit, 6 Journal of Environmental Law 19 (1994).
[165] See Chapters 33–40, Agenda 21, *supra* note 144.
[166] See Chapter 38, *id.*
[167] General Assembly Resolution 47/191, A/Res/47/191, Dec. 23, 1992.

disappointment for environmentalists who would have liked the adoption of new more stringent standards and timetables for the accomplishment of environmental objectives. In fact, many NGOs denounced the summit as a failure. United Nations officials were relieved, by contrast, that the conference did not completely break down.[168] Several of the targets and timetables that were proposed in the summit were eventually eliminated or diluted. For instance, a proposal by the European Union and some Latin American countries to adopt a numerical goal for the amount of energy to be obtained from renewable resources was opposed by the oil-producing countries and the United States. The final provision adopted provided for an increased reliance on renewable resources without providing for a specific target.

The summit adopted two documents: the Declaration on Sustainable Development[169] and the Plan of Implementation.[170]

The declaration moves the environmental agenda closer to the concerns of developing countries. Some of the provisions of the declaration include:

- the focus on human dignity;[171]
- the allusion to sustainable development as based on three pillars – economic development, social development, and environmental protection;[172]
- the focus on the reduction of poverty and on reducing the gap between the rich and the poor;[173]
- the challenge of globalization;[174]
- the focus on Least-Developed Countries and Small Island States;[175]
- the need to develop "more effective, democratic, and accountable" institutions.[176]

The Implementation Plan provides targets for social issues facing mostly developing countries and sets specific goals such as:

- halving by the year 2015 the proportion of world's people whose income is less than $1 per day,[177] and the proportion of people suffering from hunger;[178]
- achieving significant improvement in the lives of at least one hundred million slum dwellers by 2020;[179]
- halving by the year 2015 the proportion of people without access to safe drinking water;[180]

---

[168] Hilary French, From Rio to Johannesburg and Beyond: Assessing the Summit, Oct. 22, 2002, Worldwatch Institute Press Release.

[169] Sept. 4, 2002 available online at http://www.johannesburgsummit.org [hereinafter Declaration].

[170] Sept. 4, 2002 available online at http://www.johannesburgsummit.org [hereinafter Plan of Implementation].

[171] Paras. 2 & 18, Declaration, *supra* note 169.

[172] Para. 5, *id.*

[173] Paras. 3 & 12, *id.*

[174] Para. 14, *id.*

[175] Para. 24, *id.*

[176] Para. 31, *id.*

[177] Para. 6(a), Plan of Implementation, *supra* note 170.

[178] Para. 8, *id.*

[179] Para. 10, *id.*

[180] Para. 6(a), *id.*

- reducing by 2015 the mortality rates for infants and children under five by two-thirds and maternal mortality by three-quarters, using as a baseline the 2000 mortality rate;[181]
- reducing the HIV/AIDs infection among young people aged fifteen to twenty-four by 25 percent in most affected countries by 2005, and globally by 2010, and supporting a global fund to fight AIDs, malaria and tuberculosis;[182]
- ensuring that by 2015 all children will be able to complete a full course of primary schooling;[183]
- developing integrated water resources and water efficiency plans by 2005[184] (including the support of water allocation based on human needs, para. 25 (c));
- encouraging by 2010 the application of the ecosystem approach to the management of the oceans;[185]
- maintaining or restoring fish stocks to levels that produce maximum sustainable yield by 2015;[186]
- achieving significant reduction of the current loss of biological diversity by 2010;[187]
- encouraging the adoption of a harmonized system for the classification and labeling of chemicals by 2008;[188]
- aiming to achieve by 2020 the use and production of chemicals that led to the minimization of adverse effects on human health and the environment.[189]

The Implementation Plan refers to the TRIPs (Trade-Related Intellectual Property Rights) agreement, which was adopted as a subsidiary agreement to the treaty that established the WTO. The controversy that surrounded the TRIPs agreement is analyzed in more detail in Chapter 9. The TRIPs agreement was viewed by many in the developing world as an agreement designed to protect the interests of large pharmaceutical corporations residing in the North at the expense of the health of people in the developing world. The Implementation Plan, therefore, provides specifically that

> the TRIPs Agreement does not and should not prevent WTO members from taking measures to protect public health. Accordingly, while reiterating our commitment to the TRIPs Agreement, we reaffirm that the Agreement can and should be interpreted in a manner supportive of WTO's members' right to protect public health and in particular to promote access to medicines for all.[190]

Overall, the social and economic provisions included in the Implementation Plan overwhelm the strictly environmental provisions. Reading through the Plan, one

---

[181] Para. 46(f), *id.*
[182] Para. 48, *id.*
[183] Para. 109(a), *id.*
[184] Para. 25, *id.*
[185] Para. 29(d), *id.*
[186] Para. 30(a), *id.*
[187] Para. 42, *id.*
[188] Para. 22(c), *id.*
[189] Para. 22(a), *id.*
[190] Para. 94, *id.*

gets the impression of going through an economic and social declaration rather than a *stricto sensu* plan of environmental implementation.

During the WSSD, certain partnerships were fostered among NGOs. According to some commentators, the WSSD strengthened the commitment of states to provide financial sources for the cause of sustainable development.[191]

4.4. From Stockholm to Johannesburg

The Stockholm Conference, and ensuing environmental legislation, was one of the first attempts to deal with environmental problems at a global scale. The result was a number of instruments that did not offer clear standards but, nevertheless, helped create state consensus that some environmental problems need to be tackled internationally.

The Rio Conference was a first attempt to deal with the complexity that many environmental problems present. The conventions that followed the Rio Conference are decidedly more elaborate instruments than those that preceded it. The Rio Conference created an impetus to include clear and enforceable standards in international instruments that states would be held accountable to implement. The instruments adopted after the Rio Conference present more resemblance to the command-and-control legislation of many developed countries.

The Rio Conference was significant because it was an attempt to find a common ground between what developed states wanted to accomplish and what developing countries stood for. Concepts such as sustainable development and common but differentiated responsibilities sounded initially like principles deprived of concrete content. In the aftermath of the conference, they have acquired strength and have defined many subsequent international and local developments. Today, the concept of sustainable development with its three pillars articulates successfully some of the conditions of sustainable growth. The social and economic pillars are as important as the environmental pillar. The concept has had an effect even on localities within developed countries with the enunciation of the concept of "sustainable communities."[192] The principle of common but differentiated responsibilities has found articulation in the climate change and ozone regimes through the provision of payments to developing countries in order to induce their compliance with international agreements. Overall, the Rio Conference provided an opportunity for developing countries to use the environmental agenda as a means to advance their concerns about development and growth.

---

[191] During the WSSD, a number of countries made commitments for the furtherance of the goals of the summit. An agreement was made, for instance, to replenish the GEF with the amount of $3 billion. The UN received thirty-two partnership initiatives with $100 million in resources for biodiversity and ecosystem management, twenty-one partnerships for water and sanitation with at least $20 million in resources, and thirty-two partnerships for energy projects with $26 million in resources. The EU announced that it would increase its development assistance by more than 9 billion annually from 2006 onward. The United States announced $970 million in investments over the next three years for water and sanitation projects and Japan announced 250 billion donation for education over a five-year period.

[192] The concept of sustainable communities has been applied in some communities in the United States, see *infra* note 275.

The WSSD promoted issues of social and economic development with a new sense of urgency. The conference has more to do with ensuring that countries accomplish a level of development than with providing for new environmental standards. Putting issues of development at the core of what was initially conceived as an environmental summit demonstrates the difficulty involved in isolating environmental concerns from the pursuit of growth. The WSSD has posed the question of the purpose of environmental protection in a world where many people are suffering still from poverty and disease. It is question worth asking.

4.5. Case Law

The development of international environmental law has been influenced by the decisions of the International Court of Justice and other tribunals that have tried to apply in practice the principles of international law.

The *Corfu Channel* case was brought before the ICJ by the United Kingdom in the aftermath of World War II.[193] The case concerned the damage to ships and injuries to officers of the British navy by a minefield located in the Corfu Strait, allegedly planted by Albania. The United Kingdom claimed that the Albanian government knew about the minefield and failed to notify the British ships that were passing through the strait, exercising their right to innocent passage. The British government further claimed that the Albanian government should be required to make reparations because it breached its international obligation of notification. Albania, by contrast, claimed that it knew nothing about the minefield.

The Court concluded that the fact that the minefield had been recently laid and the fact that Albania had kept close watch on its territorial waters, during the time the minefield was set, rendered Albania's lack of knowledge improbable. The Court took into account, as additional evidence of Albania's knowledge, what happened after the minefield explosion – namely, that the Greek authorities had appointed a committee to inquire into the event whereas the Albanian government had not done so. The Court found that the Albanian government should have notified the British warships of the existence of the minefield. The Court mentioned that such an obligation was not necessarily based on an international treaty but:

> on certain general and well-recognized principles, namely: elementary considerations of humanity, even more exacting in peace than war; the principles of the freedom of maritime communication; and every State's obligation not to allow knowingly its territory to be used for acts contrary to the rights of other States.[194]

The pronouncement of the Court of every state's obligation not to allow its territory to be used for acts contrary to the rights of other states has been repeated frequently in cases of polluting/hazardous activities that may have adverse affects on the territory of another state. Such obligation implies a duty of a polluting state to notify other states for acts that it knows happen within its territory and can adversely affect other states. The duty of notification, which has been repeated in many international

---

[193] Corfu Channel Case, (UK v. Albania), April 9, 1949, (1949) ICJ Reports 4.
[194] *Id.* at 22.

environmental instruments,[195] was initially articulated in the *Corfu Channel* case. It must be noted also that the Court referred to "elementary considerations of humanity" that made the conduct of Albania unlawful. Thus, humanity considerations, no matter how imprecise they sound, become a criterion for judging the behavior of states.

Another case with a clearer environmental focus is the *Trail Smelter* case.[196] This case involved a dispute between the United States and Canada regarding the damage to United States territory inflicted by sulphur dioxide emissions from a smelting plant at the Consolidated Mining and Smelting Company of Canada at Trail, located in the British Columbia. In 1935, Canada and the United States agreed to submit the dispute to arbitration.

The tribunal concluded, after examining domestic and international law, that:

> under the principles of international law . . . no State has the right to use or permit the use of its territory in such a manner as to cause injury by fumes in or to the territory of another or the properties or persons therein, when the case is of serious consequence and the injury is established by clear and convincing evidence.[197]

This conclusion of the tribunal has been cited frequently in international environmental law writings as evidence of the establishment of the concept of state liability for environmental harm. However, it must be noted that the tribunal carefully stated that state liability applies only when "the case is of serious consequence" and that additionally the injury must be established "by clear and convincing evidence."[198] Furthermore, in the *Trial Smelter* case, Canada had in some way acquiesced to pay some damages by virtue of the fact that it had paid damages before 1932 and had agreed to put the issue to arbitration.[199]

The tribunal recognized the payment of damages for concrete cases of environmental harm but was not receptive of general claims for damage to the environment. The tribunal recognized damages for cleared and uncleared land using the standard established by the U.S. courts in cases of nuisance and trespass – that is, the amount of reduction in "value of use or rental value" of the land caused by the fumes.[200] The market value of the land was the criterion that was used, therefore, to establish the amount of damages and not some sort of evaluation of natural resources damage. The tribunal did not award damages for pastured lands, damage to livestock, and property damage in the town of Northport. The tribunal did not award damages to business enterprises.[201] The tribunal concluded that some of these damages were too remote and uncertain and that the parties failed to provide proof. The tribunal did

---

[195] See Chapter 3, Section 2.2.

[196] Trail Smelter Case, (United States v. Canada), April 16, 1931, March 11, 1941, 3 UN Reports of International Arbitral Awards 1905 (1941).

[197] *Id*. at 1907.

[198] See also William A. Nitze, Acid Rain: A United States Policy Perspective, in International Law and Pollution 329, 338 (Daniel Barstow Magraw, ed., 1991).

[199] Samuel Bleicher, An Overview of International Environmental Regulation, 2 Ecology Law Quarterly 1, 22 (1972).

[200] Trial Smelter case, *supra* note 196, at 1907.

[201] *Id*.

not award any damages for the injurious effects of the disposal of waste slag in the Columbia river, thus rejecting explicitly, a claim for pure environmental damages.[202]

Although the tribunal was conservative in the award of damages, it played a more decisive regulatory role. The tribunal ordered Canada to establish controls on the emissions of sulphur dioxide by providing for maximum permissible sulfur emissions including detailed requirements for hourly emissions.

The *Trail Smelter* case has launched a discourse in international law about whether a standard of state responsibility or strict state liability has been established for polluting activities. If such a standard has been established the question is what the prerequisites are for the success of a claim of strict liability in international incidents of pollution. As analyzed earlier, the tribunal required that the polluting acts must be "of serious consequence" and that the injury must be established by clear and convincing evidence. These requirements set a high threshold for the establishment of a standard of state liability. Policy makers must clarify two points:

- The polluting activities must be "of serious consequence." Because some form of pollution is part of everyday life, the amount and nature of pollution that is significant for the establishment of a strict liability claim under international law must be clearly established.
- There must be clear and convincing evidence of harm. This is a difficult requirement to meet, as the *Trail Smelter* case itself demonstrates. Most of the damage to environment is hard to establish, as the scientific evidence is often inconclusive.

The *Lac Lanoux* case[203] involved a decision taken by France (an upstream state) to build a barrage on the Carol River for the purposes of hydroelectricity production. France intended to divert the waters of the Carol River before returning them to Spain, where they would be used for agricultural irrigation. Spain claimed that the diversion of waters by France was against its interests, despite the eventual restitution of waters to their original destination. Because the restitution of waters was dependent on the will of France, Spain claimed that one party was preponderant in water management. Such preponderance was against the equality of the parties established in the water treaties that had been signed between the parties.[204]

The tribunal held that although France is entitled to exercise its rights, it cannot ignore Spanish interests. Spain is entitled to demand that its rights are respected and that its interests are taken into consideration.[205] But the tribunal held that taking into account Spain's interests does not mean that France must seek an agreement with Spain before constructing works on shared river resources. The tribunal held that subjecting a state's right to use its watercourses to the completion of a prior agreement with another state would give that other state essentially "a right to veto"

---

[202] For an extensive analysis of the Trial Smelter case, see Edith Brown Weiss et al., International Environmental Law and Policy 245–62 (1998).

[203] Lac Lanoux Arbitration, (France v. Spain), Nov. 16. 1957, 12 UN Reports of International Arbitral Awards 281 (1957).

[204] The three treaties at Bayonne on Dec. 1, 1856, April 14, 1862, May 26, 1866. According to Spain, the French scheme establishes "a preponderance which is repugnant to the spirit of equality which inspires [the treaty between the parties]." See Lac Lanoux case, pleadings of Spain, *id.*

[205] Para. 24, *id.*

that paralyzes the exercise of territorial competence of one State at the discretion of another state.[206] The tribunal further stated:

> the rule according to which States may utilize the hydraulic force of international watercourses only on condition of a *prior* agreement between the interested States cannot be established as a custom, nor even less as a general principle of law.[207]

The tribunal took into account that France held negotiations with Spain after which its positions had "undergone greater re-adaptation and even transformation." The tribunal held accordingly that no matter how inconclusive those negotiations had been France must still give "a reasonable place to adverse interests in the solution it adopts."[208]

In the aftermath of the *Lac Lanoux* case, a new bilateral treaty was signed between France and Spain. A six-member commission was established to ensure that the agreement would be implemented. If Electricité de France is not able to deliver the amount of water agreed to Spain, France can take all necessary measures to resolve the situation including making reparations.[209]

The *Lac Lanoux* case has been heralded as establishing the principle of prior consultation with another state before undertaking a project that has transboundary effects.[210] Such a principle has been repeated in a number of international instruments, including the Environmental Impact Assessment (EIA) Convention.[211] Other important legal issues are the principle of equity among coriparian states and the hypothetical conclusion of the case if Spain had argued that the French project inflicted damages on its territory. With regard to a possible environmental claim, the tribunal seems to have indicated that Spain would have had a stronger argument if it had proven that the French project was harmful – in terms of the adverse effects of the composition or temperature of waters diverted to Spain's agricultural fields.[212] With regard to the equity among coriparian states, the tribunal supported the sovereignty and ensuing rights of upstream states. But the tribunal concluded also that such sovereignty is not untrammeled as an upstream state has the duty to take into account, at least, the interests of downstream states by means of negotiation.

The *Behring Sea Seals* cases were the first cases that dealt with the protection marine mammals as early as in 1893[213] and 1902.[214] The question that was put in front of the tribunal was whether states had jurisdiction to enact conservation measures for the protection of marine mammals in the high seas. The tribunal rejected claims that states had such jurisdiction and declared the freedom of the high seas. However, the

---

[206] Para. 11, *id.*

[207] Para. 13, *id.*

[208] Para. 24, *id.*

[209] Sergei Vinogradov et al., Transforming Potential Conflict into Cooperation Potential, UNESCO, Technical Documents in Hydrology 7, PCCP Series, No. 2, 2003.

[210] Para. 24, Lac Lanoux case, *supra* note 203.

[211] See Chapter 3.

[212] Para. 6, Lac Lanoux case, *supra* note 203.

[213] Behring Sea Seals Arbitration, (Great Britain v. United States), 1 Moore's International Arbitration Awards 755 (1893).

[214] The 1902 Behring Sea arbitration involved United States claims against Russia for assuming property rights over the high seas. The United States used the same arguments that the British had used in the 1893 case.

decision is interesting in that the tribunal encouraged states to adopt regulations to protect the seals. The tribunal actually proposed regulatory measures that prompted states to conclude agreements for the management of seal stocks.[215]

The 1893 *Behring Sea* arbitration case arose out of years of controversies regarding the need to protect fur seals in the high seas in order to make conservation measures meaningful in the territorial waters. The United States decided to assert its claim against the United Kingdom for the protection of seals in the high seas by seizing British ships. The United States claimed that the industry that exploited seals had property rights over the seals and that these rights could be defended in the high seas by exercising the United States' right to self-defense. The British government claimed that seals in the high seas, like other fisheries resources, could be exploited by all according to the principle of freedom of the high seas which includes the freedom of fishing. The tribunal sided with the United Kingdom, affirming the freedom of the high seas and denying state property rights on common property resources, but the tribunal mandated regulatory standards for the protection of seals.[216] Later tribunals have been more willing to recognize more extensive rights of coastal states for the protection of high-seas fisheries.[217]

The *Oder* and *Meuse* cases involve disputes regarding the use of transboundary rivers. The *Oder* case,[218] which was brought before the Permanent Court of International Justice in 1920, examined the extent of jurisdictional reach of the International Commission of the River Oder put together by the coriparians to regulate the use of the river. According to the Polish position, the jurisdiction of the Commission stopped at the Polish border and did not extend to sections and tributaries of Oder that were situated within the Polish territory. The Court held that the basic concept that dominates this area of law, namely, navigable use of international watercourses, is that "of a community of interests of riparian States." This community of interests leads in itself to a common legal right. The basic features of such a common right "are the perfect equality of all riparian States" in the use of the whole watercourse and "the exclusion of any preferential privilege of any one riparian state in relation to the others."[219] The Court held that the jurisdiction of the International Oder Commission extended to sections of Oder located within the Polish territory. The facts of the case restrict the case to the navigational uses of

---

215 Convention Respecting Measures for the Preservation and Protection of the Fur Seals in the North Pacific Ocean, July 7, 1911. The convention has been considered successful in restoring the fur seal population. It was denounced by Japan in 1940. The convention was replaced by the Interim Convention on Conservation of North Pacific Fur Seals, Feb. 9, 1957. The convention established the North Pacific Fur Seals Commission (NPFSC). The convention was further amended, see Protocol Amending the Interim Convention on the Conservation of North Pacific Fur Seals, Oct. 14, 1980. See also Protocol Amending the Interim Convention on Conservation of North Pacific Fur Seals, Oct. 12, 1984. For the text of the treaties and brief summaries, see http://ww.intfish.net/treaties (Internet Guide to International Fisheries Law).

216 See Myres S. McDougal & William T. Burke, The Public Order of the Oceans 948–50 (1962). See also Ian Brownlie, Principles of Public International Law 232–33 (1998).

217 See, e.g., Fisheries Jurisdiction case, Chapter 6, Section 3.5

218 Territorial Jurisdiction of the International Commission of the River Oder, (Denmark, Czechoslovakia, France, Germany, the United Kingdom, and Sweden v. Poland), Sept. 10, 1929, PCIJ Series A, No 23.

219 *Id.* at 27.

international watercourses. The case has been viewed, nevertheless, as a precursor of the principle of equitable utilization of water resources that was enunciated later in the 1997 UN Watercourses Convention.[220]

Another case that deals with the apportionment of shared water resources is the *Meuse* case.[221] In 1863, the Netherlands and Belgium had signed a treaty that would settle permanently and definitely the use of the Meuse for the purposes of canal irrigation and navigation. The treaty provided for one intake in the Netherlands territory that would be the feeder for all canals situated below the town of Maastricht. As the developmental needs of the two states became more acute, the parties tried unsuccessfully to enter into a new agreement in 1925. After the failure to reach an agreement, the Netherlands proceeded with the construction of new canals and barrages on the Meuse, and Belgium did the same. In their submissions to the Court, the parties asked the Court to declare each other's works on the river to be in violation of the 1863 treaty. The Netherlands claimed that the treaty provided for the construction of only one intake that allowed it to control all intakes, including those located in the Belgian territory. The Court held that this would place the parties in a situation of legal inequality. In the absence of a treaty that establishes explicitly such inequality, the claim of the Netherlands, the Court argued, must be rejected. Eventually, the Court rejected both the claims of the Netherlands and the counterclaims of Belgium, and held that:

> As regards such canals, each of the two States is at liberty, in its own territory, to modify them . . . *provided that the diversion of water at the treaty feeder and the volume of water to be discharged therefrom to maintain the normal level and flow . . . is not affected*" [emphasis added].

The concurring opinion of Judge Hudson elucidates further the conclusions of the majority as he explicitly refers to the principle of equity between coriparian nations. The judge stated: "A sharp division between law and equity . . . should find no place in international jurisprudence."[222] Based on the principle of equity, the Netherlands cannot ask Belgium to discontinue the operation of its lock when Netherlands is free to operate its own lock.[223]

The judicial decisions on the use of watercourses demonstrate the importance of the principle of equity in the development of international law. The equity principle is certainly a fluid principle because what is equitable is determined by taking into account the circumstances of each case. Despite its fluidity, however, or because of it, the principle has played an important role in shaping perceptions of legitimacy in the allocation of common resources. Chapter 5 examines in detail the principle of equitable utilization in a number of treaties concerned with the protection of waters in specific regions.

An ICJ advisory opinion on the legality of the use of nuclear weapons has been cited frequently as an affirmation of the principles of international environmental law

---

[220] Stephen C. McCaffrey, The Law of International Watercourses 182–83 (2001).

[221] The Diversion of Water from the Meuse, June 28, 1937, (1937) PCIJ Series A/B, No. 70.

[222] *Id.* at 76.

[223] *Id.*

stated in the *Trail Smelter* case. The General Assembly of the United Nations asked the Court to give an advisory opinion on the legality of use of nuclear weapons.[224] The Court rejected the argument that the use of nuclear weapons infringed on the right to life as stated in the Covenant on Civil and Political Rights. According to the Court, the arbitrary deprivation of life cannot be judged by simply using the Covenant but by referring also to the law applicable in armed conflict.[225] States have the right to self-defense, a right that does not preclude the use of nuclear weapons.

Having said that, the Court emphasized that:

> the environment is under daily threat and that the use of nuclear weapons could constitute a catastrophe for the environment.

The Court stated that

> the environment is not an abstraction but represents the living space, the quality of life and the very health of human beings, including generations unborn. The existence of the general obligation of States to ensure that activities within their jurisdiction and control respect the environment of other States or of areas beyond national control is now part of the corpus of international law relating to the environment.[226]

The Court further stated that, although environmental treaties do not deprive states of their right to self-defense, states:

> must take environmental considerations into account when assessing what is necessary and proportionate in the pursuit of legitimate military objectives. Respect for environment is one of the elements that go to assessing whether an action is in conformity with the principles of necessity and proportionality.[227]

The Court concluded that international environmental law does not specifically prohibit the use of nuclear weapons but provides important environmental factors to be taken into account in the implementation of principles that apply to armed conflict.[228] The Court stated that it could not reach a decision with regard to the legality or illegality of the use of nuclear weapons by a state in an extreme circumstance of self-defense in which the very survival of a state would be at stake. But the Court

---

[224] Legality of the Threat or Use of Nuclear Weapons, (Advisory Opinion), July 8, 1996, (1996) ICJ Reports 226 [hereinafter Legality of Nuclear Weapons].

  The World Health Organization (WHO) asked also for the ICJ's advisory opinion with regard to the legality of the use of nuclear weapons in cases of armed conflict. The WHO asked for an advisory opinion because of its mandate as an organization concerned with health and, consequently, with the adverse effects of nuclear weapons on human health and the environment. The Court held that a specialized agency, such as WHO, could ask for an advisory opinion if three conditions are satisfied: (1) the agency is authorized under the Charter to ask for opinions; (2) the opinion requested is on a legal question; (3) the question arose under the scope of the activities of the requesting agency. The Court concluded that in the case of the WHO the first two conditions were satisfied. But the latter condition was not satisfied because the competence of the WHO to deal with the effects of the use of nuclear weapons on health "is not dependent on the legality of the acts that caused them." See Paras. 20–26, Legality of the Threat or Use of Nuclear Weapons (Advisory Opinion), July 8, 1996, (1996) ICJ Reports 66.

[225] Para. 24–25, Legality of Nuclear Weapons, *id.*

[226] Para. 29, *id.*

[227] Para. 30, *id.*

[228] Para. 33, *id.*

held that a threat of use or the use of nuclear weapons would generally be contrary to the rules of international law applicable in armed conflict, and, in particular, to the principles and rules of humanitarian law.[229] Thus, in addition to asserting the obligation of states to respect the environment of other states, when engaging in activities under their jurisdiction and control, the Court underlined the importance of environmental considerations in informing the principles of proportionality and necessity in the pursuit of armed conflict.

The *Nuclear Tests* cases have influenced the development of international environmental law, not for the eventual conclusions of the Court, but because of the *dicta* included in the Court's ordering of provisional measures and the pleadings of the parties. In the *Nuclear Tests* cases, France was challenged by New Zealand[230] and Australia[231] for conducting nuclear testing in the Pacific that had allegedly adverse effects on their territory. In more detail, the governments of Australia and New Zealand asked the Court to declare that carrying further atmospheric tests in the South Pacific was not consistent with the rules of international law[232] and violated their rights under international law.[233] France did not appear in the proceedings and did not file any pleadings. France challenged the jurisdiction of the Court. During the course of Court deliberations on the jurisdictional issue, France declared its intention to stop atmospheric testing "under normal conditions" and to shift its operations underground. New Zealand and Australia objected that France's declaration [234] on the cessation of atmospheric testing did not offer sufficient assurance that nuclear testing would cease. Despite these objections, the Court concluded that the unilateral declaration of France to stop nuclear testing constituted an undertaking of an *erga omnes* obligation to stop such testing.[235] The Court held that the dispute no longer existed[236] and that proceeding with the case would have no meaning.[237] Thus, the Court did not decide on the legality of nuclear testing.[238]

Before proceeding with the question of jurisdiction, Australia and New Zealand had asked the Court to issue provisional measures for the cessation of atmospheric testing,[239] which the Court did, putting a temporary injunction on nuclear testing. In taking these provisional measures, the Court took into account the claims of Australia

---

[229] Para. 105, *id.*

[230] Nuclear Tests Case, (New Zealand v. France), (Judgment), Dec. 20, 1974, (1974) ICJ 457 [hereinafter New Zealand case].

[231] Nuclear Tests Case, (Australia v. France), (Judgment), Dec. 20, 1974, (1974) ICJ 253 [hereinafter Australia case].

[232] Para. 11, *id.*

[233] Para. 11, New Zealand case, *supra* note 230.

[234] According to one of the statements made by the French authorities: "Thus the atmospheric tests which are soon to be carried out will, in the normal course of events, be the last of this type." See Para. 35, *id.*

[235] Para. 50, *id.*

[236] Para. 55, *id.*

[237] Para. 56, *id.*

[238] For the issue on whether unilateral declarations expressed *erga omnes* have a legally binding effect, see Ian Brownlie, Principles of Public International Law 644 (1998). See also Thomas M. Franck, Word Made Law, 69 American Journal of International Law 612 (1975).

[239] Nuclear Tests Case, (New Zealand v. France), (Interim Measures), June 22, 1973, (1973) ICJ Reports 135; Nuclear Tests Case, (Australia v. France), (Interim Measures), June 22, 1973, (1973) ICJ Reports 99.

and New Zealand regarding their right to "be free from atmospheric nuclear tests by any country." In ordering the interim measures, the Court noted the claims formulated by the government of Australia, namely:

(i) The right of Australia and its people, in common with other States and their peoples, to be free from atmospheric nuclear weapons tests by any country . . . ;
(ii) The deposit of radioactive fall-out on the territory of Australia and its dispersion in Australia's airspace *without Australia's consent*:
   (a) violates Australian sovereignty over its territory;
   (b) impairs Australia's independent right to determine what acts shall take place within its territory and in particular whether Australia and its people shall be exposed to radiation from artificial sources;
(iii) interference with ships and aircraft on the high seas and in the superjacent airspace, and the pollution of the high seas by radioactive fall-out, constitute infringements of the freedom of the high seas [emphasis added].[240]

Thus, one can detect from the claims of Australia an expectation that a state must obtain the consent of potentially injured states in the conduct of what may be perceived as ultrahazardous activities. And this is despite the claims of France that radioactive fallout from nuclear testing was so infinitesimal that it may be regarded as negligible.[241] One of the dissenting judges in the case, Judge De Castro, stated that the case involves an application of the principle articulated in the *Trail Smelter* case according to which no state has the right to use its territory for activities that would cause injury in another state.[242]

5. GLOBALIZATION AND INTERNATIONAL LAW

The notion of globalization has entered formally the vocabulary of international environmental law with the WSSD in 2002. In the Plan of Implementation, under the section "Sustainable development in a globalized world," it is mentioned that:

Globalization offers opportunities and challenges for sustainable development . . . globalization and interdependence are offering new opportunities to trade, investment capital flows and advances in technology, including information technology, for the growth of the world economy, development and the improvement of living standards around the world.[243]

It is also mentioned that:

Globalization *should be fully inclusive and equitable*, and there is a strong need for policies and measures at the national and international levels, formulated and implemented with the full and effective participation of developing countries and countries with economies in transition, to help them to respond effectively to those challenges and opportunities [emphasis added].[244]

[240] Para. 22, Interim Measures, Australia, *id*.
[241] Para. 18, Australia case, *supra* note 231.
[242] Dissenting opinion Judge De Castro, Australia case, *id*. at 388–89.
[243] Para. 45, Plan of Implementation, WSSD, *supra* note 170.
[244] *Id*.

Globalization takes place as economic globalization, cultural globalization, and communications globalization.[245] Economic globalization has been defined as the:

> integration of national economies into the international economy through trade, direct foreign investment (by corporations and multinationals), short-term capital flows, international flows of workers and humanity generally, and flows of technology.[246]

Globalization has been blamed for many of the ills of the world today. Antiglobalizers claim that globalization is responsible for the increasing gap between the rich and the poor, the unfair labor standards in the developing world, and the deterioration of the environment. They generally equate globalization with the blind faith in free markets. The World Trade Organization, the World Bank, and the International Monetary Fund have been castigated for the uncritical pursuit of free market policies, neglecting the need for the creation of a social safety net that would shield those most vulnerable in our societies from the abrupt changes that globalization entails. These institutions, the discontents with globalization claim, are imposing changes in the developing world in the style of untrammeled free market principles[247] without paying due attention to the importance of timing and sequencing reform.[248] Timing and sequencing reform could help avoid social disruption that undermines the very social fabric of developing societies.[249]

The discontent with globalization is expressed as anti–free markets and anticorporation. Free markets may have triumphed as the economic system of the twenty-first century but have failed to capture the hearts and minds of people who crave for social justice.[250]

The anticorporation strand comes from the belief that corporations have taken and will continue to take advantage of the lower labor and environmental standards in developing countries transferring, thus, pollution to other localities and engaging in inhumane labor practices. Antiglobalizers wish to level the playing field so that environmental and labor standards – as they have been established in developed countries – are respected uniformly all across the world and that the race to the bottom is avoided.[251] Furthermore, discontents with globalization have a firm belief in the limits of markets and share a fear that markets spur commercialization at the expense of value systems of societies.

Defenders of globalization have claimed, by contrast, that overall globalization has increased wealth and has served the poor in countries such as India and China with the largest poverty numbers in the world. Both the countries had followed an isolationist trade stance in the 1970s. They reverted to more open economic policies in 1980s and 1990s, having as a result a much higher growth rate.[252] With regard to environmental standards, defenders of globalization are quick to note that the race to the bottom has yet to happen. This is because environmental standards are only one

[245] Jagdish Bhagwati, In Defense of Globalization 3–4 (2004).
[246] *Id.* at 3.
[247] *Id.* at 99.
[248] Joseph E. Stiglitz, Globalization and its Discontents 57 (2003).
[249] *Id.* at 77.
[250] Bhagwati, *supra* note 245, at 13.
[251] *Id.* at 22.
[252] *Id.* at 64–66.

of the multiple considerations that multinationals take into account when pursuing investment in different countries. Other considerations may be more paramount, such as labor costs, capital costs, infrastructure development, the weather, taxes and tax breaks, and political stability.

However, even defenders of globalization admit that globalization needs to be managed well in order to produce further desirable results. Such management of globalization involves the establishment of institutions that would provide a social safety net to support those affected mostly by the abrupt changes that globalization brings. It has been claimed that developing countries should be allowed to develop adjustment programs, when jobs are lost to foreign competition, the way developed countries have done in the past to protect their industries and workers. If developing countries cannot afford such programs, it has been proposed that the World Bank could fund such programs.[253] Furthermore, some state intervention into agricultural policies should be allowed so that the farmers in the developing world are not wiped out by the vagaries of international trade.[254]

6. PRINCIPLES

6.1. Sovereignty over Natural Resources

The sovereignty of a state over its natural resources is a principle frequently iterated in international treaties. States have made conscious attempts to expand their state sovereignty into areas or over resources that previously were considered the common heritage of mankind or simply free access areas. States expanded their jurisdiction over the seas by establishing Exclusive Economic Zones. Furthermore, states are attempting to extend their jurisdiction over the high seas as states that fish in the high seas are being forced to abide with the rules of regional fisheries organizations.

In the area of biodiversity protection, the assertion of state sovereignty has not always been effective and vocal but it has not been absent, either. States have been zealous of controlling their valuable biodiversity resources despite a declaration included in the International Undertaking on Plant Genetic Resources that plant resources are the common heritage of mankind.[255] In the Convention of Biological Diversity (CBD), "common heritage" has become "common concern"[256] and states have asserted property rights over the plants and other biodiversity resources that occur naturally within their territory.

What has generated this zealous nationalism has been the publicity surrounding the development of pharmaceuticals and other products from natural substances. Developing countries have claimed that it is unfair to have to pay high prices for pharmaceuticals and biotechnology products and would have not been invented without the substances derived from resources found in their territory. In other cases, it has been claimed that pharmaceutical companies have taken advantage of the knowledge of indigenous or local people without acknowledging their contributions

---

[253] *Id.* at 228–35.
[254] *Id.* at 238.
[255] Chapter 7, Section 2.1.2.4.
[256] See Biodiversity Convention, *supra* note 146.

to the development of a new product. Today, national sovereignty and control over the collection, dissemination, and exploitation of germplasm are the norm. This norm has been institutionalized in the Treaty on Plant Genetic Resources for Food and Agriculture.[257]

6.2. Obligation Not to Cause Damage

The duty of states not to cause damage to the territory of another state is derived from the sovereignty of states. The obligation not to cause damage to the territory of another state, though, is not without qualification. Some polluting activities are bound to cause damage to the territory of other states and frequently such activities are legal. The obligation of states to prevent causing harm to other states, and liability that may ensue from the breach of that obligation, have been examined in detail by the International Law Commission and are explored in depth in Chapter 11.

6.3. Principles of Preventive Action and Precaution

The preventive approach is based on the idea that it is better to prevent environmental damage than to employ measures to restore the environment thereafter. The prevention of environmental damage has been *le raison d'être* of environmental policy.

The preventive approach has been expanded by a relatively new principle – the precautionary principle. The precautionary principle is based on the premise that action on environmental matters should be taken even if there is a lack of total scientific certainty, often reversing the burden of proof and placing it on those who claim that an activity is not damaging.[258]

In some cases, the existence of an environmental problem is evident, for instance, in the case of depletion of the ozone layer. In most cases, however, especially those that have to do with the impact of hazardous substances on human health or the environment, the scientific evidence may not be conclusive. In those cases, the precautionary principle advocates that some action is better than inaction.

The precautionary principle is an expression of the backlash against a tepid approach to environmental pollution that has often characterized international action. Many times, governments have procrastinated taking action on environmental problems and blamed their inaction on the lack of scientific certainty or faith in the assimilative capacity of the environment. This procrastinating attitude exacerbated many problems that could have been resolved had it not been "for the lack of scientific certainty" argument. One such obvious problem involves the discharge of untreated sewage at sea that polluted the Mediterranean. One would think that treatment of sewage before it is discharged into the sea would be a sensible investment option for most of the Mediterranean countries dependent on tourism, despite the lack of scientific certainly on the effects of sewage discharges into shallow

---

[257] See Chapter 7, Section 2.1.2.3.
[258] See Patricia W. Birnie & Alan E. Boyle, International Law and the Environment 98 (1992). See also James Cameroon & Juli Abouchar, The Precautionary Principle: A Fundamental Principle of Law and Policy for the Protection of the Global Environment, XIV(1) Boston College International and Comparative Law Review 1 (1991); Lothar Gündling, The Status in International Law of the Principle of Precautionary Action, 5 International Journal of Estuarine and Coastal Law 23 (1990).

waters. Also, in principle, some standards should be applied so that most industries and households do not discharge their wastes untreated in the environment.

The precautionary principle has been quite controversial because it advocates action despite the lack of scientific certainty. Taking action under such conditions could be costly or, even worse, could be proven wrong. The precautionary principle, nevertheless, has been repeated in many international conventions, and the Rio Declaration includes a precautionary approach.[259] Some commentators view the principle as a guiding principle of international environmental law,[260] but others adopt a more cautionary attitude.[261] The United States has taken a skeptical approach toward the precautionary principle viewing it almost as a protectionist principle – a new nontariff barrier to trade.[262] The European Union, at the other extreme, has transformed the principle into a constitutional principle,[263] favoring a strong version of the principle.[264]

6.4. Polluter Pays Principle and Equitable Sharing of Cost

The polluter pays principle was enunciated clearly in the international arena in the Rio Declaration. The principle basically demands for the person who is in charge of polluting activities to be financially responsible for the damage s/he causes. Some commentators have underlined that the principle has merely a rhetoric value because most polluters will be able to pass the costs of pollution onto consumers. Also, in most cases, it is difficult to identify the polluter.[265]

Although the polluter pays principle has been enunciated in many international instruments, especially those adopted after 1992, when decisions are made about who should bear the cost of polluting activities it is not always followed. The Rhine Convention on Chlorides explicitly provides that the Netherlands, the country that is the recipient of pollution, undertakes to pay for some of the costs of pollution prevention.[266] The arbitration tribunal that interpreted the convention did not endorse the polluter pays principle.[267] In the case of the Chernobyl disaster, none of the

---

[259] See *supra* Section 4.2.

[260] Cameroon, *supra* note 258.

[261] Gündling, *id.*

[262] See David Vogel, The WHO, International Trade and Protection: European and American Perspectives 13, European University Institute, Robert Schuman Centre for Advanced Studies, EUI Working Papers, RSC No 2002/34 (2002).

[263] Art. 174(2), Treaty Establishing the European Economic Community (EEC Treaty or Treaty of Rome), March 25, 1957. For an updated version of the EC Treaty as amended by the Amsterdam and Nice Treaties, see official site of the European Communities available online at http://europa.eu.int/eur-lex.

[264] See Daniel C. Esty, Thickening the International Environmental Regime 5, European University Institute, Robert Schuman Centre for Advanced Studies, Policy Paper 02/8 (2002).

[265] For instance, in the case of a landfill, where many industries have dumped their waste, it is difficult to pinpoint which company's waste has created the environmental damage. Thus, the assumption is made usually that all disposers are jointly and severally liable. For issues of liability on waste transfers, see generally Elli Louka, Bringing Polluters before Transnational Courts: Why Industry Should Demand Strict and Unlimited Liability for the Transnational Movements of Hazardous and Radioactive Wastes, 22 Denver Journal of International Law and Policy 63 (1993).

[266] Chapter 5, Section 5.4.2.

[267] *Id.*

countries affected by the radioactive fallout demanded compensation for the damages they suffered from the Soviet Union. The Soviet Union denied any responsibility, claiming that measures undertaken by the affected countries were overcautious.[268] Furthermore, the International Law Commission in its Draft Articles on Prevention of Transboundary Harm from Hazardous Activities refers to the "factors involved in an equitable sharing of interests" between the polluting party and the affected party.[269]

The International Law Commission guidelines on the prevention of transboundary harm from hazardous activities not prohibited by international law refer to the factors that must be taken into account for an equitable balance of interests between a polluting state and a state that is the recipient of transboundary pollution. In more detail, it is provided that for an equitable balance of interests between these two states to be achieved: "The degree to which the State of origin and, as appropriate, the State likely to be affected are prepared to contribute to the costs of prevention" must be taken into account.[270]

This equitable balance of interests between the polluting state and the affected states seems to contradict the polluter pays principle.[271]

6.5. Sustainable Development

The term "sustainable development" has been included in the Rio Declaration on Environment and Development to denote the need to balance environmental and development considerations.[272] The original articulation of the principle is found in the Brundtland report, which stated that sustainable development means development that satisfies the needs of present generations without jeopardizing the ability of future generations to meet their own needs.[273] In the WSSD, sustainable development was further articulated as having three pillars, namely: economic development, social development, and environmental protection.

The term "sustainable development" has been decried by some as devoid of content, as a concept used to express different and often disparate worldviews. And this is true, to some extent, as developed countries and their NGOs have used the principle to underline the importance of environmental values, whereas developing countries have used the principle to buttress their right to development.

Despite these misgivings, however, the principle has assisted in reconciling in one phrase what before seemed irreconcilable – namely, environmental protection and development. It is interesting to see how sustainable development has been used in local communities to articulate goals and indicators for future development, such

---

[268] Günther Handl, Paying the Piper for Transboundary Nuclear Damage: State Liability in a System of Transnational Compensation, in International Law and Pollution 150, 152 (Daniel Barstow Magraw, ed., 1991).

[269] Art. 10, Draft articles on Prevention of Transboundary Harm from Hazardous Activities adopted by the International Law Commission at its Fifty-third session (2001), Official Records of the General Assembly, Fifty-sixth session, Supplement No. 10 (A/56/10), chp. V.E.1., Nov. 2001.

[270] Arts. 2 & 10(d), id.

[271] Rio Declaration on Environment and Development, supra note 143.

[272] Id.

[273] World Commission on Environment and Development, Our Common Future 43 (Brundtland Report) (1987).

as the goals of equity,[274] economic vitality, strong community, quality of education, good government, decent housing, healthy people, efficient transport and land-use, protected natural resources, and minimal pollution and waste. Sustainable development has put on the negotiating table issues of economic and social development that are prerequisites for the quality of life and environmental protection.[275]

The sustainable development concept, polluter pays principle, and precautionary principle may not be the principles that would resolve future environmental disputes. Other principles, such as that of equitable sharing of costs of polluting activities and a preventive rather than a precautionary approach, may gain ground. The principles, though, articulated as such, are informing the intellectual background of decision-makers and are helping to establish a common credo among those who are involved in the everyday shaping of international environmental affairs. To dismiss these principles as too fluid and, thus, irrelevant would require a sort of imperviousness to their galvanizing effects as they reverberate from international to local agendas.

6.6. Equitable Utilization

The principle of equitable utilization of resources has been articulated in early judicial decisions regarding the sharing of freshwater resources. In the *Lac Lanoux* case, the tribunal articulated the duty of states to take into account other states interests before developing a resource by engaging, at least, in negotiations and consultation. In the *Oder* and *Meuse* cases, the PCIJ referred to the community of interests and equality of riparian states so that no state acquires preference over others. The 1997 UN Watercourses Convention refers to the principle of equitable utilization of watercourses.

The principle of equity is difficult to pin down. Some commentators have viewed equity as a defining concept of international law.[276] Other commentators have argued that equity considerations introduce an especially subjective element in the interpretation of international law.[277] To most people, equity would mean a fifty-fifty allocation of a resource; to others, that those with priority in use must be protected; to still others, equitable allocation must be based on needs independent of the extent to which a resource is located within national boundaries. The application of equity in the different regions of the world has not been the same. The interpretation of equity depends heavily on the dynamics of interrelationships among countries that happen to share a resource. Equity frequently lies in the eyes of the beholder, especially if that beholder is a relatively more powerful state that refuses to compromise. Chapter 5 examines in detail the concept of equity in the allocation of freshwater sources. In addition to the allocation of freshwaters, the principle of equity has been used in other allocation issues, such as the delimitation of the continental shelf.[278]

---

[274] The indicators are equal pay between men and women and decrease in infant mortality.

[275] Living with the Future in Mind: Goals and Indicators of NJ's Quality of Life, First Annual Update to Sustainable State Project Report (2000) (the report includes sustainability goals and indicators for New Jersey's quality of life).

[276] Franck, *supra* note 23, at 79.

[277] Higgins, *supra* note 110.

[278] See *supra* note 108.

The principle of equitable utilization of resources has found its articulation in the Biodiversity Convention. The Biodiversity Convention provides that countries must share equitably the benefits derived from the development of biodiversity resources.[279] This principle of equitable sharing of benefits derived from biodiversity resources, though, has resisted practical articulation. Developed countries and many biotechnology companies fear that equitable utilization would involve distribution of profits coming from patenting biotechnology devices. Because of such concerns, the United States has not ratified the Biodiversity Convention. More recently, state parties to the Biodiversity Convention have engaged in efforts to define what an equitable sharing of benefits from the development of biodiversity resources would mean.[280]

6.7. Common but Differentiated Responsibilities

The principle of common but differentiated responsibilities is a possible articulation of the concept of equity.[281] Countries have differentiated responsibilities with regard to environmental protection because not every country has contributed to the same extent to environmental degradation and because not all countries have the same resources to devote to environmental problems. The principle of common but differentiated responsibilities has found apt articulation in the climate change and ozone protection conventions in which it is explicitly provided that developed countries should provide additional funding to developing countries in order to ensure the implementation of these treaties.

6.8. Human Rights

Human rights standards are not explicitly referred to in international environmental instruments. The right to development is offered as a counterposition to environmental protection in the balancing of environmental and developmental goals. But, generally, there has not been an explicit reference to human rights as they may work in tandem with environmental goals. The Stockholm Conference and the WSSD refer explicitly to the goal of human dignity.[282] The Rio Conference refers to the right to development that some have viewed as the force that should drive international law.[283]

The focal point of the WSSD is the reduction of poverty. The goal of poverty reduction is not explicitly articulated in international human rights instruments but it is implicit in the right to development. It is also implicit in article 11 of the 1966 Covenant on Economic, Social and Cultural Rights, in which it is provided that parties to the covenant "recognize the right of everyone to an adequate standard of living for himself and his family, including adequate food, clothing and housing."[284]

---

[279] See art. 15, Biodiversity Convention, *supra* note 146.
[280] See Chapter 7, Section 2.1.2.4.
[281] See Franck, *supra* note 23, at 381.
[282] See also McDougal, *supra* note 8.
[283] See *supra* note 149.
[284] Art. 11(1), International Covenant on Economic, Social, and Cultural Rights, *supra* note 4.

The insertion of human rights into the environmental discourse is important not only because human rights are the prerequisite for the quality of life sought by environmental protection. Ecodevelopment, like conventional development, has entailed in some cases neglect for the needs of people whose interests do not lie within the ecodevelopment agenda. Forcible exclusions of people from what are seen as naturally pristine areas have been executed by many governments in the developing world. Environmentalism has been used by certain elites to perpetrate suppressive policies that, otherwise, would have not acquired approval in international circles. The protection of human rights should ideally provide the threshold for the pursuit of development including ecodevelopment.[285] Threshold human rights standards would involve the basic human rights standards, such as:

- the right to life, liberty, and the security of person;[286]
- the right not be subjected to torture or cruel, inhuman, and degrading punishment;[287]
- the right not be subjected to arbitrary arrest, detention, and exile;[288]
- the right to effective remedies before national tribunals.[289]

Commentators have proposed the articulation of a right not be displaced and the use of such right to oppose government policies geared toward involuntary displacement.[290]

7. SETTLEMENT OF DISPUTES

It is not uncommon for disagreements among states to escalate into international disputes and methods have been developed by the international community to resolve or, at least, to contain such disputes. Such efforts include conciliation, good offices and mediation, arbitration, and adjudication.

---

[285] Elli Louka, Biodiversity and Human Rights: The International Rules of the Protection of Biodiversity 26 (2002).

[286] Art. 3, Universal Declaration of Human Rights, *supra* note 4; Arts. 6 & 9, International Covenant on Civil and Political Rights, *supra* note 4; Art. 4, African Charter on Human and Peoples' Rights, *supra* note 4.

[287] Art. 5, Universal Declaration of Human Rights, *id.*; Art. 7 Covenant on Civil and Political Rights, *id.*; Art. 5, African Charter on Human and Peoples' Rights, *id.*

[288] Art. 7, Universal Declaration of Human Rights, *id.*; Art. 9 Covenant on Civil and Political Rights, *id.*; Art. 6, African Charter on Human and Peoples' Rights, *id.*.

[289] Art. 8, Universal Declaration of Human Rights, id; Arts. 9 & 14 Covenant on Civil and Political Rights, id; Art. 7 African Charter on Human and Peoples' Rights, *id.*

[290] Stavropoulou, *supra* note 7. See also The Forsaken People: Case Studies of the Internally Displaced (Roberta Cohen & Francis M. Deng, eds., 1998). It is mentioned in the study that, in 1997, the number of displaced people due to armed conflict and other human rights violations soared to 20 million in at least 35 countries. See also The Guiding Principles on Internal Displacement, E/CN. 4/1998/53/Add.2, 11/02/1998. These principles were issued by the special representative to the Secretary General on Internally Displaced Persons (IDPs), Francis Deng. The principles are based on human rights and humanitarian norms currently in existence. See also Walter Kalin, Guiding Principles on Internal Displacement: Annotations 17–18 (published by the American Society of International Law & the Brookings Institution Project on Internal Displacement, Studies in Transnational Legal Policy, No. 32, 2000).

Conciliation

One of the first means used for the settlement of disputes is conciliation.[291] A formal conciliation procedure involves the establishment of a Conciliation Commission. The Vienna Convention on the Law of Treaties, the Law of the Sea Convention, and a number of environmental agreements provide explicitly for a conciliation commission in case a disagreement develops among state parties to these conventions.

Good Offices and Mediation

Good offices and mediation involve further efforts to contain disputes that have span out of the control of disputants. A country or an international organization[292] may offer their good offices or offer to mediate in a dispute. The difference between good offices and mediation is not very clear. In principle, a "good offices" proposition assumes a nonnegotiating role for the party that offers good offices. In mediation, the intervening party takes part in the negotiations.

One way for a mediator to resolve an issue is by altering parties' perception of differences facing them. A mediator may break down contested issues into smaller subissues that are more easily resolved. Or a mediator may combine seemingly unrelated issues so that a compromise can be struck. As a rule, negotiating mechanisms that are flexible and relatively informal are preferable for seeking resolution of difficult disputes. Negotiation and mediation can be more effectively carried out in private rather than in public meetings. This does not mean, however, that "parliamentary diplomacy" and public statements cannot be used to help bring resolution.

Arbitration

Arbitration, in contrast to conciliation and mediation, leads to a binding settlement. The arbitral body is composed of judges who are normally appointed by the parties but who are not subject to their instructions. The arbitral body may be established *ad hoc* or it may be a continuing body set up to handle certain categories of disputes. Arbitration differs from judicial settlement in that the parties have competence, as a rule, to appoint arbitrators, to determine the procedure to be applied and to indicate the applicable law, to some extent. The Permanent Court of Arbitration deals with many types of arbitration proceedings.[293]

An undertaking to arbitrate an issue usually does not resolve all detailed questions that must be settled before arbitration takes place. It may specify the manner in which the arbitrators are to be selected. Usually, each party is to select an arbitrator and a third arbitrator is appointed by an agreement of the parties. Other detailed questions are usually answered in an agreement between the parties called *compromis d'arbitrage*.

International law does not lay down specific rules concerning the weight of evidence in arbitration proceedings. Admissibility of evidence and the weight to be attached to it are largely left to the arbitral tribunal. For the most part, the rules

---

[291] For an array of procedures that can be used for the settlement of disputes, see art. 33, UN Charter, *supra* note 9.

[292] The good offices of the Secretary General have been used often. See art. 99, UN Charter, *supra* note 9, that has been interpreted to include the concept of "preventive diplomacy."

[293] The Permanent Court of Arbitration (PCA) was established by the Convention for the Pacific Settlement of International Disputes in 1899.

followed by arbitration tribunals are more flexible than those applied generally by domestic courts.

States can sabotage arbitral proceedings by refusing to appoint an arbitrator. And it is not unusual for a country to try to avoid arbitration by frustrating the arbitration proceedings. Treaties include often clauses, therefore, about the procedure to be followed to appoint an arbitrator when a party refuses to enter into arbitration proceedings or has failed to appoint an arbitrator.

Adjudication

States are generally reluctant to use the ICJ for the resolution of their disputes. The reasons behind this reluctance have to do with the time-consuming and uncertain character of litigation. Governments resent losing control over a case that may not be resolved to their satisfaction and being bound by an outcome that they do not favor. International law is perceived as too intertwined with politics to make room for real judicial decisions. Legal issues are viewed as but an element of the political reality with trade-offs to be made that do not have much to do with legal regulations.

8. MONITORING AND ENFORCEMENT

Monitoring is the prerequisite of enforcement. Some international agreements are well monitored. For instance, states often carefully monitor treaties for the control of weapons, whereas states do not devote many resources to the monitoring of environmental treaties.[294] Because of innovative technologies, however, that allow to pinpoint the location of ships or developments in DNA technology that allow for the identification of endangered species, it is generally presumed that environmental agreements are better monitored today than in the past.

If monitoring proves that a state has violated the law and the elected dispute resolution mechanisms do not resolve the issue to the satisfaction of the offended parties, one would expect that enforcement would follow. This is not the case, however, in many international treaties. Unless a vital state interest is at stake, states generally exhibit a remarkable amount of tolerance to treaty violation.

The Vienna Convention does not give much guidance regarding treaty violation. Article 60(1) provides that: "A material breach of a bilateral treaty by one of the parties entitles the other to invoke the breach as a ground for terminating the treaty or suspending its operation in whole or in part."[295] This provision is not particularly helpful with regard to environmental treaties. If two states have signed a treaty under which they undertook the obligation to prevent waste dumping in the sea, the breach of the treaty by one of the parties – by engaging in dumping – would mean that the other party could suspend the treaty. But the suspension of the treaty would not be of any help to the nonviolating party if that party wishes to implement the treaty.

The same problematic applies to multilateral treaties, for instance, treaties that oblige parties to cut or stabilize their polluting emissions. If a state party violates such a treaty by increasing its emissions and another party retaliates by increasing its

---

[294] Abram Chayes & Antonia Handler Chayes, The New Sovereignty: Compliance with International Regulatory Agreements 174–79 (1995).
[295] See *supra* note 86.

own emissions, that retaliating action would not only be harmful to the retaliating state but also unfair to the other parties to the convention. In that case, the violating party would have achieved the demise of the international regime that other states are striving to establish.

In general, states have used an array of measures to ensure compliance by other states. Frequently, countries retaliate against a state that violated a treaty by breaching another treaty. A whole range of self-help measures – short of the threat of use of force or the actual use of force against the political independence or territorial integrity of a state – have been considered legitimate. Following the alleged breach of a particular treaty or another international obligation, diplomatic relations are ruptured, foreign assets are frozen, seized, or attached,[296] shipments of surplus food and other forms of foreign aid are discontinued, internal subversion is tacitly encouraged, and trade sanctions are initiated.[297] Resort to war is allowed also in cases of self-defense in order to counter an armed attack.[298] It has been claimed even that an armed attack does not have to be present in order for a country to engage in self-defense. It just has to be imminent. Some governments have evoked the right to preemptive or anticipatory self-defense.[299] These retaliation measures are often called self-help measures or countermeasures.

The enforcement of environmental treaties has rarely involved retaliatory measures such as those described here. However, this does not mean that all international environmental treaties are deprived of enforcement mechanisms. Certain environmental treaties, for example, the Montreal Protocol for the Protection of the Ozone Layer, authorize trade sanctions against not only parties that have not implemented the treaty provisions but also against nonparties,[300] thereby extending the jurisdictional reach of the convention to states that are not formally bound by it.

The United States has used actively trade sanctions to force the extraterritorial application of its environmental legislation. The *Tuna-Dolphin* and *Shrimp-Turtle* cases have caused a lot of acrimony in GATT/WTO fora.[301]

As a rule, however, countries have applied more carrots rather than sticks to ensure the implementation of environmental legislation. Generally, distribution issues, with regard to allocation of water, fisheries resources, and biodiversity, have generated the most disputes. Pollution matters, as long as they are not clearly defined as allocation matters, have generated less acrimony. Depending on the configuration of power in a region might or right have been used more or less convincingly for the management of environmental disputes.

---

[296] Cuban Assets Control Regulations, 31 C.F.R. §515.201 (1979).
[297] See Cuban Embargo by the United States, 22 U.S.C. §2370.
[298] Art. 51, UN Charter, *supra* note 9.
[299] See *supra* notes 13–15.
[300] See Chapter 8, Section 1.
[301] See Chapter 9, Section 3.

2 Foundations of International Environmental Law

1. FUNCTIONS OF LAW

Status Quo and Change

Institutions provide the rules of the game in a society. These are the rules concocted by humans to assist them in their cohabitation.[1] Law is an institution. One of the goals of law is to establish rules that would increase the predictability and certainty of outcomes and, thus, facilitate transactions in a society. As an economist would put it, the purpose of law is to reduce the transaction costs of cooperation among individuals or other legal entities, such as corporations and states. Transaction costs include the costs of defining and enforcing property rights and the costs of remedying the information asymmetries among parties about to enter a transaction.[2] A vast amount of society's resources is devoted to monitoring and enforcing behavior to ensure conformity with the rules of law.

The purpose of international law is to facilitate state interaction by introducing order where, otherwise, would be disorder, anarchy, and war. The primary goal of the United Nations is to safeguard peace, a precondition for cooperative outcomes. Various international organizations and treaties have been adopted with the purpose of coordinating state interaction by standardizing expected behavior.

The pursuit of order and stability perpetuates a view of a law as an institution of the *status quo*. To give an example, the principle of *stare decisis* is explicitly endorsed in Anglo-Saxon systems but also is implicitly adhered to in civil law systems. The principle of *stare decisis* perpetuates a perception of law as an institution that is unreceptive to social change. But the content of law has changed through the years. The question then is how law, an institution that serves the *status quo*, can accommodate social change.

Change in law like in any other institution can be abrupt. This is, for instance, in case of a revolution when established norms seem to be subverted overnight. In most cases, however, change in law, as in most institutions, is so gradual as to be imperceptible to people/states that experience it. Change in law may happen when a constituency of interests is able to propose counternorms to already established

---

[1] Douglass C. North, Institutions, Institutional Change and Economic Performance 3 (1990).
[2] *Id*. at 27.

norms.[3] These counternorms are initially only part of the rhetoric of certain groups.[4] If they reach a disaffected audience, however, they may become ingrained in the mainstream and subvert established norms. It may take decades or even centuries but, when circumstances are ripe (e.g., in terms of economic/technological developments or emerging new entrants), the established norms would be challenged and could be replaced by new norms. The emancipation of women and the termination of slavery are relatively newly established norms pushed forward by industrialization and the demise of traditional agricultural society. Ideas regarding the injustices done to women and the fundamental unfairness of slavery were floating around, however, for centuries.[5] Eventually, circumstances became ripe for these ideas to take hold. Colonization similarly lost the moral ground that it claimed in the nineteenth century, and the wars of decolonization brought new states in the international arena.

Formal and Informal Rules

Even as formal rules change, informal rules could remain the same. Such rules usually are unwritten. They are the codes of conduct in a society. They are customary rules that are passed from one generation to the next and are quite resistant to change. Some of these informal rules could be in direct conflict with existing rules or could violate the spirit of change brought by the new rules.[6]

Thus, the real world often involves a mixture of newly established rules and old codes of conduct. It would be misguiding for a scholar to focus on the formal rules and to neglect the informal rules of conduct. Such a focus is likely to produce a distorted picture of reality. Michael Reisman puts this eloquently when he says that one must verify words against practice before pretending to understand the norms according to which social groups, including the international society, operate.[7] Chapter 1 alluded to the importance of power and authority in shaping the rules of international law. Power is not an overt prescription in most formal rules of international law. But it definitely shapes the rules of the game as iterated among various states.[8]

Informal rules are important in the configuration of rules of the game in the international society. The international system has been described as an anarchical system in which no central authority can take decisive action that would subjugate the will of many and disparate actors. Some commentators have argued that international

---

[3] According to Jhering, change in law happens when new interests assert themselves against old interests. See Rudolph Von Jhering, The Struggle for Law 9 (1915).

[4] See Robert. C. Ellickson, The Evolution of Social Norms: A Perspective from the Legal Academy, Yale Law School, Program for Studies in Law, Economics and Public Policy, Working Paper No. 230, July 1999 available online at http://ssrn.com/abstract=191392 (Social Science Research Network Electronic Paper Collection).

[5] See, e.g., Jean-Jacques Rousseau, On the Social Contract 20 (Translated by Donald A. Cress, ed., 1987). See also Arlene W. Saxonhouse, Women in the History of Political Thought: Ancient Greece to Machiavelli (1985).

[6] The international trafficking of persons could be conceived as a perpetuation of the institution of slavery and, despite the fact that it is overwhelmingly condemned, it is still practiced.

[7] W. Michael Reisman, Law from the Policy Perspective, in International Law Essays: A Supplement to International Law in Contemporary Perspective 1, 3 (Myres S. McDougal & W. Michael Reisman, eds., 1981).

[8] Id.

law is a fiction that mirrors rather than constrains state behavior.[9] A view of international law as a system shaped as much by power as by formal rules of conduct is also echoed by international lawyers.[10] Anarchy and coercion, however, could be costly even for powerful states that view stability and predictability as advantageous in terms of cost reduction in their everyday interaction with other states.[11] Therefore, as Louis Henkin has observed, in what has become a classic line in international circles, "almost all nations observe almost all principles of international law and almost all of their obligations almost all of the time."[12]

The result is a decentralized legal system with many formal rules but also many informal rules and various patterns of consistent or inconsistent state practice. Because the international legal system is so diffuse, the notion of a "system" seems like a future ambition. Some commentators prefer to use, therefore, the notion of "international regime."

International Regimes

International regimes have been described as the convergence of expectations, patterns of behavior, and practice.[13] Regimes have been defined as international arrangements characterized by implicit and explicit principles, norms, rules, and decision-making processes around which the expectations of different actors converge.[14]

The regimes examined in this study include:

- the Marine Pollution regime as articulated in the Law of the Sea Convention (UNCLOS), the Convention on pollution from ships (MARPOL Convention), the London Dumping Convention, and various regional instruments;
- the Shared Watercourses regime that is centered on the 1997 UN Watercourses Convention and further exemplified in various regional instruments;
- the Fisheries Resources regime that is the focus of a number of instruments such as the UNCLOS and the 1995 Fisheries Agreement. A number of instruments have attempted to apply the regime in regional fora;
- the Plant Genetic Resources (PGR) regime that centers around the Convention on Biological Diversity and has to do with the protection of and property rights over "raw" germplasm resources and intellectual property rights over "worked" germplasm resources, as they may be articulated in biotechnology inventions or pharmaceutical inventions;
- the regime for the protection of the ozone layer that is articulated in a framework convention and a number of protocols, the regime for the reduction of greenhouse gases that are responsible for climate change, and the regime for

---

[9] H.L.A. Hart, The Concept of Law 217 (1994). See also Hans J. Morgenthau, Politics among Nations 278 (1960).

[10] See, e.g., Abram Chayes & Antonia Handler Chayes, The New Sovereignty: Compliance with International Regulatory Agreements, 6, 27, 41, 84 (1995).

[11] Robert Axelrod, The Evolution of Cooperation (1984).

[12] Louis Henkin, How Nations Behave 47 (1979).

[13] Oran R. Young, Regime Dynamics: The Rise and Fall of International Regimes, in International Regimes 93 (Stephen D. Krasner, ed., 1983).

[14] Stephen D. Krasner, Structural Causes and Regime Consequences: Regimes and Intervening Variables, in International Regimes 1, id.

transboundary air pollution that deals with pollutants that could have transboundary effects as they are emitted by certain states but end up in the environment of other states; and

- the waste regime as it has come into focus in the international arena through the trade (legal or illegal) of hazardous and radioactive wastes and, specifically, the unsound transfer and disposal of hazardous wastes in countries of the developing world.

Some regimes have been characterized as issue-focused, such as the regime for the protection of the ozone layer. The ozone regime is comprised of a convention and a number of protocols and has imposed specific regulations for the phasing out of ozone depleting substances.[15] Issue-focused regimes include also the transboundary air pollution regime. The climate change regime seems at this point issue-focused. However, as the regime may expand to implement the clean development mechanism, joint implementation or tradable allowances, it may increase in complexity. The waste regime is also issue-focused as it is centered basically on the Basel Convention and a limited number of regional instruments that have simply banned waste imports into particular regions.

Other regimes have been characterized as complex as they have attracted attention in various international fora that have infused these regimes with different normative directions. The Plant Genetic Resources regime developed under the Biodiversity Convention (CBD) has been characterized as such a regime. The regime is comprised of a number of soft norms and hard rules dispersed in a number of international fora, such as the WIPO, the WTO, the CBD, the FAO, the IARCs, and UN Human Rights bodies.[16] Some authors have characterized these regimes as conglomerate regimes or regime complexes. Such regimes emerge as actors dissatisfied with outcomes on an international issue in a particular forum engage in "regime shifting" or "regime shopping." Frequently, actors disaffected with the evolution of an international regime in a particular forum attempt to establish regime counternorms in another forum, hoping that such counternorms would take root and lead to regime change.[17]

Some regimes straddle the borders between issue-focused and complexity. The marine pollution regime and the fisheries regime[18] are organized around a couple of international instruments (namely, the UNCLOS, the LC, the MARPOL, and the 1995 Straddling Fisheries Agreement) but then are expounded in a number of regional instruments the purpose of which is to make these agreements implementable on the ground. Various legal bodies have created, therefore, soft norms not always synchronized with each other. Not the same hazardous substances, for instance, are controlled by regional instruments regulating sea pollution. Some

---

[15] Chapter 8, Section 1.

[16] Chapter 7, Section 2.1.2; Chapter 9, Section 4.3.

[17] For the concept of regime shopping and complex regimes, see Kal Raustiala & David G. Victor, The Regime Complex for Plant Genetic Resources, Research Paper No. 03–19, University of California, Los Angeles School of Law, Research Paper Series, Spring 2004 available online, at http://ssrn.com/abstract=441463.

[18] Chapter 4 and Chapter 6.

hazardous substances may coincide among regimes and others may differ. This makes the coordination among interrelated regimes occasionally complex as countries, for example, have to report on different substances under different regimes and to conform to different technological requirements.

The freshwater management regime is also quite complex as a quite broad international convention has been interpreted in different regions in ways that conform more with the regional balance of power rather than with consistent perceptions of equity. Many multilateral and bilateral agreements had been adopted before the convention that do not conform exactly with the spirit of the convention. The situation is so fluid that some commentators have challenged the normative value of the UN Watercourses Convention.[19]

Within the biodiversity regime, the Plant Genetic Resources subregime is quite complex, as explained earlier. Given the regional dimension of biodiversity, many regional conventions have been adopted that add substance and texture to the Biodiversity Convention. Species-specific and habitat-specific treaties also abound. Understanding and coordinating the interrelationship among all these instruments (that also claim overlapping jurisdictional boundaries) and a large number of soft norms that have been enacted is a complex task even for the expert.[20]

Overall, regimes that deal with pollution tend to be more issue-focused, whereas regimes that deal primarily with allocation issues tend to be more complex. Regimes that deal primarily with the allocation of natural resources present by definition distribution issues that tend to be the most contentious in any society. It is not surprising then that actors engage in forum shopping in an attempt to find distributive solutions that better fit their needs. All international environmental regimes are to some degree distributional regimes. In some regimes, the distributional conflict and ensuing complexity with regard to the allocation of a resource is much more pronounced.

Complexity, Redundancy, and Networks

Complexity in international regimes is sometimes seen as redundancy. Often, international lawyers lament the coexistence of regimes dealing with essentially the same matter, the multiplicity of institutions concerned with similar issues, and the number of soft norms and hard norms that have to be put together painstakingly to understand complex international regimes. This multiplicity in international law is often viewed as an undesirable redundancy and many international scholars have recommended the simplification and the streamlining of the international system.

Redundancy may not be an undesirable phenomenon, however. Scholars that have studied public law systems have commented on the beneficial effects of redundant or what otherwise could be called parallel systems.[21] It has been mentioned that parallel systems are essential in administrative structures in order to reduce serious errors, to induce healthy bureaucratic rivalry, and to implement risk management.

---

[19] Chapter 5, Section 4.
[20] Chapter 7, Section 2.1.2.
[21] See, generally, Jonathan B. Bendor, Parallel Systems (1985).

If all elements of an administrative structure hinge on a central mechanism, the collapse of that mechanism would induce the collapse of the depending administrative structure. But when multiple, parallel, and overlapping systems are at work that are not dependent on each other, the collapse of one system would not necessarily induce the demise of all systems. The importance of decentralized systems is made explicit by today's information technology, such as the Internet, that functions based on a system of organized, independent, and also overlapping networks.[22] The collapse of one of these networks is unlikely to cause the collapse of the whole system.

Commentators have noted the importance of building parallel bureaucracies that would act as a check on each other or that could, at least, take over if one of them becomes disfunctional. The importance of parallel systems is underlined also for developing countries' administrative systems where corruption is often prevalent. Because in developing countries building accountability is more important than the pursuit of efficiency, corruption is prevented by pitting parallel, yet overlapping, bureaucracies against each other.[23]

The international system could be conceived as a system of parallel and yet overlapping networks.[24] This overlapping structure has been actually the trademark of international law, despite repeated calls to reform such law after the model of centralized domestic administrative structures. The decentralized and overlapping nature of international environmental instruments and institutions is generally not viewed as efficient as resources are spent on multiple organizations dealing with more or less the same subject matter.

Decentralization coupled with overlap has been important, however, for the maintenance of minimum public order as issues, which cannot be resolved in a forum, could be shopped to another forum until the disaffected parties are satisfied. Decentralization and overlapping have played an important role in the maintenance of peace in the international system. The PGR regime is a clear example of how what could be conceived as a redundant system has helped in the diffusion of tension.[25] States dissatisfied with the Whaling Convention have transferred their concerns to other fora, therefore averting a possible crisis.[26] The number of organizations, treaties, and networks that deal with biodiversity ensure that if an issue is neglected in one forum it may find successful resolution in another forum.[27] The FAO deals with issues of agrobiodiversity. This has forced the COP of the CBD to deal more decisively with issues of resource ownership and control.[28]

---

[22] See Bobbi Low et al., Redundancy and Diversity in Governing and Managing Common-Pool Resources, Paper Presented at the 8th Biennial Conference of the International Association for the Study of Common Property, Indiana University, Bloomington, Indiana, May 31–June 4, 2000.

[23] Stephen B. Peterson, Another Path to Customs Reform: Mexico's Second Inspection, Harvard Institute for International Development, Discussion Paper No. 632, April 1998.

[24] See, e.g., Anne-Marie Slaughter, Global Government Networks, Global Information Agencies, and Disaggregated Democracy, Working Paper No. 018, Harvard Law School available online at http://papers.ssrn.com/abstract=283976.

[25] Chapter 7, Section 2.1.2. See also Chapter 9, Section 4.3.

[26] Chapter 7, Section 5.2.

[27] Chapter 9, Section 4.

[28] Chapter 7, Sections 2.1.2.3 & 2.1.2.4.

One could conclude, therefore, that institutional redundancy may not always be undesirable in international law and that some redundancy built into the international system may have some beneficial effects.

2. FOUNDATIONS

Law has been defined as an institution of *status quo* preservation but also as a means for social change. The question to be answered here is what the foundations of international environmental law are that would enable it to alternate between these two functions. The issue that needs to be examined involves the foundational purposes that, if absent, would deprive international environmental law of meaning as such law.

Dictionary definitions are useful in stripping down a concept to its basic meaning. Dictionaries define "foundations" as the fundamental principle on which something is founded, the basis.[29] Dictionaries also define "foundations" as that on which an idea or belief rests.[30]

International environmental law was initially conceived as an institution that would establish rules for the management of environmental problems that started to become all too obvious in the late 1970s. In dealing with these problems, states gradually discovered that they are not amenable to easy solutions. It was quickly apprehended that environmental issues are complex issues and that the best way to address them is to:

- define them in the midst of scientific uncertainty;
- devise management solutions that are not too costly; and
- deal with the distributive issues involved.

The pursuit of effectiveness and the pursuit of equity are the foundational purposes of international law. Effectiveness can be broken down into two pursuits: the pursuit of minimum order (the preservation of peace) and the pursuit of maximum order (the successful management of environmental issues). Equity is understood as an element of law that constitutes also the normative direction of law.

Notions of cost-effectiveness have not been paramount in international law. The development of an accountable and responsive international system has acquired precedence over an efficient one. As underlined earlier, many commentators have criticized the international system for waste of resources on what seems to be a redundant administrative structure. What may seem as an inefficient overlapping structure, however, may be, in effect, an efficient way to diffuse tension and conflict in international arenas.

Although international instruments rarely pretend to be cost-effective instruments, cost-effectiveness is examined here for the purposes of adding to the depth of understanding of international environmental issues. After all, it would be hard to characterize an excessively wasteful system as effective.

---

[29] Webster's New World Dictionary of the American Language, Second College Edition (David B. Guralnik, ed., 1986).

[30] A.S. Hornby, Oxford Advanced Learner's Dictionary of Current English (Oxford University Press, 1974).

Furthermore, effectiveness and equity are not clearly separable. Usually, an effective resolution of an issue would entail satisfactory distributive outcomes. Equity perceptions could assist in achieving effectiveness and in maintaining effective outcomes.

2.1. Minimum Order

The primary function of law is to maintain a minimum public order.[31] This minimum public order involves the maintenance of peace and the creation of rules that would increase the predictability and certainty of transactional outcomes. These rules often tend to be procedural. Basic rules of law that make possible a minimum order include: *pacta sunt servanta*, due process (or treat like cases alike), publication of laws in force, and consistency in the articulation and administration of international norms.[32]

Some authors have taken the existence of a minimum public order even further and have defined it as the existence of an organized government operating through legal instruments of command.[33] In this sense, all societies, in which some form of government is based on rules, are minimum-order societies (independent of whether this government is liberal, socialist, democratic, or despotic). A minimum order is one in which there is a hierarchy of command, rules are implemented consistently and predictably, and coercive instruments are used against those who violate the rules.

A minimum order, thus, would not necessarily entail the support of human rights but only in the fundamental sense of avoiding excessive cases of inconsistency in the administration of justice. Taking human life may be allowed, for instance, exclusively by the state apparatus as long as some procedural safeguards exist that do not threaten the existence of the minimum order and those who support it. For instance, for a common type of offense a defendant may be afforded a defense in front of a semi-independent body and be given a sentence corresponding to a violation of a rule of law published in advance.[34] For offenses designed to undermine the established order, the predictability of a serious punishment would almost always be equally fulfilled.

A minimum order is not a state of terror in which people resolve to obey because they are constantly coerced to do so. It is not a maximum order either, however, in the sense that the individual is respected. A minimum order contains rules that guide the everyday life with a considerable amount of predictability. These rules do not necessarily have to be conceived as fair or as directed towards equitable outcomes. But they have to be conceived as a fair game in the sense that if someone chooses to follow the rules, they would expect predictable outcomes and, in general, a normal life under the rules of the game as they have been defined.

Such a minimum order is often referred to in international law as peace, which is the absence of war among states. Peace does not presuppose justice but is, in essence, the absence of a Hobbesian state of affairs of perpetual and irresolvable

---

[31] See Myres S. Mc Dougal & Florentino P. Feliciano, Law and the Minimum World Public Order: The Legal Regulation of International Coercion (1961).

[32] Lon L. Fuller, The Morality of Law 39–40 (1964).

[33] Wolfang G. Friedman, Law and Social Change in Contemporary Britain 281 (1951).

[34] Even totalitarian states are willing to respect such procedural requirements in matters that do not threaten their existence.

conflict.[35] International law is based on a number of devices the purpose of which is the maintenance of peace: such as diplomacy and various more or less formal networks and organizations. The purpose of these formal and informal networks and organizations is to diffuse tension and avert war.

International environmental law, as "a branch" of international law, has similarly as its purpose the maintenance of peace among states with regard to the management of global commons. International environmental law shares the same discursive apparatus with international law, namely, diplomacy and various formal or informal organizations and networks. New organizations have been created to deal specifically with environmental problems. Such apparatus enables international law to control environmental conflict.

The fundamental purpose of international law is the maintenance of peace. Law and the maintenance of peace are, in some way, tautological expressions of the same phenomenon. Peace cannot exist without some rule of law and law cannot further develop unless peace preexists. Behind this seeming peace, though, strife is often prevalent as rivaling consistencies are battling to change the established order[36] but there is no conflict in the sense of war of all against all. An order penetrated by law has to cultivate perceptions that "things are under control."

Commentators uninitiated to international law are often taken aback by assertions of international lawyers about the effectiveness of international regimes. International lawyers often pronounce international environmental regimes effective independent of whether they have been effective at resolving the environmental problem at hand. It is enough that they manage to bring states to the table to discuss and attempt to resolve an issue.

For those who would like to see an environmental problem resolved, regimes that just manage to bring parties to the negotiating table are perceived as merely preparatory and not of high relevance. From a maintenance of the minimum-order perspective, however, the first and foremost goal of any legal order, these regimes are quite successful in that they have averted conflict and have managed to bring parties together to pursue common outcomes. This may seem a meager objective to those who would have liked to see environmental problems banished. Given the experience of two world wars, however, and the constant friction in many regions of the world over the allocation of natural resources, achieving a common ground from which collaborative efforts could be launched is by no means a negligible accomplishment.[37]

2.2. Equity

States are not equal in real terms. As mentioned in Chapter 1, states possess different degrees of power and resources. The "elite of states" is often able to induce concessions from other states. Sometimes this elite is aggressive and rapacious but – because it is too costly to rule the world by using terror – elites often make concessions in

[35] Thomas Hobbes, Leviathan 627 (C.B. MacPherson, ed., 1982).

[36] See Rudolph Von Jhering, The Struggle for Law 1, 6–7, 9 (1915).

[37] Elli Louka, Cutting the Gordian Knot: Why International Environmental Law Is Not Only about the Protection of the Environment, 10 Temple International and Comparative Law Journal 80 (1996).

matters that would not jeopardize their fundamental interests. Elites are powerful but they are not omnipotent. Unless they judiciously use their power, they could be toppled.[38]

A substantive concept of equity may involve the pursuit of various and mutually exclusive objectives. Equity could be conceived as:

- distributive equity. Distributive equity involves the pursuit of equality through equal distribution of power and resources according to a socialist ideal or a pursuit of a paradigm in which those who win in a transaction are willing to provide satisfactory compensation to losers;[39]
- survival of the fittest in various articulations of meritocracy, ability or capability rewarding systems. This idea of equity has not much to do with equality but starts with the assumption that people are unequal and, thus, rewards would have to match the level of merit, ability, and capacity; and
- corrective equity: correct the imbalance in the existence of power by providing assistance to the weaker members of society and those in need. Corrective equity is a sort of redistributive equity with the goal of addressing past inequalities. In this respect, equity may be dedicated to the pursuit of the reduction of the gap between the rich (powerful) and the poor (weak). Such notion of equity emanates from notions of solidarity among humans. In this case, equity has not much to do with the achievement of an ideal level of equality, where all people would be equally powerful and wealthy, but with the reduction of inequalities – most people achieving a minimum standard of living (food, shelter, and education).

In addition to these conceptualizations of equity, other versions include what could be called punitive equity, the tit-for-tat approach, or procedural equity – the right process. Examples of right process include elements that define a minimum order, such as *pacta sunt servanda* and due process.[40]

The notion of equity has found articulation in various areas of law and is expressed in multiple concepts, such as that of unjust enrichment (that one should not obtain unfair enrichment at the expense of others) and of estoppel or good faith and in instruments of resource allocation.[41] In general, equity has been used by courts to mitigate the effects of stringently implemented rules of law.

International law is rife with examples where the concept of equity has been used in legal instruments to achieve corrective and distributive outcomes. Corrective equity is often articulated in agreements that give preferential treatment to developing countries to correct imbalances that come from the fact that they are weaker members of the international community. Trade agreements, such as the Lomé Treaty, that grant preferential treatment to developing countries could be classified under this category.[42]

---

[38] See, e.g., Mancur Olson, The Rise and Decline of Nations (1982).

[39] This is an articulation of the Kaldor-Hicks principle in economics. For an analysis of the Kaldor-Hicks principle, see Richard A. Posner, Economic Analysis of Law 12–14 (1986).

[40] For the substantive and procedural notions of equity, see Thomas M. Franck, Fairness in International Law and Institutions 23–26 (1995).

[41] *Id*. at 50–56.

[42] *Id*. at 58–61.

Equity, as it has been articulated in international rules of water allocation,[43] biodiversity protection,[44] and sea-bed mining[45] has more of a distributive than a corrective overtone. The idea here is to establish *ex ante* some equitable distributive outcomes so that correction does not become necessary. Principles of equity also are mentioned in the United Nations Law of the Sea Convention (UNCLOS) with regard to the delimitation of the EEZ[46] and by courts in the delimitation of the continental shelf.[47]

No matter the substantive content of equity, it must be understood within the framework of the power balance in a region or in the world. Equity is not something that can be accomplished in a vacuum. Equitable outcomes that do not subvert the existing order, to become operational, must be accepted by the powerful and be satisfactory to the weak.

For equity to be executed within an established order to achieve results, it must function within the rules of the game understood as the aggregate of formal and informal rules that regulate conduct in a society. Such formal − and particularly informal − rules have to do with the power configuration in the international society.

The international system, as analyzed in Chapter 1, has acknowledged power but also has tried to constrain it through concepts such as equity. The international system has attempted to deal with distributive issues through resource transfer, knowledge transfer, and financial assistance to developing countries. International environmental issues are essentially distributional issues. International environmental law is an institution that has been used to arbitrate resource use and appropriation problems.

A common view of international environmental law is as a device to manage or, for optimists, to resolve environmental problems. As the law has evolved from Stockholm to the WSSD, however, distributional concerns are becoming more vocal. Distributional issues have been always implicit in international environmental instruments.[48] The WSSD brought distributional issues to the limelight as it specifically addressed problems pertinent to developing countries, such as poverty, sanitation, disease, and lack of drinking water. These are not "the-run-of-the-mill" environmental problems as perceived from a developed country perspective (e.g., ozone depletion, climate change, and endangered species protection). These are clear-cut problems that face developing countries.

Since the late 1980s, developing countries have attempted to usurp the environmental arena and use it as a forum to present environmental problems as essentially development problems − a classic case of forum shopping. Development problems have failed to capture the attention of developed countries and are addressed

---

[43] Chapter 5.

[44] Chapter 7.

[45] See *infra* section 5.2.

[46] Art. 59, UNCLOS, *infra* note 90. According to article 59 of UNCLOS, when conflict arises with regard to the attribution of rights and jurisdiction in the EEZ "the conflict should be resolved on the basis of equity."

[47] See Chapter 1, note 108.

[48] See, e.g., Stockholm Declaration, Chapter 1, Section 4.1.

frequently with meager handouts. Issues of poverty make headlines[49] but frequently are met with donor fatigue.

The second generation of human rights, such the right to food, shelter, education, and a minimum standard of living,[50] was an attempt to use human rights language to bring the concerns of the developing world to the forefront of the international agenda. The effort was a mixed success, as some developed countries still view rights as negative expressions of liberty that involve the abstention of state from the realm of individual freedom. Positive rights in terms of entitlements to a standard of living have not obtained the recognition that they deserve. The right to development, albeit positioned by developing countries as entitlement to wealth and prosperity, has not been recognized to the extent that would allow for its materialization.

Because development issues have not acquired much attention in international fora, developing countries attempted to use the area of environmental protection, as the new forum, to bring their claims. The cooperation of developing countries in the management of environmental issues has been considered essential. Most revered forest resources are located in developing countries. The destruction of ozone and climate change cannot be addressed without the assistance of developing countries that, because of increasing industrialization, are bound to emit most pollutants in the future. Developing countries made clear that without significant additional financial resources they should not be counted on to participate in international environmental agreements. It was a basic distributional reticence.

Environmental protection has been used as the subterfuge to bring distributive issues in the international debate. A successful rearticulation of a distributional issue as an environmental issue has been encapsulated in the notion of sustainable development. Sustainable development, for most developing countries, is a rearticulation of the right to development in "eco-speak." This rearticulation has been successful. Only one of the three pillars of sustainable development is devoted to the environment. The others have to do with social and economic development. Other articulations, such as common but differentiated responsibilities and additional financial assistance, have taken root. In the WSSD, developing countries have taken the bold step to redefine development issues as environmental issues.

Forum shifting has worked for some developing countries that have been able to extract additional resources from the developed world for the advancement of sustainable development or biodiversity protection.

2.3. Effectiveness as Equity

The purpose of rules of law is to serve order and justice. Rules of law are concocted to address issues as they emerge from social, technological, and other changes. Recently,

---

[49] Poverty has been defined as a pronounced deprivation of well-being related to lack of material income or consumption, low levels of education and health, vulnerability and exposure to risk, no opportunity to be heard, and powerlessness. See FAO, State of the World's Forests 61 (2003).

[50] See International Covenant on Economic, Social and Cultural Rights, G.A. res. 2200A (XXI), 21 U.N.GAOR Supp. (No. 16) at 49, U.N. Doc. A/6316 (1966), reprinted in 993 U.N.T.S. 3, entered into force Jan. 3, 1976.

rules of law have been developed to address the Internet and information technology, cloning, and biotechnology.

Environmental laws have been developed to deal with environmental problems. Environmental problems are understood as problems brought by industrialization that has led to the despoilment of environment in terms of diminishing air quality, water quality, and biodiversity resources. Some of the first instruments that were enacted to address environmental problems set as a goal zero pollution. Soon it was realized, however, that zero pollution was not a feasible goal for managing a phenomenon-companion to industrialization. Thus, even if statutory goals were set on zero pollution, reality involved the management and reduction of environmental problems. Because environmental legislation has been adopted to deal with environmental problems, it is not surprising that when such legislation is appraised from the perspective of effectiveness, it is judged based on whether it has managed the environmental problem with some measure of success.

For international environmental legislation to be called effective, it must meet two preconditions. First, it must establish a minimum order (convince states that cooperative solutions are better than conflict). Second, it must address successfully the distributional issues. Only after it addresses minimum-order and distributive issues with some success could it be claimed that the legislation has begun to address the environmental problem effectively.

Environmental issues are not high-conflict issues in the way that other issues could be, for instance, issues of nuclear proliferation, terrorism, or the possession of chemical weapons. Even in areas in which one would expect high conflict, such conflict has yet to materialize.[51] States have been willing to enter into agreements to protect the global commons, especially as these agreements are usually vague and nonstandard setting. Thus, one could claim that the first goal of international environmental law – that is, the maintenance of a minimum order – is usually within the reach of states.

Resource allocation issues are more difficult issues to resolve. Distributive issues are thorny for any legal system because they have to do with perceptions of fairness. Even if there is a consensus on how the appropriate allocation may be executed, parties may have difficulty in getting from words to deeds. The water management regime and the plant genetic resources regime are regimes in which the equitable distribution of resources has baffled policy makers.[52] Other times, the quest for equity may present corrective overtones. For instance, in the ozone regime there has been agreement that financial assistance is necessary to induce cooperation from developing countries.[53]

International environmental instruments work through commands or incentives. Environmental instruments usually prescribe how much pollution is to be emitted and by whom (e.g., developed countries, developing countries, economies in transition) or which fisheries and by whom are to be exploited (e.g., coastal states, distant water fishing states). These are by nature sensitive allocation decisions that

---

[51] For conflicts on the allocation of water resources, see Chapter 5.
[52] See, generally, Chapter 5 and Chapter 7.
[53] Chapter 8, Section 1.

could create disaffection and turmoil in societies. For environmental instruments to be effective, they must be perceived as resulting in:

- win–win (or Pareto optimal) situations;[54] or
- situations in which losers would be compensated whereas winners would still remain better off (Kaldor-Hicks optimal situations).[55]

Environmental instruments are unlikely to manage in an effective consensual fashion the environmental problem at hand unless they are appreciated as fair. Unless the losing constituency is compensated for concessions it makes, it is likely that it will sabotage solutions that would disadvantage it.

Understanding effectiveness as the pursuit of optimal outcomes presents effectiveness as a global welfare maximizing decision based on assessing the global social benefits versus the total social costs. Thus, efficiency concerns, in terms of societal welfare maximization, are brought to bear on the evaluation of effectiveness outcomes. Furthermore, a pursuit of a global wealth maximizing decision has in it distributive elements, at least, in terms of compensation of those who are to lose the most from the welfare maximizing outcome.

Fair distributive outcomes, for instance, are considered achieved in some international fora when certain instruments, such as those that focus on climate change and ozone protection, pursue pollution reduction, thus maximizing global social welfare while, at the same time, addressing justice concerns by compensating countries for which pollution reduction would be too costly. If that compensation is deemed to be sufficient (something that is still not clear in the ozone protection and climate change regimes), distributive justice from a Kaldor-Hicks optimality perspective would be achieved. Thus, a global wealth-maximizing outcome would be viewed simultaneously as an equitable outcome.

Assuming that Pareto optimal and Kaldor-Hicks outcomes are not attainable (and commentators agree that Pareto and Kaldor-Hicks outcomes rarely can be achieved), only coercive enforcement could convince the losers to comply. Governments are not eager to oblige with such enforcement, however, either for lack of will (unwillingness to offend other states) or way (lack of resources). Resistance from a losing constituency, combined with the lack of an effective and willful enforcement, is the reason why environmental legislation has not been implemented effectively on the ground.

The issue of enforcement is particularly sensitive in international law. This is because international law lacks an organized enforcement apparatus that would apprehend offenders and deliver punishment. As many commentators have lamented, the international system lacks an organized international police force. The international world is comprised of states that are the makers and enforcers of law. States generally are unwilling to pursue and demand of other states to obey the law, unless their vital interests are at stake.

---

[54] Posner, *supra* note 39, at 13. "A Pareto-superior transaction is one that makes at least one person in the world better off and no one worse off."

[55] According to the Kaldor-Hicks principle of optimality, a change is identified as wealth maximizing if those who gain from the change could, in principle, compensate the losers and still be better off. See *id.* at 12–13.

This unwillingness to pursue enforcement actions is due also to the origins of international law. International law was established as an institution to bring peace among belligerent states. If states were to pursue the enforcement of environmental law to the point of committing acts of aggression against other states (that could culminate from trade sanctions to reprisals), one of the fundamental pillars of international law – that is the maintenance of peace – would cease to exist and international law would begin to look incoherent. Because the fundamental purpose of international law is the maintenance of peace, environmental issues are usually not allowed to escalate to open confrontation and many environmental transgressions are tolerated, forgiven, or are traded off.

2.4. Cost-Effectiveness

The Self-Enforcing Character of International Law

Scholars who have studied the effectiveness of international regimes have expressed doubts that such regimes can be examined from the point of view of cost-effectiveness.[56] International law has been so overwhelmed with problems of minimum order and equity that dealing with the issue of achievement of benefits with the least cost appears to be overambitious.

Having said that, one should not assume that efficiency concerns are outside the ambit of international law. Efficiency concerns are, in fact, part of the rationale in decisionmaking in international law. This is because of the reliance of international law on self-enforcing rather than coercive mechanisms. Reliance on self-enforcement may create other administrative costs, but it could be justified for the purposes of equity. In international environmental law, in general, efficiency decisions cannot be neatly separated from equity considerations.[57]

Efficiency is viewed, generally speaking, as a concept that guides decision making so that the costs of an elected outcome are not higher than the benefits. If the costs are higher than the benefits, the outcome would be considered inefficient. Usually, various solutions with different cost/benefit articulations are compared with one another to determine which solution produces the most benefits with the least cost.

In the pursuit of efficiency, an assumption is made that instruments that give parties incentives to comply would generally be more efficient than instruments based on third-party enforcement. Third-party enforcement is responsible for a large chunk of costs of administering decisions. The less the need for third-party enforcement – and the more the reliance on self-enforcement, incentive-based devices – the more the likelihood that costs would be reduced, thereby creating efficient outcomes.

In domestic systems, attempts have been made to enshrine efficiency considerations in the decision-making process with mixed success. Domestic systems traditionally are based on command-and-control instruments and are heavily dependent on third-party enforcement. These domestic systems have been challenged from an

---

[56] See, e.g., Oran R. Young & Marc A. Levy, The Effectiveness of International Environmental Regimes, in The Effectiveness of International Environmental Regimes 1, 5 (Oran R. Young, ed., 1999).

[57] For the interconnection of notions efficiency and distributive fairness, see generally Posner, *supra* note 39, at 13. According to Posner: "The dependence of even the Pareto-superiority concept of efficiency on the distribution of wealth . . . suggests a serious limitation of efficiency as an ultimate criterion of social good."

efficiency perspective as failing to produce optimal outcomes (that is, the achievement of most benefits at the least cost). A whole school of law, the law and economics
approach, has as its objective to assess domestic command–and–control instruments
and propose more efficient alternatives.

From an efficiency viewpoint, international law could be characterized as a self–
enforcing institution. Enforcement is not absent in international law, but it is dispersed among a number of different actors that are usually reluctant to pull enforcement actions against recalcitrant states unless they perceive that vital interests are at
stake. Actors in international law usually make a conscious choice to avoid coercive
mechanisms and, instead, rely on persuasion. To be successful in persuasion, incentives usually are provided to induce compliance. These incentives may take the form
of financial assistance, knowledge transfer, or trade preferences. Although international environmental instruments recently have assumed an increasing command–
and–control regulatory character, the self–enforcing nature of international law has
remained, leading to efficiency results in areas where third–party enforcement would
be expensive. The self–enforcing nature of international law is demonstrated by the
fact that instruments that rely primarily on command, such as the blanket prohibition
of certain activities, have not been that successful. A prime example is provided by the
Basel regime[58] and the CITES regime.[59] Because enforcement has not been credible
in these regimes, the emergence of illegal markets is the ensuing phenomenon.

This self–enforcing nature of international law, based on a number of decentralized
incentives, saves on the costs of third–party enforcement, but it creates other costs
in terms of coordination and the running of parallel and overlapping administrative
systems that are expensive.[60] The question then is whether a more centralized system
relying more on third–party enforcement would be more desirable than the current
decentralized incentive–driven system based on a number of costly administrative
overlaps. The evolution of international law seems to point to the second direction,
as the achievement of a perception of equitable results makes an overlapping apparatus
desirable.

Cost–Effectiveness and Equity

Cost reduction issues cannot be separated neatly from equity issues. An outcome, for
instance, cannot be considered cost–effective if the initial decision reduces costs, over
the costs of competing decisions, but the eventual outcome is constantly sabotaged
by the losers. For an outcome to be efficient, it has to address concerns of equity
with some sort of effectiveness. Another option is to use coercion to force efficient outcomes, but the costs of using coercion may outdo the cost savings initially
presumed.

For decision making that involves issues of national development and environmental management, it would be misguiding to perceive efficiency as a simple calculation
of benefits and costs. Many of the benefits would resist quantification and many of
the costs may not be that obvious, especially social costs.

In terms of environmental management or development decisions that have overall global beneficial effects but also entail many losers – in terms of displacement

---

[58] Chapter 10, Section 3.
[59] Convention on the International Trade in Endangered Species (CITES), see Chapter 7, Section 2.2.
[60] See *supra* Section 1.

of populations or the wiping-out of traditional occupations – a Kaldor-Hicks criterion seems to be a more appropriate way to take into account equity concerns. This is because the criterion considers global wealth maximizing effects but recognizes, simultaneously, the need to compensate the losers. Therefore, although the criterion is presented as a criterion of efficiency, it is imbued with equity considerations. Of course, the criterion does not provide a clear guidance about the level of compensation that is considered satisfactory to the losers, because this would vary according to individual circumstances and situations, but it does provide a more organized framework concerning how to combine effective, efficient, and equitable outcomes.

A Kaldor-Hicks criterion has been applied in the climate change and ozone regimes in which achievement of global beneficial environmental effects has been pursued by providing compensation to developing countries that have the most to lose for reducing their emissions.[61] Whether the regimes would be successful would depend on whether the compensation provided would be considered satisfactory to developing countries – which means that proceeds received from compensation should outweigh the benefits of pursuing polluting technologies.

A Kaldor-Hicks criterion has yet to be applied in development/environmental management decisions in which the uprooting of populations is justified for purposes of maximizing the global welfare (e.g., in terms of global biodiversity protection). Compensation in cases of internal displacement is rarely provided and, if it does, it is rarely considered satisfactory.[62]

3. REGULATION OF NATURAL RESOURCES

The foundations of international environmental law, as analyzed in the previous section of this chapter, are the pursuit of a minimum order and sound environmental management through the satisfaction of perception of equitable outcomes. The pursuit of these goals gives international environmental law its meaning. Without the maintenance of peace, one could not even begin to discuss an international legal order. Most international environmental issues involve the management of common resources – basically, an allocative enterprise. This section explores in depth the distributional nature of environmental issues.

Environmental issues are common pool resource issues. The tragedy associated with the use of common property resources is all well known in environmental resource management. As Hardin explained, the problem with common property resources is the inability to exclude others from the use of the resource. Because all users of a common property resource are wealth maximizers, they try to get as much of the resource in an effort to outperform other users. As everybody maximizes their takings, the resource eventually collapses. Common property issues can be articulated as "taking out" problems (e.g., deforestation, fishing) or "putting in" problems (any form of pollution).[63] The rationale of a polluter is the same as that of an extractor. Because each individual polluter and resource extractor are wealth maximizers, in the minds of each of these individual wealth maximizers the costs of the sustainable

---

[61] Chapter 8, Sections 1 & 2.
[62] See Chapter 1, Section 6.8. See also Chapter 7, Section 1.2.
[63] Garrett Hardin, The Tragedy of the Commons, 162 Science 1243 (1968).

management of a resource or the costs of avoiding pollution would always outweigh the benefits. Environmental management becomes, thus, a collective action problem. That is, even if an individual polluter or extractor takes measures to diminish his/her impact on a resource, others would continue to behave as profit maximizers, leading sooner or later to the collapse of the resource.

The remedy for such common property problems is government control or private property. As Hardin expounded, taxes and property rights are examples of coercive means to escape the tragedy of commons. He admitted that taxes or private property are generally not perceived as equitable solutions. But he believed that they are "necessary evils" for the avoidance of destruction of resources.[64]

Recent commentators have elaborated on the tragedy of commons described by Hardin and have refined some elements of his account. Commentators have tried to distinguish between the nature of a resource and the system of governance of a resource. The existence of commons does not necessarily presuppose a common property system. The commons could be open-access resources, they could be under private entitlements, or they could be government property. Therefore, in order to separate the nature of a resource from the system of governance of a resource, it is more appropriate to use the term "common pool resources."[65]

Common pool resources are resources that could be accessed by all. Access to the resources by some, however, subtracts from the utility of resources to subsequent users. In this respect, common pool resources are distinguished from public goods.[66] For public goods, access by some users does not subtract from the enjoyment of future users. Air quantity, for instance, could be conceived as a public good because it is not subject to subtractibility. By contrast, air quality is a common pool resource because the pollution of air by some users would subtract from the enjoyment of other users.

Common pool problems are essentially collective action problems. Collective action problems in the management of common pool resources involve distributive decisions in terms of deciding

- who is to be included in the management of a resource (and thus, who is to be excluded);
- how to distribute the benefits to those included; and
- how to compensate the excluded.

Environmental decision making has to do with the distribution of common pool resources. The question for decision makers is often how to distribute the use of natural resources or how to distribute the burden of an externality caused by the use of a resource.

International environmental problems dealt with in this study are common pool problems. Air quality, the high seas, and high-seas fisheries are, by definition, common pool resources because they constitute global resources that could be accessed by everyone. The use of these resources by some would subtract from the use of others. Other problems have become common pool problems because of the lack

---

[64] Id.

[65] See Charlotte Hess & Elinor Ostrom, Artifacts, Facilities, and Content: Information as a Common Pool Resource 52, paper to be presented at the "Conference on the Public Domain," Duke Law School, Durham, North Carolina, Nov. 9–11, 2001.

[66] Id. at 44, 55.

of effective jurisdictional control. Such problems include biodiversity, plant genetic resources, and freshwater sources.

Air quality is a common pool resource because the pollution of the air by some affects the utility of the air for others. The high seas is also a common pool resource because the pollution of waters by some would disadvantage the use by others. High-sea fisheries are common pool resources because the depletion of fisheries by a state would affect other states that wish to fish in the high seas. Freshwater resources, such as lakes and rivers, are common pool resources among the states in a region that share those resources. Subtracting too much water by one state could affect the availability of water in another state.

One must qualify, however, that freshwater sources do not necessarily have to present the problematic of common pool systems, given that states have the power to exclude other states from the use of a resource (especially upstream states versus downstream states). States that have "physical" jurisdictional control over a resource should, in principle, have the power to exclude others from the use of the resource. The question is whether they are willing and capable to use that power (which depends on the power configuration in a region and their general level of enforcement capacity).

Many river basin systems today could be characterized as common pool resources. These resources are shared by states that are the common "owners," users of the resource because they share jurisdictional control over the resource. States often use these resources as if they are the only beneficiary, and rapacious use by many users has led to the degradation of many regional river basin systems.

Terrestrial biodiversity resources do not seem to be common pool resources as biodiversity resources are under the jurisdiction and thus, one would assume, control of states. Usually, however, the assumption that control follows jurisdictional assertion is wrong. As a matter of fact, states are not always in control of their biodiversity resources, and the lack of effective control transforms such resources to open access resources. As time has gone by, however, the vise of state control over national biodiversity resources has become tighter.

Wastes are not *prima facie* common pool resources. Actually, one could hesitate to call waste a resource. Because wastes are materials of generally perceived low or zero value, they are frequently disposed haphazardly and generators, transporters, and disposers are eager to get rid of them in a legal or an illegal fashion. For those who generate waste, waste is an externality, and they would be content if they could shift such externality to the rest of the society.

States have chosen to deal with waste, which is basically the by-product of industrial or household activity, under "you generate it you own it" mantra. This is a forced enclosure of a negatively valued resource. Without this forced enclosure, waste could lie in exposed landfill areas without safeguards on the disposal or further use, becoming in effect an open-access negative resource. The situation of abandoned landfills in developed countries is well known. This situation resulted from the lack of regulatory controls with regard to the ownership of disposed wastes.

Private corporations have been pushed to take responsibility over the waste they produce and transfer under the assumption that a conscious undertaking of responsibility would lead to sounder disposal practices and waste reduction. States have adopted the principle of self-sufficiency, namely, that each country should become self-sufficient in waste management. The purpose of the self-sufficiency principle is to enclose wastes within national borders, thus preventing the infliction of external-ities from the transfer and disposal of such wastes on third states and on the global commons. The side effect of this forced enclosure has been the development of a black market in the transfers of hazardous and radioactive wastes.

4. ENCLOSURE OF NATIONAL COMMONS

Various systems have been devised for the management of common pool resources: common property, government ownership, and private ownership. Commentators document the evolution in the management of common pool resources as follows. First, common pool resources are under a common property system. The system involves a small number of individuals or, more commonly, households that make use of a resource. These households are familiar with each other, and thus are able to monitor each other's uses and avoid excess in the use of a resource. After all, it is in their interest to prevent resource collapse.[67]

With a change in population dynamics, new users make claims on the resource. Prior users, the first claimants, are unable to assert their rights over the new users and the resource becomes a *de facto* open access resource. Then the state intervenes to prevent the collapse of the resource and appropriates the resource under a rationale that state ownership would improve management. Now users have to pay fees for use. Users that cannot afford the fees are excluded. Oftentimes, however, governments fail to maintain proper control over resources and an open access phenomenon may ensue again. A last resort option, therefore, is to develop private ownership rights or rights of use, such as quotas.[68]

The evolution in the management of common pool resources does not have to lead fatalistically to the collapse of the resource or private property or government control. Common property resource systems can work when sincere efforts are made to restrict the number of users. After all, corporations and share contracts, as well as other modern forms of ownership today, are in essence common property systems.[69]

Some preconditions for the development of common property include:

- a limited number of users;
- a community of users;
- clearly defined boundaries of a resource;
- monitoring of use;
- ability to exclude outsiders;
- graduated sanctions for violations;
- minimal recognition of the rights to self-organization;
- a common understanding about the uses of a resource; and
- good information about the resource and its potential.[70]

---

[67] Hess, *supra* note 65, at 58.
[68] *Id.*
[69] *Id.* at 57.
[70] Elinor Ostrom, Self-Governance and Forest Resources 7, Center for International Forestry Research, Occasional Paper No. 20, Feb. 1999.

Common ownership resource systems regained popularity when it was realized that private property did not remedy many of the problems encountered in the developing world with regard to the use of common pool resources. Exclusionary property rights regimes do not provide answers about what to do with the "outsiders." These are the people who live at the fringes of common pool resources and find themselves on the onset of privatization, totally excluded from the resource.[71]

Common property resource systems also attracted attention because states were unable to assert effective control over common pool resources. Problems with regard to the protection of biological diversity, have been attributed to states that as apathetic spectators or instigators have allowed the decimation of natural resources. The situation is more acute in developing countries, where it is assumed that corrupt officials let companies do anything for the right price. Sometimes, the right price would dictate support for logging/fisheries operations engaging in overharvesting. Other times, the right price would involve the preservation of protected areas for ecotourism projects.

Community resource management systems have been developed for the management of biodiversity resources. CAMPFIRE is a well-known such system that has been marred by a variety of problems.[72] An ideal Community-Based Natural Resources Management (CBNRM) system would involve: collective action defined as an action taken by a group as a whole in defense of its shared interests; an enabling environment that is legislation and an institutional structure in support of the devolution of power to the local community; property rights and /or user rights (access to resource, withdrawal (e.g., rights to take fish, plants); and control rights (including exclusion, alienation and management)). Furthermore, user groups would need access to financing and skills and linkages to other groups.[73]

CBNRM is more appropriate for small-scale resources because its enforcement – and, thus, its success – are based largely on the ability of users to observe each other's behavior.[74] Extraction activities are more easily monitored by the users of a resource. By contrast, emissions/discharges of polluting substances into the environment are not that easily monitored and, thus, are not subjected frequently to CBNRM.[75] CBNRM systems are tailored better to the management of complex resources, such

[71] See Nancy Forster & David Stanfield, Tenure Regimes and Forest Management (Land Tenure Center, University of Wisconsin-Madison, March 1993); Kathleen McNamara, Key Policy Issues, in Living with Trees: Policies and Forestry Management in Zimbabwe 1, 4 (P.N. Bradley & K. McNamara, eds., 1993).

[72] See Elli Louka, Biodiversity & Human Rights: The International Rules for the Protection of Biodiversity 79–90 (2002). CAMPFIRE is a CBNRM system that has been developed in Zimbabwe. Its purpose has been to transfer some of the management of wildlife resources to the local population under the assumption that accumulated benefits from resource use would lead to the conservation of endangered resources.

[73] See Ruth Meizen-Dick & Anna Knox, Collective Action, Property Rights, and Devolution of Natural Resources Management: a Conceptual Framework, in "Proceedings of International Conference: Collective Action, Property Rights and Devolution of Natural Resource Management: Exchange of Knowledge and Implications for Policy" 48–58, Puerto Azul, Philippines, June 21–25, 1999 (Ruth Meizen-Dick et al., eds., 1999).

[74] Carol Rose, Common Property, Regulatory Property, and Environmental Protection: Comparing Community-Based Management to Tradable Environmental Allowances, in The Drama of the Commons 233, 237 (National Academy of Sciences, Elinor Ostrom et al., eds,. 2003).

[75] Id. at 241, 245.

as wildlife. A fundamental problem with all CBNRM systems is that they are closed systems. Extensive commercialization of a resource could undermine these systems. Supporting such systems would involve shielding them from outside commercial pressures[76] – a difficult-to-meet requirement in today's globalized economies.

Despite the renewed attention paid to common management resource systems, efforts to privatize common pool resources have not relented. Flexible privatization systems with regard to the management of fisheries and air pollution have had some degree of success in developed countries. Such systems start with the establishment of a level of maximum allowable pollution or a total allowable catch (TAC) (e.g., for fisheries). Permits are assigned to users of a resource (air, fisheries) that define their quotas of allowable pollution or catch (called individual transferable permits – ITPs or individual transferable quotas – ITQs). Rules for permit trading among users are established so that those who underuse their quotas could sell them to others unable to limit their emissions or catches to their initially assigned rights.

Individual Transferable Quota (ITQs) systems could be applied to larger-scale resources than those appropriate for CBNRM systems.[77] The function of ITQs is based on trade and trading needs large markets to operate. For instance, ITQs have been successful for the management of long-range pollutants, such as sulphur dioxide, but are less successful for localized pollution.[78] In the area of resource management, ITQs have been successful in certain areas in managing fisheries that usually straddle national or subnational frontiers.[79] One disadvantage of ITQ systems is that they are less responsive to complex situations[80] that may demand a reexamination of the assumptions on which they were established. ITQs systems must be able to give quota holders a reasonable amount of security that the system would continue as established, at least for the foreseeable future. Without such an implicit guarantee, not many potential buyers would be willing to purchase quotas.[81]

The operational logistics of ITQs systems present an amount of complexity that may limit their application in the international arena. They also may be perceived as inequitable. The initial allocation of quotas in these systems usually is based on historical rights. These rights could very well be contested later by potential new entrants who believe that they have legitimate claims to access a resource.

5. ENCLOSURE OF GLOBAL COMMONS

The enclosure of common pool resources is a matter of fact within most states' boundaries. National common pool resources that are not in some way enclosed under common, private, or government ownership are more liable to become open-access resources and, thus, subject to unfettered exploitation. The enclosure of resources, since the first enclosure movement,[82] has been painful for those who have been termed "outsiders" and, thus, excluded from ownership and use of a resource.

---

[76] *Id.* at 247.

[77] *Id.* at 239.

[78] *Id.* at 240.

[79] *Id.* at 239.

[80] *Id.* at 242–43.

[81] *Id.* at 247.

[82] See, e.g., J.A. Yelling, Common Field and Enclosure in England, 1450–1850 (1977).

High seas, high-seas fisheries, transboundary freshwater resources, and biodiversity resources are common pool resources that present management challenges similar to those presented in national common pool resource systems. The management of global pool resources is even more challenging than the management of local common pool resources because it demands of states not only to manage their share of a resource but also to cooperate with other states for the management of a shared resource. If collective action is problematic with regard to common pool resource management in domestic institutional settings, the collective action problems in international law could seem insurmountable.[83]

Another issue that has been presented as a global commons issue involves what has been called "intellectual global commons." Intellectual commons are conceived as the knowledge and information derived from science, technology, information technology, cyberspace, and biotechnology. Whether knowledge and information should be free access, in the public domain, or subject to intellectual property rights has been a contentious matter in global and national arenas. Some authors have called intellectual property rights over knowledge the second enclosure movement (the first one being the enclosure of agricultural land).[84] The privatization of knowledge under an intellectual property rights regime has been rationalized for the benefits it brings by creating incentives for inventors to pursue innovative activities.

The tragedy of commons rationale that fueled the enclosure movement in domestic arenas has been used to rationalize the expansion of state jurisdictional control over what were considered before global commons. The recognition of EEZ, for instance, is an example of recent tendencies to enclose the global commons.[85]

An enclosure regime could be generally effective in international law if it is inclusionary by consensus (induced by side payments) or it is exclusionary and exclusion is ensured by various coercive mechanisms. An example of an inclusionary regime is the ozone regime. An example of an exclusionary regime is the fisheries resources regime. Enclosures based on the exclusion of many outsiders are likely to incur high enforcement costs. Without extensive enforcement, exclusionary enclosure is unlikely to be effective.

5.1. Fisheries

The high seas has been considered always an open access resource. The freedom of the high seas has been considered the cornerstone of the law of the sea.[86] This freedom has been challenged, however, by a number of regimes that have encroached on the notion of freedom of high seas.

The challenge to the freedom of high seas is most obvious in fisheries management. The freedom of high seas in terms of the freedom of fishing has been challenged since the early 1900s.[87] The preponderant issue in fisheries management is the struggle to regulate a resource that falls both within national jurisdiction and

---

[83] See, e.g., Mancur Olson, The Logic of Collective Action (1965).

[84] See James Boyle, The Second Enclosure Movement and the Construction of the Public Domain, 66 Law & Contemporary Problems 33 (2003).

[85] R.R. Churchill & A.V. Lowe, The Law of the Sea 160–61 (1999).

[86] Id. at 205.

[87] See Chapter 6, Section 3.2.

within areas considered traditionally global commons – the high seas. Fisheries also could be shared among states in a region as they straddle the EEZs of different states.

The challenge to the traditional concept of the freedom of the high seas reached its peak in the mid-1990s with the adoption of the UN Straddling Fish Stock Agreement.[88] The agreement has authorized states to enter into regional management agreements for fisheries resources that straddle the EEZs and the high seas. At the core of these agreements is an exclusionary ethic. The exclusion of states not willing to be bound by the regional management rules established by the club of states that decide to enter into a regional fisheries management agreement.

Chapter 6 examines in detail the efforts of states to enclose the high seas for the purpose of guaranteeing access to fisheries resources for their population. The enclosure of high-seas fisheries is bound to bring many benefits to states that are to become co-owners of resources of a parcel of seas they have been able to carve from the commons. From the perspective of states situated on fringe of fisheries enclosures, regional fisheries management regimes are conceived as a threat. Generally, excluded states are willing to employ all means to limit the jurisdictional reach of regional fisheries agreements. Regional fisheries agreements are not meant to produce Pareto-optimal situations, as modern fisheries management cannot be accomplished but for the creation of some losers by exclusion. Furthermore, states that belong to a regional fisheries management club are unlikely to conceive it as wealth maximizing to pay compensation to losing states. This is likely to create perpetual situations of conflict.

Countries establish Regional Fisheries Organizations (RFOs) in order to prevent unregulated fishing in high sea areas adjacent to their EEZs. RFOs are essentially clubs of states, the purpose of which is to exclude other states from the use of a resource without necessarily providing compensation or other incentives for lost access. Some RFOs have been successful in fisheries conservation, whereas others have had marginal success. The success of RFOs depends on the willingness of their members to comply themselves with the rules they enact and to enforce these rules on others. The willingness to comply and to implement enforcement measures differs from RFO to RFO and some RFOs are plagued with collective action problems. The overuse of objections to common management decisions in some RFOs is demonstrative of the collective action problems they face.[89] Generally, the more cogent and economically developed a group of countries that make an RFO, the more likely it is that rules would be respected and enforced both within the RFO and on unregulated high-seas fishing – by might or right.

As the international fisheries regime is still developing and unregulated fishing in the high seas is becoming increasingly untenable on economic and environmental grounds, the question of apportionment of fisheries resources based on the concept of equity needs to be further elucidated in the regional agreements among states. Equity is a shifting concept in regional fisheries arrangements in which the rights of states that traditionally fish an area could be challenged constantly by new entrants.

---

[88] See Chapter 6, Section 3.3.1.
[89] Therefore, some RFOs, such as the NAFO, have established that objections must be based on clear and justifiable grounds, see Chapter 6, Section 3.5.4.

The clout of these new entrants and the authority of regional organizations would determine how the allocation of fisheries resources would be resolved in particular regions.

Enclosure of fisheries resources at the international level has been accompanied with the increasing privatization of fisheries resources at the national level predominantly through Individual Transferable Quotas (ITQ) schemes. The advantages and pitfalls in the application of such schemes are examined in detail in Chapter 6.

5.2. Deep Sea-Bed Resources

The mining of deep sea-bed resources is examined here as an example of a common pool resource that countries have attempted to place *ex ante*, that is, even before the technology is perfected for its exploitation, under a common property regime. The management of deep sea-bed resources is the first such regime in which the minute details of a "common heritage" approach to the management of a global common pool resource have been worked out. The further evolution of the regime, which has yet to be fully articulated, may be indicative of the fate of common property regimes under international law.

The UNCLOS[90] has established a regime for the management of deep sea-bed resources that are outside the national jurisdiction of states. At issue here are the precious metals and nodules found in the deep sea-bed. The exploitation of these valuable resources has remained a theoretical matter as technologies have yet to be applied extensively to allow for deep sea-bed exploitation.

Prima facie deep sea-bed resources are outside the national jurisdiction of states, thus, they could be deemed open-access resources that could be accessible to any entity wishing to engage in deep sea-bed mining. Such a view of the deep sea-bed as an open-access resource would have benefited companies in developed countries that are eager to develop the technologies for sea-bed exploitation. In early 1960s, several consortia were formed to mine precious sea-bed nodules, including companies such as U.S. Steel, Amoco, and Lockheed Missile.

The developing world, however, in what could be characterized as a preemptive move, decided to push for a common heritage approach of deep sea-bed. Such a common heritage approach was not just a revamped version of open access (as it has been the case with plant genetic resources). Instead, a common property resource system was established according to which those who were to exploit the resource were to share the benefits with those unable to engage in exploitation. The details of the system are established in Part IX of the UNCLOS. The sea-bed area is declared the common heritage of mankind,[91] and no state is allowed to assert sovereignty over the area and its resources.[92] The rights to the area are "vested in mankind as a whole" on whose behalf the International Seabed Authority (ISA), the organization established under the sea-bed provisions, is to act.[93] Activities in the area are to take place for the benefit of mankind as a whole, irrespective of the geographical location

---

[90] United Nations Convention on the Law of the Sea, Dec. 10, 1982, reprinted in 21 ILM 1261 (1982).
[91] Art. 136, *id.*
[92] Art. 137(1), *id.*
[93] Art. 137(2), *id.*

of states,[94] and the ISA "shall provide for the equitable sharing of financial and other economic benefits derived from activities in the Area."[95]

The functioning of the regime is entrusted to the development of an international mining organization called Enterprise[96] that is managed under the ISA. The technology and financing for the functioning of Enterprise are to come from developed countries,[97] but the benefits from exploitation are to be shared with developing countries. Production controls[98] and various fees[99] are also included, to protect the land mining industries of the developing world.

The United States refused to go along with this version of a common heritage approach that was viewed as an ideological articulation of "the new international economic order" (NIEO) inspired by socialist ideals that undermined free markets. The mining industry in developed countries opposed the sea-bed provisions that resemble OPEC-like cartelization,[100] mandatory technology transfers that seem to negate intellectual property rights,[101] financial arrangements that resemble taxes, and the creation of an international mining enterprise.[102]

Eventually, the United States succeeded in amending the deep sea-bed provisions of the UNCLOS even after the convention was ratified. The amendments are more respectful of market principles and give more decision-making power to countries that have the technology to mine sea-bed resources. The amendments are included in an agreement[103] that is to be read as a single instrument with the UNCLOS.[104]

The agreement reflects concerns of the United States and other developed countries that international bureaucracies should be kept as minimal as possible for the purposes of cost-effectiveness.[105] Furthermore, the decision-making authority of the Assembly and the Council, the constituting bodies of the ISA,[106] were revamped

---

[94] Art. 140(1), *id.*

[95] Art. 140(2), *id.*

[96] Art. 153, *id.*

[97] Art. 11(3) of Annex IV, *id.*

[98] See art. 151, *id.*

[99] Art. 13 of Annex III, *id.*

[100] See art.151 on Production Policies, *id.*

[101] Art. 144, *id.* See also art. 5 of Annex III, *id.*

[102] See James K. Sebenious, Towards a Winning Climate Coalition, in Negotiating Climate Change: The Inside Story of the Rio Convention 277, 288 (Irving M. Mintzer, et al., 1994).

[103] Agreement Relating to the Implementation of Part XI of the United Nations Convention on the Law of the Sea of Dec. 1982, July 28, 1994 available online at http://www.un.org/Depts/los/convention_ agreements [hereinafter Sea-bed Agreement].

[104] Resolution Adopted by the General Assembly, Agreement relating to the implementation of Part XI of the United Nations Convention on the Law of the Sea of 10 December 1982, Forty-eighth session, Agenda Item 36, UN. Doc. A/RES/48/263, Aug. 17, 1994.

[105] Thus, according to the agreement all organs and subsidiary bodies to be established under the UNCLOS and the agreement must be cost-effective. See Section 1, para. 2, Annex to Sea-bed Agreement, *supra* note 103. It is mentioned also that the functioning of the Authority and other organs must be based on an evolutionary approach allowing for flexibility and adaptability and the further development of the organs. See Section 1, para. 3, Annex to Sea-bed Agreement, *id.* The agreement sets up a Finance Committee comprised of 15 members that must include representatives from the largest financial contributors to the ISA's budget. The Committee is to make decisions on financial and budgetary issues by consensus and can make recommendations to the Assembly and the Council. See Section 9, Annex to Sea-bed Agreement, *id.*

[106] The Council, the Assembly and the Secretariat are the constituting organs of the ISA, see art. 158 UNCLOS, *supra* note 90.

to give more decision-making power to the United States and other industrialized nations. One of the major reasons many industrialized countries refused to ratify the convention is that decision making was based more or less on principles of equality among states rather than those of effective power.[107] Furthermore, technology transfers to developing countries are no longer mandatory.[108] Other arrangements that have to do with market-based reform include the termination of production limits,[109] the reduction of the fee for approval of a plan of work,[110] and the termination of the obligation for the mandatory funding of Enterprise.[111]

Thus, one could state that the sea-bed agreement has amended the UNCLOS in a way that it is more favorable to developed countries and is more reflective and respectful of the distribution of power in the world. The fact that developed countries do not have to subsidize the activities of Enterprise, engage in mandatory technology transfers, and observe limits in production, in combination with decision-making arrangements that give them control over the sea-bed, should have led them to ratify the convention.

Despite the transfer of decision-making power, some preferential treatment of developing countries has remained and the fundamental premises of egalitarianism promoted by the regime are still prominent.[112] Resistance in the United States to

---

[107] For instance, the Assembly, which is constituted of all members of the ISA, can now make decisions only upon the recommendation of the Council and the Finance Committee. See art. 159, UNCLOS, *id*.

   If the Assembly does not accept the Council's recommendation, the matter must be returned to the Council for further consideration. Furthermore, the Council is now restructured. The United States is guaranteed a seat in the Council in perpetuity. The decision making of the Council is changed and now industrialized nations can form a blocking vote to a decision. Section 3, paras. 5, 9 & 15, Annex to Sea-bed Agreement, *supra* note 103.

[108] See art. 5 of Annex III, UNCLOS, *supra* note 90. Instead, the Enterprise and developing states wishing to obtain sea-bed mining technology shall seek to obtain such technology "on fair and reasonable commercial terms and conditions on the open market, or through joint-venture arrangements." See Section 5, para. 1(a), Annex to Sea-bed Agreement, *supra* note 103.

[109] According to the agreement:
   "There shall be no discrimination between minerals derived from the Area and from other sources." See Section 6, para. 1(d), Annex to Sea-bed Agreement, *id*.

[110] The agreement also does away with an expensive annual fee set at $1 million and establishes a set of principles and procedures that would guide decision making in determining fees. The application fee for the approval of a plan of work in the sea-bed is also reduced to $250,000 (from $500,000), see Section 8, Annex to Sea-bed Agreement, *id*.

[111] With regard to the Enterprise, the international mining company established under part IX of the UNCLOS, the agreement provides that the provisions of the convention that provide for the funding of the Enterprise by state parties do not apply. State parties are under no obligation to finance any of the operations or joint-venture arrangements of the Enterprise. See Section 2, para. 3, Annex to Sea-bed Agreement, *id*.

[112] For instance, articles 140 and 150 of the UNCLOS that refer to preferential treatment of developing countries and the equitable sharing of benefits have not been phased out. The Enterprise has retained its status as an international mining firm. The agreement even provides that if the Enterprise or developing states cannot obtain deep sea-bed mining technology, the Authority may request all or any of the contractors and their sponsoring states to cooperate with the Authority in facilitating the acquisition of mining technology. But the acquisition of technology must happen on fair and reasonable commercial terms and conditions consistent with the effective protection of intellectual property rights. See Section 5, para. 1(b), Annex to Sea-bed Agreement, *id*. The agreement also offers financial assistance to developing countries that are likely to suffer serious adverse impacts on their export earnings from the reduction in the price of a mineral due to sea-bed mining. See Section 7, Annex to Sea-bed Agreement, *id*.

the UNCLOS ratification has to do with the potential implications of the principles enunciated in the convention. Despite the toned-down nature of the distributive conditions in the agreement, the fundamental structure remained: an international mining enterprise exploiting the sea-bed as a common heritage of mankind.

A ratification of the UNCLOS by the United States would imply an acceptance of this fundamental principle – that the sea-bed is the common heritage of mankind – with all possible ramifications (real or imagined) for future interpretation that such a principle may entail. As some commentators have put it, the experimental nature of state-of-the-art of sea-bed mining, and, thus, the uncertain future benefits resulting from such mining, has made developed countries unwilling to provide side-payments to developing countries that would facilitate the exploitation of the deep sea-bed.[113]

5.3. Germplasm and Related Knowledge

The plant genetic resources regime initially was conceived as a common heritage regime, but common heritage in this case was understood more or less as free access. Certain countries used to place restrictions on the exports of valuable resources, but such restrictions were an exception rather than the norm. The common heritage regime for plant resources in a natural condition was a *de facto* free access regime.[114] In some ways, plant genetic resources are like fisheries. They are fugitive resources spread among various countries and continents. The sheer magnitude and nature of the resources make it difficult to place them under firm state jurisdictional control.

Some of these useful plant genetic resources, mostly agrobiodiversity resources, have been exchanged, studied, and exploited – almost without national controls – for centuries, despite the fact that they are in effect under national jurisdiction. The fact that these resources are rarely indigenous to a specific country but are usually shared among a number of countries in a continent has led to globalization in their use and exploitation. Although these resources are under areas of national jurisdiction, it is almost impossible to expect that a state, no matter its jurisdictional reach, could have effective control over the large variety of plants (and their seeds) that are within its territory. Plant genetic resources were, therefore, *de facto*, global, open access resources for decades. There have been some exceptions in cases of lucrative plant resources that some states have tried to keep under national control.[115] State effective control over lucrative plant genetic resources has aided in the legitimization of the current regime of enclosure of plant genetic resources.

By contrast, inventions, derived from plant genetic resources, have been zealously appropriated under private intellectual property rights regimes. Private intellectual property rights over "worked plant genetic resources" have been articulated as plant breeders' rights or biotechnology patents.[116]

---

[113] Gary D. Libecap et al., Public Choice Issues in Collective Action: Constituent Group Pressures and International Global Warming Regulation, July 20, 2000, available online at http://ssrn.com/abstract=235285 (Social Science Research Network Electronic Paper Collection).

[114] See Chapter 7, Section 2.1.2.2.

[115] Jack R. Kloppenburg, Jr. & Daniel Lee Kleinman, Plant Genetic Resources: The Common Bowl, in Seeds and Sovereignty 1, 5 (Jack R. Kloppenburg Jr., ed., 1988).

[116] Chapter 9, Section 4.

Thus, although resources found in nature have been free access, knowledge derived from the use of these resources has been enclosed under private intellectual property rights systems. This disparity has motivated developing countries, countries that are by definition rich in biodiversity resources, to enclose their germplasm by asserting their willingness to enforce national jurisdiction over plant genetic resources. Since the late 1980s, the assertion of national jurisdiction over plant genetic resources has replaced, earlier systems of *de jure* common heritage but *de facto* open access to plant genetic resources.

The wisdom of subjecting plant genetic resources to effective state ownership and control has been under question. Plant genetic resources are rarely indigenous to a country. There are usually found in a number of countries within the same continent. Furthermore, genetic material may be shared among plants that are spread across continents. It is unclear, therefore, that a state enclosure of plant genetic resources would be effective in practical terms, that is of actually enclosing plant genetic resources within national frontiers. Cartel-like enclosure supported by all countries in a region is likely to be more successful but international experience with cartels has not been very promising, especially given the free-rider problems that are rife in cartels.

The transformation of an open-access system to a proprietary system has to do with the desire of developing countries to obtain, at least, some compensation from third parties that are accessing their genetic resources. Developing countries are hopeful that jurisdictional control can generate Pareto-optimal opportunities as they would provide plant genetic resources in exchange for new technology, such as biotechnology. Biotechnology companies and developed countries, however, have yet to perceive the benefits of controlled access to be substantial enough to justify significant side-payments to the developing world. This may be because too much trust has been placed in resources already kept in gene banks and the breakthroughs in other technologies. Contracts that have been entered into between bioprospectors and developing countries since the initiation of formal control systems over natural resources have yet to bring to developing countries the "green gold" they initially expected to flow from plant genetic resources enclosure. The United States has yet to ratify the Biodiversity Convention, especially because biotechnology companies are reluctant to share newly developed technologies with developing countries.

At the same time that developing countries have asserted property rights over resources found in nature, they have challenged the system of intellectual property protection for "worked" plant genetic resources. Developing countries have challenged intellectual property systems over "worked genetic resources" and their fundamental assumptions. At the basis of all intellectual property systems rests a belief that intellectual property rights – and monetary and reputation benefits associated with them – would encourage inventors to engage in innovative activity.

The challenge to "the enclosure of intellectual commons" or, as it is called also, "the enclosure of intellectual public domain," is essentially a challenge to the assumption that stronger intellectual property rights will promote the advancement of the innovative enterprise.[117] Those who challenge the "enclosure of intellectual commons" have claimed that such enclosure has stifled innovation as the boundaries

---

[117] Boyle, *supra* note 84, at 57.

between discoveries and inventions are disappearing and, thus, useful discoveries are quickly appropriated whereas their unfettered use would have generated more innovation.[118] Some commentators have used the notion of "tragedy of anti-commons" in which a scarce knowledge-resource is underused because too many owners block each other.[119] Seeds of dissension concerning the validity and usefulness of intellectual property rights over genetic resources have undermined the legitimacy of the Trade-Related Intellectual Property Rights (TRIPs) agreement adopted under the WTO,[120] and have generated demands for more openness and transparency in the processes of granting intellectual property rights under national systems. Developing countries have specifically demanded that the disclosure of country of origin of a resource and prior knowledge about the use of a resource by indigenous peoples and farmers become part of the patent application process.[121]

5.4. Freshwater Resources

Freshwater resources shared by states are common pool resources. This is because the use of the resource by a state subtracts from the use by other states. The pollution of a river, for instance, by an upstream state affects the use of water downstream. Extensive use of water by upstream states means that downstream states would have to either undertake the costs of purifying the water, for drinking or agricultural use, or forfeit use all together.

Common pool freshwater resource problems have been exacerbated by what has been called demand-led scarcity of water. Most freshwater resources are under stress today because the majority of states have yet to introduce some sort of rationalization and planning in the use of their freshwater resources. Problems with water scarcity in certain regions have to do more with unsound water management rather than actual limited water supply. Countries still divert too much water to agriculture and have yet to implement systems that would ensure that users pay a fair market price for water use. By contrast, those who view freshwater as a public good refuse to accept that fees, charges, and water privatization are the way to go with regard to the proper management of water. Some further assert that the conflict between private and public management is a pseudo-debate: whether water management is in private or in public hands, cost recovery of water production and purification in a way that takes into account those who cannot afford full water pricing, may be the compromise desired.[122]

In the international arena, the 1997 UN Watercourses Convention is the first global instrument that has been adopted to deal with the management of water as a shared common pool resource among states.[123] The convention has proposed a system of management of shared freshwater resources based on equity, the needs of countries affected, and a list of other nonexclusive criteria. The convention proposes

---

[118] *Id.* at 34–42.
[119] Michael A. Heller & Rebecca S. Eisenberg, Can Patents Deter Innovation? The Anticommons of Biomedical Research, Science 698, May 1, 1998.
[120] See Chapter 9, Section 4.3.
[121] *Id.*
[122] Chapter 5, Section 2.2.
[123] Chapter 5, Section 4.

that countries should enter into regional agreements for the protection and allocation of water resources, as regional arrangements are likely to be more pertinent for the regulation of water in a region.

Countries entered into regional agreements for the management and allocation of their shared watercourses before the 1997 UN Convention. Some agreements were not based clearly on principles of equity, as it could be understood as a fifty-fifty allocation or an allocation based on needs, but more appropriately as equity based on historical rights of "first in use, first in right." The Nile Agreement has been presented as an effort by a regional power to enclose shared water resources for its exclusive use.[124]

Countries have entered into agreements to manage their common water resources. These agreements usually establish River Basin Organizations (RBOs), which, like Regional Fisheries Organizations (RFOs), are given various powers for the management of shared resources.[125] Such powers include data collection, regulation, monitoring, and dispute settlement. The degree of independence of RBOs from state influence depends on how willing states are to delegate control of a common resource to an independent regional agency. Safeguards are built frequently into these agreements to ensure that none of the states monopolizes power.

Some RBOs have been successful in the management common water resources. Others have been less successful. Some of these agreements have produced win–win situations in terms that all states affected have gotten a piece of the pie. Some states have accepted compensation for agreeing to more water use by their neighbors. Some agreements have promised more than they could deliver. Other agreements have been umbrella agreements in which the use of multiple water resources is negotiated simultaneously and concessions in the use of one resource are compensated with advantages in the use of others.

Overall regional water management agreements are a "mixed bag" that reflects, *inter alia*, the power configuration in a region. Equity in this case has much more to do with behavior that conforms to the expected rules of the game in a region than some idealized perception of equity as a fifty-fifty distribution of resources or an objective assessment of the needs of coriparians. The rules of the game generally mean that some process safeguards are followed (such as that everybody is heard and can provide information), and that the needs of hegemons are respected and needs of weaker states are not neglected.

In some cases, the enclosure of common water resources has taken place as an effort to include as many coriparians as possible. In other regions, enclosure has been forced by regional hegemons who have been able to exclude potential other users, based on prior use or backed by the threat of force.

5.5. Air

Air is generally conceived as a public good. The consumption of air by one person does not affect the availability of the air for others. With industrialization, however, it was quickly understood that the use of air by new technologies affects air quality.

[124] Chapter 5, Section 5.1.
[125] Chapter 5, Section 2.3.2.

Polluted air is not only aesthetically displeasing. It can cause respiratory and other physical ailments. The crowding of the air by polluting emissions transformed the air from a public good to an open access resource the relentless use of which – under a business as usual scenario – would lead to its degradation. The pollution of the air induced the realization that air is a common pool resource. In the absence of government regulation or property rights, a tragedy of commons was inevitable.

The first efforts for the enclosure of the air were regulatory. An overall upper limit of pollution was set and standards were established for individual sources of pollution that could not be exceeded. It was soon realized, however, that all polluters were not equally effective in reducing pollution. For smaller polluters, lacking economies of scale, pollution reduction could be costly.

Regulators, therefore, have decided to introduce tradable quota systems for certain pollutants, similar to the ITQs established in fisheries. The upper limit of pollution is promulgated by regulation and polluters are assigned permits specifying the level of pollution they could emit. If they are to emit less pollution than that assigned, they could sell some of their permits to other polluters. The system gave some flexibility to industries – that could not easily absorb the costs of adopting new technologies – to adapt. In the United States, the Environmental Protection Agency (EPA) initiated in 1982 an interrefinery trading of lead credits. The goal of the EPA was to reduce the content of lead in gasoline without undermining the profitability of small refiners that had to shoulder higher implementation costs. Thus, if some refiners could lower their emissions to levels lower than the regulatory standards, they could earn credits that they could trade with firms that could not lower their emissions. The refineries made extensive use of the program.[126] A major tradable allowance program has been initiated for sulphur dioxide emissions also. It is estimated that the cost savings from the program amount to $1 billion annually.[127]

Permits to pollute were challenged initially by environmental NGOs that viewed assigned property rights, in terms of permits to pollute the air, a public good, as *ipso facto* immoral. In some ways, the permits to pollute could be conceived as a restricted privatization of the air. The privatization of the air did not happen in terms of an unlimited license to pollute. The life span of air pollution permits has been limited and the ITPs have addressed only a small number of pollutants. The final goal has been the reduction of pollution in a fashion that would involve some cost savings for the industry. Pollution rights have made possible pollution reduction in several areas in ways that are more cost-effective than the traditional command-and-control legislation.

In terms of international law, air is certainly a shared resource among states. The initial efforts to enclose the air as a commons were regulatory. The transboundary air pollution regime, the ozone regime, and the climate change regime are efforts to enclose the commons by regulating them. A system of tradable emissions among countries has yet to be established with expanded markets where polluters could buy or sell emission credits. However, some of the concepts that have been enshrined

---

[126] Curtis Carlson et al., Sulfur Dioxide Control by Electric Utilities: What Are the Gains from Trade?, Discussion Paper 98–44-REV, April 2000 (Resources for the Future, 2000).

[127] Albert L. Nichols, Lead in Gasoline, in Economic Analyses at EPA: Assessing Regulatory Impact 48 (Resources for the Future, R. Morgenstern et al., eds. 1997).

in international conventions, such as that of joint implementation, come close to restricted privatization. Joint implementation is allowed in international agreements for regional legal entities such as the European Community. Countries in a region are viewed as an entity and it is the overall level of pollution in the region that counts for the purposes of meeting the regulatory requirements set by an international treaty rather than pollution generated by each individual country. This means, implicitly, that countries need to determine among themselves air pollution entitlements. Such determinations are usually based on the level of industrialization, needs, and availability of state-of-the-art technology. Thus, states with more advanced technology may be willing to concede pollution rights to countries with less advanced technologies in that region. Countries that experience a prolonged recession may decide to sell some of their emission credits to countries that are unable to proceed with drastic emission cutting. The transboundary air regime in Europe, the ozone regime, and the climate change regime provide for different versions of joint implementation that boil down to the same idea of establishing pollution entitlements that would be traded eventually.[128] The climate change regime has adopted the Clean Development Mechanism, which involves joint implementation projects between countries of the North and countries of the South.

The collaborative nature of joint implementation should not be blinding with regard to the underlying assumption on which it is based: that the air is a common pool resource and without regulation and some sort of privatization, in terms of assignment of restricted pollution rights, it would be degraded.

International instruments have addressed the distributional effects of controlling air pollution. Developing countries have viewed the distributional effects of air pollution control as inequitable. Developing countries have yet to achieve the level of industrialization of developed countries. As they have not significantly contributed to air pollution, they view it as unfair to shoulder emission reduction costs because so much more needs to be accomplished in terms of their industrialization. Compensation has been demanded for the forfeiture of "dirty but cheap" industrialization that was the norm for the industrialization of the North. Major air pollution control treaties provide for such compensation to developing countries as a form of side-payment for their participation in the enclosure of the commons. As some developing countries are to become the major emitters of air polluting substances in the future, the success of air pollution regime depends on their willingness to participate in the enclosure of global air resources.

5.6. Seas

The seas are a classic example of common pool resources transformed into open-access resources. States that share the sea suffer from the collective action problems of managers of common pool resources. Regulation of pollution by one state could quickly be overridden if other states continue to pollute. The free-rider mentality would eventually lead to a tragedy of commons.

States have enclosed the seas by extending their jurisdictional reach through the establishment of EEZs. Other efforts to control pollution are regulatory in terms of

[128] See Chapter 8.

limiting pollution from ships, dumping, and land-based sources. These regulatory efforts have not been that successful, however. Some states are more eager to curb pollution than others, and this creates a serious problem with defections. States in general have been more successful in regulating pollution by dumping and pollution by ships than pollution from land-based sources. Pollution by dumping is more easily controllable because what is not dumped in the seas potentially could be dumped in the land.[129]

Controlling pollution from ships is trickier. Ships are numerous and it is difficult to observe their behavior when they are traveling in the high seas. Because of the inability to monitor a large number of these diffuse sources of pollution, regulatory/technological requirements are established that all ships have to adopt. The rationale is as follows: if ships are built in a way that their mere construction would reduce polluting events, pollution should be reduced. Insurers and the resellers' market are transformed, thus, into the monitoring device for meeting these ship construction requirements. If ships do not meet the requirements set by the MARPOL Convention they cannot not obtain insurance and they are unlikely to be resold at a fair market price. Regulatory requirements are, therefore, followed by and large and this has led to the reduction of marine pollution.

The regulation of the seas in terms of marine pollution from land-based sources has not been that successful. This is because the sources of pollution are many and diffuse. Every little factory that dumps polluting substances in a river that ends up in the seas and any agricultural field in which fertilizers are used are possible culprits of such pollution. The problem is that generators of pollution cannot be easily located and standards would differ for the various industries the pollution of which ends up in the seas.

Countries have tried to address sea pollution by controlling the number and nature of substances that different industries discharge directly into the sea or to freshwater sources that end up in seas. The distributive impacts of limiting marine pollution, because of lapses in effectiveness, have yet to be explored satisfactorily in terms of side payments to developing countries that may not have the capacity to control polluting discharges.

5.7. Waste Management

Waste management is an allocation issue in terms of sharing the burden of an externality. As mentioned earlier, waste, the way it is dealt with today, could hardly be characterized as a resource. Most countries view wastes as the by-product of an industrial activity. The initial impetus, therefore, is to find ways to get rid of waste as cheaply and as quickly as possible. Waste transfers from developed to developing countries acquired attention in the late 1980s. Companies in developed countries started to transfer their hazardous wastes to developing countries because it was much cheaper and less politically controversial to dispose of their waste there. A number of instruments were adopted, therefore, based on the rationale that each country should, in principle, be responsible for its own waste. The principles of self-sufficiency and proximity are the principles on which international waste transfers

---

[129] See Chapter 4, Section 3.2.

are based (that is, each country must be self-sufficient in waste management and wastes must, in principle, be disposed of as close as possible to the point of generation). The emergence and persistence of black markets in waste trade, therefore, should not come as a surprise.[130]

The "you generate it you own it" mentality that characterizes most international instruments (and national ones) regarding waste generation could be defined as a forced enclosure. Companies are required to own their wastes and the externalities caused by them and to take measures to deal with them responsibly. Countries are requested to take control over wastes generated within their borders and to prevent, as much as possible, waste transfers to other countries. Waste is, after all, a (negative) resource that if not dealt with responsibly would cause many externalities, such as contaminated land and groundwater supplies, sea and river pollution, and air pollution. Waste, if not treated adequately, could affect all resources – air, water, and land. If land disposal facilities are not safeguarded properly, they are bound to become a source of contamination, especially in communities that are not familiar with the hazards that these facilities present. Therefore, safeguards must be applied so that these facilities are controlled and those who own them must be responsible for the proper treatment and disposal of the wastes they contain.

Forcing generators, transporters, and disposers to own their waste and be liable for the externalities it causes is the first attempt at sound waste management. The forced enclosure of this perceived negative resource (waste), in terms of expecting each country or locality to develop self-sufficiency in waste disposal and treatment, however, may not be as effective as intended. Generators must own the waste they produce and be responsible for the externalities it causes. Forcing countries to become self-sufficient in waste management could generate undesirable outcomes. Self-sufficiency could produce particularly undesirable results in developing countries that may wish to develop a recycling industry or do not generate sufficient wastes to justify the development of indigenous waste treatment and disposal facilities.

5.8. National Biodiversity Resources

In the previous paragraphs, we examined how national governments have attempted to appropriate what are considered to be global common pool resources for the purposes of averting a "tragedy of global commons." In this section, we will examine the inverse phenomenon: how the international community has tried through regulation to implement effective international control of national biodiversity resources. This still-in-progress "internationalization" of national biodiversity resources is based on arguments that many states, and particularly developing countries, are inept at or unwilling to manage in an effective fashion their biodiversity resources.

Endangered species and habitats are not generally considered global common pool resources since they are under the national jurisdiction of states. Sometimes, endangered species and habitats straddle national borders of two or more countries

---

[130] Conference of the Parties to the Basel Convention on the Control of Transboundary Movements of Hazardous Wastes and their Disposal, Fifth Meeting, Dec. 6–10, 1999, Note by the Secretariat, Prevention and Monitoring of Illegal Traffic in Hazardous Wastes and Other Wastes, UNEP/CHW.5/18, Aug. 11, 1999.

that may collaborate for the common management of a resource. But, generally, unsound management of a resource in one area does not automatically mean the degradation of a resource in another contiguous area. The view of the ecosystem as interdependent entity (everything connected to everything else) is not supported by most ecologists. Many ecosystems have remained viable, whereas other ecosystems adjacent to them have been degraded.[131]

Biodiversity resources, under the jurisdiction of one state, exhibit all the characteristics of common pool resources within that state. Pastures, forests, and semiagricultural areas often were common property resources that were later transformed, because of population pressures, into open-access resources. States have attempted to enclose these resources by using different versions of enclosure, namely through common property, government ownership, and control and private property, with mixed results. Chapter 7 provides many examples of the efforts of states to enclose their common biodiversity resources.

Despite the fact that terrestrial biodiversity resources are not what one would call global commons, efforts have been made to internationalize the issue of protection of biodiversity resources. The Biodiversity Convention, for instance, provides that biodiversity resources are a matter of global concern. The CITES regulates trade in endangered species. A number of other conventions attempt to regulate specific species and habitats located naturally within state boundaries.

The enclosure of biodiversity resources *at the global level* involves efforts to internationalize the management of such resources and then place such resources under the control of states and other constituencies that perceive to have interests in the preservation of resources. The international enclosure of biodiversity resources involves two steps: first, the internationalization of biodiversity as an issue through a number of soft global/regional instruments and media attention. The global importance of the resource is underlined (e.g., the elephant, the Amazonian rain forest). Second, stringent instruments are adopted the purpose of which is to affect the national/local management of a resource. It is not surprising, therefore, that developing countries have resisted, in principle, the international enclosure of their national commons. Occasionally, however, they have been more complacent as such enclosure comes with side-payments direly needed in many areas of the developing world.

Examples of the international enclosure of biodiversity resources include the concept of heritage sites. The concept of heritage sites attempts to transform national areas into, at least, areas of international concern. Regulation/prohibition of trade in endangered species attempts to determine the evolution of local resource management systems in developing countries. Debt-for-nature swaps involve debt forgiveness for developing countries under the undertaking by these countries to put land aside for conservation – thereby dictating land utilization decisions in these countries. It is interesting to note that environmental NGOs have been able to purchase debt and used such debt for nature swaps with developing countries, thus adding, nongovernmental involvement in the attempt to enclose national biodiversity resources internationally.

---

[131] See Bobbi Low et al., Redundancy and Diversity in Governing and Managing Common-Pool Resources 12, Paper Presented at the 8th Biennial Conference of the International Association for the Study of Common Property, Indiana University, Bloomington, Indiana, May 31-June 4, 2000.

The presumption behind attempts to internationally enclose biodiversity resources is that developing countries lack the capacity or will to preserve such resources. Without the intervention of developed countries and other interested constituencies, it is perceived that developing countries are being faced with a tragedy of commons. Because biodiversity resources of the developing world are conceived as unique and worth preserving for humanity and future generations, a tragedy of commons within a country is appreciated as a global tragedy of commons.

Generally, developing countries have resisted efforts of international enclosure of their national biodiversity resources. Developing countries have refused to adopt an international convention on forests.[132] Developing countries are trying to assume effective control over their agrobiodiversity resources.[133] Developing countries firmly insist on the inclusion, in most international environmental instruments, of the phrase (or permutations of it) – "each state is sovereign over its natural resources." In other cases, however, developing countries have been tempted by the compensation offered and have agreed implicitly to the international enclosure of their natural resources (e.g., through debt for nature swaps).[134]

6. ENCLOSURE OF GLOBAL COMMONS AND GLOBAL WELFARE

The gradual enclosure of global commons is a fact. The question that must be answered is whether this enclosure is beneficial for the global welfare or whether international policy makers should pursue a different course of action for the development of international law, a course of action more likely to increase global benefits.

Even the use of term "global welfare," however, could be looked on with distrust. An argument that enclosure instruments, or any instrument for that matter, could have some effects on "global welfare" seems to be premised on an assumption of a world that shares the same interests. As often repeated in this study the world is divided between developed and developing countries and even between developing and least-developed countries. Even within the same group of countries, developed or developing, states could very well conceive that their interests are not aligned with those of their counterparts. Many could argue, justifiably then, that global welfare is a fiction that attempts to generate unity in a world divided between the haves and the have-nots or, even worse, according to nationally conceived interests.

The notion of global welfare is examined here from the foundational perspectives of international environmental law – namely, minimum order, equity, and effectiveness. In other words, the question we attempt to answer is whether the enclosure of global commons can generally be perceived as an equitable, effective enterprise for all of those that participate in that enterprise.

---

[132] See Chapter 7, Section 3.2.

[133] Chapter 7, Section 2.1.2.2.

[134] A debt-for-nature swap is an agreement between a developing nation and its creditors. In the debt-for-nature swap, creditors agree to forgive the debts of a developing country in exchange for the environmental protection of a specific area. The target of most debt-for-nature swaps are large areas of land located in tropical rain forests. As will be seen in Chapter 7, these areas of land are often claimed by agriculturalists.

In terms of effectiveness, the instruments are judged on whether they have been able to bring a minimum order (some sort of collaboration among states) or a maximum order (the effective management of an environmental problem that could, at least, partially generate a resolution of such a problem).

From the perspective of effectiveness as a minimum order, one could easily conclude that most environmental regimes have been able to bring order in what is often conceived to be a chaotic international scene.

From the respective of the effective resolution of environmental problems, international environmental instruments have had a mixed record of achievement. This is because some of the instruments have not been able to address the distributional issues that are at stake. Dissension and disagreement, therefore, are perpetuated in international fora as countries engage in forum shopping to achieve the resolution that would best serve their interests.

International environmental regimes may become ineffective also because countries have been reluctant to invest the resources that would allow for regime monitoring, enforcement, and for the minimum infrastructure for regime development. As environmental issues compete with other issues (such as various conflicts and epidemics) considered of relatively higher importance in international agendas they rarely acquire the priority they could deserve.

International environmental regimes, thus, may lack in effectiveness either because they have not addressed distributional issues in a satisfactory fashion or because they have not acquired the importance in international arenas that would attract the attention and resources of states.

Fisheries

The enclosure movement in fisheries has produced a number of regional agreements that attempt to control the fisheries of an area by giving priority to coastal states and distant-water fishing states with historical rights in fisheries. These agreements are usually perceived as equitable among the states that agree to share a resource. For those who remain outside, however, these agreements are perceived as inequitable. The issue is, for instance, why historical rights should be given preference over newer claims. Sometimes also skirmishes develop among states that have entered the agreement – between states more attuned to preserve the resource (usually coastal states) and states more interested in the quick economic profit (usually distant water fishing states). The distributional issues in fisheries management are bound to be the most explosive issues in the future management of the resource. The success and, thus, the effectiveness of the regime would depend on its ability to generate perceptions of equitable distribution among the insiders and to compensate outsiders for nonparticipating. In the absence of means of compensation, effective and, thus, legitimate enforcement means must be put in place.

The distributive character of fisheries regime is particularly relevant in some regional fora. The Pacific fisheries resources regime has been evolving into a regime in which small island states have started to assert control over their fisheries resources and are using the regime as a mechanism to spur collective action that would generate rents from the resource. In the past, such rents were not forthcoming as better-equipped distant water fishing states tended to dominate the management of the resource.[135]

The cost-effectiveness of regional enclosures has not been examined, specifically, as the effectiveness of the regimes is still under question. The international system is by definition an incentive-based system and, thus, a cost-effective system because it avoids in principle third-party enforcement. It seems unlikely that the fisheries regime, as it develops through exclusionary enclosures, however, would avoid traditional enforcement. It is highly likely that the regime will be challenged by states that remain outside the regime. Because the compensation of losing states may not be high enough to be considered satisfactory by them, only the credible threat of enforcement would prevent unregulated fishing in the high seas.

A final question is whether regional fisheries agreements are more effective than the prior regime of freedom of fishing in the high seas. The anarchical situation in the high seas combined with threats to the sustainability of fisheries resources presented the enclosure of fisheries – in terms of regulation and assertion of jurisdictional control by coastal states – as the only reasonable outlet. It seems that, in the case of fisheries, the choice is between two evils: open access and ownership by exclusion. As open access is becoming untenable, ownership by exclusion seems to be the future evolving norm.

Germplasm and Related Knowledge

In the plant genetic resources regime, two enclosure tendencies are in place. The first one concerns the physical enclosure of resources within the territory of a state. The other has to do with the enclosure of intellectual commons.

The physical enclosure of plant genetic resources has been pursued more as the restoration of distributional equity and the tit-for-tat response to intellectual property rights over "worked genetic resources" expressed as plant breeders' rights or patent rights on biotechnology inventions. Plant breeders' rights have been protected for years and new laws have been enacted for the patented protection of biotechnology inventions.

As a response to the "enclosure of intellectual commons," countries rich in biodiversity, but not advanced in biotechnology, started to view the enclosure of their physical resources as fair and the perfect retaliation against the assertion of developed countries concerning intellectual property rights over "worked resources." It was expected that the enclosure of "raw" biodiversity resources, and the concomitant assessment of fees for accessing those resources, would bring countries economic advantages. It was further expected that new norms would emerge for sharing in the profits of intellectual property rights over resources. Although new norms have emerged that provide restricted conditions of access to unprocessed biodiversity resources, the advantages envisaged by developing counties in enclosing their germplasm resources have yet to materialize, at least, to the extent that developing countries had contemplated.

Overall, the regime for the enclosure of "raw germplasm resources" has been characterized as ineffective. Too many barriers have been placed on the access to "raw genetic resources" so as to inhibit research and innovation without making

---

[135] See, e.g., Chapter 6, Section 3.5.1.

developing countries wealthy.[136] The control of access to germplasm resources inspired by corrective justice concerns has been unable to address in an effective fashion the distributional issues of the present, namely, how resources that are found in some biodiversity rich areas of the world could be accessed by those who want to generate profitable knowledge by providing, at the same time, some measurable profitable outcomes for the developing world.

Developing countries believe that they are entitled to some compensation, given that it is knowledge extracted from *their resources* that generates wealth for international corporations. Without these "raw resources," often propagated and preserved by local populations, many of the "inventions" of multinational companies might have never happened.

Multinational companies, by contrast, do not seem willing to provide any substantial compensation for the acquisition of resources. This is because they perceive that the value they add to the resource, after many years of experimentation, is what generates profits and not the resource itself. Some bioprospecting agreements between developing countries and companies of the developed world attempt to address the concerns of developing states without, at the same time, ceding too much ground in terms of monetary benefits to such states.

Demands to open the intellectual property rights regime, at least with regard to biotechnology, are unlikely to shake the foundations of such a regime. Biotechnology is a new technology and countries (and companies) are likely to continue to be zealous of biotechnology innovations generated within their borders. It is unlikely that biotechnology would become open-access technology any time soon, as many developing countries would prefer.

Although demands to open the intellectual property rights regime are unlikely to produce the demise of the regime, they could affect the shaping of such a regime. Challenges to biotechnology patents based on the existence of prior knowledge may discourage the filing of superficial patents. Forcing the disclosure of knowledge obtained from indigenous communities, and on which a biotechnology invention may be based, could assist in some of the benefits from intellectual property trickling down to those communities.

Demands to open intellectual property, so that inventions become common property immediately after they are recognized, are unlikely to find soon a fertile ground. But demands to open the intellectual property rights regime are likely to make such a regime more responsive to claims of equity, especially with regard to the appropriation of prior knowledge, when such knowledge should have remained in the public domain as open-access knowledge. The intellectual property rights regime over "worked resources" that originate in developing countries is likely to continue to be conceived as inequitable from the perspective of countries within the territories of which such a resource is located. This is likely to be so even if the "worked resource" involves a clear "inventive step" in the isolation of valuable material within the resource.

Demands to open the intellectual property rights regime are not always based on equity concerns. They have to do with the effectiveness of the regime as well. For instance, in an era when the distinction between discoveries and inventions is

---

[136] Chapter 7, Section 2.1.2.1.

becoming blurred, it has been charged that intellectual property rights on knowledge are bound to undermine rather than to spur innovation.[137]

The fundamental premise of intellectual property rights regime is that it encourages innovation because it allows scientists to obtain monetary and reputational benefits from the fruits of their endeavors. Demands to open the intellectual property rights regime challenge this fundamental assumption. Claims are made, for instance, that the sharing of more knowledge and the appropriation of less knowledge would result in more innovation. This is because so many of the new intellectual property rights claims are made not on "inventions," as inventions were understood in past, that is some sort of device ready for application. Intellectual property rights also are made on substances found naturally, provided that a scientist has been able to isolate these substances and identify them in the laboratory. Declaration of property rights over a process to isolate a naturally occurring substance, when other competing processes of isolation have yet to be invented, essentially declares a monopoly over the use of the substance. Legitimate concerns can then be raised whether such an effective monopoly is preferable to a sharing arrangement.[138]

As technology has developed to include more than improvement in mechanical devices, the intellectual property rights regime has had to evolve to encompass the new life technologies. The debate over what should be considered patentable, and what should not, would continue as such technology is further refined and developed. The declaration of property rights over living material is unlikely to cease. Courts and legislators, however, would need to define further the parameters of protection of intellectual property ownership.

Developed countries do not intend to unravel intellectual property rights protection in order to accord biotechnology concessions to the developing world. It is also unlikely that developing countries would balk at the enclosure of their unprocessed germplasm resources. The enclosure of "raw germplasm resources" is not motivated so much by the benefits it would bring to developing countries but, rather, seen as an expression of corrective justice hard fought for and won in international arenas. The enclosure of germplasm resources is not the most effective international regime, but it is likely to continue to reign when more would have been gained for the global welfare if literally anyone interested in germplasm was allowed to collect germplasm and experiment with it to find out potential useful applications. The gene bank system and that of International Agricultural Research Centers (IARC), as it enveloped in the past, was based on the premise of free collection, use, and experimentation. Although that germplasm resources system was far from a perfect system, it had achieved much for the preservation of useful or rare seeds, the development of new cultivars, and the distribution of much needed genetic material to countries in need.[139]

The current system of enclosure of "raw germplasm resources" and intellectual property rights over "worked resources" is a system that is based on the enforcement apparatus of domestic systems and their jurisdictional reach into other systems. Countries that have enclosed "raw germplasm resources" must ensure that none of

---

[137] See Boyle, *supra* note 84.
[138] *Id.*
[139] See Chapter 7, Section 1.3.

their indigenous natural resources cross their national borders without their consent. Countries that have enclosed "worked germplasm resources" must verify that patent rights on biotechnology inventions are respected in the developing world. The costs of third-party enforcement for the enclosure of germplasm resources and the protection of intellectual property rights could be potentially quite high.

The costs of enforcement could be quite high because many developing countries do not have effective control over their territories and borders. Thus, potentially many people could infiltrate these countries who may wish to collect plants and seeds for further experimentation. The extensive piracy regarding many products produced in developed countries, especially software and various other technological devices, demonstrates that the enforcement of intellectual property rights in many countries with regard to biotechnology inventions is bound to be challenging.

It was hoped that the TRIPs agreement, as it is situated under the umbrella of an international organization, would be able to bring to the protection of intellectual property rights a new legitimacy in the developing world. Such legitimacy, however, has yet to be attained as the debate over intellectual property on pharmaceutical products has aptly demonstrated.[140]

Freshwater Resources

With regard to freshwater resources that cross national frontiers, states have to come to a common agreement on how to apportion such resources. Equity concerns are paramount in the regime for the protection and allocation of freshwater sources. The 1997 UN Convention explicitly refers to equity. Many regional agreements have claimed that they constitute an attempt to share resources equitably. The meaning of equity within the regional fora where freshwater agreements have been concluded has varied. It is rare that equity means a fifty–fifty allocation of a resource. Many times, states have decided to share their waters based on their respective needs. Other times, equity has meant negotiation on a bundle of resources. In that case, concessions with regard to a resource in the bundle are accompanied by the acquisition of advantages in another resource. One could clearly decipher, behind the equity discourse, that the needs of hegemonic states have held more weight in some cases. Sometimes, the distribution of resources reaches a Pareto optimal outcome in terms of the achievement of win-win situations. Other times, states that have heightened interests in the use of a resource are willing to provide other states what can be considered adequate compensation with the promise of renegotiation as the needs of states may change.

Because one of the purposes of law is to redress the imbalance between the powerful and the weak by searching for equitable results, the question is what equity has been translated to mean in the regional freshwater agreements. According to a dictionary definition, equity means that the rules of the game are observed: for instance, in the sense of a fair game, the rules of boxing are observed.[141] A correct appreciation of equity in regional freshwater agreements would involve an in-depth understanding of the rules of the game as they are configured and reconfigured in a specific region. Such rules of the game are not included only in formal instruments.

[140] See Chapter 9, Section 4.2.
[141] See Chapter 5, note 66.

They have to do with implicit rules that have been formed, *inter alia*, by the use of effective power in a region. To assume, for instance, that each state in a region has the same say in the distribution of a resource is to assume a world not motivated by power, a hardly realistic assumption.

Regional agreements for the allocation and protection of freshwaters vary in the degree of effectiveness they have achieved for the development and protection of freshwater resources. Some agreements just serve minimum order purposes as they are basically there to ensure that conflict does not escalate out of control. Other agreements have been more substantive and actually have led to a balance in the development of a resource. Agreements among countries in developed regions have been more effective because these countries do have the financial means to engage in the sound management of a resource. Some agreements in developing regions have been effective in bringing in line the expectations of countries with regard to the future management of a resource.

Whether such agreements have been cost-effective is something that needs further examination. Again, as in the case of regional fisheries agreements, an evaluation of efficiency of regional arrangements would have to examine these arrangements in light of a competing proposition. Such a competing proposition does not seem to exist at this point. The international management of all freshwater resources that would involve the establishment of an international authority to deal with these resources seems to be out of the question for the time being. Given that freshwater resources lie within the jurisdiction of each state, such an international authority would be unlikely to develop. Even if such an international authority were developed, it would have to work through a number of regional cooperative arrangements so that management does not become chaotic. In the absence of a competitive proposition, regional management would be the way of the future. But regional arrangements would benefit from benchmarking studies that would demonstrate best practices and how these practices could be applied to different regions to enhance efficient and effective water management.

Regional freshwater agreements are generally in tune with the self-enforcing apparatus of international law. Regional agreements often establish a commission, the purpose of which is the interpretation of the agreement in terms of the allocation of benefits from water use – but the agreement does not remain static, evolving as time passes. The establishment of an institutional framework, which deals with dispute resolution and the future management of freshwaters at stake, frequently is considered more important than the achievement of water distribution at a specific point in time. Commissions have been granted extensive powers and, when granted such powers, have been able to play the role of final arbitrator in international water disputes. The success of commissions, however, has not been uniform. In some cases, commissions have languished because state parties to an agreement were reluctant to delegate to them power and authority.

Regional water management organized around a commission usually involves the centralization of many water services and water authorities that were previously diffused among different states and regions. Commissions usually are made up of scientists who specialize in water management. These scientists often bring their expertise in water management matters and have been able to use their expertise and hard data to diffuse the political nature of a dispute. Regional commissions equipped with information could become effective organs in the management of water resources in many regions.

Air

Transboundary Air Pollution

The global enclosure of the air has taken effect through a number of regulatory and market-based instruments.

Transboundary air pollution centers around the UN/ECE Convention on Transboundary Air Pollution. The regime involves the cooperation of similarly developed countries that have decided to work together to reduce the transboundary impacts of their discharges. This regime has become increasingly more stringent with regard to the emissions of certain pollutants and now regulates effectively a number of pollutants that are responsible for transboundary air pollution.[142]

This regime has been perceived as effective in reducing emissions. Much needs to be accomplished, however, in terms of certain pollutants, such as Volatile Organic Compounds (VOCs) and Persistent Organic Pollutants (POPs). Typically, less developed countries in the region, are allowed to increase their emissions, whereas major polluters agree to reduce their emission discharges. The distributive effects of transboundary air pollution regime have not been challenged significantly by any of the participating countries.

The cost-effectiveness of the regime has to be examined thoroughly. The question is whether the regime would be less costly or more effective if, instead of command-and-control technological requirements, it had made available to its members more of incentive-based instruments. Market-based instruments have been introduced in national fora with substantial gains in efficiency. The duplication of such instruments in international fora, therefore, seems to be desirable. Some market-based mechanisms have been incorporated in the transboundary air regime. But market-based instruments have yet to be developed internationally. There are no international markets for buying and selling emission credits. The complexity of creating such markets, given the regulatory and cultural disparities among states, would probably outweigh the expected efficiency gains at this point. But it should not be excluded in the future. The transboundary air pollution regime is highly regulatory, and participants in the regime need to investigate how to manipulate the regime to take advantage of the self-enforcing nature of international law.

Protection of Ozone Layer

The ozone regime started as a regulatory enclosure of the global commons. But it was soon realized that such an enclosure could not be implemented without the consent of all potential stakeholders. Unlike the enclosure of fisheries, where a number of states can create an exclusionary ownership regime, the enclosure of air was not amenable to exclusionary ownership. Ozone-depleting substances can destroy the ozone layer independent of whether they come from developed or developing countries. The enclosure of global commons of the air had to be inclusive. Such inclusion could be coercive or consensual. The treaties that make up

---

[142] See Chapter 8, Section 3.

the ozone regime have established a number of incentives, in terms of delayed targets and timetables and in terms of financial compensation, that facilitate compliance by developing states. At the same time, however, sticks in the form of trade sanctions and noncompliance remedies are available.[143]

Theoretically, the ozone regime should be effective because those who have the most to gain from the reduction of ozone-depleting substances are willing to compensate those that are to lose in terms of forfeiting cheap industrialization made possible by ozone-depleting substances. Whether the compensation offered would be considered satisfactory so that countries would be willing, indeed, to forfeit cheap industrialization remains to be seen. The regime, in addition to compensation, provides for trade sanctions for the countries that refuse to comply. But restrictions, in terms of sanctions, are unlikely to be as successful because the smooth functioning of the regime is already threatened by the existence of black markets for ozone-depleting substances

The regime has been considered effective in terms of actually achieving some of the recovery of the ozone layer. But the effectiveness of the regime still remains under question as now developing countries have to apply specific targets. Given the potential amount of ozone-depleting substances that could emitted by newly industrialized countries, the defection of developing countries from the regime could decidedly undermine the effectiveness of the regime.

Climate Change

The climate change regime is more complex than the ozone regime. There is some uncertainty about what climate change would involve and which countries it would adversely affect. Thus, although it could be presumed that most countries would prefer to remedy the ozone problem such presumption does not necessarily hold for climate change. Some countries/regions are to benefit from climate change, whereas others are to be losers. Furthermore, certain countries have come to contest the science behind climate change making the regulation of climate change even more complex and acrimonious. The enclosure of global commons of the air in terms of climate change control started with a framework convention and was firmed by the Kyoto Protocol. The Kyoto Protocol has established a number of mechanisms, such as joint implementation, emissions trading, and the Clean Development Mechanism, to induce cooperation.[144]

Given the nature of air as global commons, an inclusionary property regime had to be established based on the coercion or consensual accord of all possible stakeholders. It remains to be seen whether the enclosure of the air, in terms of control of greenhouse gases, would become effective because major emitters, such as the United States, have refused to join in the regime, claiming that the scientific evidence behind climate change claims is faulty. Assuming that there are no enticements for the United States to participate and in the absence of a coercive mechanism against a global hegemon, the air could remain an open access resource for major CO_2 emitters. Thus, the regime would be ineffective because those who perceive themselves

---

[143] See Chapter 8, Section 1.
[144] See Chapter 8, Section 2.

as winners cannot compensate or even entice a major emitter that has much to lose in terms of current growth by the drastic reduction of greenhouse gases.

Demands for the proper allocation of costs of the enclosure of the air have been articulated by developing countries. Countries in the developing world – such as India and China, which are to become large CO_2 emitters – have refused to join in the regime. These countries claim that the benefits they would forfeit in terms of further industrialization by joining in the regime outweigh significantly any compensation that would be offered by developed countries. The implied demand behind these claims is that unless substantial compensatory measures – such as availability of cleaner state-of-the-art technology at subsidized cost – are to become available, developing countries are not to abandon the business as usual scenario for their industrialization.

The climate change regime has just entered into force.[145] This means that the market-based mechanisms included in the Kyoto Protocol that provide schemes of joint implementation among developed countries and between developed and developing countries could become soon fully operational. Experimentation with such schemes has already started.[146] The degree of participation of developed and developing countries in such schemes would determine whether regulation of greenhouse gases is to be achieved in a more cost-efficient way rather than by command-and-control measures. The market-based mechanisms included in the Kyoto Protocol need a comprehensive and quite laborious administrative apparatus to function smoothly. The development of such a well-functioning administrative apparatus would present a challenge for international institution-making.

Seas

As mentioned earlier, the effectiveness of an enclosure depends on how inclusive it is. If all potential participants agree on the rationale for an enclosure and decide to limit their takings (or discharges), then enclosure would be an effective means of managing the global commons. Another solution, the one most frequently encountered in practice, is to opt for the enclosure of a resource by a limited number of participants. The other potential stakeholders would then be bought off (compensation or side-payments) or be coerced to compliance.

The marine pollution regime is based on the rationale of inclusiveness. With regard to sea dumping and pollution from ships, states have striven to develop regimes in which the majority of polluting countries would participate. Although participation seems to be satisfactory in terms of numbers, it is still lacking in terms of substance. Many countries, for instance, fail to report on the amount of hazardous substances they dump in the seas. The regime on the control of pollution from ships seems to be more successful because it is based on construction standards. There is speculation, however, that many illegal discharges still happen in the high seas.[147]

---

[145] With the ratification of Russia, the regime entered into force on February 16, 2005.

[146] E.g., in the context of the European Community, see Directive 2003/87/EC of the European Parliament and Council of October 13, 2003, establishing a scheme for greenhouse gas emission allowance trading within the Community and amending Council Directive 96/61/EC, OJ L 275, 25.10.2003.

[147] Chapter 4, Section 3.2.

The enclosure of the seas in terms of discharges from land-based sources has been the most challenging because there are so many sources of pollution. Countries that surround specific areas of the seas have usually entered into agreements to control pollution, but such regimes have been largely ineffectual given the nature of the problem involved. As a result, many land-based sources of pollution treat the seas as an open-access area. Because pollution from land-based sources constitutes the bulk of sea pollution, the seas, in terms of pollution control, have remained open-access areas.[148]

The regime for the control of marine pollution has not been challenged significantly in terms of its distributive outcomes. Both developed and developing countries have been laggards with regard to restricting the number of substances they introduce into the seas as the regime for the control of land-based sources of pollution has demonstrated. At the same time, most developing countries are not considered to be significant polluters of the seas, as their level of industrialization is quite low.

The regime for the prevention of marine pollution acquired new steam after the 1992 Rio Conference. Many of the conventions for the protection of the seas have been revamped to include more explicit regulatory requirements. Some progress has been made in the certain regions of the developed world, as the Rhine River regime and the Danube River regime have demonstrated.[149] These regimes have included a number of decisive measures to control the harmful substances that enter into the rivers and, consequently, into the seas. Overall, however, despite the number and increasingly stringent character of international conventions, not much has been accomplished in practice for the control of entry of pollutants in the seas. Therefore, one could claim that the regime has been lacking in effectiveness, as states have not seen marine pollution as a problem of such an international magnitude that would allow for the devotion of credible resources for its implementation.

Waste Management

For international waste transfers, the notion of equity has been translated to mean self-sufficiency. At the core of the waste regime is the achievement for every country of self-sufficiency in waste management. Equity as self-sufficiency dictates that states need to become self-reliant in the management of their environmental externalities so that they do not impose such externalities on other states. Behind this notion of equity as self-sufficiency lurks the belief that, unless self-sufficiency is imposed, the more powerful states would let their environmental externalities be borne by weaker states. Self-sufficiency attempts an *ex ante* distribution of externalities rather than an *ex post facto* correction of such externalities. Notions of self-sufficiency echo notions of equity as capability. Those responsible/capable of producing pollution must bear the externalities of polluting events.

There is a competing notion of equity, with regard to the waste issue, that has do with an appreciation of the fact that waste generation is a matter of common responsibility. All countries generate some waste. Requiring each country to become self-sufficient in all types of waste treatment and disposal seems to negate the notion

---

[148] See Chapter 4, Section 1.
[149] See Chapter 5, Section 5.4.2.

of corrective equity, frequently expressed as solidarity. Furthermore, self-sufficiency undermines the function of international law as a device that cultivates cooperation among states. Corrective equity (or solidarity) has taken many forms in international law – such as assistance to countries with less capacity and resources and humanitarian intervention. Expressions of solidarity are not that infrequent in international arenas as, for instance, when countries send assistance to states hit by disasters.

The pursuit of self-sufficiency undermines cooperative behavior in international law that is so much needed in tackling issues of common concern. Self-sufficiency could threaten minimum order as it tends to promote isolationism. Notions of self-sufficiency in waste management could lead to ineffective and inefficient waste management decisions.

Furthermore, most international law, and especially international trade law, is based on the assumption that countries cannot be self-sufficient in everything. This is why it makes sense to trade with other countries. If waste could be reconceptualized as another good that states are willing to trade among themselves, the transnational management of wastes, based on the principle of sound waste management, could become a reality.

Wastes have acquired a bad name because they are by-products of industrial and household activity. Industries and households generate waste, but none of those responsible for waste generation is eager to shoulder the externalities of waste pro-duction. Altering notions of self-sufficiency with regard to waste management would require a change in assumptions about waste usability. Redefining wastes as potential sources for other material and energy production would be important in changing such perceptions.

The waste regime has been influenced by equity considerations with regard to who should be responsible for waste management and transfers and, thus, how to distribute the costs of an externality called waste. In an attempt to find an equitable solution, countries have enacted complex regulatory apparatuses. The international system for the control of waste movements, which has been replicated in regional fora (e.g., the EC context), is similarly quite burdensome. The implementation of an international waste control system has encountered difficulties. Waste generators have bypassed regulation by finding refuge in illegal markets. A stringent regulatory apparatus accompanied with the lack of credible enforcement demonstrates that, despite all rhetoric, states have not appreciated waste trade as a priority issue the way they have evaluated other matters, for instance, the control of trade in weapons of mass destruction.

National Biodiversity Resources

In principle, biodiversity resources are under the jurisdiction of a state. States often have asserted ownership over natural resources located within national borders. Thus, usually, resources not privately owned are likely to be government owned. Com-mon property regimes, as a spontaneous development, have ceased to exist in most countries, whereas some countries are now experimenting with induced common property institutions, such as the CAMPFIRE program.[150] States have been eager, otherwise, to state that they are effective sovereigns over their national resources.

---

[150] See Louka, *supra* note 72.

Given that states have been quite zealous in asserting sovereignty over their natural resources, an international enclosure of national commons does not seem to have much of a chance for success. An international enclosure of national commons would mean that governments have nominal control over their biodiversity resources and that the actual control is effectuated by states or other constituencies who have the power, will, and economic resources to play a decisive role in the management of natural resources of other states.

Government jurisdiction and control over national biodiversity resources have not always been effective. This is particularly the case in developing countries, where many governments may not have the capacity to monitor effectively the use of their resources that end up becoming open-access resources. Therefore, certain states and a number of environmental constituencies have made a conscious attempt to internationalize the management of certain national biodiversity resources.

Internationalization of the protection of biodiversity resources has been attempted more or less successfully in different international fora. Some international instruments mention that biodiversity is the common concern of the global community. There are instruments on the protection of specific habitats, species, species trade, and debt-for-nature swaps. Through these instruments, a number of states and environmental constituencies have been able to dictate management decisions in the developing world. The enclosure of biodiversity resources at the global level has been made possible through the enactment of various instruments that suggest management methods for national biodiversity resources by mandating, for instance, the establishment of protected areas and restrictions on the trade in endangered species. Some of these suggestions have been incorporated into the policies of certain developing countries under the presumption that ecodevelopment will bring more benefits than traditional development.

The international enclosure of biodiversity has been creeping into national systems under the name of effectiveness. It is assumed that if the international community intervenes in the management of national biodiversity resources of certain states such management would become more effective. International governance structures, it is assumed, more objectively gauge the benefits and costs of conservation of biodiversity resources. Governments, by contrast, are likely to be sidetracked by various short-term problems of economic development and are to neglect the preservation of resources.

The enclosure, however, has not been complete, as it has encountered resistance in developing countries. Developing countries have maintained an ambivalent attitude with regard to the internationalization of their resources. In terms of financial assistance, when the benefits are plentiful, enclosure is tolerated. But when the benefits are meager, enclosure is resisted. If those wishing to preserve biodiversity resources are able to provide satisfactory compensation to those who are willing to forfeit benefits from resource exploitation at the right price, international enclosure is successfully effectuated. In all other cases, internationalization is resisted.

In terms of effectiveness, it is hard to claim that international enclosure has worked. Despite the number of international instruments adopted and stringent measures, including trade restrictions and prohibitions, many resources remain degraded. This is because international managers (as they spring from the bureaucracy of international organizations or NGOs) do not really have the insight to substitute local knowledgeable managers. Expertise in environmental matters cannot substitute knowledge about local conditions. Environmental management decisions require some sensitivity to the social and economic conditions of local populations. Sometimes, international bureaucracies could become impervious to such concerns.

Pronouncements of international institutions on the management of local resources are frequently conceived as out of touch with the realities that developing countries face. The decision to ban the trade in ivory was viewed as damaging to local management programs for endangered species and, thus, inequitable. Pressure to create international instruments for the protection of tropical forests have been perceived as one-sided (and by some as disguised trade restrictions) if similar protection measures are not to be placed on temperate forests. It is generally perceived as inequitable that some countries should bear the costs of resources preservation, whereas other countries were not (or are not) inhibited by similar concerns in their development.

7. INTERNATIONAL INSTRUMENTS

Most international environmental regimes mentioned in this chapter are centered on a legal instrument that defines their initial articulation and influences their future evolution. Some of these international instruments, for those uninitiated in international law, would seem as empty requirements. Some of the conventions for the protection of the seas from land-based pollution, for instance, urge states to cooperate and may prohibit some forms of pollution but are deprived of strict regulatory standards. From the perspective of a domestic legal order, these instruments have no teeth.

From an international perspective, however, even broad instruments that set the parameters of cooperation among states are vital because they further the goal of a minimum order. These instruments present, at least, an agreement of states to cooperate on a specific subject matter. For most international lawyers who participate in what sometimes seem tedious negotiations, this is a significant achievement.

As international environmental instruments have progressed from the 1970s, the command-and-control character of the instruments has increased.[151] Treaties deprived of concrete obligations are supplemented by protocols that are quite specific. The institutional framework generated by international conventions is responsible for the promulgation of a number of recommendations that may not have binding force but, nevertheless, are persuasive and create expectations of performance.

One could characterize many of the recently adopted instruments for the control of pollution as command-and-control instruments. The Ozone Protocols and the Kyoto Protocol are definitely such instruments that provide detailed standards for implementation. The same is true for the protocols that have exemplified the transboundary air pollution regime.

The treaties for the control of marine pollution from land-based sources, as they have been amended in the 1990s, straddle the boundary between command-and-control regulations and more unspecified agreements. The LC and the MARPOL

---

[151] Alan Boyle, Codification of International Environmental Law and the International Law Commission: Injurious Consequences Revisited, in International Law and Sustainable Development: Past Achievements and Future Challenges 61, 63 (Alan Boyle & David Freestone, eds., 1999).

treaties are definitely command-and-control, technology-forcing instruments. The LC is a prohibitory such instrument, whereas the MARPOL rests on a number of technological standards.

In terms of natural resource management, international instruments tend to be less specific because it would not make sense to establish taking standards, such as total allowable catches (TACs) for fisheries or other species, at the international level. The promulgation of TACs is generally conceived as a national or a regional problem. Different TACs may be necessary in different regions or states depending on the availability of a resource today, future prognosis, and the needs of countries involved.

Regional instruments for the protection of fisheries resources have not yet acquired a legitimacy that would pool together states in their implementation. Regional fisheries agreements and related regulations on catches are frequently flouted even by states that subscribe to a regional agreement. Most fisheries agreements could beef up their regulatory effectiveness if they did away with the right of states to veto regulations that they do not agree with. The command-and-control character of fisheries agreements is diminished by the number and extent of opt-out clauses.

The Convention on Biological Diversity (CBD) is a framework convention that relies on interstate cooperation for the protection of national biodiversity. The convention proposes new ways to look at biodiversity as it is related with biotechnology inventions and innovations. But the convention does not provide concrete standards for international transfers of germplasm or for the transfer of biotechnology. A number of issue-specific agreements have attempted to do so. These agreements basically are trade agreements that establish the parameters of trading among participants. The Treaty on Plant Genetic Resources for Food and Agriculture is such an agreement. So is the Biosafety Protocol[152] and the CITES Convention.[153] Furthermore, a number of regional/bilateral agreements exemplify the letter of the convention. The flourishing of instruments that have attempted to clarify the Biodiversity Convention in conjunction with the TRIPs agreement and the WIPO instruments have transformed the biodiversity regime to more of a command-and-control regime. At this point, the nesting of the regime in many different international fora has created some confusion about the rules of the game proposed by the regime.[154]

The freshwater regime is centered on an international convention that is based on a number of procedural requirements of notification and the principle of equity that states are to apply when entering into regional freshwater agreements. Because the principle of equity does not provide specific standards, states are – more or less – left to their own devices in configuring the regional agreements for allocation of freshwater resources. Such agreements have acquired varying degrees of specificity and control. Most of these agreements have established RBOs the purpose of which is to interpret a regional freshwater treaty progressively. The idea behind RBOs is that regional agreements would need fine-tuning; RBOs are to undertake such fine-tuning, thus sparing states the hassle of negotiating new agreements. Regional

---

[152] See Chapter 3, note 84.
[153] See Chapter 7, Section 2.2.
[154] See Chapter 7, Section 2.1.2. See also Chapter 9, Section 4.3.

freshwater agreements are usually quite specific with regard to the amount of water allocated to each state and what would happen in situations of water scarcity. Sometimes, however, the agreements present a political compromise to avoid the escalation of conflict in a region. In an attempt to diffuse conflicting situations, for instance, parties have promised to provide water to coriparians without specifying where the water is to come from.

The waste regime is a par excellence regulatory command-and-control regime in both national and international fora. The Basel Convention on the trade in hazardous wastes controls and waste transfers is based on a system of prior notification and consent. The liability protocol has completed the regulatory character of the regime. Whether the command-and-control approach through restrictions on waste trade is the way to curb the externalities of waste production has still to be proven.

Another characteristic of the command-and-control regulation, in addition to its increasing stringency, is a phenomenon called differentiation. Increasing the number and stringency of standards beyond the implementing capacity of concerned actors may lower overall performance. This is because whether a standard would be complied with depends on the capacities of those who are to implement the standard. For instance, a new stringent standard has more chances to be implemented by a new, state-of-the-art facility than by an older facility.[155] Therefore, it may be more desirable to adopt nonuniform standards – higher standards for new facilities and less stringent standards for old facilities. In international law, differentiation means that often standards must be tailored to meet the capacity level and needs of developing countries.

This notion of differentiating standards is encountered in some of the most recent international environmental instruments. For instance, the Kyoto Protocol and the Montreal Protocol differentiate between developed countries, developing countries, and even least-developed countries. Also, many soft law instruments refer to the concept of common but differentiated responsibilities among states with regard to the abatement of pollution. The UN Framework Convention on Watercourses mentions that the needs of countries should be taken into account in shaping the notion of equitable allocation of resources. Some fisheries agreements make room for the needs of the least-developed countries in a region.

The differentiation made explicit in many international agreements is recognition of the reality that not all countries are the same; thus, they cannot be similarly bound. After differentiation is introduced, the question is how to establish mechanisms to control differentiation so that countries that are entitled to differentiating standards do not take advantage of such standards to be permanently exempted from international regimes. Mechanisms to control differentiation are becoming quite developed in regional fora, especially fora that present more or less a federal state structure (e.g., the European Union).[156] In international law, mechanisms to control differentiation are weaker because of the nature of international law as an incentive-based instrument.

---

[155] Ian Ayres and John Braithwaite, Responsive Regulation: Transcending the Deregulation Debate 107 (1992).

[156] See, generally, Elli Louka, Conflicting Integration: The Environmental Law of the European Union (2004).

However, the control of differentiation is not totally absent as some of the recent compliance proceedings have demonstrated.[157]

A side effect of increasing regulation is the creation of illegal markets. International illegal markets exist today for products coming from endangered species, ozone-depleting substances, and hazardous and radioactive wastes. The illicit trade in endangered species is estimated to be quite significant.[158] The black markets for ozone-depleting substances are expected to grow as some developing countries are acquiring the capacity to produce such substances.[159] The illegal transfers of hazardous and radioactive wastes are well documented.[160] Some commentators have challenged the effectiveness of the CITES and the Basel regimes because of the illegal markets they have generated. The effectiveness of the ozone regime has come under doubt for the same reasons. Commentators suspect that a number of banned substances may be entering the seas through illegal dumping by ships or from land-based sources.

Because regulation can be costly, market-based instruments have been proposed to address international environmental problems. Market-based instruments have worked well in some domestic systems, but their administrative complexity may thwart their application at the international level. The implementation of market-based instruments in the climate change regime should be followed closely so as to extract lessons for the future of market-based instruments in international law.

8. CONCLUSION

Figure 2.1 classifies the international regimes from 1) the perspective of the level of enclosure strived for or achieved and 2) perceptions of accomplishment of distributive equity that may be correlated with regime effectiveness. The horizontal axis denotes the classification of regimes based on whether they have generated perceptions of fair allocation of resources or of the allocation of externalities associated with the use of resources. Fair allocation of resources or of externalities is frequently associated with effective management. The vertical axis classifies the regimes based on whether they have been enclosed effectively or on whether are still perceived as open access resources.

The enclosure pursued by the fisheries regime has been perceived as inequitable from the perspective of states that are left outside regional fisheries arrangements or from the perspective of insiders whose fishing efforts would be restricted. Attempts to enclose global fisheries have been intense but such enclosure has yet to be completed due to the strong resistance of states left outside.

The enclosure of "raw genetic material" has been conceived as a tit-for-tat enclosure geared to compensate for the enclosure of "worked genetic material." Various intellectual property rights devices have been used by pharmaceutical companies and biotechnology companies for the enclosure of "worked genetic resources." Both enclosures of plant genetic resources and related knowledge (PGR) are pursued in

---

[157] See compliance procedures, Chapter 3, Section 3.
[158] See Chapter 7, Section 2.2.
[159] See Chapter 8, Section 1.3.
[160] See *supra* note 130.

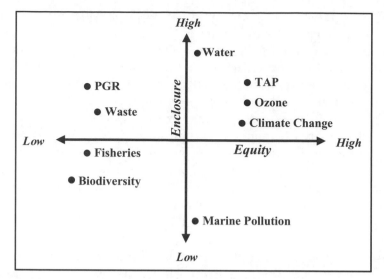

Figure 2.1. Classification of international regimes based on enclosure and equity perceptions

a rigorous manner by the states involved. Both enclosures have been perceived by states that have not been included in them as inequitable.

The enclosure of freshwater resources, in terms of effective regulation and allocation of what otherwise could become open-access resources, has not been pursued with the same vigor in all regions. Whenever this has been accomplished, the enclosure has been perceived as equitable depending on how inclusive it has been designed to be. The monopolistic enclosure of resources by a hegemonic power has been conceived rarely as equitable.

The results of the enclosure of the air are still in the making. One could claim that the ozone regime and the climate change regime could be effective. This is because the attempts to enclose the resource are inclusive. Developing countries have been promised compensation for their participation in the ozone and climate change regimes. If the compensation is deemed sufficient, the regimes could be considered equitable and, thus, could become effective in managing air quality. If the compensation is considered insufficient, the enclosure is unlikely to be finalized and the regimes could malfunction (Figure 2.1 presents an optimistic scenario for the evolution of the regimes).

The enclosure achieved by the Transboundary Air Pollution Regime (TAP) has enjoyed a high level of legitimacy. This is because the countries that participate in the regime exhibit more or less similar levels of development.

The enclosure of the seas has been less eventful in terms of distributive conflicts. This is because controlling pollution inputs in the seas has yet to materialize in an effective fashion. States still treat the seas in terms of polluting inputs as an open-access resource.

The international enclosure of national biodiversity resources is still in the works. Countries have principally resisted the international enclosure of their national biodiversity resources and have perceived such an enclosure as inequitable.

The enclosure of wastes has been motivated by concerns of equity. Some developed and developing states have assumed that it is equitable for each state to become self-sufficient in the management of its wastes. Otherwise, wastes could become an open-access negative resource. Although perceptions of equity of the regime are high, in certain circles the regime has been challenged by countries that still wish to import wastes to keep their industries afloat or to strengthen their recycling sector. Some countries view the notion of equity as self-efficiency as antithetical to corrective notions of equity and the articulation of cooperation among states.

3 Compliance and Governance Mechanisms

This chapter examines compliance and governance mechanisms as they apply to most international environmental issues. Environmental impact assessments are needed, for instance, for most development projects, independent of whether they affect air quality, water, or species diversity. The right to information and participation in decision making applies to a large number of environmental issues.

In addition to general governance mechanisms, many treaties contain requirements for the exchange of information among states or for state reporting to institutions established under a treaty – either about the level of state compliance or regarding the state of the environment. Many environmental instruments include the requirement of notification and consultation with other states, which are especially important in emergency situations. However, before 1990, it was rare for environmental treaties to establish implementation committees or independent inspection panels.

Compliance and governance mechanisms could be instrumental in addressing environment problems, provided that states are willing to comply with their obligations. For instance, prompt notification in case of an environmental emergency can save lives and lead to preventive efforts that would thwart further contamination. States reporting on the severity of their environmental problems and their compliance record could provide information that would help clarify the nature of these problems and indicate measures to address them. The importance of information must not be overlooked in environmental matters, the effective management of which is based on the availability of correct information. Improving the quality of information about the nature of a problem and the means available to address it could go a long way toward resolving some of the thorny environmental issues (e.g., fisheries management, in which accurate information has been notoriously unavailable, or climate change, in which some scientific uncertainty has prevented countries with high emissions from taking action).

1. ENVIRONMENTAL AND STRATEGIC IMPACT ASSESSMENT

The Environmental Impact Assessment (EIA) was adopted first in the United States as a way to assess the environmental implications of development projects.[1] Since

---

[1] See National Environmental Policy Act (NEPA) of 1970, 42 U.S.C. §4321.

then, a large number of national and international environmental instruments have included provisions for assessment.[2]

The United Nations Economic Commission for Europe (UN/ECE) Convention on Environmental Impact Assessment (EIA) in a Transboundary Context[3] provides for EIA for activities that are likely to cause a *significant* adverse transboundary impact,[4] leaving the definition of what constitutes a "significant" impact open to interpretation.

The convention provides for a four-step process for EIA for projects likely to have transboundary impacts. First, the state of origin must notify the affected state.[5] This notification must contain information on the proposed activity, the nature of possible decision, and an indication of a reasonable time within which a response is required.[6] If the affected state does not respond within the time set in the notification, or indicates that it does not intend to participate in the procedure, then the transboundary EIA process stops there.[7]

Otherwise, on receipt of response of the affected party, the state of origin must send information on the EIA procedure and the proposed activity.[8] The notification process can be initiated by the affected party if that party considers that it would be affected by an activity listed in Appendix I and no notification has been given by the state of origin. In that case, the treaty provides for an exchange of information between the state of origin and the affected state in order to determine whether there would be a transboundary impact. If the parties cannot agree, then they can submit the matter to an Inquiry Commission (unless they agree on another method of settling the dispute).[9] It is worth noting that an Inquiry Commission has yet to be used in a transboundary EIA.[10] Furthermore, it is provided that the public of the affected party must be informed and must be provided with possibilities of making comments on or of filing objections to the proposed activity. Such comments or objections must be transmitted to the state of origin.[11]

The second step for a transboundary EIA involves the preparation of the environmental impact assessment information.[12] Appendix II of the convention set outs the

---

[2] With regard to waste dumping and the protection of watercourses, see Patricia W. Birnie & Alan E. Boyle, International Law and the Environment 240, 327 (1994). See also article 206 of UNCLOS, Chapter 4, Section 3.1; Principle 17 of Rio Declaration refers to Environmental Impact Assessment, Chapter 1, Section 4.2. The 1992 Biodiversity Convention refers to Environmental Impact Assessment, see, e.g., art. 14(1)(a), Biodiversity Convention, Chapter 7, Section 2.1.

[3] Convention on Environmental Impact Assessment in a Transboundary Context, Feb. 25, 1991, reprinted in 30 ILM 800 (1991) [hereinafter EIA Convention]. The convention was amended in 2001 at the second meeting of the parties, see Decision II/14, 2001. The convention was amended also in 2004 at the third meeting of the parties, Decision III/7, 2004. A consolidated version of the convention can be found at http://www.unece.org/env/eia [hereinafter EIA Convention].

[4] See art. 2(2) & Appendix I, *id.*

[5] Art. 3, *id.*

[6] Art. 3(2), *id.*

[7] Art. 3(3), *id.*

[8] Art. 3(5), *id.*

[9] Art. 3(7), see also Appendix IV, *id.*

[10] See ECE, Convention on Environmental Impact Assessment in a Transboundary Context: Review of Implementation 2003, at 22, Aug. 30, 2004 [hereinafter Implementation 2003].

[11] Art. 3(8), EIA Convention, *supra* note 3.

[12] Art. 4, *id.*

minimum requirements for an EIA, which must be communicated to the affected state. The requirements must include a description of the proposed activity, alternatives to the activity, including a no-action alternative, mitigation measures, and postproject activities.[13] The state of origin of the transboundary activity is required to allow for the participation of nationals of the affected state in the decision-making process, on the same terms, as it allows for its own nationals.[14]

The third step involves consultation between the state of origin and the affected state on the basis of information supplied by the state of origin.[15] Consultations must happen within a reasonable time frame. The state of origin is not required to refrain from the proposed activity based on the failure of consultations with the affected state, but in its final decision it must take into account the comments provided by the affected state.[16]

The fourth step involves the final decision and postproject analysis.[17] The purpose of the postproject analysis is to monitor compliance with the conditions set out in the authorization or approval of the proposed activity and the effectiveness of mitigation measures.[18] Postproject analysis is undertaken if the concerned parties determine that it is necessary to do so.[19]

The record of state compliance with the convention is mixed. The implementation of the convention has encountered some problems, for examplelate notification, notification in the language of the country of origin, inadequate information in the notification, difficulty of understanding the originating party's EIA procedure and problems with processing notifications.[20] Some of the parties reported that the content of the EIA documentation they received was inadequate.[21] Most of the parties noted, though, that their comments had been taken into account by the state of origin.[22]

Regarding the participation of the public of the affected state in the EIA process, some of the common problems states describe include difficulties in interpretation, a lack of public interest, and border controls.[23] Parties reported that comments received from the public of the affected state were taken into account in decision making.[24] Some parties reported that they have been involved in EIA procedures in which the party of origin did not initiate consultations.[25] Issues regarding the translation of the EIA documents in other languages, and who should undertake the costs of these translations, also emerged.[26]

Even after reviewing the record of implementation by state parties, it is difficult to decipher whether the EIA process has any real impact on the decision-making

---

[13] Appendix II, *id.*

[14] Arts. 4(1) & 2(6), *id.*

[15] Art. 5, *id.*

[16] Art. 6, *id.*

[17] *Id.*

[18] Appendix V, *id.*

[19] Art. 7, *id.*

[20] Implementation 2003, *supra* note 10, at 10.

[21] *Id.* at 12.

[22] *Id.*

[23] *Id.* at 14.

[24] *Id.*

[25] *Id.*

[26] *Id.* at 20.

process or whether it is one more procedural requirement by which a number of steps are mechanically followed as items to check off a list. In this context, one should not underestimate the information in the hands of the state of origin and the leverage that such information gives to that state. A state may decide to divulge or bury such information, and this could affect the quality of EIA.

The EIA is especially powerful when it is used by international financial institutions as a condition for providing assistance for national projects. The World Bank adopted its own EIA procedures, the World Bank Operational Directive on EIA, in 1989, and it has been revised frequently.[27] The World Bank has performed three reviews of its own EIA procedure. The first review revealed that the EIA process was operative and was producing results, but several problems were reported. Such problems included a weak process of public consultation, insufficiently analyzed site and design alternatives, inadequately developed mitigation, monitoring, and management plans, and a limited EIA impact on project design.[28]

The second review was performed in 1997.[29] It was noted that the EIA was incorporated firmly into the Bank's policies but there were questions about the supervision of the EIA procedure and the increasing workloads regarding the performance of EIAs. The study noted that the most important improvements in the performance of EIAs occurred in the areas of mitigation, planning, and monitoring. But public consultation and analysis of alternatives remained a weak point, although some evidence of progress was reported.[30] The review recommended the employment of more environmental specialists (especially local ones) and the greater use of local NGOs.[31] The review stressed the importance of Sectoral Environmental Assessments (SEAs) as the Bank is attempting to adopt a sectorwide view of its loan policies. The review noted that SEAs were a more effective means of addressing sector-related environmental issues that were only partly addressed with project-specific EIAs.[32]

A 2002 review of the World Bank's EIA process followed up on the recommendations of the 1997 review. The Bank appeared to be beefing up its training programs on EIA and tried to improve the capacities of borrowing countries. The Bank established measures to ensure that public consultation was strengthened and that alternative projects were actually proposed during the EIA process.[33] Further efforts have been undertaken so that EIAs are executed early in the process; recommendations provided for in an EIA are transformed into precise legal requirements in the loan and credit agreements. There is an understanding that, unless EIA results are precisely incorporated into the legal loan and credit instruments, they would be disregarded.[34] Furthermore, efforts are made so that category A projects (projects with significant environmental impacts) and category B projects (projects with potential

[27] World Bank Operational Policy, OP 4.01, January 1999 (revised August 2004).

[28] World Bank, Third Environmental Impact Assessment Review (FY 96–00), at 6 (2002) [hereinafter Review 2002].

[29] World Bank, The Impact of Environmental Assessment: A Review of World Bank Experience, World Bank Technical Paper No. 363, 1997 [hereinafter Review 1997].

[30] *Id.* at xvi.

[31] *Id.* at xviii.

[32] *Id.*

[33] Review 2002, *supra* note 28, at 7.

[34] *Id.* at 8.

environmental impacts) are supervised annually by an environmental or social specialist.[35]

The World Bank has now incorporated EIA into its environmental and social safeguard policies. The purpose of these policies is to include environmental and social policy requirements in the projects undertaken by the Bank. In addition to EIA, various safeguard policies have been adopted.[36] The Bank also has established a Quality Assurance and Compliance Unit (QACU). This unit functions within the Environmentally and Socially Sustainable Development (ESSD) Network of the Environmental Department at the Bank. The QACU is making progress in ensuring the implementation of safeguard policies at the Bank.

However, several problems remain that the Bank is attempting to address. The Inspection Panel, which the Bank has established to its credit, has discovered several breaches of safeguard policies of the Bank.[37] Several other problems have been encountered in EIAs.

The initial categorization of a project as an A project guarantees that the project commands more attention. The EIAs performed on category A projects have improved. B project categorization, as a rule, generates less attention in a number of areas, including analysis of alternatives, public consultation, and supervision. Because a categorization of a project as a B project would involve "less effort," there is an inherent personnel bias to categorize all projects as B projects.

Other problems include the lack of supervision by environmental specialists and the need for better tools in identifying long-term environmental and social impacts.[38] Although public consultations have improved, in general, most of this improvement is noticeable in category A projects rather than in category B projects.[39] This has led to an incentive to categorize all projects as B projects.

In the context of bilateral donor assistance, the issue of coherent EIAs has been raised within the OECD. The OECD has attempted to devise "terms of reference" that would be common in all bilateral assistance projects, but the practicality of such an endeavor has been challenged by some donors that view EIAs as issue-specific.[40] The OECD has pointed out the complexity involved in the EIA process, namely, the involvement of multiple stakeholders, the multijurisdictional legal/regulatory framework, the complex scientific data, and sophisticated analytical methods. Because of

---

[35] *Id.*

[36] The safeguards adopted include:
  - Nature Habitats. The Bank does not support projects involving the significant conversion of natural habitats;
  - Involuntary Resettlement. The Bank adopts measures to mitigate the impact of displacement emanating from development projects;
  - Indigenous Peoples. The Bank adopts measures to ensure that indigenous peoples benefit and are not adversely affected by development projects.
       Other safeguard policies address forestry issues, the protection of cultural property, the safety of dams, international waterways, and disputed areas. See Review 2002, *supra* note 28, at 15.

[37] World Bank, Accountability at the World Bank: The Inspection Panel – 10 years on (2003).

[38] Review 2002, *supra* note 28, at 55.

[39] *Id.* at 82–83.

[40] OECD, Coherence in Environmental Assessment (1999).

this complexity, the effective management of the EIA process is a significant challenge for most states.[41]

A new instrument was adopted in 2003 as a protocol to the EIA Convention, the Protocol on Strategic Environmental Assessment (SEA).[42] SEAs have been popular nationally and internationally as a means of improving the understanding of environmental effects of development projects. The World Bank's Sectoral Environmental Assessments are, in essence, SEAs for a specific sector. The EU also has adopted a directive on SEAs.[43]

The EIA and the SEA differ in their scope. The EIA takes place after a policy has been decided for the projects that would implement the policy. The SEA takes place at the level of policy formulation. For instance, if a government decides to cover its energy needs by using more coal than other resources, EIA can be used to assess the effects of coal use on the environment for each project that implements the policy. By contrast, SEA would be applied at the sectoral level, at the point at which the government makes a decision on the methods to cover its energy needs. In practice, what differentiates SEA from EIA is that SEA is applicable before a plan or a program is adopted or submitted to legislation,[44] whereas EIA is applicable after a plan or program is adopted for the individual projects that implemented it. SEA, whenever performed, is likely to reduce the number and scope of EIAs because many of the issues and alternatives usually addressed at the EIA level would be addressed at the SEA level. Despite the possibilities of implementation of SEA at the policy level, most SEAs today are performed at the program and planning level.[45]

The 2003 protocol provides the sectors for which SEAs must be performed, which include agriculture, forestry, fisheries, energy, industry including mining, transport, regional development, waste management, water management, telecommunications, tourism, town and country planning, and land use.[46]

The World Bank has increased its use of SEAs and has performed SEAs in various countries and regions on different sectors of the economy, including energy, power, water, wastewater, and transportation. The Bank has noted several advantages with the performance of SEAs. Such advantages include the identification of key environmental issues at an early stage, a better framework for a legal agreement, and better decision making.[47] The Bank also has been involved in a limited number of Regional Environmental Assessments (REAs), which could accurately be described as strategic assessments with a regional outlook.

---

[41] The OECD has developed guidelines for EIA management in development projects, see "Guidelines" for Managing Environmental Assessment of Development Projects, Part IV, in Coherence in Environmental Assessment, *id*. See also OECD, Good Practices for Environmental Impact Assessment of Development Projects (1992).

[42] Protocol on Strategic Environmental Assessment to the UNECE Convention on Environmental Impact Assessment in a Transboundary Context, May 21, 2003 available online at http://www.unece.org/env/eia/sea protocol.htm [hereinafter SEA Convention].

[43] Directive 2001/42/EC of the European Parliament and of the Council on the assessment of the effects of certain plans and programmes on the environment, OJ L 197/30, 21.07.2001.

[44] Art. 4(1), SEA Convention, *supra* note 42.

[45] *Id.*

[46] Art. 4(2), *id.*

[47] Review 2002, *supra* note 28, at 127–28.

The execution of SEAs has been more challenging in bilateral donor assistance. Most governments have not developed the methodologies and lack experience in conducting SEAs.[48] Some commentators have characterized SEAs as the reincarnation of national/regional planning. Because such planning is performed at a higher level of government than project planning, "outside" intervention is not often welcomed (e.g., by donors or NGOs). This has to do with the degree of confidentiality that often accompanies and is expected of high-level policy decisions. Having said that, the outright exclusion of NGOs from the SEA process may not be politically feasible today.

2. STATE OBLIGATIONS

Exchange of information, prior notification, consultation, and informed consent are considered the "staples" of many international treaties. States do not hesitate to inject these procedural requirements into international agreements. These requirements are so frequently used that one could claim that they have become rules of customary international law. Other commentators argue, however, that, although states have been involved in many notification and consultation procedures, most of this involvement results from a specific treaty requirement rather than from a belief in the existence of a general rule of customary international law requiring notification and consultation. According to the same commentators, except for the requirement to notify and to consult in emergency situations, which could be considered a customary international rule, there is no general customary notification and consultation rule in international environmental law.[49]

There many reasons why states may be hesitant to exchange information, to notify another country, or to consult with another country.[50] States may be engaging in dangerous activities, and the discovery of this by other states could trigger claims of state liability or responsibility. Some activities of states or private operators located in their territory may constitute trade secrets, the revelation of which could compromise the comparative advantage of states. Information on how to monitor or best address an environmental problem could involve the exchange of commercially valuable knowledge. In other cases, the revelation of an environmental accident could adversely affect the reputation of states. For all these reasons, it seems that states have an inherent interest in hiding rather than in divulging information, let alone notifying other states about the true content of the information in their possession.[51]

In some cases, states may be more willing to reveal information, for instance, in cooperative situations in which none of the parties is perceived to hold privileged information, when the revelation of information may have positive reputation effects, or when information may assist in putting together alliances against a third state. Exchange of information also is preferred in regions in which countries have resolved to engage in collaborative efforts to address common environmental problems.

---

[48] Coherence in Environmental Assessment, *supra* note 40, Part VI (B).

[49] Phoebe N. Okowa, State Responsibility for Transboundary Air Pollution in International Law 166–67 (2000).

[50] See, e.g., Chapter 5, n. 313 (for failure to notify until after the fact).

[51] For the importance of secrecy rather than transparency in state interaction, see, e.g., Patrick Radden Keefe, Chatter: Dispatches from the Secret World of Global Eavesdropping (2005).

Thus, in order to determine whether the exchange of information, notification, and consultation requirements are emerging as rules of customary international law, one has to make some comparisons. One needs to pinpoint circumstances under which states have revealed information, even if this is not strictly required under a treaty, versus circumstances under which they did not. Because there is no knowledge on how many potential notifications states have missed – for example, when it would have been a good idea to notify – it is hard to determine how frequently notification and consultation are followed as a customary rule of international environmental law.

It must be noted, however, that some developments, for example, the general progress in technology (e.g., the information technology, or Vessel Monitoring Systems), and developments specific to the international environmental field, including:

- the right to information, participation in decision making, and access to justice convention;
- the establishment of joined monitoring systems; and
- the transparency that is necessary for the proper functioning of some environmental instruments,

indicate that more information is available in the international system with the assistance of or in spite of the resistance of states.

2.1. Exchange of Information

Exchange of information is a routine form of cooperation among states. Many treaties have provided as a matter of course for exchange of information. The UN/ECE Convention on Transboundary Air Pollution (CLRTAP) includes many articles on the exchange of information. Article 8 of the convention more specifically provides that states must exchange information on emissions and major changes in national policies and technologies for reducing transboundary air pollution.[52] Similar provisions for exchange of information are included in the protocols to the convention. The EMEP monitoring system under the CLRTAP has been instrumental in supplying parties with information about emissions and compliance by other parties.[53]

Other instruments that provide for the provision and exchange of information include the Stockholm Declaration,[54] the Rio Declaration,[55] Agenda 21,[56] the Basel Convention,[57] the 1986 IAEA Notification Convention,[58] the UNCLOS,[59] the Vienna Convention for the Protection of Ozone Layer,[60] and the Montreal Protocol for the Protection of the Ozone Layer.[61]

The Montreal Protocol is quite detailed regarding the exchange of information. State parties must exchange information on the best technologies for improving the containment, destruction, and recycling of ozone-depleting substances (ODS); on

---

[52] See also arts. 3, 4 & 9, CLRTAP, Chapter 8, Section 3.
[53] For the EMEP monitoring system, see Chapter 8, Section 3.1.1.
[54] Principle 20, Stockholm Declaration, Chapter 1, Section 4.1.
[55] Principle 9, Stockholm Declaration, *id.*
[56] Chapter 40 of Agenda 21 is titled "Information for Decisionmaking." See Chapter 1, Section 4.2.
[57] Information is an important element in the Basel Convention, see Chapter 10, Section 3.1.
[58] See Chapter 10, Section 3.2.
[59] Arts. 61, 144, 200, 244, UNCLOS, Chapter 4, Section 3.1.
[60] Art. 4, Vienna Convention, Chapter 8, Section 1.2.1.
[61] Art. 9(1), Montreal Protocol, Chapter 8, Section 1.2.2.

the possible alternatives to ODS; and on the costs and benefits of various control strategies.[62] Such exchange of information could be quite extensive, and it may involve patents and trade secrets that could be viewed as a competitive advantage of certain states. Companies usually are reluctant to release this type of information to other countries and competing companies. Because of the difficulties of enforcing the exchange of information on new technologies, the Climate Change Convention is less demanding in this respect. The convention, therefore, cannot be interpreted as forcing the release of confidential private information.[63]

The Convention on Biological Diversity urges the parties to transfer technology, and the knowledge associated with it, especially to developing countries.[64] This provision has not been well received by companies in the developed world, which are more concerned with preserving their intellectual property rights rather than with transferring technology and the knowledge associated with it.

Overall provisions for exchange of information play a pivotal role in international environmental law. Accumulating credible information can discourage states from flouting international conventions and could alert other states about potential issues of noncompliance.[65]

2.2. Notification

One way to obtain information is through notification by a state of origin of transboundary environmental issue. The EIA Convention requires the state of origin to notify the state affected. The EIA Convention goes as far as to require the response of the affected state within the time frame set in the notification.[66]

The duty of states of origin of polluting activities to notify states that may be affected is included in many treaties. The UN/ECE Convention on Transboundary Air Pollution provides for notification.[67] Many bilateral treaties on air pollution and nuclear installations provide for an obligation to notify. A number of bilateral treaties on nuclear installations contain detailed provisions on notification and the supply of information with regard to the construction, maintenance, and operation of nuclear installations, especially those that are close to frontier areas.[68]

A number of international instruments include the obligation to notify in emergency situations. The 1986 IAEA Notification Convention[69] provides for early notification in case of a nuclear accident. The treaty was adopted after the Chernobyl accident, when the then Soviet Union failed to notify affected states promptly. This treaty places on the state of origin of a nuclear accident the duty to notify

---

[62] *Id.*

[63] Art. 4(1)(h), Climate Change Convention. "Promote and cooperate in the full, open and prompt exchange of relevant scientific, technological, technical, socio-economic and legal information related to the climate system and climate change, and to the economic and social consequences of various response strategies." See Chapter 8, Section 2.2.1.

[64] Art. 17, Biodiversity Convention, Chapter 7, Section 2.1.2.2.

[65] Abram Chayes & Antonia Handler Chayes, The New Sovereignty: Compliance with International Regulatory Agreements 151 (1995).

[66] See *supra* Section 1.

[67] Art. 8(b), CLRTAP, Chapter 8, Section 3.1.1.

[68] Okowa, *supra* note 49, at 138–39.

[69] Chapter 10, Section 3.2.

all affected states. The notifying state must respond to requests from affected states for further information and consultations.[70] The IAEA Convention has some limitations because it applies in cases of accidents that pose actual or potential risk of transboundary radioactive contamination. The convention applies to accidents of "radiological safety significance"[71] but does not apply to accidents that may occur in military nuclear installations.

The duty of notification in emergency situations or when a country is to engage in an activity likely to have transboundary environmental impacts is provided in a number of other instruments, such as the Rio Declaration,[72] the UNCLOS,[73] the Basel Convention,[74] the Biodiversity Convention,[75] and the 1997 UN Watercourses Convention. The 1997 UN Watercourses Convention provides for a detailed notification procedure. A state that is to undertake measures that would affect a shared watercourse must notify the affected state and wait six months for a reply. During this period, the notifying state is not to put into effect any measures that would affect the shared watercourse. The convention provides for the reply to the notification as well as the course of action to be taken in cases in which notification is not given or there is no reply to the notification.[76]

2.3. Consultation

Consultation is the natural extension of notification. The EIA Convention provides for the obligation of a state of origin to consult with an affected state after the notification is given. It must be noted that the requirement of consultation does not give a veto power to an affected state with regard to an activity planned by a state of origin. But an obligation to consultation means that, at least, the comments of affected states are taken into account in the planning of a project. Otherwise, the obligation for consultation would be an empty requirement.

The duty of notification and consultation can be found in early cases of international environmental law, for example, the *Lac Lanoux* arbitration. In the *Lac Lanoux* case, the tribunal concluded that France had the duty to notify and to consult with Spain with regard to works planned on Lake Lanoux but that such consultations did not give Spain the right to veto France's decisions.[77] The duty of consultation is implied in the *Fisheries Jurisdiction* cases in which the ICJ concluded that a state that contemplates to extend its fisheries zone is to take the interests of affected states into consideration. This duty can be realized through consultations.[78]

Other international conventions that provide for the duty of consultation include the UN/ECE Transboundary Air Pollution Convention[79] and several bilateral treaties on nuclear installations.[80] The COPs of most conventions constitute for a

---

[70] Art. 6, IAEA Notification Convention, *id.*

[71] Art. 1(1), *id.*

[72] Principle 18, Rio Declaration, Chapter 1, Section 4.2.

[73] Art. 198, UNCLOS, Chapter 4, Section 3.1.

[74] Art. 13(1), Basel Convention, Chapter 10, Section 3.1.

[75] Art. 14(1)(d), Biodiversity Convention, Chapter 7, Section 2.1.

[76] Arts. 12–16 & 19, Watercourse Convention, Chapter 5, Section 4.

[77] Chapter 1, Section 4.5

[78] *Id.*

[79] Art. 5, CLRTAP, Chapter 8, Section 3.1.1.

[80] Okowa, *supra* note 49, at 153.

for the exchange of information and consultation of state parties to a convention. The obligation to conduct consultations is also provided in the IAEA Notification Convention, the Ramsar Convention,[81] and the UNCLOS.[82] Principle 17 of the Rio Declaration provides for the requirement of consultation.

Some more recent conventions provide, in addition to notification/consultation, for the prior informed consent of the notified party. This requirement could be considered a "consultation-plus" procedure, in which the affected party has, in effect, the power to veto the activity of the originating party. For instance, with regard to the transfers of hazardous wastes, in order for a state party to the Basel Convention to transfer wastes to another country, it must obtain the prior informed consent of that country. If the importing country refuses to consent to the waste shipment, the shipment cannot take place, at least not legally. The prior informed consent requirement is included in the Rotterdam Convention on Prior Informed Consent (PIC) Procedure for Certain Hazardous Chemicals in International Trade.[83] Even more elaborate consultation requirements are included in the 2000 Biosafety Protocol,[84] in which it is provided that, for a transboundary transfer of living modified organisms to take place, the PIC of the importing country is required in addition to an Advance Informed Agreement (AIA) procedure.[85]

2.4. Reporting/Monitoring

Data gathering is a prerequisite to lawmaking. Without data, one cannot get a concrete understanding of the nature and extent of environmental problems and, thus, cannot devise institutional means for addressing those problems. In Chapter 5, it is emphasized that accurate data have been an important precondition for the successful conclusion of regional water treaties. The absence of accurate data on the state of fisheries resources has marred international and regional fisheries management regimes.

Because of the importance of data for the proper functioning of international law, many treaties provide as a task of states to gather various types of information on issues that a treaty deals with and to report back to the treaty institutions, usually the COPs, through secretariats. Most international environmental regimes provide for the requirement of reporting. However, the record of compliance with reporting requirements is not always stellar. Reporting requirements are taken seriously in the International Labor Organization (ILO), but compliance with reporting is fair to poor in most environmental treaties. Reporting is quite problematic under many human rights instruments.[86]

---

[81]   Art. 5, Ramsar Convention, Chapter 7, Section 3.3.

[82]   Art. 142(2), UNCLOS, Chapter 4, Section 3.1.

[83]   See Rotterdam Convention on the Prior Informed Consent (PIC) Procedure for Certain Hazardous Chemicals and Pesticides in International Trade, Sept. 10, 1998, reprinted in 38 ILM 1 (1999). The convention entered into force Feb. 24, 2004.

[84]   Cartagena Protocol on Biosafety to the Convention on Biological Diversity, Jan. 29, 2000, reprinted in 39 ILM 1027 (2000).

[85]   Art. 7, *id.* (provides for a detailed decision-making process that the state of import must apply before importing biotechnology devices).

[86]   Chayes, *supra* note 65, at 23.

Some conventions require state parties to report on their performance with respect to standards established under these conventions. Other conventions require parties to report on future plans and programs to meet treaty goals. Yet other conventions require reporting in order to feed information databases established under the convention. Several international institutions have established monitoring bodies. The purpose of these bodies is to collect information on the state of environment. The UN/ECE Convention on Transboundary Air Pollution has established a monitoring program, called EMEP, which has played an important role in air quality control in Europe.[87]

Most international environmental treaties provide for reporting/monitoring requirements more or less explicitly. Such conventions include the UNCLOS,[88] the 1997 UN Watercourses Convention,[89] the Vienna Convention for the Protection of the Ozone Layer,[90] the Climate Change Convention,[91] the Biodiversity Convention,[92] the MARPOL Convention,[93] and the 1995 Fisheries Agreement.[94] Frequently, the subject matter of a treaty dictates the content of reporting. Certain treaties request parties to report on their emissions or discharges or to provide the inventories of their natural resources.[95] Other treaties concentrate on the violations of a convention by persons under the jurisdiction of states.[96] Still other conventions ask states to report on measures they have undertaken to comply with the convention.[97]

The problem with periodic reporting requirements is that they are rarely accompanied by an independent evaluation of the reports. States provide reports on the overall measures they have undertaken to address an environmental problem, but rarely do they provide information to enable a third party to determine whether these measures have been sufficient. Also, most treaties do not provide for independent evaluators who would examine reports provided by states and explore potential discrepancies. Most reporting requirements do not specify the content of reports and fail to provide for a uniform reporting format.[98]

---

[87] See Chapter 8, Section 3.1.1.

[88] Art. 204, UNCLOS, Chapter 4, Section 3.1.

[89] Art. 11, Watercourse Convention, Chapter 5, Section 4.

[90] Arts. 2 & 3, Vienna Convention, Chapter 8, Section 1.2.1.

[91] Arts. 4(1)(a) & (g) & 5, Climate Change Convention, *id.* Chapter 8, Section 2.2.1.

[92] Art. 7(b) & (c), Biodiversity Convention, Chapter 7, Section 2.1.

[93] Arts. 5(2) & 6(2), MARPOL Convention, Chapter 4, Section 3.4.

[94] Art. 14 & Annex I, 1995 Fisheries Agreement, Chapter 6, Section 3.3.1.

[95] See, e.g., Protocols to the UN/ECE Transboundary Air Pollution Convention: Art. 4, SO2 Protocol; Art. 8(1), NOx Protocol; Art. 7(b), Heavy Metals Protocol; Art. 9(b), POPs Protocol, see Chapter 8, Section 3.1.2. See also art. 3(5), Rhine Chlorides Pollution Convention, Chapter 5, Section 5.4.2. Many conventions on natural resources management request that states provide an inventory of their natural resources, see art. 7, Biodiversity Convention, Chapter 7, Section 2.1. See also art. 11(1), World Heritage Convention, Chapter 7, Section 3.1.

[96] See art. 4(3), MARPOL Convention, Chapter 4, Section 3.4; See also art. IX(4), International Whaling Convention, Chapter 7, Section 5.2.

[97] See art. 3(1), Basel Convention, Chapter 10, Section 3.1; Art. 26, Biodiversity Convention, Chapter 7, Section 2.1; See also art. 12, Climate Change Convention, Chapter 8, Section 2.2.1.

[98] Regarding the inadequacies of international reporting, see Okowa, *supra* note 49, at 232–37. The author addresses mostly the inadequacies of reporting mechanisms under the UN/ECE Convention on Transboundary Air Pollution. The author mentions that only the VOCs Protocol, within the framework of the Transboundary Air Pollution Convention, provides details on the content of reports that must

Some of the most recent conventions provide for more extensive reporting requirements. For instance, the Climate Change Convention provides that state parties must provide a national inventory of emissions of greenhouse gases and of the removal of greenhouse gases by sinks using comparable methodologies.[99] Developed countries are to provide a detailed description of policies and measures they have undertaken to address greenhouse emissions.[100] Information designated by a party as confidential, however, should be treated by the secretariat as confidential,[101] thereby removing possible fears of state parties regarding the release of sensitive information. The Kyoto Protocol, as further implemented, may provide for a most structured reporting procedure.[102]

Most compliance procedures provided for in international environmental treaties today recognize the review of compliance of a state's reporting requirements, as one of their explicit functions.[103] However, it has been noted that the requirements of reporting included in most international instruments often overwhelm the capacities of national bureaucracies to respond with adequate and meaningful reports.[104] Nonreporting, underreporting, or misreporting are, therefore, prevalent.

3. VERIFICATION AND COMPLIANCE

On-Site Inspections

On-site inspections by an international body to verify matters of compliance in areas under the jurisdiction of a state are rare, indeed, in international law. Inspections by the IAEA are the best known. The purpose of the IAEA inspections is to verify the conformance of nuclear reactors of states with international standards. However, even these inspections require that the IAEA enters into specific arrangements with the states concerned, and "surprise inspections" are not allowed.[105]

With regard to pollution from various and diffuse sources of pollution, meaningful inspections, provided that are accepted by states as legitimate, do not seem to be feasible under the current structure of international law.

Formal Compliance Procedures

International environmental instruments are increasingly incorporating nonadversarial Compliance Procedures (CPs).[106]

---

be provided by the parties. The author recommends that an independent body of experts should be able to scrutinize the reports provided by states and could point out discrepancies between the goals to be achieved under a treaty and the level of performance by state parties. The author recommends that lessons must be drawn from the practices of the Human Rights Committee and the ILO that are more aggressive in evaluating reports provided by parties.

[99] Art. 12(1)(a), Climate Change Convention, Chapter 8, Section 2.2.1.
[100] Id.
[101] Art. 12(9), id.
[102] Art. 7(4), Kyoto Protocol, Chapter 8, Section 2.2.2.
[103] Maas Goote & René Lefeber, Compliance Building under the International Treaty on Plant Genetic Resources for Food and Agriculture, Commission on Genetic Resources for Food and Agriculture, Background Study Paper No. 20, at 8–9, Jan. 2004 [hereinafter Compliance Procedure Paper].
[104] Chayes, *supra* note 65, at 172.
[105] Okowa, *supra* note 49, at 242.
[106] Compliance Procedure Paper, *supra* note 103.

Pursuant to article 8 of the Montreal Protocol, for example, parties to the ozone regime have established an Implementation Committee. The ozone implementation committee held about thirty meetings as of December 2003.

A compliance procedure has been adopted also under the UN/ECE Convention for Transboundary Air Pollution (CLRTAP). Although the convention itself does not provide for a compliance procedure, the 1991 and 1994 protocols specifically include such a procedure. A decision was made, therefore, to adopt a joint procedure that would apply to the convention and to the protocols simultaneously. Thus, a joint Implementation Committee has been established.[107]

In 2002, parties to the 1998 Aarhus Convention adopted a compliance procedure in accordance with article 15 of the convention. What is interesting about this procedure is that members of the public can initiate the compliance proceedings under certain circumstances.

Under the UN/ECE EIA Convention, a compliance procedure has been adopted, despite the fact that the text of the convention does not provide for such a procedure. The procedure is being reviewed to incorporate provisions on public participation.

Under the Basel Convention, the first meeting of the Implementation Committee was held in October 2003. The compliance procedure under the Kyoto Protocol was finalized in 2001.[108]

Furthermore, adoption of compliance procedures are being negotiated in other fora:[109] the Biodiversity/Biosafety forum; the 1998 Rotterdam Convention on the Prior Informed Consent Procedure for Certain Hazardous Chemicals and Pesticides;[110] the 2001 Stockholm Convention on Persistent Organic Pollutants;[111] the 1996 Protocol to the London Dumping Convention; and the UN Watercourses Convention.

Other procedures that do not strictly qualify as noncompliance procedures (because there is not a specialized body to deal with noncompliance) are those adopted under the CITES[112] and the Bern Convention for the Conservation of European Wildlife and Natural Habitats.[113] The procedure established under the Bern Convention, for instance, provides that, when the secretariat of the convention comes across a case of noncompliance (e.g., through information provided by a party or an NGO), it first investigates the case. If it determines that action needs to be taken, it seeks further information from the party concerned. Following the response of the party, the secretariat decides whether to put the case before the COP meeting of the Bern Convention, which may have to undertake further action if needed.[114]

Other procedures are geared more toward the initiation of a consultation process. Article 13 of the Climate Change Convention provides for a multilateral consultative process the purpose of which is to resolve questions of implementation of individual

[107] *Id.* at 1.

[108] *Id.* at 2.

[109] *Id.* at 2–3.

[110] See *supra* note 83.

[111] Convention on Persistent Organic Pollutants, May 22, 2001, 40 ILM 532 (2000).

[112] CITES Convention, Chapter 7, Section 2.2.

[113] Bern Convention, Chapter 7, Section. 4.1.

[114] Compliance Procedure Paper, *supra* note 103, at 3.

states rather than to pursue cases of noncompliance. State parties have to come to an agreement about the body that is to administer the multilateral consultative process.[115]

In addition to the procedures included in international instruments, the UNEP and the ECE have adopted general guidelines on the compliance with and implementation of environmental agreements.[116]

In general, compliance procedures do not serve the same function as dispute settlement arrangements.

- The function of a compliance procedure is to achieve uniform compliance with the provisions of an international treaty. Thus, the goal is to trigger *erga omnes* compliance from the violating state. By contrast, the purpose of a dispute settlement procedure is generally to resolve a dispute between two parties.
- The compliance procedure affects the future behavior of a noncompliant party. The purpose of a dispute settlement provision, on the contrary, is retroactive. Dispute settlement has to do with compensation and restitution of the harmed person.
- The compliance procedure is nonadversarial. Although the dialogue between an Implementation Committee and a noncompliant party may become confrontational, it cannot be characterized as adversarial. The purpose of a compliance procedure is not to declare winners and losers but to find a common ground for the implementation of international legislation. Dispute settlement, on the contrary, is adversarial.

For compliance procedures to be viewed as legitimate some procedural requirements – namely transparency, fairness, predictability, and due process – have to be followed. Due process requirements include informing a party of a submission against it; allowing time for a response; allowing participation by the noncompliant party in the procedure; and providing for the scrutiny of information submitted against a party to determine its reliability.[117]

Bodies that execute compliance procedures are usually appointed by the parties to a treaty. In some compliance procedures, it is emphasized that the individuals appointed are to serve "the common good" as understood under a specific treaty, rather than to accommodate the interests of the parties that appointed them. Another way to ensure the independent character of members of a compliance body is to lessen their dependence on state parties and to stress their expertise in the subject matter of the treaty.[118]

In terms of who should be entitled to trigger a compliance procedure, current procedures offer a variety of alternatives, including the noncompliant party itself, another state party, the secretariat of a convention, the COP, or other treaty bodies.[119]

Compliance committees have a number of remedies at their disposal; these range from cautions/warnings and declarations of noncompliance to the adoption and

[115] *Id.*
[116] *Id.* at 4.
[117] *Id.* at 8, 13.
[118] *Id.* at 10.
[119] *Id.* at 11.

application of a compulsory action plan that would address the implementation difficulties of a noncompliant state. Some procedures provide for the suspension of rights and privileges of the noncompliant party under the treaty in question, but the legal basis for the adoption of such an extreme measure is highly contested.[120]

Nonforcible Countermeasures

As retaliation to an alleged contravention of an environmental obligation, states could adopt trade sanctions. Cases that have come before the WTO involve trade sanctions imposed unilaterally by states on other states because of an alleged violation of an environmental obligation. The WTO, as discussed in Chapter 9, has frowned on unilateral sanctions for the enforcement of conservation measures. The WTO has indicated, however, that multilateral trade sanctions may be viewed more favorably. Such multilateral trade sanctions are provided for in the Montreal Protocol against nonparties to the protocol or noncompliant state parties.

4. RIGHT TO INFORMATION AND PARTICIPATION AND ACCESS TO JUSTICE

4.1. International Instruments

The Convention on Access to Information, Public Participation in Decisionmaking and Access to Justice in Environmental Matters was adopted in 1998 and entered into force in 2001.[121] The convention was adopted under the UN/ECE framework. The convention is the first international instrument that develops unequivocally the right of the public to access information, to participate in decision making, and to access justice. As such, the convention, despite all the exceptions that (if read expansively) could defeat its purpose, is considered a revolutionary instrument that recognizes in a practical manner a human right to a healthy environment.

Although the convention provides for the right to a healthy environment, it is not the only instrument to acknowledge such a right. Many other instruments implicitly or explicitly have done so in the past.[122] The convention, however, went many steps further than usually expected for international environmental law instruments by providing the procedures through which the right to information and participation can be materialized.

States as a general rule are reluctant to provide information either because they do not conceive it to be their function to do so or because they are weary about the consequences of the provision of too much information on their power to control

---

[120] *Id.* at 17.

[121] Convention on Access to Information, Public Participation in Decision-making and Access to Justice in Environmental Matters, June 25, 1998, reprinted in 38 ILM 517 (1999) available online at http://www.unece.org/env/pp [hereinafter Aarhus Convention].

[122] The oldest instrument to recognize explicitly a human right to "a satisfactory environment" is the 1981 African Charter of Human and Peoples' Rights. In 1988, an Additional Protocol to the American Convention on Human Rights established a right to a healthy environment. For other instruments, see The Aarhus Convention: An Implementation Guide 2–4, ECE/ECEP/72 (prepared by Stephen Stec & Susan Casey-Lefkowitz, 2000) [hereinafter Guide].

the electorate. Thus, the right to information appears to increase the transparency and openness of government structures, as it allows citizens to have access to information at states' disposal. At the same time, however, this seemingly democratic right empowers states because it legitimizes their role as collectors and organizers of information. This role can be taken advantage of in the collection of private information. The right to access information, the right to participation in decision making, and the right to access to justice have been called the three pillars of the convention.

Before analyzing the articles of the convention, one has to clarify the definition of public authorities against which the information and participation rights can be asserted. The definition of public authority is quite inclusive and comprises what traditionally could be considered public authorities[123] and "natural or legal persons having public responsibilities or functions, or providing public services, in relation to the environment under the control of" a traditional public authority.[124] This includes government-created or government-financed corporations that perform public functions. In the United Kingdom, for instance, public functions are performed by private companies. Such private companies, because they perform public functions, fall under the scope of the convention.[125] "Environmental information," as defined under the convention, is also quite inclusive.[126]

The convention is explicit that persons, organizations, or groups that exercise their rights under the convention:

- must be recognized and supported;[127]
- shall in no way be penalized, persecuted, or harassed for their involvement;[128] and
- shall have access to rights established under the convention without discrimination as to citizenship, nationality, or domicile.[129]

The convention supports what has been called active and passive access to information.[130] Passive access to information has to do with the right of public to gain access to information at its request.[131] Active access to information speaks of a government's duty to collect and disseminate information on its own initiative.[132]

To provide access to information, information must be collected. The state, according to the convention, has a central role in the collection and dissemination of environmental information. Public authorities not only must possess and

---

[123] See art. 2(2)(a)&(b), Aarhus Convention, *supra* note 121.

[124] Art. 2(2)(c), *id.*

[125] Guide, *supra* note 122, at 33.

[126] Environmental information means any information in written, visual, oral, electronic or any other material form. See art. 2(3), Aarhus Convention, *supra* note 121.

[127] Art. 3(4), *id.*

[128] Art. 3(8). *id.*

[129] With regard to legal persons, access to information is allowed without discrimination as to where the registered seat is or the effective center of activities is. See art. 3(9), *id.*

[130] Guide, *supra* note 122, at 49.

[131] Art. 4, Aarhus Convention, *supra* note 121.

[132] Art. 5, *id.*

update environmental information[133] but also must establish systems to ensure the adequate flow of information.[134] Public authorities must disseminate information to the public in the event of an imminent threat to human health and the environment so as to prevent and mitigate harm coming from the threat.[135]

If information is available but it is still hard to obtain, the purpose of the convention will be defeated.[136] Effective access to information can be accomplished by a variety of means: publicly accessible lists, registers and files, positive official support, and the identification of points of contact.[137] States are required to ensure that all information becomes available in electronic databases easily accessible through public telecommunications networks.[138] States are required to establish a coherent, nationwide, and publicly accessible database – compiled through standardized reporting.[139] States also are required to publish facts that affect major environmental issues and to make accessible relevant explanatory material.[140]

The requirement not only to provide information but also to organize it so that it can be effectively accessed is the innovative element of the convention. The goal is for pollution inventories to contain information on discharges and emissions of each and every polluter so that the public acquires full knowledge and could name and shame polluters. The wide publication of noncompliance – which could undermine corporate reputations – is what policy makers are relying on to foster implementation. However, as mentioned earlier, the right to information, despite its democratic credentials, could become an intimidating tool in the hands of states. States absorbed in their now legitimate role as collectors and organizers of information may be willing to collect all kinds of information based on various public interest objectives.

The convention provides explicitly that authorities must respond to requests of information "within the framework of national legislation" with copies of actual documentation[141] without requiring the public to demonstrate an interest and in the form that the public requested.[142] The convention provides explicitly that information requested must be provided within a month after a request has been received.[143]

---

133 Art. 5(1)(a), *id.*

134 Art. 5(1)(b), *id.*

135 Art. 5(1)(c), *id.*

136 The difference between making information available publicly and making it available in a user-friendly form is illustrated by a Web site set up by NGOs in the UK. The NGOs took publicly available information from the UK Environment Agency Chemical Release Inventory and put it in a new GIS-type database. The new Web site has attracted public interest that did not exist before the development of the GIS-type database. See Guide, *supra* note 122, at 71.

137 Art. 5(2)(b), Aarhus Convention, *supra* note 121.

138 The information that could be downloaded from the internet includes: reports on the state of the environment, texts of legislation referring to the environment, policies, and plans and programs relating to the environment. See art. 5(3), *id.*

139 Art. 5(9), *id.*

140 Art. 5(7), *id.*

141 The requirement to have access to "actual documents" exists already in many countries. In Portugal, for instance, the right to access information includes the right to be informed that a document exists and the right to obtain a copy of the document. See Guide, *supra* note 122, at 54.

142 Art. 4(1)(a), Aarhus Convention, *supra* note 121.

143 Art. 4(2), *id.*

There are broadly formulated exceptions, however:

- the one-month deadline can be extended to two months when the volume and complexity of information justify such an extension;[144]
- the information can be provided in a different form than that requested by the public.[145]

The request also can be refused if:[146]

- it is manifestly unreasonable or formulated in too general a manner;[147]
- it concerns material in the course of completion or internal communications of public authorities when such an exception is provided by national law or customary rights;
- it violates the confidentiality of proceedings of public authorities;
- it adversely affects international relations, national defense, or public security;[148]
- it hampers the ability to receive a fair trial or criminal/disciplinary proceedings;
- it adversely affects the confidentiality of commercial and industrial information or other legitimate economic interest[149] including intellectual property rights with the exception of information on emissions;[150]
- it corrupts the confidentiality of personal data where such confidentiality is provided for in national legislation;
- the interests of a third party would be affected and that party has not consented to the release of the information.

The sheer number and indefinite character of many of these exceptions could undermine seriously the purpose of the convention. Therefore, the text of the convention provides for grounds for refusal, which must be interpreted strictly by performing a cost-benefit analysis between the public interest served by the disclosure and the interest protected by nondisclosure.[151] Refusal must be in writing if the applicant requests it; this must state the reasons for denying information and must be provided within a month or, for complex requests, within two months after the request has been submitted. The refusal must contain information on the process of appeal.[152] A public authority that does not possess a certain kind of information must refer an

---

[144] Art. 4(2), *id.*

[145] Art. 4(1)(b), *id.* A test of reasonableness should apply if information is provided in another form than that requested. Informing the applicant about the existence of a single copy of a book, which contains the information, located far from his/her residence cannot be considered an adequate response. See Guide, *supra* note 122, at 55.

[146] Art. 4(3), Aarhus Convention, *supra* note 121.

[147] The French courts have ruled, for instance, that requests for all documents relating to a specific species and for all environmental impact assessments are too general. Requests are considered general if they would involve hundreds or thousands of documents. See Guide, *supra* note 122, at 57.

[148] The public security exception is too broad of an exception. Certain states have established steps that would help the public determine whether information should be considered a state secret. *Id.* at 59.

[149] Parties have been encouraged to define what constitutes legitimate economic interest and to establish a process that would help identify whether the nondisclosure of information serves really a specific legitimate economic interest. *Id.* at 60.

[150] The fact that emissions cannot be considered confidential is significant given that, without information on emissions, most environmental groups would be unable to target their action.

[151] Art. 4(4), Aarhus Convention, *supra* note 121.

[152] Art. 4(7), *id.*

applicant to another authority.[153] Parties can charge for supplying information, but the charges are not meant to deter access to information.[154]

Right to Participation

One of the first instruments that refers to a right to participation is the UN/ECE Convention on Environmental Impact Assessment. The convention explicitly states that the assessment of proposed activities likely to have an environmental impact should take place with the participation of the public.

The Aarhus Convention establishes three types of participation:

- public participation in decisions on specific activities, here called *specific public participation*;[155]
- public participation concerning plans, programs, and policies relating to the environment, here called *general public participation*;[156]
- and public participation in the preparation of executive regulations and of legally binding instruments, here called *normative public participation*.[157]

The general themes that run through these types of participation include:

- *reasonable time frames* – that public participation procedures should allow sufficient time to inform the public and for the public to prepare and participate effectively;
- *early in the process* – that public participation should occur early in the process when all options are still open;
- *accounting for results* – that the state must take into account the results of public participation.

For specific participation, the activities to which this type of participation applies are listed in the Annex to the convention,[158] but it is provided that other activities could be included that may have significant environmental impact[159] in accordance with national law.[160] The public must receive notice early in the process in an adequate, timely, and effective manner.[161] This means that just posting a notice in any public medium is not adequate and effective if the public concerned does not have access to the medium or the information is buried under all other sorts of information.[162] Individual notice also may be necessary, according to the circumstances.[163]

---

[153] Art. 4(5), *id.*

[154] Art. 4(8), *id.*

[155] Art. 6, *id.*

[156] Art. 7, *id.*

[157] Art. 8, *id.*

[158] Annex I provides for many of the activities included in the EIA Convention, see *supra* Section 1.

[159] Activities with significant impact on the environment are defined in Annex III of the EIA Convention. *Id.*

[160] Art. 6(1)(a)&(b), Aarhus Convention *supra* note 121.

[161] Art. 6(2), *id.*

[162] Guide, *supra* note 122, at 96.

[163] Art. 6(2), Aarhus Convention, *supra* note 121. For instance, the Polish Environmental Protection Agency requires the relevant authorities to draw a list of environmental NGOs that are interested in receiving notifications relating to EIA. When the Agency's decision involves a project that requires an EIA, the Polish authorities must notify in writing all the environmental NGOs located in the affected area. See Guide, *supra* note 122, at 96.

The convention provides that, for a notice to be effective, it must include *inter alia* the proposed activity, the nature of possible decisions and draft decisions, and the public authority responsible for making decisions. The notice also should include information about the participation procedure itself – namely, when the procedure starts; the opportunities for the public to participate; the time and venue; and an indication of the type of environmental information already available.[164] The public authority must enable the public to participate by providing all information useful for decision making. This includes the site and physical and technical characteristics of the proposed activity, the effects of the activity on the environment, the measures envisaged to prevent and to reduce adverse effects, an outline of the main alternatives, and a nontechnical summary.[165] In other words, for the countries that have adopted the EIA Convention,[166] this convention specifically requires authorities to provide the public with documentation potentially included in an EIA.[167]

General public participation in plans and programs[168] also is authorized under the convention, but the provision is broader than the provision for specific participation.[169] It is provided, however, that participation in plans and programs must take place under "a transparent and fair framework," which indicates that, at least, participation must be effective. The requirement for public participation in plans and programs links this convention to the SEA Convention that provides for the environmental assessment of plans and programs.[170] The convention becomes even more laconic with regard to participation in environmental policies.[171]

Regarding normative participation, it is underlined that the public should be given the opportunity to comment either directly or through representative consulting bodies[172] on the preparation of executive regulations and legally binding instruments. Draft rules should be published and be available publicly.[173]

Access to Justice

Access to justice is provided for in the convention when the request for information has been refused wrongfully, when it has been ignored, or when it has been answered inadequately. Under these circumstances, the convention provides that the public should have access to a review procedure before a court or an independent and impartial body.[174] The procedure provided for must be free of charge or inexpensive.

---

[164] Art. 6(2), Aarhus Convention, *supra* note 121.

[165] Art. 6(6), *id.*

[166] Most countries that belong to the Economic Commission for Europe (ECE) apply some sort of EIA.

[167] The convention explicitly refers to EIA in article 6(2)(e). See Aarhus Convention, *supra* note 121.

[168] This may include plans and programs regarding tourism, land use, transport as well as strategies on health, sanitation, and water resources. See Guide, *supra* note 122, at 115.

[169] Art. 7, Aarhus Convention, *supra* note 121.

[170] See *supra* Section 1.

[171] "To the extent appropriate, each Party shall endeavor to provide opportunities for public participation in the preparation of policies relating to the environment." See art. 7, Aarhus Convention, *supra* note 121.

[172] Art. 8(c), *id.*

[173] Many countries already have procedures on the publication of draft rules, see Guide, *supra* note 122, at 121.

[174] Art. 9(1), Aarhus Convention, *supra* note 121.

Certain countries have decided to create independent and impartial bodies to review access to information cases. For instance, France has established the Commission for Access to Administrative Documents.[175] Most countries also have administrative appeal processes that are usually free of charge.[176]

The convention provides that those who have standing to bring access to information complaints must either have sufficient interest or maintain that their rights have been impaired. For the purposes of the convention, NGOs are deemed to have sufficient interest and deemed to have rights capable of being impaired.[177]

An interesting facet of the access to justice provisions is that they are not only available for procedural and substantive violations of the access to information rights[178] but also for any violation of national environmental law.[179] Access to justice should provide adequate and effective remedies – including injunctive relief – that must be equitable and timely. Moreover, judicial decisions must be in writing and must be publicly accessible.[180]

Other Provisions

The governing body of the Aarhus Convention is the Meeting of the Parties that takes place every two to three years.[181] In the meantime, working groups are to elaborate on the different aspects of the convention.[182] The parties to the convention have established a compliance committee.[183] The compliance committee reviews cases of noncompliance through submissions by parties, referrals by the secretariat of the convention, or communications from the public. The compliance committee cannot engage in enforcement but has to report to the Meeting of the Parties on its findings. The Meeting of the Parties may take measures against a state that has breached its obligations under the convention that range from assistance and cautions to the suspension of privileges accorded under the convention.[184]

2003 Kiev Protocol

The Aarhus Convention was supplemented in 2003 by the Kiev Protocol on Pollutant Release and Transfer Register.[185] The objective of the protocol is to improve access to information through the establishment of coherent, nationwide pollutant

---

[175] Guide, *supra* note 122, at 126.

[176] *Id.* at 127.

[177] Art. 9(2), Aarhus Convention, *supra* note 121.

[178] Art. 9(2)(b), *id.*

[179] Art. 9(3), *id.*

[180] Art. 9(4), *id.*

[181] Art. 10, *id.*

[182] Working groups established under the convention include: the working group on genetically modified organisms; the working group on pollutant release and transfer registers; the task force on electronic tools; the task force on access to justice; and the task force on financial arrangements. More detail on the working groups is available online at http://www.unece.org/env/pp/tfwg.htm.

[183] See art. 15, Aarhus Convention, *supra* note 121. See also Decision I/7 Review of Compliance, Meeting of the Parties to the Convention on Access to Information, Public Participation in Decision-making and Access to Justice in Environmental Matters, First Meeting, Lucca, Italy, Oct. 31, 2002.

[184] *Id.*

[185] Kiev Protocol on Pollutant Release and Transfer Registers, May 21, 2003 available online at http://www.unece.org/env.

release and transfer registers (PRTRs) in state parties to the protocol.[186] The PRTRs are to be facility-specific with respect to reporting on point sources; could accommodate reporting on diffuse sources; are pollutant- or waste-specific as appropriate; and must distinguish among releases to air, land, and water.[187] Furthermore, PRTRs are developed based on periodic mandatory reporting; must include standardized and timely data; and must be coherent, user-friendly, and publicly accessible (this includes electronic formats).[188] PRTRs are supposed to be structured, computerized databases or several linked databases maintained by a competent authority.[189] The Kiev Protocol requires reporting on a wide range of activities and pollutants (eighty-six pollutants are covered under the protocol).[190]

Thus, although the Kiev Protocol does not regulate pollution *per se*, it is expected that, though a "name and shame" the polluter rationale, it would be able to exert pressure for the reduction of pollutants. Although the protocol has been adopted under the UN/ECE framework, it is open to all states for signature. By December 2003, thirty-six states had signed the protocol, including the European Community (EC).

4.2. Application of Right to Information

The issue of the content and amount of information that a state is required to provide under modern access to information requirements came under scrutiny in the *OSPAR* case examined by the Permanent Court of Arbitration.[191] The facts of the case are as follows.

British Nuclear Fuels (BNFL), a company owned by the United Kingdom, operates a nuclear reprocessing plant in Sellafield. In 1993, BNFL applied to a local authority to build a Mixed Oxide Fuel (MOX) plant to reprocess fuel used in nuclear reactors. The license to build the plant was given in 1994 and the construction was completed in 1996. Ireland challenged the construction of the plant, claiming that the plant would pollute the Irish sea with radioactive waste and pointing out the dangers presented by the transfers of radioactive material (to be shipped in and out of the plant).

Before bringing the case to the Permanent Court of Arbitration, Ireland attempted to bring the case before the ITLOS with no success.[192] Both the United Kingdom and Ireland are members of the European Union (EU) and, thus, the case potentially could be brought before the European Court of Justice. In addition, under article

---

[186] Art. 1, *id.*

[187] Art. 4(a)–(d), *id.*

[188] Art. 4(f)–(h), *id.*

[189] Art. 4(j).

[190] See Annex I & Annex II, *id.*

[191] Dispute Concerning Access to Information under Article 9 of the OSPAR Convention (Ireland v. United Kingdom of Great Britain and Northern Ireland) Permanent Court of Arbitration, July 2, 2003 available online at http://www.pca-cpa.org [hereinafter OSPAR case].

[192] Arbitral Tribunal Constituted Pursuant to Article 287, and Article 1 of the Annex VII of the UNCLOS for Dispute Concerning the MOX Plant, International Movements of Radioactive Materials, and the Protection of Marine Environment of the Irish Sea (MOX Plant Case), (Ireland v. United Kingdom) Order No. 4, Further Suspension of Proceedings on Jurisdiction and Merits, Nov. 14, 2003.

37 of the Euratom Treaty – of which both the United Kingdom and Ireland are signatories – it is provided that members must provide the European Commission of the EU with their plans to dispose of radioactive waste and that the European Commission must deliver its opinion within six months. Based on this provision, the United Kingdom had submitted its MOX construction plans to the European Commission, which concluded that:

> the implementation of the plan for the disposal of radioactive wastes arising from the operation of the BNFL Sellafield mixed oxide fuel plant, both in normal operation and in the event of an accident of the type and magnitude considered in the general data, is not liable to result in radioactive contamination, significant from the point of view of health, of the water, soil or air space of another Member State.[193]

Furthermore, the government of Ireland had participated in the public consultation procedures regarding the operation of the plant. During these procedures, Ireland opposed the operation of the plant on the grounds that it would perpetuate the nuclear fuel reprocessing industry in Britain. In addition, Ireland charged that potential discharges from the plant in the Irish Sea were objectionable and unacceptable.[194] Further consultations were followed because there were concerns that the BNFL did not provide the public with sufficient commercial information that would justify the commissioning and the operation of the plant. The BNFL consulted with independent firms about the information that should be submitted to the public domain and information that could be withheld because it would involve giving up its competitive advantage;[195] or because the release of information would breach safeguards and security requirements with regard to the location, quantities, and movements of plutonium.[196]

The parties agreed to bring the case before the Permanent Court of Arbitration (PCA) based on the right to information requirements included in the OSPAR Convention.[197] According to Ireland, article 9 of the OSPAR Convention provides it with the right to be informed on the following matters:

- estimated annual production capacity at the MOX facility;
- time taken to reach that capacity;
- sales volumes;
- probability of achieving higher sales volumes;
- probability of being able to win contracts for recycling fuel in "significant quantities;"
- estimated sales demand;
- percentage of plutonium already on site;
- maximum throughput figures;

---

[193] Para. 17, OSPAR case, *supra* note 191.

[194] Para. 23, *id.*

[195] For instance, information that would allow competitors to build market share or to understand the economics of the plant.

[196] Paras. 24–26, OSPAR case, *supra* note 191.

[197] See Convention for the Protection of the Marine Environment of the North East Atlantic (OSPAR Convention), Sept. 22, 1992, reprinted in 32 ILM 1069 (1993). For an analysis of the convention, see Chapter 4, Section 4.1.

- lifespan of MOX facility;
- number of employees;
- price of MOX fuel;
- the number of contracts, if any, to purchase mixed oxide fuel from Sellafield;
- arrangements to transport plutonium to Shellafield and mixed oxide fuel from Sellafield;
- the number of transfers of plutonium and mixed oxide fuel to and from Sellafield.[198]

The tribunal had to examine the following questions:

1. whether article 9(1) of the OSPAR Convention provides for an obligation of the United Kingdom to disclose the information requested by Ireland;
2. whether the information requested by Ireland was within the scope of definition of information provided for in article 9(2) of the OSPAR Convention;
3. if the information requested by Ireland was indeed within the scope of article 9 whether any of the exceptions included in article 9(3)(d) applied. Article 9(3)(d) of the OSPAR Convention provides that a party may refuse to provide information of "commercial and industrial confidentiality, including intellectual property."

The tribunal first examined whether the United Kingdom's obligation to provide Ireland with information was derived directly from article 9(1). Article 9(1) provides:

> The Contracting Parties shall ensure that their competent authorities are required to make available the information described in paragraph 2 of this Article to any natural or legal person, in response to any reasonable request, without that person's having to prove an interest, without unreasonable charges, as soon as possible and at the latest within two months.

According to the United Kingdom, article 9(1) provided for the obligation of states to establish regulations on the provision of information. The merits of an application for information were to be determined, thus, by U.K. municipal law. Ireland argued, on the other hand, that the United Kingdom's obligation derived directly from article 9(1) and, thus, the tribunal had the jurisdiction to decide on the merits of the United Kingdom's refusal to provide information.[199] The tribunal agreed with Ireland. According to the tribunal, article 9(1) "is pitched at a level that imposes an obligation of result rather than merely to provide access to a domestic regime which is directed at obtaining the required result" and concluded that the United Kingdom was under an obligation to provide information.[200]

---

[198] Para. 161, OSPAR case, *supra* note 191.

[199] Para. 124, *id.*

[200] Para. 137, *id.* But see also declaration of Professor Michael Reisman who stated that support for the Irish position would essentially involve the deletion of certain important words in article 9(1) namely the provision of "ensure that their competent authorities are required to." According to Professor Reisman the intention behind article 9(1) was not to establish "an obligation on the international plane to provide information." See paras. 5–6, Declaration of W. Michael Reisman, *id.*

The tribunal went on to examine whether the information requested by Ireland was under the purview of article 9(2). The tribunal clarified that article 9(2) identified information as:

- any available information on the state of the maritime area;
- any available information on activities or measures adversely affecting or likely to affect the maritime area;
- any available information on activities or measures introduced in accordance with the convention.

The tribunal disagreed with the Ireland that article 9(2) involves the release of all environmental information. The tribunal added that even if article 9(2) was interpreted to require the disclosure of all environmental information, the information requested by Ireland was not of the environmental type but more of the type of information on "economic justification."[201] The tribunal noted that article 9(2) was carefully crafted to include information on measures likely to have adverse effects on the maritime area and not on all measures.[202]

Furthermore, the tribunal rejected Ireland's claim that it had the authority to apply "evolving international law and practice." Ireland had cited the decision of the ICJ in the *Gabčíkovo-Nagymaros* case,[203] in which the Court stated:

> new norms and standards have been developed, set forth in a great number of instruments during the last two decades. Such new norms have to be taken into consideration, and such new standards given proper weight, not only when States contemplate new activities but also when continuing with activities begun in the past.[204]

The tribunal disagreed with Ireland that this passage from the *Gabčíkovo-Nagymaros* case gave it authority to apply law in *statu nascendi* that is still evolving rather than established law.[205] The tribunal, furthermore, did not take into account the right to information as elaborated in the Aarhus Convention. The Aarhus Convention entered into force after the tribunal heard oral arguments. Neither the United Kingdom nor Ireland had ratified the convention at the time of the proceedings.

The tribunal balked at a broad interpretation of right to information requirements as articulated in various international instruments. It would be interesting to see how international law on the provision of information would evolve now that the Aarhus Convention has been ratified and new instruments are added that include access to information provisions. The tribunal was right to distinguish that for the right to information in environmental matters to function, a balance must be maintained between the interest of the public to know and the interests of states or companies that wish to keep commercial information confidential. As what is commercially important – and, thus, better kept confidential – and what the public must know may often intersect, this would, indeed, be a difficult balance to keep.

---

[201] Paras. 180–81, *id.*

[202] Paras. 175–76, *id.*

[203] Case Concerning the Gabčíkovo-Nagymaros Project, (Hungary v. Slovakia), Sept. 25, 1997, (1997) ICJ Reports 7.

[204] Para. 140, *id.*

[205] Para. 101, OSPAR case, *supra* note 191. "The Tribunal has not been authorized to apply evolving international law and practice and cannot do so."

5. CONCLUSION

The multiple compliance and governance mechanisms analyzed in this chapter serve a number of functions including that of prevention of damage (EIAs and SEAs, notification requirements), monitoring (through accumulation of data, exchange of information and reporting), and enforcement (compliance procedures). The adoption of environmental instruments and methods that apply across environmental issues and economic sectors provides evidence of the increased sophistication of international institutions in handling environmental matters. Compliance and governance mechanisms provide a network of options to states regarding the implementation of environmental law. Overall, the provision of information under a "name, help, and, as a last resort, shame" a polluting state rationale is expected to produce more results than strict enforcement devices. In the information age, the most potent enforcement device may be the dissemination and use of information

4

Marine Environment

1. STATE OF MARINE ENVIRONMENT

Pollution enters the marine environment through dumping, through discharges from the operations of ships, through land-based sources, and through the atmosphere (pollutants end up in the atmosphere from land-based sources). The GESAMP has determined that only 10 percent of marine pollution comes from dumping and 1 percent is a result of sea-bed activities. The main culprit of marine pollution (77 percent) is pollution coming from land-based sources.[1]

Despite the plethora of national and international instruments devoted to the prevention and elimination of sea pollution, the results, in terms of environmental improvement, are mixed. According to a GESAMP study:

> Although there have been some notable successes in addressing problems caused by some form of marine pollution, and in improving the quality of certain coastal areas, on a global scale marine environmental degradation has continued and in many places has intensified.[2]

The GESAMP report has placed emphasis on the increasing global problem of eutrophication, that is, the increased biological production in coastal and near shore waters, because of the input of nutrients from sewage and agricultural fertilizers.[3] According to the GESAMP, eutrophication is "among potentially the most damaging of all human influences on the oceans, in terms both of scale and consequences."[4] The GESAMP has warned that excessive nutrient inputs "can turn marine areas into wastelands."[5] The GESAMP has determined that sewage is a problem of high priority in all regional seas.[6] After sewage, environmental issues that need to be addressed

---

[1] GESAMP, The State of the Marine Environment 88 (1990) (GESAMP Joint Group of Experts on Scientific Aspects of Marine Environmental Protection comprised of IMO, FAO ICO, WHO, WMO, IAEA, UNEP, and UNESCO).

[2] GESAMP, Protecting the Oceans from Land-based Activities 1 (Reports and Studies No. 71, Jan. 15, 2001) [hereinafter GESAMP 2001].

[3] Eutrophication involves the increased growth of phytoplankton and its eventual decay that increases the consumption of oxygen dissolved in the sea and, occasionally, causes oxygen depletion, leading to the mass mortality of fish and other organisms.

[4] GESAMP 2001, *supra* note 2, at 1.

[5] *Id*. at 2.

[6] *Id*. at 3.

with urgency include sediment mobilization, Persistent Organic Pollutants (POPs), heavy metals, and physical alteration.[7]

The sea disposal of low-level radioactive waste has become controversial. Although in the 1970s such practice was tolerated, in the 1990s the London Convention prohibited the dumping of low-level radioactive waste at sea.

The GESAMP has determined, however, that low-level radioactive wastes do not present as high a risk as other wastes, especially toxic wastes. The GESAMP results are based on a 1993 IAEA study that evaluated the comparative risks of ingesting chemical carcinogens versus those of ingesting radionuclides through seafood consumption. The study was prompted by a need to see the risks associated with the disposal of low-level radioactive waste in the appropriate context. The IAEA study concluded that the incremental risk associated with the contamination of seafood from the sea disposal of low-level radioactive waste is three or four orders of magnitude lower than the risk posed by what are considered toxic chemicals.[8] The study examined the environmental effects of reprocessing plants located in Sellafield (United Kingdom), LaHague and Marcoule (France; now shut down), Trombay (India), and Tokai-Mura (Japan). It was concluded that nuclear power reactors discharge small quantities of radioanuclides, that they are generally well regulated, and that they should not be a source of concern.[9] The GESAMP recognizes, however, that the use of nuclear power is an emotive issue and that public opinion on this topic is unlikely to change.[10]

Although low–radioactive waste is not an issue of concern, the dumping of nuclear waste that comes from the decommissioning of nuclear weapons, nuclear military installations, and obsolete nuclear vessels, is. The GESAMP has singled out Russia for the illegal disposal of high-level radioactive waste at sea, which is in violation of the London Dumping Convention that banned such practice since its adoption.[11] The dumping activities of Russia, especially those involving the dumping of reactor assemblies containing spent fuel and of entire nuclear submarines, are of concern. The GESAMP has insisted that the difficulties involved in the decommissioning of military vessels, and particularly of nuclear submarines of the Russian North Fleet, suggest that such activities pose threats to the marine environment. There have been a number of accidents involving nuclear-powered and nuclear-armed vessels[12]

The GESAMP has identified several sources of marine pollution: sewage treatment plants, development activities that lead to discharges of sediments, and mariculture facilities. Diffuse sources of pollution include agriculture, widescale forestry, and development activities that lead to increased mobilization of the soil. In terms of contaminants, substances of concern include mercury and lead, POPs, and what has

---

[7] *Id.*

[8] *Id.* at 14.

[9] *Id.* at 17.

[10] *Id.* at 22.

[11] High-level radioactive wastes belong to Annex I of the 1972 London Dumping Convention, the so-called black list that prohibited the dumping of certain wastes. See London Dumping Convention, *infra* note 62.

[12] GESAMP 2001, *supra* note 2, at 37.

been called the "dirty dozen."[13] The GESAMP has concluded that most metallic compounds should be of concern at a local level and only exceptionally at a regional scale.[14]

Salt discharged from desalination plants in high volumes and concentrations has adverse effects on regional areas, for instance, the Persian Gulf and the Red Sea.Heat discharges have detrimental effects on small and poorly flushed water bodies.[15]

Pollution from vessels is caused by the operational discharges from ships, for instance from cleaning of tanks or discharges following accidents. Although vessels contribute a small percentage of marine pollution (12 percent of the total), they are usually perceived as one of the main contributors to marine pollution because of the large publicity that oil spills generate. The GESAMP has concluded that the releases of hydrocarbon compounds from routine operations, such as oil exploitation and exploration and shipping, are relatively well regulated (through the MARPOL Convention 73/78).[16] Large oil spills create problems but are of "limited significance" on spatial and long-term scales.[17] Oil is not the worst pollutant of the seas. Heavy metals (lead, mercury, and cadmium), however, are potent pollutants. Nitrates and phosphates from agriculture could cause a significant amount of eutrophication and should become an issue of priority.

Other contaminants include polycyclic aromatic hydrocarbons (PAHs), which are likely to increase because of the increasing exploitation of the sea-bed and remain troublesome because of their appearance in seafood.[18] Litter and sediment mobilization are likely to be issues of primary concern at the local and regional levels.[19] Physical alteration of coastlines, as a result of cumulative impacts, is an issue on which the GESAMP has focused its attention. The GESAMP has warned for action to be taken to prevent impacts on coastlines from increased sediment, excavation works, forestry, agriculture, beach development, and construction of hotels and marinas. Habitat destruction, dredging, and infilling operations are considered major problems, especially in the Red Sea/Gulf of Aden. Sand and gravel extraction from the sea-bed is also a concern in the North East Atlantic and the Irish Sea.[20]

The GESAMP study has emphasized that certain marine environments are more sensitive to pollution than others and, thus, require special attention, such as coral reefs, sea-grass beds, coastal wetlands, mangrove forests, shallow coastal waters, and small islands.

---

[13] The "dirty dozen" include pesticides (aldrin, chlordane, DDT, dieldrin, endrin, heptachlor, mirex, toxaphene); industrial chemicals (hexachlrobenzene, polychlorinated biphenyls [PCBs]) and other dioxins (PCDDs), and furans (PCDFs). *Id.* at 17.

[14] *Id.* at 22.

[15] *Id.* at 20.

[16] Hydrocarbons enter the seas from a variety of activities: 850,000 tons per year from ship traffic and offshore activities; 350,000 tons per year from coastal refineries, storage, and transshipment facilities; and other unknown sources. Volatile Organic Compounds (VOCs) potentially are a major route of oil input to the oceans, as they have been estimated to be 3,750,000 tons per year, principally from tankers. *Id.* at 23.

[17] *Id.*

[18] *Id.* at 23–24.

[19] *Id.* at 25.

[20] *Id.* at 26.

Polluted groundwater can affect the marine environment adversely. Slow but persistent seepage of groundwater takes place along most of the world's coastlines and eventually may lead to pollution.[21]

2. INTEGRATED COASTAL ZONE MANAGEMENT

The need for an integrated coastal area management (ICAM) emerged from the conflicts among the different potential users of coastal areas. Tourism and fisheries, conservation and land development, and oil shipping and recreation are rarely compatible with each other.[22]

Integrated coastal management has been defined as a continuous and dynamic process by which decisions are made for marine and coastal area management. The purpose of this process is to overcome the fragmentation that underlines both a sectoral management approach (tourism/oil shipping/fishing) and departmentalization among the levels of government (local/national/regional).[23] The purpose of ICAM is to achieve intersectoral integration (e.g., among fisheries, tourism, offshore oil exploitation, and other activities); intergovernmental integration (among different levels of government); spatial integration (between the land area and the ocean side of the coastal zone); and the integration of science and management through more effective communication channels between managers and scientists; and, finally, international integration.[24]

Nations vary with regard to the geographical extension of ICAM. Most states have yet to establish the landward boundaries of their ICAMs. With regard to the seaward boundary, some countries apply ICAM to their territorial sea, whereas others apply ICAM to their Exclusive Economic Zone (EEZ) as well.[25] ICAM develops in stages that involve identification and assessment of issues; planning and preparation; formal adoption and funding; and implementation, operation, and evaluation. The turf battles among the institutions that may have overlapping jurisdiction over coastal areas can hamper the development of ICAM. The establishment of a coordinating agency often becomes a priority for the implementation of ICAM.[26]

Other issues to be considered for sound integrated coastal zone management include the level of development in a specific country, the concentration of population in coastal zones, and the political regime under which decisions are made.[27] For ICAM to become successful, integration must not be a goal in itself; it cannot replace sectoral management but only supplement it.[28]

ICAM has been endorsed by international instruments, such as Chapter 17 of Agenda 21. A number of international and regional organizations also have adopted

---

[21] *Id.* at 52–53.
[22] Biliana Cicin-Sain & Robert W. Knecht, Integrated Coastal and Ocean Management: Concepts and Practices 23–24 (1998).
[23] *Id.* at 39.
[24] *Id.* at 45.
[25] *Id.* at 51.
[26] *Id.* at 218–19.
[27] *Id.* at 122.
[28] *Id.* at 155.

ICAM, such as the World Bank,[29] the OECD,[30] the FAO,[31] the UNEP regional seas program,[32] the UNESCO,[33] the GESAMP,[34] and the IMO.

ICAM has been developed in different areas of the world. It is practiced by 447 global, national, and subnational entities in at least 95 developed and developing countries and semisovereign states. An international survey of forty-three ICAM projects, however, has found that only 12 percent of these projects are fully implemented.[35]

ICAM has been applied with mixed success within the Mediterranean Action Plan (MAP) regime. The Coastal Areas Management Programmes (CAMPs) in the Mediterranean region have been guided by the Priorities Action Programme (PAP).[36]

In the European Union, ICAM is referred to as Integrated Coastal Zone Management (ICZM). The Community has engaged in efforts to develop an ICZM. The European Environment Agency (EEA) has defined ICZM as a "dynamic, multidisciplinary and iterative process to promote sustainable management of coastal zones."[37] Many of the elements of ICZM are still in the process of being defined.

A distinguishing element between coastal zone management and river basin management is that whereas rivers could be shared by many states, coasts are clearly under an individual state's jurisdiction. Despite this technical matter, however, it would be difficult to separate coastal zone management from river basin management in areas where rivers end up in the sea and affect coastal zones. Coastal zone management has been associated more with land-use planning and marine resources management. River basin management has been associated with freshwater

---

[29] World Bank, Africa: A Framework for Integrated Coastal Zone Management, Environmentally Sustainable Development Division and Land, Water and Habitats Division, Africa Region (1995). Comprehensive guidelines for integrated management also were presented at a conference in Noordwijk, Netherlands sponsored by the World Bank. See Guidelines for Integrated Coastal Zone Management, Environmentally Sustainable Studies and Monographs Series, No.9 (Jan C. Post & Carl G. Lundin, eds., 1996); see also Integrated Coastal Zone Management of Coral Reefs: Decision Support Modeling, Environmentally Sustainable Studies and Monographs Series (Kent Gustavson et al., eds., 2000).

[30] Recommendation of the OECD Council on Integrated Coastal Zone Management, July 23, 1992, C(92)114/Final.

[31] FAO, Development of Coastal Areas and Enclosed Seas, Research Paper No. 4 (1991), paper presented at the UN Conference on Environment and Development, Rio de Janeiro, Brazil, June 8–12, 1992. See also FAO Guidelines, Integrated Coastal Area Management and Agriculture, Forestry and Fisheries (1998).

[32] See *infra* note 36.

[33] See Co-Chairs Report, The Global Conference on Oceans and Coasts at Rio+10, Ensuring the Sustainable Development of Oceans and Coasts, UNESCO, Dec. 3–7, 2001.

[34] GESAMP, The Contributions of Science to Integrated Coastal Zone Management, Reports and Studies No. 61, 1996.

[35] Robert Kay, Coastal Planning Experience from Elsewhere, in Coastal Area Management Programmes: Improving Implementation 208 (PAP/RAC, 2002).

[36] The Priority Actions Programme/Regional Activity Centre (PAP/RAC) was established in 1978 as an element of the MAP and it is also part of the UNEP. For more information on the application of ICAM in the Mediterranean region, see Elli Louka, Developing Consensus through Application: The Integrated Coastal Area Management Experience in the Mediterranean Region 143, in Contributions to International Environmental Negotiation in the Mediterranean Context (Evangelos Raftopoulos & Moira L. McConnell, eds., 2004).

[37] The definition is available in the glossary of the EEA official site available online at http://glossary.eea.eu.int/EEAGlossary.

management. But coastal zone management and river basin management cannot be neatly segregated. The UNEP–Water Branch and Priority Actions Programme Regional Activity Center (PAP/RAC) that focuses on the implementation of the Mediterranean Action Plan is exploring the application of Integrated Coastal Area and River Basin Management (ICARM).[38]

3. EVOLUTION OF INTERNATIONAL INSTRUMENTS

The international regime for the protection of the seas includes:

- a global "umbrella" convention that addresses pollution from all sources (the United Nations Convention on the Law of the Sea [UNCLOS]);[39]
- two international conventions concentrating on specific issues – sea dumping and pollution from vessels (London Dumping Convention and MARPOL Convention, respectively);
- a number of conventions concerned with the protection of regional seas;
- the Global Programme of Action (GPA)[40] for controlling pollution from land-based sources. The program is to help states to develop regional action plans and environmental impact assessments, but little specific action has been taken under the program.[41]

3.1. Law of the Sea Convention

The UNCLOS was adopted in 1982 and entered into force in 1994. The convention concentrates both on the prevention of marine pollution and the protection of marine living resources. Part XII of the convention deals with the preservation and protection of marine environment but environmental provisions are dispersed all through the text of the convention. Some of the environmental provisions include granting to coastal states jurisdiction in matters relating to the protection of marine environment;[42] the responsibility not to cause damage by pollution to other states and their environment;[43] the need to prevent, control, and abate pollution according to each state's capability;[44] and particular sources of pollution with which states must be concerned, such as pollution from land-based activities, vessels, and the atmosphere.[45]

---

[38] UNEP/MAP/PAP, Conceptual Framework and Planning Guidelines for Integrated Coastal Area and River Basin Management (Priority Actions Progamme, 1999).

[39] United Nations Convention on the Law of the Sea, Dec. 10, 1982, reprinted in 21 ILM 1261 (1982) [hereinafter UNCLOS]. The convention has been ratified by many countries except for the United States. The United States has refused to ratify the convention because of the deep-sea bed mining provisions.

[40] The GPA was adopted on November 3, 1995, and called, *inter alia*, for a clearing-house mechanism that would provide decision-makers access to current sources of information, practical experience, and scientific and technical expertise to deal with the impacts of land-based activities. See UNEP(OCA)/LBA/IG.2/7 available online at http://www.gpa.unep.org/documents/gpa.

[41] GPA 2001 Intergovernmental Review Meeting, Nov. 26–30, 2001.

[42] Art. 56, UNCLOS, *supra* note 39.

[43] Art. 194(2), *id.*

[44] Art. 194(1), *id.*

[45] Art. 194(3), *id.*

The convention provides that no dumping should take place in the territorial sea and the EEZ of a state without express authorization of that state and after deliberation with all other states that may be adversely affected.[46]

The provisions for pollution control from land-based sources are not as specific. The convention provides that states must control pollution from land-based sources including rivers and pipelines.[47] States must minimize the release of toxic and harmful substances to the marine environment.[48]

More specific requirements are included to control pollution from vessels. States are not only to prevent and to control pollution from vessels but also to adopt routing systems that minimize the possibilities of accidents that cause pollution. States must adopt rules for ships that fly their flag in accordance with rules and standards that "at least have the same effect as that of generally accepted international rules and standards."[49] Because the convention does not define the international rules and standards, this clause remains somewhat indeterminate.[50] Port states can adopt rules against pollution with regard to vessels that enter their ports or internal waters.[51] Coastal states are to combat vessel pollution from foreign vessels' passage through their territorial seas, including vessels that exercise their right to innocent passage.[52] States can adopt regulations, in accordance with international rules and standards, with regard to the protection of the environment in the EEZ area,[53] as the convention has enlarged the jurisdiction of states to include the EEZ.

Pollution from sea-bed activities is expressly recognized in the UNCLOS. At this point, pollution from sea-bed activities does not exceed 1 percent of the total pollution, but this may change in the future, depending on the intensity of sea-bed exploitation. States must prevent pollution of the marine environment arising from or connected with sea-bed activities under their jurisdiction and from artificial islands, installations, and structures under their jurisdiction.[54] As mentioned in Chapter 2, sea-bed activities beyond the national jurisdiction of states are regulated by the International Seabed Authority.[55] The Council of the International Seabed Authority must not approve sea-bed exploitation when substantial evidence indicates a risk of serious harm to the environment. In 2000, the International Seabed Authority adopted Regulations on the Prospecting and Exploration of Polymetallic Nodules, which include provisions on the protection of marine environment. In addition to the UNCLOS, other conventions concentrate on the protection of sea-bed, including the 1989 Protocol Concerning Marine Pollution Resulting from Exploration and Exploitation of the Continental Shelf in the Arabian Gulf Region[56] and the 1994 Protocol Concerning the Protection of the

---

[46] Art. 210(3) & (5), *id.*
[47] Art. 207(1), *id.*
[48] Art. 207(5), *id.*
[49] Art. 211(1) & (2), *id.*
[50] R.R. Churchill & A.V. Lowe, The Law of the Sea 346–47 (1999).
[51] Art. 211(3), UNCLOS, *supra* note 39.
[52] Art. 211(4), *id.*
[53] Art. 211(5), *id.*
[54] Art. 208, *id.*
[55] Art. 145, *id.*
[56] Mar. 29, 1989 available online at http://www.unep.org/regionalseas/Programmes.

Mediterranean Sea Against Pollution Resulting from Exploration and Exploitation of the Continental Shelf and the Seabed and its Subsoil (1994 Madrid Offshore Protocol).[57]

Flag states play a primary role in enforcing the UNCLOS provisions.[58] The enforcement power of flag states on ships that carry their flag is well recognized in international law, as ships are considered an extension of a state's territory. The enforcement authority of the coastal state is a newer concept in international law. It emanates from the belief that an extension of a state's jurisdiction (property rights) beyond its territorial sea would be beneficial for the protection of marine environment. Today, coastal states have significant enforcement powers in their EEZ when a violation results in a discharge causing a major damage or threat of damage to their coastline or related interests.[59] In those circumstances, the coastal state can even arrest an offending vessel.[60] But enforcement action by coastal states is subject to a number of safeguards.[61] Because coastal states are often port states, it may be easier for such states to exercise their jurisdiction when ships are in their ports rather than to pursue them in the high seas.

3.2. Pollution from Dumping

Wastes dumped deliberately at sea constitute only 10 percent of the overall sea pollution. Waste dumping has been regulated by the London Convention that used to be called London Dumping Convention (LDC).[62] The convention was adopted in 1972, but the 1996 amendments revamped the whole purpose of the convention. Although the goal of the 1972 convention was to regulate pollution by dumping, the goal of the 1996 convention[63] was to put a stop to waste dumping at sea.

The 1972 LDC regulated waste dumping by establishing three lists: the black, the gray, and the white. The black list – Annex I of the convention – includes wastes considered the most dangerous.[64] The dumping of these wastes is prohibited,[65] but there are exceptions. Only high-level radioactive wastes are absolutely banned. The other prohibitions are not applicable when wastes "are rapidly rendered harmless by physical, chemical, or biological processes in the sea" as long as they do not render edible marine organisms unpalatable and do not endanger the health of humans or that of domestic animals. Prohibitions do not apply to wastes, for example, sewage sludge or dredged materials, containing the black list substances as trace

---

[57] Oct. 14, 1994, *id.*

[58] See art. 217, UNCLOS, *supra* note 39.

[59] Art. 220, *id.*

[60] Art. 220(3)–(8), *id.*

[61] Arts. 223–233, *id.*

[62] Convention on the Prevention of Marine Pollution by Dumping of Wastes and Other Matter, Dec. 29, 1972, reprinted in 1046 UNTS 120 [hereinafter LDC].

[63] See *infra* note 80.

[64] These consist of: organohalogen compounds, mercury and mercury compounds, cadmium and its compounds, persistent plastics, crude oil and its wastes, materials produced for biological and chemical warfare, and high-level radioactive wastes. See LDC, *supra* note 62, Annex I.

[65] Art. IV (1)(a), *id.*

contaminants.[66] The "trace contaminants" and "harmlessness" provisions dilute to a great extent the absolute prohibitions contained in Annex I.

The gray list – Annex II – includes wastes perceived as less dangerous than the Annex I wastes.[67] The dumping of these wastes cannot take place without prior special permits issued by national governments.[68] The white list – Annex III – includes all other wastes that can be dumped after the issuance of a general permit. National authorities must issue general and special permits after taking into consideration the waste characteristics,[69] the dumping site[70] and disposal method, the effects of dumping on marine life, and other uses of the sea, as well as the possibility of application of alternative land-based solutions.

The LDC attempts to control dumping in the territorial sea[71] and the high-seas[72] but not in the internal waters of state parties.[73] The convention is silent regarding waste dumping in the Exclusive Economic Zone (EEZ) because it was concluded before the latest UNCLOS that first clearly defined the EEZ. In 1988, the LDC Eleventh Consultative Meeting decided that the scope of the convention should be extended to include the EEZ.[74] The implementation of the convention is left to flag states, port states, and coastal states in their territorial sea and EEZs.[75] For the enforcement of the convention in the high seas, state parties have agreed to cooperate.[76]

The 1972 version of LDC regulates rather than prohibits waste dumping. Even the black waste list contains exceptions, and the gray and white lists hardly contribute to the harmonization of national legislation because special and general permits

[66] Annex I, paras. 8–9, *id.*

[67] Annex II includes: (1) wastes containing significant amounts of: arsenic, lead, copper, zinc, beryllium, chromium, nickel, vanadium, organosilicon compounds, cyanides, fluorides, pesticides not included in Annex I, and low-level radioactive wastes; (2) bulky wastes such as containers and scrap metal liable to sink to the sea bottom that may seriously harm fishing and navigation; and (3) nontoxic substances which may become harmful because they are dumped in large quantities, or substances that are liable to seriously reduce amenities. See LDC, *id.*

[68] Art. IV (1)(b), *id.*

[69] These characteristics include the amount, composition, form, properties, toxicity, persistence, accumulation of wastes, susceptibility to physical, chemical and biochemical changes, interaction with the marine environment, and possibility to produce taints that reduce the marketability of marine resources. See Annex III, *id.*

[70] The characteristics of the site include location, rate of disposal, packaging, water, dispersal, and bottom characteristics. See *id.*

[71] Art. III(3), *id.* In the territorial sea, a state is sovereign, but its sovereignty is limited by the right to innocent passage.

[72] No state has jurisdiction over the high seas. See Convention on the High Seas, April 29, 1958, reprinted in 450 UNTS 82. See also International Convention Relating to Intervention on the High Seas in Cases of Oil Pollution Casualties, Nov. 29, 1969, reprinted in 9 ILM 25 (1970).

[73] In its internal waters a state is sovereign and can prescribe and enforce its domestic or international legislation.

[74] See Note by the Secretariat, Review of Proposed and Adopted Amendments to the Convention, Fifteenth Consultative Meeting of Contracting Parties to the Convention on the Prevention of Marine Pollution by Dumping of Wastes and other Matter, Agenda item 3, at 6, LDC 15/INF. 14, Oct. 23, 1992. See also UNCLOS, Dec. 10, 1982, reprinted in 21 ILM 1261 (1982). According to UNCLOS, article 210(5), dumping within the EEZ or in the continental shelf shall not take place without the prior approval of the coastal state.

[75] Art. VII (1), LDC, *supra* note 62.

[76] Art. VII(3), *id.*

are issued unilaterally by national authorities. Reports on the effectiveness of the convention have been mixed. All through the 1980s and the 1990s, extensive efforts have been undertaken to beef up the text of the convention with more stringent provisions.

- In 1982, the parties to the convention adopted a resolution for the prohibition of dumping of all radioactive material (not only high-level nuclear wastes that were already included in Annex I – black list).[77]
- In 1985, the moratorium on radioactive waste dumping was renewed.[78]
- In 1993, the convention was amended to make the moratorium on radioactive waste dumping legally binding. The moratorium is to be reviewed every twenty-five years.
- In 1993, an amendment to the convention prohibited the incineration of hazardous waste and sewage sludge at sea.[79]
- In 1993, the convention was amended to end, in principle, industrial waste dumping.

The 1993 amendments overhauled the purpose of the convention. The substances that are still permissible to dump are dredged materials, sewage sludge, fish processing wastes, and oil and gas installations and vessels. All other waste dumping is prohibited.

In 1996, the London Dumping Convention was amended by a protocol[80] that codified some of the developments incorporated in the 1993 amendments. The protocol changed drastically the orientation of the convention with regard to waste dumping. The protocol is based on:

- the precautionary approach;[81]
- the reverse listing approach, according to which states are required to prevent waste dumping with the exception of wastes that are listed in Annex I, the dumping of which requires a permit;[82]
- the prohibition of incineration at sea;[83] and
- the prohibition of waste exports to countries for dumping or incineration at sea.[84]

Article 9 requires contracting parties to designate an appropriate authority or authorities. The purpose of these authorities is to issue permits with regard to waste included in Annex I. With regard to dumping material not contained in Annex 1, parties must go through an extensive waste assessment procedure if they wish to proceed

---

[77] Resolution LDC. 14(7) (1982).

[78] Resolution LDC. 21(9) (1985).

[79] Resolution LDC. 51(16) Concerning Disposal at Sea of Radioactive Wastes and other Radioactive Matter (1993).

[80] Protocol to the Convention on the Prevention of Marine Pollution by Dumping of Wastes and Other Matter, Nov. 7, 1996, reprinted in 36 ILM 1 (1997) [hereinafter LC].

[81] Art. 3(1), *id.*

[82] Art. 4(1) & (2), *id.* Annex I includes: (1) dredged material; (2) sewage sludge; (3) fish waste; (4) vessels and platforms and other man-made structures at sea; (5) inert, inorganic geological material; (6) organic material of natural origin; and (7) bulky items of iron, steel, and concrete generated in locations with no alternative disposal facilities available, *id.*

[83] Art. 5, *id.*

[84] Art. 6, *id.*

with dumping. The details of the assessment procedure are included in Annex 2.[85] The parties to the convention have published guidelines regarding wastes that could potentially be dumped based on the Annex 2 procedure.[86]

States that can enforce the convention include the flag state; states in whose territories vessels and aircraft are loading waste to be dumped or be incinerated at sea; and any states in whose jurisdiction dumping is executed. Parties are to undertake measures to prevent and punish actions contrary to the provisions of the protocol.[87] The protocol provides for a compliance procedure that is to be fine-tuned no later than two years after the adoption of the protocol.[88] The 1996 LC Protocol is to supersede the LDC when it enters into force for states parties that ratify it.[89]

The more stringent character of the 1996 LC Protocol versus the LDC Convention is not a result of an excessive deterioration of the oceans because of dumping. Pollution from land-based sources is more overwhelming and difficult to control. The prohibition of low-level radioactive waste dumping, for instance, has a lot more to do with the politics and the emotive issues surrounding such dumping. By the time the moratorium on low-level radioactive waste was adopted, low-level radioactive waste dumping had decreased significantly.[90] Furthermore, low-level nuclear waste is not as much of an issue as high-level nuclear waste. About two-thirds of the radioactivity in the seas comes from high-level radioactive waste associated with six Russian submarine reactors and a shielding assembly from a nuclear icebreaker reactor. The remainder comes from low-level radioactive waste dumped by European countries, especially by the United Kingdom, in the northeast Atlantic.[91]

The moratorium on low-level radioactive waste was triggered by Japan's decision to dump low-level radioactive waste in the Pacific Ocean.[92] This decision was opposed by several Pacific islands led by Nauru and Kiribati and, in the absence of firm scientific evidence, the debate escalated quickly to confrontation. Countries that produce nuclear energy – Belgium, France, Japan, the United Kingdom, and the United States – preferred to leave open the option of radioactive waste dumping. Such disposal was perceived as necessary, for instance, because of the high population density in Japan and Belgium, and the public opposition in most countries against land disposal.[93] Spain, Norway, Finland, Iceland, Ireland, and the Pacific islands were opposed to dumping. The Pacific islands, with economies almost exclusively dependent on fisheries and tourism, were strong opponents of radioactive waste

---

[85] Annex 2 provides for: (1) waste prevention audit; (2) consideration of waste management options; (3) consideration of chemical, physical, and biological properties; (4) an action list; (5) dump-site selection; (6) assessment of potential effects; (7) monitoring; and (8) permit and permit conditions. See *id.*

[86] See Guidelines for the Assessment of Wastes or Other Matter that May be Considered for Dumping available online http://www.londonconvention.org/WAG.htm.

[87] Art. 10, LC, *supra* note 80.

[88] Art. 11, *id.*

[89] Art. 23, *id.*

[90] Judith Spiller et al., Radwaste at Sea: A New Era of Polarization or a New Basis of Consensus, in 19 Ocean Development and International Law 345, at 346–47 (1988).

[91] Dumping at Sea: The Evolution of the Convention on the Prevention of Marine Pollution by Dumping of Wastes and Other Matter 6, Focus on IMO, July 1997 [hereinafter Dumping at Sea].

[92] Spiller, *supra* note 90, at 347.

[93] *Id.* at 346–47.

dumping.[94] In 1993, the sixteenth Consultative Meeting of the London Dumping Convention adopted amendments to Annex I prohibiting the disposal of all radioactive waste at sea.

The prohibition of low-level radioactive waste dumping is viewed as a victory of environmental NGOs that mobilized public opinion against radioactive waste dumping. The NGOs succeeded in framing the issue of waste dumping as a value issue – that is, it is immoral to use the seas as a dumping ground. The notion that the sea should not be used as the "garbage can" of the world has permeated arguments against radioactive waste dumping[95] and has undermined the legitimacy of industrial waste dumping.[96]

The prohibition of incineration at sea happened because of extensive public opposition to end the practice. The opposition was so strong that by the end of 1989 the only company engaging still in incineration announced that it was selling its two remaining incineration vessels. The practice ended with the decommissioning of the last incineration vessel in 1991 ahead of the agreed deadline of December 31, 1992.[97] The cessation of incineration at sea reflects, to some extent, the transfer of incineration activities to land.

Even industrial waste dumping had been declining steadily since the 1980s, but countries felt that they should further restrain it.

The question that emerges is that if countries are not allowed to dump wastes at sea, where this waste will be disposed of? A total of 64 out of 101 countries have confessed that they do not have disposal facilities to deal with industrial waste. Seventeen out of the thirty-seven countries that have claimed they have disposal facilities are OECD countries.[98] Thus, the question has become, if industrial waste dumping at sea is prohibited and countries do not have land disposal facilities, where does the waste go?[99] According to the IMO: "The Global Waste Survey showed that waste treatment and disposal is still a dangerous problem in many parts of the world, and restricting the use of the sea for disposal purposes will do nothing to reduce the amount of wastes that have to be disposed of. The danger is that in some cases waste dumping would happen illegally."[100]

The current status of industrial waste dumping is as follows. In the 1970s, the quantity of industrial wastes dumped rose from eleven million to seventeen million tons because of an increase of the contracting parties to the LDC from twenty-three to forty-three. Since the early 1980s, the quantity has decreased and it is more or less eight million tons. Between 1992 and 1995, the total quantity dumped fluctuated between 4.5 million and 6 million tons.[101]

---

[94] *Id.* at 353.

[95] See Edward L. Miles, Sea Dumping of Low-Level Radioactive Waste, 1964–1982, in Environmental Regime Effectiveness: Confronting Theory with Evidence 87, 109 (Edward Miles et al., eds., 2002).

[96] Jon Birger Skjærseth, Toward the End of Dumping in the North Sea: The Case of the Oslo Commission in Environmental Regime Effectiveness: Confronting Theory with Evidence 65, 72 (Edward Miles et al., eds., 2002).

[97] Dumping at Sea, *supra* note 91, at 6.

[98] *Id.* at 10.

[99] *Id.*

[100] *Id.* at 10–11.

[101] A brief description of the London Convention of 1972 and the 1996 Protocol, available online at http://www.londonconvention.org/London_Convention.htm.

In the 1970s, the annual amount of sewage sludge dumped at sea increased from 12.5 to 17 million tons and then decreased to 14 million tons in 1985. Since 1986, quantities have remained at a steady level of about twenty million tons, before falling to twelve million tons in the early 1990s. From 1992 to 1994, the annual quantity dumped increased again from 12.5 to 16.25 million tons.[102]

About 70 percent of all dumping permits involve dredged material. The percentage of dredged material dumped has been increasing significantly. Such an increase followed the prohibition of sea incineration and of dumping of industrial waste.[103]

The cessation of dumping at sea has been largely a symbolic victory. Major land-based sources of sea pollution, such as agriculture, have yet to be adequately controlled. The effectiveness of the LC regime, therefore, should be judged not only by evaluating the impact of the regime on sea dumping but also by assessing its impact in terms of transferring pollution externalities to other media.

3.3. Regional Management

The 1972 LDC followed the model of the Oslo Convention for the prevention of waste dumping from ships and aircraft.[104] Subsequently, the model of black, gray, and white lists – on which the 1972 LDC was based – was employed by a number of regional conventions. Other conventions that attempted to control marine pollution include conventions that deal with pollution from specific sources, such as the Paris Convention,[105] which concentrates on pollution from land-based sources. Some conventions are comprehensive conventions – conventions encompassing marine pollution from all sources – such as the Helsinki Convention.[106] The LDC has influenced the development of the UNEP Regional Seas Programme.

The 1970s regional seas conventions have been characterized as ineffective. This ineffectiveness has been attributed to the lack of political will, especially in regions where developed and developing countries coexist, such as the Mediterranean region. Developing countries have strongly resisted imposition of controls on their development for the sake of environmental protection. Developed countries, by contrast, do not yet conceive marine pollution as a problem that compels financial concessions to the developing world. Another factor that may have contributed to the ineffectiveness of the conventions is the absence of a systematic approach to marine pollution. A systematic approach would dictate cooperation between the authorities regulating lakes and rivers flowing into the sea and authorities dealing with sea pollution[107] – what has been called Integrated Coastal and River Basin Management (ICARM).[108]

---

[102] *Id.*

[103] *Id.*

[104] See Oslo Convention for the Prevention of Marine Pollution by Dumping from Ships and Aircraft, Feb. 15, 1972, reprinted in 932 UNTS 3.

[105] Paris Convention for the Prevention of Marine Pollution from Land-Based Sources, June 4, 1974, reprinted in 13 ILM 352 (1974).

[106] Helsinki Convention on the Protection of Marine Environment of the Baltic Sea Area, Mar. 22 1974, reprinted in 13 ILM 546 (1974).

[107] See Barbara Kwiatkowska, Marine Pollution from Land-Based Sources: Current Problems and Prospects, 14 Ocean Development and International Law 315, at 325 (1984).

[108] See *supra* Section 2.

The paralysis of decision making, caused by scientific uncertainty regarding the presence of hazardous substances in the marine environment, also has hampered the implementation of many conventions.[109]

The conventions of the 1990s generally were more comprehensive and substantive. A good example is the North East Atlantic Convention, which replaced the Oslo and Paris Conventions. Most of the 1990s conventions ban radioactive waste dumping, but they are more permissive with regard to industrial waste dumping and pollution from land-based sources. In both developed and less-developed regions, pollution from land-based sources is the least controlled. The South Pacific Convention,[110] which has banned nuclear waste dumping, provides simply that the state parties "shall take all appropriate measures to prevent, reduce and control pollution" from land-based sources.[111] The Quito protocol[112] to the Lima Convention[113] is a regulatory instrument similar to the LC and it is in stark contrast with the protocol that bans the dumping of radioactive wastes and substances in the southeast Pacific.[114]

Other efforts to control pollution from land-based sources involve the 1995 Global Programme of Action (GPA) for the Protection of the Marine Environment from Land-based Activities. The purpose of the program is to facilitate the execution of obligations of states with regard to the control of pollution from land-based sources. The GPA has yet to deliver concrete results.

The lack of success of measures for pollution control from land-based sources, even in developed regions of the world, has been attributed to a variety of factors. First and foremost, the inability to control compliance at the local level, as many treatment plants are under the jurisdiction of local authorities and central governments do not have the authority to directly regulate them. Furthermore, countries have exhibited an opportunistic attitude, especially when endogenously generated pollution can be exported to other states or regions.[115]

3.4. Pollution from Ships

The Convention for the Prevention of Pollution from Ships (MARPOL Convention)[116] was adopted in 1973 under the auspices of the IMO. The purpose of the convention is to regulate pollution from ships with the exception of intentional dumping. The convention immediately encountered ratification problems. For the

---

[109] Roger McManus, Legal Aspects of Land-Based Sources of Marine Pollution, in New Nationalism and the Use of Common Space 90, at 97 (Jonathan Charney, ed., 1982).

[110] Convention for the Protection of Natural Resources and Environment of the South Pacific Region, Nov. 25, 1986 available online at http://www.srep.org.

[111] Art. 7, id.

[112] See Protocol for the Protection of the South East Pacific against Pollution from Land-Based Sources (Quito Protocol to the Lima Convention), July 22, 1983. available online at http://www.unep.ch/regionalseas/legal/conlist.htm.

[113] Convention for the Protection of the Marine Environment and Coastal Area of the South East Pacific (Lima Convention), Nov. 12, 1981, id.

[114] Protocol to the 1981 Convention for the Protection of the Marine Environment and Coastal Areas of the South East Pacific against Radioactive Pollution, Sept. 21, 1989, id.

[115] Skjærseth, supra note 96, at 188.

[116] International Convention for the Prevention of Pollution from Ships, Nov. 2, 1973, reprinted in 12 ILM 1319 (1973).

convention to enter into force, it needed the ratification of fifteen states with a combined fleet of not less than 50 percent of the world shipping by gross tonnage. By 1976, it had received only three ratifications (Jordan, Kenya, and Tunisia), representing 1 percent of the world's merchant shipping fleet.[117] A protocol was adopted in 1978 that amended the convention.[118] The purpose of the protocol was to lessen the regulatory burden imposed by the convention by favoring the graduated phase-in of regulatory measures. Although Annex I (regulation of oil pollution), for instance, became immediately binding after the entry into force of the protocol, Annex II (regulation of chemicals) became binding three years after the entry into force of the protocol. This gives states additional time to comply with the technical requirements of Annex II because the perceived difficulty of complying with these requirements was a major impediment to the adoption of the convention. The protocol and the convention should be understood as one document and are usually referred to as MARPOL 73/78.

The MARPOL regime has been presented as a model international regime in which the threat to proceed unilaterally was crucial in brokering an agreement among states. The United States supported MARPOL and favored segregated ballast tanks (SBTs) technology for all tankers. A group of other countries supported a system called crude oil washing (COW) as an alternative to equipping all vessels with SBTs. Most states preferred COW over SBTs as the least expensive option, but, at the same time, they wanted to prevent the defection of the United States from the regime and imposition of SBTs standards through unilateral sanctions. Eventually, both COW and SBTs were adopted as possible alternative technologies.

MARPOL 73/78 is comprised of six annexes. Annex I deals with the prevention of pollution by oil. Annex II addresses the control of pollution by noxious liquid substances.[119] Annex III deals with the prevention of pollution by harmful substances in a packaged form.[120] The prevention of pollution by sewage from ships is the subject matter of Annex IV.[121] Annex V controls pollution from garbage.[122] The prevention of air pollution from ships is the concern of Annex VI.[123]

The convention is a typical example of the 1970s instruments that were conceived as tools destined to eliminate rather than to control pollution. As stated in the preamble to the convention, parties to the convention desire "to achieve the complete elimination of intentional pollution of the marine environment by oil and other harmful substances and the minimization of accidental discharge of such substances." Furthermore, the convention is a classic example of command-and-control legislation because it provides for numerous standards of technological nature that are to be incorporated into the ship construction so as to eliminate pollution.

---

[117] MARPOL – 25 Years, Focus on IMO, at 1, October 1998.

[118] Protocol Relating to the 1973 International Convention for the Prevention of Pollution from Ships, Feb. 17, 1978, reprinted in 17 ILM 546 (1978).

[119] The convention and Annex I and Annex II entered into force on October 2, 1983. See MARPOL Convention, *id.*

[120] Annex III entered in force on July 1, 1992, *id.*

[121] Annex IV entered into force on Sept. 27, 2003, *id.*

[122] Annex V entered into force on Dec. 31, 1988, *id.*

[123] Annex VI *id.*

Annex I is concerned with the prevention of pollution by oil and includes twenty-six regulations and six appendices. It has been amended multiple times with the last amendment being adopted in 2001. Chapter I of Annex I has to do with the licensing of tankers and the issuance of certificates. Chapter II prohibits, with exceptions, the discharge of oil at sea. In areas designated as specially protected areas (including the Mediterranean Sea, Red Sea, the Gulf, and the Baltic Sea) prohibitions are stricter. An important technological provision has been regulation 13, which requires segregated ballast tanks(SBTs) for new tankers above a certain deadweight. States are to undertake obligations so that all ports have facilities for the reception of oil residues and oil mixtures remaining from oil tankers (regulation 12). A 1992 amendment of Annex I further requires ships to install double hulls. A 2003 amendment requires most single-hull oil tankers to be eliminated by 2010. For oil tankers built after 1996, the inclusion of double-hulls is a requirement.

Annex II deals with the control of noxious liquid substances carried in bulk. About 250 substances have been evaluated and included in this Annex II. The discharge of residues of such substances is allowed only in reception facilities provided that certain concentrations are met and certain measures are taken.[124] No discharge of residues containing noxious substances is allowed within twelve miles from the nearest land.[125] More stringent provisions are applied to specially protected areas.

Annex III provides regulations for the prevention of pollution from harmful substances in packaged form. This is an optional annex, similarly to Annexes IV, V, and VI. The optional character of these annexes has delayed their entry into force. Annex III contains requirements for the packing, marking, labeling, and documentation of the sea transport of harmful substances. The International Maritime Dangerous Goods (IMDG) Code includes similar substances.

With regard to the pollution by garbage from ships, Annex V provides for the distances from land that are required for a ship to dispose of its waste and methods of waste disposal. The regulation of air pollution in Annex VI controls pollution from sulphur oxide (SOx), nitrogen oxide (NOx), and it provides for the control of ozone depleting substances.

The IMO's committee is working further on mandatory regulations covering the management of ballast water to prevent the spread of unwanted aquatic organisms and the banning of antifouling paints that are harmful to the environment.[126]

Some 1.47 million tons of oil infiltrate the oceans as a result of shipping operations. Most of this oil comes from the routine operations of ships (discharges of machinery wastes and tank washings from oil tankers [the latter contributing seven hundred thousand tons]). Accidental pollution contributes less than 30 percent of the total.[127]

It appears that the MARPOL Convention, once it entered into force, made a contribution toward reducing deliberate discharges from ships. The amount of oil entering the marine environment has been reduced from 2.13 million tons in 1973 to 0.57 million tons in 1989, a decrease of about 75 percent.[128] However, it is unclear

---

[124] Annex II, Regulation 5, *id.*

[125] Annex II, Regulation 5 (1)(c), *id.*

[126] MARPOL − 25 years, Focus on IMO, *supra* note 117, at 10.

[127] *Id.*

[128] Churchill & Lowe, *supra* note 50, at 341.

how correct this figure is, because the dimensions of illegal disposal are unknown. The MARPOL Convention includes provisions for facilities that receive wastes at ports. Many ports, however, have yet to provide for such disposal facilities. This is because ship operators are reluctant to pay for such facilities and are most likely to illegally dispose of wastes at sea. Parties to the convention do not regularly report on their implementation and only a small percentage of countries provide annual reports.[129]

Some oil producing and exporting nations have failed to ratify the MARPOL Convention[130] because doing so would necessitate the construction of port disposal facilities, and such construction could be costly.[131] The IMO is currently looking into ways of financing waste reception facilities in countries that are unwilling to shoulder the costs themselves. The implementation of Annex II, which deals with the disposal of hazardous substances, is more costly than the implementation of Annex I. Reception facilities for chemicals are more expensive and complicated to build than those designed for the reception of oily wastes. This is because chemical wastes are more differentiated than oil wastes. Technological developments in ship construction at the beginning of the 1990s meant that shipping tanks would have fewer residues to dispose of after unloading noxious substances.[132]

The convention contains specific provisions on enforcement. It is provided that:

> Any violation of the requirements . . . [of the convention] within the jurisdiction of any Party to the Convention shall be prohibited and sanctions shall be established therefore under the law of that Party.[133]

Ships to which the convention applies must carry with them certificates. Such certificates provide proof that a ship is in compliance with the provisions of the convention.[134] Therefore, inspections on ships that carry certificates are restricted to ensuring that the certificate is valid. However, if a ship's condition and equipment do not correspond substantially with the particulars of the certificate, or if a ship does not hold a valid certificate, the inspecting state must ensure that the ship is detained. Such detention will cease when it is ensured that the ship does not present an unreasonable threat of harm to the marine environment.[135]

The convention provides for extensive reporting requirements. Under article 11 of the convention, labeled "Communication of Information," the parties to the convention are to communicate to the IMO their progress in implementing the convention. Such progress includes the laws and other regulations they have adopted with regard to the implementation of the convention, a list of reception facilities, including their location and capacity, and an annual statistical report of penalties imposed for infringements to the convention.

A 1990 report of the United States General Accounting Office demonstrated, however, that reporting under the MARPOL Convention on infringements to the

---

[129] *Id.* at 342.
[130] MARPOL – 25 years, Focus on IMO, *supra* note 117, at 11.
[131] *Id.*
[132] *Id.* at 17.
[133] Art. 4(2), MARPOL Convention, *supra* notes 116, 118.
[134] Art. 5(1), *id.*
[135] Art. 5(2), *id.*

convention has been inadequate.[136] Furthermore, questionnaires on the availability of reception facilities, where tankers can discharge residue ballast water, have not produced the information desired. As a result, the IMO has decided to finance data collection through a private association of tanker owners known as International Chamber of Shipping or INTERTANKO.[137] Recent reports indicate that reporting under the MARPOL regime has improved as the secretariat of the convention has adopted a comprehensive reporting form.[138]

In order to allow for rapid adjustment to technological improvements, the convention provides for "tacit acceptance" of the amendments to the annexes of the convention. The annexes of the convention provide all technical details for the application of the convention and they have to be updated frequently to conform to new technological developments.[139] Most amendments to the MARPOL Convention have attempted to simplify the convention. The purpose of the 1985 amendments to Annex II of the convention[140] was to reduce the need for reception facilities for chemical wastes and to allow for most performance to be executed through technological ship adjustments. Other amendments include the requirement for ships to carry marine pollution emergency plans for noxious and liquid substances, and there have been frequent amendments regarding the construction and equipment of ships.

The MARPOL regime has been considered an effective regime. This is because of the technological standards established that are made obligatory. Violations to the MARPOL Convention have to do with the equipment put in place to prevent discharges (e.g., segregated ballast tanks, double-hulls). For these standards to be evaded, the ship builder, classifier, and insurer would have to conspire to perform an illegal act. Assuming that ship construction proceeds in an illegal fashion, a ship that does not comply with current regulatory requirements, would not command much for resale value.[141] The command-and-control approach of the MARPOL regime has pushed the technological requirements in the construction and equipment of ships in a manner that better protects the environment. The key to the success of the regime has been the assignment of the monitoring function of these requirements to the builder, insurance agent and the reseller market. Command-and-control regulation seems to have worked in this case, because it provided for straightforward technological requirements and a number of efforts have been performed to ease the adoption of those requirements.

Other related instruments with the regard to the transfer of dangerous substances are the International Maritime Dangerous Goods (IMDG) Code and the International Convention on Liability and Compensation for Damage in Connection with the Carriage of Hazardous and Noxious Substances.[142]

---

[136] See GAO Report, International Environment: International Agreements Are Not Well Monitored 26–27 GAO/RCED-92–43 (Jan. 1992).

[137] Abram Chayes & Antonia Handler Chayes: The New Sovereignty: Compliance with International Regulatory Agreements 171–72 (1995).

[138] Id. at 260.

[139] Art. 16(2)(f), MARPOL Convention, supra notes 116, 118.

[140] The amendments were adopted on December 5, 1985 and entered into force on April 6, 1987.

[141] Elaine M. Carlin, Oil Pollution from Ships at Sea: The Ability of Nations to Protect a Blue Planet, in Environmental Regime Effectiveness: Confronting Theory with Evidence 331, 348 (Edward L. Miles et al., ed., 2002).

[142] See Chapter 11, Section 2.

3.5. Emergency Situations

The International Convention Relating to Intervention on the High Seas in Cases of Oil Pollution Casualties was adopted in 1969.[143] The purpose of the convention is to legitimize the intervention of coastal states in the high seas, in case of oil pollution or a threat of oil pollution in areas outside their jurisdiction, which would cause grave and imminent threats to their coastline or related interests.[144] Unless there is an extreme emergency, the coastal state is to consult with the flag states, other affected states, and independent International Maritime Organization (IMO) experts.[145] The measures taken must be governed by the principle of proportionality and a party that goes beyond what is required by the convention and causes damages to others is liable to pay compensation.[146] The 1969 convention was supplemented by a 1973 Protocol on Intervention on the High Seas in cases of marine pollution by substances other than oil.[147]

Oil pollution disasters and pollution by hazardous substances can best be addressed by international cooperation. The 1990 Convention on Oil Pollution Preparedness, Response and Co-operation (OPRC Convention),[148] the 2000 Protocol to the OPRC Convention,[149] and a number of regional instruments provide for the specifics of such cooperation,

3.6. Safety Regulations

A high percentage of accidents at sea are a result of human error. Because the human factor is vital in the operation of ships, both the IMO and the ILO have devised standards for training, certification, and watchkeeping of seafarers. In 1978, the ILO and the IMO adopted the International Convention on Standards of Training, Certification and Watchkeeping of Seafarers (STCW Convention).[150] The Annex to the convention contains several chapters on what each and every operation of a ship requires in terms of knowledge and expertise. To obtain STCW certificates, masters of ships must be physically fit, must have some seagoing experience, and must complete a syllabus that contains a variety of subjects including navigation, fire prevention, medical care, and maritime law.[151] The convention provides for retraining of seafarers at least every five years.[152] Port states should inspect the certificates of seafarers and ships that enter their ports if have they some grounds of suspicion

---

[143] International Convention Relating to Intervention on the High Seas in Cases of Oil Pollution Casualties, Nov. 29, 1969, reprinted in 9 ILM 25 (1970).

[144] Art. I(1), *id.*

[145] Arts. III & IV, *id.*

[146] Arts. V & IV, *id.*

[147] Protocol on Intervention on the High Seas in Cases of Marine Pollution by Substances other than Oil, Nov. 2, 1973, reprinted in 1313 UNTS 3 (1983).

[148] International Convention on Oil Pollution Preparedness, Response and Co-operation, Nov. 30, 1990, reprinted in 30 ILM 735 (1991)

[149] Protocol on Preparedness, Response and Co-operation to Pollution Incidents by Hazardous and Noxious Substances, Mar. 14, 2000 (not yet in force).

[150] July 7, 1978 available online at http://www.imo.org/Conventions/contents.

[151] N.J.J. Gaskell et al., Chorley and Giles' Shipping Law 119 (1996).

[152] *Id.*

triggered by an incident, such as an illegal discharge of oil or collision. If problems are uncovered during inspection, the master and the flag state must be informed in writing. If there is failure to correct the deficiencies and such deficiencies pose a threat to persons, property, or the environment, the ship can be detained in the port of inspecting state until the deficiencies are cured.[153]

The Safety of Life at Sea Convention (SOLAS), adopted in 1974 and entered into force in 1984, is considered central for the establishment of minimum requirements of safety at sea.[154] The convention establishes minimum standards for the safe construction, equipment, and functioning of ships. The flag state is to supervise the minimum standards and issue the appropriate certificates. State parties to the convention have the right to inspect the ships carrying the flag of other state parties if they have doubts on whether the minimum SOLAS standards are complied with.

The International Management Code for the Safe Operation of Ships and for Pollution Prevention (ISM Code) is a further development that strengthens the requirements of safety at sea.[155] The ISM Code provides for an exhaustive list of requirements for the maintenance of safety at sea. The ISM Code attempts to ensure the safe management of ships through the establishment of a safety management system (SMS) that must be established by the ship's management. A copy of the SMS must be carried on board of ships.

The safety instruments adopted, including the STCW Convention, the SOLAS Convention and the ISM Code, could increase the safety at sea. The problem is that they are not implemented in practice consistently and not all flag states have signed or ratified these instruments. Competition among carriers often makes them oblivious to the standards of the STCW Convention or the ISM Code. Many shipowners have flagged out to flag of convenience (FOC) states and, thus, are not bound by safety standards.

The comparative advantage of FOC states is based exactly on their intentional failure to enforce international standards. Many states fail to meet the educational standards for seafarers rendering their competitive advantage contingent on the provision of a cheap and an uneducated labor force to the maritime industry.

After the *Amoco Cadiz* disaster in 1978, certain European countries have put in place a regional arrangement for the inspection of ships. According to the 1982 Paris Memorandum on Port State Control (MOU), ships are to be inspected for their application of the IMO and the ILO Conventions whenever they enter the ports of a state party to the MOU, at that state's discretion. If ships are inspected and deficiencies are found, the ultimate "punishment" is for the ship to be detained in the port state until the deficiencies are rectified. Information about the inspections and deficiencies found are shared among port state authorities in an attempt to isolate substandard ships.

Initially, port state control concentrated primarily on technical issues, and living and working requirements were not inspected thoroughly. But the Paris MOU

---

[153] *Id.*

[154] The convention was amended multiple times from 1978 to 2003. See International Convention for the Safety of Life at Sea, Nov. 1, 1974, reprinted in 1184 UNTS 3.

[155] The code was adopted in 1993 and entered into force in 1998.

started to stress the importance of checking the living and working conditions in ships as they are essential for the safety at sea.[156]

In addition to the Paris MOU, other MOUs among states have been signed, and there is a movement to adopt procedures for the harmonization of the various regional MOUs. In addition to the harmonization of regional MOUs, more standardization is needed of the inspecting practices of states that are parties to the same MOU. It is not infrequent for a substandard ship to sail fairly undisturbed until it reaches the port of a state that applies more stringent controls and may be more thorough in its inspection procedures than other states.

4. SELECTED REGIONAL INSTRUMENTS

4.1. Protection of the Northeast Atlantic

The Convention for the Protection of the Marine Environment of the North East Atlantic (OSPAR) Convention[157] was adopted by the Oslo and Paris Commissions in 1992. The OSPAR Convention is a more intrusive instrument than the conventions it replaced. The convention has adopted the precautionary principle,[158] the polluter pays principle,[159] and has endorsed the application of the best available technique (BAT) and the best environmental practice (BEP).[160] The convention has prohibited incineration at sea[161] and has included provisions for access to information.[162]

The convention has banned the dumping of low- and intermediate-level radioactive wastes but with exceptions.[163] The dumping of wastes from offshore installations also is prohibited, but discharges from offshore sources are still allowed, subject to permits issued by the contracting parties.[164]

The OSPAR Convention focuses on one of the least tractable sources of marine pollution – that is, pollution from land-based sources. The convention aims to eliminate pollution from such sources by encouraging the use of best available techniques and best available practices. Discharges from point sources are allowed only if the discharger has a legal permit.[165] In particular, the discharges of dangerous substances into the sea are an issue that has preoccupied the parties to the convention. The reduction and eventual elimination of pollution from substances that are toxic, persistent, and

---

[156] ILO, The Impact on Seafarers' Living and Working Conditions of Changes in the Structure of the Shipping Industry 24 (Report for discussion at the 29th Session of the Joint Maritime Commission, JMC/29/2001/3, 2001).

[157] Convention for the Protection of the Marine Environment of the North East Atlantic, Sept. 22, 1992, reprinted in 32 ILM 1069 (1993) [hereinafter 1992 OSPAR Convention].

[158] Art. 2(2)(a), id.

[159] Art. 2(2)(b), id.

[160] Annex I, art. 1(1), id.

[161] Annex II, id.

[162] Art. 9, id. For the interpretation of this provision, see Chapter 3, Section 4.2.

[163] Exceptions are granted to the United Kingdom and France until 2008, provided that they undertake to report by 1997 on steps they have taken to explore alternative land options. For the exceptions that may be granted beyond 2008, scientific evidence would be required that the continued dumping is not harmful to the other uses of the sea. See Annex II, art. 3(3), id.

[164] Annex II, id.

[165] Annex I, art. 2(1), id.

liable to bioaccumulate is the primary goal of the OSPAR Commission established under the convention.[166] The OSPAR Commission has developed a number of strategies to deal with environmental problems, such as hazardous[167] and radioactive substances[168] and eutrophication.[169]

4.2. Protection of the Baltic Sea

The Helsinki Convention for the Protection of the Baltic Sea (HELCOM Convention) was adopted in 1974. The convention, like the OSPAR Convention, was amended in 1992[170] with modernizing provisions, such as the precautionary principle[171] and the polluter pays principle,[172] and the application of BAT and BEP.[173] The first Helsinki Convention established the Baltic Marine Environmental Protection Commission – HELCOM Commission. Although contributions for the running of the HECLOM are supposed to be shared equitably among countries, in practice most contributions are made by the wealthier Western states. Most of the work of the HELCOM is executed by a number of highly specialized working groups. The basic policy instruments are Ministerial Declarations and Recommendations. About 200 recommendations have been adopted, of which 134 are still valid. A large number of recommendations have dealt with the control of discharges of dangerous substances from point and diffuse sources. For instance, recommendations have been issued for the control of pollution from industrial point sources, municipal waste treatment, agriculture, forestry, and transport.[174]

The convention has prohibited incineration at sea.[175] Explicit provisions with regard to the regulation of dangerous substances have been adopted.[176] In 1998, the parties to the convention decided to reduce the discharges of dangerous substances by 50 percent by 1995.[177] However, only a small number of parties were able to reach that goal. Eventually parties decided to set more specific targets with the goal

---

[166] Annex I, art. 3, *id.*

[167] OSPAR Strategy with regard to Hazardous Substances, Ministerial Meeting of the OSPAR Commission, Reference Number: 1998–16, Annex 34, Ref:§B-6.3, July 22–23, 1998.

[168] OSPAR Strategy with Regard to Radioactive Substances, Ministerial Meeting of the OSPAR Commission, Reference Number: 1998–17, Annex 35, Ref:§B6.5, July 22–23, 1998.

[169] OSPAR Strategy to Combat Eutrophication, Ministerial Meeting of the OSPAR Commission, Reference Number: 1998–18, Annex 36, Ref:§B-6.6, July 22–23, 1998.

[170] Convention on the Protection of the Marine Environment of the Baltic Sea, April 9, 1992 available online at http://www.helcom.fi/Convention.htm [hereinafter 1992 HELCOM Convention].

[171] Art. 3(2), *id.*

[172] Art. 3(4), *id.*

[173] Art. 3(3), *id.*

[174] Recommendations on the control of pollution from point sources include reduction of emissions from: the pulp and paper industry, the iron and steel industry, metal surface treatment, oil refineries, pesticide production, the chemical industry, the leather industry, and the textile industry.
    Other recommendations address discharges of dangerous substances, such as DDT, antifouling paints, and mercury from dentistry. For a summary of HELCOM Recommendations and their implementation, see Helsinki Commission, Summary Report on Implementation of HELCOM Recommendations under HELCOM TC, HELCOM 21/2000, Feb. 24, 2000.

[175] Art. 10, 1992 HELCOM Convention, *supra* note 170.

[176] Annex I, *id.*

[177] See Henrik Selin & Stacy D. VanDeveer, Hazardous Substances and the Helsinki and Barcelona Conventions: Origins, Results and Future Challenges 7, paper presented at the Policy Forum Management of Toxic Substances in the Marine Environment: Analysis of the Mediterranean and the Baltic, Javea, Spain, Oct. 6–8, 2002 [hereinafter HELCOM & MAP].

the elimination of hazardous substances by 2020.[178] Such hazardous substances are included in a list of 280 substances, of which 43 substances are declared to be of priority status.[179]

The HELCOM regime is comprised of diverse states with different approaches to regulation. For instance, the western Baltic states rely heavily on emission limit values, whereas the eastern Baltic states prefer environmental quality standards because these standards usually are not based on the application of state-of-the-art technology . Most of the HELCOM recommendations have focused on emission limit values rather than quality standards.[180]

4.3. UNEP Regional Seas Program

The UNEP Regional Seas Programme was launched with the 1975 adoption of the Mediterranean Action Plan (MAP). The MAP has served as a model for the development of plans and programs in other regions. The regimes adopted under the aegis of the UNEP are characterized by two phases: pre-UNCED and post-UNCED phases. The pre-UNCED period is characterized by vaguer instruments that have hardly contributed to the abatement of pollution. The post-UNCED instruments are stricter and could – with proper implementation – play a role in pollution abatement. The problem is that most states have yet to use these instruments to achieve the goal of pollution reduction.

The regional seas regimes, developed under the auspices of the UNEP, cover the following areas:

- the Arabian Gulf (POMPE area);[181]
- the Black Sea and North East Pacific;[182]
- the Caribbean (WCR);[183]

---

[178] *Id.* at 8.

[179] *Id.* at 9.

[180] *Id.* at 5–6.

[181] Regional Convention for Co-operation on Protection of the Marine Environment from Pollution (1978 Kuwait Convention), April 24, 1978, reprinted in 1140 UNTS 133.

Protocols include:

Protocol Concerning Cooperation in Combating Pollution by Oil and other Harmful Substances in Cases of Emergency, July 1, 1979, reprinted in 17 ILM 526 (1978).

Protocol Concerning Marine Pollution Resulting from the Exploration and Exploitation of the Continental Shelf, Mar. 29, 1989 available online at http://www.rompe.net.

Protocol Concerning Pollution from Land-based Sources, Feb. 21, 1990, *id.* Protocol on the Control of Marine Transboundary Movements and Disposal of Hazardous Wastes, Mar. 17, 1998, *id.*

[182] Convention on the Protection of the Black Sea against Pollution, April 21, 1992, reprinted in 32 ILM 1101 (1993). The convention was adopted simultaneously with protocols on land-based sources of pollution, emergency situations, and dumping. In 2002, a comprehensive convention on the Protection and Sustainable Development of the Marine and Coastal Environment of the North East Pacific was adopted. See Convention for Co-operation in the Protection and Sustainable Development of the Marine Environment of the North East Pacific, Feb. 18, 2002 available online at http://www.cep.unep.org.

[183] Convention for the Protection and Development of the Marine Environment of the Wider Caribbean Region (1983 Cartagena Convention), Mar. 24, 1983, reprinted in 22 ILM 221 (1983).

Protocol Concerning Co-operation in Combating Oil Spills, Mar. 24, 1983, reprinted in 22 ILM 240 (1983) (Cartagena Oil Spills Protocol).

Protocol Concerning Specially Protected Areas and Wildlife in the Wider Caribbean Region (Kingston Specially Protected Areas Protocol), Jan. 18, 1990 available online at http://www.cep.unep.org.

- the West and Central Africa;[184]
- the East Africa;[185]
- the Red Sea and the Gulf of Aden (PERSGA);[186]
- the South Pacific (SPREP);[187]
- the South East Pacific, (SE/PCF);[188]
- East Asian Seas (EAS).[189]

These regional programs are usually structured around a framework convention. The convention is then refined by protocols that deal with the specific problems in a region, such as pollution from land-based sources, ship pollution, and dumping. Some regions have adopted protocols with regard to the creation of specially protected areas. The UNEP conventions contain monitoring mechanisms and provide for exchange of information and reporting. In some programs, the secretariat functions are carried by the UNEP. In other programs, regional commissions are assigned the role of secretariat. For instance, the Permanent Commission of the South Pacific is assigned the role of secretariat under the 1981 Lima Convention for the Protection of South East Pacific.

GESAMP Priorities

The GESAMP has investigated measures required in terms of addressing environmental priorities in all regions. Domestic sewage is or should be a top priority in

---

Protocol on the Prevention, Reduction and Control of Land-Based Sources and Activities to the Convention for the Protection and Development of the Marine Environment of the Wider Caribbean Region, Oct. 6, 1999 available online at http://www.cep.unep.org.

[184] Convention for Co-operation in the Protection and Development of the Marine Environment of the West and Central African Region (Abidjan Convention), Mar. 23, 1981, reprinted in 20 ILM 746 (1981). Protocol Concerning Co-operation in Combating Pollution in Cases of Emergency, Mar. 23, 1981, reprinted in 20 ILM 756 (1981).

[185] Convention for the Protection, Management and Development of the Marine and Coastal Environment of the Eastern African Region (Nairobi Convention), June 21, 1985 available online at http://sedac.ciesin.org/entri. See also Protocol Concerning Protected Areas and Wild Fauna and Flora, June 21, 1985, id. Protocol Concerning Cooperation in Combating Marine Pollution in Cases of Emergency, June 21, 1985, id.

[186] Convention for the Conservation of the Red Sea and Gulf of Aden Environment (Jeddah Convention), Feb. 14, 1982, available online at http://www.persga.org; Protocol Concerning Regional Cooperation in Combating Pollution by Oil and other Harmful Substances in Cases of Emergency, Feb. 14, 1982, id.

[187] Convention for the Protection of the Natural Resources and Environment of the South Pacific Region (Noumea Convention), Nov. 25,1986, reprinted in 16 ILM 38 (1987); Protocol Concerning Co-operation in Combating Pollution Emergencies, Nov. 25, 1986 available online at http://www.sprep.org. Protocol for the Prevention of Pollution of the South Pacific Region by Dumping, Nov. 25, 1986, id.

[188] Convention for the Protection of the Marine Environment and Coastal Areas of the South East Pacific (Lima Convention), Nov. 12, 1981 available online at http://sedac.ciesin.org/entri.
    See also Agreement on Regional Co-operation in Combating Pollution of the South East Pacific by Hydrocarbons or other Harmful Substances in Cases of Emergency (Lima Agreement), Nov. 12, 1981, id. Protocol for the Protection of the South East Pacific against Pollution from Land-based Sources, July 22, 1983, id. Protocol for the Conservation and Management of Protected Marine and Coastal Areas of the South East Pacific, Sept. 21, 1989, summary available online at http://www.cpps-int.org. Protocol for the Protection of the South East Pacific against Radioactive Contamination, Sept. 21, 1989 summary available online at http://www.cpps-int.org.

[189] The region covers the coastal and marine areas of Australia, Cambodia, China, Indonesia, Malaysia, Philippines, the Republic of Korea, Singapore, Thailand, and Vietnam.

all regions. However, the Mediterranean program is the only program that addresses explicitly the need to develop sewage infrastructure. The regulation of agricultural runoff and industrial facilities is either a second or third priority in most regions. Habitat modification is ranked as a third or fifth priority area for all seven regions.[190] Persistent Organic Pollutants (POPs) are listed as of high priority but, in reality, they are not a serious problem, for the time being, in all regions.[191] The regulation of oil substances is highly ranked in most programs but oil substances do not pose a serious problem in most seas. Instead, sediment mobilization deserves more attention.[192]

The GESAMP points out that most regions place emphasis on POPs and heavy metals, although they report low levels of contamination. On the contrary, physical alteration, which should be viewed as a serious issue, is not accorded the importance it deserves.[193] The undue attention paid to hazardous substances in areas that are not highly industrialized has been attributed to the "high public and international profile" of such substances.[194] Furthermore, some of the problems that the GESAMP perceives as important, such as physical alteration, require integrated management.[195] Integrated management procedures are complicated and costly and many governments still try to grapple with what integrated management would involve. In comparison, prohibiting the discharges of some chemicals seems like a straightforward regulation to adopt.[196]

MAP Regime

The regulation of pollution in the Mediterranean Sea started in the early 1970s when many states in the region lacked the expertise to enact pollution regulation and to apply monitoring controls. The first instrument that was adopted was the Mediterranean Action Plan (MAP), which provided the general guidelines for the protection of the Mediterranean. The MAP was adopted along with the Barcelona Convention, and was administered by the UNEP Regional Seas Office. The Barcelona Convention was adopted in 1976,[197] and was amended in 1995.[198] The amendment of the convention necessitated the amendment of the protocols.[199] The amended version of the Barcelona Convention contains all the relatively new concepts of

---

[190] GESAMP 2001, *supra* note 2, at 62.

[191] *Id*. at 69.

[192] *Id*. at 71.

[193] *Id*. at 73.

[194] *Id*.

[195] *Id*. at 82.

[196] *Id*. at 85. Banning certain persistent organic pollutants has not produced the desired results – because of the continuing input of these substances from secondary sources of pollution, such as land disposal sites and the atmosphere. Remediation of land disposal sites is necessary to address this problem effectively.

[197] Convention for the Protection of the Mediterranean Sea against Pollution (Barcelona Convention), Feb. 16, 1976, reprinted in 15 ILM 290 (1976).

[198] Convention for the Protection of the Marine Environment and the Coastal Region of the Mediterranean, June 10, 1995, reprinted in OJ L 322/34, 14.12.1999, available online at http://www.unep.ch/seas/main/med/medconvi.html [hereinafter 1995 Barcelona Convention].

[199] The protocols include:

> The Mediterranean Dumping Protocol (Protocol for the Prevention of Pollution of the Mediterranean Sea by Dumping from Ships and Aircraft), signed in 1976 and entered into force in 1978. The Protocol was amended in 1995. The Dumping Protocol has banned the disposal of hazardous substances. See Protocol for the Prevention of Pollution of the Mediterranean Sea

international environmental law such as the precautionary principle, the polluter pays principle, the BAT, and the BEP. Other provisions include the protection of biological diversity[200] and the provision on the transboundary movement of wastes and their disposal.[201]

Comparatively, the MAP regime is more decentralized than the HELCOM regime. The Barcelona Convention is administered by the UNEP Regional Seas Office. As the convention evolved, a sort of secretariat has developed. The parties have established six regional activity centers (RACs) to coordinate regional activities on different issues.[202] Overall, the MAP regime has relied on a number of scientific organizations and UN bodies. NGOs have not played an important role in the development of the MAP regime.[203] Financial contributions for the execution of the convention are put into a trust fund to which $10 million is meant to be contributed annually. The amount contributed, however, is never as much as this.[204] Some state parties to the convention could be major financial contributors, but most countries do not seem eager to assist in the implementation of the convention.

The MAP regime has not functioned very well, not because of the lack of good intentions but because of the lack of administrative and financial capacity. In order to address the causes of implementation deficit, the parties set up a Strategic Action Program (SAP) with the financial assistance of the Global Environment Facility (GEF). The purpose of the SAP is to help parties develop their national programs with the goal the elimination of pollution from land-based activities by the year 2025.[205]

Other issues that need to be addressed urgently involve the lack of data and poor reporting. No clear and specific data exist on the discharges of polluting substances in the Mediterranean Sea. Because of the lack of data, it is difficult to compare compliance among countries and to establish quantitative baselines from which the reduction of pollution will be calculated.[206] The lack of data has been used as an excuse not to take action under the regime. For instance, the parties to the convention

by Dumping from Ships and Aircraft or Incineration at Sea, June 10, 1995 available online at http://www.unep.ch/seas/main/med/mdumpii.html.

The Emergency Protocol (Protocol Concerning Co-operation in Combating Pollution of the Mediterranean Sea by Oil and other Harmful Substances in cases of Emergency), signed in 1976 and entered into force in 1978. The Protocol was amended in 2002 by the Prevention and Emergency Protocol. See Protocol Concerning Co-operation in Preventing Pollution from Ships and, in cases of Emergency, Combating Pollution of the Mediterranean Sea, Jan. 25, 2002.

The Mediterranean Land-Based Sources Protocol (Protocol for the Protection of the Mediterranean Sea against Pollution from Land-Based Sources), signed in 1980 and entered into force in 1983. It was amended in 1996. See Protocol for the Protection of the Mediterranean Sea against Pollution from Land-Based Sources and Activities, Mar. 7, 1996, available online at http://www.unep.ch/seas/main/med/mlbspii.html.

[200] Art. 10, 1995 Barcelona Convention, *supra* note 198.

[201] Art. 11, *id.*

[202] HELCOM & MAP, *supra* note 177, at 15. Such RACs include: the Specially Protected Areas RAC, the Environmental Remote Sensing RAC and the Cleaner Production RAC (which promotes the reduction of industrial wastes).

[203] *Id.* at 15–16.

[204] Amounts contributed in 1990 were $5.45 million. In 1996, the amount reached $6.75 million. *Id.* at 16.

[205] *Id.* at 20.

[206] *Id.* at 23.

had known that 80 percent of their sewage that was entering the Mediterranean was not treated, but they failed to adopt treatment technologies.[207]

The issue of ICAM entered officially the MAP regime through the 1995 update of the Barcelona Convention. Article 4(3) of the convention provides that parties are committed to the integrated management of coastal zones. ICAM has been emerging as an issue within the MAP regime since 1988 when the Priority Action Programme/Regional Activities Center (PAP/RAC) adopted a Methodological Framework for Integrated Planning and Management in the Mediterranean Coastal Areas.

5. CONCLUSION

The control of marine pollution has had mixed results. The UNCLOS is an umbrella convention that provides some guidance for the control of marine pollution. The UNCLOS is a comprehensive convention, but it does not provide the specifics of pollution prevention and the restoration of degraded marine ecosystems.

The LDC was one of the first conventions that tried to address a specific environmental problem, namely pollution by dumping. The model supplied by the LDC has had some arguable success. The LDC has provided a flexible regime that gives significant latitude to national governments and allows for exceptions even for wastes included in the black list. Its arguable success has been attributed to the fact that it addresses only 10 percent of marine pollution, for which there exist alternatives on land. A proposal to ban both ocean and land waste disposal would have been opposed by most countries concerned. The LDC regime is indicative of the shortcomings of prohibitions. Russia has admitted that it dumped high-level radioactive wastes in the sea for years in contravention of the explicit prohibition of the LDC. The LDC had banned sea disposal of high-level radioactive wastes with no exceptions since the early 1970s.

The 1996 version of the LDC, called now the London Convention (LC), could be successful, provided that states are willing to transfer some pollution from the seas to the land. It is unlikely, however, that the simple ban of waste dumping at sea would be sufficient to create capacity for the proper waste disposal on land. Countries may find refuge in illegal sea disposal or unsound land disposal. The ban and the reverse listing mechanisms would probably create an uneasy regime in which countries would try to find some breathing space under exceptions that would legitimize sea disposal.[208]

The MARPOL regime has been effective in controlling pollution from ships. This is a case of command-and-control legislation that succeeded in creating transparency in international law with regard to the implementation of international standards. The regime demonstrates the power of hegemonic states in imposing standards of

---

[207] Jon Birger Skjærseth, The Effectiveness of the Mediterranean Action Plan, in Environmental Regime Effectiveness: Confronting Theory with Evidence 314, 323 (Edward Miles et al., eds., 2002).

[208] See, e.g., Information Received from the Government of Papua New Guinea (PNG) concerning the disposal of hard rock mine waste from the Lihir Goldmine in its internal waters, Submission to the Twenty-fifth Consultative Meeting of the LC, LC.2/Cir. 433, Dec. 17, 2003. In 2002 Greenpeace charged that PNG was dumping wastes from Lihir Goldmine in violation of the LDC. The wastes were dumped as uncontaminated geological material by PNG, but Greenpeace claimed that the wastes should have been labeled industrial wastes.

their choice on other states under the threat of defection or sanctions. The safety standards regime (comprised of the SOLAS Convention, the ISM Code, and the STCW Convention) is still half-heartedly implemented. How seriously states take their role of exercising control over their ports is instrumental in the implementation of the regime.

Integrated coastal zone management has been studied and applied in various national and regional fora with mixed success. Although interesting theoretical frameworks have been developed for ICAM, the specifics of its application have yet to be grasped completely by policy makers.

Regarding regional regimes, the compliance under the HELCOM and the OSPAR regimes has been better than the compliance under the MAP regime. The better record of compliance under the HELCOM and the OSPAR regimes has been attributed to the parties that are driving the process behind the two conventions. The disappointing compliance record under the MAP regime is not caused by the lack of will but by the lack of ability in developing the institutions that would administer environmental policy. This is so despite the fact that certain countries that belong to the MAP regime are member states of the EC and the fact that other countries have applied for membership.

5 Water Resources

1. STATE OF WATER RESOURCES

Facts and Recent Trends

The fair and efficient management of water resources and the protection of water quality are some of the most pressing issues in international policy making. Today, 1.1 billion people do not have access to safe water and 2.4 billion people lack access to basic sanitation.[1] In developing countries, 90 percent of all wastewater still goes untreated into local water streams. An estimated forty-seven countries are classified as suffering medium to high water stress.[2] Some five million deaths a year are caused by polluted drinking water.[3] It is estimated that $75 billion will be needed per year to expand water service infrastructure beyond the costs required for maintaining existing systems, whereas, at present, the total development assistance allocated to the water sector is only about US$3 billion per year.[4]

A joint study executed by WHO and UNICEF has found that in low-income countries, the reliable and consistent provision of water supply is lacking. On the sanitation front, further challenges have to be met, as many cities are not equipped with appropriate sanitation facilities.[5] The issue of water and proper sanitation was one of the most important issues during the WSSD, when the goal was set to halve by 2015 the number of people without access to safe drinking water and basic sanitation.[6] It was in the 1970s, with the full swing of the environmental movement, that the intensive manipulation of water (i.e., dams, canals) came under criticism. Major river works such as dams led to the displacement of local populations[7] and, thus, social justice issues were added on to environmental issues to militate against

---

[1] OECD, Improving Water Management – Recent OECD Experience: Executive Summary 1 (2003) [hereinafter OECD Improving].

[2] *Id.* at 1.

[3] *Id.* at 4.

[4] *Id.*

[5] Global Water Supply and Sanitation Assessment 2000 Report (WHO/UNICEF, 2000).

[6] WSSD, Plan of Implementation, Section 7, see Chapter 1, Section 4.3.

[7] Volkmar Hartje, International Dimensions of Integrated Resource Water Management, Working Paper on Management in Environmental Planning, Institute for Landscape and Environmental Planning, Technical University of Berlin 1–2 (2002).

large infrastructure projects. Today, many water infrastructure projects are postponed or are subject to demanding EIA requirements.

Developed countries have reduced sewage and industrial discharges into their waters by investing in wastewater treatment plants. Developed countries have cleaned up some of the most polluted waters – the Rhine River is a notable example – and have attempted to increase their water use efficiency.[8] Countries are increasingly cognizant of the implications of the simultaneous recognition of water as a public good and as a commodity that must be priced appropriately. Developed countries have experimented with water pricing schemes that reflect the full costs of providing water services.[9] Countries have started to integrate water quality and water quantity considerations under what has been called Integrated Water Resources Management (IWRM).

International assistance agencies have pushed for water privatization in developing countries with mixed results. Certain privatization efforts in developing countries have been resisted. Access to water, it has been argued, is a human right. A full recovery of costs of water production would place an undue burden on poor communities. Developing countries also are faced with obstacles pursuing IWRM, as they often lack strong institutions that would make integrated water management possible.[10]

Regulating water demand or supply is not an easy endeavor. Water is a fugitive resource. Attempts to regulate water supply (e.g., floods or droughts) through dams and canals are costly. The storage and transportation of water could be expensive relative to the economic value of water at the point of use. Economies of scale have been instrumental for the provision of water at acceptable prices and water traditionally has been provided by state monopolies in the pursuit of public interest.[11]

Instead of controlling demand through pricing, most countries have dealt with water scarcity through regulation, prohibition of certain uses, and cutting off water supply. Water metering has been introduced in most developed countries, but the reallocation of water from one use to another has been resisted.[12]

Groundwater

Groundwater is an important source of drinking water for many areas and its allocation often has been a source of tension. The 1997 UN Watercourses Convention deals with groundwater to the extent that it is related to surface waters.[13]

Thus, internationally, large bodies of independent aquifers remain unregulated. Groundwater constitutes 97 percent of the freshwater on earth. Groundwater aquifers may be shared between countries, and mismanagement or depletion of aquifer supplies in one state may affect the aquifers of another state. Because groundwater is confined under the earth, it is more difficult to understand its flows, regulate it,

---

[8] OECD Improving, *supra* note 1, at 1.

[9] *Id.* at 2.

[10] Hartje, *supra* note 7, at 11–12.

[11] FAO, Reforming Water Resources Policy – A guide to Methods, Processes and Practices 2 (FAO Irrigation and Drainage Paper 52, 1995).

[12] *Id.*

[13] See *infra* note 127.

and protect it. It is more difficult to remedy polluted groundwater. A great threat to groundwater is salinization. Out of the regional agreements, examined later, only the agreement on the Jordan River and the U.S.-Mexico Agreement deal with the regulation of groundwater supplies. The Genevese Agreement is specifically dedicated to the allocation and protection of groundwater.[14]

After the adoption of the 1997 UN Watercourses Convention, the International Law Commission devoted its efforts to the regulation of transboundary groundwater. As was the case with transboundary freshwaters, the commission dropped the term "shared" in favor of "transboundary" groundwater. Some states expressed concerns that the notion of "shared resources" may imply a reference to the "shared heritage of mankind" or to notions of shared ownership.[15] Some states have proposed the principles of equitable use and reasonable utilization for their application to groundwater management. Other states have argued that these principles cannot be applied automatically to the regulation of groundwater just because they have been adopted for the allocation of surface freshwaters. This is because some groundwaters may not be renewable and further restrictions need to be placed on their use.[16] The draft article on the obligation not to cause significant harm has encountered fewer objections, however. Some states even advocated omitting the term "significant" because some groundwaters are likely to be more fragile than surface freshwaters.[17] Draft article IX provides that, in the absence of agreement or custom to the contrary, no use of groundwater should be granted "inherent priority" over other uses. It is advised that, in case of conflict between the uses of a transboundary aquifer, the issue must be resolved by giving priority to the requirements of vital human needs.[18]

Transboundary Water Resources

As many freshwaters are under the jurisdictional control of more than one country, the allocation of water supplies has been a thorny issue in international law. There are about 263 river basins in the world, of which one-third is shared by more than two countries and nineteen involve five or more states. One hundred forty-five nations have portions of their territory located in international river basins.[19] There have been as many as 1,831 interactions between states regarding their shared waters both conflictive and cooperative during the past fifty years.[20] And cooperative interactions have outnumbered conflicting ones. During the last fifty years, there have been only

---

[14] See Groundwater and Its Susceptibility to Degradation: A Global Assessment of the Problem and Options for Management (UNEP, Department for International Development, Belgian Development Cooperation & British Geological Survey, 2003); See also Internationally Shared (Transboundary) Aquifer Resources Management (ISARM): A Framework Document (UNESCO, 2001).

[15] Para. 3, Second Report on Shared Natural Resources: Transboundary Groundwaters by Chusei Yamada, Special Rapporteur, International Law Commission, Fifty-sixth session, May 3–June 4 and July 5–Aug. 6, 2004, A/CN.4/539, Mar. 9, 2004.

[16] Paras. 21–23, id.

[17] Para. 25, id.

[18] Para. 33, id.

[19] Meredith A. Giordano & Aaron T. Wolf, Sharing Waters: Post-Rio International Water Management, 27 Natural Resources Forum 163, 164 (2003).

[20] Id. at 164.

thirty-seven acute disputes (involving violence) but, at the same time, 150 treaties have been adopted.[21] Most disputes between states have to do with the allocation of water quantity or with infrastructure development.[22] Treaties and the institutions created by them – usually in the form of river basin commissions – have helped in averting conflicts. Coriparian countries have better relations in basins regulated by international treaties than in basins that function outside the international regulatory framework.[23]

2. ISSUES IN WATER MANAGEMENT

2.1. Allocation and Equity

2.1.1. Substantive Equity

Allocation Doctrines
The allocation of transboundary water resources among states has been one of the first issues to be adjudicated at the international level.[24] To understand the issue of water allocation, one has to understand the dynamics of the upper-lower riparian relationship as it may be influenced by the hegemonic tendencies of specific coriparians.

An upper riparian, by virtue of its geographical position, is in physical control of a river basin. Any action of an upper riparian has the potential to reduce water quantity and affect water quality downstream. A classic example of an upstream state with veto power is Turkey, with regard to the downstream states of Syria and Iraq. Turkey, militarily and economically more sophisticated than Syria and Iraq, has been able to impose its vision of the river basin on the downstream states, but not without sustaining some collateral damage itself.[25]

Physical control of the river basin, however, does not always translate into effective control. There have been cases in which downstream states have been able, by virtue of the inaction of upper riparians, to acquire effective control of water flow downstream. Because of the lack of action by upper-riparians and their geographical position at the end of a watercourse, downstream states develop usually into states with agriculture-driven growth. Downstream states claim, thus, prior rights to the watercourse, by virtue of their *de facto* agricultural development and prior use, and veto future development of upstream states. This veto is effective if a downstream state is militarily or economically more powerful than upstream states. A classic example of a downstream state with effective veto on upstream development is Egypt. Egypt has claimed that its prior use of the Nile River waters should prevent upstream development that would harm its agricultural expansion. Because of the political and economic weaknesses of upstream states – Sudan and Ethiopia – Egypt's veto has been an effective veto.

---

[21] *Id.* at 165.
[22] *Id.*
[23] *Id.* at 166.
[24] See *Lac Lanoux, Oder,* and *Meuse* cases, Chapter 1.
[25] See *infra* Section 5.3.

Overall, coriparians have invoked four doctrines with regard to the rights to transboundary watercourses:

- Absolute territorial sovereignty – an upstream state can manipulate the water resources according to its interests, without regard to the concerns of downstream states.[26]
- Absolute territorial integrity – an upstream state can do nothing that would affect the natural flow of a watercourse downstream.[27]
- Limited territorial sovereignty (or obligation not to cause significant harm) – states can use transboundary watercourses provided that no significant harm is imposed on other nations.[28]
- Community of interests and equitable use – concepts that have been developed in some of the early decisions of the ICJ[29] and the 1997 UN Watercourses Convention.[30] These concepts are derived from the hydrological unity of a watercourse and imply that a variety of factors must be taken into account with regard to the community of coriparians in deciding what would constitute a fair allocation of water resources.

The principles of equitable utilization of water resources and the obligation not to cause significant harm are embodied in the 1997 UN Watercourses Convention.[31] The principle of prevention of significant harm on the territory of other states supports the interests of downstream states. Downstream states usually demand that infrastructure development upstream must not undermine their use of water resources.

The principle of equitable utilization is more favorable to upstream development, as it stresses equity considerations that put past and future uses on the same level. The 1997 UN Watercourses Convention includes a number of factors that must be taken into account in determining equitable utilization.[32] However, given that no weights are assigned to these factors, states are at liberty to decide which factors are more salient for the specific allocation of their shared watercourse. Moreover, given that these factors are articulated in an open-ended fashion, it seems that anything states could agree on could constitute the basis of equitable utilization.[33] Some commentators have underlined that equitable utilization does not necessarily imply a fifty-fifty allocation of water resources, but it could imply the equitable utilization of the benefits derived from water use.[34]

---

[26] For example, India, with regard to the Ganges River, before the completion of the 1996 agreement with Bangladesh. See *infra* Section 5.2. This is known as the Harmon doctrine in the United States. Attorney General Judson Harmon articulated the absolute territorial sovereignty doctrine with regard to the diversion of the Rio Grande by the United States, which adversely affected Mexican interests. See Stephen C. McCaffrey, The Law of International Watercourses: Non-Navigational Uses 114–15 (2001).

[27] *Id.* at 128. Egypt with regard to the Nile River. See *infra* Section 5.

[28] *Id.* at 137.

[29] See *Oder* and *Meuse* cases, Chapter 1.

[30] See *infra* note 127.

[31] Arts. 6, 7, Watercourse Convention, *infra* note 127.

[32] Art. 6(a)–(g), *id.*

[33] For an analysis of the factors, see *infra* Section 4.

[34] McCaffrey, *supra* note 26, at 331.

In addition to the loose articulation of the concept of equitable utilization, the UN Watercourses Convention does not clarify the relationship between equitable utilization and the obligation not to cause significant harm. Equitable utilization and the obligation not to cause significant harm are mentioned without an evaluative criterion about which one should prevail in case of conflict. Because equitable utilization seems to favor upstream riparians and the obligation not to cause significant harm favors downstream riparians, the issue that remains unresolved is whether downstream traditional uses should be given priority over upstream new uses. Some commentators have interpreted the obligation not to cause significant harm as subordinate to the concept of equitable utilization.[35] However, the opposite interpretation is not precluded by the text of the convention.

Regional Context

In regional contexts, the principle of equitable utilization and the obligation not to cause significant harm have been interpreted to mean the realistic apportionment of benefits of water uses. This apportionment is sensitive to the power configuration in a region.[36] The differences in economic development and infrastructure readiness further shape the relationships among coriparians.[37] Countries with weak institutions and minimal infrastructure are usually not ready to enter into multilateral agreements with other coriparians, as they do not have the resources to collect the data to support their negotiating positions.[38] Separating water issues from the general balance of power in a region would produce an artificial understanding of water conflicts and compromises. In the Middle East, for instance, it is obvious that an agreement on water utilization cannot be easily separated from the broader security concerns in the region. The Tigris-Euphrates water conflict would probably resist resolution as long as Syria continues to be suspected for its alleged support for the Kurdish movement.[39]

Some agreements have been enabled by developments that are not directly linked with water use and allocation. For instance, the 1959 treaty between Sudan and Egypt was brokered after the change of government in Sudan that maintained a friendlier predisposition toward Egypt.[40] The final adoption of the agreement on the river Ganges between Indian and Bangladesh was facilitated eventually by the change in government in both countries as well as by issues not specifically related to water use.[41]

---

[35] *Id.* at 345–47.

[36] For the role of power in international law, see W. Michael Reisman, Law from the Policy Perspective, reprinted in International Law Essays 1, 6 (Myres S. McDougal & W. Michael Reisman, eds., 1981).

[37] Aaron T. Wolf, Conflict and Cooperation: Survey of the Past and Reflection for the Future, UNESCO-Green Cross International Project: "From Potential Conflict to Cooperation Potential (PCCP): Water for Peace" (2002) [hereinafter Wolf (Conflict and Cooperation)].

[38] Anthony Richard Turton, The Political Aspects of Institutional Development in the Water Sector: South Africa and its International River Basins 243 (dissertation thesis, Faculty of Humanities, University of Pretoria, May 31, 2003).

[39] See *infra* Section 5.3.

[40] See *infra* Section 5.2.

[41] John Waterbury, Between Unilateralism and Comprehensive Accords: Modest Steps toward Cooperation in International River Basins, 13(3) Water Resources Development 279, at 282, n. 2 (1997).

Regional agreements demonstrate the flexibility of the concept of equitable utilization as countries have been innovative in adapting the principle to circumstances that affect their region. Commentators have noted that the successful negotiation of international water allocation treaties often involves a quick passage from a rights discourse to a needs discourse.[42] For instance, the water agreement between Israel and Jordan recognizes the sovereign rights of Jordan over certain wells but allows, simultaneously, the lease of these wells to Israel for water pumping.[43] The water needs of Jordan are equally recognized, but they are relegated to the future discovery of additional water resources, therefore creating tension in the execution of the agreement as these resources have not been forthcoming. The 1959 treaty between Egypt and Sudan provides for a loan of Sudan's water allocation to Egypt until Sudan is able to make use of all its water allocation under the treaty.[44]

It seems that in most international agreements the interests of the downstream state are protected, but not in the sense of receiving water equal to the water allocated to the upstream state. Downstream uses are outlined specifically in the regional agreements and are protected.[45] Furthermore, some international agreements have been made possible because they have connected water allocation to other benefits. For instance, the Mahakali Treaty between India and Nepal is not only about water allocation but also about the production of energy.[46] Some agreements may not have been realized without the promise of specific benefits of international assistance. The promise of financial assistance by the World Bank was the catalyst for the adoption of the Indus Treaty.[47] The impetus generated by the financing offered by international institutions has ignited the motivation for the Mekong cooperation.[48]

2.1.2. Procedural Equity and Institutional Development

All regional agreements provide for an institution, usually a commission, the purpose of which is to collect information, execute studies, induce consensus, and provide a framework for dispute settlement. Commissions rarely are charged with resolving disputes among parties or with deciding the reallocation of water and its uses. However, commissions, through the collection and interpretation of data and the provision of advice, can facilitate consensual arrangements among parties. Commissions are usually comprised of an equal number of representatives from all riparians signatories of a regional freshwater agreement. Commissions are often technical bodies comprised of engineers rather than politicians.

In more detail, commissions established under regional agreements are of three types: (1) commissions involved in the joint management of water resources that have regulatory character (e.g., Rhine Commission and Danube Commission); (2) commissions limited to the execution of studies and programs (Zambezi Commission, Mekong Commission); and (3) bodies searching for consensus (the bodies that have

---

[42] Wolf (Conflict and Cooperation), *supra* note 37.

[43] See *infra* Section 5.3.

[44] See *infra* Section 5.1.

[45] Aaron T. Wolf, Criteria for Equitable Allocations: The Heart of International Water Conflict, 23(1) Natural Resources Forum 3 (1999).

[46] See *infra* Section 5.2.

[47] *Id.*

[48] Wolf (Conflict and Cooperation), *supra* note 37.

spearheaded the Nile initiative).[49] Common characteristics of commissions provided for in regional agreements are that they are created for long periods of time; they promote projects; and they have a permanent secretariat comprised of nationals of member states. Usually, commissions have technical responsibilities (collecting data, planning projects, maintaining infrastructure, monitoring of water use and quality), financial responsibilities (obtaining and using funding); and administrative responsibilities.[50] Commissions have various functions: advisory functions (providing opinions and advice); consensus-building functions; operational functions (ensuring the smooth operation of an agreement); normative functions (issuing regulations); and, occasionally, dispute settlement functions.[51]

An optimal organization for an international commission would involve an assembly composed of state representatives, a board of trustees, an authority responsible for the settlement of disputes, working groups responsible for technical work, and a secretariat responsible for administrative matters. A commission organized in an optimal manner would involve user participation, appropriate financing, and networking arrangements with other commissions.[52]

The development of institutions that are resilient and empowered to manage shared water resources constitutes the essence of the process through which equity is materialized. It is through a commission that the concerns and interests of all riparians are voiced. Commissions provide the procedural safeguards for the implementation of water management. Commissions further cultivate perceptions that such management, and ensuing allocations, is equitable. The technical expertise provided by commissions enables the removal of issues from the political domain, thus desensitizing conflict. Commissions in more developed stages of integration among coriparians (e.g., at the level of the European Union) facilitate cooperative arrangement not only among coriparian states but also among the actual resource users. The basin commissions, envisioned in the Water Framework Directive of the European Union, are required to facilitate the participation of citizen groups in the decision-making process.[53]

The institutionalization of water management, through commission-type organizations or other River Basin Organizations (RBOs), is more important than the agreed water allocations among state parties, as it is the institutional framework and the authority granted to it by states that determine the smooth functioning of coriparian relationship. Commentators have attributed the malfunctioning of regional agreements to changes in the circumstances of the basin or in the circumstances of riparians that cannot be managed effectively by the institutional apparatus in place.[54] When change in a river basin overwhelms the ability of institutions to absorb and

---

[49] Proposal for a Strategic Guide to Assist in the Constitution of International Inter-State Commissions for Shared Water Resources 38, French Académie de l'Eau, April 2002 [hereinafter Inter-State Commissions]. See also George E. Radosevich & Douglas C. Olson, Existing and Emerging Basin Arrangements in Asia: The Tarim River Basin Water Resources Commission and the Mekong River Commission 3, in Third Workshop on River Basin Institution Development, World Bank, June 24, 1999 [hereinafter World Bank 1999].

[50] Inter-State Commissions, *id.* at 39.

[51] *Id.* at 40.

[52] *Id.* at 51.

[53] See *infra* Section 5.4.1.

[54] Wolf (Conflict & Cooperation), *supra* note 37, at 9.

accommodate change, tensions and conflict ensue and the need to renegotiate the institutional framework becomes imperative.

Other procedural equity requirements included in regional agreements[55] and the UN Watercourses Convention are the requirements of notification in the event of planned measures that are to have significant adverse effects on the territory of other watercourse states. The notification requirements explicitly provide what is to be included in a notification; the period required for a reply to a notification; and the procedure to be followed in the absence of a reply.

2.1.3. Principled Equitable Utilization or *Ad Hoc* Regionalism?

Because the law, as articulated in the 1997 UN Watercourses Convention, is indeterminate and countries have concocted different solutions to allocation problems, the question that emerges is whether transboundary water allocation is an unprincipled, *ad hoc* development based on the political, economic, and authoritative configurations in a region, or whether equity considerations and the "no harm" principle, embodied in international instruments, have played a role in the allocation of water resources.

Most regional agreements, even some of those articulated before the adoption of the 1997 UN Watercourses Convention, refer to the principles of avoidance of significant harm and equitable utilization. The principle of no significant harm to downstream uses is mentioned in international agreements, but it has not played a decisive role in water allocation. The needs of coriparians have assumed, instead, the center stage in the negotiation of most agreements. The most eloquent example is provided by the Nile basin agreement between Sudan and Egypt. The Nile regime has been viewed as the classic case of the application of the no harm principle – where a downstream riparian has been able to effectively claim the principle of no harm to thwart development upstream. The 1929 water agreement between Egypt and Sudan (when Sudan was under the colonial control of Great Britain) hardly took into account the future development needs of Sudan. The 1959 Egypt-Sudan Agreement negotiated between sovereign governments, however, is more oriented toward a needs-based approach to equity, as it is more generous in its water allocation based on Sudan's needs. The agreement provides compensation to populations adversely affected by Nile development projects. The agreement further provides for a loan of Sudan's water to Egypt for as long as Sudan cannot make use of its allocated water. The agreement has not been contested because of an unstable political situation in Sudan that undermines ambitious national development.[56]

The Incomati-Maputo Agreement among South Africa, Mozambique, and Zimbabwe clearly takes into account the needs of the downstream state, Mozambique.[57] The Indus River regime between India and Pakistan has dictated the geographic separation of entitlements to the river basin based on the needs of coriparians because any integrated river arrangement would have been unable to address the concerns of the downstream state (Pakistan).[58] The Ganges Agreement

---

[55] SADC Agreement, see *infra* Section 5.1.
[56] See *infra* Section 5.1.
[57] *Id.*
[58] See *infra* Section 5.2.

between India and Bangladesh has been viewed as a demonstration that India has abandoned the absolute territorial sovereignty doctrine and is now more inclined toward the equitable water resources apportionment.[59] The Mahakali Agreement explicitly mentions that prime consideration in the utilization of waters of Mahakali must be given to Nepal, the downstream state. Overall, most of the agreements seem to be inspired by a notion of equity based on water needs. Some agreements have been made possible based on a broader notion of equity that has to do more with the exchange of a bundle of benefits among parties rather than just with strict water allocations.[60]

Thus, regional agreements cannot be characterized as unprincipled, *ad hoc* arrangements, as they have been influenced by a needs-based version of equity and have been affected – but not determined – by the exigencies of prior rights. At the same time, however, the development of regional water agreements cannot be expected to transform the relationships between coriparians into relationships between equal sovereigns. Equity is not the same as equality. On the contrary, the power configuration among coriparians in a region and, especially, the existence of a state with hegemonic tendencies have shaped many of the agreements and their execution. The Nile Treaty, for instance, between Egypt and Sudan provides that if it becomes necessary to allocate waters to other coriparians the water allocated must be deducted in equal parts from the shares of Sudan and Egypt. Such reallocation has yet to happen. Furthermore, after their independence from colonial rule, and despite declarations of nonrecognition of the Sudan-Egypt Agreement, the other Nile coriparians have been unable, because of internal institutional weakness, to present a unified front against Egypt. Egypt has threatened to retaliate against countries that harm its downstream use of Nile.[61] The Nile basin initiative, promoted as an initiative among all Nile coriparians, has yet to produce any concrete results.

The Incomati-Maputo Agreement guarantees the protection of the needs of Mozambique after years during which these needs were neglected. It is interesting to note, however, that these needs are to be fulfilled with additional water rather than with current water supplies. It is worth questioning how the agreement would have been formulated if such additional supplies were not forthcoming. The agreement between Israel and Jordan guarantees the fulfillment of the water needs of Israel, a regional nuclear power, but relegates the fulfillment of the needs of Jordan to the future discovery of water supplies. The Ganges Agreement was brokered after India decided unilaterally to build a dam in Farakka, despite the objections of Bangladesh (then East Pakistan) against such construction. Nepal has expressed dissatisfaction over the execution of the Mahakahi Agreement.[62] And the Indus regime is probably sustained because it effectively divides the entitlements to the river under the precept of equitable utilization. The Mekong regime, despite its success, still

---

[59] *Id.*

[60] *Id.*

[61] Olaf Westermann, Interstate Collaboration, Local Conflicts and Public Participation in the Nile River Basin, Working Paper 2004/6, in Proceedings of the International Conference, "From Water-wars to Water-riots? Lessons from Transboundary Water Management" 113, 122, Danish Institute for International Studies (DIIS) (Jannik Boesen & Helle Munk Ravnborg, eds., Dec. 2003).

[62] Damodar Bhattarai et al., Water and Risk, Asia High Summit 2002, at 18, May 6–10, 2002.

faces an uncertain future because a hegemonic upstream riparian, China, has refused to be bound by the regime.

In other words, equity in regional water agreements is not the pursuit of some abstract ideal of equity based on an initial condition of ignorance about future configurations of power.[63] It is, rather, equity as it could possibly be shaped under a given context of power configuration. It is a pragmatic articulation of equity in which the more powerful states have agreed to accommodate the needs of weaker states in order to avoid constant irritation and when such accommodation does not jeopardize vital national interests. The United States, for instance, has tried to accommodate the downstream requests of Mexico[64] because it does not perceive water as a matter of national security and has the technological and other resources that make compromise preferable to confrontation.

The strategy of weaker states is to confine their demands to more or less short-term water needs rather than to put forward aggressive future growth plans that would be water intensive. Furthermore, weaker states have tried to present a unified front against a regional hegemon. The Mekong initiative is an attempt by the lower riparians to present a unified front against China.[65] The Zambezi River regime was inspired by the desire to erect a unified front against the apartheid regime of South Africa.

In conclusion, it could be said that the notion of equity pursued in the international agreements is an equity under some predefined, often unspoken, code of conduct in a region. In the Oxford dictionary "fair" is defined as "in accordance . . . with the rules of the game." The example given is: "It was a fair fight, e.g. the rules of boxing were observed."[66] In water agreements, a similar perception of fairness applies. Regional water agreements are appraised as fair not because they are above the rules of the game – that has been played for years, even for centuries, in some regions – but because they have followed the rules of the game to extract the optimal outcomes for coriparians, based on these rules. Water agreements are based on a notion of fairness that is guided by the foresight that the circumstances of states may change. Institutions are needed, therefore, to attune or further redefine the currently achieved compromise.

2.2. Efficiency and Quality

Most international agreements on water allocation are scarcely concerned with issues of water quality. Water quality, though, is inextricably related with allocation issues. Lots of water of doubtful quality (because of the increasing levels of salt or pollution) is unlikely to alleviate the water needs of riparians.

---

[63] See, e.g., John Rawls, A Theory of Justice (1971).

[64] See *infra* Section 5.5.2.

[65] This has not been a successful effort in its entirety. For instance, certain countries are the dominant nations of the Lower Mekong basin, and Vietnam and Cambodia have preferred to follow consensual solutions than challenge them. A treaty between China, Myanmar, Laos, and Thailand on the commercial navigation of the Mekong River was adopted without the notification of Cambodia and Vietnam and without prior consultation with the Mekong Commission. For a description of the incident, see *infra* Section 5.2.

[66] A. S. Hornby, Oxford Advanced Learner's Dictionary of Current English (Oxford University Press, ed., 1974).

Commentators have argued that water scarcity in some regions is a demand-led scarcity. States have been blamed for wasting water resources in agricultural development by commissioning expensive irrigation projects when food supplies could actually be imported at significantly cheaper prices.[67] The Middle East region has been characterized as a region of demand-led scarcity since states in the region have considered agricultural development as a matter of national security and have tried to achieve self-sufficiency in food supply – often to no avail despite significant diversions of water to agriculture.[68]

Water quality issues are interlinked with issues of water efficiency. Water of poor quality for a specific use is bound to lead to wastage of water resources. Because of the heavy subsidies that support agricultural development in most countries, agriculture is considered a wasteful use of water resources. Agriculture is also considered one of the major diffuse sources of water pollution because of the nitrates and fertilizers that end up in lakes and rivers. Farmers, however, have viewed the provision of water as an entitlement and have resisted efforts to price water according to the true costs of its production. Those devoted to efficient water allocation have favored the allocation of water to industrial uses because industry, which is less inclined to view water provision as an entitlement, is more willing to pay higher water prices than agriculture.

Efficient water allocation has involved the privatization of public utilities and the use of pricing to recuperate the costs involved in water production (e.g., the costs of water extraction, purification, and distribution). Increasing the price of the water to reflect the true costs of its production[69] has been considered, in some circles, as the mechanism that would effectively allocate water to users who are more willing and able to pay for it (most often industrial users). It has been contended, further, that strategic planning and management (SPM)[70] and various forms of water trade can be used to alleviate water scarcity and the ensuing conflict in certain regions.[71]

This economic view of water as a commodity suitable for pricing and profit – what has been called demand-led management of water resources[72] – has been resisted

---

[67] Some commentators have called water needed for agricultural commodities virtual water. It usually requires one thousand cubic meters of water to produce a ton of grain. If the ton of grain is imported through trade, the economy would not have to produce one thousand cubic meters of water. See J.A. Allan, Virtual Water – the Water, Food, and Trade Nexus: Useful Concept or Misleading Metaphor?, 28(1) Water International 4,5, Mar. 2003.

[68] Some countries in the region, however, have sought to reform their water practices. Israel, for example, has been involved in a number of micro-irrigation projects.

[69] See, e.g., Peter H. Gleick, The Changing Water Paradigm: A Look at the Twenty-First Century Water Resources Development, 25(1) Water International 127, Mar. 2000.

[70] See Douglas Webster & Ti Le-Huu, Draft Guidelines on Strategic Planning and Management of Water Resources, June 30, 2003 (paper prepared for Water Resources Section, Environment and Sustainable Development Division, United Nations Economic and Social Commission for Asia and the Pacific [UNESCAP]).

[71] Diane Segal, Singapore's Water Trade with Malaysia and Alternatives, John F. Kennedy Scholl of Government, Harvard University, Mar. 30, 2004. The paper explores the water trade between Singapore and Malaysia. The author points out that Singapore has to find alternative methods to increase its water supply because imports from Malaysia may become more uncertain in the future. The author maintains that Singapore must diversify its water supply while still trying to maintain trade with Malaysia as the cheapest option. Water trade with other countries and the construction of submarine pipelines are proposed as alternatives.

[72] In contrast with supply-led management that is concerned with the supply of water without regulating demand.

by groups that view the provision of water as a human right. The indiscriminate internalization of the costs of water production and the passing on of these costs to the consumer have been viewed as yet another method to undermine the survival of the poor of the world. It has been argued that poor constituencies would not be able to afford the water prices charged by private companies. Water, as a social good, has been counterpositioned against water as an economic good.[73]

A recent incident that underlines the conflict between water as a human right and water as an economic good involves the efforts of the Bolivian government to privatize water supply. The government, following a recommendation by the World Bank, passed a law in 1999 allowing for the privatization of water supply and the cessation of subsidies to municipal utilities. Water management was taken over by International Water, a subsidiary of the Bechtel corporation. Soon after the privatization, water prices reached $20 per month in a city where the minimum salary is $100 per month. Demonstrations against the price increases led to street conflict and a number of people were killed. In 2000, Bechtel left Bolivia and the government retracted the privatization legislation. In 2001, Bechtel filed a suit against Bolivia for $25 million at the International Center for the Settlement of Investment Disputes, an international tribunal housed at the World Bank.

Those who disfavor water pricing have claimed that efficient water allocation does not necessarily mean fair water allocation. According to notions of fairness, water allocations to disadvantaged users must be subsidized and protected.[74] For instance, the reallocation of water from agriculture to industry is more efficient but it is not necessarily fair. Those who view water as a human right have claimed that universal access to water is one of the fundamental conditions of human development and have proposed the pursuit of the right to water as an implicit component of the right to food, health, and life. The human right to water has been quantified as water sufficient to serve basic human needs – such as drinking, cooking, and basic domestic uses.[75] Some countries are far behind even of meeting this basic requirement.[76]

The 1997 UN Watercourses Convention recognizes extensively issues of water pollution[77] but does not really tackle issues of efficiency in water allocation. It is provided that one of the factors to be taken into account in determining equitable utilization is "conservation, protection, development and *economy* [emphasis added]" of water use and "the costs of measures taken to that effect."[78] The provision seems, thus, to provide some primitive articulation of a cost-benefit analysis of water use, but it is hardly clearly articulated.

Most regional agreements that concentrate on water allocation are usually deprived of environmental provisions, but there are notable exceptions, such as the SADC Agreement,[79] which has been influenced by the 1997 Watercourses Convention, the Incomati-Maputo Agreement,[80] and the Mekong

---

[73] Hubert Savenije & Pieter var der Zaag, Water as an Economic Good and Demand Management: Paradigms with Pitfalls, 27(1) Water International 98, 99, Mar. 2002.

[74] See Vandana Shiva, Water Wars: Privatization, Pollution and Profit (2000).

[75] Peter H. Gleick, The Human Right to Water, 1 Water Policy 487, 490, 495–96 (1998).

[76] *Id.* at 496 (50 l per person per day).

[77] See arts. 20–26, UN Watercourse Convention, *infra* note 127.

[78] Art. 6(1)(f), *id.*

[79] See *infra* Section 5.1.

[80] *Id.*

Agreement.[81] Agreements between developed states, on the contrary, whose resources have been marred by pollution, could be exclusively devoted to environmental problems such as the Rhine Convention,[82] the Danube Convention,[83] and the United States-Canada Agreements.[84] The issue of water pricing has yet to be included in regional arrangements with the exception of the Incomati-Maputo Agreement[85] and the Water Framework Directive[86] of the European Union. With regard to the Water Framework Directive, explicit obligations to introduce water pricing have been resisted by member states of the European Union with a strong agricultural sector. This demonstrates how politically charged water pricing has become even in some of the most integrated areas of the world.

2.3. Integrated Water Resources Management

Integrated water resources management (IWRM) or integrated river basin management (IRBM) is an attempt to manage water in an integrated fashion by taking into account:

- physical, ecological, and chemical characteristics of the water;
- the interests of all different users as they may collide or intercept;
- environmental components of water use (i.e., management of pollution);
- the participation of stakeholders in the decision-making process;[87]
- the intersectoral management of water resources through the coordination of different central/local departments and agencies.[88]

Integrated water management conceives the river basin as a hydrological unit that must be managed in a consistent fashion by taking into account all various impacts and uses (e.g., fishing, pollution by industry and agriculture, impacts from tourism). At the core of integrated river basin management is the River Basin Organization (RBO), usually a commission, the purpose of which is to coordinate the national/local water policies and to manage the river basin in an integrated fashion.

2.3.1. National

Most countries have recognized the importance of integrated river basin management and have experimented with different forms of river basin organizations both

---

[81] See *infra* Section 5.2.

[82] See *infra* Section 5.4.2.

[83] *Id.*

[84] See *infra* Section 5.5.1.

[85] See *infra* Section 5.1.

[86] See *infra* Section 5.4.1.

[87] For the importance of stakeholder participation, see Richard McNally & Sylvia Tognetti, Tackling Poverty and Promoting Sustainable Development: Key Lessons for Integrated River Basin Management, WWF Discussion Paper, July 2002 [hereinafter Poverty and IRBM].

[88] Hubert Savenije & Pieter var der Zaag, Water as an Economic Good and Demand Management: Paradigms with Pitfalls, 27(1) Water International 98, Mar. 2002. See also Recommendations and Guidelines on Sustainable River Basin Management, Workshop report of "International Workshop on River Basin Management," The Hague, Oct. 27–29, 1999 (Organized by the RBA Centre, Delft University of Technology, the Netherlands).

for planning and allocation purposes.[89] The names of these organizations and the functional independence of these organizations differ from country to country, but there are common characteristics such as: a mandate of the organization that is based on the hydrological unit; the inclusion of public participation; and coordination and management functions.[90]

The World Bank has classified river basin organizations into river basin committees or councils that have a merely coordinating function; river basin commissions that focus on planning and management; and river basin authorities that have regulatory authority.[91]

River basin councils or committees have a limited role and limited supporting staff. They meet irregularly and are comprised of the heads of government departments concerned with natural resource management. Committee-type bodies were developed in the United States in 1960s but were abolished in the 1980s. In Germany, committee-type bodies are charged with coordination of management in the rivers of Rhine, Weser, and Elbe.[92]

A river basin commission is essentially a government agency with more personnel at its disposal than a committee and is engaged in planning, monitoring, and reporting. River basin commissions can be found in Spain, France, Germany, and the United Kingdom.[93]

The designation of an organization as a river basin commission usually implies the development of an institution with regulatory authority and the power of that institution to enforce its decisions. The mandate of the organization usually expands beyond water allocation and management and may involve the coherent management of a region that is dependent on a hydrological unit. Because of its extensive authority, the organization usually absorbs some already existing organizations.[94]

An example of a river basin authority is the Tennessee Valley Authority (TVA) in the United States. The TVA has more extensive functions than pure water management. The authority was charged initially with the mandate to alleviate poverty in the entire region under its oversight (encompassing the states of Tennessee, Kentucky, Virginia, North Carolina, Georgia, Alabama, and Mississippi). Its powers, therefore, extend beyond mere water regulation and allocation. The TVA was established in 1933 with the mandate to transform one of the poorest regions in the United States into an economic success. The TVA built and operated fifty-four dams and it is well known for its water resources management programs and a large multipurpose reservoir system. Today, it provides 5 percent of electric energy in the United States.

Although the TVA faces many challenges, it has been proposed as a model RBO for other countries' river basin management. This is because it provides an example of interstate collaboration in water management and because of its broad mandate – that

---

[89] R. Maria Saleth & Ariel Dina, Water Challenge and Institutional Response: A Cross Country Perspective 36 (World Bank, 1999) [hereinafter Water Challenge].

[90] Id. at 37–38.

[91] See World Bank 1999, supra note 49, at 4.

[92] Id.

[93] Id. at 5. See also Hartje, supra note 7, at 18.

[94] World Bank, id.

is, the eradication of poverty.[95] The TVA model was used as a paradigm by the Johnston plan that attempted to mediate the Arab-Israeli water conflict and has influenced water management in the Middle East region.[96] The model of TVA had been proposed for the resolution of the conflict between India and Pakistan with regard to Indus waters, but it was eventually rejected as the riparians opted for the actual segregation of entitlements to the river.[97]

Another RBO, that has been considered a model for emulation, is the Murray-Darling Basin Commission (MDBC) in Australia. The MDBC covers the territories of a number of states (South Wales, Victoria, Queensland, South Australia, and the entire Australian Capital Territory) under a federal system that has been called cooperative federalism. The MDBC was created in the early 1980s with a mandate to manage water quantity, but its mandate was expanded later to encompass issues of water quality and the land-based management of the river basin.[98] Some of the measures adopted by the MDBC have been the placement of caps on water diversions[99] and the creation of rights on water that are separate from the rights on land. This has allowed owners of rights to water to sell their surplus of water without selling their land. Some of the states in the region, including South Wales and Victoria, have developed sophisticated water markets.[100] The development of interstate water markets, however, has proven more challenging as states have yet to harmonize their regulations.[101]

2.3.2. International

The concept of IWRM has been proposed as a principle of international water policy – a principle pursued by UN agencies and international development assistance programs. The concept of integrated water management has been the focus of Agenda 21 and is the mantra of many environmental NGOs.

Chapter 18 of Agenda 21 provides for the integrated management and development of water resources by adopting a "catchment management approach."[102] Agenda 21 calls for a number of other measures that imply the comprehensive management of water resources, such as mandatory environmental impact assessment, risk management, and measures for the protection of groundwater.[103] Agenda 21 asks states to cooperate in order to harmonize their strategies and action programs.[104] The WSSD Implementation Plan refers explicitly to integrated water resources management and water efficiency plans.[105]

---

[95] Comprehensive River Basin Development: The Tennessee Valley Authority, World Bank Technical Paper No. 416, at 1–5 (Barbara A. Miller & Richard B. Reidinger, eds., Nov. 1998) [hereinafter TVA].

[96] See *infra* Section 5.3.

[97] See *infra* Section 5.2.

[98] A Case-Study of the Murray-Darling Basin: Final Report for the International Management Institute 20, CSIRO Land and Water (Darla Hatton MacDonald & Mike Young, eds., 2001) [hereinafter MBDC].

[99] *Id.* at 28.

[100] *Id.* at 45.

[101] *Id.* at 47.

[102] Paras. 18.35–18.36, Agenda 21, Chapter 1, Section 4.2.

[103] Para. 18.40(d), *id.*

[104] Para. 18.10, *id.*

[105] Para. 25, WSSD, Plan of Implementation, Chapter 1, Section 4.3.

Although states have generally cooperated in the management of their shared watercourses, one could not claim that the concept of IWRM has been the guiding principle of state practice in transboundary water arrangements.[106] On the contrary, most agreements are purely allocation agreements or endorse developmental goals, such as hydroelectric energy production. Only some of the agreements deal partially with pollution control.[107] Water quality has been the focus of water agreements in developed regions (i.e., the Rhine regime and the United States-Canada Great Lakes Agreement). Comprehensive agreements that deal with water quality and quantity in an integrated fashion are rare.

It could be claimed actually that some agreements are antithetical to the notion of integrated water management. Integrated water management is based on an understanding of the river basin as a hydrological unit. Some agreements have sidelined totally the hydrological unit and merely attempt to manage water resources at the border (1909 U.S.-Canada Border Agreement). Other agreements attempt to deal with more than one hydrological unit with the expectation that concessions made in one river basin will be offset by advantages received in others (Jordan-Yarmouk Agreement, Incomati-Maputo Agreement). Certain agreements are dependent on increasing water quantities becoming available in the future (Incomati-Maputo Agreement, Jordan-Yarmouk Agreement) or on formulas that provide for allocations that are larger than the water flow (Aral Sea Agreements). The Indus Agreement has provided a viable regime for India and Pakistan, exactly because it abandoned the concept of integrated management and segregated river management.

Similarly, the International River Basin Organizations (IRBOs), usually commissions that have been formed, have monitoring, reporting, and data gathering powers but rarely have regulatory and enforcement powers. It could hardly be claimed that IRBOs, at present, deal comprehensively with IWRM. Some of the recent agreements could be characterized as attempts to implement IRBM, such as the SADC Protocol or the new Mekong Agreement. It must be noted, however, that the notion of the watercourse as a "system" that implies notions of integrated management was dropped from both the 1997 UN Watercourses Convention and the 2000 SADC Protocol. States are apprehensive that notions of integrated water management embodied in international agreements would be a threat to their sovereignty. The notion of IWRM involves the control of land activities as they may affect adversely water resources.

3. CASE LAW

Some of the early cases that have been internationally adjudicated involve the allocation of water among coriparians. In the *Oder* and *Meuse* cases analyzed in Chapter 1, the Permanent Court of International Justice (PCIJ) declared the perfect equality of all riparian nations and the exclusion of any preferential privilege of any riparian in relation to others. The cases have been considered a precursor of the

---

[106] See, e.g., John Waterbury, Between Unilateralism and Comprehensive Accords: Modest Steps toward Cooperation in International River Basins, 13(3) Water Resources Development 279 (1997).

[107] See also Hartje, *supra* note 7, at 24–25.

concept of equitable utilization of resources adopted in the 1997 UN Watercourses Convention.[108]

The *Lac Lanoux* case has been heralded as establishing the obligation of negotiation and consultation before undertaking a project that is likely to have adverse effects on the territory of other states. This means that upstream states, for instance, would have to consult with downstream states before constructing a major project – such as a dam – on their side of the river. Although this requirement of prior consultation is considered by some a principle of international law it has not been followed consistently by all states.[109] It must be noted that the tribunal in the *Lac Lanoux* case pointed out that the requirement of prior consultation does not mean that there is an obligation to conclude an agreement with adversely affected states. The requirement to conclude an agreement, before the undertaking of a project likely to have adverse effects, was considered by the tribunal as a right to veto by the affected state. Such a right to veto compromises the territorial competence of the initiating state.[110]

A more recent case that clarifies the management of shared watercourses is the *Gabčíkovo-Nagymaros* case.[111] The dispute arose out of a 1977 agreement between Hungary and Slovakia (then Czechoslovakia) on the construction of two barrages on the Danube River for the purposes of hydroelectricity production, prevention of flooding, and improvement of navigation. The parties undertook an obligation to ensure that the quality of waters of the Danube River was not to be impaired.[112]

In 1988, Hungary, giving in to public pressure regarding the environmental soundness of the project, decided to withdraw from the project. After unsuccessful negotiations with Hungary, Slovakia decided to engage in the unilateral execution of the project on its territory called "Variant C." Hungary objected to the unilateral diversion of the river by Slovakia, and the parties decided in 1993 to submit the dispute to the ICJ by a special agreement.

The Court was asked to decide the following questions:

- whether Hungary could withdraw from the 1977 treaty; and
- whether Slovakia was entitled to proceed with the provisional unilateral solution in its territory.

Hungary invoked the doctrine of "a state of ecological necessity" for the breach of its obligations under the 1977 treaty. A state of necessity is considered a legitimate ground for the abrogation of an international obligation under article 33 of the Draft Articles on International State Responsibility prepared by the International Law Commission. According to article 33, a state of necessity can be invoked by a state, as a ground for the breach of its international obligations, only when the breach of the international obligation is the only way to safeguard an essential interest of the state against a grave and imminent peril.[113]

---

[108] See *infra* note 127.
[109] See *infra* note 313. The issue of prior consultation was raised also in the context of the U.S.-Mexico Agreement regarding the increasingly salinity of the waters of the Colorado River. The parties undertook to consult with each other before undertaking projects that would affect the salinity downstream.
[110] See Chapter 1, Section 4.5.
[111] Case Concerning the Gabčíkovo-Nagymaros Project, Sept. 25, 1997, (1997) ICJ Reports 7.
[112] Para. 15, *id.*
[113] Para. 50, *id.*

The Court examined the Hungarian claim and stated that it found no difficulty in identifying Hungary's concerns as "an essential interest of the state."[114] However, the Court concluded that the potential environmental problems cited by Hungary do not constitute "a grave and imminent peril." A grave and imminent peril must entail a threat to a state's interests "at the actual time" and not by the mere possibility of future developments.[115] The Court stated that many of the adverse environmental impacts cited by Hungary could be addressed within the context of the 1977 treaty, especially the application of articles 15, 19, and 20. According to the Court, these articles do not contain specific conditions of performance but require parties, in performing their obligations, to ensure that the quality of water in the Danube is not impaired, that nature is protected, and to take new environmental norms into consideration.[116]

Hungary claimed further that its inability to perform, in accordance with the 1977 treaty, was due to an unforeseen change in circumstances. Such change in circumstances was demonstrated by the project's diminishing economic viability and the development of new norms of international environmental law. The Court pointed out that the new developments in the state of environmental law and environmental knowledge were not completely unforeseen in the 1977 treaty between the parties. The 1977 treaty provided avenues through specific articles (articles 15, 19, and 20) to accommodate change.[117]

Furthermore, the Court held that the provisional solution adopted by Slovakia failed to respect the principle of proportionality required by international law. The Court said that Slovakia, by unilaterally assuming the control of a shared watercourse, deprived Hungary of its right to an equitable and reasonable share of the resources of Danube.[118] In this context, the Court made reference to the *Oder* case. The Court cited the passage that mentions "the perfect equality of all riparian States in the use of the whole course of the river and the exclusion of any preferential privilege of any one riparian State in relation to the others."[119] The Court mentioned that this principle, of perfect equality of states, has been strengthened by the 1997 UN Watercourses Convention.[120] It is worth noting that the convention was just adopted at the time.

The Court instructed the parties to continue negotiations based on the principles of international environmental law and the law of international watercourses. The Court instructed the parties to pay damages to one another – Slovakia because the countermeasures it had undertaken were not proportionate and, thus, it was in breach of international law; and Hungary, because it had breached its obligations under an international treaty.[121]

Overall, the ICJ clearly upheld the sanctity of treaties because it refused to discharge Hungary of its obligations under the treaty and disapproved the unilateral actions by Slovakia that would have further undermined the execution of the treaty.

---

[114] Para. 53, *id.*
[115] Para. 54, *id.*
[116] Para. 112, *id.*
[117] Para. 104, *id.*
[118] Para. 85, *id.*
[119] *Id.*
[120] *Id.*
[121] Para. 152, *id.*

The Court considered the concerns of the disputing states as legitimate but refused to accept that those concerns could not be resolved within the treaty framework. The Court made some statements *in dicta* that demonstrate that environmental considerations are playing an influential role in the Court's reasoning. The Court repeated its conclusions in the *Legality of the Threat or Use of Nuclear Weapons* case:[122]

> The environment is not an abstraction but represents a living space, the quality of life and the very health of human beings, including generations unborn. The existence of the general obligation of States to ensure that activities within their jurisdiction and control respect the environment of other States or of areas beyond national control is now part of the corpus of international law relating to the environment.[123]

The Court did not refer to the precautionary principle itself but made reference to the fact that both parties agreed "on the need to take environmental concerns seriously and to take the required *precautionary measures* [emphasis added] ... "[124] The Court stressed that "the awareness of the vulnerability of the environment and the recognition that environmental risks have to be assessed on a continuous basis have become much stronger" since the conclusion of the 1977 treaty between the parties.[125]

The Court made reference to the concept of sustainable development and declared that:

> new norms and standards have been developed, set forth in a great number of instruments during the last two decades. Such new norms have to be taken into consideration, and such new standards given proper weight, not only when States contemplate new activities but also when continuing with activities begun in the past. The need to reconcile economic development with protection of the environment is aptly expressed in the concept of sustainable development.[126]

These statements made by the Court demonstrate that environmental considerations have influenced the Court's reasoning. However, although the Court has taken into account the environmental imperative, it has been reluctant to bow unequivocally to environmental concerns that are not fully substantiated. The Court instructed the parties to go back to the negotiating table and try to find solutions within the framework of the 1977 treaty. The text of that treaty, according to the Court, allowed for interpretations that could take into account environmental protection.

4. INTERNATIONAL INSTRUMENTS

The 1997 Watercourses Convention[127] is largely based on the efforts of the International Law Commission and the Institute of International Law to codify the law of Non-Navigational Uses of International Watercourses. It establishes the framework

---

[122] Legality of the Threat or Use of Nuclear Weapons, Advisory Opinion, see Chapter 1, Section 4.5.
[123] Para. 53, *Gabčíkovo-Nagymaros* case, *supra* note 111.
[124] Para. 113, *id.*
[125] Para. 112, *id.*
[126] Para. 140, *id.*
[127] Convention on the Law of Non-Navigational Uses of International Watercourses, May 21, 1997, reprinted in 36 ILM 700 (1997) [hereinafter Watercourse Convention].

for the use of watercourses and principles to guide the agreements of states with regard to the use of international watercourses. The convention is a framework convention to be executed by regional or bilateral agreements among states.[128] The convention encompasses both surface waters and the groundwater connected with surface water.[129] Certain countries have refused to sign the convention because they are concerned about the implications of equitable use on the relationship with their coriparians.

Article 5 of the convention provides that a watercourse state must utilize a watercourse in a reasonable and equitable manner. This reasonable and equitable manner requires the optimal use but, at the same time, sustainable use of the watercourse and must be consistent with the adequate protection of the watercourse. Article 5 is referring, thus, to allocation issues, as parties are to utilize the water in a reasonable and equitable manner. Article 5 also addresses quality considerations by providing that the optimal use of the watercourse must be sustainable and "consistent with the adequate protection of the watercourse."[130]

Article 6 includes an account of nonexhaustive factors that states must take into account for the equitable and reasonable use of watercourses. The convention does not prescribe weights for these factors but provides that all of these factors are to be considered together and "a conclusion must be reached on the basis of the whole."[131] The factors to be taken into account in determining whether the use of waters is equitable and reasonable are:

- the geographic, climate, hydrological, and ecological conditions;
- the social and economic needs of states concerned;
- the population dependent on the watercourse in each watercourse state;
- the effects of the use of the watercourse on other watercourse states;
- the existing and potential uses of the watercourse;
- conservation, protection, development, and economy of use of the watercourse and costs of measures taken;
- the availability of alternatives, of comparable value, to a particular planned or existing use.[132]

Thus, the factors to be taken into account in determining reasonable and equitable utilization are broad enough to encompass any concern of a coriparian. This, in combination with the fact that no weights are attached to these factors, has driven some commentators to conclude that the convention does not provide normative guidance for the allocation of international watercourses.[133]

The obligation not to cause significant harm adds to the indeterminate nature of the convention.[134] Article 7(2) provides that when a significant harm occurs to another watercourse state, the state that causes the harm is responsible for taking

---

[128] Art. 3, *id*. See also McCaffrey, *supra* note 26, at 303.
[129] Art. 2(a), Watercourse Convention, *supra* note 127.
[130] Art. 5(1), *id*.
[131] Art. 6(3), *id*.
[132] Art. 6(1), *id*.
[133] See, e.g., Waterbury, *supra* note 41.
[134] Art. 7, Watercourse Convention, *supra* note 127.

appropriate measures to "eliminate or mitigate" such harm and even discuss the issue of compensation.

Commentators have claimed that the obligation not to cause significant harm is implied in the principle of reasonable and equitable utilization and that adding the no significant harm obligation, as a separate principle, only fuels confusion and undermines the normative character of the convention.[135] The determination of the threshold at which harm becomes "significant" harm could be subject to debate and could add to the perplexity of allocation decisions.

Commentators have tried to make sense of the reasonable and equitable use provision as it compares with the no significant harm provision. Causing *any* harm, it is argued, does not nullify *per se* a reasonable and equitable arrangement for the sharing of water resources. Therefore, the convention provides that the harm must be *significant*, that is, it must affect a legal interest of the affected state. Any use of a water resource is likely to cause some harm to another state. Therefore, it is important to underline that not any harm but harm that is *significant* and has to do with a legally protected right or interest is the harm states must avoid in their exploitation of a water resource.[136] The distinction between actual harm and legal injury is crucial in understanding the principle of equitable utilization as it informs the no significant harm principle.[137] What the convention does not allow is harm that would deprive a state of its equitable share of use of resources.[138]

It has been maintained, furthermore, that equitable share does not mean an entitlement to an actual equal apportionment of water resources. Equitable share means that each state has a right to an equitable share of the uses and benefits of a shared watercourse.[139] Equitable utilization, in other words, is a dynamic process and when a new use is proposed negotiations should be conducted to determine how such use is to be accommodated.[140]

The convention provides for an elaborate procedure of notification when a new use of a watercourse is proposed. A state that needs to undertake measures that would affect a shared watercourse needs to notify the affected state and to wait for six months for a reply to its notification.[141] During this six-month period, the notifying state is not permitted to undertake the planned measure without the consent of the affected state.[142] The convention provides for all the minute details of this notification procedure, including the reply to the notification and steps to be followed in the absence of notification or reply. Procedures to be followed in order for a state to implement urgent measures are clarified in the convention.[143]

The requirements for notification were the least controversial during the negotiations.[144] This lack of controversy has been interpreted as a demonstration of the

---

[135] McCaffrey, *supra* note 26, at 300, 308, 379.
[136] *Id.* at 310.
[137] *Id.* at 329.
[138] *Id.*
[139] *Id.* at 331.
[140] *Id.* at 345.
[141] Arts. 12 &13, Watercourse Convention, *supra* note 127.
[142] Art. 14 (b), *id.*
[143] Arts. 15, 16, 18, & 19, *id.*
[144] McCaffrey, *supra* note 26, at 312.

solidification of notification requirements as principles of customary international law.

The primary focus of the convention is the allocation of water resources. The principle of IRBM is not included in the convention. It could be said actually that IRBM was consciously sidelined as states were reluctant to include the term "watercourse system" even in the title of the convention. However, in recognition of the fact that water quantity, by itself, may not be of much consequence, when water is unsuitable for a specific consumptive use, the convention includes specific provisions on the "protection, preservation and management" of water.[145] Pollution that is to cause "significant" harm to other watercourse states must be prevented, reduced and controlled.[146] States need to cooperate to establish lists of substances the discharge of which in a watercourse should be prohibited, limited and monitored.[147] Furthermore, state parties recognize the close interrelationship between the protection of watercourses and the preservation of marine environment.[148]

The convention encourages states to enter into negotiations with regard to the management of a shared watercourse that may include the establishment of a joint management mechanism.[149] Part VI of the convention provides for detailed dispute settlement provisions. In these provisions, there is the requirement that when negotiations on a specific dispute fail, one of the parties to the dispute could submit the contested issue to a fact-finding body.[150] This provision was controversial, during the negotiations of the convention, because it provides for compulsory fact-finding at the request of any party to a dispute without requiring the consent of other parties.[151]

The treaty purports to protect the groundwater but more work needs to be done to protect the groundwater effectively.[152] Actually, the treaty, in its definition of waters to be protected, includes groundwater connected to surface water but not confined groundwater.[153] Thus, confined groundwater remains unregulated. The International Law Commission has engaged in efforts to devise rules for the regulation of groundwater.[154]

The 1997 UN Watercourses Convention has been derided, particularly, for failing to provide simple and effective criteria for the allocation of water sources and uses. It has been claimed that the requirement of reasonable and equitable utilization is not really taken into account in regional agreements and states articulate *ad hoc* arrangements particular to their situation.

Before sidelining the convention, however, one must consider carefully the situation that decision makers were faced with when negotiating the convention. There are many watercourses shared by states, and various regimes were in force before

---

[145] See arts. 20–26, Watercourse Convention, *supra* note 127.
[146] Art. 21(2), *id.*
[147] Art. 21(3)(c), *id.*
[148] Art. 23, *id.*
[149] Art. 24, *id.*
[150] Art. 33(3), *id.*
[151] McCaffrey, *supra* note 26, at 313.
[152] *Id.* at 414–45.
[153] Art. 2(a), Watercourse Convention, *supra* note 127.
[154] See *supra* note 15.

the adoption of the convention. The configuration of power in a region tends to provide an additional complicating factor in water allocation. A convention with clear criteria and specific weights for factors to be balanced for equitable utilization would not have a serious chance to be accepted by states. For the allocation of sensitive resources, which some consider national security resources, the convention had to maintain a considerable amount of flexibility in order to become acceptable. Rigidity is not always an enviable requirement in law. By being flexible, but nonetheless proposing the principle of equity, the convention provided a basis for discourse among states. In allocation matters, when certain states would outplay weaker states, the law can attempt to tinker with a given power configuration by injecting the element of equity into allocation deliberations. The law cannot substitute bargaining in allocation decisions. But, by interjecting the requirements of reasonableness, equity, and no harm the law can, at least, attempt to influence deliberation outcomes and provide the weak with a more substantiated articulation of their interests.

5. REGIONAL INSTRUMENTS

Various agreements have been adopted by states on the allocation of water resources and benefits associated with these resources. The agreements that have been adopted are not necessarily efforts to incorporate integrated river basin management or environmental concepts into the management of a river basin unit. They are, rather, attempts to reconcile bitter conflicts over resource management. Therefore, some agreements cover:

- a single river basin (i.e., Mekong and Nile Agreements);
- border waters (the 1909 U.S.-Canada Agreement);
- a whole region, that is umbrella agreements, such as the SADC Agreement, the UN/ECE Agreement and the U.S.-Mexico Agreement on all shared rivers;
- more than one river basin so that certain concessions a state makes on a river basin can be offset by advantages it obtains in another river basin (Jordan–Yarmouk Agreement and Incomati–Maputo Agreement).

Most agreements mention the concepts of equitable utilization of water resources and the no harm principle and some of them make allusions to environmental concepts and to integrated river basin management. In practice, what most agreements have adopted is a needs version of equitable utilization. Integrated river basin management, although mentioned occasionally in the agreements, hardly has been applied in reality. In fact, some agreements have been successful because they have not incorporated the concept of integrated river basin management, such as the Indus Agreement, which has proceeded on the assumption that it is better to separate the river for the sake of maintenance of peace between belligerent neighbors.

The 1909 U.S.-Canada Agreement is an attempt to regulate the disputes between Canada and the United States with regard to their border waters. It is less concerned with river regulation based on integrated management.[155] It was hoped that

---

[155] Itay Fischhendler, Can Basin Management Be Successfully Ignored? The Case of the US-Canada Transboundary Water 3, Occasional Paper 52, School of Oriental and African Studies (SOAS)/King's College London, May 2003.

concentrating on border waters would reduce the issues and transaction costs of dealing with all shared waters in one treaty.

Water management in South Africa is based on interbasin water transfers (which are somewhat antithetical to the concept of management of the river as an integrated unit) and this has had an influence on the agreements that South Africa has signed with its neighbors.

The suprabasin umbrella agreements of the SADC and the UN/ECE demonstrate that, although water problems may be different in various regions, a framework approach could make sense as an initial attempt to resolve these problems. For instance, the problems in the SADC region are related to droughts and water scarcity, but in Europe most issues have to do with flooding and water quality. In both regions, however, framework agreements made sense in defining the problems encountered in these regions and in propelling action for the future.[156]

With the exception of some agreements (i.e., the 2002 Incomati-Maputo Agreement and the EU Water Framework Directive), most agreements are still based on supply management of water resources rather than on demand management. Regulating water quantity, by regulating demand through pricing or through other market-based mechanisms, is rarely mentioned in international agreements. Actually, some agreements are based on the possibility of making more water available through development projects. The Jordan-Yarmouk Agreement (between Israel and Jordan) is notable in this respect because it provides for more water for Jordan but fails to specify where this water is to come from.

5.1. Africa

Nile

Nile is referred to as the longest river of the world. Its major source is Lake Victoria in East Central Africa, Uganda. From there, what has been called the White Nile flows into Sudan, where it meets the Blue Nile. Subsequently, the river flows into Ethiopia and Egypt and from there into the Mediterranean Sea. From Lake Victoria to the Mediterranean Sea, the length of the river is 5,584 km (3,470 miles). The Nile has been known since ancient times as the river that fueled the growth of the ancient Egyptian civilization. Today, the Nile continues to contribute to the agricultural development of Egypt, but upstream states have started to assert their claims. States that are demanding equitable utilization of the Nile waters include Burundi, Congo, Eritrea, Ethiopia, Kenya, Rwanda, Sudan, Tanzania, and Uganda. Most of these states face serious domestic problems, such as poverty, political upheavals, and separatist movements. For instance, Eritrea became a state after an ugly war with Ethiopia. Sudan is still marred by a number of political problems and the regime has been infamous for violations of human rights. These states, because of their internal institutional problems, have had a difficult time in inducing Egypt – a more politically stable and economically independent country – to subscribe to a binding regime for the fair allocation of water resources in the region.

---

[156] Hubert H.G. Savenije & Pieter van der Zaag, Conceptual Framework for the Management of Shared River Basins with Special Reference to the SADC and EU, 2 Water Policy 9 (2000).

The first treaty to define the utilization of the Nile was a 1902 treaty between Great Britain and Ethiopia. According to Article III of the treaty, Ethiopia is not to construct or allow to be constructed in its territory any work on the Nile except in agreement with Britain and Sudan.[157]

The 1929 treaty between Egypt and Sudan (ruled at the time by Great Britain) provided for allocation of water resources based on what seem to be blatantly inequitable shares: four BCM/year[158] were allocated to Sudan and forty-eight BCM/year were allocated to Egypt. Egypt acquired inspection rights at the Sennar Dam, and it was agreed that no works would be developed along the river that would threaten Egypt's interests. In the exchange of notes between Egypt and the United Kingdom, Egypt specifically refers to its "natural and historical rights in the waters of the Nile and its requirements for agricultural extension"[159] and the need to safeguard its interests. It is explicitly provided that unless there is an agreement with the Egyptian government:

> no irrigation or power works or measures are to be constructed or taken on the River Nile and its branches, or on the lakes from which it flows, so far as all these are in the Sudan or in countries under British administration, which would, in such a manner as to entail any prejudice to the interests of Egypt, either reduce the quantity of water arriving in Egypt, or modify the date of its arrival, or lower its level.[160]

Egypt's coriparians, which were under British administration when the 1929 treaty was signed, renounced the treaty following their independence. They have been hesitant, however, to openly engage in action that could directly challenge Egypt's interests.

Despite what seems to be an inequitable allocation of water, the 1929 agreement between Egypt and Sudan was prompted by a realization that Sudan's water needs had to be addressed. It was realized by Great Britain that water quantities greater than those that had been utilized so far by Sudan were necessary for the future development of Sudan.[161] A Commission was established in 1925 by the United Kingdom and Egypt to examine the allocation issue. The commission issued a detailed report on the apportionment of Nile waters. The commission concluded, *inter alia*, that it: "felt that in the circumstances it was impossible either, on the one hand, to postpone indefinitely all access in the Sudan, or, on the other, to damage seriously ... the basin of Upper Egypt." It was decided that the development of Sudan should not

---

[157] Art. III, Treaties between Great Britain and Ethiopia, relative to the frontiers between Anglo-Egyptian Soudan, Ethiopia, and Erythroea, May, 15, 1902 available online at http://ocid.nasce.org (Transboundary Freshwater Dispute Database). The Transboundary Freshwater Dispute Database is one of the databases available by the Oregon Coalition of Interdisciplinary Databases (OCID) and the Northwest Alliance for Computational Science and Engineering (NACSE). It is hosted by Oregon State University.

[158] BCM = billion cubic meters. One BCM equals one thousand mcm (million cubic meters).

[159] Art. (2), Exchange of Notes between His Majesty's Government in the United Kingdom and the Egyptian Government in regard to the Use of the Waters of the River Nile for Irrigation Purposes, Note by Mohamed Mahmoud Pasha to Lord Lloyd, May 7, 1929, available online at http://ocid.nacse .org.

[160] Art. 4(b), *id.*

[161] Art. 2, *id.*

be curtailed but only "to the point of setting a limit to the extent and rate of this development."[162]

After independence, Sudan declared that it was not bound by the 1929 agreement. Egypt at the time was eager to proceed with the construction of the Aswan High Dam. Because of its dispute with Sudan, however, Egypt was not able to obtain financing from the World Bank.[163] The first negotiations with Sudan took place in 1954, but they broke off, resuming in 1956. It was the coming to power of a military regime more friendly toward Egypt that helped to push through the negotiations. According to the Egyptian negotiating position, the Nile waters, which were estimated to be at eighty BMC/year were to be divided as follows: sixty-two BCM/year for Egypt and eight BCM/year for Sudan (assuming ten BCM/year evaporation losses allocated equally). Sudan's position was articulated as follows: total water in the Nile was estimated to be eighty-four BCM/year, of which fifty-nine BCM/year would be allocated to Egypt and fifteen BCM/year to Sudan (and evaporation losses of ten BCM/year to be subtracted from Egypt's share).

The 1959 agreement between Egypt and Sudan[164] seems to have adopted a middle position by assigning 55.5 BCM/year to Egypt and 18.5 BCM/year to Sudan. It is remarkable to note that Sudan is allocated more water than what it asked for when negotiating its position.

The agreement gave Egypt the green light to construct the Aswan High Dam (Sudd el Aali Dam) and – given the increased water flow expected from the Aswan and the Roseires Dam to be constructed by Sudan – allocates water as follows: forty-eight BCM/year for Egypt and four BCM/year for Sudan (as allocated in the 1929 treaty), to which are added 7.5 BCM/year for Egypt and 14.5 BCM/year for Sudan. This makes for a final allocation of 55.5 BCM/year to Egypt and 18.5 BCM/year to Sudan.[165]

The allocation of water in the 1929 treaty negotiated between Great Britain and Egypt was 12:1. The allocation of water in the 1959 treaty negotiated between Sudan and Egypt seems to be more equitable, at the ratio of 3:1. Furthermore, Egypt agrees to pay compensation to Sudan for the destruction of existing property resulting from the construction of Aswan canal,[166] and Sudan undertakes the obligation to transfer the population affected by the stored water at Aswan.[167] To prevent evaporative losses of waters in swamps, the parties agree further to undertake works, the costs of which are to be shared equally between the parties. It is provided that Egypt could start unilaterally those works and, when Sudan is ready to utilize its share of water, it must pay Egypt "a share of all the expenses in the same ratio as the Sudan's share in benefit."[168] The agreement provides for a loan of water from Sudan to

[162] Para. 38, Report of the Nile Commission (1925). The report of the Nile Commission was incorporated in the 1929 agreement between Egypt and Sudan.

[163] McCaffrey, *supra* note 26, at 242.

[164] Agreement between the Government of United Arab Republic and the Republic of Sudan for the Full Utilization of the Nile Waters, Nov. 8, 1959, reprinted in 453 UNTS 51, available online at http://ocid.nacse.org.

[165] Art. First; Art. Second (4), *id.*

[166] Art. Second (6), *id.* See also Annex II, *id.*

[167] Art. Second (7), *id.*

[168] Art. Third (2), *id.*

Egypt of fifteen hundred MCM/year in order to enable Egypt to proceed "with her planned programmes for Agricultural Expansion."[169] A Permanent Joint Technical Commission is established that is to be formed by equal number of members from both parties. One of the functions of the commission is to allocate water in times of water scarcity. During periods of water scarcity, the commission is charged with the requirement "of devising a fair arrangement for the two Republics to follow."[170] If other riparian states are to claim a share of Nile waters, Sudan and Egypt have agreed to adopt "a unified view."[171] If it becomes necessary to allocate waters to other states water to be allocated "shall be deducted from the shares of the two Republics in equal parts . . ."[172]

It has been claimed that the 1959 Egypt-Sudan Agreement falls more within the lines of equitable utilization as articulated in 1997 UN Watercourses Convention. The 1929 Egypt-Great Britain Agreement is more in accordance with the principle of established/historical rights. Some commentators have characterized the 1959 agreement as a needs-based agreement.[173] The allocations were decided on the basis of local needs and, specifically, agriculture. Egypt argued for a larger share of waters because of its irrigation and extensive agriculture. The agreement even includes the innovative element of the provision of a water loan from Sudan to Egypt because Sudan could not consume all the water allocated to it by the agreement. The focus of the agreement is still, however, on the agricultural expansion of Egypt, whereas Sudan's development seems to be placed further into the future. Today, a politically unstable Sudan is unlikely to prioritize fair water allocations.[174]

The 1959 agreement incorporates historical uses and allocates additional water based on development needs. The agreement contains innovative elements such as: allowing Egypt to proceed unilaterally with Nile projects but providing Sudan with the possibility to acquire up to 50 percent of the water in the future (provided it is willing to pay for 50 percent of the costs). It is remarkable that the agreement has endured since 1959 and that, despite the constant turbulence in the region, none of the parties has repudiated it.

The agreement is not inclusive of all riparian states. States that were not included in the agreement repudiated the agreement after their independence from Great Britain.[175] Ethiopia has repudiated a 1902 agreement according to which, it was not allowed to undertake works along the Nile River without concluding a prior agreement with Great Britain and Sudan.[176]

---

[169] Annex I, *id.*

[170] Art. Fourth, *id.*

[171] Art. Fifth (1), *id.*

[172] Art. Fifth (2), *id.*

[173] Wolf (Conflict and Cooperation), *supra* note 37, at 9.

[174] Olaf Westermann, Interstate Collaboration, Local Conflicts and Public Participation in the Nile River Basin, Working Paper no 2004/4, in Proceedings of the International Conference, "From Water-wars to Water-riots? Lessons from Transboundary Water Management" 113, 122, Copenhagen, 2003, Danish Institute for International Studies (DIIS) (Jannik Boesen & Helle Munk Ravnborg, eds., 2004) [hereinafter from Water-wars to Water-riots].

[175] McCaffrey, *supra* note 26, at 246.

[176] *Id.* at 244–45.

More recent agreements[177] concluded among coriparians in the Nile are the Framework Agreement between Egypt and Ethiopia on cooperation,[178] the agreement on the management of resources of the Lake Victoria,[179] and the Convention on the Establishment of the Lake Victoria Fisheries Organization.[180]

The 1993 agreement between Egypt and Ethiopia does not provide specific details of cooperation between the state parties to the agreement. It provides, however, that each party must refrain from engaging in any activity that may cause "appreciable harm" to the interests of the other party.[181] It is prescribed that the use of Nile waters is to be worked out "on the basis of the rules and principles of international law."[182] It is interesting that environmental considerations are included in the agreement because parties refer to "the necessity of the conservation and protection of the Nile waters" and agree to cooperate "through comprehensive and integrated development schemes."[183]

The 1994 Lake Victoria Fisheries Organization was established by the governments of Kenya, Uganda, and Tanzania. The purpose of this organization is to provide the institutional forum for the management of fisheries resources in the lake. The 1994 Lake Victoria Agreement on the management of common resources attempts to introduce the concept of integrated management.[184] Fisheries management[185] and land-use management are specifically addressed.[186]

The allocation of Nile waters has remained the sore point in the region for decades. In 1999, the coriparians in the region (Burundi, Congo, Egypt, Ethiopia,

---

[177] A series of agreements were concluded during colonial times with regard to the construction of Owen Fall Dams in Uganda.

    See Exchange of Notes Constituting an Agreement between the Government of the United Kingdom of Great Britain and Northern Ireland and the Government of Egypt regarding the Construction of the Owen Falls Dam, Uganda, May 30, May 31, 1949, reprinted in 226 UNTS 274, available online at http://ocid.nasce.org.

    It is provided that this agreement is executed within "the spirit of the Nile Waters Agreement of 1929" and that the Uganda Electricity Board can take action with regard to the Owen Falls Dam provided that such action "does not entail any prejudice to the interests of Egypt in accordance with the Nile Waters Agreement of 1929." During the construction of the dam, the interests of Egypt are to be represented by an Egyptian resident engineer.

    See also Exchange of Notes Constituting an Agreement between the Government of the United Kingdom of Great Britain and Northern Ireland and the Government of Egypt regarding the Construction of the Owen Falls Dam in Uganda, July 16, 1952, reprinted in 226 UNTS 288, available online at http://ocid.nasce.org . According to this agreement, Egypt agrees to undertake a portion of the costs for the construction of the dam that would be needed to use Lake Victoria for water storage. Egypt agrees further to pay the Uganda Electricity Board £980,000 for the loss of hydroelectric power.

[178] Framework for General Co-operation between the Arab Republic of Egypt and Ethiopia, July 1, 1993 [hereinafter 1993 Agreement Egypt-Ethiopia].

[179] Agreement to Initiate a Program to Strengthen Regional Coordination in Management of Resources of Lake Victoria, Aug. 5, 1994, available online at http://ocid.nasce.org.

[180] Convention for the Establishment of the Lake Victoria Fisheries Organization, June 30, 1994, reprinted in 36 ILM 667 (1997).

[181] Art. 5, 1993 Agreement Egypt-Ethiopia, *supra* note 178.

[182] Art. 4, *id.*

[183] Art. 6, *id.*

[184] Attachment 1 (Components and Preparatory Activities for a Lake Victoria Environmental Management Program), para.2, 1994 Lake Victoria Agreement, *supra* note 179.

[185] Component 1 (Fisheries Management and Control of Water Hyacinth and Other Invasive Weeds), *id.*

[186] Component 2 (Management of Water Quality and Land Use (Including Wetlands)), *id.*

Eritrea, Rwanda, Sudan, Tanzania, and Uganda) have spearheaded the Nile Basin Initiative (NBI) and have agreed on a common vision:

> To achieve sustainable socio-economic development through the equitable utilization of, and benefit from, the common Nile Basin water resources.[187]

The Nile Basin initiative has been supported by international donors, such as the World Bank and the UNDP. Countries have agreed on a number of projects in the region totaling a potential $2 billion in investment. In 2004, the Nile Transboundary Environmental Action Project was launched comprised of eight basin-wide projects. The purpose of the project, which is to be financed by the GEF, the UNDP, and the Canadian International Development Agency (CIDA), is to strengthen regional institutions, increase environmental education and awareness, support land, forest and water conservation, foster biodiversity protection, and provide for water quality monitoring on a basin-wide basis.

Coriparians of the Nile have proceeded with subregional programs, for instance, the Eastern Nile Subsidiary Action Program (ENSAP) bringing together Egypt, Ethiopia, and Sudan, and the Nile Equatorial Lakes Subsidiary Action Program (NELSAP) bringing together Burundi, Congo, Kenya, Rwanda, Tanzania, Uganda, Egypt, and Sudan. The purpose of subregional programs is to reduce the complexity and transaction costs involved in negotiating simultaneously with nine riparians. It is a divide-and-conquer strategy that puts momentarily the issue of integrated river basin management aside in order to achieve some level of minimum cooperation. The Nile Basin initiative has established its own institutional framework with the Council of Ministers (Nile-COM), a Secretariat (Nile-SEC), and a Technical Advisory Committee (Nile-TAC).[188]

At this point, many proposals have been put on the table regarding the integrated management of the Nile. But none of the proposals has reached the stage of actual execution. Ethiopia and Egypt need to engage in negotiations to redefine water allocations. Ethiopia provides 86 percent of the waters of the Nile that flow into Egypt. Ethiopia wants to increase the volume of water it retains in order to abate serious problems of soil erosion. Recent proposals that involve the unilateral development of the Nile, through a series of micro-dams in Ethiopia, and the New Valley Project in Egypt are likely to increase tensions in the region.

Tanzania reportedly has launched a project to build a pipeline to withdraw water from Lake Victoria without consulting with Sudan and Egypt.[189] In 2002, Egypt threatened to take action against Sudan, Ethiopia, and Uganda for illegally tapping the waters of the Nile. Egypt blamed the low water level of the river on hydroelectricity plants in Uganda and Ethiopia and on Sudan's illegal taking of water.[190]

The outcome of the Nile initiative is difficult to predict. Some international commentators have claimed that the Nile initiative is an example that international

---

[187] Joint Statement of the Nile Basin Council of Ministers, Mar. 18, 2004, available online at http://www.nilebasin.org.

[188] For more details about the Nile Basin Initiative, see *id.*

[189] Faustine Rwambali, Tanzania Ignores Nile Treaty, Starts Victoria Water Project, AllPuntland.com, Feb. 13, 2004.

[190] Nile Waters at Record Lows, Egypt Irked, African Environmental News Service, Nov. 15, 2002.

law matters in the relations among the coriparians.[191] The new agreement between Ethiopia and Egypt, for instance, explicitly refers to the no harm principle and the importance of the rules of international law.[192] The interpretation that seems to have been endorsed by the Nile parties with regard to the principle of equitable utilization is that prior uses matter and that further allocations can be made on the basis of need. It is seems that the principle of no appreciable harm, that favors downstream states, is likely to play a significant role in the further development of the regime. Given the dire situation of the many countries in the region, it has been suggested that one of the focal areas of the Nile regime should be the reduction of poverty through development.[193]

SADC Region

The Zambezi River agreements have been the regional arrangements in Southern Africa that have prepared the ground for the comprehensive Southern African Development Community (SADC) regime. This regime covers all shared watercourses in the SADC. The Zambezi River regime seems to be more in tune with the principle of equitable allocation of river resources conceived as a fifty-fifty allocation among equally positioned states. The Zambezi regime is more in tune with a modern position in water management that water quality is as important as water quantity. The regime was launched by a bilateral agreement on sharing hydropower. It was followed by a more comprehensive agreement on the quality of Zambezi ecosystem resources but it was barely executed. Despite its shortcomings, the Zambezi regime is considered the precursor of the SADC regime.

The 1987 agreement between Zambia and Zimbabwe[194] deals with the utilization of hydropower and provides unequivocally that the power from hydroelectric dams will be equally shared. The agreement establishes the institutional framework for its administration comprised of a council,[195] an authority, the Zambezi River Authority (which is replacing the Central African Power Corporation),[196] and a board of directors, which is to be responsible for the policy, management, and control of the authority.[197] The purpose of the authority is, *inter alia*, to undertake studies to determine the desirability of new dams on the Zambezi River. The construction of such dams is subject to approval by the council.[198] The agreement provides explicitly that parties must ensure the "efficient and equitable" allocation of resources.[199] Article 23 provides some of the specifics of equitable allocation such as: "States

---

[191]   Jutta Brunnée et al., The Changing Nile Basin Regime: Does Law Matter?, 43 Harvard International law Journal 105 (2002).

[192]   See *supra* note 178.

[193]   See *supra* note 187.

[194]   Agreement between the Republic of Zimbabwe and the Republic of Zambia Concerning the Utilization of the Zambezi River, July 28, 1987, available online at http://ocid.nacse.org. The agreement replaced earlier agreements concluded in 1963, 1977, 1985 and 1986.

[195]   Art. 4, *id.* The Council is a Council of Ministers: two ministers come from Zambia and two ministers come from Zimbabwe.

[196]   Art. 7, *id.*

[197]   Art. 8, *id.*

[198]   Art. 9, *id.*

[199]   Art. 18, *id.*

undertake to share all the available energy from the Kariba Dam equally."[200] It is provided, however, that water allocated annually by the authority that is not utilized would be deemed forfeited.[201] The parties agree to share the energy from future dams provided that they pay their share of construction costs. If a state bears more than half of construction costs, the other party has the right to make a further contribution, not exceeding half of the costs. The other party, thus, becomes entitled to the portion of the energy corresponding to this additional contribution.[202] Parties can sell portions of their energy and, in the event a party wishes to sell its energy surplus, the other party has the right of first refusal.[203]

The 1987 Agreement on the Environmentally Sound Management of the Common Zambezi River[204] is more inclusive in terms of the countries involved[205] and in terms of the issues it addresses. The agreement was adopted under the auspices of the SADC. The purpose of the agreement is to establish an Action Plan for the Environmentally Sound Management of the Common Zambezi River System, the Zambezi Action Plan (ZACPLAN).[206] Both the agreement and the Action Plan emerged from consultations between the UNEP and the SADC countries in early 1984. The quick adoption of the agreement has been credited to the leadership role played by the UNEP.[207] This was the time during which South Africa was under the apartheid regime, and the agreement was viewed as an effort to unite the majority of the SADC countries against South Africa.[208]

The agreement sets up an institutional framework for its functioning that includes an Intergovernmental Monitoring and Coordinating Committee, a trust fund, and national focal points.[209] The development of an independent secretariat was resisted during the agreement negotiations, as certain countries insisted that the existing SADC institutions undertake the secretariat functions.[210] The Action Plan provides for environmental assessment, environmental management, and environmental legislation.[211] The Action Plan is conservative in its articulation of the goals of environmental management. It is noted that "such management should take account of the assimilative capacity of the environment, the development goals as defined by national authorities and the economic feasibility of their implementation."[212] Overall, the plan notes the deficiencies in the management of river resources, including lack of adequate drinking water supply and proper sanitation facilities, degradation of natural resource base, soil erosion, and inadequate health education.[213] The

---

[200] Art. 23(1) and Annexure II, *id.*

[201] *Id.*

[202] Art. 23(2), *id.*

[203] Art. 23(3), *id.*

[204] Agreement on the Action Plan for the Environmentally Sound Management of the Common Zambezi River System, May 28, 1987, reprinted in 27 ILM 1109 (1988), available online at http://ocid.nasce.org [hereinafter Zambezi Agreement].

[205] Botswana, Mozambique, Tanzania, Zambia, and Zimbabwe are signatory states of Zambezi Agreement, *id.*

[206] Art. 1 & Annex I, *id.*

[207] Mikiyasu Nakayama, Politics Behind Zambezi Action Plan, 1 Water Policy 397, 406 (1998).

[208] *Id.* at 399–400.

[209] See arts. 2 & 3, Annex II, Zambezi Agreement, *supra* note 204.

[210] Nakayama, *supra* note 207, at 404.

[211] Para. 20, Annex I. The Action Plan is attached to the 1987 Agreement as Annex I, see *supra* note 204.

[212] Para. 29, *id.*

[213] Para. 14, *id.*

Action Plan emphasizes that the major stumbling block in the management of natural resources is the lack of information about the environment and its resources.[214] The plan proposes the adoption of the concept of integrated river basin management in the region.[215] The Action Plan covers funding required for the implementation of phase I of the plan and, explicitly, provides that contributions to the total cost of the plan must be equally shared among all participating countries.[216]

The Zambezi Agreement and the Action Plan were not very successful. Some countries resented the anti–South African underpinnings of the agreement as they contemplated water sharing schemes with South Africa.[217] The reaction from international donors also was tepid, and the agreement and Action Plan did not really get implemented.[218] The agreement has been credited, however, for paving the road to the 1995 SADC Agreement.

The 1995 SADC Protocol[219] is clearly an attempt to merge into a single protocol the concept of integrated river management and equitable allocation of resources. The agreement refers in its title to the "shared watercourse systems" and the issue of equitable resource allocation permeates many of the articles of the agreement.

The 1995 Protocol was signed by many more states than the 1987 Zambezi Agreement on its adoption[220] and is concerned with the shared watercourse systems of the SADC region. The SADC Agreement is the umbrella agreement under which other agreements, including the Zambezi Agreement and the Incomati-Maputo Agreement, fall.

The protocol includes a number of principles that must be followed by member states. One such principle is the principle "of community of interests in the equitable utilisation"[221] of water systems and related resources that combines aptly in one phrase the language used by the Permanent Court of International Justice[222] and the terminology of 1997 Watercourses Convention.[223] In order to achieve equitable utilization in an optimal manner, the following factors must be taken into account: (1) geographical, climatic, hydrological, and other factors of a natural character; (2) social and economic needs; (3) the effects of the use of the watercourse by one state on another state; (4) existing and potential uses of the watercourse; and (5) agreed standards and guidelines.[224]

Other principles that the protocol establishes are:

- the maintenance of a proper balance between resource development for the achievement of a higher standard of living and conservation and enhancement of the environment;[225]

---

[214] Para. 17, *id.*

[215] Para. 24, *id.*

[216] See Appendix I & Appendix II, Action Plan, *id.*

[217] Nakayama, *supra* note 207, at 406.

[218] *Id.*

[219] Protocol on Shared Watercourse Systems in the Southern African Development Community (SADC), Aug. 28, 1995, reprinted 34 ILM 854 (1995) [hereinafter 1995 SADC Protocol].

[220] Signatory countries include: Lesotho, South Africa, Mozambique, Tanzania, Zimbabwe, Botswana, Malawi, Namibia, Swaziland, and Zambia.

[221] Art. 2(2), 1995 SADC Protocol, *supra* note 219.

[222] *Oder* and *Meuse* cases, see Chapter 1.

[223] Art. 2(2), 1995 SADC Protocol, *supra* note 219.

[224] Art. 2(6) & (7), *id.*

[225] Art. 2(3), *id.*

- the provision of permits for the discharge of wastes into waters that would be issued only if a state determines that the discharges will not have adverse effects on the watercourse system;[226]
- notification in cases of emergency;[227]
- the inviolable character of watercourse systems and installations in times of international and internal conflicts.[228]

The agreement provides, specifically, for the establishment of river basin management institutions[229] and for the objectives[230] and functions of such institutions.[231] River basin institutions are to develop monitoring systems, to promote equitable utilization, to formulate strategies for development, and to promote the execution of integrated water resource development plans.[232]

The 1995 Protocol was amended in 2000.[233] The amendment was necessary in order to adapt the Protocol to the 1997 UN Watercourses Convention. Consequently, the title to the agreement does not refer any longer to "watercourse systems" but simply to "watercourses" with the goal to advance the SADC agenda of regional integration and poverty alleviation.[234] Many of the provisions of the 2000 Protocol are identical to the provisions of the 1997 Watercourses Convention. The 2000 version of the protocol expands on the provisions of the 1995 Protocol with more specific requirements. For instance, equitable utilization is analyzed in more detail[235] when reference is made to the equitable and reasonable use of a watercourse. Three additional factors are added for the determination of equitable utilization that are similar to the factors mentioned in the 1997 Watercourses Convention.[236] The protocol further provides, in a manner similar to the 1997 Watercourses Convention, that in determining equitable and reasonable use, "all relevant factors

---

[226] Art. 2(8), *id.*

[227] Art. 2(9)–(10), *id.*

[228] Art. 2(13), *id.*

[229] Art. 3, *id.*

[230] Art. 4, *id.*

[231] Art. 5, *id.*

[232] Art. 4, *id.*

[233] Revised Protocol on Shared Watercourses in the Southern African Development Community (SADC), Aug. 7, 2000, reprinted in 40 ILM 321 (2001). The protocol was signed by Angola, Botswana, Congo, Lesotho, Malawi, Mauritius, Mozambique, Namibia, Seychelles, South Africa, Swaziland, Tanzania, Zambia, and Zimbabwe. The protocol was ratified in 2002.

[234] Art. 2, *id.*

[235] Article 3(7) provides:

> 3(7)(a) "Watercourse states shall in their respective territories utilise a shared watercourse in an equitable and reasonable manner. In particular, a shared watercourse shall be used and developed by Watercourse States with a view to attain optimal and sustainable utilization thereof and benefits therefrom, taking into account the interests of the Watercourse States concerned, consistent with adequate protection of the watercourse for the benefit of present and future generations."
>
> 3(7)(b) Watercourse states shall participate in the use, development and protection of a shared watercourse in an equitable and reasonable manner. Such participation, includes both the right to utilise the watercourse and the duty to co-operate in the protection and development thereof, as provided in this Protocol." *Id.*

[236] Art. 3(8)(a), *id.*

are to be considered together and conclusion must be reached on the basis of the whole."[237]

The protocol addresses the obligation not to cause significant harm in a similar fashion as the 1997 UN Watercourses Convention does. State parties must utilize their watercourses in a manner that would prevent causing "significant harm to other Watercourse States."[238] When significant harm is caused to other watercourse states the state that caused the harm must take appropriate measures to eliminate or mitigate such harm and, when appropriate, "to discuss the question of compensation."[239] With regard to natural or legal persons who have suffered or are under a serious threat of suffering significant transboundary harm as a result of activities related to a shared watercourse, the protocol provides as follows: the watercourse state must not discriminate – on the basis of nationality or residence or place where the injury occurred – in granting to persons harmed access to its judicial proceedings and a right to claim compensation or any other sort of relief.[240]

Although the 1995 SADC Protocol provided for a mere requirement of notification in cases of emergency, the 2000 SADC Protocol provides for specific requirements of notification, in line with the 1997 UN Watercourses Convention, in case of planned measures that may have *significant* adverse effects on other watercourse states. The notification requirements are specific with regard to:

- what is to be included in the notification;
- the period required for a reply to the notification;
- the procedure to follow in case there is no reply;
- the procedure to follow in case a watercourse state needs to adopt urgently a planned measure (to protect public health, safety, or other equally important interests) and the proper notification path cannot be followed.[241]

Finally, the protocol includes specific environmental provisions[242] and the institutional framework for its implementation. A number of institutions are devoted to the implementation of the protocol including the Committee of Water Ministers, the Committee of Water Senior Officials, the Water Sector Coordinating Unit and the Water Resources Technical Committee and subcommittees.[243] State parties could enter into agreements for the implementation of the provisions of the protocol in a specific water basin.[244]

The adoption of the 1995 and 2000 SADC protocols was one of first steps needed for the spearheading of water management in the SADC region. As mentioned earlier, the SADC regime is the umbrella regime for a number of other agreements concluded in the region including the Incomati-Maputo Agreement examined later. Much needs to be accomplished, however, in terms of the alignment of the SADC Agreement with the national laws of SADC members. Practical solutions must be

---

[237] Art. 3(8)(b), *id.*
[238] Art. 3(10)(a), *id.*
[239] Art. 3(10)(b), *id.*
[240] Art. 10(c), *id.*
[241] Art. 4(1), *id.*
[242] Art. 4(2), *id.*
[243] Art. 5, *id.*
[244] Art. 6, *id.*

found for a number of issues, namely: how to weigh existing uses over future uses; how to compensate subsistence farmers who are *de facto* sidelined by new uses; what water transfers are legitimate and who should be compensated and how; and how to deal with conflict resolution in the region.[245]

Incomati–Maputo

The Incomati River Basin Agreement falls under the umbrella of the SADC Agreement. The agreement incorporates some of the most recent developments in international environmental law as it was adopted at the time of the WSSD. Incomati is one of the rivers that was included in the attempts at regional integration in the Southern African region through the "peace park" concept.[246]

The Incomati and Maputo River basins are managed as one entity because the same riparians share both the basins. The Incomati River is more developed than the Maputo River and the Incomati–Maputo basin is the smallest one in South Africa.[247] South Africa, as the most economically developed state in the region, has been instrumental in influencing the development of watercourse law in the region. The South African approach to river management defies, in some ways, integrated river basin mangement in which a single hydrological unit is proposed as a basis for management.[248] The South African approach has relied, instead, on interbasin transfers (IBT) of waters.[249] From the perspective of interbasin water transfers, both

---

[245] Joanne Heyink-Leestemaker, An Analysis of the New National and Sub National Water Laws in Southern Africa: Gaps between the UN Convention, the SADC Protocol and National Legal Systems in South Africa, Swaziland and Mozambique, Institutional Support Task Team of the Shared River Initiative on the Incomati River, Southern Africa (2000).

[246] The peace park concept involves the merging of national parks in the three countries located in the Incomati and Limpopo river basins: the Gaza Park in Mozambique, the Kruger Park in South Africa, and the Ghonarezhou Park in Zimbabwe. It is hoped that merging national parks in the region would precipitate regional integration. See Álvaro Carmo Vaz & Pieter van der Zaag, Sharing the Incomati Waters: Cooperation and Competition in the Balance, UNESCO, Technical Documents in Hydrology, PCCP Series, No. 14, at 13 (2003). For further details on the national park concept and the concept of transboundary parks, see Chapter 7, Section 1.2.

[247] Another basin is the Orange River Basin that is shared between South Africa and Namibia. The basin was under a number of bilateral agreements before the signing in 2000 of the ORASECOM Agreement that established the Orange-Senqu River Commission (ORASECOM). The agreement recognizes the 1997 UN Watercourses Treaty. An interesting feature of the agreement is that it includes Botswana as a signatory despite the fact that Botswana contributes no water to the basin and makes no use of water from the basin. This is obviously a result of the friendly relationships between Botswana and South Africa. The agreement grants negotiating privileges to Botswana. Botswana could grant concessions to the other riparians in this regime in turn for concessions in regimes where it holds more interests (e.g., in the Limpopo Basin). See Turton, *supra* note 38, at 207–13.

    The Limpopo River Basin is a highly developed basin with forty-three dams (three in Botswana, two in Mozambique, twenty-six in South Africa, and twelve in Zimbabwe). The basin is the donor and recipient of many interbasin water transfers. The first agreement to include all the riparians in the region was signed in 1986 by Botswana, Mozambique, Zimbabwe, and South Africa and established the Limpopo Basin Permanent Technical Committee (LBPTC). But the committee did not function well because of the tensions between the parties. As a result, South Africa concluded a number of bilateral agreements with Swaziland. *Id.* at 220–21.

[248] *Id.* at 188.

[249] *Id.* at 185. Interbasin water transfers between surplus Water Management Areas (WMAs) and deficit WMAs is part of South Africa's National Water Resource Strategy.

the Incomati and the Maputo Rivers were underdeveloped at time of the adoption of the agreement.

The Incomati River is the second most important river in Mozambique after the Limpopo River. And both the Incomati and Maputo rivers are very important to another riparian, Swaziland.[250]

The development of the Incomati/Maputo regime has gone through a tumultuous process. Mozambique sabotaged the apartheid regime in South Africa and this affected its interbasin relationship with South Africa, an upstream state with control of the water flow downstream. By contrast, Swaziland has benefited from its friendly relationship with South Africa.

A 1983 agreement concluded after the colonial period established a Tripartite Permanent Technical Committee (TPTC).[251] The committee did not function as planned and an attempt was made to revive the committee in 1991 in the Piggs Peak Agreement.[252] The Piggs Peak Agreement was not successful in resurrecting the committee. It was important, however, in launching the Joint Incomati Basin Study (JIBS),[253] the purpose of which was to provide the data for a water sharing agreement among the states. The JIBS concluded that if developments planned by South Africa and Swaziland were put into effect, the water available for the development of Mozambique would be inadequate.[254] Mozambique, subsequently, withdrew its support from the study. South Africa did not abide with its obligation in the agreement to provide two cubic meters of water per second ("averaged over a cycle of three days") to Mozambique.[255] Given the failure of multilateral arrangements, South Africa entered into a bilateral agreement with Swaziland that established a Joint Water Commission.[256] But that commission was ineffectual.

The demise of the apartheid regime in South Africa assisted in the resumption of friendlier relationships among the coriparians. The reduction of tensions between coriparians, in combination with the impetus provided by the WSSD (that took place in South Africa), led to the development of the Tripartite Interim Incomati-Maputo Agreement (TIIMA).[257]

---

[250] *Id.* at 228–31.

[251] Agreement between South Africa, Swaziland and Mozambique relative to the Establishment of a Tripartite Permanent Technical Committee, Feb. 17, 1983, available online at http://ocid.nasce. org.

[252] Tripartite Permanent Technical Committee Ministerial Meeting of Ministers Responsible for Water Affairs, Feb. 15, 1991, available online at http://ocid.nacse.org [hereinafter Piggs Peak Agreement].

[253] Section 1, *id.*

[254] Turton, *supra* note 38, at 236.

[255] Section 3(a), Piggs Peak Agreement, *supra* note 252. See also Vaz, *supra* note 246, at 42–43.

[256] Art. 1, Treaty on the Establishment and Functioning of the Joint Water Commission between the Government of the Republic of South Africa and the Government of the Kingdom of Swaziland, Mar. 13, 1992, available online at http://ocid.nacse.org. Another bilateral agreement between South Africa and Swaziland that established the Komati Basin Water Authority (KOBWA) responsible for the development of Komati River Basin Development Project was more successful and assisted in the construction of the Maguga Dam in Swaziland. See Turton, *supra* note 38, at 235.

[257] Tripartite Interim Agreement between the Republic of Mozambique and the Republic of South Africa and the Kingdom of Swaziland for Co-operation on the Protection and Sustainable Utilisation of the Water Resources of the Incomati and Maputo Watercourses, Aug. 29, 2002 [hereinafter 2002 Interim Agreement].

The TIIMA revives the TPTC[258] and it is based on the hydrological data collected during JIBS process. From the perspective of conflict resolution, the agreement guarantees the water rights of Mozambique, as parties recognize, in particular:

> The strategic importance to Mozambique of augmenting the water supplies to the city of Maputo and its metropolitan area from one or both of the Incomati and Maputo watercourses.[259]

Annex I of the TIIMA provides for the specifics of the water allocation among the three countries.[260] The agreement provides additionally for the water requirements of ecosystems and for water conservation.[261] In what could be viewed as a pure allocation agreement, state parties have included plenty of environmental provisions. For instance, article 6 is devoted to the "protection of the environment." Article 7 is concerned with sustainable utilization and provides that countries are entitled to "optimal and sustainable utilisation of and benefits from the water resources" taking into account "the interests of the other Parties concerned, consistent with adequate protection of the watercourses for the benefit of present and future generations."[262] The principles on which the agreement is based are influenced both by environmental prerogatives and the 1997 UN Watercourses Convention. The parties decided, for instance, to adhere to the principles of "equitable and reasonable utilisation and participation," "cooperation," and "sustainable utilization."[263] Provisions also are included to address "significant transboundary impacts"[264] and "capacity building."[265] Unlike most allocation agreements – which are concerned with the management of water supply – the TIIMA makes reference to demand-led water management by including references to water conservation measures and pricing policies.[266]

Another important element of the agreement, and an ingredient for the successful functioning of international watercourse regimes, is the institutionalization of exchange of and access to information.[267] This exchange of information would be crucial within the context of the TIIMA because, as mentioned even in the title of the agreement, this is to be an interim agreement between the parties. The collection of data is, therefore, necessary for the conclusion of a permanent agreement at a later date.[268] The collection of accurate information during the execution of this agreement could play a pivotal role in the process of allocation of water resources in the region.

Regarding the issue of water allocation, the most innovative element of the agreement is that it overcame a potential allocation conflict by providing for a series of

---

[258] Art. 5, *id.*

[259] Art. 9(4)(a), *id.*

[260] See also art. 6, *id.*

[261] Arts. 7–8, Annex I, *id.*

[262] Art. 7(1). See also art. 8 on "water quality and prevention of pollution," *id.*

[263] Art. 3, *id.*

[264] Art. 13, *id.*

[265] Art. 14, *id.*

[266] Annex I, art. 8, *id.*

[267] Art. 12, *id.*

[268] The agreement is to remain in force until 2010 or until another agreement is negotiated, see art. 18 (2), *id.*

projects mostly dams[269] that would increase the availability of water (by 30 percent), including water reserved for the city of Maputo.[270] The agreement provides explicitly for priority of uses. Domestic, livestock, and industrial uses as well as ecological water requirements are granted priority over other uses.[271] There are provisions on procedures to be followed in case of drought.[272] It has been claimed that although the provision of additional water – through the further development of the basin – was instrumental in breaking a potential deadlock in the negotiations, it prevented the parties from critically evaluating some of the current uses (e.g., expensive afforestation projects).[273] Overall, however, the agreement has been heralded as a success in translating the concept of equitable utilization into concrete obligations undertaken by the parties to the agreement.[274] The inclusion of the Maputo basin in the Incomati Agreement has been considered a useful approach. Including two river basins in the agreement provided the parties with the possibility of being more flexible on their requirements in one basin in order to obtain more concessions on the other basin.[275]

The agreement places itself under the regional cooperative structure of the SADC regime. Disputes are to be settled by an arbitration panel. If one of the disputing parties refuses to appoint an arbitrator, the president of the SADC tribunal is to appoint that arbitrator.[276]

Niger

Nine countries share the Niger Basin, namely, Burkina Faso, Benin, Cameroon, Chad, Ivory Coast, Guinea, Mali, Niger, and Nigeria. The 1960s Niger Basin regime[277] was replaced, in the 1980s, by a regime administered by the Niger Basin Authority.[278] The function of the new regime is to ensure the integrated development of the Niger Basin in all fields including energy, water resources, agriculture, animal husbandry, fisheries, forestry exploitation, transport, communications, and industry.[279] More particularly, the objectives of the Niger Authority include: statistics and planning; infrastructure development; water control and utilization; environmental control and preservation; navigation control and regulation and financing of projects and works.[280] The treaty provides the details of the institutional structure of the authority and financial provisions influenced by the model of integrated river basin management.

---

[269] See Annex II, Reference Projects, id.

[270] Vaz, supra note 246, at 46. See Annex I, Art. 6(4), 2002 Interim Agreement, supra note 257.

[271] Annex I, Art. 1(2), id.

[272] Annex I, Art. 4(5) and (6), id.

[273] Vaz, supra note 246, at 47.

[274] Id.

[275] Id. at 51.

[276] Art. 15(3)(c), 2002 Interim Agreement, supra note 257. Pending the entry into operation of the SADC tribunal, the appointment of the arbitrator is to be made by the President of the International Court of Justice.

[277] Act regarding the Navigation and Economic Co-operation between the States of the Niger Basin, Oct. 26, 1963, reprinted in 587 UNTS 9. See also Agreement concerning the Niger River Commission and the Navigation and Transport on the River Niger, Nov. 25, 1964, reprinted in 587 UNTS 21.

[278] Convention creating the Niger Basin Authority, Nov. 21, 1980, available online at http://ocid.nacse.org.

[279] Art. 3(1), id.

[280] Art. 4, id.

Another agreement in the region that sheds light on the equitable utilization of resources is the agreement between Niger and Nigeria on the equitable development of resources at their common frontier (namely, the Maggia/Lamido, Gada/Goulbi, Tagwai/El Fadama, Komadougou/Yobe river basins).[281] The agreement specifies the factors that must be taken into account in determining equitable utilization. Some of these factors are particular to the region and are inclusive of environmental considerations. The factors that must be taken into account in determining equitable utilization include:

- the climate of the region and its dependence on rainfalls and the general hydrology;
- existing water uses;
- reasonably planned water development requirements;
- economic and social development needs of the parties;
- dependence of local populations on water for their livelihood;
- the availability of alternative sources of water to satisfy competing demands;
- the practicability of compensation as a means of adjusting water demands;
- maintaining an acceptable environmental balance around a body of water;
- avoidance of unnecessary waste in the utilization of water; and
- the proportion according to which each party contributes to the water balance in the basin.[282]

In addition, it is provided that these factors are to be considered together and a determination must be arrived on the basis of all the factors.[283] The factors included in the Niger-Nigeria Agreement, in delineating equitable use, are more detailed than those included in the 1997 UN Convention. The requirement of prevention of unnecessary waste in water use places environmental requirements on an equal footing with allocation issues. It is interesting to note that the parties included the proportion of each party's contribution to water balance as a factor to be taken into account for equitable utilization.

Regarding established/historical claims, the parties propose to deal with them in the following fashion: an active water use would take precedence over a competing active use that came into being at a later time, provided that:

1. the prior use is beneficial to both parties and is reasonable under the circumstances; and
2. the factors enumerated in article 5 do not lead to a conclusion that favors the later in time use.[284]

The institutional administration of the agreement is to be performed by the Nigeria-Niger Joint Commission and a Permanent Technical Committee of Water Experts.[285]

A Niger Basin Authority (NBA) has been established but many ailments have plagued the authority, such as insufficiency in technical and operational capacities;

---

[281] Art. 1, Agreement between the Federal Republic of Nigeria and the Republic of Niger Concerning the Equitable Sharing in the Development, Conservation and Use of their Common Water Resources, July 18, 1990, available at online http://ocid.nasce.org.
[282] Art. 5(1), *id.*
[283] Art. 5(2), *id.*
[284] Arts. 6–7, *id.*
[285] Arts. 11 & 12, *id.*

lack of dialogue and coordination with member countries; and lack of concerted and joint action to test the legal and institutional mechanisms. The situation in the region is so bleak that the World Bank ordered an audit of the NBA in order to refine its mandate and assess its resources.[286]

5.2. Asia

Mekong

The Mekong River Basin cooperation was one of the first efforts for integrated river basin organization. China, Myanmar, Laos, Thailand, Cambodia, and Vietnam are the coriparians in the region, states that have faced a significant number of political and economic challenges during the last decades. China and Myanmar have not been actively involved in the concerted efforts of other coriparians to manage the river basin but have not meddled significantly either – at least until recently – in the efforts of other states.

The region on the average receives plenty of water and water shortages have not been responsible for tensions and conflicts among coriparians. The international community has played a pivotal role in supporting the Mekong initiative.[287] The first Mekong Committee established in 1957 received international financial assistance. One of the first projects of the committee was to establish a number of hydrometeorological stations. A total of four hundred stations were built by 1975.[288] The committee undertook a vast array of studies in the region, including hydrographic surveys, special studies on fisheries, agriculture, forestry, minerals, transportation, and power markets. By the end of 1965, twenty countries, eleven international agencies, and private organizations had pledged $100 million to the Mekong Committee. Responding to concerns that its mission was too technocratic and that it paid scant attention to the social impacts of engineering works, the Mekong Committee ordered a number of social studies.[289]

International support for the committee started to wane in the 1970s as bringing planned projects to life proved more difficult than was initially thought. The coriparians adopted in 1975 a declaration of principles for the utilization of the waters of the Mekong River. The declaration contains one of the earliest versions of the elements that comprise "equitable utilization" of resources.[290] The objectives of the

---

[286] International Network of Basin Organizations (INBO) Newsletter, No. 12, Dec. 2003–Jan. 2004.

[287] For the early attempts to cooperate in the basin, see Ti Le-Huu & Lien Nguyen-Duc, Mekong Case Study, UNESCO, Technical Documents in Hydrology, PCCP series, No. 10, at 27–29 (2003).

[288] Id. at 5.

[289] For the early institutional framework of the Mekong River Basin, see the case study, available online at http://www.transboundarywaters.orst.edu/projects/casestudies/mekong.html (Transboundary Freshwater Dispute Database).

[290] Joint Declaration of Principles for Utilization of the Waters of the Lower Mekong Basin, Jan. 31, 1975 available online at http://ocid.nasce.org [hereinafter Joint Declaration]. The principles are similar to the principles included in the 1966 Helsinki Rules. See International Law Association, Helsinki Rules on the Uses of the Water of International Rivers, International Law Association, Report of the fifty-second conference (1966). The 1966 Helsinki Rules are the product of the International Law Association, an organization that provides recommendations for the future development of international law. The Helsinki rules have had significant influence on the development of international watercourse law. See McCaffrey, supra note 26, at 320.

declaration are to ensure conservation, development, and control of water resources at the basin level.

The declaration contains several factors that are to be considered:

- the comparative costs of alternative means of satisfying the economic and social needs of each basin state and the availability of other resources;[291]
- the avoidance of unnecessary waste in the utilization of water;[292]
- the practicability of compensation as a way to adjust conflicts among users;[293] and
- the cost–benefit ratio of each project, taking into account social, economic, and financial costs and benefits, both downstream and upstream from the project.[294]

The obligation not to cause significant harm does not constitute a separate obligation but is one of the elements to be taken into account in deciding the parameters of equitable use. It is provided that one of the elements that must be taken into account in determining equitable use is "the degree to which the needs of a Basin State may be satisfied, without causing substantial injury to another Basin State."[295]

The declaration seems to adopt the principle of integrated management of the basin. The declaration provides that individual projects must be implemented "in a manner conductive to the system development of the Basin's water resources" and that each state within its territory must be entitled to "a reasonable and equitable share."[296]

Another interesting feature of the declaration is that it elaborates in detail on the existing utilization of the basin. The use of water for domestic and urban purposes must have priority over any other use. A riparian state may not be denied an existing reasonable water use in order to preserve water for other riparians' future use.[297] The declaration goes into specific details in defining existing uses[298] and proposes means of accommodation between existing uses and later in time competing uses.

> A reasonable use in existence as of any given date may continue in operation unless the factors justifying its continuance are outweighed by other factors, referred to in Article VI, leading to the conclusion, confirmed by an international tribunal of competent jurisdiction, that it be modified or terminated so as to accommodate a concurrent or competing incompatible use, but in such event its modification or termination shall entitle the holder of the right to such use to reasonable, prompt and adequate compensation, assured prior to the curtailment of such use.[299]

---

[291] Art. VI (7)–(8), Joint Declaration, *id.*

[292] Art. VI (9), *id.*

[293] Art. VI (10), *id.*

[294] Art. VI (12), *id.*

[295] Art. VI (11), *id.*

[296] Art. V, *id.*

[297] Arts. XII & XIII, *id.*

[298] Art. XIV, *id.* "A use is deemed to be existing from the first act of implementation followed, with use of reasonable diligence, by initiation of construction, and application to use of the full quantity claimed, with like due diligence, within a reasonable period of time, related to the magnitude of the use, and continuing until such time as such use ceases to be effective."

[299] Art. XIV, *id.*

The declaration defines equitable use not as

> the right to an equal division of the use of these waters among riparian States, but as the equal right of each riparian State to use these waters on the basis of its economic and social needs consistent with the corresponding rights of the others.[300]

The declaration provides for the process that a state needs to follow in order to undertake a project in the region. Parties who wish to undertake a project must present it "well in advance" to other states to obtain formal prior agreement. A detailed study, inclusive of all the detrimental effects of the project, including ecological impacts on other states, must be undertaken. And the amount of compensation due to the affected states must be determined.[301]

Parties are encouraged to adopt measures to minimize detrimental effects on the ecological balance of the basin[302] and must take measures to ensure that displaced populations are "suitably relocated or equitably compensated, or both."[303] It also is provided that the compensation must be paid before the taking of land.[304]

Despite the bold provisions of the declaration, that clearly set the parameters of equitable water management in the region, the Mekong Committee eventually languished. The committee was revitalized in 1995 as the Mekong Commission. In the meantime, the river basin management in the Mekong region was based on *ad hoc* planning.[305] The 1995 Agreement on the Sustainable Development of the Mekong River Basin, which established the Mekong Commission, was launched by the states of Laos, Vietnam, Cambodia, and Thailand. China and Myanmar maintain an observer status and are not formal members of the commission.[306]

The objective of the agreement is to achieve the optimal use of waters of the Mekong river "though a dynamic and practical consensus" in conformity with the rules of utilization to be set out by the Mekong Commission.[307] It is clarified that "prior consultation" with other coriparians for undertaking a project constitutes neither a right to veto nor a right to use water unilaterally in disregard of the rights of other riparians. Article 5 provides for the procedures that are to be followed to undertake a project during a wet or dry season based on whether a project is a single-state project or an interbasin project.[308] Article 26 provides for the "rules for water utilization and interbasin diversions." States are to avoid, minimize, and mitigate adverse effects of their water use on other states. When a state is notified that it is causing "substantial damage" to other states, the state that causes the harm "shall cease immediately the alleged cause of harm until such cause of harm is determined in accordance with Article 8."[309] Article 8 provides for state responsibility

[300] Arts. X & XI, *id.*

[301] Art. XVII, *id.*

[302] Art. XXIV, *id.*

[303] Art. XXV, *id.*

[304] Art. XXV, *id.*

[305] See Le-Huu, *supra* note 287, at 37.

[306] Agreement on Co-operation for the Sustainable Development of the Mekong River Basin, April 5, 1995, reprinted in 34 ILM 864 (1995), available online at http://ocid.nasce.org.

[307] Art. 26 (more specifically the rules are set by the Joint Committee and approved by the Council. Both the Joint Committee and the Council are organs of the Mekong Commission. See also art. 12, *id.*).

[308] See arts. 5B(1) & 5B(2), *id.*

[309] Art. 7, *id.*

for harmful effects that cause substantial damage to coriparians. The Mekong River Commission is established that has the status of an international body and can enter into agreements with donors and international organizations.[310] The Mekong Commission is comprised of three permanent bodies: the Council, the Joint Committee, and the Secretariat.[311]

The Mekong Commission has been criticized for concentrating on dam construction and large infrastructure projects without sufficient elaboration on the environmental impacts of such projects. A recent controversy involves the Upper Lancang-Mekong Navigation Project, which has to do with the development of a series of dams in the region. The project is expected to provide 17 percent of China's electricity and to facilitate navigation.[312] The project was the result of an agreement among China, Myanmar, Laos, and Thailand on the commercial navigation on the Lancang-Mekong River. It is interesting to note that the agreement was adopted without notifying the Mekong Commission and the lower riparian states of Cambodia and Vietnam, which were not given prior notification before they were invited to witness the reef blasting ceremony.[313] A weakness of the Mekong Commission is that it has been unable to bring all parties under its auspices. Countries have defected the commission in situations in which such defection would serve better their interests.

Indus

The sharing of Indus river waters percolated from an interprovince dispute (during the period that India was under the control of Great Britain) to an international dispute after India's independence and the creation of Pakistan. In 1947, India and Pakistan decided to sign an agreement to allocate the waters of the Indus river, called the Standstill Agreement, which allowed for water allocations to Pakistan. Pakistan additionally agreed to make payments for the provision of water. India claimed that such payments were recognition of its water rights, whereas Pakistan claimed that they were payments for operation and maintenance works. The issue escalated in 1948 when, because of the lack of an international agreement – the 1947 agreement had just expired –[314] India (the upper riparian) decided to curtail the flow of the river into Pakistan. The water flow was resumed a month later, but the India-Pakistan relationship was scarred by the incident. The incident fueled fears in Pakistan of its precarious dependence on India for water.[315]

In 1951, India invited David Lilienthal, a former chairman of the Tennessee Valley Authority (TVA) – who also visited Pakistan – to provide proposals for the resolution of the dispute. The TVA was viewed, at the time, as one of the most

---

[310] Art. 11, *id.*

[311] For the specific functions of these organs, see arts. 15–33.

[312] Poverty and IRBM, *supra* note 87, at 11.

[313] Paul Erik Lauridsen, Transboundary Water Management in the Mekong: River of Controversy or River of Promise, in From Water-wars to Water-riots 47, 62, *supra* note 174.

[314] The standstill agreement expired in April 1, 1948.

[315] Indus Water Treaty, Case Study, available online at http://www.transboundarywater.orst.edu/projects/casestudies/indus.html.

successful examples of integrated river basin management.[316] Lilienthal proposed
the application of the concept of integrated water management through the development of an "Indus Engineering Corporation." The corporation was to include
representatives from India and Pakistan and from the World Bank. The plan proposed
by Lilienthal called for financing by the World Bank.[317]

The World Bank was involved in the Indus dispute from the initial stages of the
conflict but a solution remained elusive. Two major stumbling points remained: the
unwillingness of Pakistan to be dependent for its water supply on India; and India's
refusal to finance the works that would guarantee the independent water supply of
Pakistan.[318]

The issue was resolved based on the pragmatics of the situation rather than what
would ideally be prescribed under the principles of integrated river basin management. The Indus Water Treaty eventually was signed in 1960.[319] The mutual suspicions of the parties dictated the separation of the entitlement to the river resources
with all waters of the eastern rivers (namely, the Sutlej, Beas, and Ravi) allocated
to India, with minor exceptions, and all western rivers (namely, the Indus, Jhelum,
and Chenab) allocated to Pakistan, with some exceptions.[320] The issue of funding
the additional development needed to achieve the division of the river was to be
undertaken by India for a specific amount of £62,062,000.[321] The rest of the money
needed was to be provided by the World Bank. Arrangements for a transitional
period of ten years were provided for in the treaty, during which time the works
necessary for the separation of river resources were to be effectuated.[322]

As the Indus Basin regime demonstrates, integrated river basin management may
not be a realistic option for certain regions, specifically regions characterized by
belligerent relationships among coriparians. In the case of the Indus River basin,
the separation of water entitlements was a more realistic resolution to the dispute
than an insistence on integrated river management. The unequal power of states in
the region (with India considered the stronger party) delayed the negotiations and
influenced the final outcome. That a financial institution with the leverage of the
World Bank was willing to assist the parties in reaching agreement and in providing
the financing, that would make agreement possible, could be considered the catalyst
in this case. The specific negotiating steps that the World Bank took in its attempt
to resolve the Indus dispute (such as its request for each party to provide its own
Indus allocation plan) have been replicated in other fora.[323]

The fact that the Indus River regime has been able to survive – despite tensions
in the region – is a demonstration that realistic arrangements, although not optimal,
may be more durable than integrated management.

---

[316] See *supra* note 95.
[317] For a detailed account of Lilienthal's proposal and the negotiations that took place, see Undala Z. Alam,
Water Rationality: Mediating the Indus Water Treaty 97 (dissertation thesis, submitted to the Geography
Department, University of Durham), Sept. 1998.
[318] *Id.* at 144.
[319] Indus Waters Treaty, Sept. 19, 1960, reprinted in 419 UNTS 126.
[320] Arts. II & III, Art. I (5)–(6), *id.*
[321] Art. IV, *id.*
[322] Art. II (5)–(9), *id.*
[323] Indus Waters Treaty, Case Study, *supra* note 315.

Ganges and Mahakali

Ganges

The Ganges River regime presents another interesting case between an upper riparian (India) and a lower riparian (Bangladesh) regarding the use of a shared river where one of the countries involved is the dominant power. Negotiations with regard to the use of the river started in the early 1950s when Bangladesh, at that point still East Pakistan, found out that India was about to construct a barrage at Farakka. India used various negotiating tactics to avoid reaching an agreement with Bangladesh, including the absence of data presented as an obstacle to the conclusion of a substantial agreement.[324] After Bangladesh acquired its independence in 1971, various negotiating rounds were held and a final agreement was reached in 1977.[325] The agreement is a demonstration, according to some commentators, that India accepted the principle of reasonable and equitable share of water resources and abandoned the Harmon doctrine, which it had espoused earlier.[326]

The agreement was considered an interim arrangement for the sharing of the Ganges waters at Farakka. The allocation of the waters is based on 75 percent availability of the Ganges flow, as the historical records indicate.[327] The agreement allocates waters to India and Bangladesh for specific months and for specific dates in the month according to a detailed schedule.[328] The agreement allocates an average 60 percent of the total available water to Bangladesh. The treaty also provides that if, in any ten-day period, the share of Bangladesh's water falls below 80 percent, the release of water to Bangladesh should never fall below the 80 percent of its share.[329] Potential abundance of water – above what has been predicted in the treaty – is to be shared proportionally between the parties.[330]

A Joint Committee is established under the agreement. If the Joint Committee cannot resolve an issue between the parties, the issue must be referred to a panel of an equal number of Bangladeshi and Indian experts. If the panel fails to reach a decision, the matter must be referred to the two governments, which "shall meet urgently at the appropriate level" to resolve further the issue by mutual discussion.[331]

The issue of allocation was so crucial in the undertaking of this agreement that environmental matters were not even touched upon by the parties. On the contrary, as the title of the treaty indicates,[332] the parties were more concerned with finding a technical solution for increasing the flows of the Ganges River during dry seasons.[333]

---

[324] Ganges, River Controversy, Case Study, available online at http://www.transboundarywaters.orst.edu/ projects/casestudies/ganges.html.

[325] Agreement between the Government of the People's Republic of Bangladesh and the Government of the Republic of India on Sharing of the Ganges Waters at Farakka and on Augmenting Its Flows, Nov. 5, 1977, reprinted in 17 ILM 103 (1978), available online at http://ocid.nasce.org [hereinafter Ganges Agreement].

[326] McCaffrey, *supra* note 26, at 252.

[327] Art. II(i), Ganges Agreement, *supra* note 325.

[328] Art. II (i) and attached Schedule, *id.*

[329] Art. II (ii), *id.*

[330] *Id.*

[331] Art. VII, *id.*

[332] *Id.*

[333] Art. VIII, *id.*

The 1977 agreement was an interim agreement valid for five years, after which time it could be extended for another mutually agreed period.[334] Dissatisfaction with the agreement emerged quite quickly and in 1982 the parties, in a joint memorandum of understanding, declared that the agreement "had not proved suitable for finding a satisfactory and durable solution and that with its termination fresh efforts were necessary" to arrive at a solution.[335] The governments agreed that the problem rested with the "inadequate flow of waters" available at Farakka that imposed sacrifices on both countries. The memorandum refers to the need to "arrive at equitable sharing of waters available" at Farakka and provides for a renewed schedule.

The parties eventually entered into a new treaty in 1996[336] "desirous of finding a fair and just solution without affecting the rights and entitlements of the either country" or establishing any general principles of law or precedent.[337] The treaty makes explicit reference to the concepts that were incorporated later into the 1997 UN Watercourses Treaty. Article IX provides that: "guided by the principles of equity, fairness and no harm to either party" both governments agree to conclude water sharing Treaties/Agreements with regard to their common rivers.[338]

The treaty provides for a formula according to which parties are to share waters at Farakka and an indicative Schedule on allocations per ten days in every month (from January to May).[339] The formula prescribed essentially translates the concept of equitable allocation to a concept of equal allocation establishing more or less a fifty-fifty allocation of waters available at Farakka.[340] If water availability falls below a certain threshold (50,000 cusecs in any ten-day period), the two governments are to enter into "immediate consultations to make adjustments on an emergency basis, in accordance with principles of equity, fair play and no harm to either party."[341]

The treaty includes provisions for its review. Every five years, or even earlier, any party can request adjustments to the treaty "based on principles of equity, fairness and no harm" to either party. Either party can ask for a first review of the treaty two years after its signature to assess the impact of the treaty and the workings of the sharing arrangements.[342] When negotiating future adjustments to the treaty, India must release to Bangladesh, at least 90 percent of Bangladesh's share of waters as prescribed in the formula provided for in article II.[343]

---

[334] Art. XV, *id.*

[335] Indo-Bangladesh Memorandum of Understanding on the Sharing of Ganga Waters at Farakka, Oct. 7, 1982, available online at http://ocid.nasce.org.

[336] Treaty between the Government of the Republic of India and the Government of the People's Republic of Bangladesh on Sharing of the Ganga/Ganges Waters at Farakka, Dec. 12, 1996, reprinted in 36 ILM 519 (1997), available online at http://ocid.nasce.org.

[337] Preamble, *id.*

[338] See also article X, *id.*

[339] See Art. II, Annexure I and Annexure II, *id.*

[340] Annexure I. When the water available at Farakka is at 70,000 cusecs or less → 50% for India, 50% for Bangladesh; at 70,000–75,000 cusecs → balance of flow for India, 35,000 cusecs Bangladesh; at 75,000 cusecs or more → 40,000 to India, balance of flow to Bangladesh. See *id.*

[341] Art. II (iii), *id.*

[342] Art. X, *id.*

[343] Art. XI, *id.*

A Joint Committee, in which both countries are represented in equal numbers, is charged with dispute settlement.[344] If the Joint Committee cannot resolve an issue, then the issue can be referred to the Indo-Bangladesh Joint Rivers Commission, which was established by the parties in 1972. If that body cannot resolve the issue either, the two governments must meet urgently at the appropriate level to resolve the issue by mutual discussion.[345]

Problems with the implementation of the agreement were already evident in 1997 when the water at Farakka dropped below the minimum provided for in the treaty. This prompted Bangladesh to request a review of the state of river.[346] A review of the agreement two years after its adoption demonstrated that it had performed reasonably well, even when water reaches a very low level during the months of March and April.[347]

Mahakali

The Mahakali River Agreement has been adopted by India and Nepal for the "integrated development of the Mahakali River" including a number of barrages and projects to be executed on the river.[348] The agreement is not only about water sharing but also about the apportionment of energy resources associated with the development of the river. Ecological concerns[349] and the principle of equitable sharing[350] are scarcely referred to in the agreement where the "water requirements of Nepal shall be given prime consideration."[351]

The agreement makes the following apportionment of resources between Nepal and India.

- With the regard to the waters of the Sarada barrage, Nepal gets 1,000 cusecs in the wet season and 150 cusecs in the dry season.[352] India gets 350 cusecs to maintain its river ecosystem.[353]

---

[344] Art. IV, *id.* The Joint Committee is also responsible for data collection and it is to provide the two governments with yearly reports. See arts. V & VI, *id.*

[345] Art. VII, *id.*

[346] Case Study, *supra* note 324.

[347] A. Nishat & M.F.K Pasha, A Review of the Ganges Treaty of 1996, paper presented at AWRA/IWLRI-University of Dundee International Specialty Conference, "Globalization and Water Resources Management: The Changing Value of Water," Aug. 6–8, 2001. But see also Mohammand Ehteshamul Hoque, Hydropolitics: an Overview with Special Focus on the Farakka Barrage, Paper Presented at the South Asian Forum for Young Researchers (SAFYR), Dhaka, Bangladesh, (Proceedings of the "Workshop on Water and Politics: Understanding the Role of Politics in Water Management," August 2004, Published by the World Water Council).

[348] Treaty between His Majesty's Government of Nepal and the Government of India Concerning the Integrated Development of the Mahakali River including Sarada Barrage, Tanakpur Barrage and Pancheshwar Project, Feb 12, 1996, reprinted in 36 ILM 531 (1997), available online at http://ocid.nasce.org [hereinafter Mahakali Treaty].

[349] But see art. 1(2), in which it is provided that India is to maintain the flow of the water downstream of the Sarada Barrage "to maintain and preserve the river eco-system." *Id.*

[350] It is provided, however, that the Mahakali River Commission established under the agreement is to be guided by the "principles of equality, mutual benefit and no harm to either party." See art. 9(1), *id.* Some commentators have noted that the reference made to the principle of equality rather than equity may be attributed to the fact that the Mahakali is a border river where equitable utilization may mean equal utilization, whereas the Ganges River is a successive river. See McCaffrey, *supra* note 26, at 255.

[351] Art. 5(1), Mahakali Treaty, *supra* note 348.

[352] Art. 1(1), *id.*

[353] Art. 1(2), *id.*

- With regard to the Tanakpur barrage, Nepal gives its consent to use a piece of its land for the construction of the barrage.[354] In exchange for its concession of land, Nepal receives 1,000 cusecs of water in the wet season and 300 cusecs of water in the dry season.[355] It receives also seventy million kilowatt-hour of energy "on a continuous basis annually, free of cost" from the date of the entry into force of the treaty.[356] Nepal has the option to receive additional energy from the Tanakpur Power Station, equal to half of the energy produced there, if it bears half of the operational cost and half of the capital cost of the project.[357]
- With regard to the Pancheshwar project, it is provided that the countries agree to "have equal entitlement in the utilization of the waters" from this project without prejudice to their existing uses of water.[358] The project shall be implemented with power stations of equal capacity located at each side of the border and "the total energy generated shall be shared equally between the Parties."[359] The cost of this power generation project is to be shared by the parties in proportion to the benefits they receive from the project.[360]
- Finally, it is provided that India is to provide Nepal with 350 cusecs of water for irrigation purposes, but the details of this arrangement are to be executed at a later date.[361]

It is further mentioned that any other project to be executed on the Mahakali River border area must be designed and implemented by an agreement between the parties.[362] A subtle reference is made to the no harm principle. It is provided that, unless there is an agreement between the parties, each party must refrain from using or obstructing or diverting the waters of the river in a manner that would affect its natural flow and level.[363]

The treaty establishes a commission – guided by the principles of equality, mutual benefit, and no harm to either party – that must be comprised of an equal number of representatives from both parties.[364] The purpose of the Mahakali Commission is to collect information, make recommendations, and provide expert evaluation, monitoring, and coordination.[365] The commission is to act as a dispute settlement mechanism of first resort.[366] If, in the course of settling a disagreement between the parties, the commission makes recommendations with which one of the parties disagrees, that party can refer the dispute to arbitration after giving a three-month notification to the other party.[367]

[354] Art. 2(1), *id.*
[355] Art. 2(2)(a), *id.*
[356] Art. 2(2)(b), *id.*
[357] Art. 2(3)(b), *id.*
[358] Art. 3, *id.*
[359] Art. 3(2), *id.*
[360] Art. 3(3), *id.*
[361] Art. 4, *id.*
[362] Art. 6, *id.*
[363] Art. 7, *id.*
[364] Art. 9(1)–(2), *id.*
[365] Art. 9(3), *id.*
[366] Art. 9(3)(e), *id.*
[367] Art. 11, *id.*

The purpose of the Mahakali and Ganges agreements is to settle disputes with regard to the allocation of river resources. Provisions with regard to water quality are not prevalent in the agreements. Both agreements are using, to a greater or lesser extent, some terminology of equitable utilization or the principle of equality of riparians and the no harm principle that had permeated the negotiations of the 1997 UN Watercourses Convention. As a matter of fact, in the Mahakali River regime equitable utilization becomes equal utilization, at least in terms of phraseology. In practical terms, Nepal has expressed some concerns about the equitable implementation of the agreement.

5.3. Middle East

Jordan

The question of the apportionment of waters of the Jordan River and tributaries dates back to the 1950s when the riparian states – Israel, Jordan, Lebanon, and Syria – attempted to conclude an agreement on integrated water management in the region. The Jordan River originates in three countries – Lebanon, Israel, and the Golan Heights region of Syria. Israel has effective control of the Golan Heights since the 1967 war. Israel occupied Lebanon until 2000, thus, it was in total control of the upstream until 2000.[368] Since 2000, Israel has been in control of two of the three tributaries to the river.

The occupation of the West Bank by Israel, after the 1967 war, means that Israel is in control of important aquifers located there. Thus, after the 1967 war, Israel was able to take control over the water resources crucial for its survival as an independent state. It comes as no surprise, therefore, that commentators have viewed the 1967 war as motivated in part by concerns regarding the water security of Israel. It has been argued that, although water was not the primary reason for the war, it was one of the major driving forces behind the war. The dependence of Israel on drinking supplies from the West Bank, and the perception that incorrect drilling practices by Jordanians and Palestinians would affect adversely Israel's water supplies, led allegedly to the war and the occupation of the West Bank.

One of the tributaries of the Jordan River is Yarmouk which starts from Syria and forms the border between Syria and Jordan and some of the boundary between Israel and Jordan. When all waters of the Jordan river are taken into account, 77 percent of these waters originate in Arab countries.[369]

In 1953, the United States tried to mediate the conflict in the region by sending a special envoy, Eric Johnston. Johnston tried to mediate a settlement in the region regarding the apportionment of water resources by designing a regional development plan. Johnston's proposals were based on a similar plan devised by the TVA focusing on integrated river management, ignoring the political boundaries of the region, and taking into account the needs of respective countries, especially irrigation and agricultural development. Israel proposed its version of allocations and the Arab nations, organized as an Arab League technical committee (under the leadership of Egypt), proposed their own plans. Reconciliation was not achieved and the Johnston

---

[368] McCaffrey, *supra* note 26, at 267–68.
[369] *Id.* at 268.

plan was abandoned.[370] It has been argued, however, that the provisions of the Johnston plan have become the customary law in the region because coriparians often refer to the plan to justify their water appropriations.[371]

One of the reasons that the Johnston plan fell short of bringing the parties together was that it ignored the Palestinian question. Egypt, as a regional power, was granted a leading role in the negotiations. The inclusion of other states, however, for instance, Iraq and Saudi Arabia, could have made a difference in the completion of successful negotiations.

The Johnston agreement did not address the issue of groundwater, an issue that was later ignited during the Israeli–Palestinian conflict. By not addressing the ground water issue and its relationship with surface water, the proposed agreement neglected the hydrological reality of the region.[372]

Eventually in 1994, Israel and Jordan signed a peace treaty that addresses water allocation, among other issues.[373] The treaty is notable because, unlike most regional agreements, it deals not only with surface water (Jordan/Yarmuk) but also with groundwater (the Araba/Arava groundwater). Article 6 of the treaty provides that the parties recognize the necessity of finding "a practical, just and agreed solution" to their water problems and understand that "their water resources are not sufficient to meet their needs."[374] The parties pledge to address water issues along their entire boundary "in their totality" including the possibility of transboundary water transfers.[375] The parties agree to alleviate water shortages by:

- the development of new and existing water resources and the minimization of wastage of water;
- the prevention of contamination of waters;
- mutual assistance in the alleviation of water shortages; and
- the transfer of information and joint research.[376]

Annex II of the agreement deals with the details of the apportionment of waters. With regard to the waters of the Yarmouk River, Israel obtains 12 MCM in the summer and 13 MCM in the winter with the possibility of pumping an additional 20 MCM in the winter.[377] Jordan receives the rest. With regard to the waters of the Jordan river:

- Israel is entitled to maintain its current uses of the Jordan River between the confluence of Yarmouk and Tiral Zvi/Wadi Yabis.[378]

---

[370] For a detailed account of the negotiating history, see Jordan River: Johnston negotiations, 1953–55; Yarmuk mediations, 1980s, Case Study, available online at http://www.transboundarywaters.orst.edu/projects/casestudies/jordan_river.html.

[371] McCaffrey, *supra* note 26, at 270.

[372] See Case Study, *supra* note 370.

[373] Treaty of peace between the state of Israel and the Heshemite Kingdom of Jordan, done at Arava/Araba crossing point, Oct. 26, 1994, reprinted in 34 ILM 43 (1995), available online at http://ocid.nasce.org [hereinafter Israel/Jordan Peace Treaty].

[374] Art. 6(1)&(2), *id.*

[375] Art. 6(4), *id.*

[376] *Id.*

[377] Annex II, art. I, *id.*

[378] Annex II, art. I(2)(c), *id.*

- Jordan is entitled to an annual quantity from the Jordan River, equivalent to that of Israel but Jordan's use must not harm the quantity and quality of the Israeli use. The Joint Committee established under the treaty is to examine the prevention of appreciable harm.[379]

- Jordan is to receive 20 MCM from the Jordan River in the summer in return for the 20 MCM it provides for Israel during the winter from the Yarmouk River. Jordan is to bear the operation and maintenance costs for such a transfer and the total costs of any new transmission system. This particular water transfer is to be regulated further by a protocol.[380] At the time the agreement was signed, however, Jordan did not have a storage system for the water to be received under this provision.

- Jordan is entitled also to a minimum average of 20 MCM of the floods of the Jordan south of Yarmouk.[381]

- Jordan is entitled to another 10 MCM from the desalinization of springs that Israel is undertaking to pursue under the treaty. Israel is to explore the possibility of financing the supply of desalinated water to Jordan.[382]

Regarding arrangements for additional water, Jordan and Israel will cooperate "in finding sources" for supplying Jordan an additional quantity of 50 MCM per year of water of drinkable standards.[383] This proved to be one of the most controversial provisions of the agreement because it did not provide how the water was to be supplied and who was to pay for the additional supplies of water.[384]

The treaty provides that the operation and maintenance of systems that are located in the Israeli territory and supply Jordan with water and electricity are Israel's responsibility. The operation and maintenance of new systems that serve only Jordan are to be contracted out by Jordan. Israel is to guarantee easy and unhindered access, through its territory, to personnel for the installation of such new systems.[385]

The agreement contains further provisions on water storage, where additional works on the river are envisaged,[386] and water quality and protection.[387] The parties are to protect the rivers and the groundwater from pollution, contamination, and unauthorized withdrawals of each other's allocations.[388] The parties are to jointly construct monitoring stations.[389] And the discharge of untreated municipal and industrial wastewater into the river is prohibited within three years after the entry into force of the treaty.[390] Israel and Jordan agreed that the saline springs diverted

---

[379] *Id.*

[380] Annex II, art. I(2)(a), *id.*

[381] Annex II, art. I(2)(b), *id.*

[382] Annex II, art. I(2)(d), *id.*

[383] Art. I(3), *id.*

[384] Munther J. Haddadin & Uri Shamir, Jordan River Case Study, Part II: The Negotiations and Water Agreement between the Heshemite Kingdom of Jordan and the State of Israel, UNESCO, Technical Documents in Hydrology, PCCP Series, No. 15, at 12 (2003).

[385] Annex II, Art. I(4), Israel/Jordan Peace Treaty, *supra* note 373.

[386] Annex II, art. II, *id.*

[387] Annex II, art. III, *id.*

[388] Annex II, art. III(1), *id.*

[389] Annex II, art. III(2), *id.*

[390] Annex II, art. III(3), *id.*

to the Jordan river would be marked for desalination. The two countries are to cooperate so that the brine, resulting from desalination, is not disposed of in the Jordan River and its tributaries.[391]

Jordan claimed sovereignty over a piece of land in the Arava/Araba Valley that was, when the treaty was signed, under the control of Israel. Israel had drilled fourteen wells in the area and used the water for irrigation purposes.[392] With regard to these groundwaters, the treaty recognizes that some of the wells that are drilled in Israel fall on the Jordanian side of the border. It is explicitly provided in the treaty that these wells are under Jordan's sovereignty. Israel, however, is to retain the use of these wells in the quantity and quality specified and neither country is to take measures to reduce the yield or the quality of these wells.[393] Furthermore, Israel can increase the pumping of these wells up to 10 MCM/year but only after the Joint Committee, established under the treaty, determines that this additional pumping is "hydro geologically feasible and does not harm existing Jordanian uses."[394] By providing, thus, Israel with the use of groundwater, although recognizing simultaneously Jordan's sovereignty, the agreement found an innovative way to resolve the conflict over the groundwater.

The parties further agreed that any change in the use of Jordan and Yarmouk rivers is to be made by mutual agreement. Israel and Jordan are to notify each other within six months of intended river projects.[395] Furthermore, the countries are to cooperate to increase water supplies and improve water use efficiency.[396] Finally, the agreement establishes a Joint Water Committee to act as an arbitrator in matters that could cause appreciable harm to either of the parties.[397]

The allocation of water in the Israel-Jordan peace treaty has been derided as unrealistic. It is interesting to note that the concept of equitable utilization is not mentioned. The concept of appreciable harm, however, is mentioned in two circumstances: one regarding the use of waters by Jordan that may cause appreciable harm to Israel;[398] and the other regarding the additional pumping of groundwater by Israel that may not harm Jordan.[399] Overall, the parties are more concerned with finding more water than with pursuing the equitable allocation of water currently available.[400]

Israel achieved safeguarding its existing water use and, potentially, additional rights, whereas some important needs of Jordan are to be addressed by future projects of water desalination.[401] Some commentators have criticized the treaty for its attempt to deal with water scarcity through future projects. It does not come as surprise that, shortly after the conclusion of the treaty, Jordan complained to Israel that

[391] Annex II, art. III(5), *id.*
[392] Haddadin, *supra* note 384, at 9.
[393] Annex II, art. IV(1), Israel/Jordan Peace Treaty, *supra* note 373.
[394] Annex II, art. IV(3), *id.*
[395] Annex II, art. V, *id.*
[396] Annex II, art. VI(2), *id.*
[397] For the role of the Committee, see Annex II, arts. I(2)(c) & IV(3), *id.*
[398] Annex II, art. I(2)(c), *id.*
[399] Annex II, art. IV(3), *id.*
[400] Annex II, arts. VI (2) & I(3), *id.*
[401] Annex II, art. I(2)(d) & (3), *id.*

promised water quantities had yet to be delivered.[402] The provision of the additional 50 MCM of water to Jordan is a continuous source of consternation between the parties.[403]

Despite these shortcomings, the regime seems to be robust and the treaty has lasted despite the constant animosity between the parties. The regime was particularly challenged during the period of 1998–2000, when a severe drought brought up renewed disagreements over water allocation. The agreement does not specifically address drought. Despite the absence of a specific provision on drought, the regime created under the agreement has been able to assist in the resolution of the dispute between the parties.[404]

Another inflammatory issue in the region concerns the West Bank aquifer and the water withdrawals from this aquifer by Israel. It has been claimed that Israel's withdrawals jeopardize the survival of Palestinians. After the 1967 war, Israel issued an order on the development of groundwater of the West Bank. The law provided that no legal person was to own or administer water in the region without prior license. Such license could be revoked without any explanation. Palestinian wells were not allowed to exceed a depth of 140 meters, whereas wells belonging to Jewish settlers could go as far as 800 meters in depth. Israel has classified the hydrological data in the region as secret and has removed them from the public domain. An interim agreement signed in 1995 between Israel and the Palestinians[405] recognized the water rights of Palestinians and provided for additional allocations of water to Palestinian territories. The agreement further established a Joint Water Committee (JWC). However, many issues remain unresolved. There are constant recriminations that Israel is appropriating much of the water for its own benefit leaving for Palestinians the leftovers.[406]

It has been argued that the implementation of a demand-led approach to water management could help diffuse the water crisis in the region. Israel has increased its water efficiency by switching to drip irrigation. A potential decision of the states in the region to abandon agricultural self-sufficiency may provide the key to the alleviation of a constant sense of water crisis.

Tigris–Euphrates

The allocation of water in the Tigris-Euphrates Basin in the Middle East is severely contested. The dispute involves two downstream riparians, Syria and Iraq, who claim historical rights on the rivers. Turkey, the upstream riparian, refuses to recognize these historical rights. Turkey insists on developing the Tigris-Euphrates Basin in a manner that serves its needs.[407]

---

[402] McCaffrey, *supra* note 26, at 275.

[403] Andres Jägerskog, Why States Cooperate over Shared Water: The Water Negotiations in the Jordan River Basin 146, Department of Water and Environmental Studies, Linköping University, Sweden (2003).

[404] *Id.* at 47.

[405] Israeli-Palestinian Interim Agreement on the West Bank and the Gaza Strip, Sept. 28, 1995, reprinted in 36 ILM 551 (1997) available online at http://ocid.nacse.org.

[406] For an analysis of the dispute, see McCaffrey, *supra* note 26, at 275–79.

[407] For the views of Turkey on the dispute, see http://www.mfa.gov.tr (Web site of ministry of foreign affairs of Turkey).

The issue became particularly inflammatory in 1975 when Turkey's construction of two dams reduced significantly water availability downstream. Another incident in the 1990s, that had to do with the filling of Atatürk reservoir, stopped the Euphrates flow for a month.[408] When all projects planned by Turkey on Tigris-Euphrates are in place the natural flow to Syria will be reduced by 30–55 percent and the flow to Iraq will be reduced by 80 percent.[409] By contrast, the development of Anatolia is extremely important to Turkey as the area is considered underdeveloped and has been lagging behind in economic prosperity.[410] Turkey is not self-sufficient in energy and energy production, thus, by using the hydropower of the river could reduce its dependence on oil imports.[411] International donors, however, have refused to finance Turkey's projects without the consent of the coriparians.[412]

The issue has been complicated further as a result of the alleged Syrian support for the Kurdish rebels in Turkey. Syria's alleged support for the rebels has been viewed as way for Syria to obtain more concessions from Turkey on the water issue.[413] For Syria and Iraq, water is important for national security. Both countries wish to lessen their dependence on food imports.[414] As long as the situation in Iraq remains fluid following the 2003 war, the Tigris-Euphrates dispute is unlikely to be resolved in a quick manner.

5.4. Europe

In Europe, interbasin agreements are more focused on pollution and are more influenced by the concept of integrated water management. Europe's environment has withstood many impacts from industrial and other polluting activities. As a result, many rivers and lakes became severely polluted. In the 1990s, states engaged in concerted efforts to restore the ecological viability of some of the river systems, with some success.

The integration efforts propelled by the European Union have created new dynamics for water management. The Water Framework Directive that was adopted by the European Union[415] is a conscious attempt to implement the concept of integrated water management all across the European Union. The Water Framework Directive (WFD) is unique because it does not only prescribe the legislation that states must adopt but also because it dictates the administrative structure that states must establish to engage successfully in integrated water management.

---

[408] Patrick MacQuarrie, Growing Conflict over Development in the Euphrates-Tigris Basin 14 (dissertation thesis, Trinity College, Dublin, Ireland, Feb. 26, 2004). The incident triggered the signing of a treaty between Syria and Iraq for the equitable sharing of water between them. Of course, without water coming from Turkey, the treaty would have minimal effect. *Id.* at 53.

[409] *Id.* at 15.

[410] *Id.* at 16.

[411] *Id.* at 26.

[412] *Id.* at 24.

[413] *Id.* at 21.

[414] *Id.* at 30, 41 (for instance 90 percent of Iraq's withdrawal is for agriculture. Iraq's water supplies face also significant quality problems).

[415] See *infra* note 439.

5.4.1. Suprabasin Instruments

The 1992 Watercourses Convention

The 1992 Watercourses Convention[416] was adopted within the framework of the United Nations Economic Commission for Europe (UN/ECE). The convention is concerned primarily with the control of water pollution that may have transboundary impacts. The parties to the convention undertake the obligation to prevent, control, and reduce the transboundary impacts of polluting activities.[417] The convention encourages the control of pollution at the source[418] and endorses the precautionary[419] and polluter pays[420] principles. The convention endorses the use of the best environmental practice (Annex II) and the best available technology (Annex I). Annex III provides that states must set guidelines for water quality objectives and criteria. The convention includes provisions for monitoring and encourages states to adopt rules on responsibility and liability.[421]

Indicative measures that parties can adopt include environmental impact assessment, the reduction of nutrient inputs from industrial and municipal sources, and the use of nonwaste or low-waste technologies.[422] The convention includes a clause on the exchange of information between riparian parties,[423] warning and alarm systems about critical situations that may have transboundary impacts,[424] and public information (on water quality objectives, permits issued, and results on water sampling for purposes of monitoring and enforcement).[425] The convention, like the 1997 UN Watercourses Convention, encourages riparian states to develop joint bodies for the management of their shared water resources.[426]

In 1999, the parties to the Watercourse Convention adopted a Protocol on Water and Health.[427] This protocol puts emphasis on the quality of drinking water, including the protection of drinking water supplies and adequate sanitation. This is one of the first international agreements that addresses explicitly the quality of drinking water. The purpose of the protocol is to protect human health.[428]

The protocol provides that parties must establish targets and target dates in order to achieve access to drinking water and adequate sanitation.[429] Such targets and timetables must cover, *inter alia*:

- the quality of drinking water supplied (by taking into account the guidelines of the World Health Organization);

---

[416] Convention on the Protection and Use of Transboundary Watercourses and International Lakes, Mar. 17, 1992, reprinted in 31 ILM 1312 (1992).

[417] Art. 2(1) (2), *id.*

[418] Art. 2(3), *id.*

[419] Art. 2(5)(a), *id.*

[420] Art. 2(5)(b), *id.*

[421] Art. 7, *id.*

[422] Art. 3, *id.*

[423] Art. 13, *id.*

[424] Art. 14, *id.*

[425] Art. 16, *id.*

[426] Art. 9 (1) & (2), *id.*

[427] Protocol on Water and Health to the 1992 Convention on the Protection and Use of Transboundary Watercourses and International Lakes, June 17,1999, reprinted in 38 ILM 1708 (1999).

[428] Art. 1, *id.*

[429] Art. 6(1), *id.*

- the reduction of outbreaks and incidents of water-related diseases;
- the level of performance to be achieved by each collective system of water supply; and
- the discharges of untreated wastewater.[430]

Parties are encouraged to establish local or national arrangements for coordination among their competent authorities.[431] State parties are encouraged to develop water management plans on the basis of catchment areas or on the basis of groundwater aquifers.[432] States must make arrangements for public participation within a transparent and fair framework. States must ensure, further, that the outcome of public participation is taken into account.[433]

The protocol includes provisions on the development of response systems to deal with disease outbreaks[434] and on public awareness, research, training, and information.[435] The protocol contains extensive provisions on joint and coordinated international action and cooperation in relation to transboundary waters.[436] The protocol establishes that, "on the basis of equality and reciprocity," states must adapt their agreements on transboundary waters in order to eliminate contradictions with the protocol.[437] Regarding compliance, the protocol provides that "multilateral arrangements of a non-confrontational, non-judicial and consultative nature for reviewing compliance shall be established by the Parties at their first meeting."[438]

Water Framework Directive

The adoption of the Water Framework Directive is one of the first attempts to establish the principle of integrated water management on a regional scale. The adoption of the Water Framework Directive (WFD)[439] has to do with the realization that a more systematic approach to water management is needed based on the principles of Integrated River Basin Management (IRBM).[440] However, given that the WFD is developed within the mature context of an organization, that straddles the boundaries of a federal state and an international entity, it is unclear whether the WFD could provide a realistic model for other regions.

Purposes

- Prevention of Deterioration and Achievement of Good Status

The WFD attempts to regulate the entire water ecosystem in each and every region of the European Union and beyond. The directive requires that waters of high ecological status remain undisturbed but for the rest of waters protection and

---

[430] Art. 6(2), *id.*

[431] Art. 6(5)(a), *id.*

[432] Art. 6(5)(b), *id.*

[433] *Id.*

[434] Art. 8, *id.*

[435] Art. 9, *id.*

[436] Arts. 12 & 13, *id.*

[437] Art. 13(1)(c), *id.*

[438] Art. 15, *id.*

[439] Directive 2000/60/EC of the European Parliament and of the Council of 23 October 2000 establishing a framework for Community action in the field of water policy, OJ L 327/1, 22.12.2000 [hereinafter WFD].

[440] See, e.g., Strategies for River Basin Management: Environmental Integration of Land and Water in a River Basin (Jan Lundqvist et al., eds., 1985). See also *supra* Section 2.3.

sustainable use is the goal. According to the directive, all waters must achieve good ecological status either through the prevention of further deterioration or restoration. The directive provides that waters must preserve, at least, their current status – which means that waters of high status should not become waters of good status and that waters of good status should not end up as waters of moderate status.[441]

- Regulation and Elimination of Hazardous Substances

The purpose of the directive is to contribute to the goals of international agreements, including the HELCOM and OSPAR Conventions,[442] on the prevention and elimination of discharges of hazardous substances. The goal is to achieve concentrations close to background values for naturally occurring substances and close to zero for man-made substances.[443] This provision explicitly mentioned as one of the goals of the directive was resisted by the chemical industry. With regard to the regulation of hazardous substances, the European Commission adopted in 2001 a list of thirty-three priority substances.[444]

- Regulation of Water Supply/Demand Management

Although timidly mentioned, one of the goals of the directive is to provide the starting framework for the control of water supply.[445] With this goal in mind, it is provided that the River Basin Management Plans must ensure a balance between the abstraction and recharge of groundwater. The directive introduces also the cost-recovery principle. According to the principle of cost-recovery, states must take into account the costs of water services, including environmental and resource costs, by conducting an economic analysis.[446]

The principle of cost-recovery was more aggressively articulated in the draft version of the directive. The European Commission had proposed that farmers, households, and industry should be charged for the full price of water. The price was to include all costs of abstraction and distribution and the costs of wastewater treatment. Southern countries, led by Spain, objected to full pricing. Full pricing is a controversial issue in the South because of the large quantities of water used in agriculture. Overall, the pricing of water is a divisive issue because it has to do with perceived entitlements to use water without paying for the costs of its production and purification. As a matter of fact, some countries charge nothing for water, whereas others pass the full costs of water production to the consumer.

Organization

Establishment of River Basin Districts. The directive provides that member states must identify the water basins lying within their territory and must assign them to

[441] Art. 1(a), WFD, *supra* note 439.

[442] See Chapter 4.

[443] Art. 1(e), WFD, *supra* note 439.

[444] Decision No 2455/2001/EC of the European Parliament and of the Council of 20 November 2001 establishing the list of priority substances in the field of water policy and amending Directive 200/60/EC, OJ L 331/1, 15.12.2001.

[445] Art. 1(e) provides that the aim of the directive is to contribute to the "provision of sufficient supply of good quality surface water and groundwater...," WFD, *supra* note 439.

[446] The parameters for such an analysis are located in Annex III, WFD, *id.*

river basin districts. Groundwater and coastal water must be assigned to the nearest and most appropriate river basin district.[447] If a river basin district expands beyond the territory of a state, the state is supposed to cooperate with other member states to establish international river basin districts.[448]

Member states are supposed to cooperate with nonmember states when the river basin district extends beyond EU territory.[449]

After establishing the river basin districts, states must analyze their characteristics, review the impact of human activities, and perform an economic analysis of water use.[450] States must identify within each river basin district the water intended for human consumption and must ensure that this water complies with the requirements of the 1998 Water for Human Consumption Directive.[451] States also must establish the appropriate monitoring programs by 2006.[452]

River Basin Management Plans. States are to provide the European Commission with a list of their competent authorities and the competent authorities of international bodies with which they are to cooperate six months after the entry into force of the directive.[453] Once a competent authority is designated, it is responsible for the production of the River Basin Management Plan (RBMP). By 2009, states must have ready their RBMPs.[454] States are encouraged to devise a single RBMP for each international river basin district but, when this is not achievable, they are supposed to devise, at least, a RBMP for the portion of the international river basin district that falls within their territory.[455] Thus, a lack of cooperation cannot provide the justification for not going ahead with the development of RBMPs.

What must be included in the RBMPs is detailed in Annex VII of the directive. RBMPs usually include: a general description of the characteristics of the river basin district; a summary of pressures from human activity; the mapping of protected areas; a list of environmental objectives for all types of water included; and an analysis of the economic usage of water. Each RBMP must include also a "programme of measures"[456] required to meet the objectives of the directive as delineated in article 4. The objectives have to do with the nondeterioration of the status of water bodies and the restoration of all water bodies to good ecological status (when such restoration does not entail excessive costs). The list of measures involves basic and compulsory measures and optional supplementary measures. Basic measures are required to meet the standards of specific directives.[457]

---

[447] Art. 3(1), WFD, *id.*
[448] Art. 3(3), *id.*
[449] Art. 3(5), *id.*
[450] Art. 5(1), *id.*
[451] Art. 7, *id.*
[452] Art. 8(2), *id.*
[453] Art. 3(8), *id.*
[454] Art. 13(7), *id.*
[455] Art. 13(2)–(3), *id.*
[456] Art. 11, *id.*
[457] Such directives include the Wastewater Directive, the Nitrates Directive, the Bathing Water Directive, the Drinking Water Directive, the Environmental Impact Assessment Directive, and the Habitats Directive.

Water Classification. The classification of waters is an important element of the directive. Annex V divides surface waters into five categories: rivers, lakes, transitional waters, coastal waters, and artificial and heavily modified waters. Numerous types of water are found all across Europe with different ecological conditions.

Furthermore, states must classify their waters based on ecoregions (Annex II). After waters are classified according to the ecoregion in which they belong, further differentiation is necessary based on their ecological status.[458] Based on their ecological status, waters are classified as of high, good, moderate, poor, and bad status.[459] In order to determine the proper status of water quality, elements such as chemical and physiochemical elements are to be considered. For instance, for the classification of rivers[460] into an ecological status an examination of quality elements, including biological,[461] hydromorphological,[462] chemical, and physiochemical elements, is required.[463] Similar elements are used to categorize lakes, transitional waters, coastal waters, and heavily modified or artificial water bodies. Establishing water quality to be something more than chemical quality is an innovative element of the directive. The discretion, however, given to states to classify their waters may create incentives to place waters under the least demanding category. This is the category of artificial or heavily modified waters. Member states are not required to restore these waters to good ecological status.

The directive establishes parameters for the classification of the quantitative status and chemical status of groundwater.[464]

Monitoring. The directive provides for three types of monitoring: surveillance monitoring, operational monitoring, and investigative monitoring. The purpose of surveillance monitoring is to facilitate the classification of waters prescribed under the directive – that is, the classification of waters into different ecoregions and the classification of waters based on their status.[465] The purpose of operational monitoring is to identify the waters that are at risk of failing to meet environmental objectives.[466] The purpose of investigative monitoring is to uncover the reasons behind the failure of some waters to meet environmental objectives.[467] The directive also provides for the frequency of monitoring[468] and for additional monitoring

---

[458] Annex V, WFD, *supra* note 439.

[459] Annex V, para. 1.2., *id.*

[460] Annex V, para. 1.1.1., *id.*

[461] Natural ecological variability makes it impossible to establish absolute biological standards all through the Community. Biological quality has to be assessed, therefore, based on the degree of differentiation between the current status of water and what that status would have been without human influence.

[462] Hydromorphological elements include: the hydrological regime, river continuity, and morphological conditions.

[463] The chemical and physiochemical elements have to do with temperature, salinity, oxygenation, acidification, and a number of pollutants.

[464] Art. 4(1)(b)(ii), WFD, *supra* note 439.

[465] Annex V, para. 1.3.1., *id.*

[466] Annex V, para. 1.3.2., *id.*

[467] Annex V, para. 1.3.3., *id.*

[468] Annex V, para. 1.3.4., *id.*

requirements for protected areas.[469] All monitoring programs must be operational by 2006.

Public Participation. The institutionalization of public participation.[470] distinguishes this directive from the other water directives. More specifically, the directive provides that states must encourage the participation of all interested parties in implementation, that is, the production, review, and updating of RBMPs. Public participation is encouraged in each and every step of the RBMPs, for instance, in producing the timetable and work program, conducting the interim overview of significant management issues, and drafting the first version of the plan.[471] States must supply interested parties with all background documents and information used in the preparation of the plans and must give interested parties six months to comment on the documents they receive.[472] Each and every update of RBMPs must go through the same procedure.[473]

Timetable and Derogations. The directive guides states step-by-step on what they need to accomplish and by what deadline to be considered in conformance with the directive. When states request a deadline extension they must provide an explanation for such a request.

Assessment. The directive is an innovative piece of legislative work because it concentrates on the development of a methodology that would make possible the achievement of environmental objectives. Prior EU directives rarely focused on developing a system that would drive implementation. The organization of the river basin districts and the power they would eventually wield will determine the success of this directive.

An important element in the administrative organization of water protection is that it provides a forum for public participation. Administrative organization controls the flexibility provided under the directive. States that wish to request exceptions must state the reasons for such a request. It is hoped that the process of explanation and publication in the RBMPs would discourage superficial requests for derogations.

It remains to be seen how successful the directive is. The question is whether this planned and methodological approach to regulation would be better than the sole prescription of targets, the implementation of which is left to states' own devices. Given the lack of implementation, and especially the causes of nonimplementation, the EU had no other option but to try a different approach. If successful, this approach could be transcribed into other areas of regulation.

Water management in Europe is highly fragmented. Coordination, therefore, would be needed among the different bodies that manage waters and land-use

---

[469] Annex V, para. 1.3.5., *id.*
[470] Art. 14, *id.*
[471] Art. 14(1), *id.*
[472] Art. 14(2), *id.*
[473] Art. 14(3), *id.*

planning boards. Coordination with countries outside the sphere of the European Union is extremely important.

Because the deadlines imposed are quite challenging, existing institutional arrangements are likely to be used but most of them need to be reformed and structurally redefined. Participation is to be a challenge if it is to involve more than consultation. Abundant funding and a clear mandate would smooth the functioning of RBMPs.

5.4.2. Basin-Specific Instruments

Franco–Swiss Genevese Aquifer Agreement

The Genevese aquifer is exploited for drinking water by Swiss and French localities – the Caton of Geneva and the Prefect of Haute-Savoie. Between 1940 and 1960, water extractions from the Genevese aquifer were very close to the average natural recharge. The groundwater level was slowly lowering but without serious effects. Between 1960 and 1980, the aquifer was overpumped, with extractions reaching up to fourteen million cubic meters in 1971, almost twice its potential yield. This overpumping lowered the water table by more than seven million cubic meters in twenty years, reducing the total groundwater storage to about one-third.[474]

In 1977, the Canton of Geneva in Switzerland and the Prefect of Haute-Savoie in France signed an "arrangement" on the protection, utilization, and recharge of the Franco-Swiss Genevese aquifer.[475] The "arrangement" is an honest effort to resolve conflicts and follows a pragmatic approach based on a yearly technical water extraction and recharge program aimed at rational management of the resource. The arrangement makes no reference to the fact that France is the only contributor to the aquifer.[476] But, in indirect fashion, the arrangement acknowledges France's contribution by allowing France to extract free water, equal to the amount of its current consumption (two million cubic meters)[477] and making the Canton of Geneva solely responsible for the construction and operation of the artificial recharge installation.[478]

Considering the state of the aquifer at the time when the arrangement was negotiated, a general limitation on water extraction was included until the aquifer was restored to an acceptable level.[479] Monitoring of extractions is to be done by metering – regular readings are performed and recorded jointly in two originals, one for the Swiss authorities and the other for the French authorities.[480] Authorized users are granted permits by their national authorities. Every year, each group of users

---

[474] Bernard J. Wohlwend, An Overview of Groundwater in International Law – A Case Study: The Franco-Swiss Genevese Aquifer 2, paper presented for the Workshop III on "Harmonization of Diverging Interests in the Use of Shared Water Resources," organized by the United Nations Economic and Social Commission for Western Asia (ESCWA) in cooperation with the German Technical Cooperation (GTZ), Dec. 17–19, 2002.

[475] Arrangement on the Protection, Utilization, and Recharge of the Franco-Swiss Genevese Aquifer, June 9, 1977 [hereinafter Genevese Aquifer Agreement].

[476] Wohlwend, *supra* note 474, at 11.

[477] Art. 9(2), Genevese Aquifer Agreement, *supra* note 475.

[478] Art. 8(1), *id.*

[479] Art. 22, *id.*

[480] Arts. 6 & 11(2), *id.*

is to present the commission, established under the agreement, with a forecast of the volume of water it plans to extract in the next twelve months.[481] Regarding water quality, pollution abatement evaluations are to be regularly conducted on each side of the aquifer based on standard criteria.[482] Because a groundwater recharge installation was constructed, the arrangement deals with the apportionment of costs between the Swiss locality and the French locality.[483]

The arrangement establishes a commission composed of three Swiss and three French members, two of which are to be specialists in water matters.[484] The commission's role is only consultative. The mandate of the commission is to propose a yearly management program for the Genevese aquifer after taking into account the needs of various users. In this context, the commission can take measures to ensure the protection of waters in the aquifer and remedy possible causes of pollution.[485]

The Franco-Genevese aquifer agreement is in line with other aquifer agreements the purpose of which is to limit groundwater extractions so as to reduce the possibility of groundwater salinization. Limitations on the extractions of groundwater are mentioned in other agreements such as the United States-Mexico Agreement on the Permanent and Definitive Solution to the Salinity of the Colorado River Basin, which provides limitations on the pumping of groundwater in the region.[486] Another such treaty is the 1994 Treaty between Israel and the Kingdom of Jordan, which limits the extraction rate from wells.[487]

Rhine

The Rhine regime is one of the oldest[488] and, comparatively, most successful international regimes for the protection of rivers. The regime was launched in 1963 with the Convention on the Creation of an International Commission for the Protection of Rhine (ICPR) against Pollution. It was supplemented thirteen years later by the Convention on the Protection of Rhine against Chemical Pollution[489] and the Convention on Chlorides Pollution.[490]

One of the early challenges that the Rhine regime was faced with was that of chloride pollution generated principally by the French Mines de Potasse d'Alsace

---

[481] Art. 10, *id.*

[482] Art. 16, *id.*

[483] Arts. 12–14, *id.*

[484] Art. 1, *id.*

[485] Art. 2(1), *id.*

[486] See *infra* Section 5.5.2.

[487] See *supra* Section 5.3.

[488] For the history of the development of the regime, see Ine D. Frijters & Jan Leentvaar, Rhine Case Study, UNESCO, Technical Documents in Hydrology, PCCP series, no. 17, at 4–6 (2003). See also Pieter Huisman et al., Transboundary Cooperation in Shared River Basins: Experiences from the Rhine, Meuse and North Sea, 2 Water Policy 83 (2000).

[489] For the history of the regime, see History – ICPR on its own behalf, available on the ICPR Web site at http://www.iksr.org/hw/icpr/1uk.htm. See also Agreement on the International Commission for the Protection of the Rhine against Pollution, April 29, 1963. The agreement was adopted by the European Community in OJ L 240/50, 19.09.1977. See also Agreement on the Protection of Rhine against Chemical Pollution (with annexes), Dec. 3, 1976, reprinted in 16 ILM 242 (1976). The Rhine flows through France, Germany, Switzerland, and the Netherlands, and its basin affects eight countries.

[490] See *infra* note 492.

(MDPA). The MDPA is responsible for 54 percent of the total chloride levels of the Rhine.[491] Instead of dumping the chlorides in the river, other alternatives for MDPA include dumping the chlorides at sea or injecting them into the ground or temporarily storing them on land.

France contested initially that it was solely responsible for the increased salinity of Dutch waters. A number of studies were commissioned that provided evidence that the Alsace mines were indeed the primary contributors of the increased salinity found in the Dutch waters.

The first convention to address chloride pollution in the Rhine was signed in 1976.[492] The purpose of the convention was to improve the quality of Rhine waters at the German–Netherlands border so that the chloride content is not greater than 200 mg/l.[493] In order to achieve that goal, it was provided that the discharge of chlorides should be reduced by an annual average of 60kg/s "gradually and in French territory."[494] To achieve this reduction, France was to install a system for the injection of chlorides into the Alsace subsoil.[495] The costs of the undertaking were to be shared by France, Germany, Switzerland, and the Netherlands, according to a formula:

Germany:	30 percent
Switzerland:	6 percent
France:	30 percent
Netherlands:	34 percent.

This cost-sharing formula is not quite in agreement with the polluter pays principle. The polluter pays principle would have dictated that France undertakes the bulk of costs for the removal of chlorides. Actually, the Netherlands, which is a recipient of pollution from other states, bears a high portion of the costs.[496]

The Chlorides Treaty was signed in 1976, but it was not ratified by France until 1985. The reluctance to ratify the convention had a lot to do with opposition in the state of Alsace against underground storage. In the meantime, a private action was brought against the MDPA that was settled in 1988 for 3.75 million Dutch guilders.[497]

In 1991, an additional Protocol to the Chlorides Convention was adopted.[498] The cost-sharing formula is similar to the one included in the 1976 Chlorides Convention.[499] The parties agree to reduce the chloride content of Rhine waters so that 200 mg/l is not exceeded but "by a limited amount and for a limited period of time."[500] The protocol does away with the controversial in-ground injection

---

[491] McCaffrey, *supra* note 26, at 256.

[492] Convention on the Protection of the Rhine against Pollution by Chlorides, Dec. 3, 1976 (the convention was amended by an exchange of letters dated April 29, 1983, May 4, 1983, and May 14, 1983), reprinted in 16 ILM 265 (1977).

[493] Preamble, *id.*

[494] Art. 2(1), *id.*

[495] Art. 2(2), *id.*

[496] See also McCaffrey, *supra* note 26, at 257.

[497] *Id.* at 257.

[498] Additional Protocol to the Convention on the Protection of the Rhine Against Pollution by Chlorides, Sept. 25, 1991, reprinted in 1840 UNTS 372.

[499] Art. 4, *id.* See also Annex III, *id.*

[500] Preamble, *id.*

and provides for the temporary storage of chlorides on land.[501] The chlorides that are stored temporarily can be discharged into the Rhine in an ecologically sound manner "once the production in the Alsace Potassium Mines reaches a lower level, and subject to conditions to be determined by the Contracting parties at a later date on the basis of a proposal by the International Commission."[502] Even when chlorides are discharged into the Rhine, the guideline of 200 mg/l must be maintained.[503]

Furthermore, the protocol provides that the Netherlands must take some measures that would contribute to the decrease in the salinity of the Rhine waters.[504] The costs of these measures are to be apportioned by the parties according to the cost-sharing formula of the 1976 convention.

Even the additional protocol, however, did not resolve the problem of the salinity of Rhine waters. In the meantime, the parties brought the issue in front of the Permanent Court of Arbitration (PCA).[505] The Netherlands contended that the purpose of the Chlorides Protocol was to improve the quality of drinking water and that France should bear the costs of chloride pollution according to the polluter pays principle.[506] France, by contrast, contended that the purpose of the protocol is to build solidarity among the riparians of the Rhine and that France should not pay more than the other parties. France based its contention on the financing method used to control pollution. The financing method is based on contributions by all state parties to the protocol.[507]

The PCA was not receptive to the application of the polluter pays principle in its interpretation of the Rhine Chlorides Protocol. The PCA noted the importance of the polluter pays principle in treaty law, but it did not consider the principle as part of the general international law. According to the tribunal:

> 103. Le Tribunal observe que ce principe [polluter pays] figure dans certains instruments internationaux, tant bilatéraux que multilatéraux, et se situe à des niveaux d'effectivité variables. Sans nier son importance en droit conventionnel, le Tribunal ne pense pas que ce principe fasse partie du droit international général.[508]

The tribunal cited the *Oder* case[509] and, specifically, the notion of "community of interests" among riparians. The tribunal concluded that the notion of solidarity of coriparians is an element of their community of interests.[510] The tribunal found that the amounts of waste discharged by France into the Rhine far exceeded the amount provided for in the Chlorides Protocol. The tribunal concluded that France must

[501] Art. 1(1), *id.*
[502] Art. 2, *id.*
[503] *Id.*
[504] Art. 3, *id.*
[505] Arbitration in Application of the Convention of December 3, 1976 on the Protection of Rhine against Pollution by Chlorides and the additional Protocol of September 25, 1991 (March 12, 2004), available online at http://www.pca-cpa.org [hereinafter Chlorides case].
[506] Para. 102, *id.*
[507] Para. 96, *id.*
[508] Unofficial translation: The Tribunal observes that this principle [polluter pays principle] is found in certain international instruments, bilateral and multilateral, and has variable levels of effectiveness. Without negating its importance in treaty law, the Tribunal does not think that this principle is part of general international law.
[509] See Chapter 1, Section 4.5.
[510] Para. 97, Chlorides case, *supra* note 505.

compensate the other parties for the excess amount it has discharged. The amounts of compensation should be calculated in two phases:

1. France must pay to the Netherlands the amount that Netherlands has paid in excess of France's expenditures; and
2. accrued interest that is to be distinguished between interest accrued until December 31, 1998, and interest that accrued afterwards.

The final award of damages to the Netherlands was €18,119,353. France must put aside €1,524,490 for the future control of chlorides pollution in the Rhine.

Several other problems face the riparian nations of the Rhine, such as flood control, the management of fisheries and chemical pollution, and the tackling of emergency situations.[511]

In the late 1990s, many of the instruments that made up the Rhine regime were updated to conform to new developments in international environmental law. The 1999 Rhine Convention[512] was influenced by the Convention on the Protection of North East Atlantic[513] and the 1992 Convention on the Protection and Use of Transboundary Watercourses and International Lakes.[514]

The goals of the 1999 Rhine Convention are to pursue sustainable development in the Rhine ecosystem, to ensure the production of drinking water and flood prevention, and to assist in the restoration of the North Sea.[515] The convention is based on the precautionary principle,[516] the polluter pays principle[517] and the principle of compensation in the event of major technical measures.[518] The principles of application of the state of the art and best environmental practice also are mentioned in the convention.[519]

Thus, the ICPR regime goes even further than the other international regimes; for instance, the international regimes for the protection of the seas. It directly establishes a principle of compensation, not encountered in many other regional instruments and, instead of proposing the use of best available technology (not entailing excessive costs), it boldly endorses the state of the art technology.

The obligations undertaken by the parties are similar to the obligations encountered in other international regimes. The discharges of hazardous substances should be reduced and eventually eliminated.[520] The discharges of wastewater must be subject to authorization.[521] Compliance with permits must be monitored and permit requirements must be reviewed frequently.[522]

---

[511] Frijters, *supra* note 488, at 23–29.
[512] Convention on the Protection of the Rhine, April 12, 1999, reprinted in OJ L 289/31, 16.11.2000 [hereinafter 1999 Rhine Convention].
[513] See Chapter 4, Section 4.1.
[514] See Convention on the Protection and Use of Transboundary Watercourses and International Lakes, Mar. 17, 1992, reprinted in 31 ILM 1312 (1992).
[515] Art. 3, 1999 Rhine Convention, *supra* note 512.
[516] Art. 4(a), *id.*
[517] Art. 4(d), *id.*
[518] Art. 4(f), *id.*
[519] Art. 4(h), *id.*
[520] Art. 5(4)(b), *id.*
[521] Art. 5(4)(a), *id.*
[522] Art. 5(4)(c)–(d), *id.*

The Rhine water quality has been improved. The majority of hazardous substances, for which monitoring information exists, exhibit concentrations below the target values set by the parties.[523] But few hazardous substances, such as mercury, cadmium, and PCBs, are still found in high concentrations. Most of these difficult-to-control substances originate from diffuse sources.[524] Wastewater discharges into the Rhine have been reduced significantly, as 90 percent of the households in the Rhine catchment area are connected to municipal sewage treatment plants.[525]

The success of the regime has to do with the resources of the signatory state parties that are affluent Western European countries.[526] The small number of state parties also facilitates monitoring and compliance.

Danube

The Convention for the Protection of the Danube River[527] was adopted two years after the adoption of the Convention for the Protection of Transboundary Watercourses.[528] The Danube is the second longest river in Europe, running through a large number of countries including Germany, Austria, Bosnia and Herzegovina, Bulgaria, Croatia, the Czech Republic, Hungary, Moldova, Romania, the Slovak Republic, Slovenia, Yugoslavia, and Ukraine. Thus, unlike the Rhine regime, the Danube regime is to face challenges not only because of the large number of countries whose policies need to be coordinated, but also because of the issues[529] that most of these countries are facing as they are restructuring their institutions and economies.

One of the objectives of the Danube Convention is to achieve the goals of "sustainable and equitable water management"[530] and to "at least maintain and improve the current environmental and water quality conditions of the Danube River."[531] The convention is based on the precautionary principle and polluter pays principle[532] and recommends the application of the best available techniques and best environmental practices.[533] The convention allows for both emission limit values[534] and water quality objectives.[535] Annex II of the convention lists a number of industrial sectors that must be regulated and the substances whose discharges should be prevented or reduced considerably.[536] The International Commission for the Protection of the Danube River (ICPDR), established under the convention, updates the

---

[523] See State of Rhine: yesterday-today-tomorrow 9, Conference of Rhine Ministers, Jan. 29, 2001.

[524] State of the Rhine, *id.* at 3.

[525] *Id.* at 2, 7.

[526] State parties include: Germany, France, Luxembourg, the Netherlands and Switzerland.

[527] Convention on Cooperation for the Protection and Sustainable Use of the Danube River, June 29, 1994, reprinted in OJ L 342/19, 12.12.1997, available online at http://www.icpdr.org [hereinafter Danube Convention].

[528] See *supra* note 514.

[529] See, e.g., Aaron Schwabach, The Tisza Cyanide Disaster and International Law, 30 Environmental Law Reporter 10509 (2000).

[530] Art. 2(1), Danube Convention, *supra* note 527.

[531] Art. 2(2), *id.*

[532] Art. 2(4), *id.*

[533] Annex I, *id.*

[534] Art. 7(1), *id.*

[535] Art. 7(4), *id.*

[536] Art. 7(3), *id.*

list of substances at regular intervals. Additional emphasis is put on the importance of keeping emission inventories,[537] harmonizing monitoring programs and methodologies,[538] and reporting to the ICPDR on laws, activities, institutions, and financial expenses related to the protection of the Danube River.[539] Providing information to the public on request[540] has assumed the center stage under the obvious influence of the Aarhus Convention.[541]

Water quality in the Danube has been improving. Further infrastructure projects, including the development of wastewater treatment plants, are likely to contribute even more to the improvement of water quality. Hazardous substances, and especially heavy metals, have been more resistant to controls and some concentrations are actually increasing. The ICPDR has identified the chemical, food, pulp, and paper industries to be the major industrial polluters of the Danube River Basin.[542] The ICPDR has issued Recommendations on the best available techniques to be applied by these sectors.[543]

Pollution from diffuse sources, especially agriculture and animal farming, has yet to be adequately monitored and controlled. The establishment of inventories of pollutants from diffuse sources is one of the future goals of state parties to the convention.

Most parties to the Danube treaty are member states of the European Union or candidate countries. Therefore, efforts have concentrated on the implementation of the Water Framework Directive and the development of an International River Basin Management Plan.

Aral Sea

The Aral Sea region is comprised of the former states of the Soviet Union – Kazakhstan, Kyrgyzstan, Tajikistan, Turkmenistan, and Uzbekistan – as well as Northern Afghanistan and China's Xinjiang Uighur Autonomous Region. During the Soviet Union era, the management of the Aral Sea was a problem internal to the Soviet Union. After the breakup of the Soviet Union, water distribution issues assumed international dimensions.

Two major rivers flow in the region and end up in the Aral Sea: Amu Darya and Syr Darya. The mismanagement of the Aral was infamous during the Soviet era, and many commentators have considered the Aral Sea Basin an environmental disaster. Once one of four largest lakes in the world, the Aral Sea has shrunk to half its original size. Even today, the water quality is considered quite poor, with high amounts of salt, fertilizers, and pesticides. The groundwater is considered equally contaminated. Irrigation agriculture is one of the major activities in the region and

---

[537] Art. 8, *id.*

[538] Art. 9, *id.*

[539] Art. 10, *id.*

[540] Art. 14, *id.*

[541] See Chapter 3.

[542] See Recommendation on Best Available Techniques in the Chemical Industry (IC/34), Sept. 5, 2000; Recommendation on Best Available Techniques in the Food Industry (IC/33), Sept. 5, 2000; Recommendation on Best Available Techniques in the Chemical Pulping Industry (IC/35), Sept. 5, 2000; Recommendation on Best Available Techniques in the Papermaking Industry (IC/36), Sept. 5, 2000.

[543] *Id.*

the rivers that end up in the sea have been heavily managed and built upon. Between the 1960s and 1980s, an extensive network of canals, dams, and reservoirs had been built in the basin.[544]

Most waters that end up in the Aral Sea originate in the upstream states of Tajikistan and Kyrgyzstan, whereas the downstream states of Uzbekistan, Turkmenistan, and Kazakhstan experience water shortages. Most of the water in these downstream states is consumed in cotton fields, because cotton is the major export item for these states.

The first treaty to regulate the water distribution among the states in the region, after the breakup of the Soviet Union, was the Almaty treaty of 1992.[545] The treaty provisions were more or less a replica of the allocations prevalent during the Soviet era that distributed most of the available water to downstream states. Under the 1992 treaty, the management of the water allocations was assigned to the Interstate Water Management Coordination Commission (IWMC).

Other agreements have been put into effect since 1992. An agreement with an environmental focus was signed in 1993.[546] The agreement focuses, *inter alia*, on "restoring the balance of the destroyed ecosystems in the region," "enhancing the discipline of water usage in the basin," "addressing the urgent problem of clean drinking water supply" and meeting "the requirements of environmental safety for the people in the region."[547] The agreement provides that the Russian Federation is to work as an observer "in addressing the Aral Sea crisis and the rehabilitation of the disaster zone."[548] The agreement establishes an Interstate Council and an Executive Committee.[549]

A further resolution was adopted in 1999 on the clarification of legal status of the International Aral Sea Fund (IASF) that was initially established in 1993.[550] Yet another resolution was adopted in 1995, which provided for the implementation of an action plan on the improvement of the ecological situation in the Aral Sea "with consideration for social and economic problems of the region."[551]

Many commentators have criticized the institutional overlap among the different organizations established under the different treaties and have emphasized the need to clarify the roles of the IWMC, the Interstate Council, the IASF, and their subsidiary

---

[544] Valery Votrin, Transboundary Water Disputes in Central Asia: Using Indicators of Water Conflict in Identifying Water Conflict Potential (thesis, Vrije Universiteit Brussel, 2003).

[545] Agreement on Co-operation in the Field of Joint Management and Conservation of Interstate Water Resources, Almaty, Feb. 18, 1992.

[546] Agreement between the Republic of Kazakhstan, Kyrgyz Republic, Republic of Tajikistan, Turkmenistan, and Republic of Uzbekistan on Joint Activities in Addressing the Aral Sea and the Zone Around the Sea Crisis, Improving the Environment, and Ensuring the Social and Economic Development of the Aral Sea Region, Mar. 26, 1993.

[547] Art. I, *id.*

[548] Art. III, *id.*

[549] Art. II, *id.*

[550] Resolution of Heads of States of Central Asia on the Agreement between Kazakhstan, Kyrgyz Republic, Tajikistan, Turkmenistan, and Uzbekistan on the Status of the International Aral Sea Fund and its Organizations, April 9, 1999.

[551] Resolution of the Heads of States of Central Asia on Work of the EC of ICAS on Implementation of Action Plan on the Improvement of Ecological Situation in the Aral Sea Basin for the Three to Five Years to come with Consideration for Social and Economic Development of the Region, Mar. 3, 1995, available online at http://ocid.nacse.org.

organs.[552] Some of the institutional overlap has been attributed to donor programs that operate in the region totally disconnected from each other.[553]

The issue of water allocation has been acute, as upstream states are eager to develop their hydroelectricity potential, whereas the downstream states insist on water allocations based on past distributions. In order to achieve both goals, the states of the central Asia have entered into barter agreements. Irrigation water is provided by upstream states, whereas downstream states are to provide electricity in exchange. An agreement among Kazakhstan, Kyrgyzstan, and Uzbekistan provides for exchanges of water for electricity.[554] According to the agreement, the downstream states are to cooperate in providing electric power to the upstream state, Kyrgyzstan. Kyrgyzstan's water delivery is made conditional on such cooperation.[555] Kyrgyzstan is the only party that agrees to reduce its energy consumption by 10 percent, but no equivalent reductions are undertaken by downstream states in terms of water conservation.

A further agreement was pursued among Kazakhstan, Kyrgyzstan, and Uzbekistan "on cooperation in the area of environmental and rational nature use."[556] The agreement refers, *inter alia*, to the protection and rational use of natural resources on the basis of equality of rights and mutual benefit,[557] the harmonization of environmental legislation,[558] and the requirement of prior notification for projects that may have "ill effects" on the adjacent countries.[559]

Despite the flamboyant rhetoric, however, most of the environmental agreements have not been implemented and the situation in the Aral Sea remains as dire as ever. The barter agreements are hardly applied in practice because of suspicions among the parties that, after they execute their obligations, their coriparians would refuse to execute their share of the agreement. Privatization of water and energy sources has increased the uncertainty regarding the execution of barter agreements.[560] Attempts by international agencies to mediate conflicts and disagreements between the parties are not always welcomed. Problems in the region could become even more explosive, as Afghanistan could, in the future, assert its water rights.[561]

---

[552] Syr Darya River Basin Transboundary Technical Assistance on Cooperation in Regional Water Management 5 (Prepared by PA Consortium Group and funded by U.S. Agency for International Development), Aug. 31, 2001.

[553] Erika Weinthal, Central Asia: The Aral Sea Problem, 5(6) Foreign Policy in Focus, Mar. 2000.

[554] Agreement between the Governments of the Republic of Kazakhstan, the Kyrgyz Republic, and the Republic of Uzbekistan on the Use of Water and Energy Resources of the Syr Darya Basin, Mar. 17, 1998, available online at http://ocid.nasce.org. An agreement in 1999 added Tajikistan in the arrangement. See Protocol on Inserting Amendments and Addenda in the Agreement between the Governments of the Republic of Kazakhstan, the Kyrgyz Republic, and the Republic of Uzbekistan on the Use of Water and Energy Resources of the Syr Darya Basin, May 7, 1999, available online at http://ocid.nasce.org.

[555] Art. 6, *id.*

[556] Agreement between the Governments of the Republic of Kazakhstan, the Kyrgyz Republic and the Republic of Uzbekistan on Cooperation in the Area of Environment and Rational Nature Use, Mar. 17, 1998, available online at http://ocid.nasce.org.

[557] Art. 1, *id.*

[558] Art. 2(a), *id.*

[559] Art. 3, *id.*

[560] Weinthal, *supra* note 553.

[561] Votrin, *supra* note 544.

5.5. American Region

5.5.1. United States–Canada

The United States and Canada have had disputes with regard to their shared water resources, which they have tried to resolve through a number of bilateral agreements. The first such agreement was the 1909 U.S.-Canada Boundary Water Treaty.[562] The treaty does not address the shared waters of the two countries on a river basin basis but regulates only the use of waters at the border area between the United States and Canada. The treaty is both a suprabasin agreement, because it deals with all border waters, and a subbasin agreement, because it has restricted itself to waters in the border area.[563] Because of the many issues involved, and the transaction costs of negotiating a treaty that would deal with all shared river basins, it was more expedient to proceed initially with a boundary treaty.[564] The treaty specifically provides that it does not constitute a river basin agreement because the parties have "exclusive jurisdiction and control over the use and diversion, whether temporary or permanent, of all waters on [their] own side of the line."[565] This provision was interpreted by Canada, with regard to the shared Columbia River, as the embodiment of the Harmon doctrine of absolute territorial sovereignty.

The treaty provides, however, that any interference or diversion of waters that causes harm on the other side would give injured parties the same rights and legal remedies as if the injury took place in the country where the diversion or interference occurred.[566] The parties are not to construct works on the shared water resources, the effect of which would be to raise the natural level of waters on the other side of the boundary, unless such construction is approved by the International Joint Commission (IJC) established under the treaty.[567] Furthermore, the treaty provides that that boundary waters "shall not be polluted on either side to the injury of health or property on the other,"[568] which is remarkable for an agreement signed in 1909.

Regarding the allocation of water resources, the treaty makes allusion to the concept of equitable utilization by providing that parties must have "equal and similar" rights in the use of the waters.[569] It provides "an order of precedence" for the use of water (placing water use for domestic and sanitary purposes first). The existing use of boundary waters is not to be disturbed.[570]

The convention establishes a Joint Commission comprised of six commissioners (three from the United States and three from Canada).[571] The commission has several

---

[562] Treaty Relating to the Boundary Waters and Questions Arising along the Boundary between the United States and Canada, Jan 11, 1909, available online at http://www.ijc.org (international joint commission website) [hereinafter Boundary Waters Treaty].

[563] See Itay Fischhendler, Can Basin Management be Successfully Ignored?, The Case of the US-Canada Transboundary Water, Occasional Paper No. 52, at 16, School of Oriental and African Studies/King's College London, University of London, May 2003.

[564] *Id.* at 8.

[565] Art. II, Boundary Waters Treaty, *supra* note 562.

[566] Art. II, *id.*

[567] Art. IV, *id.*

[568] *Id.*

[569] Art. VIII, *id.*

[570] *Id.*

[571] Art. VII, *id.*

tasks including approval of governmental applications for development projects in the transboundary area, monitoring, and dispute settlement. Regarding the settlement of disputes between the parties, however, the role of the commission is advisory. It is clearly provided that the reports of the commission on dispute settlement matters shall not have the character of arbitral awards.[572] Despite its limited official role in settling disputes between the parties, the commission has been able to reconcile over 130 contested matters since its establishment.

A boundary water treaty, as expected, could not address all the issues between the riparians. The United States and Canada, therefore, had to go back to the negotiating table to conclude agreements and address issues that the boundary treaty could not by its nature address. Subsequently, two other agreements were adopted: an agreement that addressed the shared waters of the Columbia River on a river basin scale and a treaty that provided measures for the restoration of waters of the Great Lakes.

The Columbia River Basin Agreement was adopted as a result of a dispute with regard to the diversion of the waters of the Columbia River. Canada used the provision of the 1909 Boundary Treaty[573] and claimed that the Harmon doctrine applied to the waters of Columbia. Canada is the upstream state and United States, via its position as a downstream state, is dependent on Canada. The dispute over the waters of Columbia became acute when Canada decided to build a dam to divert the waters of the Columbia River to an area wholly within the jurisdiction of Canada in order to produce hydroelectricity. In this attempt, Canada did not take into account the needs of the United States.[574] Eventually, the parties adopted a river basin agreement encompassing all potential uses of water on a river basin scale.[575] The agreement is one of the first agreements that alludes to the concept of integrated river basin management.

The United States and Canada adopted a 1972 agreement on water quality[576] that was replaced in 1978 by the United States-Canada Great Lakes Quality Agreement.[577] The 1978 agreement was further amended in 1983[578] and 1987.[579] The Great Lakes Quality Agreement is in essence an agreement the primary purpose of which is the restoration of some of the degraded areas of the Great Lakes. The purpose of the 1987 version of the agreement is to maintain and restore the chemical, physical, and biological integrity of Great Lakes waters,[580] thereby adopting an ecosystem approach to the management of those waters. The agreement provides

---

[572] Art. IX, *id.*

[573] See *supra* note 565.

[574] Fischhendler, *supra* note 563, at 11.

[575] Treaty relating to Cooperative Development of the Water Resources of the Columbia River Basin, Jan. 17, 1961, and exchange of notes Jan. 22, 1964, and Sept. 16, 1964, reprinted in 542 UNTS 244.

[576] Agreement between the United States and Canada Concerning the Water Quality of the Great Lakes, April 15, 1972, reprinted in 11 ILM 694 (1972).

[577] Agreement between the United States and Canada on the Water Quality of the Great Lakes, Nov. 22, 1978, reprinted in 30 UST 1383.

[578] Oct. 16, 1983, available online at http://sedac.ciesin.columbia.edu/entri/ (environmental treaties and resource indicators (ENTRI)).

[579] The 1987 text of the agreement is available at the United States Environmental Protection Agency Web site at http://www.epa.gov.

[580] Art. II, *id.*

for the control of polluting activities, the elimination or reduction of the release of hazardous substances into the waters, and the establishment of areas of concern.[581] Annex II of the agreement provides for remedial action plans and lakewide management plans in areas of concern that aim, as a general principle, to apply the ecosystem approach[582] and to assist in the virtual elimination of persistent toxic substances.[583]

The Joint Commission, established under the 1909 Boundary Agreement, is responsible for the execution of the Great Lakes Quality Agreement. The commission is to collect and to analyze data and to deal with various issues presented under the agreement.[584] The commission has more powers than a typical international commission since it can conduct public hearings and demand testimony and documentation.[585] The commission has the mandate to verify the data provided to it.[586] A Water Quality Board and a Science Advisory Board assist the commission in the execution of its tasks.[587] Remedial action for areas of concern must be submitted to the commission in three stages:

1. when a definition of the problem to be addressed has been completed;
2. when the remedial and regulatory measures have been identified; and
3. when monitoring indicates that the desired results have been achieved.[588]

The parties are to report to the commission on their progress.[589]

In 1987, the parties designated forty-two areas of concern (twenty-five areas in the United States, twelve in Canada, and five shared areas). The commission has provided governments with reports on the progress of the restoration of Great Lakes and has published guidelines for the listing and delisting of areas of concern. Based on the information provided by the parties, the commission has been able to construct a map with the areas of concern and a matrix of restorative activities. The commission has urged governments to provide continuously updated information in order to help quantify past efforts and to identify future needs.[590]

5.5.2. United States–Mexico

One of the first allocation issues between the United States and Mexico had to do with the waters of Rio Grande. The dispute was eventually resolved by a 1906 treaty.[591] The convention clearly refers to the concept of equitable utilization of

---

[581] Arts. III, V & VI, *id*. See also Annexes to the convention for more details on measures required regarding the control of dangerous substances, activities, and the undertaking of monitoring and surveillance.

[582] Annex 2, Sec. 2(a), *id*.

[583] Annex 2, Sec. 2(c), *id*.

[584] Art. VII(1), *id*.

[585] Art. VII(2), *id*.

[586] Art. VII (4) & (5), *id*.

[587] Art. VIII, *id*.

[588] Annex 2, Sec. 4(d), *id*.

[589] Annex 2, Sec. 7(b), *id*.

[590] For the current efforts of the Commission, see http://www.ijc.org.

[591] Convention between Mexico and the United States for the Distribution of Waters of Rio Grande, May 21, 1906, available online at http//ocid.nasce.org.

resources.[592] The treaty provides for the construction of a storage dam in the United States and the delivery by the United States to Mexico of sixty thousand acre-feet of water annually based on a monthly schedule.[593] The water delivery is to be made "without cost to Mexico and the United States agrees to pay the whole cost of storing the said quantity of water to be delivered to Mexico."[594] It is provided, however, that the delivery of water must not be construed "as a recognition by the United States of any claim on the part of Mexico to the said waters" and Mexico waives all claims to the waters of Rio Grande.[595]

Further water issues between the countries were eventually addressed in a 1944 treaty (on the Colorado River, the Rio Grande, and the Tijuana River).[596] The treaty apportions the water resources between the countries[597] and, more important, establishes an International Boundary and Water Commission (IBWC). The purpose of the commission is to regulate the rights and obligations of the parties and to arrange for the settlement of disputes. The commission consists of both U.S. and Mexican members. The head of each representation must be an Engineer Commissioner.[598] The treaty is devoted to the allocation of water resources and does not deal with the problems, such as water salinity, that became acute in 1960s.

A number of works executed on the Colorado River by the United States increased the natural salinity of the river to levels that made the waters unacceptable for irrigation in Mexico. After years of negotiations, the United States and Mexico entered into an agreement in 1973 (Minute 242) for a "permanent and definitive solution to the salinity of the Colorado River Basin."[599] The agreement provides that 1.36 million acre-feet of water out of 1.5 million acre-feet to be delivered to Mexico (under the 1944 Treaty) are to have an annual average salinity of no more than 115 ppm ($\pm$ 30 ppm) over the annual average salinity of the Colorado River waters.[600]

Minute 242 attempts to regulate the groundwater that was neglected in 1944 Treaty. Minute 242 provides that, pending a conclusion of a comprehensive agreement on groundwater, each country must limit the abstraction of groundwater to specific amounts.[601] In order to avoid future problems, the countries must consult with each other with regard to new developments of their groundwater and surface waters.[602] The United States is to supply "nonreimbursable assistance," on a basis

---

[592] The preamble mentions that the United States and Mexico are "desirous to provide for the equitable distribution of the waters of the Rio Grande for irrigation purposes." *Id.*

[593] Arts. I & II, *id.*

[594] Art. III, *id.*

[595] Art. IV, *id.*

[596] Treaty between the United States and Mexico Relating to the Waters of the Colorado and Tijuana Rivers and of the Rio Grande (Rio Bravo) from Fort Quitman, Texas, to the Gulf of Mexico, Feb. 3, 1944, reprinted in 3 UNTS 314. The treaty was supplemented by a protocol signed on Nov. 14, 1944, available online at http://ocid.nasce.org.

[597] Art. 4 (Rio Grande (Rio Bravo)), Art. 10, 11 (Colorado), Art. 16 (Tijuana), *id.*

[598] Art. 2, *id.*

[599] Mexico-U.S. Agreement on the Permanent and Definitive Solution to the Salinity of the Colorado River Basin (International Boundary and Water Commission Minute 242), reprinted in TIAS No. 7708, 12 ILM 1105 (1973) available online at http://www.ocid.nasce.org.

[600] Section 1(a), *id.*

[601] Section 5, *id.*

[602] Section 6, *id.*

accepted to both countries, exclusively for the rehabilitation of the Mexicali Valley relating to the salinity problem.[603]

The agreement between the United States and Mexico demonstrates that issues of water quantity and water quality are nonseparable in practice. Mexico received the water promised by the United States, but it was of such poor quality that it caused more damage than good. The agreement also demonstrates that the management of groundwater and surface waters cannot be neatly separated.

6. CONCLUSION

The examination of the case studies demonstrates that integrated water management, although it has been offered as a model for regional agreements, is not the norm in state practice. Water allocation has been the paramount issue in most regions, especially those that deal with water scarcity. When allocation is the issue of paramount concern, water quality is often sidelined.

Water quality issues have been pronounced on continents that have made heavy use of their waters when the pollution of certain rivers seems to reach the point of no return. Efforts to restore rivers have been undertaken, however, and are bound to continue in a more organized fashion as the Water Framework Directive adopted by the EU presents the ambition to implement integrated water management in Europe.

Most agreements have established commissions, the purpose of which is to collect data, monitor the shared resources, and propose solutions in case of conflict. Most of these commissions do not have legislative or dispute resolution authority, but their recommendations, because they are based on scientific data, are influential on policy making in different regions.

The notion of equity, as expressed in most regional agreements, is an equity that has to do with the fair allocation of benefits and costs that come from water management. A fifty-fifty allocation of the water resources *per se* is rarely found in regional agreements. The application of equity must not be understood as an attempt to render states equal but as an effort to address the needs of states under the dynamics of power configuration in a region. In most cases, the needs of coriparians are taken into account, especially when this is allowed by water abundance. Even countries that could be considered regional hegemons often have opted for cooperative solutions in water management.

---

[603] Section 7, *id.*

6 Fisheries Resources

1. STATE OF WORLD FISHERIES

The state of world fisheries is considered under threat with reports forecasting the depletion or collapse of fisheries resources. The FAO has documented that of all major fisheries, 35 percent are subject to severe overfishing, 25 percent are fully exploited, and 40 percent present scope for further development.[1] Furthermore, more than 90 percent of fish stocks are under national jurisdiction, and efforts at the national level are crucial for their protection.

In 2002, the FAO reported that, following a decline to 79.2 million tons in 1998, the total production of fisheries increased to 84.7 million tons in 1999. The production of fisheries increased further to 86 million tons in 2000, recovering to the historical maximum levels recorded in 1996 and 1997.[2] According to the FAO, as fishing pressure increases, underexploited resources continue to decline, fully exploited fisheries remain relatively stable, and overexploited, depleted, or recovering stocks increase slightly.[3] Catches from the northwest and southwest Atlantic have remained relatively stable for the last five to ten years. But the failure of cod, redfish, and haddock to rebound in the northwest Atlantic has been a source of concern.[4] Most tuna stocks are fully exploited in all oceans and some are overfished or even depleted.[5] The major cause for the depletion of fisheries has to do with the overcapacity of fishing fleets, which do not allow for the recovery of the resource.

In addition to fisheries, many marine species are claimed to be endangered. The overharvesting of whales, it has been claimed, has led to the decline of species, which justifies a moratorium on whale harvesting. Dolphins and other marine mammals are claimed to be driven gradually to extinction by nonselective gear, such as large driftnets.

Evidence that determines with certainty how fisheries perform under different threats is rarely incontrovertible. Errors in the data provided or unforeseeable events

---

[1] Ministerial Meeting on the Implementation of the Code of Conduct for Responsible Fisheries, The Management of Fishing Capacity: A New but Crucial Issue for Sustainable World Fisheries, Rome, Italy (FI:MM/99/2), March 10–11, 1999.

[2] FAO, State of the World's Fisheries and Aquaculture 21 (2002) [hereinafter FAO Fisheries].

[3] Id. at 22–23.

[4] Id. at 23.

[5] Id. at 26.

that have adverse effects on fisheries have often confounded estimates and have led to over-harvesting.

In 1992, the United States reported that the northern cod population had declined to the point that it was on the verge of extinction. A moratorium was declared, thus, on the entire northern cod fishery. In 1995, it was decided, further, that the northern cod should remain closed for the next ten to fifteen years.[6] The crisis was attributed to overfishing fueled by optimistic Total Allowable Catches (TACs) permitted by policy makers and founded on erroneous scientific evidence.[7] In addition to the genuine problem of forecasting the growth of fisheries population,[8] the fact that scientists were isolated from policy makers and from the fishers who operate in the seas did not help the overall situation. The TACs that were established were not of much assistance because they were based on data provided by industry, data that were often distorted because of unreported discards and illegal practices.[9]

Attempts to regulate fisheries have faced many challenges that have to do with the nature of the resource that, since ancient times, has been viewed as an open access resource. Because fisheries cannot be contained in order to be soundly managed, it is easy, for those willing and able, to engage in illegal activities by flouting national and international regulations. The situation is so acute that the FAO published in 2002 an International Plan of Action to Prevent, Deter and Eliminate Illegal, Unreported and Unregulated (IUU) Fishing.

It is difficult to abate illegal fishing because, to begin with, it is hard to estimate the extent and location of fishery resources. Frequently, fishers are unwilling to report their data under the fear of disclosing fishing grounds to competitors. Thus, in addition to illegal fishing, for which reliable data does not exist, there is intentional misreporting and nonreporting.[10] Furthermore, illegal fishing is exacerbated by the large numbers of vessels that are registered in countries with open registries. These countries have no substantial interest in fisheries and frequently fail to exert effective control on fishing vessels that carry their flag. Flag of convenience (FOC) vessels have undermined international efforts to regulate fisheries.[11]

2. NATIONAL MANAGEMENT OF FISHERIES RESOURCES

2.1. Regulation

The regulation of fisheries resources has had the following evolution: in the 1950s, the first quota regimes were introduced. During the same period, some fisheries were closed because of overharvesting, and gear and size controls gradually were

---

[6] Bonnie J. McCay & Alan Christopher Finlayson, The Political Ecology of Crisis and Institutional Change: The Case of the Northern Cod, Presented to the Annual Meeting of the American Anthropological Association, Nov. 15–19, 1995.

[7] Id.

[8] James Wilson, Scientific Uncertainty, Complex Systems, and the Design of Common-Pool Institutions, in The Drama of the Commons 327 (National Academy of Sciences, Elinor Ostrom et al., eds., 2003). (The author reminds us that complex and adaptive systems do not lend themselves to long-term predictions because of the changing and often nonlinear casual relationships).

[9] McCay, *supra* note 6.

[10] FAO Fisheries, *supra* note 2, at 60.

[11] Id. at 65.

imposed. In the 1960s, most states started to issue licenses to a limited number of qualified fishers. Eventually, in the late 1970s, the first Individual Tradable Quota (ITQ) systems were introduced in the hope that transforming fishers into owners would help in the self-regulation of fishery resources.

The rights granted to fishers for the exploitation of fisheries have been divided into access rights and withdrawal rights. Access rights could be Territorial Use Rights in Fishing (TURFs), which involve the assignment of rights to individuals or groups to fish in certain areas usually based on customary usage. Access rights also could be expressed as Limited Entry Rights in the form of a limited number of licenses available to all potential fishers.[12]

Withdrawal rights (also called effort rights) have to do with limitations on the inputs (such as time for fishing, vessel size, and gear type) or limitations on outputs (such as annual quotas or trip limits). An annual quota is usually expressed as a Total Allowable Catch (TAC) and is distributed to persons or communities in the form of Individual Quotas (IQs). These quotas could be subject to trading (ITQs) or no trading (IQs). The initiation of quotas in fisheries, which are distributed to persons or communities, in essence creates property rights over fisheries resources. The privatization of fisheries resources under IQs systems was a calculated response to the failure of traditional regulatory methods to induce the sound management of fisheries. However, privatization has not entailed in this case the lack of regulation. On the contrary, before they become self-enforcing, IQs need to be intensely regulated.[13]

Whether withdrawal rights or access rights are appropriate for the management of specific fisheries depends on the type of fisheries under question and the societal goals that policy makers wish to achieve. For instance, sedentary fishery resources could be amenable to TURFs, whereas for highly mobile fisheries – for which extensive monitoring is required – effort rights may be in order.[14]

ITQs could be assigned to communities or individual fishers depending on societal priorities. Whether ITQs would be assigned to a community has to do with how cohesive this community is and how experienced it is or it can become in fisheries management. A more fundamental question has to do with whether ITQs should be applied at all or whether a strategic planning approach is more preferable. ITQs are usually preferable when the fishery under exploitation is industrial, capital intensive, and profit-driven. For ITQs to become an effective regulatory mechanism, substantial trade markets must be smoothly functioning. But if equity concerns, such as local employment and the basic standards of living of a local community, are at issue strategic planning may be preferable.[15]

Fishery resources are managed usually at the regional level. The central government, however, sets the general guidance and mandates. For instance, in the United States, the 1976 Fishery Conservation and Management Act transferred the rights to manage fishery resources to eight Regional Fishery Management Councils.

---

[12] Anthony T. Charles, Use Rights in Fishery Systems, in "Conference: Property Rights: Design Lessons from Fisheries and Other Natural Resources," 1, 2, International Institute of Fisheries Economies and Trade (IIFET), Oregon State University, 2000.

[13] *Id.* at 3.

[14] *Id.* at 4.

[15] *Id.*

These councils, in cooperation with the appropriate federal agency (the National Marine Fisheries Service), prepare the Fishery Management Plans, that is, total allowable catches and other regulatory requirements, such as gear, vessel size, and quotas.[16]

In the European Union, the Common Fisheries Policy is based on two policy mechanisms: the Multi-Annual Guidance Programme (MAGP) and the TACs. The International Council for the Exploration of Sea (ICES) assesses the global stocks and provides its assessment to the Advisory Committee on Fishery Management (ACFM), which decides what the official ICES advice would be. The European Commission drafts proposals based on the advice of ACFM. The proposals then go to the Council of Ministers for approval. Once the Council of Ministers has adopted the proposal, the TAC is allocated among member states according to the principle of "relative stability," a principle that has to do with the historical allocation of fishery resources.[17]

The EU has engaged in attempts to improve its Common Fisheries Policy by taking into account environmental considerations and by addressing problems such as overcapacity of fishing vessels, inspection, and enforcement.[18] With regard to its external fisheries policy, the EU is increasingly realizing that compliance with the Regional Fisheries Agreements would be fundamental in preserving its fishing rights in areas of high seas outside the EEZ of developing countries. Compliance with the UNCLOS and the 1995 Fisheries Agreement has been urged by the European Commission.[19]

The EU has tried to address fisheries within the concept of Integrated Coastal Zone Management (ICZM) that involves integrating fisheries concerns into the overall management of coastal areas.[20] The European Commission has discussed the establishment of a Community Joint Inspection Structure to coordinate national and EU inspection policies and activities.[21]

2.2. Privatization

Attempts to regulate fishery resources have not been always successful. Fisheries are, by definition, an open access, fleeting resource difficult to supervise. The activities of fishers in the high seas are equally hard to monitor. Privatization, thus, has been presented as an alternative option to command-and-control regulation that dictates specific gear, catches, or timing of fishing activities. The rationale for privatization seems to be incontrovertible: if fishers acquire property rights over fisheries resources, they could refrain from treating the resource as an open-access resource, resulting in

---

[16] Steven F. Edwards, An Elemental Basis of Property Rights to Marine Fishery Resources, in "Conference: Property Rights: Design Lessons from Fisheries and Other Natural Resources," International Institute of Fisheries Economies and Trade (IIFET), Oregon State University, 2000.

[17] Patty L. Clayton, Using Fishermen's Expertise to Improve Fisheries Management, in "Conference: Property Rights: Design Lessons from Fisheries and Other Natural Resources," International Institute of Fisheries Economies and Trade (IIFET), Oregon State University, 2000.

[18] Council Regulation (EC) No 2371/2002 of 20 December 2002 on the conservation and sustainable exploitation of fisheries resources under the Common Fisheries Policy, OJ L 358/59, 31.12.2002.

[19] Green Paper on the Future of the Common Fisheries Policies 18, 32, 35, COM (2001)135 final.

[20] *Id.* at 28.

[21] *Id.* at 31.

a tragedy of commons. Privatization of fisheries resources has taken place in many national fora through the introduction of Individual Tradable Quotas (ITQs).

Six steps need to be completed for the establishment of an Individual Tradable Quota (ITQ) or, as it is otherwise called, Individual Tradable Permit (ITP) system:

1. provision of the upper limit for the overall use of the resource (e.g., TAC);
2. initial allocation of tradable permits;
3. establishment of rules for the trade of quotas;
4. decision on the legal nature of quotas;
5. monitoring procedures; and
6. enforcement.

Each step presents its own level of difficulty, rendering ITQs challenging in countries that do not have a history of regulating effectively private markets. Even in developed countries, such as Germany and the United Kingdom, with competent regulatory institutions, tradable permit regimes have not been as successful as expected.[22] Furthermore, the regulatory and monitoring costs of applying ITQs are quite high. Because of these high costs, ITQs have been used when other regulatory systems have failed.[23]

The upper limit of the use of the resource is usually set by regulation and it is rarely uncontestable. In the case of air pollution (another area in which ITPs have been applied extensively), the upper limit is based on the best scientific evidence of the amount of a pollutant that would not have adverse effects on human health.[24] For natural resources management, the upper limit is set based on the available scientific evidence on the maximum exploitation that a resource can take without being driven to extinction. These estimates are frequently inaccurate and the reason why resources have been often overexploited.

The initial allocation decision is never easy. This is because of the equity issues involved regarding the spread of the TAC among a number of potential users. The question is whether a lottery system would be more successful than a first-come, first-served system or whether historical use patterns should be respected. In the case of fisheries, historical use patterns have been invariably respected because doing otherwise would have made allocation politically untenable.[25]

Whether quotas should be tradable is a matter of contention. Proponents of tradable permits argue that trade in permits grants fishery resources to those who place the highest value on them. Those who want to exit fisheries exploitation get compensation in terms of the money they receive from selling their fishing permits. For the opponents of tradable permits, trade could eventually lead to the concentration of permits in the hands of the few wealthy, for instance, when small fishing businesses are bought out by larger ones.[26] States have addressed the problem of potential monopoly of fishing permits by putting a limit on the number of permits that a legal person could accumulate. Other countries have totally prohibited the transfer of

---

[22] Tom Tietenberg, The Tradable Permits Approach to Protecting the Commons: What Have We Learned?, in The Drama of Commons 197, 216, *supra* note 8.

[23] *Id.*

[24] See Chapter 1, notes 114, 115.

[25] Tietenberg, *supra* note 22, at 207.

[26] *Id.* at 209.

quotas that violates public interest, for instance, the preservation of certain community values. Still other countries have opted for the allocation of quotas directly to communities. These communities retain control over transferability requirements.[27]

Tradable quotas allocate property rights to a resource but with strings attached that are usually tighter than the strings attached to traditional property rights. Tradable permits are not fully articulated property rights. This is because states have been ambivalent about whether fishery resources should remain in the public domain or owned privately. The public trust doctrine dictates that common pool resources belong to the public and that the government is holding them in trust for the public.[28] Under a public trust doctrine, tradable permits should be set to expire after conservation or other goals, for which they have been granted, are not longer relevant (although the possibility of expiration has been quite contentious).[29] Furthermore, tradable permits are rarely banked or borrowed.[30]

Tradable permits present many monitoring problems. In the absence of appropriate monitoring, fishers are tempted to engage in illegal fishing, highgrading (discarding fish of low value to make room for quota fish), and discarding bycatch (non-targeted species discarded after they are caught).[31] To avoid compliance problems, reliable data should exist about the state of fisheries before a decision to issue tradable permits is made. The data should be reviewed frequently, after permits are issued, to identify how the new system is influencing the development of the resource. The institution in charge of fisheries management should keep records of permits issued and to whom they are issued as well as of all permit transfers. An easier way to track the permit system is through computerization. The adoption of software, that would be user friendly (e.g., card swipe systems) and that would give fishers the flexibility to trade, even when they are at sea and have caught more than their quota, has been recommended.[32] Another method to track the data is to establish a paper trail. For instance, to require that fish sales are made to registered buyers and that both buyers and sellers sign the landing entries. The buyers therefore undertake the responsibility of monitoring the sellers and the paperwork that is created may become available for audits.[33] On-board observers and random ship searches also are encouraged when the fisheries bring enough profits to justify such monitoring costs.

The penalties imposed in case of violations should be commensurate with the offense. High penalties, disproportionate with the offense, can generate reluctance on the part of the local authorities to actually enforce them.[34] The imposition of strict penalties by a zealous enforcement agency may generate even more disobedience.

---

[27] Id. at 210.

[28] Id. at 205.

[29] Sevaly Sen et al., ITQs and Property Rights: A Review of Australian Case Law, "Conference: Property Rights: Design Lessons from Fisheries and Other Natural Resources", International Institute of Fisheries Economies and Trade (IIFET), Oregon State University, 2000.

[30] Tietenberg, *supra* note 22, at 211. The Emissions Trading Program in the United States, for instance, has allowed for some banking but not borrowing. Banking or borrowing involves the potential of creating temporarily a high concentration of pollutants. Borrowing and banking complicate further monitoring and enforcement.

[31] Id. at 213.

[32] Id. at 214.

[33] Id.

[34] Id. at 215.

Organized communities, such as fishers, may resist what they conceive as a punitive enforcement system. Whether a tradable permit system is conceived as fair would determine its effectiveness in protecting a resource.

Tradable permits have been effective in controlling air pollution.[35] In the area of fisheries, the evidence is more mixed. For instance, some fisheries experience temporary declines right after a tradable permit system is introduced. This is probably because the TAC is based on unreliable data and the lack of monitoring that leads to illegal activity.[36]

A tradable permit system may be challenged because it produces undesirable distributive effects. Tradable permits usually involve a reduction in fishing effort. Thus, they may reduce employment in a locality. Processing plants may be disadvantaged as they lose their negotiating power over fishers who now have to pace their production. Smaller fishers may be bought out by larger fishers. And fishing communities may disappear completely.[37]

These unequal distributional effects, including the arbitrary character of the initial allocation of quotas, fuel objections against ITQs. Further objections derive from ideological grounds, for instance, a belief that, because the markets are at the source of an environmental problem, they cannot be part of the solution.[38]

3. INTERNATIONAL MANAGEMENT OF FISHERIES RESOURCES

3.1. Law of the Sea Convention

The freedom of high seas, associated with the freedom to navigate the high seas and the freedom of fishing in the high seas, has been one of the cornerstones of international law. However, as issues of overexploitation of fisheries resources crowded the international agenda, the freedom of high seas, at least for the purposes of fisheries exploitation, is being increasingly challenged: by the creation of the Exclusive Economic Zone (EEZ)[39] and by attempts to expand coastal state jurisdiction even in areas beyond the EEZ.

Articles 61 and 63 of the United Nations Law of the Sea Convention (UNCLOS)[40] assign to coastal states the management of marine resources. The burden of proof of whether a fishing activity would have damaging effects on resources now falls on the states that wish to engage in such activity.[41] In regulating such activities the coastal state must take into account the best scientific evidence and resource exploitation must not exceed the maximum sustainable yield.[42]

---

[35] See Chapter 2, n. 126–27.

[36] Tietenberg, *supra* note 22, at 219.

[37] *Id.* at 220–21.

[38] *Id.* at 197–98.

[39] See arts. 55–59, United Nations Convention on the Law of the Sea (UNCLOS), Dec. 10, 1982, reprinted in 21 ILM 1261 (1982). See art. 57: "The exclusive economic zone shall not extend beyond 200 nautical miles from the baselines from which the breadth of the territorial sea is measured."

[40] See *id.*

[41] Francisco Orrego Vicuña, The Changing International Law of High Seas Fisheries 26–27 (1999).

[42] Art. 61(3) & (4), UNCLOS, *supra* note 39.

The convention provides that the responsibility for the management of catadromous stocks must be assigned to states in the waters of which the stocks spend the majority of their time.[43] The harvesting of catadromous stocks should happen only in the waters landward of the outer limits of the EEZ favoring, thus, the coastal state.[44]

Anadromous stocks are stocks that originate in the rivers of states and often end up in the seas, such as salmon. The convention provides that states in whose rivers anadromous stocks originate have the primary interest and responsibility for the management of these stocks.[45] Cooperation with other states is encouraged, however, especially if other states are to become economically dislocated when deprived of the exploitation of such stocks.[46] States must try to reach an agreement with regard to the fishing of anadromous stocks in areas beyond the outer limits of the EEZ.

Highly migratory fish stocks, including tuna, are more difficult to regulate since, as their name indicates, these stocks migrate between the high seas and the EEZ of coastal states. The issue becomes often confrontational because coastal states assert exclusive jurisdiction over the management of these stocks, but distant water fishing states (DWFS) refuse to resign from fishing these stocks in the high seas, claiming the doctrine of freedom of the high seas. Because the exploitation of highly migratory fish stocks has yet to be resolved by consistent state practice, the UNCLOS provisions on the management of these stocks are more tentative. For instance, article 65 refers vaguely to the need of cooperation between coastal states and distant water fishing states. Commentators have noted, however, that high-sea fishing activities should not flout conservation measures of coastal states. Lack of compliance with conservation measures would be incompatible with the spirit of the UNCLOS.[47]

The overall appraisal of the UNCLOS with regard to fisheries management has been positive.[48] For the most part, the convention tries to strike a compromise between the interests of coastal states and the needs of distant water fishing states. The compromise, however, has been difficult to work out in the everyday affairs of states. Flag states are still resenting the extension of coastal state jurisdiction. And regional fisheries management organizations that now have extended their jurisdictional reach to high seas areas have to deal with accommodation issues as a number of new entrants are eager to join in regional fisheries management organizations.

3.2. Case Law

The international regulation of fisheries and marine mammals has been the subject of international attention since 1893, when the first arbitration case, the *Behring Sea Seals* case was decided.[49] The case involved a dispute between the United States and the United Kingdom regarding the taking of fur seals in the Behring Sea. The

---

[43] Art. 67, *id.*
[44] Art. 67(1), *id.*
[45] Art. 66(11), *id.*
[46] Vicuña, *supra* note 41, at 35–36. See also art. 66(3)(a), UNCLOS, *supra* note 39.
[47] Vicuña, *supra* note 41, at 44.
[48] *Id.* at 48.
[49] See *Behring Sea Seals* case, Chapter 1.

question that was put before the tribunal was whether a state has the jurisdiction to take measures for the protection of species outside its territorial waters. The tribunal sided with Great Britain and upheld the freedom of high seas. The tribunal stated, however, that the freedom of high seas should not impede the adoption of regulations that would be protective of species. The tribunal proposed a conservation plan that included protected areas, closed seasons, limitations on inputs, and exchange of information. The tribunal also recommended a three-year ban on the hunting of seals.

The *Behring Sea Seals* arbitration case was the precursor of a series of conventions adopted in 1911, 1942, and 1957 for the protection of seals.[50] The *Behring Sea Seals* arbitration case is important because it shows that, early on, in the evolution of law of the sea, coastal states ventured to impose enforcement of conservation measures beyond their traditionally confined jurisdictional area.

Coastal state jurisdiction has been the subject of two additional cases decided by the ICJ: the *Fisheries Jurisdiction* cases.[51] Both of these cases included similar facts and were decided simultaneously by the ICJ.

One of the *Fisheries Jurisdiction* cases involved a dispute between Iceland and Germany over Iceland's extension of its fishing zone to fifty nautical miles. The ICJ rejected the extension of the fisheries zone but held that Iceland, as a coastal state, had preferential rights over the fisheries just beyond its territorial zone.[52] According to the Court,

> in order to reach an *equitable solution* of the present dispute it is necessary that the preferential fishing rights of Iceland, as a State specially dependent on coastal fisheries, be reconciled with the traditional fishing rights of the Applicant [emphasis added].

The Court repeatedly underlined the preferential rights of coastal states and the importance of conservation measures. The Court stated that

> State practice on the subject of fisheries reveals an increasing and widespread acceptance of the concept of preferential rights for coastal States, particularly in favor of countries or territories in a situation of special dependence on coastal fisheries.[53]

The Court took notice of "the exceptional dependence of Iceland on its fisheries" and of "the need of conservation of fish stocks."[54]

---

[50] Convention Respecting Measures for the Preservation and Protection of the Fur Seals in the North Pacific Ocean, July 7, 1911. The convention has been considered successful in restoring the fur seal population. It was denounced by Japan in 1940. The convention was replaced by the Interim Convention on Conservation of North Pacific Fur Seals, Feb. 9, 1957. The convention established the North Pacific Fur Seals Commission (NPFSC). The convention was further amended, see Protocol Amending the Interim Convention on the Conservation of North Pacific Fur Seals, Oct. 14, 1980. See also Protocol Amending the Interim Convention on Conservation of North Pacific Fur Seals, Oct. 12, 1984. For the text of the treaties and brief summaries, see http://ww.intfish.net/treaties (Internet Guide to International Fisheries Law).

[51] Fisheries Jurisdiction Case, (UK v. Iceland), (Merits), July 25, 1974, (1974) ICJ 3. See also Fisheries Jurisdiction Case, (Federal Republic of Germany v. Iceland), (Merits), July 25, 1974, (1974) ICJ 175.

[52] Paras. 44–45, (Germany v. Iceland), *id*.

[53] Para. 50, *id*.

[54] Para. 37, *id*.

The Court underlined further the importance of the reasonable use of fisheries and the obligation of states to negotiate[55] an equitable solution to the problem.[56] According to the Court:

> It is one of the advances in maritime international law, resulting from the intensification of fishing, that the former *laissez-faire* treatment of the living resources of the sea in the high seas has been replaced by a recognition of a duty to have due regard to the rights of other States and the needs of conservation for the benefit of all.[57]

According to the Court, both parties have an obligation to keep under review the fisheries resources. The parties must examine together, based on scientific evidence and other information, the measures required for "the conservation and development, and equitable exploitation"[58] of resources taking into account international agreements.

The Court concluded that the task before the parties is to conduct negotiations:

> on the basis that each must in good faith pay reasonable regard to the legal rights of the other ... bringing about an *equitable apportionment of the fishing resources* based on the facts of the particular situation, and having regard to the interests of other States which have established fishing rights in the area [emphasis added].[59]

The Court repeated its pronouncement in the *North Sea Continental Shelf* cases that the point is not simply of finding "an equitable solution, but an equitable solution derived from the applicable law." The Court repeated phraseology included in the *North Sea Continental Shelf* cases:

> ... it is not a question of applying equity simply as a matter of abstract justice, but of applying a rule of law which itself requires the application of equitable principles.[60]

The Court's pronouncement of equity is further elucidated by its *dicta* in the *North Sea Continental Self* cases. In those cases, the Court mentioned with regard to equity:

> There can never be any question of completely refashioning nature, and equity does not require that a State without access to the sea should be allotted an area of continental shelf, any more than there could be a question of rendering the situation of a State with an extensive coastline similar to that of a State with a restricted coastline. Equality is to be reckoned within the same plane, and it is not such natural inequalities as these that equity could remedy.[61]

---

[55] Para. 65, *id.*

[56] According to the Court, "The most appropriate method for the solution of the dispute is clearly that of negotiation. Its objective should be the delimitation of the rights and interests of the Parties, the preferential rights of the coastal State on the one hand and rights of the Applicant on the other, to balance and regulate equitably questions such as those of catch limitation, share allocation" and other related issues. *Id.*

[57] Para. 64, *id.*

[58] *Id.*

[59] Para. 69, *id.*

[60] *Id.* See also para. 85, North Sea Continental Shelf cases, (Federal Republic of Germany/Denmark; Federal Republic of Germany/the Netherlands), (Judgment), Feb. 20, 1969, (1969) ICJ Reports 3.

[61] Para. 91, *id.*

In other words, the Court stated that equity does not mean equality. The law is not the institution that would bring conditions of equality among states. It is, instead, an institution that, taking into account "natural" inequalities, attempts to even the level playing field among states. That is, although the inequalities between states would continue to exist, the law provides devices that could help remedy some of the inequality. But the law could not possibly place states in an abstract condition of absolute equality.

Recent disputes over fisheries have to do with the different priorities of states parties to regional fisheries organizations. A regional fisheries organization often sets the TAC within a region. It then allocates the TAC among state parties. Regional organizations often give state parties the right to object to the assigned quota and, thus, to engage in unilateral fishing programs. Such programs have been brought before international tribunals that usually decline jurisdiction in such cases but have issued statements of caution about the importance of prudent management under situations of uncertainty.

In the *Southern Bluefin Tuna* case, for instance, Australia and New Zealand contested, before International Tribunal for the Law of the Sea (ITLOS), the lawfulness of Japan's decision to engage in a unilateral fishing program. All three countries are parties to the Convention for the Conservation of Southern Buefin Tuna[62] but could not agree on a TAC. Before the ITLOS proceeded on the merits, Australia and New Zealand asked the tribunal to issue provisional measures. The tribunal issued provisional measures asking all parties to resort to the quotas in force before the dispute erupted. The ITLOS urged the parties that, in the absence of scientific certainty, they should proceed with prudence and caution.[63] But the tribunal established eventually concluded that it did not have jurisdiction to decide on the merits of the case.[64]

The *Estai* case[65] involved a dispute between Canada and the European Community over the TAC established by the North Atlantic Fisheries Organization (NAFO). In 1995, the European Community disputed the quota set by the NAFO and set its own quota. On March 9, 1995, the Spanish fishing vessel *Estai* was boarded by Canadian inspectors and charged with violating Canada's fisheries protection laws. Spain brought the issue before the ICJ, but the Court held that it had no jurisdiction to decide the case because Canada invoked a reservation clause with regard to conservation measures taken within the NAFO area. Despite the lack of jurisdiction, the Court did not agree with Spain's position that the Canadian measures did not qualify as conservation measures.

In the *Monte Confurco* case,[66] Seychelles, Belize, and Panama challenged France's seizure of their vessels in the latter's EEZ. The case involved the interpretation of article 73 of the UNCLOS that deals with enforcement of laws and regulations of coastal states in their EEZs. According to article 73:

1. The coastal State may, in the exercise of its sovereign rights to explore, exploit, conserve, and manage the living resources in the exclusive economic zone, take

---

[62] May 10 1993, reprinted in 1819 UNTS 360.

[63] *Southern Bluefin Tuna* cases, (New Zealand v. Japan; Australia v. Japan), ITLOS Provisional Measures, reprinted in 38 ILM 1624 (1999).

[64] *Southern Bluefin Tuna* Arbitral Award, Aug. 24, 2000, reprinted in 39 ILM 1359 (2000).

[65] Fisheries Jurisdiction Case, (Spain v. Canada), (Estai Case), Dec. 4, 1998, (1998) ICJ Reports 432.

[66] The *Monte Confurco* case, (Seychelles v. France), (Application for Prompt Release), Dec. 18, 2000, List of cases No. 6, ITLOS 2000, available online at http://www.itlos.org.

such measures, including boarding, inspection, arrest and judicial proceedings, as may be necessary to ensure compliance with the laws and regulations adopted by it in conformity with this Convention.

2. Arresting vessels and their crews shall be promptly released upon the posting of reasonable bond or other security.
3. Coastal State penalties for violations of fisheries laws and regulations in the exclusive economic zone may not include imprisonment, in the absence of agreements to the contrary by the States concerned, or any other form of corporal punishment.
4. In cases of arrest or detention of foreign vessels the coastal State shall promptly notify the flag State, through appropriate channels, of the action taken and of any penalties subsequently imposed.

The interpretation of article 73 was brought before the ITLOS based on article 292 of the UNCLOS. Article 292 provides that the ITLOS has jurisdiction over cases that involve the prompt release of vessels and crews detained by a party to the UNCLOS – on the posting of a reasonable bond or other financial security.

The plaintiff states in this case did not challenge the enforcement authority of the coastal state. They questioned, however, the extent of that authority in terms of imposing reasonable sanctions. Seychelles did not contest the enforcement authority of France in terms of article 73(1) but asked the tribunal to declare that France had violated:

• article 73(4) with regard to giving notice to the flag state;
• article 73(3) by engaging in the unlawful detention of the master of the vessel; and
• article 73(2) with regard to the posting of "reasonable" bond. According to Seychelles, the bond requested by France was not reasonable.[67]

The tribunal declared the claims of Seychelles not admissible with regard to articles 73(3) and 73(4) because article 292(1) does not explicitly provide for the tribunal's jurisdiction over the implementation of these articles.[68] With regard to the posting of a reasonable bond, the tribunal revisited its decision in the *Camouco* case and declared the bond demanded by France unreasonable.

More specifically, in the *Camouco* case,[69] the ITLOS had held that a number of factors are relevant in the assessment of the reasonableness of bonds and other financial security. Such factors include: the gravity of the alleged offense, the penalties imposed under the circumstances by the law of the detaining state, the value of the detained vessel and of the cargo seized, and the amount and form of the bond imposed by the detaining state. These factors, though, the tribunal held, are not exclusive and their function is to complement rather than replace the criterion of reasonableness.[70] The

---

[67] Paras. 3–6, *id.*

[68] Paras. 61–63, *id.*

[69] The *Camouco* case involved a dispute between Panama and France along the same lines as the *Monte Confurco* case. For the discussion of reasonableness of bond, see paras. 64–68 of the *Camouco* case. In the *Camouco* case, the tribunal reduced the amount of bond from 20 million FF to 8 million FF. See *Camouco* case, (Panama v. France), (Application for Prompt Release), Feb. 7, 2000, List of cases No. 5, ITLOS 2000, available online at http://www.itlos.org.

[70] Para. 76, *Monte Confurco* case, *supra* note 66.

tribunal stated that it did not intend to establish rigid rules and the exact weight to be attached to each of these factors.

France, to strengthen its claims, asked the tribunal to take into account the general context of unlawful fishing in the region. According to France, the illegal fishing in the region was a threat to resources and violated the measures taken by the Commission for the Conservation of Antarctic Marine Living Resources (CCAMLR) for the conservation of the Patagonian toothfish.[71]

The tribunal referred to the French law,[72] the value of the vessel,[73] and the value of the cargo and fishing gear. The tribunal noted that the parties did not dispute the value of the cargo, which was estimated at 9,000,000 FF (158 tonnes of toothfish).[74] The tribunal relied on the presumption that all fish found on board of the vessel was fished in the EEZ of France, taking into account, therefore, the factual circumstances of the case as requested by France.[75]

The tribunal concluded that the bond of 56.4 million FF imposed by France was unreasonable and reduced the amount of the bond to 18 million FF (9 million FF in cargo value already held by the French authorities and 9 million FF in the form of a bank guarantee).[76]

The *Grand Prince* case[77] involved the seizure of a Belize vessel by French authorities. The case had to do with illegal fishing of Patagonian toothfish in the EEZ of France, which prompted France to detain the vessel. Belize requested the prompt release of the vessel based on the posting of a reasonable bond.

The case is of particular interest because the tribunal did not decide on the merits of the case. The tribunal declined jurisdiction based on the fact that Belize had not proven adequately that it was the flag state of the vessel detained by French authorities. The tribunal based its decision on article 292(2) of the UNCLOS that the application for the prompt release of a vessel may be made "only by or on behalf of the flag state of the vessel." By declaring that it did not have jurisdiction over the case, the tribunal, in effect, denied Belize the possibility to protect the vessel that now, with no nationality, was left at the mercy of the French authorities.

Some commentators have deplored the tribunal's decision as introducing uncertainty in maritime law. If Belize was willing to assume responsibility as the flag state, the argument goes, the tribunal should not have engaged in exploration of whether this was actually the case. The parties wanted the tribunal to decide the case and the tribunal, instead, based on technicalities, decided to deny to adjudicate the case.[78] The decision has been applauded by environmental groups, however, as it strikes a blow to FOC states that fail not only to supervise the vessels that use their flag but also to register such vessels properly.[79] The tribunal's refusal to

[71] Para. 79, *id.*

[72] Para. 83, *id.*

[73] Para. 84, *id.*

[74] Paras. 85–88, *id.*

[75] *Id.*

[76] Para. 93, *id.*

[77] The *Grand Prince* Case, (Belize v. France), (Application for Prompt Release), April 20, 2001, List of Cases No. 8, ITLOS 2001, available online at http://www.itlos.org.

[78] Ted L. McDorman, Case note: The *Grand Prince* (Belize v. France), (2001) International Fisheries Bulletin, No. 15.

[79] *Id.*

adjudicate the case legitimized, in effect, the enforcement authority of the coastal state.

The *Volga* case[80] is yet another case brought before the ILTOS regarding the illegal exploitation of the Patagonian toothfish. The case was brought by the Russian Federation against Australia for the release of the vessel *Volga* and three members of its crew that were caught fishing illegally in the EEZ of Australia. Australia emphasized that "continuing illegal fishing in the area covered by the Convention for the Conservation of Antarctic Marine Living Resources ("CCAMLR") has resulted in a serious depletion of the stocks of Patagonian toothfish and is a matter of international concern."[81] Australia invited the tribunal to take into account

> the serious problem of continuing illegal fishing in the Southern Ocean and the dangers this poses to the conservation of fisheries resources and the maintenance of the ecological balance of the environment.[82]

The tribunal shared the concerns of Australia about illegal, unregulated, and unreported fishing, and appreciated the measures taken by states to deal with the problem.[83] However, the tribunal insisted that, in this case, the issue that it had to decide had to do with the reasonableness of the bond requested based on articles 292 and 73(2) of the UNCLOS.[84]

In rendering its decision, the tribunal revisited its judgment in the *Monte Confurco* case. According to that judgment, the reasonableness of the bond for the release of a vessel is not based solely on the mechanical application of rigid criteria. Certain criteria, however, such as: the gravity of the alleged offenses, the penalties imposed under the laws of the detaining state, the value of the detained vessel and cargo seized, are some of the factors to be taken into account in determining the reasonableness of bond requested by the detaining state.[85]

Australia had requested AU$1,920,000 for the release of the vessel, which reflected the full value of the vessel, fuel, lubricants, and fishing equipment. This was not disputed by Russia.[86] The tribunal, however, observed that Australia made the release of the vessel conditional on the installation of a Vessel Monitoring System (VMS) and a request that information about the ship owners be submitted to the Australian authorities.[87] The tribunal concluded that these additional nonfinancial conditions could not justifiably be considered as part of the bond. The tribunal determined that the bond for the release of the vessel should be set at the amount of AU$1.92 million, an amount to which both parties had agreed before, and that no additional nonfinancial conditions should inhibit the prompt release of the vessel.[88]

---

[80] The *Volga* Case, (Russian Federation v. Australia), (Application for Prompt Release), Dec. 23, 2002, List of Cases No. 11, ITLOS 2002, available online at http://www.itlos.org.

[81] Para. 67, *id*.

[82] *Id*.

[83] Para. 68, *id*.

[84] Para. 69, id

[85] Paras. 63–64, *id*.

[86] Para. 67, *id*.

[87] Para. 75, *id*.

[88] Para. 90, *id*.

The exploitation of the swordfish in the South Pacific was brought both before the ITLOS and the WTO Dispute Settlement Body. The exploitation of the swordfish by the EU in the waters adjacent to the EEZ of Chile had prompted claims by Chile that the EU had failed to respect the UNCLOS. The UNCLOS called for cooperation between coastal states and other states (e.g., distant water fishing states) for the conservation of fish stocks (article 64 of the UNCLOS).[89]

Because of the failure of the EU to cooperate, Chile prohibited the unloading of swordfish in its ports, thereby creating logistical problems for the EU. The EU uses Chilean ports for its exports of swordfish to NAFTA countries and, particularly, to the United States.

The EU brought the import prohibition before the WTO Dispute Settlement Body on the grounds that the Chilean import prohibition violated articles V (freedom of transit for goods) and XI (quantitative restrictions on imports and exports) of the GATT.[90]

Chile brought the case before the ITLOS. Chile asked the ITLOS to declare that the EU had failed to fulfill its obligations under article 64 of the UNCLOS. Chile claimed that the EU was in violation of articles 116–119 (conservation of living marine resources of the high seas), article 297 (dispute settlement) and article 300 (underlining the importance of good faith and no abuse of rights).[91]

The EU based its claims before the ITLOS on article 87, that has to do with the freedom of high seas, and article 89 that prohibits any state from asserting its sovereignty over the high seas. The EU contended that Chile had imposed unilaterally its EEZ conservation requirements on the high seas.[92]

Eventually, the parties decided to suspend the proceedings before the ITLOS and the WTO. They agreed to establish a bilateral technical commission, port access for fish captured under a new scientific fisheries program, and the creation of a multilateral conservation forum for the South East Pacific.[93]

3.3. International Instruments

3.3.1. Agreement on Fisheries Management

General Provisions

The management of straddling fish stocks (stocks that straddle the EEZ and the high seas) and highly migratory fish stocks is a constant source of irritation between coastal states and distant water fishing states. An agreement was adopted in 1995 to elucidate further the appropriate management of these stocks.[94]

---

[89] Marcos Orellana, The EU and Chile Suspend the Swordfish Case Proceedings at the WTO and the International Tribunal of the Law of the Sea, American Society of International Law Insights, Feb. 2001.

[90] Id.

[91] Id.

[92] Chile had negotiated the Calapagos Agreement under the auspices of the Commission of the South Pacific without attempting to include all interested states. Id.

[93] Id.

[94] Agreement for the Implementation of the Provisions of the United Nations Convention on the Law of the Sea of 10 December 1982 Relating the Conservation and Management of Straddling Fish Stocks and Highly Migratory Fish Stocks, Dec. 4, 1995, reprinted in 34 ILM 1542 (1995) [hereinafter 1995 Fisheries Agreement].

The agreement, by definition, applies to areas that are outside national jurisdiction.[95] The agreement emphasizes the precautionary approach,[96] which is viewed as a weaker version of the precautionary principle, but also the importance of scientific evidence.[97] The agreement refers to all the issues that have plagued the management of fisheries resources, such as pollution, waste, discards, lost or abandoned gear, and catches of nontargeted species. The goal of the agreement is to minimize such issues so that they do not have adverse impacts on the management of fisheries resources.[98] The agreement urges states to collect data regarding fishing activities[99] and to promote the conduct of scientific research so as to support fisheries conservation and management.[100]

The agreement mandates that regional organizations are to take measures with regard to fisheries. And, in a manner more obligatory than the UNCLOS, it provides that, with regard to highly migratory fish stocks, state cooperation is mandatory,[101] whereas, for straddling fish stocks, state cooperation is desirable.[102] Article 7 of the agreement is devoted to the issue of compatibility between conservation and management measures established in the high seas and those adopted for areas under national jurisdiction. For states to determine the compatibility between measures taken in the high seas and those adopted in areas under national jurisdiction, a number of factors have to be taken into account:

1. the effectiveness of measures undertaken by coastal states in accordance with article 61 of the UNCLOS[103] must not be undermined by measures taken in the high seas;
2. previously agreed, UNCLOS-compatible measures established in the high seas for the same stock by coastal states and states fishing in the high seas;
3. previously agreed, UNCLOS-compatible measures for the same stock adopted by regional fisheries arrangements;
4. the biological unity of stocks, the distribution of stocks, and the geographical particularities of the region including the extent to which stocks are found and fished within areas under national jurisdiction; and
5. the respective dependence of coastal states and distant water fishing states on stocks.[104]

States must ensure that measures do not result in harmful impacts on living marine resources as a whole.[105]

---

[95] Art. 3(1), *id.*
[96] Arts. 5(c) & 6, *id.*
[97] Art. 5(b), *id.*
[98] Art. 5(f), *id.*
[99] Art. 5(j), *id.*
[100] Arts. 5(k) & 14, *id.*
[101] Art. 7(1)(b), *id.* According to the article states "shall cooperate . . . with a view to ensuring conservation . . ."
[102] Art. 7(1)(a), *id.* According to the article states "shall seek . . . to agree upon the measures necessary for the conservation . . ."
[103] Article 61 of the UNCLOS provides that a coastal state must determine the allowable catch of living resources in its EEZ based on the best scientific evidence and the attainment of the maximum sustainable yield. See UNCLOS, *supra* note 39.
[104] Art. 7(2)(a)–(e), 1995 Fisheries Agreement, *supra* note 94. See also art. 11(d)–(e), *id.* See also article 24 on the recognition of special requirements for developing states.
[105] Art. 7(2)(f), *id.*

The criteria, thus, that the convention proposes to be used in order to determine the compatibility between measures taken under national jurisdiction and those proposed for the high seas do not dictate the exact nature of these measures. It has been proposed, therefore, that equity considerations – as defined in the *Fisheries Jurisdiction* cases and the *North Sea Continental Shelf* cases – should be applied in balancing the criteria provided for in article 7(2).[106] If states cannot reach consensus within a reasonable period of time, they can invoke the procedures for dispute settlement.[107] Pending a final agreement on conservation and management measures, state parties may adopt provisional measures of practical nature. If the adoption of such provisional measures is not feasible, the dispute settlement provisions can be used.[108] The convention does not provide much guidance on the considerations that parties must take into account in order to adopt provisional measures.[109]

Who should participate in a regional management organization is not, in principle, contested. The agreement provides that coastal states and states fishing in the high seas must pursue cooperation in relation to straddling fish stocks and highly migratory fish stocks either directly or through regional or subregional fisheries management organizations or arrangements. In doing so, they must take into consideration the specific characteristics of the region or subregion.[110] Pending the conclusion of regional fisheries arrangements, states must observe the provisions of the 1995 Fisheries Agreement and must act in good faith with regard to the rights, interests, and duties of other states.

All states with a real interest in a fishery could enter into an already existing RFO or establish a new RFO.[111] Commentators have interpreted this clause to mean that states that actually conduct fishing operations in a region may possibly enter an RFO.[112] It has been claimed that the agreement is drafted in a way that participation in a regional organization becomes the prerequisite for fishing in a region beyond areas of national jurisdiction.[113] The agreement provides that only states that are parties to a regional fisheries organization, or agree to apply conservation and management measures prescribed by such an organization, shall have access to fisheries resources regulated by that organization.[114] If a regional organization is not in place, coastal states and distant water fishing states are to cooperate to establish such an organization.[115]

---

[106] Alex G. Oude Elferink, The Impact of Article 7(2) of the Fish Stocks Agreement on the Formulation of Conservation & Management Measures for Straddling & Highly Migratory Fish Stocks, FAO Legal Papers Online #4, Aug. 1999 available online at http://www.fao.org/Legal/prs-ol/full.htm.

[107] Art. 7(4), 1995 Fisheries Agreement, *supra* note 94.

[108] Art. 7(5), *id.*

[109] See art. 7(6) which provides that "provisional arrangements . . . shall take into account the provisions of this Part, shall have due regard to the rights and obligations of all States concerned, shall not jeopardize or hamper the reaching of final agreement on compatible conservation and management measures and shall be without prejudice to the final outcome of any dispute settlement procedure." *Id.*

[110] Art. 8(1), *id.*

[111] Art. 8(3), *id.*

[112] Vicuña, *supra* note 41, at 207.

[113] *Id.* at 209.

[114] Art. 8(4), 1995 Fisheries Agreement, *supra* note 94.

[115] Art. 8(5), *id.*

The agreement provides for the elements that are necessary to establish a regional fisheries organization (i.e., the definition of the fisheries concerned, the area of application, and the establishment of a scientific advisory body).[116] The agreement enumerates the functions that are to be fulfilled by regional and subregional organizations (i.e., conservation measures, TACs, data collection, scientific advice).[117]

The parameters of accommodation of new entrants are further defined in the agreement. In determining the extent of rights of new entrants, regional organizations must take into account:

- the status of stocks and the existing fishing effort;
- the fishing patterns, practices, and interests of participants;
- the contributions of new and old members in the management and conservation of stocks;
- the needs of coastal fishing communities that are dependent mainly on fishing;
- the needs of coastal states that are "overwhelmingly" dependent on the exploitation of marine living resources; and
- and the interests of developing countries in whose national jurisdiction fisheries stocks also occur.[118]

Three out of these six factors have to do with the needs of developing states or fisheries-dependent regions (needs of coastal fishing communities dependent on fishing; needs of coastal states overwhelmingly dependent on fishing; interests of developing states). The preferential treatment given to states and regions dependent on fisheries, also underscored in many regional agreements, suggests a needs-based orientation in the allocation of fisheries resources.

The 1995 Fisheries Agreement provides that NGOs must be given the opportunity to participate in regional and subregional organizations, as observers[119] addressing current demands for transparency in international organizations. Further details are provided for the collection of information and cooperation in scientific research.[120] Article 15 provides for implementation of the agreement in enclosed and semienclosed areas.

Enforcement

The agreement is clear that states that are not parties to regional fisheries organizations are not discharged from the obligation to cooperate in the conservation and management of relevant fish stocks.[121] Furthermore, states that are members of regional and subregional organizations must take measures – consistent with the 1995 agreement and international law – to deter activities of vessels that undermine the effectiveness of regional and subregional arrangements.[122]

It is a well-known rule of international law that flag states have jurisdiction over vessels that carry their flags. An explicit exception to this general rule is found

---

[116] Art. 9, *id.*
[117] Art. 10, *id.*
[118] Art. 11, *id.*
[119] Art. 12(2), *id.*
[120] Art. 14, *id.*
[121] Art. 17(1), *id.*
[122] Art. 17(4), *id.*

in article 111 of the UNCLOS. Article 111 provides that coastal states can always undertake the hot pursuit of a vessel in the high seas that committed a violation in their jurisdictional area.

The 1995 agreement does not nullify flag state jurisdiction. On the contrary, it strengthens such jurisdiction by providing detailed requirements for the obligations of flag states to enforce regional management rules on their vessels.[123] However, because of problems presented by the flagging and reflagging of vessels and the perennial issues with flags of convenience, the agreement broadens the jurisdictional reach of state parties to regional organizations.

State parties to a regional management organization are empowered to take action (that is, board and inspect a vessel) when flag states are unwilling or unable to assert their jurisdiction. What is even more empowering is that vessels can be boarded and inspected by members of a regional fisheries organization even if the flag state under question is not a member of the fisheries organization. The caveat is that both the inspecting state (member of the regional organization) and the flag state (either a member or nonmember of the regional organization) have to be parties to the 1995 agreement.[124]

The agreement provides detailed provisions regarding the inspection and boarding of vessels by states parties to regional organizations in case of a serious violation,[125] including unauthorized fishing in areas under national jurisdiction[126] and fishing by vessels of no nationality.[127] It is provided, *inter alia*, that inspecting states, when boarding a vessel, must respect the regulations for the safety of the vessel and the crew, minimize interference with fishing operations, and avoid the use of force (except in cases of self-defense).[128]

The inspecting state, however, may not be able to finalize its inspection if the flag state exercises its peremptory right to take over the inspection.[129] For a flag state to take over an inspection, it must be notified by the inspecting state. The flag state must respond to the notification within three working days after its receipt or in accordance with the requirements of the specific regional organization. If the flag state decides to fulfill its obligation to enforce the regional agreement, the inspecting state must release the vessel to the flag state.[130]

The lack of response by the flag state to the notification of the inspecting state triggers the enforcement responsibilities of the inspecting state. The inspecting state can authorize its enforcement personnel to remain on board to secure evidence and may require the ship's master to bring the vessel to the nearest appropriate port so

---

[123] Arts. 18 & 19, *id.* These articles provide that flag states must ensure the compliance of their vessels with regard to regional and subregional rules for fisheries management. A flag state can enforce such rules through investigation and prosecution, including the physical inspection of vessels. The vessel is required to give information regarding its fishing gear, fishing operations, and related activities. The flag state must impose sanctions, if needed, and such sanctions must be stringent enough to deter future illegal behavior.

[124] Art. 21(1), *id.*

[125] Art. 21(11), *id.*

[126] Art. 21(14) *id.*

[127] Art. 21(17), *id.*

[128] Arts. 21 & 22, *id.*

[129] Art. 21(5), *id.*

[130] Art. 21(12)–(13), *id.*

as to proceed with the inspection.[131] This provision is a watered-down version of an earlier provision that categorically provided for the right of the inspecting state to seize and arrest a vessel that committed a serious violation.[132] Flag states objected to the blatant recognition of the right of inspecting states to seizure and arrest. The fact that the inspecting state can keep enforcement personnel on the vessel to secure evidence and can ask for the vessel to be brought to the nearest appropriate port amounts to significant powers of seizure and arrest. These powers granted to inspecting states break new ground; before, only flag state jurisdiction reigned.

The 1995 agreement also has strengthened port state enforcement. The MAR-POL Convention was one of the first conventions to recognize port state jurisdiction with regard to reporting and prosecuting violations.[133] The Law of the Sea Convention under article 218 significantly extended port state jurisdiction.

Port states have jurisdiction over their ports and, as a matter of course, frequently enact provisions requiring fishing vessels that enter their ports to hold licenses or they can prohibit landings or transshipments.[134] The agreement takes advantage of these inherent jurisdictional powers of port states and provides that a port state can take measures – including the inspection of documents, fishing gear, and catch on board – when vessels voluntarily use its ports and terminals.[135] It is provided that port states can institute prohibitions or impose restrictions on landings or transshipments if it is determined that catches are taken in contravention of regional or subregional arrangements.

The agreement provides for detailed dispute settlement provisions and seeks to clarify the role of the dispute settlement provisions under the UNCLOS.[136]

3.3.2. FAO Code of Conduct for Responsible Fisheries

The 1995 Fisheries Agreement was adopted at a time when the debate about responsible fisheries management was prominent in national and international fora. The agreement was adopted almost simultaneously with the 1995 FAO Code of Conduct for Responsible Fisheries (CCRF).[137]

The spirit that permeates the 1995 agreement – namely, the expansion of coastal state jurisdiction and the regionalization of fisheries management – is evident in the FAO Code of Conduct. Furthermore, in the Code, fisheries issues are interlinked with food security and the alleviation of poverty.[138] The Code requires flag states to have effective control over vessels that carry their flag and to ensure the application of the Code.[139] Even if a state is not a member of a regional or subregional organization, it is encouraged to cooperate with regional and subregional arrangements.[140] States are required to maintain the appropriate monitoring and enforcement

---

[131] Art. 21(8), *id.*

[132] Vicuña, *supra* note 41, at 253.

[133] See Chapter 4, Section 3.4.

[134] Vicuña, *supra* note 41, at 263.

[135] Art. 23(2), 1995 Fisheries Agreement, *supra* note 94.

[136] Art. 30, *id.*

[137] FAO Code of Conduct for Responsible Fisheries, adopted by the twenty-eighth session of the FAO Conference, Oct. 31, 1995, available online at http://www.fao.org.

[138] Section 6.2, *id.*

[139] Section 6.11, *id.*

[140] Section 7.1.5, *id.*

mechanisms[141] and to ensure transparency by welcoming the involvement of NGOs.[142] States are encouraged to apply recovery measures for stocks that are near depletion.[143]

The Code of Conduct provides specific requirements for flag states. It requires that flag states maintain records of vessels that are allowed to carry their flags. These records must include all information about the vessel (for instance, ownership and authorization to fish).[144] No vessel should be allowed to fish within the jurisdiction of other states or in the high seas unless such a vessel has been issued a Certificate of Registry. The Certificate of Registry and the authorization to fish must be carried always on board of a vessel.[145] Furthermore, fishing vessels that are authorized to fish in the high seas or under the jurisdiction of another state must always be internationally recognizable by using a marking system, such as the FAO Standard Specifications and Guidelines for Marking and Identification of Fishing Vessels.[146] The safety requirements for fishing vessels must meet the standards set by international conventions and voluntary guidelines. States must encourage the owners of fishing vessels to obtain insurance.[147] Furthermore, the integration of fisheries into coastal area management, so that it does not compete but complements other coastal area activities, has been recommended.[148] To ensure the implementation of the Code of Conduct, the FAO has asked states to sign compliance agreements.

3.4. Regional Agreements

The implementation of the 1995 Fisheries Agreement is left to regional fisheries organizations and the entrepreneurship and willingness of states to adopt and enforce sound management measures.

Some fisheries organizations are affiliated with the FAO. These organizations are not very influential because they have no independent funding and their role is more or less advisory. The lack of funding for the functioning of these bodies has become so acute that certain meetings are canceled because of lack of resources.

Non-FAO regional organizations, on the contrary, have better budgets – ranging from $500,000 to $1 million – that are supported by member state contributions. Proposals have been made, therefore, to render FAO-related bodies more independent in order to enhance their role in international fisheries management. Regional Fisheries Organizations (RFOs) affiliated with the FAO include: the Indian Ocean Fishery Commission (IOFC), the Western Central Atlantic Fishery Commission (WECAFC), the Regional Fisheries Advisory Commission for the South West Atlantic (CARPAS), the Committee of the Eastern Central Atlantic Fisheries (CECAF), the Asia Pacific Fishery Commission (APFIC), and the General Fisheries Council of the Mediterranean (GFCM).

---

[141] Section 7.1.7, *id.*
[142] Section 7.1.6, *id.*
[143] Section 7.6.10, *id.*
[144] Section 8.2.1, *id.*
[145] Section 8.2.2, *id.*
[146] Section 8.2.3, *id.*
[147] Sections 8.2.5 & 8.2.8, *id.*
[148] Section 10, *id.*

Some RFOs were developed before the adoption of the 1995 agreement, whereas others came into being as a result of the 1995 agreement. Some organizations concentrate on overall fisheries management in a region, whereas others may focus on the management of a lucrative species.

For instance, tuna, a highly migratory fish stock, has been regulated by a number of regional organizations as early as in 1949. The 1949 Convention on the development of an Inter-American Tropical Tuna Commission (IATTC)[149] was established to manage tuna in the eastern Pacific Ocean. But the jurisdictional reach of the commission was challenged after recognition of the EEZ. Many coastal states in the region have challenged the rights of distant water fishing states to fish in the eastern Pacific. El Salvador, Mexico, Nicaragua, and Peru have adopted the Eastern Pacific Tuna Convention, which has yet to enter into force.[150]

Other agreements for the regulation of tuna that were adopted before 1995 include: the 1991 Western Indian Ocean Tuna Organization Convention;[151] the 1993 Agreement on the Establishment of the Indian Ocean Tuna Commission (IOTC) open to FAO members situated within the jurisdictional delimitation of the agreement and to other states with the permission of coastal states;[152] and 1993 Convention for the Conservation of Southern Bluefin Tuna.[153] The Bluefin Tuna Convention has four parties only (Australia, New Zealand, Japan, and South Korea). The convention established a Commission for the Conservation of Southern Bluefin Tuna with the purpose to set and to allocate the TAC among the parties. Japan's undertaking of an experimental program that would have violated the TAC allocation led to a dispute that was brought before the ITLOS.[154]

A recent convention for the regulation of tuna is the 1996 Atlantic Tuna Convention.[155] The convention provides for an International Commission for the Conservation of Atlantic Tuna, a Council, and an Executive Secretary.[156] The commission established under the convention can make recommendations that become effective six months after the date of notification unless more than one-fourth of the majority of states objects.[157] Because the Commission has imposed quotas many fishers have moved to the north Pacific Ocean. In the north Pacific Ocean, fishing activities remain more or less unregulated – demonstrating that lack of coordinating action, even in what may be perceived to be a regional problem, transfers resource exploitation to other regions of the world.

---

[149] Convention for the Establishment of an Inter-American Tropical Tuna Commission, May 31, 1949, reprinted in 80 UNTS 3.

[150] Convention Establishing the Eastern Pacific Tuna Organization (OAPO), July 31, 1989, available online at http://www.intfish.net/treaties (Internet Guide to International Fisheries Law).

[151] Western Indian Ocean Tuna Organization Convention, June 19, 1991, available online at http://www.intfish.net/treaties.

[152] Agreement on the Establishment of the Indian Ocean Tuna Commission, Nov. 25, 1993, available online at http://www.intfish.net/treaties.

[153] Convention for the Conservation of Southern Bluefin Tuna, May 10, 1993, reprinted in 1819 UNTS 360.

[154] The *Southern Bluefin Tuna* case, see *supra* note 63.

[155] International Convention for Conservation of Atlantic Tuna, May 14, 1996, reprinted in 637 UNTS 63.

[156] Art. III(1), (2) & (4), arts. V & VII, *id.*

[157] Art. VIII, *id.*

Other valuable stocks that have been regulated by regional organizations include anadromous stocks, such as salmon. Anadromous fish stocks have not been regulated as extensively as highly migratory fish stocks. Anadromous stocks originate in the rivers of states and end up in the sea. In the UNCLOS, the state of origin is given primary responsibility for the management of these stocks. Coastal states are given also some role in the management of these stocks.[158] Agreements for the protection of anadromous fish stocks include the North Pacific Anadromous Stocks Commission (NPAFC), the North Atlantic Salmon Conservation Organization (NASCO), and the United States-Canada Pacific Salmon Commission.

Other RFOs that deal with fisheries resources include the Northwest Atlantic Fisheries Organization (NAFO), the North East Atlantic Fisheries Commission (NEAFC), the South East Atlantic Fisheries Organization (SEAFO), the International Baltic Sea Fishery Commission, the South Pacific Forum Fisheries Agency (SPFFA), and the Commission for the Conservation of Antarctic Marine Living Resources (CCAMLR).

The regional fisheries agreements exhibit certain common elements.[159] Most of the agreements provide for the establishment of a commission that is to be assisted by a scientific body. Other assisting organs also may be provided, such as councils, panels, and working groups. Although commissions are usually assigned regulatory functions – for instance, they can establish the TAC and other conservation and management measures – their recommendations remain optional. Most regional agreements include provisions on an objection procedure that, if followed, would mean that the decisions of the commissions are not binding on the objecting parties. Not all agreements provide for dispute settlement provisions.[160] The budget contributions[161] for the running of the regional organization are clearly defined in some of the agreements but not in all agreements. Budget contributions are based usually on catches and fixed fees or some equal sharing formula. Certain agreements, in which developing states constitute the majority of participants, provide for voluntary contributions (expected by the developed countries in the region).[162] Thus, the needs and capabilities of states inform the provisions for budget contributions in regional agreements.

An evaluation of the regional arrangements demonstrates that they have yet to meet their full potential. Regional arrangements have not been successful for a

---

[158] Vicuña, *supra* note 41, at 85.

[159] See also Judith Swan, Decision-Making in Regional Fishery Bodies or Arrangements: The Evolving Role of RFBs and International Agreement on Decision-Making Processes, Fisheries Circular No. 995 (FAO, 2004).

[160] With regard to the agreements examined in this study, the SEAFO (art. 24), the WCPC (art. 31), the CCAMLR (art. XXV), the GFCM (XVII) provide for dispute settlement procedures.

[161] Agreements that give details on budget contributions include the WCPC (arts. 17 and 18), the NEAFC (art. 17), the SEAFO (art. 12), the CCAMLR (art. XIX), the GFCM (art. IX), the NAFO (art. XVI) and the ICCAT (X).

[162] E.g., the SEAFO. The NEAFC Agreement limits the contributions of countries with low population numbers to a maximum of 5 percent of the total budget. The WCPC agreement provides for contributions based on an equal basic fee, national wealth (reflecting the level of development), and the total catch taken. It provides also for voluntary contributions and a fund is established for the needs of effective participation of developing countries (arts. 17, 18, art. 30(3)).

number of reasons including: inadequate information for decision making; lack of capacity in collecting data; the inability to reach consensus on conservation measures;[163] and the relentless tug of war between coastal states and distant water fishing states. The inability to reach consensus has undermined the regulatory might of these organizations.

Most treaties on which RFOs are based contain provisions that provide that if a member state objects to the recommendations of the regulatory body of the treaty that state is exempt from applying the recommendations. Provisions for objections – which are politically expedient because their purpose is to encourage states to join an organization (and defect later by objecting to regulatory measures) – eventually create an *à la carte* regime. This *à la carte* regime provides flexibility for the participants, but its normative functions are severely reduced. The question for policy makers here is whether to allow potential detractors to create regimes within a regime by providing for objections or to discourage participation by eliminating permissive objection procedures. Other measures that have been proposed for the empowerment of RFOs include allowing such organizations to conduct inspections of suspected vessels.

RFOs have attempted to control illegal landings by introducing catch documentation schemes. The ICCAT has introduced one of the first catch documentation schemes. According to the scheme, any bluefin tuna imported into an ICCAT member state has to be accompanied by a document that identifies the country of origin. The catch documentation scheme has revealed that several countries with flag of convenience vessels were catching up to 30 percent of the total tuna resources in the region. Members of the ICCAT have decided to impose sanctions against states that did not comply with the ICCAT regulations. As a result of the scheme, Panama, Honduras, and Belize, all flag of convenience states, are rethinking their strategies.[164]

The CCAMLR regime, similarly, has experimented with a catch documentation scheme. The implementation of the scheme within the CCAMLR jurisdiction is bound to be more challenging because of the extent of the area and number of resources covered by the CCAMLR. For now, the scheme has concentrated on the regulation of Patagonian toothfish fishing. All toothfish landings in the ports of member states must be accompanied by a catch document authorized by the flag state and verified at the port of landing. Since the scheme was introduced, eighteen attempts to land fish illegally have been reported.[165]

Another well-known scheme involves the 1998 Agreement on the International Dolphin Conservation Program. The goal of the agreement is to authorize the issue of certificates the purpose of which is to verify that canned tuna is dolphin safe. Dolphin-safe tuna is tuna harvested without dolphin mortality or serious injury.[166]

Other RFOs are envisioning the development of catch documentation schemes. The increase in the number of such schemes prompted the International Coalition of Fisheries Associations (ICFA) to request their standardization. The FAO has been

---

[163] Vicuña, *supra* note 41, at 216.
[164] FAO Fisheries, *supra* note 2, at 66.
[165] *Id.* at 67.
[166] *Id.*

working on the development of a standardized catch documentation scheme.[167] Extending catch documentation schemes from small fisheries to large ones, where regulation of more than one species is at stake, will encounter difficulties in implementation.[168]

3.5. Case Studies

3.5.1. South East Atlantic Fisheries Organization (SEAFO)

The Convention on the Conservation and Management of Fishery Resources in the South East Atlantic Ocean was finalized in November 2000 but was not signed until 2001.[169] This convention, along with the Western and Central Pacific Convention,[170] was the first convention to be adopted after the 1995 Fisheries Agreement. The state parties to the convention include the coastal states of Angola, South Africa, Namibia, and the United Kingdom, and distant water fishing states including Iceland, Norway, the Republic of Korea, the United States, and the EU.

The adoption of the convention was in the works since 1997, when coastal states started negotiations to establish a regional fisheries agreement for the high seas fisheries of the Atlantic. The negotiating process was opened, thereafter, to distant water fishing states with historical fishing rights in the region and other states interested in future participation. Certain distant water fishing states, notably Japan, were not particularly happy with the convention because of references it contained to the 1995 Fisheries Agreement,[171] which Japan has yet to ratify.[172]

The convention is inspired by the rationale of the 1995 Fisheries Agreement. What is notable about the convention is that it explicitly covers areas of the high seas. The convention applies to "all waters beyond areas of national jurisdiction" as delimited by the geographical boundaries included in the convention.[173]

The convention covers a large number of species. The convention defines fishery resources as fish, mollusks, crustaceans, and other sedentary species within the Convention Area. Species that are excluded are species under the jurisdiction of coastal states and species regulated by the International Commission for the Conservation of Atlantic Tunas (ICCAT).[174] The convention covers also living marine resources, defined to include seabirds.[175]

The convention is administered by the South East Atlantic Fisheries Organization (SEAFO). The SEAFO is comprised of a commission, a compliance committee, a scientific committee, and a secretariat.[176]

---

[167] *Id.* at 67–68.

[168] *Id.* at 68.

[169] Convention on the Conservation and Management of Fishery Resources in the South East Atlantic Ocean, April 20, 2001[hereinafter SEAFO].

[170] See *infra* note 207.

[171] See Preamble and art. 1(b), SEAFO, *supra* note 169.

[172] See The South East Atlantic Fisheries Organization (SEAFO) Convention: an initial review, 2001 International Fisheries Bulletin No. 12, available online at http://www.oceanlaw.org.

[173] Art. 4, SEAFO, *supra* note 169.

[174] Art. 1(l), *id.*

[175] Art. 1(n), *id.*

[176] Art. 5, *id.*

The commission is the primary regulatory body of the convention and each state party to the convention must be represented in the commission.[177] The commission formulates the conservation and management measures,[178] including TACs and fishing effort,[179] and adopts measures for the "control and enforcement within the Convention Area."[180] The commission compiles and disseminates accurate and complete statistical data to ensure that the best scientific advice is available and must maintain confidentiality of information when appropriate.[181] The commission is to apply the precautionary approach and must be "more cautious when information is uncertain, unreliable or inadequate."[182] The absence of scientific information must not be used as a reason for failing to adopt conservation measures.[183]

The convention provides for a number of criteria that must be taken into account in allocating fisheries resources in the Convention Area. It is unclear whether these criteria would provide the normative guidance needed for the allocation of fisheries resources. The criteria are stated in an open-ended manner and no weights are attached to them.

The criteria include:

- the state of fisheries resources including other living marine resources in combination with existing levels of fishing effort;
- interests, past and present fishing patterns, including catches and practices in the convention area;
- the state of development of fisheries;
- the interests of developing states in whose national jurisdiction the stock occurs;
- contributions of states to conservation and management of fishery resources in the convention area;
- contributions of states to new and exploratory fisheries;
- the needs of coastal fishing communities that are dependent on fishing in the southeast Atlantic; and
- the needs of coastal states whose economies are overwhelmingly dependent on the exploitation of fishery resources.[184]

Although the criteria are broad and open-ended, three out of the eight criteria refer to the interests of coastal developing states, the needs of coastal fishing communities, and the needs of coastal states that are dependent on fisheries. Furthermore, article 21 of the convention is exclusively dedicated to the "recognition of the special requirements of developing States in the region," especially developing states that are dependent on fisheries. Thus, although one could not conclusively articulate how the criteria should be balanced for the allocation of fisheries resources, it is obvious that the needs of developing states dependent on fisheries are assigned a certain amount of priority in the allocation of fisheries resources.

---

[177] Art. 6(1)–(2), *id.*
[178] Art. 6(3)(b), *id.*
[179] Art. 6(3)(c), *id.*
[180] Art. 6(3)(h)–(i), *id.*
[181] Art. 6(3)(l), *id.*
[182] Art. 7(2), *id.*
[183] Art. 7, *id.*
[184] Art. 20, *id.*

The convention provides specific requirements for contracting parties, and more specifically for flag states, and for noncontracting parties.[185] More specifically, flag states must meet the following requirements:

- the immediate investigation of violations of SEAFO measures;
- the establishment of national records of fishing vessels;
- the marking of fishing vessels and gear;
- the provision of information to the commission including catches, landings, transshipments, and fishing effort;[186] and
- the control over their fishing vessels by providing authorizations for fishing.[187]

With regard to noncontracting parties, the convention provides that either they should become parties to the convention or respect the regulations enacted by the SEAFO.[188]

In order to strengthen implementation by flag states that are parties to the convention, a system of observation, inspection, compliance, and enforcement called "the System" is established.[189] The System is comprised of the following elements:

- control measures, including vessel authorization, the marking of vessels and fishing gear, and the recording of fishing activities;
- an inspection program (boarding and inspection of vessels on a reciprocal basis);
- an observer program (placing observers on vessels); and
- procedures for following up on infringements, including sanctions and other enforcement actions.

The annex to the convention provides details on vessel registration and the marking of vessels and gear. But the inspection and observer programs are not defined clearly.

The dispute settlement provisions provided for by the convention make room for the settlement of a dispute by the mere initiative of one of the parties. When a dispute regarding the implementation of the convention emerges among the parties, the parties must cooperate among themselves in order to resolve the dispute by means of negotiation, inquiry, mediation, conciliation, arbitration, and judicial settlement.[190]

If the dispute is of a technical nature, and the parties cannot resolve the dispute among themselves, the parties may refer the dispute to an *ad hoc* panel established in accordance with procedures put in place by the commission at its first meeting.[191]

If a dispute is not resolved within a reasonable time frame, any of the parties can request binding adjudication either under Part XV of the UNCLOS or – in the case of straddling fish stocks – under Part VIII of the 1995 Fisheries Agreement.

The convention clearly is an ambitious instrument that seeks to regulate many of the aspects of fisheries resources in the southeast Atlantic. The success of the convention would be determined by the availability of resources that would make "the System" operational. An effective monitoring and enforcement system supported

---

[185] Arts. 13, 14, 22, *id.*
[186] Art. 14(3), *id.*
[187] Art. 14(3)(b), *id.*
[188] Art. 22, *id.*
[189] Art. 16, *id.*
[190] Art. 24(2), *id.*
[191] Art. 24(3), *id.*

by coastal states and distant water fishing states could go a long way toward ensuring the implementation of the convention.

3.5.2. South Pacific Forum Fisheries Agency (SPFFA) and Western and Central Pacific Commission (WCPC)

SPFFA

The Convention on the Conservation and Management of Highly Migratory Fish Stocks in the Western and Central Pacific Ocean[192] was not the first attempt to organize states in the Pacific Ocean. Several attempts have been made to organize regional fisheries management since 1979 with the development of the South Pacific Forum Fisheries Agency (FFA). State parties to the FFA are Australia, New Zealand, the Cook Islands, Fiji, Kiribati, Nauru, Niue, Papua New Guinea, the Solomon Islands, Tonga, Tuvalu, and the Western Samoa. Overall, the area includes twenty-two island states and territories, of which fifteen are either atolls or small islands. The extension of the EEZ of these states to two hundred miles amounted to an actual enclosure of the high seas, with the exception for some areas that are not covered by the extended jurisdiction of states.[193] The FFA started as a weak organizational arrangement, and the distant water fishing states – primarily Japan and the United States – were able to negotiate bilateral agreements with individual coastal states under a divide and conquer strategy.[194]

Eventually, some states decided to take control over their resources and signed the Nauru Agreement,[195] the purpose of which is to control the fishing activities of distant water fishing states. State parties to the agreement that emerged as leaders in the region include the states of Micronesia, Kiribati, the Marshall Islands, Nauru, Palau, Papua New Guinea, and the Solomon Islands. An offshoot of the Nauru Agreement was the adoption of monitoring, control, and surveillance (MCS) requirements that include minimum terms and conditions (MTCs) for Foreign Fishing Vessels (FFVs) access to the South Pacific Fisheries Resources. The MTCs have been reviewed in 1990 and again in 1997 and 2003. They now include minimum vessel identification requirements, catch and position reporting, and the reporting of transshipment activities. Furthermore, for FFVs to participate in the Pacific Ocean fisheries, they must be included in the regional register and be in good standing. Good standing is automatically granted unless the vessel or its operator has committed a serious fisheries offence. When good standing is suspended, the vessel is prevented from fishing in the region. The country that licenses a foreign vessel has the right to place observers on that vessel to perform compliance, monitoring, and other functions. FFVs also must be equipped with a Vessel Monitoring System (VMS).[196]

---

[192] Convention on the Conservation and Management of Highly Migratory Fish Stocks in the Western and Central Pacific Ocean, Sept. 5, 2000, available online at http://www.ffa.int.

[193] Edward L. Miles, The Management of Tuna Fisheries in the West Central and Southwest Pacific, in Environmental Regimes Effectiveness: Confronting Theory with Evidence 117, 121 (Edward L. Miles et al., eds., 2002).

[194] *Id.* at 127–31.

[195] Nauru Agreement concerning Cooperation in the Management of Fisheries Resources of Common Interest, Feb. 11, 1982, available online at http://www.intfish.net/treaties.

[196] Fisheries Monitoring, Control and Surveillance in the Western and Central Pacific Ocean available online at the FFA Web site, http//www.ffa.int [hereinafter Control and Surveillance].

Distant water fishing states initially resisted the efforts of the Pacific Islands to take control over their fisheries resources. The United States and Japan, in particular, were not receptive to the idea of a register for FFVs, but eventually both countties decided that it was in their best interests to acquiesce to the idea.[197]

In 1987, the United States entered into an agreement with certain Pacific Island states for the regulation of its fishing activities in the area.[198] In 1993, the operation of this treaty was extended for another ten years, until July 2003. Then, the United States and the Pacific Islands decided to extend the treaty for another ten years until 2013. The tuna harvested by U.S. vessels in this area of the Pacific has a landed value of $100 to $150 million annually. Most of this fish is landed in American Samoa, where it is processed in two canneries that provide 80 percent of the employment in that state. The value of the tuna to the U.S. economy, as it goes through the processing and distribution chain, is two or three times its landed value, and amounts to $250–$400 million annually. In exchange for its fishing rights in the region, the United States pays licensing fees to the Pacific Islands of $4 million. It also provides $14 million in related economic assistance.[199] Because of its active involvement in the fisheries of the region, the United States participated in the adoption of the 2000 Western and Central Pacific Fisheries Convention (WCPFC).

The United States is not the only distant water fishing state that has entered into a multilateral agreement with the Pacific Island states. Japan has entered into eight bilateral fishing agreements. The access fee, calculated on a per-trip basis, is paid by the Japanese fishing industry; it amounts to 5 percent of the catch value (using the previous three years' catches to calculate the fee level). Similar bilateral agreements have been concluded with Korea and Taiwan.[200]

Related Treaties

Other treaties that have been adopted in the region are the Convention on the Prohibition of Fishing with Long Driftnets[201] and the Niue Treaty on Cooperation in Fisheries Surveillance and Law Enforcement.[202] The Niue Treaty proposes to strengthen implementation by the conclusion of subsidiary or bilateral agreements between the Pacific countries that provide for concrete ways of cooperation. Such cooperation may involve the sharing of surveillance and enforcement equipment or the enabling of officers of parties to perform enforcement duties on each other's vessels. The Niue Treaty has not been extensively used, however, and countries

[197] Miles, *supra* note 193, at 137.

[198] Treaty on Fisheries between the Government of Certain Pacific Islands and the Government of the United States of America, (1988) Australian Treaty Series, No. 42, April 2, 1987.

[199] Statement of Ambassador Mary Beth West, Deputy Assistant Secretary for Oceans, Bureau of Oceans and International Environmental and Scientific Affairs, United States Department of State, Before the Subcommittee on East Asia and the Pacific, Committee on International Relations, House of Representatives, "Pacific Island Nations: Current Issues and U.S. Interests," July 23, 2002.

[200] See Sandra Tarte, The European Union and the Western and Central Pacific Tuna Fishery, Paper Prepared for the Thirteenth Europe Pacific Solidarity Seminar, Strasbourg, France, Oct. 11–13, 2002.

[201] Convention for the Prohibition of Fishing with Long Driftnets in the South Pacific (Wellington Convention), Nov. 29, 1989, reprinted in 29 ILM 1454 (1990).

[202] Treaty on Cooperation in Fisheries Surveillance and Law Enforcement in the South Pacific Region (Niue Treaty), July 9, 1992, available online at http://www.intfish.net/treaties. The treaty entered into force in 1993 and all FFA members have signed the treaty, but three of them have yet to ratify it.

have not rushed to enter into bilateral agreements as the treaty requested. Only a bilateral agreement between Tonga and Tuvalu, and a multilateral agreement among the Federated States of Micronesia, Marshall Islands, and Palau have been signed.[203]

The Arrangement for the Management of Western Pacific Purse Seine Fisheries was adopted in 1992.[204] The purpose of the arrangement is to both protect tuna fisheries and to increase the economic benefits to the Pacific Islands from tuna exploitation. In 1993, in an effort to control fishing effort based on the nationality of ships, vessel numbers per national fleet were capped at 205 vessels. Currently, a vessel day scheme has been proposed to limit the total allowable effort based on the number of fishing days.

The parties have encouraged new entrants. The fishing effort of existing vessels has been limited so as to allow for new entrants willing to abide with the regional arrangements and to pay higher fees.[205] Today, distant water fishing states are responsible for most of the purse seine fishing (twenty-nine U.S. vessels, forty-one Taiwanese vessels, thirty-five Japanese vessels, twenty-seven Korean vessels, fourteen Spanish vessels, and ten Filipino vessels).[206] The Spanish entry is a new entry based on a bilateral agreement between Spain and Kiribati.

WCPFC

The Western and Central Pacific Fisheries Convention (WCPFC)[207] establishes principles and measures for conservation and management of fisheries resources including the best scientific evidence,[208] the precautionary approach,[209] the elimination of overfishing and excess fishing capacity,[210] effective monitoring, control, and surveillance.[211] The convention provides that the principles of conservation and management must be applied by coastal states in areas under national jurisdiction within the Convention Area.[212] Conservation measures prescribed for the high seas and those adopted for areas of national jurisdiction must be compatible in order to achieve the management of fish stocks in their entirety.[213] This is especially so because there are areas of the high seas entirely surrounded by the EEZs of states' parties.[214]

The convention establishes a commission that has extensive data collection and regulatory powers and the capacity to put in place monitoring and surveillance mechanisms.[215] Subsidiary bodies to the commission are a scientific committee and

---

[203] Control and Surveillance, *supra* note 196, at 5.

[204] The parties to the arrangement are the Federated States of Micronesia, Kiribati, the Marshall Islands, Nauru, Palau, and Papua New Guinea.

[205] Control and Surveillance, *supra* note 196, at 6.

[206] See Tarte, *supra* note 200.

[207] Convention on the Conservation and Management of Highly Migratory Fish Stocks in the Western and Central Pacific Ocean, Sept. 5, 2000, available online at http://www.ffa.int. The convention entered into force June 19, 2004.

[208] Art. 5(b), *id.*

[209] Arts. 5(c) and 6, *id.*

[210] Art. 5(g), *id.*

[211] Art. 5(j), *id.*

[212] Art. 7, *id.*

[213] Art. 8, *id.*

[214] Art. 8(4), *id.*

[215] Art. 10, *id.*

a technical and compliance committee.[216] The technical and compliance committee monitors and reviews compliance, but it is not authorized to impose sanctions.[217] The budget of the commission consists of assessed and voluntary contributions.[218] Voluntary contributions have been made by New Zealand, Australia, Canada, the United States, and the GEF.

The convention elaborates on the duties of flag states, including the requirement to maintain a record of their fishing vessels in the convention area[219] and the installment of real-time satellite position fixing transmitters.[220] The convention includes elaborate provisions on compliance and enforcement (which is entrusted to state parties)[221] including boarding and inspection[222] and compliance measures taken by port states.[223] The convention provides further for the establishment of a regional observer program and the regulation of transshipments.[224] Each state party must deter vessels carrying the flag of nonstate parties and undermining the effectiveness of the convention.[225] Parties to the convention are to request nonstate parties to cooperate fully.[226] In order to encourage collaboration, cooperating nonparties are to enjoy benefits in the fishery commensurate with their commitment to comply. They may, under certain circumstances, be granted observer status in the deliberations of the Conference of the Parties.[227] It is further stipulated that the convention is to be executed in good faith and that the rights recognized must not be exercised in a manner that constitutes an abuse of right.[228]

Regarding the allocation of fisheries, the convention provides, in addition to the provisions of the 1995 Fisheries Agreement,[229] further requirements more specific to the Pacific region. Such requirements include the historic catch in the area,[230] the record of compliance by participants,[231] the special circumstances of a state that is surrounded by the EEZs of other states and has a limited EEZ of its own,[232] and the circumstances of small island developing states that are made up of a noncontiguous group of islands separated by areas of high seas.[233] One of the provisions included in article 11 of the 1995 Fisheries Agreement has been altered to reflect better the concerns of developing nations. Article 11(b) of the 1995 Fisheries Agreement provides that some of the factors to be taken into account for the allocation of fishery resources are "the respective interests, fishing patterns and fishing practices of new

---

[216] Art. 11, *id.*
[217] Art. 14, *id.*
[218] Art. 17, *id.*
[219] Art. 24(4), *id.*
[220] Art. 24(8), *id.*
[221] Art. 25, *id.*
[222] Art. 26, *id.*
[223] Art. 27, *id.*
[224] Arts. 28–29, *id.*
[225] Art. 32(1), *id.*
[226] Art. 32(4), *id.*
[227] Art. 32(5), *id.*
[228] Art. 33, *id.*
[229] Art. 11, *id.*
[230] Art. 10(3)(c), *id.*
[231] Art. 10(3)(f), *id.*
[232] Art. 10(3)(h), *id.*
[233] Art. 10(3)(i), *id.*

and existing members and participants." Article 10(3)(b) of WCPFC Convention provides that some of the elements to be taken into account for allocation purposes are

> the respective interests, fishing patterns and fishing practices of participants *and the extent of the catch being utilized for domestic consumption* [emphasis added].

Thus, although the criteria provided for allocation are generally broad, six out of the ten criteria provided for making allocation decisions under the convention are preoccupied with the needs and interests of developing nations. The historic catch in the area and the record of compliance of participants are mentioned also as criteria for allocation. Such criteria are not included explicitly in the 1995 Fisheries Agreement.

It remains to be seen whether the WCPFC is to be implemented. The European Union has attempted to enter into this agreement, as it declared its desire to participate in the negotiations that led to the WCPFC. The EU's full participation in the negotiations was declined initially, but eventually the EU was granted a seat at the negotiating table. The EU, however, could not become party to the WCPFC until after the convention entered into force.

Because becoming a player in the multilateral WCPFC forum has not been that successful, the EU has pursued bilateral arrangements with several Pacific nations. The first such agreement was signed with Kiribati. As a consequence of the agreement with Kiribati, other Pacific states are anxious to sign bilateral agreements with the EU. The Pacific Islands view the Kiribati-EU agreement as advantageous in many respects: the inclusion of generous access fees; the development of shore-based fishing facilities; the enhancement of domestic fishing capacity; and the employment of local seamen on EU vessels.[234]

The failure to complete a multilateral access agreement with the EU has been attributed to the reluctance of the Pacific Islands to give up potential advantages they perceive they can secure through bilateral agreements. The Pacific Islands may be more interested in increasing the financial benefits they receive from distant water fishing states rather than in cultivating their own domestic fishing capacity.[235] In this respect, the allocation criteria may simply provide the smokescreen for the allocation of fishing rights to the highest bidder.

3.5.3. North East Atlantic Fisheries Commission (NEAFC)

The NEAFC is one of the oldest regional instruments for the regulation of fisheries. As early as in the 1930s, conferences were held in Europe to address the issue of overexploitation of fishery resources. The first commission – considered the predecessor of the NEAFC – was established in 1953. In 1959, a North East Atlantic Fisheries Convention was adopted that supported the efforts of the first NEAFC. As early as in 1967, the NEAFC had established a Scheme of Joint Enforcement, which contained provisions for mutual inspection and control in areas outside national jurisdiction. The commission adopted recommendations that limited the catches of overexploited species, such as herring. In 1977, when states in the region extended their

---

[234] Tarte, *supra* note 200.
[235] *Id.*

jurisdiction to the two-hundred-mile EEZ, stocks and areas under the jurisdiction of the NEAFC came under national jurisdiction.

The commission was relaunched in 1980 by the Convention on Future Multi-lateral Co-operation in North East Atlantic Fisheries.[236] The parties to the 1980 Convention include Cuba, Denmark,[237] the EU,[238] and Russia. Today's NEAFC Regulatory Area includes three large areas of international waters. Article 5 of the North East Atlantic Fisheries Convention provides explicitly that the commission must make recommendations concerning fisheries located in areas beyond the juris-diction of contracting parties.[239]

The commission has extensive regulatory powers, including the regulation of fishing effort and equipment and the establishment of TACs.[240] In addition to reg-ulating fisheries in areas beyond national jurisdiction, the commission can make recommendations on fisheries management in areas under national jurisdiction.[241]

The recommendations of the commission on the regulation of fish stocks in the high seas are binding unless a contracting party objects.[242] If a state party objects, the recommendation has no binding effect on it. If three or more parties object, the recommendation has no binding effect on any of the parties.[243] This objection procedure is basically a device that allows for the adoption of the lowest common denominator in terms of the development of standards protective of fish stocks. At the same time, the objection procedure encourages wide participation in the convention, as states can opt out when conformity with the convention is not desirable.

In its 1998 annual meeting, the NEAFC adopted a recommendation on a scheme of control and enforcement with respect to vessels fishing in areas beyond the limits of national jurisdiction. The scheme entered into force in 1999 and was amended multiple times since then.[244] The scheme provides the definition of the regulatory area under the convention.[245] It includes detailed procedures on the authorization to fish in the area,[246] notification of fishing vessels,[247] vessel requirements,[248] mark-ing gear,[249] catch and fishing effort,[250] the use of a vessel monitoring system,[251] and inspection and surveillance.[252] The scheme includes a number of annexes that

---

[236] Convention on Future Multilateral Co-operation in North East Atlantic Fisheries, Nov. 18, 1980, available online at http://www.neafc.org [hereinafter NEAFC Convention].

[237] For the Faroe Islands and Greenland.

[238] Norway, Sweden, Spain, Portugal, Germany, the United Kingdom, Iceland, and Poland have fishing interests in the region.

[239] Art. 5(1), NEAFC Convention, *supra* note 236.

[240] Art. 7, *id.*

[241] Art. 8(2), *id.*

[242] Art. 12, *id.*

[243] Art. 12(2), *id.*

[244] North East Atlantic Fisheries Commission, Recommendation on a Scheme of Control and Enforcement in Respect of Fishing Vessels Fishing in Areas beyond the Limits of National Fisheries Jurisdiction in the Convention Area ("The Scheme"), Nov. 20, 1998. Entered into force July 1, 1999 as amended in November 1999, March 2001, November 2001, November 2002, and November 2003.

[245] Art. 1(a), *id.*

[246] Art. 3, *id.*

[247] Art. 4, *id.*

[248] Art. 5, *id.*

[249] Art. 6, *id.*

[250] Arts. 7 & 8, *id.*

[251] Art. 9, *id.*

[252] Arts. 13–20, *id.*

provide the forms and documents required for inspections. These standardized documents help to streamline and unify inspection and reporting requirements.

Another scheme was adopted in 2003 to promote compliance by noncontracting parties.[253] The scheme starts with the presumption that flag states that have not been accorded the status of cooperating noncontracting party, as provided for in article 10 of the scheme, undermine the effectiveness of the convention. For a noncontracting party to acquire the status of cooperating noncontracting party, it must submit a request to the commission containing the following information:

- full data on its historical fisheries in the NEAFC region, including catches, vessels, fishing effort, and fishing areas;
- details on current fishing effort, including the number of vessels and vessels characteristics; and
- details on research programs conducted in the area, the results of which it must share with the NEAFC.[254]

Furthermore, cooperating noncontracting parties must undertake to respect all recommendations issued by the commission; must inform the NEAFC of measures taken to ensure compliance; and must communicate annually to the NEAFC their catch and effort data.[255]

The status of noncontracting parties as cooperating is to be decided by the commission on a year-to-year basis. Cooperating nonparties can participate in the meetings of the commission as observers.[256]

In order to engage in fishing activities in the NEAFC area, a vessel of a cooperating nonparty must notify the Secretary of the commission by a registered letter of its intention to fish on a cooperation quota during the following year.[257] Cooperating nonparties that engage in illegal, unreported, and unregulated (IUU) fishing would be placed on an list. Noncooperating nonparties are also included in this list by virtue of the fact that they undermine the effectiveness of the convention. Each year, the list is reviewed and vessels engaging in IUU activities could be removed from the list and be transferred to a confirmed IUU list.[258] The lists are published on the NEAFC Web site.[259] Vessels included in either list could remove themselves if they meet certain conditions:

- if their flag states have taken effective action to respond to illegal IUU activities (including prosecution and the imposition of sanctions);
- if their flag states can demonstrate to the commission that vessels that have committed violations have changed ownership and the new owner has not participated in IUU fishing activities; or
- if their flag states can prove that the vessel has not engaged in IUU activities.[260]

[253] North East Atlantic Fisheries Commission, Scheme to Promote Compliance by Non-Contracting Party Vessels with Recommendations Established by NEAFC, Nov. 14, 2003. The scheme entered into force Jan. 12, 2004.
[254] Art. 10(1), *id.*
[255] *Id.*
[256] Art. 10(2), *id.*
[257] Art. 10(3), *id.* The letter must be received by October 31 of the previous year.
[258] Art. 9(1) and (2), *id.*
[259] Art. 9(5), *id.*
[260] Art. 9(3), *id.*

Sanctions are provided for states that are included in the confirmed IUU list. Vessels that appear on the IUU list that enter ports of contracting parties are not authorized to land or transship any goods and must be inspected.[261] Fishing vessels of contracting parties are not to assist in any way IUU vessels or to participate in any transshipment or joint operation with vessels included in the IUU list.[262] Contracting parties are not to supply in their ports IUU vessels with provisions, fuel, or other services.[263] Additional enforcement is envisioned against vessels included in the confirmed IUU list, including: the prohibition of such vessels to fish in waters under the national jurisdiction of contracting states; the prohibition of chartering of such vessels; trade sanctions (such as banning of fish imports); and the collection of information in order to prevent false import/export certificates.[264]

As a method of last resort against noncontracting parties that have not rectified their practices, states parties may decide to take multilateral agreed trade sanctions in order to prevent, deter, and eliminate IUU fishing activities.[265] Whether such sanctions would be upheld by the WTO Dispute Settlement Panel, however, is debatable.

The trade sanctions imposed by the regime may deter the entry of rogue fishing vessels in the region. One of the state parties to the convention is the EU and trade sanctions imposed by the EU would mean that a substantial market, for those who elect to pursue illegal fishing, could cease to exist.

3.5.4. Northwest Atlantic Fisheries Organization (NAFO)

The Convention on Future Multilateral Cooperation in the Northwest Atlantic Fisheries was signed in 1978 and was amended in 1979 and 1996.[266] Current parties to the convention include: Bulgaria, Canada, Cuba, Denmark (for the Faroe Islands and Greenland), the EU, France (for St. Pierre and Miquelon), Japan, the Republic of Korea, Latvia, Lithuania, Norway, Poland, the Russian Federation, Ukraine, and the United States of America.

The Canadian-EU relationship has been quite confrontational, as the EU has refused to cooperate with quotas set by the Northwest Atlantic Fisheries Organization (NAFO). The *Estai* case[267] provides a glimpse into the disputes between the parties. The incident provided the impetus for regularizing the regime with mechanisms that would strengthen monitoring and enforcement.

The Northwest Atlantic Fisheries Convention (NAFC)[268] has provided the framework for the regulation of fisheries in the region. The convention mentions explicitly that the "Regulatory Area" is part of the convention area that lies beyond the areas

---

[261] Art. 11(1)(a), *id.*

[262] Art. 11(1)(b), *id.*

[263] Art. 11(1)(c), *id.*

[264] Art. 11(2), *id.*

[265] Art. 12, *id.*

[266] Convention on Future Multilateral Cooperation in the Northwest Atlantic Fisheries, Oct. 24, 1978, available online at http://www.nafo.ca. The convention was amended three times between 1979 and 1996 with respect to Annex III and with regard to the scientific and statistical subareas, divisions, and subdivisions. The convention replaced the 1949 International Convention for the Northwest Atlantic Fisheries (ICNAF).

[267] See *supra* note 65.

[268] See *supra* note 266.

in which coastal states exercise fisheries jurisdiction.[269] The convention establishes NAFO, which is comprised of a general council, a scientific council, a fisheries commission, and a secretariat. The functions of the council are to coordinate the activities under the convention and, most important, to review and to determine membership in the fisheries commission.[270] The fisheries commission, like commissions in all other fisheries agreements, is responsible for the regulatory functions under the convention.[271] The convention provides explicitly that the commission must seek to ensure consistency between measures that apply within the regulatory area and measures and decisions taken by coastal states for the management and conservation of fish stocks.[272]

The convention provides, predictably, for an objection procedure to proposals made by the commission. State parties that object to a proposal by the commission are not bound by that proposal. If objections have been presented and maintained by the majority of commission members, the proposal loses its binding character, unless state parties agree among themselves to be bound by it by an agreed date.[273] The convention even provides for a procedure that states parties could employ in circumstances in which they wish not to be further bound by a regulatory measure that has entered already into force.[274]

Regarding the enforcement of the convention, state parties have agreed to "take such action, including the imposition of adequate sanctions for violations, as may be necessary to make effective the provisions of the Convention . . ."[275] The NAFO enforcement measures have included detailed provisions on TACs, vessel registration and fishing authorization, vessel equipment and vessel monitoring, and joint inspection and surveillance. An observer program has been established that requires that all vessels fishing in the regulatory area have on board an independent and impartial observer. Observers monitor whether actually a vessel complies with the regulatory requirements. Observers must report after each trip to their countries' appropriate authorities and to the NAFO Executive Secretary.[276]

The parties have agreed to put into effect a scheme of joint international enforcement. This scheme is to include provisions for reciprocal rights of boarding and inspecting vessels by the parties and for flag state prosecution and sanctions on the basis of evidence resulting from such boarding and inspections.[277] The purpose of the scheme is to promote compliance by noncontracting states.[278] As was the case in the NEAFC region, noncontracting parties engaging in fishing activities in the regulatory area are presumed to be undermining the effectiveness of the convention. Any contracting party that sees a noncontracting party must attempt to inform such vessel that it has been sighted to engage in fishing activities and that it is presumed,

---

[269] Art. I(2), *id.*

[270] Art. III, *id.*

[271] Art. XI(1), *id.*

[272] Art. XI(3), *id.*

[273] Art. XII (1)–(2), *id.*

[274] Art. XII(3), *id.*

[275] Art. XVII, *id.*

[276] For the enforcement measures in the NAFO, see Northwest Atlantic Fisheries Organization Conservation and Enforcement Measures, NAFO/FC Doc. 04/1, Serial No. N4936 [hereinafter Scheme].

[277] Art. XVIII, NAFO Convention, *supra* note 266.

[278] See Annex I. A, Scheme, *supra* note 276.

accordingly, to be in violation of the provisions of the convention. This information is to be distributed to all contracting parties and the flag state of the vessel.[279] Furthermore, contracting states are to ensure that their vessels do not receive transshipments of fish from noncontracting states that have engaged in fishing activities in the regulatory area.[280] Further provisions include inspections at sea, in case a noncontracting party's vessel consents to such an inspection,[281] and mandatory inspections in the ports of contracting parties.[282] Vessels of noncontracting parties must not land or transship any fish at the port of a contracting state unless they have gone through a thorough inspection. Such inspections include any matter that relates to the activities of a vessel in the Regulatory Area.[283] The enforcement measures do not provide, as it was the case with the NEAFC, for lists of violators and explicitly for trade sanctions.

The allocation of the fisheries in the region has been a matter of contention between Canada (the state with the largest coast in the region) and the EU. The convention provides the following guidance with regard to the allocation of catches. In allocating TACs, the commission must take into account the interests of commission members whose vessels have traditionally fished within the area; and the interests of communities that are dependent on fishing stocks in the Grand Bank and Flemish Cap.[284]

An allocation that has been a subject of contention concerns the shrimp fishery. According to the 2004 allocation, Canada receives 83 percent of the total allowable shrimp catch and several European nations share the remaining 17 percent. The NAFO has decided to divide the 17 percent equally among the 15 European nations, which means that the Faroe Islands, represented by Denmark, would receive only 144 tons. The Faroe Islands have set their own quota at 1,344 tons. They claim that such a quota is sustainable, and that it represents their historical share of fishery in the region.[285]

The flouting of regulations in the NAFO area has been attributed more to state parties to the convention rather than to noncontracting parties. Portuguese and Spanish vessels allegedly are involved in illegal fishing in the area (by catching larger fish than allowed or by breaking the moratorium on certain fisheries). Canada has closed its ports to Danish vessels and has seized such vessels that are allegedly engaging in illegal fishing activities. Denmark, by contrast, has claimed that it has no choice but to overfish because the NAFO quota is unreasonable.[286] The local communities of Newfoundland and Labrador in Canada have asked the Canadian government to reject its participation in the NAFO and to announce its intention to become custodian of fish stocks beyond its EEZ.[287]

---

[279] Art. 40, *id*.

[280] Art. 41, *id*.

[281] Art. 42, *id*.

[282] Art. 43, *id*.

[283] Art. 43(1), *id*.

[284] Art. XI (4), NAFO Convention, *supra* note 266.

[285] Dene Moore, Another Shot Fired in Shrimp War, Canadian Press, Sept. 1, 2004.

[286] Canadian Ultimatum for Danish Grand Banks Shrimpers, CBC News Online, Aug. 27, 2004.

[287] Trevor Taylor, Foreign Overfishing Must Be Stopped, National Post, Aug. 25, 2004.

3.5.5. International Commission for the Conservation of Atlantic Tuna (ICCAT)

The International Convention for the Conservation of Atlantic Tunas (ICCAT) was adopted in 1966.[288] The purpose of the convention is to regulate the management of tuna and tunalike species.[289] Thus, about thirty species fall under the ambit of the convention. The convention established the ICCAT. Institutions that are to facilitate the work of the commission include a council[290] and panels established on the basis of a species or a group of species.[291] The commission may issue recommendations based on scientific evidence. But state parties could issue objections to such recommendations. Recommendations objected to by state parties do not have binding effects on such parties. Objections supported by the majority of state parties do not become effective for all parties.[292]

Parties are to take all measures to enforce the convention and must report to the commission biannually, or at the request of the commission, on their enforcement action. Parties, on request, must provide the commission with statistical, biological, and other scientific information. The convention provides, interestingly, that when the official agencies of state parties are not able to provide the information requested by the commission, the commission can obtain such information by contacting the parties and, on a voluntary basis, from companies and individual fishers.[293]

The ICCAT Commission is affiliated with the FAO and has been plagued by problems of FAO-related bodies, including the lack of funding.[294] Recognizing that the lack of funding has impeded the effective functioning of the commission, in 1992 the parties adopted a revised formula for the calculation of contributions. Such formula is based on fixed basic fees for commission and panel membership per state party; the total weight of catch and net weight of canned products of Atlantic tuna and tunalike fishes assessed for each party; and the degree of economic development of contracting parties.[295]

The management of tuna fisheries has not been easy for ICCAT. In recent decades, for instance, the management of bluefin tuna was based on the assumption of the existence of two distinct stocks: the western Atlantic stock and the eastern Atlantic stock. New research has pointed out that the western and eastern stocks are not as distinctive as was assumed. The recovery of the western stock, thus, would be unlikely unless efforts are undertaken to curtail fishing effort on the eastern stock.

---

[288] International Convention for the Conservation of Atlantic Tunas, May 14, 1966, available online at http://www.intfish.net/treaties. The current parties to the convention are: Angola, Brazil, Canada, Ivory Coast, France, Gabon, Ghana, the Republic of Guinea, Japan, the Republic of Korea, Morocco, Portugal, Sao Tome and Principe, South Africa, Spain, and the United States.

[289] Preamble, *id.* The convention refers to "maintaining the populations of these fishes at levels which will permit the maximum sustainable catch for food and other purposes."

[290] Art. V, *id.*

[291] Art. VI, *id.*

[292] For the objection procedure, see Art. VIII, *id.*

[293] Art. IX, *id.*

[294] See also art. XI.

[295] See Protocol to Amend Paragraph 2 of Article X of the International Convention for the Conservation of Atlantic Tunas, June 5, 1992.

Pursuant to this new scientific understanding, the ICCAT is launching an effort for the integrated management of eastern and western bluefin tuna.[296]

Illegal fishing pursued by flag of convenience vessels, particularly with regard to bluefin tuna, has been prevalent in the region. To abate illegal fishing, the ICCAT has introduced a catch documentation scheme. According to this scheme, bluefin tuna imported into an ICCAT member state has to be accompanied by a document that identifies the country of origin. The scheme revealed that several flag of convenience vessels were catching up to 30 percent of the total bluefin tuna. The ICCAT members decided to impose sanctions against states that flouted the ICCAT regulations. Panama, Honduras, and Belize were among the violators.[297] As a consequence, because of fears of further retaliatory trade sanctions, several states, such as the Netherlands, Antilles, Belize, Cuba, Egypt, and Guatemala, have applied for ICCAT cooperating party status. The issue of illegal fishing, however, may run deeper than initially thought. In addition to flag of convenience ships, vessels that do not even display a flag of identification often engage in unauthorized shipping in the area.

3.5.6. General Fisheries Commission of the Mediterranean (GFCM)
The General Fisheries Council of the Mediterranean (GFCM) Agreement was adopted in 1949[298] and came into force in 1952. Since then, it has been amended three times.[299] The 1997 version of the agreement[300] incorporates many of the concepts of the 1995 Fisheries Agreement. Furthermore, the name of the GFCM was changed from General Fisheries Council of the Mediterranean to General Fisheries Commission of the Mediterranean, and an autonomous budget (from the FAO budget) was adopted.[301]

The GFCM still operates within the framework of the FAO.[302] The GFCM Agreement is open to coastal states and states whose vessels engage in fishing in the region as well as to regional economic integration organizations (i.e., the EU).[303] The region covered by the agreement is defined loosely as the Mediterranean Sea and Black Sea and connecting waters.[304] The commission established under the agreement has multiple functions, such as "the development, conservation, rational management and best utilization of living marine resources," thus opening the ambit of the convention to include not only fisheries but also any other management of

---

[296] See Report of the 2nd Meeting of the Working Group to Develop Integrated and Coordinated Atlantic Bluefin Tuna Management Strategies, May 17–20, 2004.

[297] FAO Fisheries, *supra* note 2, at 66. See also Council Regulation (EC) No 2092/2000 of 28 September 2000 prohibiting imports of Atlantic blue-fin tuna originating in Belize, Honduras, and Equatorial Guinea, OJ L 249/1, 4.10.2000.

[298] Agreement for the Establishment of a General Fisheries Council for the Mediterranean, Sept. 24, 1949.

[299] The agreement was amended in 1963, 1976 and 1997.

[300] Agreement for the Establishment of a General Fisheries Commission for the Mediterranean, Nov. 6, 1997, available online at http://www.infish.net/treaties. Parties to the agreement are: Albania, Algeria, Bulgaria, Croatia, Cyprus, Egypt, the European Community, France, Greece, Israel, Italy, Japan, Lebanon, Libya, Malta, Monaco, Morocco, Romania, Spain, Syria, Tunisia, Turkey, and Yugoslavia.

[301] Art. IX, *id.*

[302] Art. I(1), *id.*

[303] Art. I(2), *id.*

[304] Preamble, *id.*

living resources.[305] The commission is to take into account the precautionary approach and "the need to promote the development and proper utilization of marine living resources."[306] The commission is to issue recommendations on the management measures that need to be adopted in the region. But these recommendations are subject to an objection procedure.[307]

The commission has dispute settlement functions. If a dispute is not settled by the commission, it must be referred to a committee comprised of members appointed by each of the parties to the dispute and an independent chairman chosen by the members of the committee. If the committee fails to resolve a dispute, the dispute must be referred to the ICJ or to an arbitration proceeding, unless another method has been agreed on by the parties for dispute settlement.[308]

The commission is supported in its work by a Committee on Aquaculture, a Scientific Advisory Committee, and *ad hoc* technical panels. The EC is involved in the management of fisheries in the GFCM, but its involvement has not led to better implementation. The strengthening of the procedures of the GFCM is proceeding slowly, and the measures adopted suffer from internal compliance problems.[309]

3.5.7. Commission for the Conservation of Antarctic Marine Living Resources (CCAMLR)

The depletion of resources of the Antarctic region has been a subject of concern since the mid-1970s, when it was realized that certain species in the region were overexploited. The Convention for the Conservation of Antarctic Marine Resources was adopted in 1980 and entered into force in 1982.[310] The convention covers all the living resources of Antarctic including seabirds except for seals (partially, south of 60° S) that are regulated by the Convention on the Conservation of Antarctic Seals (CCAS), and whales regulated by the International Whaling Commission.[311]

The conservation of species is not the only goal of the convention. Another important goal is to attend to the concerns of nations that do not have harvesting interests in the region but are concerned with keeping the Antarctic Treaty System intact.[312] Several articles of the convention are devoted to this second goal.

The convention includes articulations of a preventive/precautionary approach. The convention attempts to apply an ecosystem approach.[313] Article II of the

---

[305] Art. III(1), *id.*

[306] Art. III(2), *id.*

[307] Art. V, *id.*

[308] Art. XVII, *id.*

[309] Green Paper on the Future of the Common Fisheries Policy 19, 38, COM(2001) 135 final.

[310] Convention on the Conservation of Antarctic Marine Living Resources, May 20, 1980, available online at http://www.ccamlr.org [hereinafter CCAMLR].

[311] See, e.g., art. VI, *id.*

[312] For instance, article IV provides that all contracting parties to the CCAMLR would be bound by articles IV and VI of the Antarctic Treaty and that nothing taking place in the context of the CCAMLR shall constitute a basis for asserting, supporting, or denying a claim to territorial sovereignty in the Antarctic Treaty. See art. IV, *id.* See also arts. III, V, *id.*

[313] See Catherine Redgwell, Protection of Ecosystems under International Law: Lessons from Antarctica, in International Law and Sustainable Development: Past Achievements and Future Challenges 205, 217 (Alan Boyle & David Freestone, eds., 1999).

convention provides that any harvesting in the convention area must be conducted in accordance with the principles of conservation that include, *inter alia*:

> prevention of changes or minimization of the risk of changes in the marine ecosystem which are not potentially reversible over two or three decades taking into account . . . the effects of associated activities on the marine ecosystem . . .[314]

This adoption of the ecosystem approach was considered to be ahead of its time. Not much was known, however, when the convention was adopted, about the functioning of ecosystems that could be implemented in practice. The convention includes simultaneously provisions on the rational use of resources. Terminology, such as "the greatest net annual increment" or "stable recruitment" of harvested population is found in the convention as well.[315]

The convention is run by a Commission for the Conservation of Antarctic Marine Living Resources (CCAMLR), a scientific committee,[316] and an Executive Secretary.[317] State parties are to provide the commission with information (including statistical and biological information) so that the commission can exercise its functions.[318] The functions of the commission involve analysis of the data collected and the enactment of conservation measures.[319] An objection procedure is provided for and conservation measures do not have binding effects on states parties that object to them.[320]

State parties are responsible for the enforcement of the convention[321] and have to establish a system of observation and inspection. The system is to include boarding on vessels and inspections, procedures for flag state prosecution, and sanctions based on evidence emanating from boarding and inspections.[322] The parties established a system of inspection in 1988, which became effective in 1989.[323] The parties have adopted a scheme of international scientific observation that became effective in the 1992/93 fishing season.[324] According to the scheme, each state party is to designate observers, and state parties are expected to conclude bilateral arrangements that would place scientific observers on board of vessels of other state parties.

Monitoring measures have not been very effective, however, and issues remain with regard to illegal catches, especially those of Patagonian toothfish. During the 1995/96 season more than one hundred vessels were observed engaging in unregulated fishing of toothfish in the region, with an estimated catch of more than ten times the harvest reported by CCAMLR members.[325] Many of the parties to the

---

[314] Art. II(3)(c), CCAMLR, *supra* note 310.

[315] Art. II(3)(a), *id.*

[316] Arts. XIV & XV, *id.*

[317] Art. XVII, *id.*

[318] Art. XX, *id.*

[319] Art. IX, *id.*

[320] Art. IX(6), *id.*

[321] Arts. XXI & XXII, *id.*

[322] Art. XXIV, *id.*

[323] The CCAMLR System of Inspection, available online at http://www.ccamlr.org.

[324] Scheme of International Scientific Observation, available online at http://www.camlr.org.

[325] See Steinar Andersen, The Convention for the Conservation of Antarctic Marine Living Resources (CCAMLR): Improving Procedures but Lacking Results, in Environmental Regime Effectiveness: Confronting Theory with Evidence 405, 419 (Edward L. Miles et al., eds., 2002).

convention are allegedly engaging in illegal harvesting operations by registering their vessels with flag of convenience states.[326]

The CCAMLR regime has been more successful when dealing with issues that are not related to the profitability of catches. Measures that have been enacted for the protection of seabirds, for instance, have been considered more successful[327] than measures to protect the Patagonian toothfish.

The shortcomings of the regime have been attributed to the resistance of laggard states (particularly of the Soviet Union) and to the lack of interest of nonharvesting nations in confronting the laggards. It has been argued that if nonharvesting nations had been more interested in conservation than keeping the Antarctic Treaty System (ATS)[328] in place, the chances of the CCAMLR becoming a more successful regime would have been greater.[329] The relative lack of interest of state parties in environmental issues has much to do with reluctance of the CCAMLR Commission to adopt conservation measures. The CCAMLR has used the lack of scientific evidence[330] as subterfuge for indecision. The ecosystem approach has been considered also an obstacle to implementation. Some commentators have characterized the ecosystem approach as an impractical approach and have proposed that a "traffic lights" approach would have been a more desirable management technique (red light – no harvesting; amber light – take some measures; green light – harvest).[331]

The CCAMLR recently adopted a Catch Documentation Scheme (CDS) that applies especially to the Patagonian toothfish.[332] The purpose of the scheme is to monitor international toothfish trade; identify the origins of toothfish imports and exports; determine whether toothfish catches have been executed in accordance with conservation measures; and gather data for the scientific evaluation of toothfish stocks. The CDS consists of a document that must accompany all landings, imports, exports, and transshipments of toothfish.[333] In order to promote compliance with the CDS – and because many fishers consider their fishing areas, catches, and techniques to be confidential information – rules for access to CDS data have been adopted. These rules provide, *inter alia*, that all data concerning landings and trading of individual companies would be aggregated or encrypted as appropriate to protect the confidentiality of information. After the data is encrypted, it can become available to

---

[326] *Id.* at 423.

[327] In 1989, CCAMLR took measures to minimize the incidental mortality of seabirds as a result of long-line fishing. The measures reduced albatross deaths by 80 percent (however, about one hundred thousand birds are still caught by IUU vessels and in areas outside the convention area). The CCAMLR has taken measures to reduce the impact of fishing on nontarget species. The CCAMLR proposed that TACs for targeted species must be linked to the allowable by-catch. A fishery, therefore, may be closed if it reaches the TAC for the by-catch even if the TAC for the targeted species has not been met. See CCAMLR's Management of the Antarctic, available online at http://www.ccamlr.org.

[328] See Antarctic Treaty, Dec. 1, 1959, reprinted in 402 UNTS 71.

[329] Andersen, *supra* note 325, at 424.

[330] Redgwell, *supra* note 313, at 216.

[331] *Id.* at 217, n. 63.

[332] CCAMLR's Management of the Antarctic, available online at http://www.ccamlr.org. See also Catch Documentation Scheme for Dissostichus Spp., Conservation Measure 10-05 (2003), available online at http://www.ccamlr.org.

[333] The document includes all information about the issuing authority, the vessel, the recipients, the license to fish, the dates within which a catch is taken, the date, and the port of landing. For more details, see Section 6, Conservation Measure 10-05, *id.*

working groups of the commission or to the scientific committee. Noncontracting parties are to be given only limited access to the data.[334]

It remains to be seen whether the CDS would be successful or whether state parties to the convention would continue to flout the rules despite monitoring and enforcement provisions. An obvious problem with the CDS is that it can be subjected to falsification. For this reason, the documents for Patagonian toothfish are to be checked in order to verify that the information contained in the catch document is consistent with the data derived from an automated satellite-linked Vessel Monitoring System (VMS).[335] The use of technology, as it becomes cheaper and more affordable, is likely to play an important role in ensuring implementation with regional fisheries agreements.

4. CONCLUSION

The fisheries regime is a classic case of an enclosure of previously global commons. The enclosure is accomplished by leaving many states outside profitable fisheries areas. The enclosure is based on a tragedy of commons rationale. That is, if coastal states develop property rights over the full range of a resource, they would have more chances to succeed in the conservation and rational management of the resource. The perpetuation of an open-access regime, on the contrary, would eventually lead to the degradation and depletion of the resource. That coastal states may be better managers of fisheries resources may be true depending on the level of development of such states and the willingness to undertake a custodian attitude with regard to fishery resources.

The enclosure of fisheries resources, as with most enclosures, is primarily exclusionary. Many recent agreements, such as the 1995 Fisheries Agreement, legitimize fishery enclosures as the future method of fisheries management. Exclusionary enclosures, however, pose fundamental questions of fairness. The enclosure of fisheries resources has as an effect that a limited number of states – those belonging to regional organizations – take advantage of and profit from those resources. Other states that have no historical rights to the resource and no clout in international negotiations are to stay out. Compensation is rarely offered to these outsider states that may, in return, engage in clandestine activities. States left out of regional arrangements tend to revolt when, what they have perceived as an open-access resource, is increasingly appropriated by coastal states or by the first-movers in a region. Some outsiders attempt to find compromises, especially, in areas of high seas that have been severely restricted due to EEZ extensions.[336]

For the insiders, the establishment of RFOs has been far from easy. How fisheries resources would be allocated among the insiders in different regimes is bound to remain controversial. The overuse of the objection procedure has the possibility of transforming regime insiders into *de facto* outsiders and to undermine the general

---

[334] See Rules of Access to Catch Documentation Scheme Data, available online at http://www.ccamlr.org.

[335] See Resolution 17/XX, Use of VMS and other Measures for Verification of CDS Catch Data for Areas Outside the Convention Area, in particular, in FAO Statistical Area 51, available online at http://www.ccamlr.org.

[336] Olav Schram Stokke et al., The Barents Sea Fisheries, in The Effectiveness of International Environmental Regimes 91, 109 (Oran R. Young, ed., 1999).

legitimacy of regulatory controls on fisheries. The regional fisheries agreements, nevertheless, are a bold attempt to regulate the "freedom of fishing in the high seas" – an attempt that has been legitimized for the purposes of conservation. States generally have been eager to participate in regional agreements, even distant water fishing states, in order to render legitimate their fishing in a particular region. Participation in regional arrangements also guarantees the possibility of placing objections on TACs established and quotas assigned.

The participation in regional fisheries agreements, as a way to legitimize fishing in the high seas, provides evidence of the erosion of the sacrosanct principle in international law, which is the freedom of the high seas. And this is not theoretical erosion based on a number of agreements. Technological devices such as VMS, as they are increasingly installed in new ships, would gradually render unobserved navigation and fishing quite difficult. Not all vessels are equipped today with VMS and there is resistance to institutionalize the installment of such devices. As things evolve, however, VMS increasingly would become the device that enhances the legitimacy of vessels to engage in high seas fishing activities. Shipowners, then, would have to decide whether they want their vessels to obtain a *carte blanche* for navigation, fishing, transit, and landing by the incorporation of state-of-the-art equipment, or if they would prefer to retain an ambiguous status that would increase the transaction costs of fishing (through repeated inspections, detentions, and fines by coastal states and port states).

7 Biodiversity

1. BIODIVERSITY MANAGEMENT

1.1. State of Biodiversity Resources

There is a general understanding that species are becoming extinct and that biodiversity is diminishing at an alarming rate primarily because of forest destruction as well as because of the disappearance of many other habitats, such as wetlands, and the pollution of seas and oceans. Because of the reported species loss and habitat destruction, measures have been taken, both in national and international arenas, to protect biodiversity.

How much biodiversity exists and how much is lost or diminishing every day is a subject of contention.[1] For those who believe that all nature as it exists today must be preserved as is, biodiversity loss is acute, and every ecosystem conversion (e.g., the conversion of forests into agricultural lands) is identical to ecosystem destruction and, thus, extinction.[2]

Other commentators, however, do not equate all habitat loss with species destruction.[3] Most ecosystems, they point out, are not so fragile that any alteration will precipitate species loss.[4] For instance, rainstorms, floods, fire, and other natural phenomena that are viewed, from a human perspective, as destructive are, in essence, part of ecosystem regulation.[5] Human actions that affect the environment do not necessarily have to have adverse impacts. Shifting agriculture, for instance, practiced

[1] E. O. Wilson, The Current State of Biological Diversity, in Biodiversity 3,13 (E. O. Wilson, ed., 1988).

[2] See D. Simberloff, Do Species-Area Curves Predict Extinctions in Fragmented Forest?, in Tropical Deforestation and Species Extinction 75, 76 (T. C. Whitmore & J. A. Sayer, eds., 1992); Graig L. Shafer, Nature Reserves: Island Theory and Conservation in Practice 11–33 (1990).

[3] David M. Raup, Diversity Crises in the Geological Past, in Biodiversity 51, 57, *supra* note 1.

[4] Some ecologists debate whether we can actually talk about "ecosystems." According to one view, nature is comprised of a community of species that are organized together as a system. According to an opposing view, nature is comprised of collections of species whose habitats happen to coincide. See David M. Raup, Extinction: Bad Genes or Bad Luck? (1991).

[5] See Richard J. Vogl, The Ecological Factors that Produce Perturbation-Dependent Ecosystems, in The Recovery Process in Damaged Ecosystems 63 (John Cairns Jr., ed., 1980).

for years in tropical rainforests by indigenous peoples, has been viewed as constructive in ecosystem evolution.[6]

When biodiversity is raised as an issue, the first image that comes to mind is the tropical rainforest. Biodiversity protection has started as a campaign to protect the tropical rainforest and especially that of the Amazon region in Brazil. In general, forest ecosystems are viewed as major sites of biodiversity supporting 50 to 70 percent of the world's terrestrial species.[7] Recent FAO estimates suggest a slow-down of deforestation in developed countries because of forest plantations. By the same token, however, the deforestation in the developing world continues to be significant. It is estimated that 15.2 million hectares of forest are decimated annually in the tropical areas. The highest deforestation areas are in Africa and South America. In Asia, the loss of primary forest is high, but it is counterbalanced by the development of plantations.[8]

The causes of biodiversity loss are often identified in a number of legal or illegal activities undertaken by companies, communities, and individuals that attempt to secure profits or just survival in biodiversity-rich areas without regard to the conservation of ecosystems. Recent studies, however, have attempted to distinguish between the causes of biodiversity loss and the indicators of biodiversity loss. Habitat destruction, overharvesting, pollution, and illegal use of resources are the indicators of biodiversity loss. The root causes of biodiversity loss have to do with poverty, land tenure issues, population changes, and national policy failures.[9]

1.2. National and Transnational Protected Areas

National Protected Areas

One of the most frequently used methods to protect biodiversity is the creation of protected areas. Such areas are usually established by evicting the populations who happen to live there, often through the use of forcible measures and without offering any compensation for the loss of the use of the area. The establishment of strict protected areas where nature would be allowed to take its course without human intervention has been advocated in many countries and by many international organizations. It has had disastrous effects, however, on the poor of the developing world, including indigenous peoples and communities that happen to make a livelihood in these areas.

---

[6] Darrell Addison Posey, Interpreting and Applying the "Reality" of Indigenous Concepts, in Conservation of Neotropical Forests 21, 28–29 (Kent H. Redford & Christine Padoch, eds., 1992). See also William Balée, People of the Fallow, in Conservation of Neotropical Forests 35, id.; Jean-Louis Guillaumet, Tropical Humid Forest Food Plants and their Domestication, in People and Food 55 (UNESCO Man & The Biosphere Series, C. M. Hladik et al., ed., 1993); Doyle McKey et al., Evolution and History in Tropical Forests in Relation to Food Availability, in People and Food 17, id.

[7] Food and Agriculture Organization (FAO), State of the World's Forests 46 (2003) [hereinafter FAO Forests].

[8] For the difficulties of estimating the rates of deforestation, see id. at 1–3.

[9] Rowan Martin, Biological Diversity: Diverging Views on its Status and Diverging Approaches to its Conservation, in Earth Report 2000, at 237 (Ronald Bailey, ed., 2000); The Root Causes of Biodiversity Loss 75 (Alexander Wood, ed., 2000).

There are thirteen hundred marine protected areas covering 1 percent of the oceans. There are one hundred thousand designated protected land areas covering about 12.7 percent of the earth's surface. This expansion of protected areas has been called by some the largest conscious land change in history.[10]

Colonial governments were the first to impose protected area management accompanied with strict enforcement in areas that previously had free access. These areas were isolated, called "nature reserves," and removed from productive use.[11] The regimes that followed colonialism implemented similar policies, realizing that the revenues generated from the consumptive uses of protected areas, such as safari hunting and tourism, are a good source of foreign exchange. Revenues from the consumptive uses of protected areas also are a good supplement to the revenues provided by agriculture, mining, and forestry. When nature reserves can pay for their preservation, through the profits generated by the wildlife industry,[12] enforcement, in terms of exclusion of local populations from these areas, is so relentless that some commentators have characterized it "coercive conservation."[13]

Africa provides an example in which protected areas and strict enforcement have been overused. In fourteen African countries, more land is set aside for conservation than for cultivation.[14] Coercive conservation methods have been applied in other areas of the world, notably Asia. Seventy percent of all protected areas worldwide are inhabited,[15] and most of the inhabitants are indigenous peoples. The estimates of the number of people that conservation efforts have displaced from protected areas range from 900,000 to 14.4 million people.[16] These invisible refugees have practically no say in conservation efforts.[17]

Marine protected areas (MPA) have been proposed for the recovery of valuable fisheries and the protection of endangered marine ecosystems and species. The establishment of marine protected areas creates as much controversy as the establishment of terrestrial protected areas because, for MPAs to be established, fishing and other productive activities would have to cease. Some MPAs are created as reserve zones in which the removal or disturbance of resources is absolutely prohibited. These reserve zones are characterized as closed, "no-take" zones.[18] Many fishers view the establishment of MPAs as "taking" of their traditional fishing grounds under an eminent domain policy and demand compensation. A whole or partial closure of a fishing ground for the creation of MPAs is likely to affect an entire fishing industry

---

[10] Protected Areas, WWF Position Paper (Aug. 2003).

[11] Producing Nature and Poverty in Africa: Continuity and Change (Vigdis Broch-Due & Richard A. Shroeder, eds., 2000).

[12] The wildlife industry – which includes ecotourism, mass tourism, safari hunting, sale of live game, meat, and other products – is viewed as a growing industry in three southern African countries (Zimbabwe, Namibia, and South Africa).

[13] Nancy Peluso, Coercive Conservation: the Politics of State Resource Control, 3 Global Environmental Change – Human and Policy Dimensions 199 (1993).

[14] Charles C. Geisler: Endangered Humans: How Global Land Conservation Efforts Are Creating a Growing Class of Invisible Refugees, Foreign Policy 80 (May/June 2002).

[15] Id.

[16] Id.

[17] Id.

[18] United States National Academy of Sciences, Marine Protected Areas: Tools for Sustaining Ocean Ecosystems 1 (2001).

including, processors, industry suppliers, and fish dealers.[19] In addition to the social costs associated with MPAs, environmental impacts on other areas as a result of fishing or other activities dislocated from MPAs are to be expected.

Large marine reserves, like nature reserves, present overall significant monitoring and enforcement problems. MPAs are not exempt from attempts at coercive conservation. In the Clumbe coral reef park in Tanzania, conflict between park rangers and local people reached its peak in 1994/95 when fishers entered the waters of a protected area in defiance of the authorities. Eventually, a conscious decision was made to offer local people employment as park rangers. It seems, at this point, that the effort has paid off, keeping fishers outside the MPA by means of persuasion rather than through enforcement.[20]

Because the creation of protected areas often involves the involuntary resettlement of people who happen to live in these areas, international organizations, including the World Bank, have developed guidelines on the involuntary displacement of people when various development projects, including ecodevelopment, are initiated.

The World Bank adopted an operational directive on internal displacement that was further revised in 2004.[21] In that directive, the World Bank recognizes that involuntary resettlement, if not mitigated, gives rise to severe economic and social problems and environmental risks as production systems are dismantled and people face impoverishment as their productive assets and income are lost. This is especially so if people are relocated to places where their productive skills are not applicable or the competition for resources is greater.[22] The World Bank provides explicitly that its policy applies to involuntary displacement with regard to involuntary restriction of access to designated parks and protected areas.[23]

The World Bank's guidelines provide that displaced people should be assisted so that they restore or even improve their standard of living.[24] Displaced people should be supported during the transition period with compensation measures, such as land preparation, credit facilities, training, and job opportunities.[25] Additional attention must be placed to those below the poverty line, such as landless people, indigenous peoples, and ethnic minorities.[26]

Other commentators have argued that the right not to be displaced should be conceived as a right deriving from the fundamental human rights[27] and have proposed

---

[19] *Id.* at 58.

[20] Sibylle Riedmiller, Private Sector Management of Marine Protected Areas: The Chumbe Island Coral Park Project in Zanzibar/Tanzania, available online at http://www.unesco.org/csi/pub/papers2/mapp14.htm.

[21] World Bank, Involuntary Resettlement, OP 4.12., as revised in April 2004.

[22] Para. 1, *id.*

[23] Para. 3(b), *id.*

[24] Para. 2(c), *id.*

[25] Para. 6(c), *id.*

[26] Para. 8, *id.*

[27] Maria Stavropoulou, The Right Not To Be Displaced, 9 American University Journal of International Law & Policy 689 (1994). See also Guiding Principles on Internal Displacement UN Doc. E/CN.4/1998/53/Add.2, Annex, Feb. 11, 1998, presented by Francis M. Deng, the Representative of the UN Secretary-General on Internally Displaced Persons. See also Walter Kälin, Guiding Principles on Internal Displacement: Annotations (American Society of International Law & Brookings Institution Project on Internal Displacement, 2000).

that conservation instruments should be linked to human rights instruments. Bio-diversity conservation should not take place through the violations of human rights of people that live in protected areas no matter the conservation interest at stake.[28]

Comanagement

Comanagement of a protected area between the government and the local com-munities has been proposed as a method to overcome monitoring and enforcement problems in protected areas.[29] The strict nature reserve model is far from acceptable in the developing world because of the large numbers of landless people.[30] Reserves that are inadequately monitored are constantly infiltrated by local people who view them as arbitrary violations of their natural rights to forests.

Even under a modern approach to nature reserves that attempts to exclude humans only from core reserve areas,[31] local people remain dissatisfied. The bio-sphere reserves proposed by the United Nations Educational, Scientific, and Cultural Organization (UNESCO) often are cited as an example of this modern approach. The biosphere reserves contain a core conservation area and buffer zones in which different uses are allowed.[32] The distinction between core areas and buffer zones, however, is not followed in reality. Most biosphere reserves today consist of a combi-nation of preexisting national parks with no separation between core areas and buffer zones.[33] Wild animals enter buffer zones destroying crops and property.[34] Core areas are often fertile and buffer zones are degraded generating demands to open core areas to use.

Some attribute the lack of success of comanagement schemes to their organi-zational structure. It is argued that comanagement programs are not structured to provide answers to the problems of local people, as the international environmen-tal interests that fund them are not ultimately accountable to local people. Studies undertaken by the FAO have confirmed that the costs of conservation are borne by the people who are the least able to bear these costs, whereas the benefits are enjoyed

---

[28] See, generally, Elli Louka, Biodiversity and Human Rights: The International Rules for the Protection of Biodiversity (2002).

[29] See Rudolf Hermes, Key Sustaining Factors to Effective Implementation of Marine Protected Areas in the Philippines, in Proceedings of the INCO-DC International Workshop on Policy Options for the Sustainable Use of Coral Reefs and Associated Ecosystems, Mombasa, Kenya, June 19–22, 2000, reprinted in ACP-EU Fisheries Research Report, No. 10, at 174 (Heidi Wittmer et al., eds., 2001) [hereinafter Coral Reefs].

[30] See, e.g., R.H.V. Bell, Conservation with a Human Face: Conflict and Reconciliation in African Land Use Planning, in Conservation in Africa 79, 88 (D. Anderson & R. Grove, eds., 1987).

[31] The modern approach to forest area management presupposes the involvement of local communities by providing incentives to maintain the reserve rather than to destroy it for the quick economic benefit. The International Union for Conservation of Nature (IUCN) in a revision of protected areas added a category of "managed resource protected areas," areas managed for the "sustainable use" of the ecosys-tem. See IUCN, Guidelines for Protected Area Management Categories 23 (1994). For other attempts to classify protected areas, see United States National Academy of Sciences, Managing Global Genetic Resources (1991); United States Office of Technology Assessment, Technologies to Sustain Tropical For-est Resources (1994); ITTO, Guidelines on Conservation of Biological Diversity in Tropical Production Forests (ITTO Policy Development Series No. 5, 1993).

[32] For a good description of a biosphere reserve, see FAO, Tropical Forest Management 41–44 (FAO paper 107, 1993).

[33] See Craig L. Shafer, Nature Reserves: Island Theory and Conservation Practice 77 (1990).

[34] See, generally, R. Sukumar, The Asian Elephant: Ecology and Management (1989).

by the wealthy nature lovers residing in developed countries.[35] In most instances, the most communities can obtain from "sharing" in the benefits of resource use is access to medicinal plants, fibers, and drinking water.[36] This is in exchange for undertaking the onerous task of patrolling, monitoring, and reporting illegal park behavior.[37]

There is often a genuine conflict of interests between conservation interests and the interests of local people.[38] Such conflict defies immediate resolution and needs to be managed in a constant fashion.[39]

Community-Based Natural Resources Management

Because of the failures of different comanagement schemes, community-based natural resources management (CBNRM) has been proposed for the management of many common pool resources, such as forests. CBNRM is based on the idea that local communities will be in charge of the management of their resources. An ideally functioning CBNRM system would involve:collective action defined as an action taken by a group as whole in defense of its shared interests;[40] an enabling environment – that is legislation and an institutional structure in support of the devolution of power to the local community; property rights and/or user rights (access to the resource, withdrawal [e.g., rights to take fish, plants]) and control rights (including exclusion, alienation and management). Furthermore, user groups would need access to financing, skills and linkages to other groups.[41] CBNRM is more appropriate for small-scale resources because its enforcement – and, thus, its success – is based largely on the ability of people to observe each other's behavior.[42] A fundamental problem with all CBNRM systems is that they are closed systems. Extensive commercialization of a resource could undermine and eventually wipe out such systems. Supporting such systems would make it necessary to shield them from outside commercial pressures[43] – a difficult-to-meet requirement in today's globalized world.

---

35   Tom Blomley, Natural Resource Conflict Management: The Case of Bwindi Impenetrable and Mgahinga Gorilla National Parks, Southwestern Uganda, in FAO, Natural Resource Conflict Management Case Studies: An Analysis of Power, Participation and Protected Areas 231, 239 (A. Peter Castro & Erik Nielsen, eds., 2003).

36   Id. at 240.

37   Id. at 242–44.

38   Zvidzai Chidhakwa, Managing Conflict around Contested Natural Resources: a Case Study of Rusitu Valley Area, Chimanimani, Zimbabwe, in FAO, Natural Resource Conflict Management Case Studies: An Analysis of Power, Participation and Protected Areas 183, 200 (A. Peter Castro & Erik Nielsen, eds., 2003).

39   Sara Singleton, Cooperation or Capture? The Paradox of Co-management and Community Participation in Natural Resource Management and Environmental Policymaking, in "Conference: Property Rights: Design Lessons from Fisheries and Other Natural Resources," 1, 4–5, International Institute of Fisheries Economies and Trade (IIFET), Oregon State University, 2000.

40   See Ruth Meizen-Dick & Anna Knox, Collective Action, Property Rights and Devolution of Natural Resources Management: a Conceptual Framework, in "Proceedings of International Conference, Collective Action, Property Rights and Devolution of Natural Resources Management: Exchange of Knowledge and Implications for Policy" (Ruth Meinzen-Dick et al., eds., 1999).

41   Id. at 48–58.

42   Carol Rose, Common Property, Regulatory Property, and Environmental Protection: Comparing Community-Based Management to Tradable Environmental Allowances, in The Drama of the Commons 233, 237 (National Academy of Sciences, Elinor Ostrom et al., eds., 2003).

43   Id. at 247.

CBNRM systems are generally based on nonconsumptive uses of biodiversity, such as bioprospecting, extractive reserves, and small ecotourism projects.

A CBNRM program has been developed in Zimbabwe with mixed success. Namibia also has experimented with conservancy systems that are a kind of privatization schemes for communal resources.[44]

Individual Transferable Quotas (ITQs), applied in fisheries management, also have been proposed for the management of wildlife in protected land areas. It has been proposed that such ITQs are feasible because wildlife is a common pool resource and the differences between wildlife and other common pool resources are of degree rather than of substance.[45] The application of ITQs, however, can encounter many practical difficulties, especially in countries that lack the institutions and preparedness to supervise private markets. Some of advantages and pitfalls of ITQs were detailed in Chapter 6.

In general, attempts at community management encounter many problems:

- unanticipated conflicts when the community in which CBNRM is attempted is not as homogenous as it was initially assumed;[46]
- parochial and separatist tendencies that provide more excuses for suppressive authoritarianism;
- additional regulatory complexity as central governments refuse to relinquish power but, at the same time, add local regulations in support of an alleged decentralization;[47] and
- further dominance by local elites as decentralization efforts are often captured by such elites in weak democratic settings.[48]

It is expected overall that decentralization, in terms of community management, would work better if it addresses the distribution issues before it deals with the natural resource management issues. Addressing distribution issues, however, as a means to resolve conservation issues has rarely occurred in practice.

Transnational Protected Areas

A relatively new trend in international circles involves interstate agreements for the creation transboundary protected areas – what has been called Transboundary

---

[44] For more details on these systems, see Louka, *supra* note 28, at 79–90.

[45] All common pool resources, including wildlife, share similar characteristics. They are quite mobile, usually defy administrative and national frontiers and are difficult to monitor. Because of these characteristics, it is difficult for individuals or communities to acquire clear property rights and to effectively exclude outsiders. See Amar Inamdar et al., What's Special About Wildlife Management in Forests?, Concepts and Models of Rights-Based Management, with Recent Evidence from West-Central Africa, Natural Perspectives, Number 44, June 1999 (issued by the Overseas Development Institute).

[46] Sobona Mtisi & Alan Nicol, Water Points and Water Policies: Decentralisation and Community Management in Sangwe Communal Area, Zimbabwe 1, Sustainable Livelihoods in Southern Africa Research Paper 15, Institute of Development Studies, Brighton (2003).

[47] P. W. Mamimine, Administration by Consensus: A Quest for Client-centered Institutional Structures for Land Administration in Zimbabwe, in Delivering Land and Securing Rural Livelihoods 365, 379, Centre for Applied Social Sciences, University of Zimbabwe & Land Tenure Center, University of Wisconsin-Madison (Michael Roth & Francis Gonese, eds., 2003). See also Elinor Ostrom, Vulnerability and Polycentric Governance Systems, Update, Newsletter of the International Human Dimensions Programme on Global Environmental Change Nr. 3/2001.

[48] Sustainable Livelihoods in Southern Africa (SLSA Team), Decentralisation in Practice in Southern Africa 25–26, Programme for Land and Agrarian Studies, University of Western Cape, Cape Town, 2003.

Natural Resource Management (TBNRM) or Integrated Conservation and Development Management (ICDM). In 2000, the governments of Zimbabwe, South Africa, and Mozambique signed an agreement creating a protected area encompassing the Gonarezhou, Kruger, and Gaza national parks – a total conservation area of 99,800 square kilometers. In 2001, the area was given the name Limpopo Transfrontier Park.[49]

At WSSD, the governments of South Africa and the United States, in cooperation with Conservation International, the World Wildlife Fund (WWF), and the Wildlife Conservation Society, announced the establishment of the Congo Basin Forest Partnership. The purpose of the partnership is to alleviate poverty and protect biodiversity through a network of protected areas. Assistance to local communities that depend on forests in the Central African countries, including Cameroon, the Central African Republic, Congo, Equatorial Guinea, and Gabon, is to be provided.[50]

Efforts to manage biodiversity across borders are not limited to terrestrial areas. France, Italy, and Monaco concluded an agreement in 1999 establishing a marine mammal sanctuary in the Mediterranean.[51] The agreement establishes a sanctuary for whales and dolphins in the Mediterranean Sea off the coasts of state parties. This is the largest marine protected area in the Mediterranean. Other transnational marine protected areas include the Indian Ocean Sanctuary and the protected area established under the Torres Strait Treaty between Australia and Papua New Guinea.

International agreements to protect biodiversity across national borders are hard to evaluate because of the multiplicity of goals involved. The purpose of these agreements is initially to build alliances among neighboring countries that would increase regional cohesion. It seems like an ideal situation, that countries cooperate to build alliances to protect forests and to alleviate the poverty of their inhabitants. Such international alliances, it is believed, could help bring peace in a belligerent region. As a matter of fact, the premises on which theses protected areas have been established include:

- a belief in bioregionalism – that is, a conviction that ecosystems are preserved better in bigger areas than in fragmented landscapes;[52]
- a belief in cultural harmonization by removing artificial national boundaries and by bringing together cohesive groups; and
- a presumption that peace and security would flourish through transboundary conservation areas.[53]

In matters of management, however, transnational conservation areas have not been all that different from national protected areas. From a state perspective, TBNRM would bring better enforcement by abating illegal migration, poaching,

---

[49] William Wolmer, Transboundary Conservation: the Politics of Ecological Integrity in the Great Limpopo Transfrontier Park 9, Sustainable Livelihoods in Southern Africa Research Paper 4, Institute of Development Studies, Brighton (2003).

[50] FAO, State of the World's Forests 57 (2003).

[51] Agreement Concerning the Creation of a Marine Mammal Sanctuary in the Mediterranean (France, Italy, Monaco), Nov. 25, 1999, available online at http://www.oceanlaw.net/texts.

[52] See, e.g., C. Llewellyn et al., Moving to Large-Scale Marine Conservation: Ecosystem and Global Approaches, in Coral Reefs, *supra* note 29, at 217.

[53] Wolmer, *supra* note 49, at 2–7.

smuggling, and rebel activity. But local people do not necessarily view more enforcement as a benefit.[54] Local people are apprehensive that transboundary protected areas would mean infringements on their free cross-border movements. The free (often illegal) movement of people from Zimbabwe to South Africa, for instance, has been credited for the survival of many households in Zimbabwe.[55] Local people are fearful that more coordinated enforcement in protected areas would mean more violations of what they see as their natural right to a resource.

The question of whether transnational conservation areas would bring, through the spill-over effect, free trade in a region has yet to be answered. Although there have been efforts to associate the Limpopo Transnational Park with the 1992 Southern African Development Treaty and, thus, to open the area to free trade, this has not yet happened.[56] Moreover, the Limpopo Park has been established with virtually no local participation (many local people are not even aware of its existence).[57] Local participation has been used as a rhetorical device and genuine attempts to democratic emancipation have been resisted.[58]

The need to manage resources in a transnational fashion is prominent in most international and regional conventions. Many treaties require state parties to consult with each other if they plan to create a protected area close to a common frontier.[59] Some conventions go even further and ask parties to comanage resources that transcend national frontiers. The Ramsar Strategic Plan of 1997–2000, for instance, advocates the development of transfrontier wetlands in accordance with article 5 of the Ramsar Treaty.[60]

Some adjacent transnational protected areas have been declared transboundary World Heritage sites[61] and the World Heritage Convention welcomes the designation of other such areas. Transboundary biosphere reserves also have been proposed as a way to enhance the management of national reserves.

1.3. Gene Banks

National and Regional Gene Banks

Gene banks were developed mainly in the 1970s and the 1980s to preserve biodiversity that would otherwise disappear. The first gene banks were developed in Europe[62] for the same reason that makes them now indispensable in developing

[54] Anna Spencely, Tourism, Local Livelihoods and the Private Sector in South Africa: Case Studies on the Growing Role of the Private Sector in Natural Resources Management 92, Sustainable Livelihoods in Southern Africa Research Paper 8, Institute of Development Studies, Brighton (2003).

[55] Id.

[56] Wolmer, supra note 49, at 7.

[57] Spencely, supra note 54, at 93.

[58] Id. at 100.

[59] See, e.g., article 13(6) of the 1985 ASEAN Agreement on the Conservation of Nature and Natural Resources, infra Section 4.3 "Contracting Parties shall co-operate in the development of principles, objectives, criteria and guidelines for the selection, establishment and management of protected areas in the Region with a view to establishing a co-ordinated network of protected areas throughout the Region, giving particular attention to those of regional importance."

[60] See infra Section 3.3.

[61] Clare Shine, Legal Mechanisms to Strengthen and Safeguard Transboundary Protected Areas, in Parks for Peace 37 (International Conference on Transboundary Protected Areas as a Vehicle for International Co-operation, September 1997, Conference Proceedings, Draft of Jan. 30, 1998).

[62] See Ottto H. Frankel et al., The Conservation of Plant Biodiversity 98 (1995).

countries – the scarcity of land. Farmers, applying modern agricultural techniques to feed a rising population, were quick to discard traditional varieties.[63] The diversity of traditional crops was in danger and needed to be preserved.[64]

The purpose of gene banks is to keep the seeds of traditional landraces and other varieties safe and in good condition so that they can be used for future breeding and genetic engineering. Gene banks concentrate on traditional and advanced agricultural varieties and their wild relatives that are either underused or under the threat of extinction.[65] Gene banks have been instrumental in the preservation of food crops. When wars decimate indigenous germplasm, gene banks intervene to rehabilitate the farming sector of the war ravaged country. For instance, the International Agricultural Research Centers (IARCs) have provided assistance when seeds of a variety of sorghum called zera zera was destroyed in an attack on a gene bank in Ethiopia during a political upheaval. Similar assistance was provided to Nicaragua and Cambodia after periods of social disruption.[66]

Many gene banks have been established worldwide. Worldwide holdings of crop germplasm amount to 4.4 million accessions, but the number of unique samples are likely to be smaller because many accessions are duplicated.[67] Germplasm collections have been established in 130 countries, and the most unique collections are located in the IARCs.[68]

In order to ensure against national gene bank failure, efforts have been made to internationalize gene bank management through the IARCs. Efforts also have been made to ensure against the destruction of collections. Most gene banks today, to be on the safe side, save a large number of seeds to the point of creating excessive overlap and sacrificing valuable space.[69]

Gene banks have been instrumental in preserving food crops but not in preserving wild species. This is because the value of many wild species is not known and the techniques to maintain and regenerate wild species are not very advanced. Botanic gardens are geared more toward the protection of wild species.

The seeds kept in gene banks are the subject of controversy. Some developing countries seek to repatriate these seeds, and they also attempt to control the transfer of these seeds and to avert the assertion of intellectual property rights over the modification of seeds. Such efforts and their repercussions on innovation and food security are explored in detail later in this chapter.

IARCs

The Consultative Group on International Agricultural Research (CGIAR) was established in 1971[70] as an informal group of private and public donors. The CGIAR

---

[63] Miguel A. Alteri & Laura C. Merrick, Agroecology and In Situ Conservation of Native Crop Diversity in the Developing World, in Biodiversity 361 (E.O. Wilson, ed., 1988).

[64] See, generally, Donald L. Plucknett et al., Gene Banks and the World's Food (1987).

[65] Id. at 17–18.

[66] Fred Powledge, The Food Supply's Safety Net, 45 (No. 4) Bioscience 235, April 1995; H. Carrison Wilkes, Plant Genetic Resources Over Ten Thousands Years, in Seeds and Sovereignty 67, 86 (Jack R. Kloppenburg Jr., ed., 1988).

[67] Report on the State of World's Plant Genetic Resources, CGRFA-EX2/96/2, April 22–27, 1996.

[68] Id.

[69] See Plucknett, *supra* note 64, at 81.

[70] Before the birth of the CGIAR in 1971, the Ford and the Rockefeller foundations had already established four international agricultural research centers: the International Rice Research Institute (IRRI), the

supports the International Agricultural Research Centers (IARCs). The CGIAR is cosponsored by the FAO, the United Nations Development Program (UNDP), the UNEP, and the World Bank.

The CGIAR began operations with four centers, but many more centers were developed in the ensuing years.[71] The centers operate from year to year because their funding is determined on an annual basis. In general, the CGIAR system has worked well and the centers' relationships with their host countries have been good.[72] As mentioned earlier, the centers have played a crucial role in the preservation of food and agricultural resources. Well over one hundred thousand samples of materials held in the CGIAR collections were distributed in 1990 for use worldwide.[73]

Some centers, including the CIMMYT, the IRRI, and the International Potato Center (CIP), focus on one commodity for which they have a global mandate. Other centers have a regional or a global mandate for more than one commodity.[74] Yet other centers perform specialized functions in food policy research, such as the International Food Policy Research Institute (IFPRI) and the International Service for National Agricultural Research (ISNAR). In recent years, the CGIAR has sponsored centers that work in the area of agroforestry and forestry.[75]

The International Plant Genetic Resources Institute (IPGRI), formerly known as International Board for Plant Genetic Resources (IBPGR), is one of the most significant policy-making centers. The IBPGR was established in 1974, when the loss of valuable landraces became so widespread that it was recognized that an international network of gene banks was indispensable. In the first years of its life, the IBPGR was involved in collecting germplasm from all around the world and depositing it in gene banks. It also assisted in gene bank development in the third world.[76] Today, the principal objective of the IPGRI is to assist the national and regional programs

---

Center for the Improvement of Maize and Wheat (CIMMYT), the International Institute for Tropical Agriculture (IITA), and the International Center for Tropical Agriculture (CIAT). These institutions helped create optimism about the future of the world food. Except for serving as gene banks, these institutions are involved in breeding high-yield rice and wheat varieties. See M. S. Swaminathan, Seeds and Property Rights: A View from the CGIAR System, in Seeds and Sovereignty, *supra* note 66, at 231–32.

[71] Selcuk Ozgediz, Governance and Management of the CGIAR Centers 139 (CGIAR Study Paper Number 27, World Bank, 1991) [hereinafter CGIAR Governance].

[72] *Id*. at xx.

[73] IPGRI, Diversity for Development: The Strategy of the International Plant Genetic Resources Institute 16 (1993) [hereinafter IPGRI Strategy].

[74] For example, the International Center for Tropical Agriculture (CIAT), the International Center for Agricultural Research in Dry Areas (ICARDA), the International Institute for Tropical Agriculture (IITA), the International Crops Research Institute for the Semi-Arid Tropics (ICRISAT), and the International Livestock Research Institute (ILRI).

[75] International Center for Research in Agroforestry based in Kenya (ICRAF) and the Center for International Forestry Research based in Indonesia (CIFOR).

[76] In the first decade of its life the IPGRI focused on collecting threatened germplasm and facilitating long-term conservation in the base collections maintained by forty international and national gene banks. By the year 1991, almost two hundred thousand samples had been collected by missions sponsored by the IBPGR. An important contribution of the IPGRI is the introduction of a standardized system for characterizing germplasm. This system has been adopted by institutions all over the world. See IPGRI Strategy, *supra* note 73, at 6.

of developing countries. Another objective is to build crop and regional networks.[77] The IPGRI has been transformed from an organization heavily involved in plant collection to an organization playing a supportive role in national and regional programs.

The IARCs could be viewed as institutions created to strengthen the agricultural superiority of the North. The clientele relationship between the donors – which frequently are developed countries – and the centers has perpetuated these perceptions. The Lucerne Action program,[78] therefore, specifically provides that the CGIAR must broaden its membership to include more developing countries and must increasingly participate in the National Agricultural Research Systems (NARS)[79] of developing countries. The agricultural research institutions of the host countries gradually have become important clients of the IARCs located in those countries. The majority of the ICRISAT's activities in India are in conformity with the needs of Indian research institutions. The IRRI has filled most of the needs for a national program in the Philippines.[80]

The centers aim to become more open and to encourage participation in their activities of private and nongovernmental organizations. Today, private companies are not significant clients of the centers, but this is expected to change in the future.[81] It is increasingly realized that more centralization and coordination is needed in the centers' activities.

2. INTERNATIONAL INSTRUMENTS

Most of the initial treaties for the protection of biodiversity dealt with specific species and particular ecosystems. Most treaties also were regional treaties. The Biodiversity Convention adopted during the 1992 UNCED Conference was the first attempt to address biodiversity as a global issue. The convention deals not only with protection issues but also with the allocation of benefits from the exploitation and the commercialization of biodiversity resources.

2.1. Biodiversity Convention

2.1.1. Biodiversity Protection

The Biodiversity Convention[82] is the first attempt to deal globally with biodiversity protection. The convention is a framework convention. It does not establish biodiversity protection standards but attempts to create the outline of a regime for

---

[77] One such successful network has been established in Europe, the European Cooperative Program for Crop Genetic Resources Networks (ECP/GR), and has stimulated the development of twenty-two European crop databases. See IPGRI Strategy, *id.* at 7.

[78] See Lucerne Action Programme, CGIAR Ministerial-Level Meeting Feb 9–10, 1995, available online at http://www.worldbank.org/html/cgiar/publications/declara.html.

[79] Public sector agricultural research is particularly important in developing countries. In most developing countries there is not much private agricultural research activity and national agroindustries are in their infancy. Most agricultural products are sold to developing countries by transnational corporations. See Why is Public Agricultural Research Needed? CGIAR Newsletter, May 1996.

[80] CGIAR Governance, *supra* note 71, at 91.

[81] *Id.* at 89.

[82] Convention on Biological Diversity, June 5, 1992, reprinted in 31 ILM 822 (1992) [hereinafter CBD].

biodiversity protection by focusing on *in situ* conservation and, marginally, on the restoration of deteriorated ecosystems and gene bank management. Declaration of national sovereignty over natural resources, intellectual property rights, and technology transfers become the vehicles for the establishment of such a regime.

The convention emphasizes that states must preserve biodiversity "as far as possible and as appropriate"[83] by undertaking measures that would protect biodiversity in nature or in gene banks. The convention clearly places biodiversity resources under national sovereignty.[84] The convention places emphasis on national[85] and bilateral action based on the presumption that biodiversity can be protected more effectively at the national/bilateral level.[86]

Gene bank development is a supplemental goal in the overall scheme of biodiversity protection.[87] The convention explicitly provides that states must adopt measures of gene bank development "for the purpose of complementing *in situ* measures."[88] *Ex situ* conservation measures should preferably take place in the country of origin.[89] Because most genetic resources are located in developing countries and gene banks are located in developed countries, the convention calls for an increase in the number of gene banks in the developing world. The convention also proposes that it is best for each country to have its own gene banks,[90] an approach that is too limited and not very practicable. Given the possibilities presented by developing regional and even international gene banks, it is not cost-efficient for many developing countries to keep their own gene banks.[91] In the area of gene bank development, self-sufficiency is costly, and collaboration is certainly a more cost-effective means to conserve germplasm.[92]

The article on *in situ* conservation presents this type of conservation as the most fundamental method of protecting biodiversity. States must "as far as possible and as appropriate" establish a system of protected areas;[93] develop guidelines for the selection and management of protected areas;[94] regulate and manage biological resources both within and outside protected areas;[95] promote "environmentally sound and sustainable development" in areas adjacent to protected areas;[96] and adopt the necessary regulatory measures for the protection of endangered species.[97] States must manage

---

[83] This terminology is repeated in many of the articles of the convention: arts 5, 6, 7, 8, 9, 10, 11, 14, *id.*

[84] Art. 15(1), *id.*: "Recognizing the sovereign rights of States over their natural resources, the authority to determine access to genetic resources rests with the national governments and is subject to national legislation."

[85] See, *e.g.*, art. 6(a), *id.*

[86] Lyle Glowka *et al.*, A Guide to the Convention on Biological Diversity, Environmental Policy and Law Paper No. 30 (IUCN, 1994).

[87] Art. 9, CBD, *supra* note 82.

[88] *Id.*

[89] Art. 9(a), *id.*

[90] Art. 9(b), *id.*

[91] Donald L. Plucknett et al., Gene Banks and the World's Food (1987).

[92] *Id.* at 191.

[93] Art. 8(a), CBD, *supra* note 82.

[94] Art. 8(b), *id.*

[95] Art. 8(c), *id.*

[96] Art. 8(e), *id.*

[97] Art. 8(k), *id.*

and control the risks associated with the release of bioengineered organisms[98] and prevent the introduction of exotic species that may have adverse impacts on endemic species and habitats.[99]

Overall, the article on *in situ* conservation seems intentionally vague so as to give states some latitude in designing their conservation programs. Because in practice *in situ* conservation often has meant total preservation of protected areas based on evictions of the people who inhabit those areas, it would have been desirable if the provisions on *in situ* conservation included a clause that ensured that *in situ* conservation will not be pursued by violating human dignity and human rights.

It must be acknowledged, however, that the Biodiversity Convention is one of the first international treaties[100] to recognize the rights of indigenous peoples and local communities to their "knowledge," "innovations," and "practices."[101] The Biodiversity Convention provides that the consent of indigenous peoples is needed to utilize their knowledge and that there should be equitable sharing of the benefits derived from such knowledge. The specifics of equitable sharing, however, still resist practical application. Parties must submit to the Conference of the Parties (COP) the measures taken to implement the convention. Parties must also submit an evaluation of the effectiveness of these measures in accomplishing the convention's objectives.[102] Reporting on the effectiveness of measures to preserve biodiversity must be based on an accurate assessment of the existing biodiversity. Many attempts have been made to assess the world's biodiversity resources and to value these resources so that the goals of biodiversity protection become more concrete.[103]

More than ten years have elapsed from the signing of the Biodiversity Convention, but not much has happened in terms of making the convention a functional instrument for the protection of biodiversity. Most of the debate on implementation focuses on the issue of access to genetic resources and equitable sharing of benefits derived from biotechnology that is based on such resources. Other issues that have preoccupied the Conference of the Parties include:

- the protection of coral reefs;[104]
- the protection of agricultural biological diversity;[105]

---

[98] Art. 8(g), *id*.

[99] Art. 8(h), *id*.

[100] Other post-UNCED agreements contain references to indigenous peoples. These references, however, sound still paternalistic. According to the Rio Declaration, indigenous peoples have a role to play in environmental conservation because "of their knowledge and traditional practices." But it is not the peoples themselves – it is the state that must support the "identity, culture and interests" of indigenous peoples. See Principle 22, Rio Declaration on Environment and Development, June 14, 1992, reprinted in 31 ILM 874 (1992).

[101] Art. 8(j), CBD, *supra* note 82.

[102] Arts. 26 & 23(4)(a), *id*.

[103] See Millennium Ecosystem Assessment (Volumes I-V, 2005). See also United States National Research Council, Valuing Ecosystem Services: Toward Better Environmental Decision-Making (Committee for Assessing and Valuing the Services of Aquatic and Related Terrestrial Ecosystems, National Research Council, 2004).

[104] SBSTTA recommendation VI/2: Marine and coastal biological diversity: progress report on the implementation of the programme of work, including the integration of coral reefs, COP 6, April 7–19, 2002.

[105] Decision VI/5: Agricultural biological diversity, COP 6, April 7–19, 2002.

- conducting EIAs and SEAs;[106]
- the global taxonomy initiative;[107]
- the implementation of article 8(j) regarding the rights of indigenous peoples to their knowledge. The COP 5 invited the World Intellectual Property Organization (WIPO) to examine and to consider mechanisms for the protection of indigenous knowledge including the establishment of a clearing-house mechanism that would enable governments to monitor the implementation of article 8(j);[108]
- the development of an ecosystem approach;[109]
- the establishment of incentive measures for the protection of diversity by taking into account the distributional impacts of such measures;[110]
- the integration of biodiversity protection into sectors of the economy;[111]
- the protection of forest biodiversity;[112] and
- the protection of coastal areas and integrated coastal zone management.[113]

2.1.2. Resource Allocation

The Biodiversity Convention has to pursue three objectives:

- the conservation of biological diversity;
- the sustainable use of its components; and
- and the fair and equitable sharing of benefits arising out of the utilization of genetic resources.[114]

The convention affirms national sovereignty over biodiversity resources. The convention sidelines prior regimes[115] that generated perceptions that biodiversity resources located under the jurisdiction of a state can be freely accessed.

The convention provides that access to genetic resources must be subject to the prior informed consent of the country of origin.[116] The convention requires state parties to develop legislative and administrative measures in order to share "in a fair and equitable way . . . the benefits arising from the commercial and other utilization of genetic resources" with state parties that provide genetic resources. Although the convention does not give the specifics of fair and equitable sharing, it provides that such sharing must occur on mutually agreed terms.[117] The convention provides for access to and transfer of technology, such as biotechnology, to developing countries

---

[106] Decision VI/7: Identification, monitoring, indicators and assessments, COP 6, *id.*
[107] Decision VI/8: Global Taxonomy Initiative, COP 6, *id.*
[108] Decision VI/10: Article 8(j) and related provisions, COP 6, *id.*
[109] Decision VI/12: Ecosystem approach, COP 6, *id.*
[110] Decision VI/15: Incentive measures, COP 6, *id.*
[111] Decision VI/21: Annex to the Hague Ministerial Declaration of the Conference of the Parties to the Convention on Biological Diversity, COP 6, *id.*
[112] Decision VI/22: Forest biological diversity, COP 6, *id.*
[113] Decision V/3: Progress report on the implementation of the programme of work on marine and coastal biological diversity, COP 5, May 15–26, 2000.
[114] Art. 1, CBD, *supra* note 82.
[115] See Undertaking on Plant Genetic Resources, *infra* notes 139, 144.
[116] Art. 15(5), CBD, *supra* note 82.
[117] Art. 15(7), *id.*

"under fair and most favourable terms."[118] Article 19 provides that each party must take measures to provide for the participation in technological research activities by parties, especially developing countries, which provided the genetic resources for such research.[119] State parties must take measures to advance priority access, on a fair and equitable basis, by developing countries, to benefits coming from technology. Such access is provided, however, if the technology is based on the genetic resources found in these developing countries.[120]

The convention clarifies that new and additional financial resources are needed to enable developing countries to meet "the agreed full incremental costs" of implementing the convention.[121] The extent to which developing countries are to implement the convention depends on developed countries executing their commitments with regard to the provision of financial resources and transfer of technology.[122] In this context, the convention elucidates – in a spirit echoing concerns vocalized during the WSSD summit – that the implementation of the convention by developing countries "will take fully into account the fact that . . . development and eradication of poverty are the first and overriding priorities of the developing country Parties."[123] A financial mechanism is to be established that would provide resources to developing countries.[124]

The convention recognizes the rights of indigenous peoples in their knowledge and innovations. The convention provides that states must encourage the equitable sharing of benefits arising from the utilization of knowledge, innovations, and practices of indigenous peoples.[125]

2.1.2.1. Market Value of Biodiversity

Bioprospecting involves the extraction of plants and other products from forests for the purpose of scientific exploration or commercialization. Previously, bioprospecting was not regulated, and companies and scientists could, as a matter of course, enter into a country and freely collect plants and seeds. The Biodiversity Convention has ensured, however, that those who engage in bioprospecting must get the consent of the authorities of the countries concerned. To obtain consent, potential users must pay a fee for the issuance of a permit.

The National Cancer Institute of the United States, the New York Botanical Garden, and private corporations have paid fees or promised royalties for the purposes of accessing biodiversity resources.[126] An agreement between the INBio institute, a nonprofit organization created by the government of Costa Rica, and Merck, a U.S. pharmaceutical company, was one of the first initiatives to establish processes and fees

---

[118] Art. 16(2), *id.*
[119] Art. 19(1), *id.*
[120] Art. 19(2), *id.*
[121] Art. 20(2), *id.*
[122] Art. 20(4), *id.*
[123] *Id.*
[124] Art. 21, *id.*
[125] Art. 8(j), *id.*
[126] See Sarah A. Laird, Contracts for Biodiversity Prospecting, in Biodiversity Prospecting 99, 113 (Walter V. Reid et al., ed., 1993). See also Edgar J. Asebey & Jill D. Kempenaar, Biodiversity Prospecting: Fulfilling the Mandate of the Biodiversity Convention, 28 Vanderbilt Journal of Transnational Law 703, 721 (1995).

for access to biodiversity resources. Merck paid an initial $1.1 million fee and agreed to transfer technology, train scientists, and pay royalties in case an INBio extract produced a viable product. The agreement was heralded as a victory for developing countries because it recognized that the acquisition and use of germplasm should be compensated.

At the same time, however, the agreement signaled that biodiversity resources are not as lucrative as they have been presented to be. INBio has to provide Merck with two thousand product extracts within two years. Given that Merck laboratories need to process five thousand samples per week to be effective, the amount provided by the INBio is too small to be significant and proves that Merck places little emphasis on resources collected from nature.[127] According to the experts at Merck, the effort put into screening "tropical samples is fragmented and not adequate for a significant chance of success."[128]

In other biodiversity agreements, the royalties negotiated are too small, usually within the range of 1 to 2 percent, and only if the final product incorporates the plant extract, or if the final product is used for the same purposes the plant extract was used traditionally. In addition, some of the royalty is usually paid back to the collaborating institution for its research costs.[129] Of all the investment opportunities forests provide, bioprospecting returns are the least predictable and the slowest to materialize. On average, at least ten years elapse between finding a promising compound and developing a successful drug. Investors are deterred by the low market value of what is called "unprocessed biodiversity" – plants and animals of unknown use. Markets for untested germplasm do not really exist.

2.1.2.2. Bilateral Redistribution

The CBD[130] asserted national control over biodiversity resources. The genetic resources covered under the convention are not inclusive of resources acquired before the entry into force of the convention.[131] Resources preserved before the entry into force of the convention include the most profitable resources safeguarded in the International Agricultural Research Centers and other gene banks. The non-retroactive application of the CBD has created a two-tiered system for the transfer of resources: *de facto* free access to gene bank resources acquired before the entry into force of the CBD, and restricted access to all other resources discovered or acceded to international collections after the adoption of the convention.

The CBD provides that access to natural resources is not allowed without some equitable sharing of the benefits derived from the manipulation of resources. According to the convention, access to germplasm resources cannot take place

[127] Asebey, *id.* at 725–28.

[128] Georg Albers-Schonberg, The Pharmaceutical Discovery Process, in Intellectual Property Rights and Biodiversity Conservation 67, 91 (Timothy M. Swanson, ed., 1998).

[129] Asebey, *supra* note 126, at 730–32. A recent agreement between Novartis and Brazil seems to be more generous in terms of initial outlays but still not that generous in terms of royalties. Novartis is required for pay two million Swiss francs, as an initial outlay, and then 250 Swiss francs for every selected promising organism. However if Novartis decides to commercialize an invention, Brazil will get a mere 0.5 percent of annual sales. See S. Peña-Neira et al., Equitably Sharing Benefits from the Utilization of Natural Genetic Resources: The Brazilian Interpretation of the Convention on Biological Diversity, 6(3) Electronic Journal of Comparative Law (Oct. 2002).

[130] Convention on Biological Diversity, June 5, 1992, reprinted in 31 ILM 826 (1992).

[131] Art. 15(3), *id.*

without a prior agreement on the equitable sharing of technology that manipulates the resources – that is, biotechnology. This provision, which calls for bilateral agreements regarding the transfer of resources and technologies, has provoked the opposition of the biotechnology industry that is reluctant to share its applications with developing countries and has prevented the United States from ratifying the convention.

In accordance with the CBD, countries have adopted legislation that provides procedures for access to their resources. Countries typically require that bioprospectors provide a letter of intent before engaging in collection, including: the number of specimens required, the manner of collecting those specimens, and their final destination. In some cases it is not only the consent of the national government that is required but also the local and indigenous communities' consent.[132]

Countries adopted restrictive access regulations in the hope of obtaining substantial monetary benefits from access fees. This type of legislation, however, has not brought the desired monetary benefits to the South and has unnecessarily curbed the interest of the North in unexplored resources. As some commentators have put it, bioprospecting "profits have been elusive, and win–win opportunities have been few and far between."[133] Technology transfers and capacity building are the most that countries should expect from bioprospecting agreements. Bioprospecting agreements rarely bring to developing countries the "green gold" for which they initially hoped.

Few countries have tried to ensure that preconditions for access to their resources do not amount to prohibitions and that access to germplasm resources remains more or less flexible. Countries have tried, for instance, to reduce the number of stakeholders with which a company has to negotiate.[134] Some countries have provided for bioprospecting rights in areas where property rights are clear[135] and have treated noncommercial research more favorably. Technology transfers and capacity building have been the preferred tradeoffs for resource access rather than large inflows of cash compensation.

Bioprospecting agreements or Material Transfer Agreements (MTAs), although not very profitable, are becoming the means for transferring germplasm. Bilateral MTAs could allow for access while prohibiting any assertion of intellectual property rights over germplasm; these agreements also could allow for the assertion of intellectual property rights under an obligation to share the royalties or could leave contentious matters to future negotiations.

Because of the high costs of negotiating and enforcing MTAs, MTAs are relatively rare. To avoid the costs associated with negotiating bilateral MTAs, it has been

---

[132] Most national laws today distinguish between commercial and academic research even if the borderline between these two types of research is often blurred, for instance, when a corporation is funding a research program of an academic institution. See Conference of the Parties to the Convention on Biological Diversity, Third Meeting, November 4–15, 1996, UNEP/CBD/COP/3/20, at 13, Oct. 5, 1996 [hereinafter National Legislation]. See also Ana Sittenfeld & Rodrigo Gamez, Biodiversity Prospecting by INBio, in Biodiversity Prospecting: Using Genetic Resources for Sustainable Development 69, 82 (Walter V. Reid et al., eds., 1993).

[133] Access to Genetic Resources: An Evaluation of the Development and Implementation of Recent Regulation and Access Agreements, at v (Prepared for the Biodiversity Action Network by the Environmental Policy Studies Workshop, School of International and Public Affairs, Columbia University, 1999).

[134] *Id*. at 23.

[135] *Id*. at iii.

proposed that a multilateral system for the transfer of germplasm is needed.[136] Such a system was adopted in 2001 for food and agriculture resources. The Treaty on Plant Genetic Resources for Food and Agriculture was adopted under the auspices of the FAO, the organization that deals with the protection of agrobiodiversity.[137]

2.1.2.3. Transnational Redistribution

The Treaty on Plant Genetic Resources for Food and Agriculture was adopted after nine years of negotiations on November 3, 2001.[138] The treaty has its roots in the International Undertaking on Plant Genetic Resources.

The International Undertaking on Plant Genetic Resources (the Undertaking) was one of the first instruments to deal with germplasm resources for food and agriculture and it was not a legally binding instrument.[139] In the 1983 version of the Undertaking, it was mentioned that plant genetic resources are a heritage of mankind and should be available without restriction.[140] This version of the Undertaking was an expression of the frustration of developing countries with the increasing protection of plant breeders' rights. Developing countries, using the common heritage rule, asserted that access to germplasm should be free. Developing countries therefore created what has been called a "strategic legal inconsistency" in the hope of acquiring access to improved germplasm.[141] The declaration did not change the international reality, however, and − although germplasm found in the wild continued to be available free of charge − improved breeder varieties remained costly for many of the farmers of the developing world. In fact, eight industrialized countries issued reservations to the Undertaking.[142]

The Undertaking was modified in 1989, under the pressure of developed countries, to clarify that "free access does not mean free of charge."[143] It was modified also in 1991,[144] when developing countries realized that bioprospecting could be profitable and monetary and other benefits could be derived from plant genetic resources. The 1991 amendment turned on its head the principle of free access by asserting that, although plant genetic resources are the heritage of mankind, they are subject to the sovereignty of states over plant genetic resources.

---

[136] IPGRI, Access to Plant Genetic Resources and the Equitable Sharing of Benefits 33 (Issues in Genetic Resources, No. 4, June 1996).

[137] Although biodiversity, in general, is now under the preview of the CBD and the governance system of that convention, the protection of agrobiodiversity has been the prerogative of the FAO. This bifurcated system has been the source of contention as the FAO is concerned that the COP of the CBD intervenes in matters that should be under its control. And the COP of the CBD is compelled, because of the broad mandate of the Biodiversity Convention, to exercise jurisdictional control over most biodiversity resources, especially those perceived to be at risk.

[138] International Treaty on Plant Genetic Resources for Food and Agriculture, Nov. 3, 2001, available online at http://www.fao.org/Legal/TREATIES. The convention entered into force in 2004.

[139] Resolution 8/83, Twenty-Second Session, FAO Conference, Nov. 5–23, 1983.

[140] Article 1, id.

[141] See Kal Raustiala & David G. Victor, The Regime Complex for Plant Genetic Resources, International Organization 37, 38, Spring 2004, available online at http://ssrn.com/abstract=441463 (Social Science Research Network Electronic Paper Collection).

[142] Id. at 19.

[143] Resolution 4/89, Twenty-Fifth Session, FAO Conference, Nov. 11–29, 1989. The amended Undertaking also recognized plant breeders' rights

[144] Resolution 3/91, Twenty-Sixth Session, FAO Conference, Nov. 9–27, 1991.

With the 1991 amendment of the Undertaking, plant genetic resources ceased to be public domain resources and developing states asserted property rights over them. Bioprospecting played a catalyst role in the enclosure of plant genetic resources based on a widespread belief that plant resources, as found in the wild, could be extremely valuable.

After the adoption of the CBD – which subjected the transfers of germplasm to bilateral controls – the need to clarify the status of agricultural and food resources that were freely exchanged for years became obvious. At issue here were the resources kept in gene banks and the IARCs. These resources were collected before the adoption of the Biodiversity Convention and were considered to be *de facto* free access resources. Because they were accumulated before the adoption of the Biodiversity Convention, they were not subject to the prior informed consent and other restrictive access requirements included in the convention. This is because the CBD does not have retroactive effects. Thus, after the Biodiversity Convention was adopted two systems applied for access to plant genetic resources:

- the post-1992 system, which controls access to biodiversity based on the consent of the country of origin; and
- the pre-1992 system, in which unprocessed genetic resources were in essence open-access resources.

Resources kept in international gene banks and the IARCs were subject to separate access requirements: one for the resources acceded before 1992 (open access) and another for resources acceded after 1992 (restricted access). This segregation between pre-1992 and post-1992 resources in the IARCs increased transaction costs and was institutionally foreign because the prevailing culture at the IARCs is free access. The IARCs could not ignore the provisions of the CBD based on a rationale that the convention was a separate institutional arrangement. Ignoring the CBD would have enraged developing countries that sought to capture some of the rents from plant genetic resources and to curb biopiracy.[145] Biopiracy – that is, the unauthorized access to plant genetic resources – was reported to be rife in the developing world.[146]

In 1993, the FAO adopted a nonbinding Code of Conduct for Plant Germplasm Collecting and Transfer.[147] The code recognizes state sovereignty over plant genetic resources. The code provides that states have the sovereign right to establish a system for the issuance of permits to germplasm collectors.[148] For that purpose, governments are to set an authority competent for issuing permits and must inform collectors about the government's rules and regulations and the permit approval process.[149] The Code of Conduct provides for the information that collectors should include in the permit application and the procedure for granting permits. The permits granted, must include, *inter alia*, "any special arrangement or restriction placed on the distribution or use of the germplasm, or improved materials derived from it."[150]

---

[145] Raustiala, *supra* note 141, at 40.

[146] See Chapter 9, Section 4.3.

[147] International Code of Conduct for Plant Germplasm Collecting and Transfer, adopted by the FAO Conference, Nov. 1993.

[148] Art. 6.1, *id.*

[149] Art. 6.2, *id.*

[150] Art. 8(e), *id.*

In 1996, the FAO adopted the Leipzig Declaration and the Global Action Plan for the Protection of Biodiversity.[151] Both of these instruments are influenced by the rhetoric of the Biodiversity Convention. However, the Global Action Plan, instead of emphasizing national *in situ* conservation, promotes more of an international outlook on global biodiversity management. The Global Action Plan provides for international cooperation in disaster situations and encourages the safeguarding of biodiversity resources in international gene banks. The plan clearly recognizes that the evaluation, regeneration, and characterization of plant collections contained in gene banks cannot happen without international cooperation and the economies of scale put together by international efforts.

A new version of the Undertaking was put forward on July 1, 2001,[152] but many important provisions were still bracketed. The issues contested included the list of crops that would be free access. Some developing countries wanted to keep crops off the list in the hope of making money by charging fees bilaterally for access to these crops.[153] Other contested provisions included patents on derived material[154] and the relationship between the amended Undertaking and the World Trade Organization, and, especially, the Trade–Related Intellectual Property Rights (TRIPs) Agreement adopted under its auspices.[155]

The negotiations on a new mandate for the International Undertaking progressed slowly because of lack of interest and lack of clarity about the value of plant genetic resources:

- Developing countries wish to keep tight control over biodiversity resources because they believe that such resources are or could become valuable.
- The North assumes that the best germplasm is already duplicated in its national gene banks. The South may still provide valuable material, but the interest of the North in such material is low. Many companies espouse that more is to be accomplished by rearranging already collected genetic material than by renewing efforts in bioprospecting.

Eventually an agreement was reached on November 2001, and the Treaty on Plant Genetic Resources for Food and Agriculture was adopted.[156] The treaty aims to establish "an efficient, effective and transparent" multilateral system to facilitate access to germplasm for the purposes of food and agriculture,[157] and to share "in a fair and equitable way" the benefits from the utilization of resources.[158] The facilitated access provided for by the agreement will be accomplished through a

---

[151] Leipzig Declaration on Conservation and Sustainable Utilization of Plant Genetic Resources for Food and Agriculture, June 17–23, 1996, adopted by International Technical Conference on Plant Genetic Resources, available online at http://www.fao.org/ag/AGP.

[152] See Report of the Commission on Genetic Resources for Food and Agriculture, Sixth Extraordinary Session, CGRFA-Ex 6/01/REP, June 25–30, 2001.

[153] *Id.*

[154] Art. 13(d), *id.*

[155] Art. 4, *id.*

[156] See *supra* note 138.

[157] Art. 12.3(a), *id.* The treaty does not address "chemical, pharmaceutical and/or other nonfood/feed industrial uses." *Id.*

[158] Art. 10.2, *id.*

standard Material Transfer Agreement (MTA), the provisions of which are to be adopted by the governing body.[159] It also is stated that:

- access shall be granted expeditiously and free of charge;[160]
- recipients must not claim intellectual property rights on the plant genetic resources or their components "in the form received from the Multilateral System"[161] (implying possibly that modification, isolation, or purification could be subject to intellectual property rights);
- access to genetic resources protected by intellectual property rights will be subject to national regulation consistent with the relevant international agreements;[162] and
- access to resources found *in situ* should be subject to national legislation and, in the absence of such legislation, to standards set by the governing body established under the treaty.

The treaty clearly covers the resources held in the *ex situ* collections of the IARCs and other international institutions[163] and invites all other holders of plant genetic resources to include their resources in the multilateral system.[164] The governing body reserves the right to take action – in terms of continuing to allow access to the system resources – against the legal and natural persons that fail to include their resources within the system.[165]

Facilitated access is preconditioned on the equitable sharing benefits. Such benefits may include exchange of information,[166] access to and transfer of technology,[167] and capacity building.[168] The most contentious issue during the negotiations was that of sharing the benefits from the commercialization of germplasm resources. The treaty provides that the Multilateral Material Transfer Agreement must provide that the recipient of a product must pay to a Trust Account[169] an equitable share of the benefits arising from the commercialization of the product. This is so if the commercialization of the product incorporates the material transferred by the multilateral system.[170] Sharing of benefits is only voluntary in the case the product is still available without restriction to others for further research and breeding.[171] The governing body must decide, in its first meeting, the "level, form and manner of payment" in accordance

---

[159] Art. 12.4 (the Governing Body of the treaty is composed of all Contracting Parties), *id*. See arts. 19.1 and 19.2 (all decisions of the Governing Body shall be taken by consensus unless, by consensus, another method of arriving at a decision on certain measures is reached), *id*.

[160] Art. 12.3(b), *id*.

[161] Art. 12.3(d), *id*.

[162] Art. 12.3(f), *id*.

[163] Art. 11.5, *id*.

[164] Arts. 11.2 and 11.3, *id*.

[165] Art. 11.4, *id*.

[166] Art. 13.2(a), *id*.

[167] Art. 13.2(b), *id*.

[168] Art. 13.2(c), *id*.

[169] Art. 13.3(f), *id*.

[170] Art. 13.2(d)(ii), *id*.

[171] Art. 13.2(d)(ii) (however, the governing body may decide to make such contributions mandatory, even when the product is still available to others for research and breeding), *id*.

with commercial practice.[172] The benefits from these payments must flow to the farmers of all countries, including the farmers of developing countries and countries with economies in transition.[173]

The treaty covers farmers' rights, leaving their protection up to national law.[174] The treaty emphasizes the importance of the Global Plan of Action[175] and the *ex situ* collections of the IARCs.[176] In this respect, the treaty calls for the development of international plant genetic resources networks[177] and for a global information system on plant genetic resources for food and agriculture.[178]

An issue that remained contentious until the final round of negotiations involved the annex to the convention, which covers the list of crops that are subject to the multilateral system. Developing countries, assuming that bilateral contracts would be more financially rewarding, succeeded in keeping many important crops and forages off the annex. The convention covers thirty-five crops and twenty-nine forages out of one hundred food crops and eighteen thousand forages important for food security. Food crops, such as soya, sugar cane, oil palm, and groundnut, are missing from the annex.[179] This omission is bound to create uncertainty about the proper means of accessing those resources given that such resources are already located in the IARCs and national gene banks.

Another issue that caused heated debate was that of a potential assertion of intellectual property rights over germplasm resources. The compromise provision provides that intellectual property rights cannot be declared on plant genetic resources for food and agriculture and their genetic parts or components "in the form received by the Multilateral System."[180] This should mean that modified resources, by bioengineering and breeding, could be patented shifting the burden of proof to the patent system to determine whether a modification is innovative enough to qualify for protection. The provision, however, still does not clarify whether derived material, such as varieties, genes, and gene sequences, can be patented. A related proposal that subordinated the treaty to the TRIPs agreement[181] – as a means for guaranteeing the protection of intellectual property rights – was not adopted. It was decided, instead, to include in the Preamble a provision that recited that all international agreements should be mutually supportive and that there must not be "a hierarchy between this treaty and other international agreements."

The treaty was adopted with 116 votes in favor, no votes against, and two abstentions, by the United States and Japan. Both countries cited concerns about the breadth of the protection of intellectual property rights under the treaty. The treaty entered into force in June 2004. The EU ratified the convention but entered reservations with regard to article 12.3(d). Article 12.3(d), as mentioned earlier,

---

[172] The governing body may decide to exempt from such payments small farmers in developing countries and in countries with economies in transition. *Id.*

[173] Art. 13.3, *id.*

[174] Art. 9, *id.*

[175] Art. 14, *id.*

[176] Art. 15, *id.*

[177] Art. 16, *id.*

[178] Art. 17, *id.*

[179] P. Mulvany, Global Seed Treaty Hangs in the Balance, 46 Biotechnology and Development Monitor 20 (2001).

[180] Art. 12.3(d), International Treaty on Plant Genetic Resources, *supra* note 138.

[181] For the TRIPs Agreement, see Chapter 9, Section 4.1.

provides that private companies cannot obtain intellectual property rights over plant genetic resources for food and agriculture "or their genetic parts or components in the form received from the multilateral system." According to the interpretative statement of the EU, article 12.3(d) must be interpreted as recognizing that

> plant genetic resources for food and agriculture or their genetic parts and components which have undergone innovation may be subject of intellectual property rights provided that the criteria relating to such rights are met.

Some commentators have characterized the treaty as a multilateral system of "communal seed treasury"[182] composed of twenty-five food and twenty-nine feed crops held by states and IARCs. To gain access to the common gene pool, private parties that produce commercial applications that incorporate plant genetic resources received from the multilateral system must pay a portion of their profits to the fund established under the treaty. The fund money is to be used, *inter alia*, to benefit the farmers of the developing world.

The First Meeting of the Commission on Plant Genetic Resources for Food and Agriculture, acting as the Interim Committee of the International Treaty on Plant Genetic Resources, took place in 2002.[183] During that meeting, the commission developed the terms of reference for the expert group that is to devise the provisions to be included in the Standard Material Transfer Agreement. The commission asked the expert group to establish the level, form, and manner of payments to be made to the multilateral system and the definition of commercialization under article 13.2d(ii).

Article 13.2d(ii) provides that the Standard Material Transfer Agreement must include a requirement for the recipient, who commercializes a product that incorporates the material accessed from the multilateral system, to pay to the trust fund an equitable share of the benefits arising from commercialization. Contributions to the fund are not required if the product is available to others, without restriction, for research and breeding. In that case, the recipient should be encouraged merely to make a contribution to the trust fund. The circumstances under which a product is considered available to others without restrictions for research and breeding is also an issue that has been assigned to the expert group to explore.

Furthermore, the expert group has to define how the Material Transfer Agreement is to incorporate all the terms provided for in article 12.3. Of course, the thorny issue here would be article 12.3(d) – that recipients shall not claim intellectual property rights on plant genetic resources for food and agriculture or their genetic parts and components "in the form" received by the multilateral system. It is possible that the interpretation of this provision by the expert group would follow closely the declaration made by the European Union on the ratification of the international treaty.

Overall, the multilateral system, if it functions as envisioned and provided that the ambiguities are resolved, could help curb the administrative costs of the bilateralism

---

[182] Lawrence R. Helfer, Regime Shifting: The TRIPs Agreement and New Dynamics of International Intellectual Property Lawmaking, 29 Yale Journal of International Law (2004), available online at http://ssrn.com/abstract=459740.

[183] Report of the Commission on Genetic Resources for Food and Agriculture Acting as the Interim Committee for the International Treaty on Plant Genetic Resources for Food and Agriculture, First Meeting, CGRFA/MIC-1/02/REP, Oct. 9–11, 2002.

embodied in the Biodiversity Convention. Some commentators have viewed the multilateral system as an attempt to revive the common heritage approach for important food crops. A common heritage approach seems to be more sensible given the high transaction costs involved in enforcing property rights on common food crops.[184]

2.1.2.4. Institutionalized Redistribution

The issues of access to genetic resources and the equitable sharing of benefits have preoccupied the COP of the CBD since the adoption of the convention.[185] Bilateral agreements, it was soon realized, are not a long-term solution because of the transaction costs they impose in comparison with the benefits.[186] A global agreement such as the International Treaty on Plant Genetic Resources for Food and Agriculture or, at least, some global guidelines are necessary for the transfer and exchange of biodiversity resources.

In a 2002 meeting of the COP, a set of guidelines were adopted, known as the Bonn Guidelines, which provide some of the parameters of equitable sharing and access.[187] The Bonn Guidelines were further buttressed by a Decision, adopted in 2004, the purpose of which was to further explain and amplify the guidelines for their implementation in the developing world.[188]

The Bonn Guidelines, as their name implies, have voluntary character and present an evolutionary approach to rule-making because of the intent to review them and to revise them as more experience is gained from access to resources and benefit sharing.[189] The guidelines include the following elements:

- national focal points the purpose of which is to facilitate the application process for access to genetic resources;[190]
- the responsibilities of contracting parties – namely, the responsibility of the country of origin to ensure that the commercialization of genetic resources would not prevent traditional use,[191] and the responsibility of users to seek the informed consent of the country of origin, to respect indigenous communities and to comply with the terms of use of resources;[192]

---

[184] Raustiala, *supra* note 141, at 27.

[185] See Decision II/11: Access to Genetic Resources & Decision II/12: Intellectual Property Rights adopted by the Second Meeting of the Conference of the Parties, Nov. 6–17, 1995; Decision III/15: Access to Genetic Resources adopted by the Third Meeting of the Conference of the Parties, Nov. 4–15, 1996; Decision IV/8: Access and Benefit Sharing adopted by the Fourth Meeting of the Conference of the Parties, May 4–15, 1998.

[186] See, e.g., Ted Agres, Biodiversity Treaty Called Disastrous, Scientist, Sept. 10, 2003.

[187] Decision VI/24: Access and benefit-sharing as related to genetic resources adopted by the sixth meeting of the Conference of Parties, April 7–19, 2002 [hereinafter Bonn Guidelines].

[188] Decision VII/19: Access and benefit sharing as related to genetic resources (Article 15) adopted by the seventh meeting of the Conference of Parties, Feb. 9–20 and 27, 2004.

[189] Art. 7(f), Bonn Guidelines, *supra* note 187.

[190] Art. 13, *id.*

[191] Art. 16(a)(iii), *id.*

[192] Art. 16(b), *id.*

It is further emphasized that providers of resources should strive "to avoid the imposition of arbitrary restrictions on access to genetic resources." See art. 16(c), *id.*

It is further provided that countries may want to introduce "voluntary certification schemes" for institutions abiding with the rules of access and benefit sharing. See art. 16(d)(v), *id.*

- the participation of stakeholders;
- procedures for access and benefit sharing – the parameters of the informed consent of the country of origin are identified in great detail;[193]
- the basic requirements for "mutually agreed terms" that are designed to minimize transaction costs;[194]
- the types of benefits including monetary and nonmonetary benefits;[195]
- national monitoring, reporting, and verification procedures;[196] and
- dispute settlement suggestions and possible remedies.[197]

It is unclear what the Bonn guidelines offer in terms of streamlining and simplifying the process of access to resources and benefit sharing. Even the requirements for the application process itself are daunting. Applicants do not only have to provide information about the resources they wish to access and the dates and place of access. They also must provide information on how the research and development is to be carried out, as well as the purpose of collection, research, and expected results. It is doubtful that private companies and research institutions will be willing to divulge confidential information about their methods of research and analysis or their expectations about research outcomes.

The 2004 Decision of the seventh COP established an open-ended working group on access and benefit sharing that is to collaborate with the Ad Hoc Working Open-Ended Inter-Sessional Working Group, the purpose of which is to clarify the implications of article 8(j). The purpose of collaboration is to assist in the elaboration and negotiation of an international regime on access to genetic resources and benefit

---

[193] See art. 24 et seq., *id.* It is provided, for instance, that prior informed consent must be obtained "adequately in advance" and that decisions on a prior informed consent application must be taken within "a reasonable period of time." See art. 33, *id.*

Prior informed consent is to be obtained also for a specific use and any change in use, including transfer to third parties, must require a new application for prior informed consent. See art. 34, *id.*

In order for a potential user to obtain prior informed consent, s/he must include in the application the following information:
- the legal entity of the applicant and that of the collector;
- the type and quantity of genetic resources to be accessed;
- starting date and duration of activity;
- the impact on conservation and sustainable development so as to determine the benefits and costs;
- accurate information regarding intended use (e.g., research, commercialization);
- information on how the research and development is to be carried out;
- identification of local bodies for collaboration and development;
- possible third-party involvement;
- purpose of the collection, research, and expected results;
- kinds of benefits that could come from obtaining access to the resource;
- indication of benefit-sharing arrangements;
- budget; and
- treatment of confidential information. See art. 36, *id.*

[194] Arts. 42–43, *id.* Article 44 includes an indicative list of typical mutually agreed terms. The list includes, *inter alia*, limitations on the possible use of the material; whether genetic resources can be transferred to third parties; provisions on the sharing of benefits; capacity building; respect for the knowledge of indigenous peoples. *Id.*

[195] Art. 46 et seq., *id.*

[196] Art. 52 et seq., *id.*

[197] Art. 59 et seq., *id.*

sharing in accordance with the provisions of the Biodiversity Convention (articles 15 and 8(j)).[198]

A concern of developing countries has been to ensure that the country of origin of germplasm is recorded, at least, in international transactions so that potential monetary benefits from the exploitation of germplasm could be traced back to that country of origin. Many developing countries have proposed a "Certificate of Legal Provenance," which would certify not only the country of origin of germplasm resources but also compliance with the access and benefit sharing requirements (e.g., prior informed consent). Such a certificate of legal provenance, developing countries claim, must become part of the patent application process. This means that official bodies that grant patents in different countries would need to require the Certificate of Legal Provenance[199] and to ensure that this certificate includes the relevant information.

The World Intellectual Property Organization (WIPO) has investigated the legal systems of different countries. The purpose of the investigation is to gather information on whether disclosure of the country of origin of germplasm and of prior traditional knowledge, on which an invention may be based, are mandatory or optional under these systems. The WIPO has attempted to grapple with the question of whether the disclosure of the country of origin of a resource or the traditional knowledge related to a resource should simply be encouraged in the patent application process or whether such disclosure should become a legal formality, the violation of which would trigger sanctions.[200]

2.2. Trade and Biodiversity

The Convention on International Trade in Endangered Species of Wild Flora and Fauna (CITES) was drafted in 1963 by the International Union for the Conservation of Nature as a result of concerns that trade in wildlife was causing significant species losses. The convention was eventually adopted in 1973 and entered into force in 1975.[201]

Structure

The CITES lists species in three annexes. Appendix I includes the most endangered species. Appendix II includes the species threatened to become endangered. Appendix III includes endangered species in the territory of state parties to the

---

[198] See Decision VII/19, COP VII meeting, *supra* note 188.

[199] Or an international certificate of origin or an international certificate of source. See Report of the Ad Hoc Open-Ended Working Group on Access and Benefit Sharing on the Work of its Second Meeting, UNEP/CBD/COP/7/6, Dec. 10, 2003.

[200] Intergovernmental Committee on Intellectual Property and Genetic Resources, Traditional Knowledge and Folklore, Fourth Session, Initial Report on the Technical Study on Disclosure Requirements Related to Genetic Resources and Traditional Knowledge, WIPO/GRTKF/IC/4/11, at 27–28, Dec. 9–17, 2002 [hereinafter WIPO-TK]. The questions that the WIPO is attempting to resolve are the following:
- whether it is reasonable to require disclosure of country of origin for all patent applications or for just those which involve exotic or rare material;
- whether traditional knowledge needs to be disclosed in case it is fundamental to the understanding of an invention or also in other occasions; and,
- which elements determine the "inventive contribution" of traditional knowledge.

[201] Convention on International Trade in Endangered Species of Wild Flora and Fauna (CITES), Mar. 6, 1973, reprinted in 12 ILM 1085 (1973).

convention. The convention prohibits trade in species included in Appendix I, regulates trade in species included in Appendix II, and encourages states to bring endangered species in their territory under Appendix III of the convention.

Species are traded based on import and export permit requirements that become less demanding the less strict the classification of species is. For instance, species classified in Appendix I are subject to both an import and an export permit while species classified in Appendix II are subject only to an export permit.[202] At present, Appendix I prohibits commercial trade in about nine hundred species and Appendix II regulates trade in four thousand animal and twenty-two thousand plant species.[203]

The listing and delisting of species has been a subject of contention. During the first meeting of the parties, criteria were adopted for the listing and delisting of species known as the Bern criteria. However, the delisting, down-listing, or up-listing of species has been controversial. For instance, the upgrade of the elephant to an Appendix I species, and ensuing trade prohibitions, divided the parties as Zimbabwe and South Africa, countries with successful wildlife management programs, decided to sabotage the ban on the trade in ivory.

Monitoring/Enforcement

The enforcement of the convention is left to state parties. States are required to take measures to punish those who violate the convention and to confiscate items that are illegally traded or possessed.[204] States must maintain detailed records of the trade in species and share them with the Secretariat of the convention through annual reports that summarize the trade.[205] The COP reviews the implementation of the convention and examines proposals to amend the lists of species in Appendix I and in Appendix II.

The work of the Conference of the Parties is facilitated by the work of four permanent committees: the Standing Committee, the Animals Committee, the Plants Committee,[206] and the Nomenclature Committee.[207] The purpose of the Standing Committee is to provide assistance in implementing the convention and in overseeing the Secretariat's budget. One of the major issues that the Standing Committee has dealt with was whether to reopen the trade in elephant products.

Despite the mechanisms in place, the enforcement of CITES has encountered many problems. Many of the exceptions[208] to the convention, for instance, the

---

[202] Arts. III and IV, *id.*

[203] FAO, State of the World's Forests 51 (2003).

[204] Art. VIII(1)(a) and (b), CITES, *supra* note 201.

[205] Art. VIII(7)(a), *id.*

[206] The Animals Committee and Plants Committee provide specialized expertise regarding the species that are under CITES control.

[207] The Nomenclature Committee was established in recognition of the need to standardize names used for animal and plant species.

[208] For the exceptions to the CITES and how they have been used to breach the convention, see Simon Lyster, International Wildlife Law 256–62 (1985). Exemptions can be obtained for: (1) transit or transshipment of species (art. VII(1)); (2) specimens that have personal or household effects (art. VII(3)) – tourist souvenirs; (3) specimens acquired before the provisions of the CITES applied to that specimen (art. VII(2)) – this provision has been abused as usually traders stockpile specimens before they are listed; (4) the noncommercial trade between scientists and scientific institutions; (5) specimens that are part of a circus or a traveling zoo. See CITES, *supra* note 201.

tourist-souvenir exception[209] and the transshipment[210] exception and state reservations,[211] have hampered monitoring and enforcement. Exceptions have been used to smuggle species under the pretense that the exceptions apply. Reservations[212] have allowed states to opt out of the provisions of the convention and have legitimized trade otherwise considered illegal under the convention.

These loopholes, cultural beliefs that have kept up demand and a fearless network of poachers, supported by the poor of the developing world, have undermined the effectiveness of the convention. Many of the species that the CITES was supposed to "save" remain endangered and others are added to the list while countries still quibble over whether trade prohibitions/restrictions are the best way to save the species. Certain commentators claim that the CITES has failed on two fronts: restricting or prohibiting international trade in species is not the way to stop species loss that is predominantly a result of habitat destruction. Furthermore, to effectively control species trade, one has to change the attitudes of hundreds of thousands of individuals involved in the harvesting, processing, and marketing of species. The task is huge and not less onerous than the control of illegal trade in drugs.[213]

CITES has perpetuated a lucrative black market in which many of the species are now traded. States are reluctant to commit the resources to back up the enforcement and monitoring of the convention. The trade in endangered species is demand-led rather than supply-led. Many east asian countries are avid importers of body parts of endangered species, such as tigers and rhinoceroses, because of their importance in traditional medicine. Some developing states have viewed the regime as reflective of the interests of developed states and therefore have resisted the application of the regime.[214]

3. PROTECTION OF HABITATS

3.1. World Heritage Sites

The World Heritage Convention was in the first wave of environmental instruments adopted in the same year that the Stockholm Declaration was endorsed. The idea of

---

[209] Art. VII(3) of the CITES provides that the regulations of the convention do not apply to specimens that have personal or household effects. Some state parties apply this exception liberally. See Lyster, *id.* at 258.

[210] Art. VII(1) of the CITES provides that the regulations of the convention do not apply "to the transit or trans-shipment of specimens through or in the territory of a Party while the specimens remain in Customs control." This provision has been abused because middlemen can import species from nonparties, hold them "in transit" in a state party (without, thus, having to obtain a permit) and then export them to a nonparty. *Id.* at 257.

[211] According to article XXIII(3) of the CITES, states that have taken reservations on certain items are considered nonparties with regard to those items. Reservations dilute the normative character of the convention because reserving parties often trade legally with nonparties and illegally with parties violating the letter and the spirit of the convention. *Id.* at 263.

[212] Arts. XXIII & X, CITES, *supra* note 201.

[213] Laura H. Kosloff & Mark C. Trexler, The Convention on International Trade in Endangered Species: No Carrot, But Where's the Stick? 17 Environmental Law Reporter 10222 (1987).

[214] Maaria Curlier & Steinar Andersen, International Trade in Endangered Species: The CITES Regime, in Environmental Regime Effectiveness: Confronting Theory with Evidence 357 (Edward L. Miles et al., eds., 2002).

combining the protection of cultural areas and natural areas was born in the United States and was later pursued by the International Union for the Conservation of Nature (IUCN). Even today, the convention is presented as a unique instrument for its combination of protection of natural and cultural sites.

The World Heritage Convention[215] includes two lists: the "World Heritage List," where nature reserves are to be listed, and the "List of World Heritage in Danger." State consent is required for the inclusion of a state territory in any of these lists.[216] The purpose of the convention is to direct international cooperation to the conservation of heritage sites through the training of specialists, interest-free loans, and the establishment of a World Heritage Fund that provides financial assistance to countries in need.[217] Most contributions to the fund come from state parties – and amount to 1 percent of their UNESCO contributions – and voluntary contributions. The total amount received each year is about $4 million, a small amount given the number and nature of needs that the fund needs to provide for.

The convention is administered by a World Heritage Committee. The executive body of the World Heritage Committee is the World Heritage Bureau. A small Secretariat facilitates the work of the committee. The committee has issued a set of operational guidelines[218] that provide the criteria for inclusion in the World Heritage List,[219] procedures for deletion from the World Heritage List, and the format and content of nominations. The guidelines provide analytical details on the type of assistance provided under the convention.[220] States that are interested in nominating a site for the World Heritage List must supply not only the laws that they have enacted to protect such sites but also information on the actual operation of such laws.[221]

The operational guidelines, in addition to natural and cultural sites, have included, since 1992, mixed sites or cultural landscapes. Cultural landscapes represent the "combined works of nature and of man."[222] The notion of cultural landscapes has not been used, however, to amend the exclusionary ethos that dominates the

---

[215] UNESCO Convention for the Protection of the World Cultural and Natural Heritage, Nov. 16, 1972, reprinted in 11 ILM 1358 (1972).

[216] Art. 11, *id.*

[217] Art. 16, *id.*

[218] The Operational Guidelines for the Implementation of the World Heritage Convention, available online at hppt://www.unesco.org.

[219] For instance, for sites to be nominated as World Heritage sites they must:
be outstanding examples representing major stages in earth's history; be outstanding examples representing significant on-going ecological and biological processes; contain superlative natural phenomena or areas of exceptional beauty and aesthetic importance; contain the most important and significant natural habitats for *in situ* conservation of biological diversity including those containing threatened species of outstanding universal value. See para. 44, Operational Guidelines, *id.*
Other criteria that are important for the nomination of sites as heritage sites include: a management plan for the site. When such plan is not available at the time of nomination, the state party must specify when such plan will become available and how it plans to mobilize resources for the preparation of the plan. Furthermore, the site must have "adequate long-term legislative, regulatory, institutional or traditional protection." See para. 44 (b)(v-vi), Operational Guidelines, *id.*

[220] Such as preparatory assistance, emergency assistance, training, technical cooperation, and assistance for educational, information, and promotional activities.

[221] Para. 11, Operational Guidelines, *supra* note 218.

[222] Art. 1, World Heritage Convention, *supra* note 215. See also para. 36, Operational Guidelines, *id.*

management of natural sites. The provisions on nature reserves still emphasize the strict separation of nature from human activity.[223]

At the time of writing, the World Heritage List contains 611 cultural sites, 154 natural sites, and only 23 mixed sites. It would be interesting to examine how many of the so-called natural sites contain indigenous or local cultural elements worthy of their characterization as cultural landscapes.

The procedure that applies for the inclusion of a site in the World Heritage List includes: a nomination by an interested state and an investigation by NGOs about whether the site qualifies as a World Heritage Site. The World Heritage Committee meets annually and examines applications on the basis of technical evaluations. These evaluations are supplied by the International Council on Monuments and Sites (ICOMOS) and the IUCN. Not all of the sites that are nominated are approved.

Monitoring under the convention is performed as periodic reporting or reactive monitoring. Periodic reporting involves reports of state parties on legislative, administrative, and other measures they have adopted for the application of the convention; and reports on the condition of the World Heritage properties located within their territories.[224] Reactive reporting involves "intelligence" collected by local NGOs, other sectors of the UNESCO and advisory bodies, for instance, the IUCN, on the real conditions of World Heritage sites.[225]

The convention could be characterized as a success in terms of the number of state parties that have subscribed to it (178 state parties in 2004), the involvement of environmental NGOs, and the fact that it has focused international attention on sites worthy of protection. The problem with the convention is that it has not been able to disassociate itself from conservation models that mandate the separation of natural sites from the populations that live in them. This artificial separation of human activity from the "natural environment" continues to propagate myths of pristine natural areas. These myths have been responsible for the evictions of local populations and human rights violations in the developing world.

3.2. Forests

The global forest regime revolves around a number of international organizations and instruments. The thrust of the global forest regime is not centered on forest conservation *per se* but, rather, on forest use under the principle of sustainable management and use. States have not been eager to adopt binding instruments for the protection of forests. Generally, states are not at ease with environmental instruments that would dictate specific forest use practices.

---

[223] For instance, one of the criteria to be used for the designation of natural sites is that:

> "The boundaries should include sufficient areas immediately adjacent to the area of outstanding universal value in order to protect the site's heritage values from direct effects of human encroachment and impacts of resource use outside of the nominated area." See para. 44 (b)(vi), Operational Guidelines, *id.*

[224] Paras. 69–76, Operational Guidelines, *id.* See also art. 29, World Heritage Convention, *supra* note 215.
[225] Para. 68, Operational Guidelines, *id.*

In 1992, the forest principles were adopted for the protection of forests. During the 1992 UNCED proceedings, the possibility of the adoption a forest convention was discussed. Developing countries resisted efforts to adopt a forest convention. Because forests are in national territories, a forest convention was considered too intrusive into national sovereignty, especially, if that convention were to focus on the deforestation in the developing world. A set of principles on the protection of all forests was more palatable.[226]

The principles affirm the sovereignty of countries over their natural resources.[227] The principles provide that states "have the sovereign and inalienable right to utilize, manage and develop their forests in accordance with their development needs."[228] But, at the same time, the principles provide that

> the agreed full incremental costs of achieving benefits associated with forest conservation and sustainable development requires increased international cooperation and should be equitably shared by the international community.[229]

The consistent affirmation of national sovereignty in the principles constitutes a reaction of developing countries against efforts to "internationalize" forest management under a conservation mandate. The quest for the international community to undertake the agreed full incremental costs of conservation implies, that if it is important for developed countries to pursue conservation goals in forests of the developing world, they must financially provide for those conservation goals. The need to finance forest conservation by developed countries is repeated frequently in the principles.[230]

The principles include provisions for participation of local communities, indigenous peoples, forest dwellers, and NGOs.[231] Furthermore, the rights of indigenous peoples are recognized in the principles more extensively than in other instruments but still under paternalistic overtones. It is provided that:

> National forest policies should recognize and duly support the identity, culture and the rights of indigenous people, their communities and other communities and forest dwellers. Appropriate conditions should be promoted for these groups to enable them to have an economic stake in forest use, perform economic activities, and achieve and maintain cultural identity and social organization . . . [232]

The principles, in accordance with the spirit of the CBD, provide that "[b]enefits arising from the utilization of indigenous knowledge should be . . . equitably shared with such people."[233]

The principles recognize the important economic and conservation role of plantations in taking pressures off old-growth forests and in providing for regional

---

[226] Non-Legally Binding Authoritative Statement of Principles for a Global Consensus on the Management, Conservation and Sustainable Development of All Types of Forests, June 13, 1992, A/CONF.151/26 (Vol. III), reprinted in 31 ILM 881 (1992).

[227] Principle 1(a), *id.*

[228] Principle 2(a), *id.*

[229] Principle 1(b), *id.*

[230] Principles 7(b), 9(a) & 10, *id.*

[231] Principle 2(d), *id.*

[232] Principle 5(a), *id.*

[233] Principle 12(d), *id.*

employment.[234] Other provisions of the principles refer to the EIA for actions likely to have adverse impacts on forest resources;[235] scientific research and forest inventories and assessments;[236] open and free international trade in forest products;[237] and the sharing of benefits from products derived from forest resources with the country from which these resources have been extracted.[238]

The International Tropical Timber Organization (ITTO) focuses on the management of tropical forests. As its name indicates, the organization deals with trade in tropical timber. The impetus for the creation of the organization[239] goes back to the 1983 International Tropical Timber Agreement (ITTA), adopted under the auspices of United Nations Conference on Trade and Development (UNCTAD). The ITTA that was adopted in 1983 has been superseded by a later ITTA.[240]

Membership in the ITTO consists of fifty-nine countries that represent 80 percent of the world's tropical forests and 90 percent of global timber trade. There are two categories of membership: producing and consuming countries of tropical timber.[241] Annual contributions and votes are distributed equally between these groups, which are called caucuses. The dues and votes are based on the value of tropical timber trade and, for producing countries, on the extent of tropical forests within their territory.[242]

The ITTO has engaged in efforts to promote sustainable timber harvesting, as demonstrated by the ITTO Action Plan (2002–06). It has worked on the development of criteria and indicators for sustainable forest management. The ITTO has issued a number of technical papers on the sustainable management of tropical forests.[243]

Proposals have been made to ban tropical timber trade as a means to protect tropical rainforests. It has been proposed, more specifically, that developed countries must ban tropical timber imports from developing countries to save tropical forests. If a total ban is unacceptable, a partial ban on the trade of "unsustainably" collected timber could be imposed. Sustainably collected timber should be certified as such to facilitate transactions.

But both a total ban and a partial ban present significant problems. Whether timber has been harvested sustainably depends on the harvesting method applied. Given the large number of timber concessions, monitoring harvesting methods would be costly. Thus, partial bans on unsustainably harvested timber are difficult to apply. A total ban has been resisted by developing countries because timber extraction is a significant source of revenue. In consideration of the current timber trade trends, a

---

[234] Principle 6(d), *id.*

[235] Principle 8(h), *id.*

[236] Principle 11, *id.*

[237] Principle 13(a), *id.*

[238] Principle 8(g), *id.*

[239] The organization was established in 1986.

[240] International Tropical Timber Agreement (ITTA), Jan. 26, 1994, reprinted in 33 ILM 1014 (1994) [hereinafter 1994 ITTA].

[241] Art. 4, *id.*

[242] Art. 10, *id.*

[243] ITTO, Principles, criteria and indicators for the sustainable management of African natural tropical forests (2003); ITTO, Guidelines for the restoration, management and rehabilitation of degraded and secondary tropical forests (2002).

ban on timber imports into developed countries may not affect overall trading. Most tropical wood is projected to be consumed in the developing world and it has been claimed that the South-to-South trade is to replace the South-to-North trade.[244] Trade prohibitions imposed by developed countries, therefore, may have minimal impact on global tropical wood consumption.

The 1994 ITTA includes certain environmental provisions. The preamble of the agreement refers to the environmental instruments adopted at the UNCED and to the goal of achieving sustainable management of tropical timber by the year 2000. Overall, it could be said that the 1994 agreement maintains a balance between environmental considerations and the concerns of developing countries, the primary exporters of tropical timber. It is provided, for example, that the objectives of the ITTO are to:promote the expansion and diversification of international trade in tropical timber;[245] provide additional financial resources to developing countries;[246] improve market transparency;[247] promote timber processing in producing countries so as to contribute to their industrialization and increase their employment opportunities and export earnings;[248] promote the rehabilitation of forest land with due regard for the interests of local communities.[249]

As the 1994 agreement is about to be replaced, issues that preoccupy policy makers have to do with timber certification; trade in nontimber forest products; transparency of subsidies; fair prices for tropical timber; and community forests. Some states have proposed to rename ITTO; the new name proposed is International Tropical Forests Organization.

In addition to the FAO and the ITTO, other bodies that deal with forests include the United Nations Forum on Forests (UNFF), which was established by the Economic and Social Council of the United Nations (ECOSOC) in 2000. The purpose of the UNFF is to continue the work of the Intergovernmental Panel on Forests (IPF) that functioned between 1995 and 1997 and the Intergovernmental Forum on Forests (IFF) that took place between 1997 and 2000. One of the mandates of the UNFF is to promote an environment that would be conductive to international negotiations for the adoption of a legally binding instrument on the protection of forests.[250]

In 2001, a new effort was undertaken to support the work of UNFF: the Collaborative Partnership on Forests (CPF). The CPF is an informal network with diverse membership including the IARCs, the World Bank, the ITTO, the FAO, the Secretariat of the CBD, the UNEP, and the UNDP.[251]

In fact, the CBD has identified forest biological diversity as one of its five thematic areas. The COP of the Biodiversity Convention has been dealing more with the management of forests as a natural resource rather than the protection of biodiversity creating misgivings within the FAO circles for duplication of efforts and a waste

---

[244] Louka, *supra* note 28, at 48.
[245] Art. 1(e), 1994 ITTA, *supra* not 240.
[246] Art. 1(g), *id.*
[247] Art. 1(h), *id.*
[248] Art. 1(i), *id.*
[249] Art. 1(j), *id.*
[250] FAO Forests, *supra* note 7, at 42.
[251] *Id.* at 45.

energy and resources as the FAO is dealing with similar issues.[252] But because the GEF supports the Biodiversity Convention, the convention has been able to fund eighty forest-related projects worth more than $500 million in 2001.[253]

Other initiatives for the protection of forests include the Programme on Forests (PROFOR), which was transferred from the UNDP to the World Bank as an element of the World Bank's new forest strategy. The National Forest Programme Facility is an initiative undertaken by the FAO, PROFOR, institutions from developing countries, and NGOs in response to calls to develop strong national forest programs as a means to address successfully forest management issues.[254]

3.3. Wetlands

The Ramsar Convention[255] provides that each state must designate suitable wetlands[256] for inclusion in the List of Wetlands of International Importance.[257] The Ramsar Convention has over 130 parties and now protects 1,229 sites covering an area of 105.9 million hectares. Each party must designate one wetland on signature or ratification.[258] Designation is unilateral and not subject to approval. The deletion or restriction of wetlands is permitted when an urgent national interest is at stake[259] as long as compensatory measures are taken, for instance, the establishment of additional protected areas.[260] The convention refers to the "wise use"[261] of wetlands that the Sixth Conference of the Parties in 1996 has interpreted to mean sustainable use. The convention exhibits strict conservation overtones since it provides that state parties "shall promote the conservation of wetlands . . . by establishing nature reserves on wetlands . . . and provide adequately for their wardening."[262] The convention provides for the possibility of transnational wetlands.[263]

The Conference of the Parties has adopted criteria for the designation of wetland sites as Wetlands of International Importance. Group A criteria help establish sites containing representative, rare, or unique wetland types and Group B criteria help to select sites of international importance for conserving biological diversity (for instance, waterbirds and fish).[264]

---

[252] *Id.* at 48.

[253] *Id.*

[254] *Id.* at 55.

[255] Convention on Wetlands of International Importance (known as Ramsar Convention), Feb. 2, 1971, reprinted in 996 UNTS 245.

[256] The definition of wetlands is quite broad. According to article 1: "For the purpose of this Convention wetlands are areas of marsh, fend, peatland or water, whether natural or artificial, permanent or temporary, with water that is static or flowing, fresh, brackish or salt, including areas of marine water the depth of which at low tide does not exceed six meters." *Id.*

[257] Art. 2(5), *id.*

[258] Art. 2(4) and (5), *id.*

[259] Urgent national interest is not determined in the convention. See art. 2(5), *id.*

[260] Arts. 2(5)–(6) and 4(2), *id.*

[261] Art. 3(1), *id.*

[262] Art. 4(1), *id.*

[263] Art. 5, *id.*

[264] The criteria are now integrated into the Strategic Framework and guidelines for the future development of the List of Wetlands of International Importance, Resolution VII. 11, Seventh Meeting of

Discussions are underway for sites that have ceased to fulfill the criteria for their designation on the Ramsar List. The Conference of the Parties may make changes in the List of Wetlands and has established procedures for wetland inventory and assessment. The current budget of the convention amounts to US$3.8 million. The COP adopted a Wetland Conservation Fund in 1990, now called Ramsar Small Grants Fund for Wetland Conservation and Wise Use.

4. REGIONAL INSTRUMENTS

4.1. Europe

Convention on the Conservation of European Wildlife and Natural Habitats
The purpose of the Convention on the Conservation of European Wildlife and Natural Habitats,[265] known as the Bern Convention, is: to promote national policies for the protection of wild flora, wild fauna and natural habitats; to integrate conservation into national planning; and to promote education and to disseminate information on the need to conserve species and their habitats.[266]

The Bern Convention includes three annexes. The exploitation of wild flora species included in Annex I is totally prohibited. Annex II prohibits "the deliberate" destruction of wild fauna species. Annex III species are to be regulated to keep their populations out of danger.

States can ask for exceptions to the provisions of the treaty "in the interests of public health and safety, air safety or other overriding public interests."[267] Other exceptions include the prevention of serious damage to crops, livestock, forests, and fisheries, or other forms of property and the service of research and education.[268] Although these exceptions seem reasonable, their wide interpretation could dilute the regulatory character of the treaty.

A network of Areas of Special Conservation Interest (ASCIs), called the Emerald network, has been established under the convention. The network includes Central and Eastern European countries and EU states. The Emerald network was launched in 1989.

The standing committee established under the convention plays an important role in the implementation of the convention. The standing committee issues recommendations and guidelines. States are to follow up the guidelines with reports on their implementation measures. A quite unique implementation procedure has been established under the convention for the examination of complaints,[269] which could become quite effective in deterring infringements to the convention.

the Conference of the Contracting Parties to the Convention on Wetlands, San José, Costa Rica, May 10–18, 1999.

[265] Convention on the Conservation of European Wildlife and Natural Habitats, Sept. 19, 1979, European Treaty Series No. 104, reprinted in IV European Conventions and Agreements 181 (Council of Europe, 1993).

[266] Art. 3, *id.*

[267] Art. 9(1), *id.*

[268] *Id.*

[269] The Secretariat examines the complaints sent to the standing committee for failure of state parties to comply with the goals of the convention. The Secretariat informs the state parties concerned and decides whether or not to intervene based on the seriousness of the complaint.

Further recommendations to enhance the role of the Bern Convention were made under the Monaco Declaration.[270] The declaration stated that the standing committee should increase its efforts to coordinate the divergent strategies for the protection of biodiversity[271] and that the appropriate coordination mechanisms should be established with the CBD.

The EU has adopted legislation that is modeled after the Bern Convention.[272] The EU also has adopted a Biodiversity Strategy.[273]

European Landscape Convention

The European Landscape Convention provides a refreshing perspective on conservation. The European Landscape Convention[274] was adopted under the auspices of the Council of Europe in 2000. The convention was the outcome of the work of Europe's Congress of Local and Regional Authorities (CLRAE). The CLRAE started a process of drafting a Landscape Convention in 1994 and completed it in 1997. It then submitted the convention to the Council of Europe for adoption. The Council of Europe adopted the convention in 2002.

The purpose of the convention is to provide a framework for the protection of all types of landscapes in Europe through the cooperation of national, regional, and local authorities and NGOs.

The convention defines landscapes as areas resulting from the interaction of natural and human factors.[275] This definition distinguishes landscapes from nature reserves. Nature reserves, as discussed earlier, have been defined as areas virtually undisturbed by humans. The definition of landscapes proposed in the convention establishes a view of landscapes that evolve with time and human needs.

The convention distinguishes between landscape protection, landscape management, and landscape planning. Landscape protection[276] has to do with the conservation of landscapes and must include both cultural and natural aspects. Landscape management involves the regular upkeep of landscapes as they evolve to meet, *inter alia*, social and economic needs.[277] Landscape planning has to do with the creation

---

If the Secretariat decides that action is appropriate, it informs the contracting parties concerned. The Secretariat then decides, based on the answer received, whether to place the complaint on the agenda of the standing committee.

If a matter is put on the agenda of the standing committee, the standing committee will have to make a decision whether to pursue it. If it decides to pursue the case, the committee has to make a choice between issuing a recommendation or conducting an on-the-spot inquiry. Depending on the outcome of the recommendation or on-the-spot inquiry, the standing committee may decide to close the file. If a state continues to violate the convention consistently, the standing committee may consider inviting one or more contracting parties to put the matter to arbitration.

[270] Council of Europe, Directorate of Environment and Local Authorities, Monaco Declaration on the role of the Bern Convention in the implementation of worldwide international instruments for the protection of biodiversity, Sept. 28, 1994.

[271] *Id.*

[272] Council Directive 92/43/EEC on the conservation of natural habitats of wild fauna and flora, OJ L 206/7, 22.07.1992.

[273] For the Strategy, see Elli Louka, Conflicting Integration: The Environmental Law of the European Union 297–98 (2004).

[274] European Landscape Convention, July 19, 2000, European Treaties Series (ETS) no. 176.

[275] Art. 1(a), *id.*

[276] Art. 1(d), *id.*

[277] Art. 1(e), *id.*

of new landscapes and the policies for reshaping and restoring current landscapes.[278] The convention establishes what is called "landscape quality objective." This quality objective must be formulated based on the aspirations of the public with regard to desirable landscape features.[279]

The convention's scope is quite large because it covers the entire territory of state parties and all kinds of landscapes – natural and urban landscapes all over land, inland water, and marine areas. The convention is not only focused on preserving outstanding landscapes but also on revitalizing degraded landscapes, thereby emphasizing the role of restoration in the European environmental agenda.

The convention clearly provides that landscape protection can be accomplished through national measures but has left the level at which these measures must be taken to the discretion of states. The convention is one of the first treaties to suggest that the principle of subsidiarity[280] must apply for its implementation. The principle of subsidiarity allows for the involvement of local and regional authorities if this involvement would facilitate the implementation of the convention.[281]

The convention encourages state parties to:

- recognize landscapes in their legislation;
- implement landscape policies through specific measures;
- establish procedures for the participation of general public, local, and regional authorities; and
- integrate landscape management into regional and town planning policies, cultural, environmental, agricultural, social, and economic policies.[282]

States are required to take specific measures that concentrate on awareness–raising, training and education, identification and assessment of landscapes, and establishment of landscape quality objectives and implementation.[283] Training and education are of paramount importance because the contribution of specialized professionals is a prerequisite for the implementation of any coherent landscape policy.[284]

International cooperation is encouraged through the establishment of transfrontier landscapes[285] but also through technical and scientific assistance, the exchange of landscape specialists, and the exchange of information.[286]

An innovative element of the convention is that, instead of creating another committee, it relies on the organs of the Council of Europe for implementation. Such organs involve the committee for the activities of the Council of Europe in the field of biological and landscape diversity (CO-DBP) and the Cultural Heritage Committee (CC-PAT).[287]

The convention provides for a landscape award given by the Council of Europe to local or regional authorities or NGOs that introduce measures for landscape

---

[278] Art. 1(f), *id.*

[279] Art. 1(c), *id.*

[280] Subsidiarity dictates that a central authority should have a subsidiary function, performing only those tasks that cannot be performed effectively at a more immediate or local level.

[281] Art. 4, Landscape Convention, *supra* note 274.

[282] Art. 5, *id.*

[283] Art. 6, *id.*

[284] *Id.*

[285] Art. 9, *id.*

[286] Art. 8, *id.*

[287] Art. 10, *id.*

protection that have a lasting effect and can serve as examples for other authorities throughout Europe.[288]

4.2. Africa

Convention on the Conservation of Nature and Natural Resources

From colonial times, the model of conservation in the African region has been that of strict conservation. The 1968 African Convention[289] concentrates on the protection of endangered species. Species belonging in Class A "shall be totally protected" throughout the territory unless authorization is given by "the highest competent authority" when the national interest is at stake or for the purposes of scientific research.[290] Class B species will be "totally protected" but also could be hunted, killed, captured, or collected under a license granted by a competent authority.[291] State parties are required to regulate hunting, capturing, and fishing and certain hunting and capturing methods are prohibited.[292] The convention makes trade in listed species subject to authorization and, as such, it functions as a regional supplement to the CITES Convention.[293]

The African Convention refers to the needs of people. The African Convention provides that conservation measures should be taken "with due regard to the best interests of people"[294] and that states must take measures to reconcile customary rights with the goals of the convention.[295] But the convention substitutes people's will with government discretion when it mentions that states must ensure that their people understand the need and rules for the rational utilization of resources through conservation education.[296]

Despite a permissive language[297] that allows for significant state discretion, the overall tone of the convention supports the premises of strict preservation. The convention, for instance, includes three categories of protected areas from which human use is more or less excluded. The convention provides that, throughout nature reserves, any form of activity, such as fishing, hunting, excavation, prospecting, and agriculture "are strictly forbidden."[298] Residing, entering, traversing, or camping is forbidden in strict nature reserves.[299] National parks include areas "exclusively set aside for the propagation, protection, conservation and management" of species "for the benefit and enjoyment of the general public."[300] In national parks, hunting

---

[288] Art. 11, *id.*

[289] African Convention on the Conservation of Nature and Natural Resources, Sept. 15, 1968, reprinted in 1001 UNTS 3 [hereinafter African Convention]. The Convention was preceded by the 1933 Convention Relative to the Preservation of Fauna and Flora in their Natural State, Nov. 8, 1933.

[290] Art. VIII(1)(1), African Convention, *id.*

[291] Art. VIII(1)(2), *id.*

[292] Art. VII, *id.*

[293] Art. IX, *id.*

[294] Art. II, *id.*

[295] Art XI, *id.*

[296] Art. XIII, *id.*

[297] See, e.g., exceptions for the convention that could be read expansively, art. XVII, *id.*

[298] Art. III(4)(a)(ii), *id.*

[299] Art. III(4)(a)(ii)–(iii), *id.*

[300] Art. III(4)(b)(ii), *id.*

and killing are prohibited except for scientific management purposes and under the control of the competent authority.[301] In special reserves, such as game reserves, "settlement and other human activities shall be controlled or prohibited."[302] In partial reserves or sanctuaries set aside to protect threatened species "all interests and activities shall be subordinated to this end."[303]

The convention does not provide for an institutional structure for its implementation. It is simply provided that reports on national measures undertaken must be transmitted to the Organization of African Unity (OAU).[304] Because there is no institution devoted to the monitoring and enforcement of the convention, states have "turned on and off" conservation measures according to the availability of international funding.

Lusaka Agreement

In 1994, the governments of certain African countries adopted an agreement that concentrates on the enforcement of the CITES.[305] In the preamble of this agreement, it is stated that an enforcement agreement is necessary as illegal trade in wildlife has become more sophisticated through the use of superior technology in transboundary transactions. The objective of the agreement is to reduce and ultimately eliminate illegal trade in wildlife,[306] an ambitious objective given the important role that black markets play in the economies of developing countries.[307]

The institutional execution of the agreement is trusted to a task force. The task force established under the agreement is composed of field officers seconded by each contracting party from the national law enforcement authority, a director, and an intelligence officer.[308] The governing council of the agreement is comprised of delegations sent by state parties headed by a government minister or an alternate. The parties are encouraged to include in their delegations high-ranking officials in the enforcement of wildlife law and relevant specialists.[309] The purpose of the governing council is to determine the general policies of the task force.[310]

The first task force was established at the first governing council in 1997. The task force has had some success in intercepting illegal wildlife transactions.[311] It suffers, however, from low participation. Parties to the Lusaka Agreement as of 2004

---

[301] Art. III(4)(b)(iii), *id.*

[302] Art. III(4)(c)(i), *id.*

[303] Art. III(4)(c)(ii), *id.*

[304] Art. XVI, *id.*

[305] Lusaka Agreement on Co-operative Enforcement Operations Directed at Illegal Trade in Wild Fauna and Flora, Sept. 9, 1994.

[306] Art. 1, *id.*

[307] Douglass C. North, Institutions, Institutional Change and Economic Performance 67 (1990). Because of insecure property rights and lack of enforcement the most profitable business in developing countries may be trade, redistributive activities or the black market.

[308] Art. 5(2)–(3), Lusaka Agreement, *supra* note 305.

[309] Art. 7(2), *id.*

[310] Art. 7(8), *id.*

[311] See, e.g., Another Milestone Attained in Operationalizing the Lusaka Agreement, Dec. 21, 1999, available online at http://www.unep.org/Documents; Largest Illegal Ivory Seizure Ever Leads to Criminal Investigation, June 3, 2004, available online at International Fund for Animal Welfare (IFAW), http://www.ifaw.org/ifaw/general/default.aspx?oid=96231.

are Kenya, Lesotho, Tanzania, Uganda, Congo, Brazzaville, and Zambia. But major players in wildlife trade do not participate. For instance, South Africa has signed but not ratified the agreement. Zimbabwe has not participated in the agreement, either. Asian countries that are major recipients of wildlife have been invited to participate, but they have declined.

Eastern African Region Protocol

The 1985 Protected Areas Protocol is an attempt to bolster conservation efforts in the Eastern African region following the model of protected areas.[312] The protocol, in addition to provisions for endangered and threatened species,[313] provides guidance for the management of protected areas. The protocol provides for the establishment of buffer zones in which human activities "are less severely restricted while remaining compatible with the purposes of the protected area."[314]

The protocol's language contains overtones that are sympathetic to the needs of local populations. But the tenets of strict conservation have had significant influence on the protocol. Contracting parties must, in taking measures protective of the environment, take into account "traditional activities of their local populations." But considering traditional activities must not endanger the ecosystems protected or cause the extinction or substantial reduction of individuals that make up a species.[315]

SADC Protocol on Wildlife Conservation and Law Enforcement

Other subregional conservation efforts involve the SADC Protocol on Wildlife Conservation and Law Enforcement.[316] The agreement has a wider ambit than the Lusaka Agreement because it deals with the harmonization of national legal instruments, enforcement of wildlife laws, the building of national and regional capacity, the establishment of transfrontier conservation areas, and the facilitation of community-based natural resources management.[317] The agreement demonstrates more sophistication in its understanding of conservation dilemmas in the developing world. Conservation is defined, for instance, as

> the protection, maintenance, rehabilitation, restoration and enhancement of wildlife and includes the management of the use of wildlife to ensure the sustainability of such use.[318]

---

[312] Protocol Concerning Protected Areas of Wild Fauna and Flora in the Eastern African Region, June 21, 1995 [hereinafter Eastern Africa Protocol]. This is a protocol to the Nairobi Convention for the Protection, Management and Development of the Marine and Coastal Environment of the Eastern African Region, June 21, 1985.

[313] Three annexes are established. Annex I deals with protection of wild flora (art. 3). Annex II focuses on species and wild fauna that must be ensured the "strictest protection" (art. 4). Annex III deals with harvestable species (art. 5), Eastern Africa Protocol, *id.*

[314] Art. 11, *id.*

[315] Art. 12, *id.*

[316] The SADC (Southern African Development Community) Protocol on Wildlife Conservation and Law Enforcement, Aug. 18, 1999. It entered into force in 2003.

[317] Art. 4, *id.*

[318] Art. 1, *id.*

It is also provided that states parties

> shall in recognition of the important role played by rural communities in the con-
> servation and sustainable use of wildlife, promote community-based conservation and
> management of wildlife resources.[319]

2003 African Convention

The 2003 African Convention,[320] which revised the 1968 African Convention,
seems to have been influenced by the new rhetoric in international environmental
law. For instance, the principles on which the convention is based are:the right of
all people to a satisfactory environment favorable to their development; the duty of
states to ensure the enjoyment of the right to development; and the duty of states
to ensure that developmental and environmental needs are met in a sustainable, fair
and equitable manner.[321] The convention still provides for strict nature reserves but
provides also for landscapes and managed resource protected areas.[322] The essence of
incompatibility between human habitation and environmental protection is maintained, though, throughout the convention.[323] Furthermore, the definitions and
management goals of different categories of protected areas propagate the idea of
uninhabited protected areas.[324]

The convention repeats provisions of the Biodiversity Convention with regard
to the fair and equitable access to genetic resources on mutually agreed terms and
the fair and equitable sharing of benefits from technology that is based on genetic
resources and related to traditional knowledge.[325] The convention devotes a whole

---

[319] Art. 7(8), *id.*

[320] African Convention on the Conservation of Nature and Natural Resources, July 11, 2003, available
online at http://www.africa-union.org/official documents/Treaties.

[321] Art. III, *id.*

[322] Art. V(6), *id.*

[323] For instance, it is mentioned that parties must promote the establishment by local communities of
protected areas managed by them primarily for the conservation and sustainable use of natural resources.
See art. XII(3), *id.*

[324] See Annex II, *id.* The objective of management of strict nature reserves is to preserve habitats, ecosystems
and species "in as undisturbed a state as possible."

 Wilderness areas are defined as large areas "without permanent or significant habitation," where one
of the objectives of management is "to enable local communities living at low density and in balance
with the available resources to maintain their life style" but not change it or improve it.

 One of the objectives of managing *national parks* is to "take into account the needs of local communities, including subsistence resource use, in so far as these will not adversely affect the other objectives
of management."

 One of the purposes of preserving *natural monuments* is "to eliminate and thereafter prevent exploitation or occupation inimical to the purpose of designation."

 One of the purposes of *habitat/species management area* is "to eliminate and thereafter prevent exploitation and occupation inimical to the purposes of designation."

 Even the management of landscapes seems to emphasize static preservation models rather than
human development needs. Some of the objectives of management include:
- "the continuation of *traditional* land uses," "the *preservation* of social and the cultural fabric," the
elimination of activities "inappropriate in scale and/or character," and the "development of public
support for environmental protection of such areas." [emphasis added].
- Managed resource protected areas are also to be areas containing "predominantly unmodified natural
systems" which could contribute to national and regional development.

[325] Art. IX(2)(j)–(k), *id.*

provision to the traditional rights of local communities and indigenous knowledge. According to the convention, the parties must take legislative and other measures to ensure that traditional rights and intellectual property rights of local communities, including farmers' rights, are respected.[326] Access to indigenous knowledge shall take place after the prior informed consent of the concerned communities.[327]

The agreements concluded in the African region demonstrate the strong influence of a strict conservation ethic on African countries. This is a continent that faces severe problems of poverty, disease, and institutional instability. It is not surprising, therefore, that these instruments have been either neglected, when resources are not available, or have been used by governments, when convenient, to suppress disobedient electorates.

4.3. South East Asia

ASEAN Agreement

Under the auspices of ASEAN,[328] an ambitious biodiversity conservation agreement, the Agreement on the Conservation of Nature and Natural Resources has yet to enter into force.[329] This may be because the agreement was quite advanced for its time both in terms of rhetoric and of substance. The agreement includes concepts, such as sustainable development and genetic diversity, that are encountered much later in international instruments.[330]

The agreement includes substantive provisions on the protection of species and ecosystems and provisions on conservation of ecological processes. The agreement refers to the integrated management of natural resources because it provides that "conservation and management of natural resources are treated as an integral part of development planning at all stages and all levels."[331]

The agreement requires the parties to maintain, wherever possible, "maximum genetic diversity."[332] Unlike many other conservation agreements, the agreement makes extensive references to gene bank development[333] and restoration including reforestation and afforestation.[334] Trade in specimens or products is to be regulated "whenever such regulations meaningfully contribute to the implementation of the harvesting regulations."[335]

The agreement includes measures for the protection of endangered species through prohibitions on the takings of species, trade regulation, and the protection

---

[326] Art. XVII(1), *id.*

[327] Art. XVII(2), *id.*

[328] The Association of South East Asian Nations (ASEAN) is a subregional organization comprised of the states of Brunei, Indonesia, Malaysia, Philippines, Singapore, and Thailand.

[329] See Agreement on the Conservation of Nature and Natural Resources adopted by the Association of South East Asian Nations, July 9, 1985, available online at http://sedac.ciesin.org/entri (Center for Science Information Network, Environmental Treaties and Resource Indicators).

[330] Art. 1(1), *id.*

[331] Art. 2(1), *id.*

[332] Art. 3(1), *id.*

[333] Art. 3(3)(d), *id.*

[334] Arts. 4(1)(c), 4(2)(d)–(f) and 6(2)(d), *id.*

[335] Art. 4(2)(g), *id.*

of habitats.[336] The development of forestry management plans based on the principle of optimal sustainable yield and the avoidance of depletion of resource capital must be supported.[337] Other substantive provisions include the protection of soil, water, and air.[338]

The agreement refers to the promotion of sound agricultural practices,[339] pollution control,[340] and adequate economic or fiscal incentives.[341] The agreement contains one of the earliest articulations of the polluter pays principle.[342] Other provisions include environmental land use measures[343] and protected areas.[344] With regard to protected areas, the agreement follows the traditional path of defining national parks as areas that "have not been substantially altered by human occupation or exploitation,"[345] and of providing that in reserves "any activity inconsistent with [conservation] . . . purposes shall be prohibited."[346] Protected areas must be managed in accordance with a management plan that would provide for buffer zones around protected areas in which activities that have harmful consequences on protected areas will be prohibited.[347] The agreement provides for a network of protected areas[348] and the promotion of conservation measures in natural areas by private owners, communities, and local authorities.[349]

One of the most innovative provisions of the agreement, for the period it was adopted, is the requirement for the participation of the public in the decision-making process. States "shall, as far as possible, organize participation of the public in the planning and implementation of conservation measures."[350] The agreement provides for notification and consultation among parties for activities that may have adverse transboundary environmental effects.[351] A conference of parties,[352] a secretariat,[353] and national focal points of coordination are to administer the agreement.[354]

The Agreement on Transboundary Haze Pollution

The Agreement on Transboundary Haze Pollution was adopted to address a specific environmental problem in the region.[355] This agreement was adopted in 2002 and

---

[336] Art. 5, *id.*
[337] Art. 6(2)(g), *id.*
[338] See arts. 7, 8, and 9, *id.*
[339] Art. 10(a), *id.*
[340] Art. 10(b), *id.* See also art. 11, *id.*
[341] Art. 10(c), *id.*
[342] Art. 10(d), *id.*
[343] Art. 12, *id.*
[344] Art. 13, *id.*
[345] Art. 13(3)(a)(i), *id.*
[346] Art. 13(3)(b)(iii), *id.*
[347] Art. 13(4)(a)–(b), *id.*
[348] Art. 13(6), *id.*
[349] Art. 13(7), *id.*
[350] Art. 16(2), *id.*
[351] Art. 20, *id.*
[352] Art. 21, *id.*
[353] Art. 22, *id.*
[354] Art. 23, *id.*
[355] ASEAN Agreement on Transboundary Haze Pollution, June 10, 2002, available online at http://www.aseansec.org.

entered into force in 2003. The purpose of the agreement is to prevent haze pollution generated from forest fires by strengthening fire fighting capability, early warning systems based on satellite imagery, and enforcement mechanisms for arsonists who are frequently plantation owners.

ASEAN Agreement on Access to Genetic Resources

An ASEAN Framework Agreement on Access to Genetic Resources is under preperation. The ASEAN Regional Center for Biodiversity Conservation established in Philippines is to play an important role in the exchange of germplasm among states in the region, and the exchange of germplasm between these states and third countries.

Soft Law Instruments

A number of soft environmental instruments have been adopted in the region such as the ASEAN Declaration on Heritage Parks;[356] the Yangon Resolution on Sustainable Development, which provides, *inter alia*, for the development of an ASEAN Environment Fund;[357] and the Jakarta Declaration on Environment and Development.[358]

4.4. Antarctica

Environmental protection in the Antarctic region is executed primarily through the Protocol to the Antarctic Treaty on Environmental Protection.[359] The protocol is governed by the notion of Antarctica as a pristine area unspoiled by humans. According to the environmental principles included in the protocol:

> The protection of the Antarctic environment . . . and the intrinsic value of Antarctica, including its wilderness and aesthetic values and its value as an area for the conduct of scientific research, in particular research essential to understanding the global environment, shall be fundamental considerations in the planning and conduct of all activities in the Antarctic Treaty Area.[360]

The protocol provides for the prohibition of mining.[361] A Committee for Environmental Protection[362] and a system of inspections by observers are established.[363] The parties must provide the committee with annual reports on the steps they have undertaken to implement the protocol. These reports must be circulated to all parties.[364] Annex I of the protocol provides extensive provisions for environmental impact assessment. Annex II includes provisions for the protection of fauna and flora. Annex III establishes waste disposal and management methods. Annex IV deals with marine pollution. Annex V provides for the establishment of protected

---

[356] Dec. 18, 2003, available online at http://www.aseansec.org.
[357] Dec. 18, 2003, available online at http://www.aseansec.org.
[358] Sept. 18, 1997, available online at http://www.aseansec.org.
[359] Protocol on Environmental Protection to the Antarctic Treaty, Oct. 4, 1991, reprinted in 30 ILM 1461 (1991).
[360] Art. 3(1), *id.*
[361] Art. 7, *id.*
[362] Arts. 11 & 12, *id.*
[363] Art. 14, *id.*
[364] Art. 17, *id.*

areas. As Antarctica remains a continent where human impact is the least evident, the establishment of protected areas appears to be more credible than the development of protected areas in other continents. It is clear, however, from the focus of the annexes that even in Antarctica protected areas would need to be managed extensively to maintain their "pristine" status.

4.5. Other Regional Instruments

South Pacific Convention on the Conservation of Nature

Other regional agreements include the 1976 Convention on the Conservation of Nature in the South Pacific.[365] The convention emphasizes the establishment of regional reserves.[366] The convention provides that, notwithstanding the strict protection of nature reserves, customary uses of areas and species in accordance with traditional cultural practices may be permitted.[367] In practice, the convention does not provide much on the development of monitoring capability. The secretariat functions are undertaken by the South Pacific Regional Environment Program (SPREP).[368]

The Western Hemisphere Treaty

The Western Hemisphere Convention,[369] contains references to "strict wilderness reserves" and obligations of state parties to "maintain the strict wilderness reserves inviolate."[370] The convention includes general provisions establishing restrictions on trade in wildlife, such as those provided for in the CITES.[371]

The Treaty for Amazonian Cooperation

The Treaty for Amazonian Cooperation[372] could be seen as an attempt to coordinate transboundary development in the Amazonian region. The treaty is a realistic instrument that attempts to combine, at least in rhetoric, the goals of development and environmental goals. Reading through the convention, one comes to appreciate the Amazonian region as an area inhabited and developed by people rather than as a pristine protected area.

As stated in the Preamble, the purpose of the agreement is to promote the harmonious development of the Amazon region, to permit an equitable distribution of benefits from development among parties, and to improve the standard of living of people. The agreement underlines the importance of rational planning for the exploitation of flora and fauna, the proper exchange of information on

---

[365] Convention on Conservation of Nature in the South Pacific (Apia Convention), June 12, 1976, (1990) Australian Treaty Series, No. 41.

[366] Art. IV, *id.*

[367] Art. VI, *id.*

[368] The SPREP was formalized as an intergovernmental organization in 1993, see Agreement Establishing the South Pacific Regional Environmental Programme (SPREP), June 16, 1993.

[369] Convention on Nature Protection and Wildlife Preservation in the Western Hemisphere, Oct. 12, 1940, reprinted in 161 UNTS 193.

[370] Arts. II(1) and IV, *id.*

[371] Art. VIII, *id.*

[372] Treaty for Amazonian Cooperation, July 3, 1978, reprinted in 17 ILM 1045 (1978). State parties to the treaty are: Bolivia, Brazil, Colombia, Ecuador, Guyana, Peru, Suriname, and Venezuela.

conservationist measures, and the promotion of scientific research.[373] The agreement deals with issues of improvement of sanitary conditions and methods of combating epidemics in the Amazon and this, in retrospect, places the agreement closer to the spirit of the WSSD adopted twenty-four years later.[374] States are to increase the flow of tourists in the region but without prejudicing the protection of indigenous cultures and natural resources.[375] The convention emphasizes the importance of conservation of the ethnological and archeological wealth of the Amazon.[376]

The Amazon Cooperation Treaty has been dormant for many years. In 2002, state parties to the treaty decided to give it a new impetus by establishing the Amazon Cooperation Treaty Organization (ACTO). The ACTO is based in Brazil and its purpose is to act as a catalyst for sustainable development in the region.

Protocol on Protected Areas in the Caribbean Region

The Protocol on Specially Protected Areas for the Wider Caribbean Region[377] provides for a variety of measures that must be undertaken in protected areas from the regulation of dumping, fishing, and hunting to the regulation of trade in endangered species and tourism.[378] The protocol does not just provide that parties should establish protected areas, but it is ambitious enough to put forward a cooperation program for the listing of protected areas.[379] The purpose of the program is to assist parties in the selection, establishment, and management of protected areas and the initiation of a network of protected areas.[380]

The procedure for the establishment of protected areas includes the nomination of protected areas by a state party based on certain selection criteria.[381] The scientific and technical advisory committee established under the convention is to review the nomination and should advise whether the site fulfills the selection criteria.[382] The protocol provides for the establishment of buffer zones[383] and the establishment of protected areas and buffer zones in areas neighboring international borders.[384]

The protocol gives guidance for the adoption of national and cooperative measures for the protection of flora and fauna.[385] Protective regulatory measures could include exceptions for the pursuit of traditional activities. These exceptions are limited, however, as concerns about the integral character of protected areas are prevalent.[386]

---

[373] Art. VII, *id.*

[374] Art. VIII, *id.*

[375] Art. XIII, *id.*

[376] Art. XIV, *id.*

[377] Protocol Concerning Specially Protected Areas and Wildlife (SPAW) to the Convention for the Protection and Development of the Marine Environment of the Wider Caribbean Region (Kingston Protocol), Jan. 18, 1990, available online at http://www.cep-unep.org/laws.

[378] Art. 5, *id.*

[379] Art. 7, *id.*

[380] Art. 7(2), *id.*

[381] Art. 21, *id.*

[382] Art. 7(3), *id.*

[383] Art. 8, *id.*

[384] Art. 9, *id.*

[385] Arts. 10 & 11, *id.*

[386] Art. 14, *id.*

5. PROTECTION OF SPECIES

5.1. Protection of Migratory Species

The Bonn Convention on the Conservation of Migratory Species of Wild Animals (CMS) was adopted in 1979.[387] Today, it has seventy-nine parties. The purpose of the convention is the conservation of migratory species including birds, mammals, reptiles, and fish. There are many types of migratory species: stock that breeds on the territory of a state and then migrates into the sea (seals, sea turtles, anadromous fish); highly migratory species that travel between EEZs, and between the EEZ and the high seas (tuna, whales); and territorial species that live in border areas and usually cross jurisdictional boundaries (e.g., gorillas, elephants).

The convention requires the immediate protection of endangered migratory species included in Appendix I and the conclusion of additional agreements for the protection of migratory species included in Appendix II.[388]

States must ensure that species protected under Appendix I are provided appropriate habitats, including habitat restoration if feasible, that would reduce the risk of extinction.[389] State parties are to remove or minimize the circumstances that would impede or prevent the migration of species and are to reduce or control the factors that may endanger species.[390]

The taking of animals listed in Appendix I is subject to exceptions that include taking for:

- scientific purposes;
- the purpose of enhancing the propagation and survival of species; and
- the purpose of accommodating the needs of traditional subsistence.[391]

Other extraordinary circumstances may justify the taking of animals.

To restrict the latitude provided to states under these broad exceptions, the convention emphasizes that the content of exceptions must be precise and be limited in space and in time and that it should not undermine the protection of species. If states decide to apply the exceptions, they must notify the Secretariat as soon as possible.

Appendix II species are to be protected by specific agreements.[392] The convention provides guidelines on what these agreements are to include.[393] The agreements that have been adopted under the convention attempt to preserve: seals in the Wadden

---

[387] Convention on the Conservation of Migratory Species of Wild Animals (Bonn Convention), June 23, 1979, reprinted in 19 ILM 15 (1980) [hereinafter Migratory Species Convention]. The convention entered into force in 1983. Today, the convention includes seventy-nine parties from five geographic regions: Africa (25), America and the Caribbean (6), Asia (9), Oceania (3), Europe (36). See Guide to the Convention on the Conservation of Migratory Species of Wild Animals (Secretariat of the UNEP, Jan. 2002) [hereinafter Guide].

[388] Arts. III and IV, Migratory Species Convention, *id.*

[389] Art. III(4)(a), *id.*

[390] Art. III(4)(b)–(c), *id.*

[391] Art. III(5), *id.*

[392] Art. IV, *id.*

[393] Art. V, *id.*

Sea,[394] bats in Europe,[395] small cetaceans in the Baltic and North Seas,[396] cetaceans of the Mediterranean and the Black Seas,[397] the Siberian crane,[398] slender-billed curlews,[399] the African–Eurasian migratory waterbirds,[400] and marine turtles.[401]

The convention is administered by the Conference of the Parties,[402] which is assisted by a Secretariat[403] and a Scientific Council.[404] In order to implement the convention, states need to establish a focal point, usually a national institution, to ensure that communication between the national and international authorities is maintained at all times.[405]

Overall, the CMS Convention has not enjoyed the attention devoted to other international conventions, such as the CBD. This is because the convention is a highly specialized tool and many of the issues it addresses are not politically charged (which cannot be said for the Biodiversity Convention).[406]

A directive modeled after the Bonn Convention has been adopted by the EU.[407]

---

[394] Agreement for the Conservation of Seals in the Wadden Sea adopted in 1990 that includes prohibitions on takings with limited exceptions. Parties to the agreement are Denmark, Germany, and the Netherlands. The agreement was adopted after an epidemic that wiped out thousands of seals in 1988. Today, seals seem to be rebounding as a result of the measures taken. See Guide, *supra* note 387, at 5.

[395] Agreement on the Conservation of Bats in Europe (EUROBATS). The agreement was adopted in 1991. Bats are protected strictly under this agreement. For instance, the deliberate capture, killing, or keeping of bats are prohibited unless licensed by a competent authority. *Id.* at 7.

[396] Agreement on the Conservation of Small Cetaceans of the Baltic and North Seas (ASCOBANS). The agreement was adopted in 1991. The advisory committee, established at the first meeting of the parties, has already stimulated international cooperation that includes cooperation on the reduction of by-catch by fishing nets. *Id.* at 6.

[397] Agreement on the Conservation of Cetaceans of the Mediterranean and the Black Seas (ACCOBAMS). The agreement was adopted in 1996 and entered into force in 2001. Three Black Sea countries (Bulgaria, Georgia, and Romania) and seven Mediterranean countries (Albania, Croatia, Malta, Monaco, Morocco, Spain, and Tunisia) have ratified the agreement so far. This is the first agreement of its kind to bring countries of the two regions together on an environmental problem. *Id.* at 9.

[398] Memorandum of Understanding concerning Conservation Measures for the Siberian Crane adopted in 1993 and revised in 1998. The agreement is successful in terms of, at least, helping to maintain the population stable. *Id.*

[399] Memorandum of Understanding concerning Conservation Measures for the Slender-billed Curlew adopted in 1994. By 2001, eighteen range states signed the agreement as well as the Birdlife International, the International Council for Game and Wildlife Conservation, and the UNEP/CMS Secretariat. The slender-billed curlew is a migratory shorebird estimated to have declined to fewer than fifty birds. *Id.* at 10.

[400] The Agreement on the Conservation of African Eurasian Migratory Waterbirds (AEWA) was adopted in 1995. It entered into force in 1999. Despite the late entry into force a number of countries and the GEF have already devoted funds for its implementation. *Id.* at 8.

[401] See Memorandum of Understanding on the Conservation and Management of Marine Turtles and their Habitats of the Indian Ocean and South-East Asia adopted in 2000. See also Memorandum of Understanding Concerning Conservation Measures for Marine Turtles of the Atlantic Coast of Africa adopted in 1999. *Id.* at 12. Conservation Plans have been attached to both these Memoranda of Understanding.

[402] Art. VII, Migratory Species Convention, *supra* note 387.

[403] Art. IX, *id.*

[404] Art. VIII, *id.*

[405] Guide, *supra* note 387, at 4.

[406] Biodiversity Convention, *supra* note 82.

[407] Council Directive 79/409/EEC of 2 April 1979 on the conservation of wild birds, OJ L 103/1, 25.04.1979.

5.2. Protection of Whales

One of the most controversial agreements for the protection of mammals is the 1946 International Convention for the Regulation of Whaling.[408] The purpose of the whaling convention is to regulate the development of the whaling industry. As explicitly provided for in the Preamble, the purpose of the convention is to "make possible the orderly development of the whaling industry" through "the proper conservation of whale stocks."[409] The convention has a quite large jurisdictional coverage as it applies to factory ships, land stations, and whale catchers, and it is effective in all waters in which whale hunting is exercised.[410]

The whaling convention established the International Whaling Commission (IWC). The regulatory powers of the IWC are extensive. The IWC can regulate whaling by opening and closing seasons, developing sanctuary areas, and regulating effort activities including size limits for species and methods and equipment used for whaling.[411] When taking regulatory action, the IWC is to take into account the interests of consumers and the whaling industry.[412]

An IWC regulation is binding on state parties unless the parties object within the time limit provided for in the convention. In case state parties object, regulations adopted are not binding on the states that have objected.[413] States can be granted exemptions for scientific purposes. In that case, the party authorized to engage in whale hunting needs to report to the commission on the results of the research accomplished.[414] This scientific exception provision has been used by some whaling countries to evade regulatory measures imposed by the commission.

The international whaling regime drastically changed in 1982 when a moratorium on commercial whaling was adopted. The moratorium was adopted after it was determined that a number of instruments that regulated the allowable quotas of whale taking had failed. From the 1940s to the 1960s, whaling was more or less a *laissez-faire* activity. Several regulatory failures caused a significant decline in stocks undermining, thus, the competitiveness of the whaling industry. From the 1960s to 1970s, measures were introduced for the management of whale hunting, but they were not deemed very successful.[415]

Regulatory failures gave the impetus for the adoption of the moratorium. That the moratorium became politically feasible, however, cannot be simply explained by the failure of regulation. As seen in Chapter 6, other fisheries regimes have experienced regulatory lapses, but the solution hardly has been the adoption of a moratorium.

---

[408] International Convention for the Regulation of Whaling, Dec. 2, 1946, reprinted in 161 UNTS 72.

[409] Preamble, *id.*

[410] Art. I, *id.*

[411] Art. V(1), *id.* See also Schedule as amended by the IWC at the 55th Annual Meeting, Berlin, Germany, June 16–19, 2003.

[412] Art. V(2)(d), Whaling Convention, *supra* note 408.

[413] Art. V(3), *id.*

[414] Art. VIII, *id.*

[415] Steinar Andersen, The International Whaling Commission (IWC): More Failure than Success?, in Environmental Regime Effectiveness: Confronting Theory with Evidence 379 (Edward L. Miles et al., eds., 2002).

The rationale for the adoption of the moratorium can be traced to the changing composition of the IWC that is now comprised not only of whaling states but also of states that have no specific interests tied to whaling. The whaling convention is open to all states. Thus, states with no interest in whaling joined the convention and formed alliances with NGOs that pursued the ban on commercial whaling. Membership in IWC increased from the initial fifteen members to forty members, in what it has been characterized as a *coup d'état* in the IWC.

Some commentators have attributed the support of nonwhaling states to the cause of moratorium as an easy way for these states to bolster their environmental credentials. Countries that had quitted commercial whaling, such as the United States and New Zealand, were strong supporters of the moratorium.[416] Sweden and Finland joined in to improve their environmental images.[417] The leadership of the United States played a successful role in discouraging whaling countries to use the objection procedure provided for in the convention. Japan's administration decided to go along with the moratorium because of U.S. threats that whaling nations would see their fisheries allocations halved in U.S. waters.[418] As a result of a strong backing by a large number of countries, the moratorium effectively stopped commercial whaling. In 1986, there were twelve nations that were involved in whaling and, in 1988, Japan was the last nation to abandon commercial whaling.[419] Today, the term "whaling nation" is equivalent to aboriginal nation.[420]

Japan has continued whaling, using the scientific purposes exception, which other state parties have viewed as a pretext for the continuation of commercial whaling by Japan. Norway resumed whaling in 1993. Because some whale stocks have rebounded, whaling countries have demanded the reopening of commercial whaling. Japan proposed an amendment that would allow for the resumption of "community-based whaling." But the IWC has been unable to move in that direction claiming scientific uncertainty and the lack of an observation scheme that would make feasible the credible monitoring of commercial whaling. Japan's proposal was not successful in the 2003 IWC meeting.[421]

To counterbalance the conservationist bias in IWC, in 1992, Norway, Iceland, Greenland, and the Faroe Islands established the North Atlantic Marine Mammals Commission (NAMMCO).[422] Acceptance of new members in the NAMMCO depends on the approval of old members. This is to avoid the entry of interests that are predisposed against the whaling industry.

Since the enactment of the moratorium, the IWC has been working on a Revised Management Procedure (RMP), the purpose of which is to propose an effective inspection and observation scheme that includes a number of international observers

---

[416] *Id.* at 392.

[417] *Id.* at 397.

[418] *Id.* at 395–96.

[419] *Id.* at 388.

[420] Aboriginal subsistence whaling is allowed for Denmark (Greenland), Russia (Siberia), St. Vincent and the Grenadines, and the United States (Alaska). The IWC is currently striving to establish an Aboriginal Whaling Scheme that would set the standards for aboriginal whaling.

[421] Annual Report of the International Whaling Commission 2 (2003).

[422] Agreement on Cooperation in Research, Conservation and Management of Marine Mammals in the North Atlantic, April 9, 1992, available online at http://www.oceanlaw.net/texts.

and national inspectors for monitoring whaling; a vessel monitoring system; reporting on whales killed; maintaining a register of DNA profiles of whales killed; monitoring the origins of whale products in the market; and funding.

The IWC has supported the development of the Indian Ocean Whale Sanctuary, which was established in 1979 as an area where commercial whaling is prohibited. Two other sanctuaries have been proposed: the South Atlantic sanctuary and the South Pacific sanctuary. But the establishment of these sanctuaries has not been possible because of lack of state support. France, Italy, and Monaco signed an agreement for the establishment of a sanctuary in the Mediterranean Sea for dolphins and whales.[423]

In 2003, the commission noted the increase in the number of whale stocks, especially of Antarctic minke whales and of Antarctic blue whales, but has not undertaken decisive action to lift the moratorium with regard to these stocks. The commission similarly noted its intention to reduce the anthropogenic mortality of North Atlantic whales to zero.[424]

The whaling convention is considered a success in the environmental NGO community, where the moratorium on whale hunting was initially proposed and is still very popular. Environmental NGOs have been able to change the focus of the whaling regime from that of the regulation of the whaling industry to that of a moral obligation to protect whales as marine mammals worthy of conservation. This change in focus of the regime has been resented by whaling states that view the current articulation of the regime as an attempt to impose convictions of morality, prevalent in certain countries, on their nations.

Whether a regime could be characterized as successful is in the eye of the beholder. For a regime established to regulate the whaling industry, the subsequent demise of such industry (and disruption of communities dependent on it) and the alienation of states that are now setting up a competing regulatory regime, are not clear indicators of success.[425]

5.3. Protection of Seals

The protection of seals has been the subject of international attention since the *Behring Sea Seals* arbitration case,[426] which affirmed the freedom of fishing in the high seas but, at the same time, favored the adoption of regulatory measures for the protection of seals. The first treaty to regulate the management of seals was adopted in 1911 among the states of Japan, Russia, the United Kingdom, and the United States. The treaty banned pelagic sealing and established a certification system to prevent illegal trade in seal skins.

The 1911 treaty lapsed in 1941 and a new treaty was adopted in 1957 as an interim treaty among the states of Canada, Japan, Russia (then Soviet Union), and

---

[423] Agreement Concerning the Creation of a Marine Mammal Sanctuary in the Mediterranean, Nov. 25, 1999, available online at http://www.oceanlaw.net/texts.

[424] Annual Report of the International Whaling Commission 3 (2003).

[425] See also Andersen, *supra* note 415, at 380.

[426] See Chapter 1.

the United States.[427] The treaty prohibited pelagic sealing but, for the purposes of research, allowed for the takings of twenty-five hundred seals in the eastern Pacific Ocean and twenty-two hundred seals in the western Pacific Ocean.[428] The treaty expired in 1984.[429]

Today, the taking of Pacific fur seals is prohibited except for aboriginal subsistence purposes. The United States has set up a fund for the Pribilof Islands, the purpose of which is to promote development in the islands that is not dependent on sealing. In general, however, the prohibition of commercial sealing, and the negative publicity associated with the fur industry, has jeopardized the livelihoods of aboriginal people who are dependent on sealing.

Commercial sealing in the Antarctic is also prohibited. A convention was adopted in 1972[430] to regulate commercial sealing in the Antarctic amid fears that the resumption of commercial sealing was eminent. The fears did not materialize and the convention has not been applied. If commercial sealing were to resume, the convention provides regulatory limits on the taking of seals (175,000 crabeater seals, 12,000 leopard seals, and 5,000 weddell seals), but these numbers are subject to scientific assessment.[431] The convention does not provide for the establishment of a commission but instructs the parties to establish a commission if commercial sealing begins.[432]

In addition to the Antarctic Seals Convention, seals in the Antarctic are protected by the Protocol to the Antarctic Treaty on Environmental Protection.[433] The protocol devotes Annex II to the conservation of Antarctic fauna and flora. According to the annex, the taking of native flora and fauna is prohibited except in accordance with a permit. Permits are granted for scientific purposes only or for the provision of specimens to museums, botanical gardens, zoos, and other educational and cultural institutions.[434] Species listed in Appendix A of Annex II – which includes fur seals and ross seals – are designated a specially protected species. A permit for the harvesting of these species cannot be issued but for a compelling scientific purpose and as long as it will not jeopardize the survival or recovery of species.[435]

5.4. Other Agreements

Other agreements that concentrate on the protection of marine mammals include the ASCOBANS Agreement, which has been adopted under the auspices of the Bonn Convention.[436] The purpose of the agreement is to regulate the management

---

[427] Interim Convention on the Conservation of North Pacific Fur Seals, Feb. 9, 1957 amended in 1963, 1969, 1976, 1980. A 1984 protocol did not become effective since the convention expired before the ratification of the protocol.

[428] Arts. III and II(3), *id.*

[429] See Chapter 1, note 215.

[430] Convention for the Conservation of Antarctic Seals, Feb. 11, 1972, available online at http://www.oceanlaw.net/texts.

[431] Annex I, *id.*

[432] Art. 6, *id.*

[433] Protocol on Environmental Protection to the Antarctic Treaty, see *supra* note 359.

[434] Annex II, art. 3(1)–(2), *id.*

[435] Annex II, art. 3(4)–(5), *id.*

[436] See *supra* note 396.

of cetaceans in the Baltic and North seas. The annex to the agreement establishes a conservation and management plan that includes obligations of state parties to develop conditions that would help the survival of animals. The intentional killing of small cetaceans is prohibited and animals caught alive and in good health as by-catches must be released.

The ACCOBAMS Agreement,[437] adopted under the auspices of the Bonn Convention, regulates the conservation of cetaceans in the Black Sea, the Mediterranean Sea, and the contiguous Atlantic area. The annex to the agreement provides for an indicative list of species protected, but the jurisdictional reach of the agreement is not restricted to this list and includes any cetacean that may be in the agreement area accidentally or occasionally.

In order to prevent the capture of small cetaceans as by-catches, efforts have been undertaken to control fishing efforts including the use of long driftnets. In 1989, the Convention for the Prohibition of Fishing with Long Driftnets was adopted in the South Pacific.[438] In 1991, the UN General Assembly adopted a resolution that called for a moratorium on all large-scale pelagic driftnet fishing in the high seas and the semienclosed areas.[439] In 1999, the countries in the eastern Pacific signed an agreement on dolphin conservation, the purpose of which is to reduce the incidental dolphin mortality in the tuna fisheries of the eastern Pacific Ocean to levels close to zero.[440]

Other agreements for the protection of endangered species include several agreements on protection of turtles in different regions of the world.[441] Conventions that deal with specific species include the 1973 Polar Bear Agreement[442] and the 1979 Vicuna Convention. The Convention on Polar Bears prohibits the taking of polar bears unless for scientific or conservation purposes or for the purpose of traditional use by local people using traditional methods.[443] The taking of polar bears is allowed also for the prevention of "serious disturbance of the management of other living resources."[444]

The Convention for the Conservation and Management of Vicuna[445] recognizes boldly that the conservation of vicuna provides an "economic production alternative

---

[437] See *supra* note 397.

[438] Convention on the Prohibition of Fishing with Long Driftnets in the South Pacific, Nov. 23, 1989, reprinted in 29 ILM 1454 (1990).

[439] General Assembly Resolution 46/215, Large-scale pelagic drift-net fishing and its impact on the living marine resources of the world's oceans and seas, A/RES/46/215, Dec. 20, 1991.

[440] Agreement on the International Dolphin Conservation Program, May 15, 1998, available online at http://www.oceanlaw.net/texts. Parties to the agreement are: the United States, Costa Rica, Ecuador, El Salvador, Honduras, Mexico, Nicaragua, Panama, Peru, and Venezuela.

[441] See agreements under Bonn Convention, *supra* note 401. See also Action Plan for the Conservation of Mediterranean Marine Turtles adopted in 1989 and revised in 1999, available online at http://www.oceanlaw.net/texts. See also InterAmerican Convention for the Protection and Conservation of Sea Turtles, Dec. 1, 1996; Cooperative Agreement for the Conservation of Sea Turtles of the Caribbean Coast of Costa Rica, Nicaragua and Panama, May 8, 1998, available online at http://www.oceanlaw.net/texts.

[442] Polar Bear Agreement, Nov. 15, 1973, reprinted in 13 ILM 13 (1973).

[443] Art. III (a)–(b), (d)–(e), *id.*

[444] Art. III(c), *id.*

[445] Convention f.or the Conservation and Management of the Vicuna, Dec. 20, 1979. Parties to the convention are Bolivia, Chile, Ecuador, and Peru.

for the benefit of the Andean population" which makes important "the gradual use [of vicuna] under strict State control."[446] The convention regulates the trade in vicuna as long as the population reaches a level that would allow for meat production and the processing of skins and wool into cloth.[447] Any form of transaction related to vicuna that happens without state authorization is considered illegal.[448] The parties undertake to establish protected areas for vicuna populations and to extend protected areas for the purposes of repopulation.[449]

6. CONCLUSION

Most conservation efforts have concentrated on the protection of nature reserves and most international legislation targets similarly *in situ* conservation. Often, international biodiversity legislation is one-sided. Although many provisions are provided for protected areas, rarely are there provisions to ensure that conservation efforts do not violate the human rights of people who live in and make use of resources of such protected areas. Conservation projects, as with other development projects, often involve the evictions of people from certain areas. Sometimes the evictions are involuntary. Most of the time, the involuntary resettlement of populations is executed without compensation. The infusion of human rights standards into the biodiversity protection regime is, therefore, essential.

Allocation issues are paramount in the Biodiversity Convention. Developing countries have decided to exercise effective control over their biodiversity resources by imposing restrictions on access to those resources. The strategy of removing biodiversity resources from the common heritage regime, which had ended up becoming an open-access regime, was a tit-for-tat response to the intellectual property rights afforded to processed biodiversity. Developing countries decided to assert proprietary rights over their resources in the hope that biotechnology companies, which need these resources for future innovations, will be more willing to share the profits coming from biotechnology inventions. These hopes have yet to materialize, and the restrictions on access to resources have increased the complexity and transaction costs of international seed transfers. An international regulatory instrument is needed that would develop a clear and multilateral approach to the international transfers of germplasm. *Ex situ* conservation, in gene banks and the IARCs, is dependent on these transfers.

---

[446] Art. 1, *id.*
[447] Art. 3, *id.*
[448] Art. 9, *id.*
[449] Art. 5, *id.*

8   Air Pollution

The unrestricted access to the air, a common pool resource, has generated global externalities.[1] Air could be perceived as a public good where no subtractability applies (consumption of air by one person does not affect air consumption by the next person). This is not the case, however, when air quality rather than air quantity is at issue. Air quality is a common pool resource, as the use of the air by polluting industries and technologies diminishes the quality of air available for the average consumer.

With regard to long-range transboundary pollution, the issue of air quality has been addressed on a regional basis among a number of similarly developed countries. A robust regime has been established, therefore, in which there are low incentives for parties to defect.

The effectiveness of ozone regime and climate change regime is not that clear. This is because of the asymmetry between costs and benefits as they are distributed among countries with different priorities, as well as because of the scientific uncertainty and cooperation difficulties fueled by the different socioeconomic conditions of states. The ozone and climate change regimes would not have been articulated but for "side-payments," in the form of additional funding and treaty exemptions, that developed countries agreed to concede to ensure developing countries' cooperation.[2] This is a classic case of the application of the Kaldor-Hicks principle, in which the "winners" have chosen to compensate the "losers" to induce their participation.

The problem with international regimes, based on providing compensation to "losers," is that they would have a tendency to unravel unless the collective net benefits received by developed countries are substantial enough to justify the subsidies paid for the cooperation of developing countries.[3] Such regimes would tend to malfunction if developing countries perceive that the side-payments are not substantial enough to buy their allegiance to the regime and decide against participation. In this chapter, we will examine how divergent perceptions of what is in the interest of each party could threaten to sabotage the ozone and climate change regimes.

---

[1] Joseph R. Bial et al., Public Choice Issues in International Collective Action: Global Warming Regulation at 3, July 20, 2000 available online Social Research Network Electronic Paper Collection http://www.ssrn.com/abstract_id=235285.

[2] *Id.* at 6, 15.

[3] *Id.* at 32.

1. OZONE DEPLETION

The ozone regime sprung from a series of events that led to the indisputable belief that chlorofluorocarbons (CFCs) and other ozone depleting substances are destroying the ozone layer, thereby allowing dangerous levels of ultraviolet radiation to reach the earth. Some of the serious consequences of ozone depletion involve increase in skin cancer, eye cataracts, immune system suppression, and damage to plants. CFCs are the well-known substances that destroy the ozone shield. But other substances could have damaging effects, including carbon tetrachloride, methyl chloroform, and hydrochlorofluocarbons (HCFCs).

CFCs are stable, nontoxic, and nonflammable substances and, thus, useful for a variety of industrial applications. CFCs have been used as replacement for other more dangerous chemicals (such as ammonia in refrigeration). CFCs have been used as coolants in refrigerators and air conditioners, as propellants in air sprays, and in a variety of other household and industrial products. They are also cheap to produce.[4]

Carbon tetrachloride (CT) initially was not considered a substance that required regulation because of misperceptions about its use. Its consumption in 1986 was greater than that of CFCs and halons combined. CT was banned or reduced in most industrialized countries by the time of the adoption of the Vienna Convention and Montreal Protocol because of its toxic and carcinogenic properties. But it was still used in many developing countries in various small operations as solvent, cleaner, or pesticide.[5]

Methyl Chloroform (or *trichloroethane*) initially was not regulated by the Montreal Protocol. It was increasingly understood, however, that it was used widely in many industries, such as aerospace, electronics, and automotive, as solvent or adhesive, and that it was destructive to the ozone layer.

HCFCs initially were perceived as the perfect substitutes for CFCs. HCFCs do not contain significant amounts of chlorine and, therefore, they were not conceived to pose a threat to the ozone layer. Eventually, however, it was realized that HCFCs vary in their chlorine content and ozone-depleting capacity and that some of them exhibit atmospheric lifetimes up to twenty years.

From 1987, the year of the adoption of the Montreal Protocol, to 2002, various other substances have been added to the list of Ozone Depleting Substances (ODS), including hydrobromofluorocarbons (HBFCs), bromochloromethane, methyl bromide, and halons.

1.1. Negotiating Process

Increasing scientific certainty that certain substances do indeed harm the ozone layer provided the impetus for the quick development of the ozone regime. During the adoption of the Vienna Convention, many parties were still quite complacent about the effects of certain chemicals on the ozone layer.

A 1986 joint WMO/UNEP report found that CFC concentrations in the atmosphere had doubled between 1975 and 1985. This report, in conjunction with public

---

[4] Richard Elliot Benedick, Ozone Diplomacy: New Directions in Safeguarding the Planet 10 (1991).
[5] *Id.* at 12.

opinion that grew wary of the ozone hole over the Antarctic, focused the attention of policy makers on the issue of ozone depletion.[6]

In addition to the scientific evidence, industry favored international regulations for the protection of the ozone layer. Industry was concerned that if international regulations were not adopted, competitors in other countries could gain a competitive advantage, as some countries could decide to regulate Ozone Depleting Substances (ODS) but others would not.[7]

Another factor that facilitated the adoption of the international regime is that companies that were to be regulated were small in number and, thus, easy to monitor and supervise. At the time of the adoption of the Montreal Protocol, the CFC industry was very concentrated. There were five major companies in the United States, five in Japan, and nine in the European Community. Du Pont, the largest CFC producer, was responsible for 50 percent of U.S.–CFC production and 25 percent of international production. Imperial Chemical Industries was the largest producer of CFCs in Europe.[8]

The negotiating process as a whole was focused, especially during the Montreal negotiations, when many small informal groups provided the impetus for negotiating action.[9] The Executive Director of the UNEP played a leadership role in the development of the regime. Impediments to negotiations, for instance, the importance of confidentiality of information, were addressed swiftly and effectively.[10] It was quickly realized that developing countries could free-ride on a regime that functions exclusively as a club of developed countries.[11] The involvement of developing countries, therefore, was secured.

The ozone regime negotiations had all the elements that could lead to success:

- issues that could be resolved easily by a multiparty-negotiated contract;
- possible outcomes that all states could accept as equitable;
- simple and clear solutions that are easy to adopt;
- clear-cut and effective compliance mechanisms;
- exogenous shocks and crises; and
- effective leadership.[12]

In the ozone regime, there was a clear identification of industries and products that destroyed the ozone layer. Moreover, the polluting industries were located in a small

---

[6] *Id.* at 14–18.

[7] *Id.* at 31.

[8] Edith Brown Weiss, The Five International Treaties: A Living History, in Engaging Countries: Strengthening Compliance with International Environmental Accords 89 (Edith Brown Weiss & Harold K. Jacobson, eds., 1998).

[9] Benedict, *supra* note 4, at 47.

[10] EC countries claimed that releasing information on CFC production by country would reveal too much information to competitors because there were only a couple of companies that produced CFCs in Europe. The consensus that developed was that countries would report information individually but that information would be released to the public in an aggregate form. See Benedict, *supra* note 4, at 126.

[11] *Id.* at 134.

[12] Oran R. Young, The Politics of International Regime Formation: Managing Natural Resources and the Environment, in Foundations of Environmental Law and Policy 315 (Richard L. Revesz, ed., 1997).

number of states. These industries had found alternatives to CFC production even before the adoption of the Montreal Protocol.

The requirements to cut CFC production with special provisions for developing countries seemed like an equitable, clear, and simple solution for all parties. Compliance was not that difficult to verify because it concentrated on a small number of substances and a small number of producers. In addition, the hole in the ozone layer and the attention it commanded in various media provided the exogenous shock that precipitated the negotiating process. Key individuals exhibited substantial leadership qualities all through the negotiating process.

As the regime has moved into a "second phase" of implementation by developing countries, however, there have been some indicators that it could unravel. Some countries may opt for illegal CFC production and trade as long as the side-payments received from developed countries are not substantial enough to justify forfeiting profits from illegal activities.

1.2. Legislative Instruments

1.2.1. Protection of Ozone Layer

The first instrument adopted to deal with ozone depletion was the 1985 Vienna Convention.[13] This convention is a framework convention, which means that it sets the parameters of action rather than establishes targets and timetables for the phasing out of Ozone Depleting Substances (ODS). The lack of urgency is reflected in the articles of the convention that focus on the exchange of information and the accumulation of scientific evidence rather than the regulation of a specific behavior.

The convention encourages parties to cooperate by using systematic observations, research, and information exchange to "better understand and assess the effects of human activities on the ozone layer."[14] The convention further requests the parties to adopt the appropriate legislative and administrative measures and to ensure the harmonization of such measures.[15] Parties are urged to cooperate in formulating standards and procedures under the convention and the protocols to be adopted[16] and to cooperate with the appropriate international bodies.[17] States are encouraged to undertake research and systematic observations on a number of issues including the physical and chemical processes that may affect the ozone layer, the ensuing human health and biological effects, the climate effects, alternative substances and technologies, and the "related socio-economic matters."[18] Parties undertake the responsibility to establish programs for the systematic observation of ozone layer for the purposes of exchanging information obtained through world data centers in a regular and timely fashion.[19] The parties are encouraged to cooperate in the legal, scientific, and technical fields and to ensure the confidentiality of information

---

[13] Convention for the Protection of the Ozone Layer, Mar. 22, 1985, reprinted in 26 ILM 1529 (1985) [hereinafter Vienna Convention].

[14] Art. 2(2)(a), *id.*

[15] Art. 2(2)(b), *id.*

[16] Art. 2(2)(c), *id.*

[17] Art. 2(2)(d), *id.*

[18] Art. 3(1), *id.*

[19] Art. 3(2) and (3), *id.*

regarded as confidential.[20] Parties are urged to assist with the development and transfer of technology and knowledge.[21]

Parties must report to the Secretariat on measures that they have undertaken to implement the convention.[22] The purpose of the conference of the parties, established under article 6, is to review the implementation of the convention.

At the time of the adoption of the Vienna Convention, the transition from the Vienna provisions to the targets and timetables of the Montreal Protocol[23] seemed to require a leap of faith. It happened, however, and the transition took place much more quickly than was initially expected.

1.2.2. Regulation of Ozone-Depleting Substances

An interesting feature of the Montreal Protocol is that it functions as a protocol in a constant evolution. The protocol was amended several times in 1990 (London Adjustments and Amendments),[24] in 1992 (Copenhagen Adjustments and Amendments),[25] in 1995 (Vienna Adjustments),[26] in 1997 (Montreal Amendments),[27] and in 1999 (Beijing Amendments).[28] The difference between adjustments and amendments is that adjustments accelerate phase-out dates and reductions of already regulated substances.[29] Amendments usually add new substances to the substances already regulated.[30]

Regulatory Measures

The 1987 Montreal Protocol was the first international regulatory effort to control ODS through restrictions in production, consumption, and trade. The first question that had to be addressed was whether to control the production or consumption of ODS.

Some countries argued for control of CFC production. It is easier to regulate production because not that many industries produce CFCs. Because of the wide CFC use, it was claimed, consumption would be more difficult to regulate. Cutting down on production, however, without restricting consumption would not directly affect demand. A robust demand for ODS could give incentives for illegal production.[31]

Article 1(5) defines production as the amount of controlled substances produced minus the amount of substances to be destroyed, by technologies to be approved by the parties, and minus the amount entirely used as a feedstock in the manufacture of

---

[20] Art. 4(1), id

[21] Art. 4(2), *id.*

[22] Art. 5, *id.*

[23] Protocol on Substances that Deplete the Ozone Layer (Montreal Protocol), Sept. 16, 1987, reprinted in 26 ILM 154 (1987).

[24] Adjustments and Amendments to the 1987 Montreal Protocol (London Adjustments and Amendments), June 29, 1990, reprinted in 30 ILM 537 (1991).

[25] Adjustments and Amendments to the 1987 Montreal Protocol (Copenhagen Adjustments and Amendments), Nov. 25, 1992, reprinted in 32 ILM 874 (1993).

[26] Dec. 7, 1995, available online at http://www.unep.org/ozone (UNEP, Ozone Secretariat).

[27] Sept. 17, 1997, *id.*

[28] Dec. 3, 1999, *id.*

[29] Art. 2(9), Montreal Protocol as amended and adjusted, *supra* note notes 23–28.

[30] Art. 9(4), Vienna Convention, *supra* note 13.

[31] Weiss, *supra* note 8, at 138.

other chemicals. The amount of recycled and reused substances is not to be considered as production. Furthermore, under article 1(6), the concept of adjusted consumption was adopted that equals production plus imports minus exports. Beginning in 1993, however, exports to nonparties cannot be subtracted but would have to be counted against domestic consumption.[32] Furthermore, the London amendments added that the amount of recycled and reused substances is not to be considered against domestic consumption.[33]

The 1987 Montreal Protocol basically regulated CFCs and halons.[34] With the additional adjustments and amendments, more substances were put under regulatory control, while, at the same time, the schedule for the elimination of substances was accelerated.

The London amendments placed under control more substances, such as fully halogenated CFCs (Annex B, Group I substances),[35] carbon tetrachloride (Annex B, Group II substances),[36] and methyl chloroform (Annex B, Group III substances).[37] During the negotiations of the London amendments, HCFCs were still viewed as transition substances that were subject to mandatory reporting on production and consumption.[38]

The 1992 Copenhagen amendments promulgated the direct regulation of HCFCs (Annex C, Group I substances).[39] The amendments proceeded to regulate a new group of substances HBFCs (Annex C, Group II substances)[40] and methyl bromide (Annex E).[41]

The 1997 amendments were the only amendments that did not introduce the regulation of new substances. Instead, they sought to strengthen regulatory measures by providing for controls on the trade in ODS[42] and licensing procedures.[43] Even before the 1997 amendments, the protocol contained provisions regarding trade with nonparties. These provisions provided for the gradual elimination of trade between parties to the ozone regime and nonparties to the regime.[44] Additionally, the 1997 amendments provide that if a party is unable to phase out production of a substance for domestic consumption, it must ban the export of the substance to other state parties for purposes other that its destruction.[45] The 1997 amendments provide for licensing procedures to take effect beginning January 1, 2000. It is provided that, by January 1, 2000, or by the date of entry into force of the protocol, each party must establish and implement a system for licensing the import and export of

[32] Art. 3(c), Montreal Protocol as amended and adjusted, *supra* notes 23–28.

[33] Art. 2(6) and art. 1(4), *id.*

[34] Arts. 2A & 2B, *id.*

[35] Art. 2C, *id.*

[36] Art. 2D, *id.*

[37] Art. 2E, *id.*

[38] Art. 7(2), London Adjustments and Amendments, *supra* note 24. See also Annex C, London Adjustments and Amendments, *id.*

[39] Art. 2F, Montreal Protocol as adjusted and amended, *supra* notes 23–28.

[40] Art. 2G, *id.*

[41] Art. 2H, *id.*

[42] Art. 4A, *id.*

[43] Art. 4B, *id.*

[44] Art. 4, *id.*

[45] Art. 4A, *id.*

new, recycled, and reclaimed ODS.[46] Each party must also report to the Secretariat regarding the operation of this licensing system.[47] But there are some exceptions for developing countries.[48]

The Beijing amendments adopted in 1999 introduced even more controls for HCFS (Annex C, Group I substances)[49] and introduced controls on a new substance called bromochloromethane (Annex C, Group III).[50]

The measures established under the Montreal Protocol, as amended and adjusted, regulate ninety-six chemicals. Developed countries must:

- have phased out halons by 1994;
- have phased out CFCs, carbon tetrachloride, methyl chloroform, and HBFCs by 1996;
- have reduced methyl bromide by 25 percent by 1999, 50 percent by 2001, and 70 percent by 2003. Methyl bromide must be phased out completely by 2005;
- reduce HCFCs by 35 percent by 2004, 65 percent by 2010, 90 percent by 2015, and 99.5 percent by 2020, with 0.5 percent permitted for maintenance purposes only until 2030; and
- phase out bromochloromethane immediately.

These deadlines, however, do not apply for uses that parties deem essential.[51] Parties have struggled to define what "essential uses" entail. Providing ODS for "essential uses" must not become the vehicle that would legitimize the wide use of substances otherwise outlawed. The "essential uses" exemption has been applied primarily for laboratory and analytical uses.[52] Requests for "essential use" exemptions have fallen significantly since 1987.[53]

As mentioned earlier, developing countries have been granted exemptions from the stringent provisions of the protocol. A delay of ten years applies for the implementation of the protocol in a developing country whose annual level of consumption of the controlled substances in Annex A is less than 0.3 kilograms per capita until (the latest) January 3, 1999.[54] But this delay applies in order to meet basic domestic needs.

The "basic domestic needs" exemption does not involve production targeted to ODS exports.[55] The Seventh Meeting of the Parties in 1995 provided detailed trade regulations to control better the use of the "domestic use" exception. The parties established "that in order to prevent oversupply and dumping of ozone-depleting substances, all Parties importing and exporting ozone-depleting substances

---

[46] Art. 4B, *id.*

[47] Art. 4B(3), *id.*

[48] Art. 4B(2), *id.*

[49] Art. 2F (8), *id.*

[50] Art. 2I, *id.*

[51] See, e.g., arts. 2A(4), 2B(2), 2C(3), 2D(2), 2E(3), 2G, 2H(5), and 2I, *id.*

[52] See Annex II, Report of the Sixth Meeting of the Parties, Oct. 6–7, 1994.

[53] See UNEP, Handbook for the International Treaties for the Protection of the Ozone Layer 285 (Ozone Secretariat, 2003).

[54] Art. 5(2) (or 0.2 kilograms per capita for substances included in Annex B), Montreal Protocol as adjusted and amended, *supra* notes 23–28.

[55] See Decision I/12C: Clarification of terms and definitions: Basic Domestic Needs, First Meeting of the Parties, May 2–5, 1989.

should monitor and regulate this trade by means of import and export licenses." In order to control trade in regulated substances parties are encouraged to establish, by 1997, a licensing system including a ban on unlicensed imports and exports. Imports and exports, thus, are allowed only between parties to the protocol that have reported on their data and have demonstrated their compliance with the provisions of the protocol. The licensing system was eventually incorporated into the 1997 amendments to the Montreal Protocol.[56]

Another provision that was factored in involved the side-payments that developed countries had to pay to ensure developing countries' cooperation.[57] Developed countries were initially reluctant to make the compliance of developing countries contingent upon financing and technology transfers. But developing countries refused to sign the protocol unless some sort of compensation was provided for their abandoning cheap ODS production and substituting such production with more expensive technology. The protocol provides, therefore, that developing countries that are unable to meet their commitments under the protocol, because of lack of funding or of technology transfers, should notify the Secretariat. The Secretariat must, in turn, notify the Conference of the Parties on the measures to be taken. During the time that the situation in the developing country is evaluated, the non-compliance procedure cannot be initiated.[58]

Joint Implementation

The protocol provides explicitly for the possibility of transferring production of ODS from one party to another so that their "joint production levels" meet the standards established by the protocol.[59] Such transfers of production, however, can happen only after the Secretariat is notified by each of the parties involved in the transfer stating the terms of the transfer and the period for which the transfer applies.

The transfer of production happens under the rubric of "industrial rationalization" endorsed in article 1(8) which provides that:

> Industrial rationalization means the transfer of all or a portion of the calculated level of production of one Party to another, for the purposes of achieving economic efficiencies or responding to anticipated shortfalls in supply as a result of plant closures.

Therefore, Canada, which produces less than 20 percent of the levels allowed for by the protocol, transferred its allowance to the United States.[60]

Article 2(8) of the protocol provides further that state parties that are members of a regional economic integration organization, such as the EU, may decide to fulfill their obligations under the protocol jointly. This "bubble approach" is allowed only if the total combined consumption levels of countries involved do not exceed the levels provided for by the protocol. Members of the regional organization also must fulfill procedural requirements, such as informing the Secretariat of the terms of the agreement for joint implementation.

---

[56] Decision VII/9: Basic Domestic Needs, Seventh Meeting of the Parties, Dec. 5–7, 1995.
[57] Art. 5(6), Montreal Protocol as adjusted and amended, *supra* notes 23–28.
[58] Art. 5(7), *id.*
[59] See art. 2(5), *id.*
[60] Weiss, *supra* note 8, at 139.

Trade Measures

In addition to regulating the production and consumption of ODS, the parties have engaged in efforts to control trade with nonparties to the protocol. Allowing trading with states nonparties to the protocol would have provided a way to evade the provisions of the protocol. Article 4 prohibits the imports and exports of controlled bulk substances,[61] the imports of products containing controlled substances,[62] and the imports of products produced with controlled substances.[63] It is further provided that each party undertakes, "to the fullest practicable extent," to discourage exports to states nonparties of ozone-depleting technology.[64] Nonparty states include states or regional economic organizations that have not agreed to be bound by the control measures in effect for an ODS.[65]

The main issue with trade prohibitions is that they may contravene the articles of the General Agreement on Tariffs and Trade (GATT) incorporated into the WTO. The WTO is based on free trade principles, and trade prohibitions would generally be viewed as antithetical to trade liberalization enunciated by the WTO.[66] Proponents of the ozone trade prohibitions have claimed that prohibitions do not violate free trade principles and that they should be viewed, instead, as exceptions to these principles. Exceptions to free trade are allowed for measures necessary to protect human, animal, or plant life and health and relating to the conservation of exhaustible natural resources.[67] Whether the WTO exceptions apply with regard to trade prohibitions of ODS is still debatable and the Appellate Body has not ruled on this matter.

The Multilateral Fund

Financial assistance was a prerequisite for the developing countries' implementation of the protocol. Article 5(3) of the 1987 version of the Montreal Protocol provided that parties must facilitate bilateral and multilateral aid to developing countries. Article 10 of the London amendments expanded on this obligation by providing for the establishment of a Multilateral Fund, the purpose of which is to finance the "incremental costs" required for compliance with the protocol. The term "incremental costs" caused interpretation problems because it suggests that not all costs of a project are to be financed by the fund, only those incremental costs that would contribute to the control of ozone-depleting substances. The Fourth Meeting of the Parties provides a nonexhaustive list of incremental costs:

1. cost of producing substitutes (e.g., cost of conversion of existing facilities, cost of patents and designs, capital costs of conversion, cost of retraining personnel, and costs of research to adapt technology to the local circumstances);
2. costs arising from premature retirement or enforced idleness of productive capacity;

---

[61] Art. 4(1)&(2), Montreal Protocol, as adjusted and amended, *supra* notes 23–28.
[62] Art. 4(3), *id.*
[63] Art. 4(4), *id.*
[64] Art. 4(5), *id.*
[65] Art. 4(9), *id.*
[66] See Chapter 9, Section 3.
[67] *Id.*

3. costs of establishing new production facilities for substitutes equivalent to the capacity lost when plants were converted or scrapped;
4. costs of adapting manufacturing facilities that used ODS as intermediate goods;
5. costs of premature retirement or replacement of user equipment; costs of collection, recycling, and destruction of ozone-depleting substances; costs of providing technical assistance to reduce consumption and unintended emissions of ozone-depleting substances.

Because this list is nonexhaustive, if parties identify incremental costs other than those mentioned in the indicative list, the executive committee that runs the fund must determine whether they are legitimate costs to be covered by the fund.[68]

The fund is run by an executive committee that is composed of representatives from fourteen countries (seven developed countries and seven developing countries).[69] The executive committee is to discharge its responsibilities in cooperation with the World Bank, the UNDP, and the UNEP.[70] The office of the chairman of the committee is to rotate on an annual basis between developed and developing countries.[71] The functions of the committee are to develop the budget for the multilateral fund and to supervise and guide the administration of the fund. The committee must review at regular intervals the performance reports on the implementation activities undertaken by the fund.

Further bilateral arrangements exist between the fund's executive committee and the World Bank, the UNEP, and the UNDP. The UNEP is to assist "in the political promotion of the objectives of the Protocol," in research and data gathering.[72] The World Bank is the operator of the activities of the fund (to be overseen by the executive committee) and the UNDP undertakes technical and feasibility studies.[73]

Decisions on funding must be made by consensus but, if consensus cannot be reached, by a two-thirds majority comprised of separate majorities of developed countries and developing countries.[74] In order for a country to receive funding, it must complete a report on the domestic effects of its phase-out efforts and list all individual project proposals and their incremental costs. Contributions to the fund are made only by developed countries on the basis of the UN scale of assessment. Contributions by other parties are welcomed.[75]

The fund's operation has encountered difficulties, especially in the implementation of the concept of incremental costs. The fund needs to further develop verification mechanisms that would allow it to uncover potential inaccuracies of states' reporting of incremental costs. The fund must further develop its capacity to determine whether funding received by developing countries is actually channeled to projects financed by the fund.

---

[68] Indicative list of categories of incremental costs, Annex VIII, Report of the Fourth Meeting of the Parties, Nov. 23–25, 1992.

[69] Annex V, para. 2, Report of the Ninth Meeting of the Parties, Sept. 15–17, 1997.

[70] Art. 10(5), Montreal Protocol as adjusted and amended, *supra* notes 23–28.

[71] Annex V, para. 3, Report of the Ninth Meeting of the Parties, Sept. 15–17, 1997.

[72] The Fund functions also as a clearing-house mechanism for the distribution of information and technology. See art. 10(3)(b), Montreal Protocol as adjusted and amended, *supra* notes 23–28.

[73] Annex IX, Report of the Fourth Meeting of the Parties, Nov. 23–25, 1992.

[74] Art. 10(9), Montreal Protocol as adjusted and amended, *supra* notes 23–28.

[75] Art. 10(6), *id.*

Today, the fund finances many projects and the number of projects eligible for funding outnumbers the funding available. Developed countries have been slow to make their contributions to the fund. But the fund procedure for approving projects seems to be rigorous and not particularly subject to political influence.[76]

Technology Transfers

Technology transfers to developing countries to facilitate their phasing-out of ozone-depleting substances were already mentioned in the 1987 version of the Montreal Protocol.[77] The London amendments adopted a stronger language to mandate that parties must "take every practicable step" to transfer technology to developing countries under "fair and most favourable conditions."[78] It is questionable, however, how this provision would be applied in practice because technologies are not in the hands of states but under the control of private companies. Technology transfers have encountered difficulties in the past because of issues of intellectual property rights (e.g., patented technology) that make private companies reluctant to transfer technology and, especially, the know-how that accompanies such technology. Because of the reluctance of private companies to release state-of-the-art technology to developing countries at a low cost, there is a fear that developing countries would revert to ODS technologies.

Monitoring/Administration

Monitoring the ozone regime means self-monitoring. Parties are to provide the Secretariat with reports including statistical data of their production, imports, and exports of all controlled substances. When such data are not available states must supply, at least, the best possible estimates.[79]

The issue of reporting was quite thorny during the negotiations as states realized that companies consider ODS production confidential. The lingering suspicions about false intentional reporting of the data by the industry were verified as a number of companies deliberately understated their 1986 data.[80]

Reporting under the protocol was initially far from exemplary, especially as many countries did not provide any reports, or as the reports they provided were not comprehensive. But the reporting effort has improved over time.[81]

The industry increasingly is taking an active role in monitoring implementation.[82] The construction of ODS producing plants in the developing world, for instance, would undermine the competitive advantage of companies manufacturing new technologies in developed countries. Environmental NGOs have been quite active in monitoring but not as active as in the monitoring of other conventions that are not as technical. Most environmental NGOs lack the expertise and data collection capabilities to independently monitor the agreement. Monitoring by the interested

---

[76] Weiss, *supra* note 8, at 152.

[77] Arts. 5(2), 9, and 10, Montreal Protocol as adjusted and amended, *supra* notes 23–28.

[78] Art. 10A, *id.*

[79] Art. 7, *id.*

[80] These 1986 data were then revised upward when the industry realized that 1986 would be the base year for cut-downs in production and consumption.

[81] Weiss, *supra* note 8, at 153.

[82] *Id.* at 148.

public also would be difficult, as the production of ozone-depleting substances is considered a trade secret and is not released to the public.[83]

The administrative functions of the convention are handled by a Secretariat.[84] The continuous monitoring of the convention is left to the Conference of the Parties. The COP is to clarify the articles of the convention; to review the implementation of the convention and of the protocols; to decide on the removal or addition of controlled substances; and to establish guidelines for reporting.[85]

Implementation

The Copenhagen amendments have introduced a noncompliance procedure,[86] according to which[87] state parties, having reservations about another party's implementation of the protocol, or the noncompliant party itself, may submit their concerns to the Secretariat. The Secretariat, in turn, informs the implementation committee.[88] The implementation committee can undertake, on the invitation of the party concerned, information gathering in the territory of the party.[89] The implementation committee must report to the COP and make recommendations.[90] The report, which does not contain information received in confidence, must be made available to any person on request.[91] All the other information exchanged by or within the committee may be made available to any party on request, but the party must ensure the confidentiality of information received in confidence.[92]

The noncompliance procedure includes an "Indicative List of Measures that Might be Taken by a Meeting of the Parties in Respect of Non-Compliance with the Protocol." These measures encompass appropriate assistance, cautions and suspension of specific rights and privileges associated, for example, with industrial rationalization, production, consumption, trade, transfer of technology, financing, and institutional arrangements.[93] Therefore, the implementation committee can apply both sticks and carrots to ensure compliance with the protocol.

The committee has decided to deal with developing countries' nonimplementation as nonimplementation related to the lack of capacity rather than the intentional flouting of international obligations.[94] Measures, therefore, that would encourage

---

[83] *Id.* at 149.

[84] Art. 12, Montreal Protocol as adjusted and amended, *supra* notes 23–28.

[85] Art. 11, *id.*

[86] The noncompliance procedure is an extension of the procedure that was adopted at the Second Meeting of the Parties. See Report of the Second Meeting of the Parties to the Montreal Protocol on Substances that Deplete the Ozone Layer, Decision II/5, UNEP/OzL. Pro.2/3, at 11, June 1990; Annex III, UNEP/OzL. Pro.2/3, at 40.

[87] Report of the Fourth Meeting of the Parties to the Montreal Protocol on Substances that Deplete the Ozone Layer, Agenda Item 9, Annex IV, UNEP/OzL.Pro.4/15, at 46, Nov. 25, 1992.

[88] *Id.* (the implementation committee consists of ten parties elected by the meeting of the parties for two years based on equitable geographical distribution).

[89] *Id.*

[90] *Id.*

[91] *Id.*

[92] *Id.*

[93] Annex V, *id.*

[94] Albania, for instance, was granted $215,060 to facilitate its compliance with the protocol. See Decision XIV/18: Noncompliance with the Montreal Protocol by Albania, Fourteenth Meeting of the Parties, Nov. 25–29, 2002; Argentina was granted $43,287,750, see Decision XIII/21: Compliance with the

implementation by these countries are often proposed. But the committee has been more aggressive regarding the failure of members of the EU to report (Belgium, Greece, Italy, and Portugal) and has voiced concerns with regard to the reliability of data provided by the Russian Federation.[95]

The Vienna Convention[96] provides further for a dispute settlement mechanism. If the parties fail to agree to arbitrate or adjudicate their disputes, a conciliation commission may be established on the request of one of the parties. The commission will render "a final and recommendatory award, which the parties shall consider in good faith."[97]

1.3. Conclusion

The first phase of implementation of the Montreal Protocol, which involved compliance by developed countries, has proceeded more or less smoothly. The issue today is how the protocol would be implemented by developing countries. Developing countries must begin their phase-out of CFCs, halons, and carbon tetrachloride. This may be particularly onerous for Asian countries that have increased their CFCs consumption as a result of a high rate of economic growth. These countries must now stabilize and reverse their CFC consumption. Given that most developed countries are still selling CFC-based products to developing countries (products that are illegal in the developed world), these sales are likely to affect the dependence of developing countries on CFC products and, actually, fuel future demand for CFCs to maintain these products.[98]

Issues of compliance also emerge as some countries have yet to ratify any of the ozone treaties and certain countries have not ratified the London, Copenhagen, Montreal, and Beijing amendments.[99] Because many countries have not ratified the Copenhagen amendment, the production of methyl bromide could continue uninhibited and spread to even more countries.

In 1996, Russia and countries with economies in transition declared that they were unable to meet the timetable for the phasing-out of CFCs. The GEF allocated $160 million to these countries and the phase-out was completed by 2002. Another $60 million was approved by the GEF to assist Russia and countries with economies in transition in the phasing out of HCFCs and methyl bromide.[100]

A related issue has to do with the illegal trade in CFCs. There has been evidence that new CFC production, under the disguise of recycled CFCs, is smuggled from developing countries into the United States and Europe. Throughout the 1990s, there were reports of rising CFC production in developing countries, the Russian

---

Montreal Protocol by Argentina, Thirteenth Meeting of the Parties, Oct. 16–19, 2001; Bosnia and Herzegovina was granted 1,308,472, see Decision XIV/21: Noncompliance with the Montreal Protocol by Bosnia and Herzegovina, Fourteenth Meeting of the Parties, Nov. 25–29, 2002. By the end of 2002 implementation proceedings had been brought against about 32 countries. Some countries had multiple proceedings brought against them.

[95] Weiss, *supra* note 8, at 153.

[96] See *supra* note 13.

[97] Art. 11, Vienna Convention, *id*.

[98] UNEP, Ozone Secretariat, available online at http://www.unep.org/ozone.

[99] For instance, Russia and China have not ratified the Copenhagen, Montreal, and Beijing amendments.

[100] UNEP, Ozone Secretariat, available online at http://www.unep.org/ozone.

Federation, and other economies in transition. A provision that allows developed countries to keep producing CFCs to meet their own essential uses has been used to legitimize some of this trade. Because CFCs are taxed heavily in most industrialized countries, illegal trading often replaces legal trade. It is estimated that illegal traders smuggle about twenty thousand tons of new CFCs into the industrialized countries every year in the guise of recycled substances.[101] The issue of illegal trade has been addressed by the COP. The COP has examined the need and scope of a universal labeling and classification system for ozone-depleting substances.[102]

Companies that have viewed the ozone regime as a means to level the playing field and secure export markets for their newer technologies are apprehensive of possible regime defections in the developing world. Du Pont reported, before a Congressional Subcommittee on Stratospheric Ozone, that at least six CFC plants have started up or are under construction in less developed countries since the Montreal Protocol was available for ratification. The migration of CFC intensive industries to less regulated countries reduces the benefits of the protocol to developed countries.[103]

If developing countries defect, the regime built around the Montreal Protocol will collapse. Developing countries' compliance has been pursued through financial incentives and transfers of technology. Thus, the question is for how long developed countries will be willing to provide financing to thwart ODS production in the developing world. One should assume that buying out the compliance of potential violators can neither be at any cost nor be perpetual.

2. CLIMATE CHANGE

Climate change involves the change in earth's atmospheric temperature because of emission of various pollutants and, especially, carbon dioxide (CO_2). It is claimed that climate change would cause significant environmental problems, such as increased desertification, the flooding of small islands and other unforeseeable environmental disasters. Most scientists agree today that the earth's temperature has been affected in a discernible manner[104] by various pollutants, but the extent of the change or whether it would bring global or regional detrimental effects is still severely contested.

Large emitters of carbon dioxide, such as the United States, have contested the severity of the greenhouse problem and have proposed to address it not only by cutting emissions of pollutants but also by regulating land use (such as decreasing the amount of deforestation in developing countries, or planting new trees). At the other extreme, the EU has attempted to deal with the problem as a source problem by pursuing emissions reductions.

The greenhouse effect, to which the climate change is attributed, is a natural phenomenon. It happens because naturally occurring greenhouse gases in the

---

[101] *Id.*

[102] See Decision XIV/7, Monitoring of trade in ozone-depleting substances and preventing illegal trade in ozone-depleting substances, Fourteenth Meeting of the Parties, Nov. 25–29, 2002. See also Decision XII/10: Monitoring of International Trade and Prevention of Illegal Trade in Ozone-depleting Substances, Mixtures and Products Containing Ozone-depleting Substances, Twelfth Meeting of the Parties, Dec. 11–14, 2000.

[103] Bial, *supra* note 1, at 23.

[104] Intergovernmental Panel on Climate Change (IPCC), Third Assessment Report, Climate Change 2001 (2001).

atmosphere absorb heat and then emit it back to the earth. As such, the phenomenon is beneficial because, without it, the earth could be a cold planet deprived of life as we know it. The problem is that the increase in the anthropogenic sources of greenhouse gases has destabilized the natural balance between the emissions of greenhouse gases and their removal by sinks (e.g., forests), thereby creating fears of climate change.

Not all countries are expected to be impacted similarly by climate change. Countries that are most threatened include those that are close to the sea – therefore, vulnerable to the rise in sea levels – and countries prone to flooding. Thus, small island states, Bangladesh, and the Netherlands could be affected substantially. China, Russia, Northern European countries, and Canada might benefit through increases in agricultural production. Some studies have indicated possible increase in agricultural production in the United States as well. The costs of abating climate change would be felt mostly in countries that produce greenhouse gases, such as the United States, Canada, China, India, Russia, Japan, and Germany. By 2015, China would be the largest producer of CO_2 and India the second.[105]

Taking action against the consequences of climate change would be costly. Significant technological improvements are required to abate greenhouse gases. Because of the certainty and magnitude of costs but uncertainty of benefits, which would not materialize for decades, countries have not been eager to undertake obligations for the abatement of greenhouse gases. Furthermore, and contrary to the ozone regime, there are no large constituencies (except for environmental NGOs and natural gas companies) in developed countries that favor drastic means to abate climate change. In the ozone regime, by contrast, companies producing ODS demanded global regulatory standards.

For many developing countries, the benefits from the abatement of climate change are long term and uncertain, but the costs are real and seem insurmountable. Thus, developed countries, as in the ozone regime, have made available a number of sidepayments to developing countries. Such side-payments – that include more lenient provisions, different base years and financial assistance – give an opportunity to developing countries to "free-ride" on the cuts performed by developed countries, at least for some time. Given that certain developed countries, notably the United States, however, have refused to participate in the climate change regime, the question is whether these side-payments would be sustainable into the future or whether they would collapse under the weight of other international problems.[106]

2.1. Negotiating Process

The Way to the Climate Change Convention

Awareness with regard to the climate change issue has been developing in international community since 1985. In 1988, governments took action by asking the WHO and the UNEP to establish an Intergovernmental Panel on Climate Change (IPCC). In 1990, the IPCC issued its first report that stated clearly that if states

---

[105] Bial, *supra* note 1, at 25.
[106] *Id.* at 27–30.

continue business as usual, the global temperature will rise in the next century by an average of 0.3 degrees C per decade – a rate of change that has never been encountered before in human history. The report of the panel provided the scientific impetus for the adoption of the Climate Change Convention.

The first dilemma, faced by those who wanted a legal instrument to regulate climate change, was whether to adopt an umbrella legislative instrument – an equivalent to the UNCLOS[107] – Law of the Atmosphere. The other approach was to create a legislative apparatus similar to the ozone regime. In the latter case, a framework convention would be followed by protocols that would increasingly toughen the commitments and impose more demanding timetables. Eventually, the second approach was endorsed because states were apprehensive of the long negotiating cycles suggested by the UNCLOS negotiating process.[108]

The negotiating dynamics that surrounded the climate change regime were quite different from those that shaped the ozone negotiations. Scientific uncertainty with regard to climate change shadowed the negotiations of the Climate Change Convention and the Kyoto Protocol. Furthermore, the costs of preventing or reducing climate change paled vis-à-vis the estimated costs of repairing the ozone hole.[109] Although the ozone negotiations involved a small number of companies located primarily in the developed world, the climate change negotiations involved a wide variety of activities (fossil fuel–dependent industries, automobiles, deforestation, and agriculture) and affected a variety of states with diverse interests. For instance, oil-producing states are quite reluctant to adopt any controls, whereas small island states, fearful of being inundated, are for decisive cutbacks or, at least, greenhouse gases stabilization. Developing countries, that usually present a unified front in international negotiations, were further split into forest-rich countries (for instance, Brazil), reluctant to decrease their deforestation rates, and countries willing to adopt more decisive measures (primarily, small island states).

Developed countries were equally divided among those who advocated stringent controls – represented mainly by the countries of the European Union – and those who were in support of a process instrument with no specific commitments and phase-out timetables – represented primarily by the United States.[110]

The Framework Climate Change Convention was the result of the negotiating wrangling among states. The convention, an outcome of efforts to include, in a single document, diverse outlooks and interests of states, is an opaque international instrument. It suffices to say that after the adoption of the convention both the EU and the United States declared that their negotiating stance had prevailed – the

---

[107] For the UNCLOS, see Chapter 4, Section 3.1.

[108] See Daniel Bodansky, The United Nations Convention on Climate Change: A Commentary, 18 Yale Journal of International Law 451 (1993).

[109] For instance, the costs of repairing the ozone hole were estimated to be $2.7 billion, whereas the costs of reducing greenhouse gases are estimated to be between $800 billion to $3.6 trillion; some project them at much lower levels. See James K. Sebenious, Towards a Winning Climate Coalition, in Negotiating Climate Change: The Inside Story of the Rio Convention 277, 292 (Irving M. Mintzer et al., eds., 1994).

[110] Delphine Borione & Jean Ripert, Exercising Common but Differentiated Responsibilities, in Negotiating Climate Change: The Inside Story of the Rio Convention 77, 82 (Irving M. Mintzer et al., eds., 1994).

EU because of its interpretation of the convention as including commitments, the United States for the exact opposite reason.

The Way to the Kyoto Protocol

The adoption of the framework convention was followed up by a protocol that set up specific targets and timetables for reducing specific greenhouse gases. The Kyoto Protocol tackles the emissions of six greenhouse gases: carbon dioxide (CO_2), methane (CH_4), nitrous oxide (N_2O), hydrofluorocarbons (HFCs), perfluorocarbons (PFCs), and sulphur hexafluoride (SF_6). The commitments made under the Kyoto Protocol were fleshed out during the Marrakesh Accords that provided explicit details on the joint implementation mechanism, the clean development mechanism, and emissions trading.

Negotiations during Kyoto involved some of the same dynamics that characterized the negotiations that led to the Climate Change Convention. However, some states had softened their stance. Oil-exporting states, for instance, resolved that some regulatory measures would be taken so they sought to keep such measures as lenient as possible. Mandatory targets and timetables remained the prerogative of the European Union. The United States advocated the inclusion of market-based mechanisms in meeting the targets. The United States was backed by a number of countries whose revenues are dependent on oil exports.[111] To allow for as much flexibility as possible in meeting targets, the United States sought to regulate as many substances as possible in addition to carbon dioxide. Putting more substances under regulation, however, was technically and politically difficult. First of all, the effects of different greenhouse gases as they interact with each other are not quite clear. Furthermore, the emissions of certain gases, such as agricultural methane, are difficult to monitor because their sources are many and diffuse.

These technical objections, however, to the regulation of more greenhouse gases were overridden as the United States made the adoption of stringent emission targets dependent on an agreement on the regulation of a basket of polluting substances. Eventually, the substances included in the basket of regulated substances were: HFCs, the "substitutes" for CFCs, perfluorocarbons (PFCs), sulphur hexafluoride (SF_6), nitrous oxide (N_2O), methane (CH_4), and CO_2.

Another issue that was quite divisive was the inclusion in the regulatory framework of sinks (forests that absorb large quantities of carbon dioxide emitted). New Zealand, Sweden, and Latvia had estimated that their total net sinks absorbed more than half of their total emissions. Such countries viewed that they could not meet stringent targets without the inclusion of sinks.[112] The United States had proposed to include sinks as part of its comprehensive approach to climate change. Other countries with large sinks, such as developing countries, viewed the regulation of sinks as an intervention into the management of their land-use patterns and, as consequence, an infringement on their sovereignty. Therefore, they resisted the inclusion of sinks. Eventually, sinks were included in the protocol, but with some qualifications.

Joint implementation was contested during the negotiations. The question was whether to allow countries to meet their obligations jointly either by establishing a

---

[111] Michael Grubb et al., The Kyoto Protocol: A Guide and Assessment 64–65 (1999).
[112] *Id.* at 76–79.

bubble for emissions (an ideal candidate for such a bubble was the EU) or through emissions trading. The issue had to do with the pragmatics of emissions. As a matter of fact, and despite the adoption of the Climate Change Convention, emissions had increased for the most part in the industrialized world. Within the OECD countries, between 1990 and the time of protocol negotiations, only two countries had managed to reduce their emissions – Germany and the United Kingdom – for reasons that had nothing to do with a conscious desire to abate carbon dioxide emissions. Emissions in France and Switzerland had remained basically stable, but in other EU countries emissions had increased. In the United States, at the time of protocol negotiations, emissions had risen by 9 percent above 1990 levels.

Against these increases in the Western world, in Eastern Europe the reverse phenomenon was taking placing. A decline in emissions as production collapsed after the recession that followed the demise of communist regimes. Much of the technology used in Eastern Europe was quite outdated and needed to be replaced with new technology. New replacement technology could be state-of-art technology that would assist in the global reduction of greenhouse gases. In the former Soviet Union, declines in greenhouse gases were even more significant, with the most serious reductions experienced in Ukraine and the Baltic states.[113]

For those countries that experienced higher emissions than those in 1990 (1990 was the baseline year), an easy way to meet their emissions targets would be to buy emission credits for countries that had enough to spare them. Such emissions trading would help many developed countries meet their targets in an inexpensive way and would transfer much needed modern technology to Eastern European countries. No wonder then that, after skillful persuasion by the United States, Russia and Eastern European countries strongly favored emissions trading. Other countries quickly caught up with the implications of an emissions trading scheme. Japan, for instance, was fearful that the United States would use its political muscle on Russia and monopolize the credit surplus of that country.[114] By contrast, developing countries opposed emissions trading because such trading would assist the United States in avoiding taking significant abatement action within its borders.[115] Eventually, a simple article on emissions trading was adopted that basically stated that emissions trading was an alternative that could be applied under the protocol.

Joint implementation was resisted initially, both as applied among developed countries and, as it could be implemented, between developed and developing countries. It was eventually adopted, under the rubric of "joint implementation," for collaborative efforts among developed countries and, under the name Clean Development Mechanism, for joint implementation projects between developed and developing countries. Whether joint implementation would be included in the protocol was probably a foregone issue. This is because the Climate Change Convention included already provisions for joint implementation and many countries were eager to obtain cheap emission credits (by doing projects in developing countries or creating bubbles with neighboring countries). Thus, ethical considerations (that is, whether it is ethical for a country to reduce its emissions by buying credits in a developing country)

---

[113] *Id.* at 83.
[114] *Id.* at 94.
[115] *Id.* at 95.

and technical concerns (that is, protection against potential abuse of baselines in developing countries) were pushed aside.

At Kyoto, the industry appeared even more divided than during the Climate Change Convention negotiations. The BP and the Royal/Dutch Shell, because of their gas reserves, supported efforts to curb greenhouse gas emissions. Other energy companies, however, such as Exxon/Mobil, were still putting pressure to resist firm commitments. Other sectors of the economy, such as the insurance sector, potentially adversely affected by abrupt weather phenomena, gas companies, and even some auto manufacturers saw more benefits in establishing targets and timetables than in procrastinating further the adoption of regulatory measures.[116]

2.2. Legislative Instruments

2.2.1. Convention on Climate Change

Obligations

The Climate Change Convention is a framework convention. Its purpose is to set the general tone for the future climate change discussions and to compromise in a single text the often irreconcilable interests and ideologies of state parties. Because of this reality – a reality for every framework convention – the convention straddles the world of firm commitments and vague hortatory articulations.

Article 4 surprisingly contains in its title the word "commitment." Article 4 is overall a procedural article, but it is not deprived of substance. It provides, for instance, that state parties must establish national inventories for greenhouse gas emissions and removals by sinks by using comparable methodologies.[117] The inclusion of the term "comparable methodologies" was subject to controversy during the negotiations, as developing countries were aware of not having at their disposal methodologies comparable with methodologies available in developed countries.

Other provisions include the obligation of parties to formulate, implement, and publish national and regional programs designed to mitigate climate change and climate change effects,[118] to promote the transfer of technology,[119] and to promote the development of sinks.[120] Another provision, that would potentially affect compliance, is the requirement to "communicate to the Conference of the Parties" information related to the implementation of the convention.[121]

Article 4(2) has been interpreted by some to include specific commitments on sources and sinks. More specifically, the convention provides that Annex I countries – that is, developed countries – must report on national policies and measures to limit emissions and to increase the number of sinks[122] within six months after the entry into force of the convention.[123] Policies must be adopted "with the aim [for states] of

---

[116] *Id.* at 257–59.
[117] Art. 4(1)(a), United Nations Convention on Climate Change, May 9, 1992, reprinted in 31 ILM 849 (1992)[hereinafter Climate Change Convention].
[118] Art. 4(1)(b), *id.*
[119] Art. 4(1)(c), *id.*
[120] Art. 4(1)(d), *id.*
[121] Art. 4(1)(j), *id.*
[122] Art. 4(2)(a), *id.*
[123] Art. 4(2)(b), *id.*

returning individually or jointly to their 1990 levels" of the emissions of greenhouse gases.[124] This provision, in combination with the requirement to return by the year 2000[125] to earlier levels of emissions, was used by European countries to make the argument that the convention actually included a commitment to cut back emissions by the year 2000 to 1990 levels.

However, because article 4 is drafted in an opaque fashion, with no strong connection between paragraphs 4(2)(a) and 4(2)(b), whether the convention establishes a real enforceable commitment was contestable.

The Conference of the Parties must review these contested targets and timetables. The review must be based on the best scientific information and "appropriate action" must be taken after the review has taken place. No details are provided, however, about what this appropriate action may entail.[126]

Overall, article 4(2), which is the closest to a specific commitment, applies only to developed countries as specified in Annex I. Annex I includes also countries with economies in transition that expressed difficulties in meeting commitments under article 4(2). Therefore, further provisions were adopted that expressly allow countries with economies in transition "a certain degree of flexibility" in meeting the requirements of article 4(2).[127]

Some have characterized the Climate Change Convention as a comprehensive convention, in that it attempts to regulate all greenhouse gases and not just carbon dioxide.[128] The convention is comprehensive also because it focuses on net emissions – that is total emissions by sources minus the removal by sinks.[129]

Joint implementation is included timidly in the convention[130] because it is provided that parties can implement the convention jointly with other parties. The convention alludes to the fact that the Conference of the Parties must review decisions on joint implementation.[131] Article 3(3) also provides that "[e]fforts to address climate change may be carried out cooperatively by interested Parties."

Regarding the costs of complying with the convention, it is provided that "the agreed full costs incurred" by developing countries under article 12 – that is, the reporting costs – are to be covered by developed countries.[132] With regard to other implementation costs, the convention is not as clear. Developed countries must provide the financial resources to meet "the agreed full incremental costs of implementing measures" by developing countries.[133] Thus, for implementation costs to be funded, they have to be mutually agreed on by developed and developing countries. However, what full incremental costs would involve could be debatable. For instance, the additional costs of building a renewable energy plant, instead of a coal-run facility, should be covered, but the opportunity costs of not decimating a

---

[124] *Id.*
[125] Art. 4(2)(a), *id.*
[126] Art. 4(2)(d), *id.*
[127] Art. 4(6), *id.*
[128] Art. 3(3), arts. 4(2)(a) and 4(1)(a), *id.*
[129] Art. 3(3), arts. 4(1)(b) and 4(2)(c), *id.*
[130] Art. 4(2)(a), *id.*
[131] Art. 4(2)(d), *id.*
[132] Art. 4(3), *id.*
[133] *Id.*

rainforest are not clearly covered. According to a generous interpretation, any activity that has as aim to reduce emissions, which would have not happened under a business-as-usual scenario, should be covered. From another point of view – one that was endorsed by international institutions – for a project to be eligible for funding it has to demonstrate some global environmental benefit.

It must be mentioned that article 4(3) covers reporting and other implementation costs but not adaptation costs, as adaptation costs are considered to have local benefits. Adaptation costs may include the removal of populations from coastal areas caused by rising sea levels. Coastal states and small island states wanted to adopt specific provisions on compensation against future disasters as a result of climate change. But eventually their concerns were addressed rather cursorily.[134] Technology transfer provisions were diluted significantly from those initially proposed by developing countries. Technology transfers were adopted eventually as an obligation of developed states to facilitate transfers of technology to developing countries.[135]

Some treaty provisions address the concerns of the most vulnerable countries which include small island countries,[136] the least–developed countries,[137] and the countries that are likely to be affected by measures to combat climate change – that is, fossil fuel–producing countries.[138]

Administrative Provisions

The convention is administered by a Conference of the Parties (COP), which is the supreme body of the convention.[139] The purpose of the COP is to keep under regular review the implementation of the convention. This review takes place by assessing, *inter alia*, all information provided by the parties on the implementation of the convention and the effects observed, as a result of measures undertaken, including environmental, economic, and social effects.[140] The COP must additionally coordinate the measures adopted by the parties[141] and guide the development and refinement of comparable methodologies for the assessment of greenhouse emissions and removals by sinks.[142] The COP "shall consider and agree on methodologies [for greenhouse emissions and removals by sinks] at its first session and review them regularly thereafter."[143] The COP must further agree on methodologies for the development of national inventories[144] and agree on criteria for joint implementation.[145] NGOs can maintain an observer status at the COP.[146]

The Secretariat is appointed by the Conference of the Parties and has general administrative functions as in most international environmental conventions.[147] The

---

134 See art. 4(4) and (8), *id.*
135 Art. 4(5), *id.*
136 Art. 4(8)(a), *id.*
137 Art. 4(9), *id.*
138 Art. 4(10), *id.*
139 Art. 7(2), *id.*
140 Art. 7(2)(e), *id.*
141 Art. 7(2)(c), *id.*
142 *Id.*
143 Art. 4(2)(c), *id.*
144 Art. 4(1)(a), *id.*
145 Art. 4(2)(d), *id.*
146 Art. 7(6), *id.*
147 Art. 8, *id.*

Secretariat cannot comment on states' implementation but can help to disseminate the information contained in the reports submitted by states and can report on its own activities.

A Subsidiary Body for Scientific and Technological Advice (SBSTA) assists the COP in the execution of its functions. The purpose of this body is to provide scientific information and advice and is comprised of government representatives that are experts in climate change issues.[148] A subsidiary body is established for implementation the purpose of which is to assist the COP in assessing and reviewing implementation.[149]

The negotiations on the administration of the financial mechanism, established under the convention, caused some skirmishes between developed and developing countries. Developed countries wanted the mechanism, which was provisionally to be included under the auspices of the GEF, to be as independent as possible from the COP. Developing countries desired the opposite. Eventually, it was agreed that the financial mechanism would have "an equitable and balanced representation of all Parties within a transparent system of governance."[150] The degree of independence of the financial mechanism remains unclear. The financial mechanism is to function under the guidance of the COP and must be accountable to the COP. The COP must decide on the policies, programs, criteria, and eligibility criteria that the financial mechanism would apply.[151] However, if another entity, such as the GEF or the World Bank, is entrusted with the fund, such entity would have decisive authority over its functioning.[152]

Principles and Guidelines

In addition to the semiregulatory and administrative provisions examined here, the convention is important because it rearticulates in a binding text some principles of international law that – although included in other instruments – had yet to be fully fledged. Such is the principle of common but differentiated responsibilities that is articulated in the preamble[153] and also in the principles section.[154]

Other principles that are articulated have less of a weight in terms of producing concrete outcomes. The provision that countries must protect the climate system for the present and future generations is more of a guiding wish rather than an applicable principle.[155] The convention includes a diluted version of the precautionary principle stating that the lack of total scientific certainty should not be used as a reason for postponing action; and providing, simultaneously, that policies and measures to deal with climate change should be cost-effective.[156] The rest of the principles focus on sustainable development and the fears of developing countries that measures to curtail climate change could become an arbitrary restriction on trade.[157]

[148] Art. 9, *id.*
[149] Art. 10, *id.*
[150] Art. 11(2), *id.*
[151] Art. 11(1), *id.*
[152] Art. 11(3), *id.*
[153] Para. 6, Preamble, *id.*
[154] Art. 3(1), *id.*
[155] *Id.*
[156] Art. 3(3), *id.*
[157] Art. 3(4) and (5), *id.*

Despite all the wrangling and recriminations that surrounded the Climate Change Convention by the end of 1993 – merely one and a half years after its adoption – the convention was ratified by fifty countries. This was the number of countries required to have the convention enter into force.

2.2.2. Regulation of Greenhouse Gases

The Kyoto Protocol brings to the climate change regime the specific commitments that were obfuscated in the Climate Change Convention. Developed countries (included in Annex I) of the protocol shall ensure that their carbon dioxide and other greenhouse gas emissions do not exceed their assigned amounts (prescribed in Annex B).[158] The goal here is a reduction of emissions by, at least, 5 percent below the 1990 emission levels for the commitment period between 2008 and 2012.[159] The year 1990 is used as a base year for CO_2, methane and nitrous oxide. The year of 1995 is used as the base year for industrial trace gases (HCFs, PFCs, and SF6).[160] The gases controlled under the protocol are included in Annex A of the protocol.

The protocol provides, but not in terms of a specific obligation, that each developed country must have achieved by 2005 "demonstrable" progress toward meeting the objectives of the protocol. "Demonstrable" progress, however, is not further clarified.[161]

The parties can meet their obligations either by reducing their emissions or increasing their removals by sinks or both. The protocol seeks to limit, however, the type of sinks that could be used to offset emissions to "direct human-induced land-use change and forestry activities," that is, afforestation, reforestation, and deforestation. Both emissions by sources and removals by sinks are to be reported "in a transparent and verifiable manner" to be reviewed by expert teams pursuant to the decisions of the Conference of the Parties.[162] The Conference of the Parties must decide how land-use, land-use change, and forest (LULUCF) activities could be used as credits against the Assigned Amounts (AAs) of emissions prescribed in Annex I. According to SBSTA, an adjustment to a state's AAs shall be equal to verifiable changes in carbon stocks during the period between 2008 and 2012 resulting from direct human-induced activities of afforestation, reforestation and deforestation undertaken since January 1, 1990.[163]

In further meetings of the parties, it was defined that the "assigned amounts of emissions"[164] would be calculated in terms of assigned amount units (AAUs) or in terms of removal units (RMUs). Removal units could be further expressed as Emission Reduction Units (ERUs) (for joint implementation reductions among developed countries) or as certified emission reductions (CERs) (for reductions accomplished within the CDM). All the AAUS and RMUS (including ERUs and

---

[158] Art. 3(1), Protocol to the United Nations Framework Convention on Climate Change, Dec. 11, 1997, 37 ILM 22 (1998) [hereinafter Kyoto Protocol].
[159] *Id.*
[160] Art. 3(8), *id.*
[161] Art. 3(2), *id.*
[162] Arts. 3(3) & 4(4), *id.*
[163] Grubb, *supra* note 111, at 120. See arts. 7–8, Kyoto Protocol, *supra* note 158. See also art. 3(10), (11) and (12), *id.*
[164] Art. 3(1), *id.*

CERs) are practically the accounting equivalents of assigned amounts of emissions (AAs). Each unit is equal to one metric ton of emissions in CO_2-equivalent terms. The difference is that AAUs are issued based on the assigned amount of emissions, whereas RMUs are issued on the basis of sink activities.

Flexibility for countries with economies in transition to establish a year different from 1990 as a base year is explicitly provided for in the protocol.[165] Furthermore, countries can use extra reductions in emissions – above those prescribed by the protocol – to meet their obligations in subsequent commitment periods.[166] However, countries cannot borrow against subsequent periods.

The "bubble concept" is extensively articulated in the protocol and is particularly relevant to the EU countries that wished to be viewed as a single implementation unit.[167] Countries that have agreed to meet their commitments jointly shall be considered to have met their commitments if their total emissions do not exceed the assigned emissions.[168] The protocol assigns uniform emission reductions for all EU countries at 8 percent. But, given the acceptance of the "bubble concept," these reductions could be reassigned among the EU countries based on their capacities, current emissions, and willingness to move on with abatement technologies. An agreement of countries to enter into a "bubble arrangement" must remain in effect for the commitment period.[169] Any change in the composition of the regional organization, after the adoption of the protocol, must not affect the commitments undertaken under the protocol.[170] In other words, the inclusion of new members from Eastern Europe under the umbrella of the European Union does not mean that the reduced emissions of Eastern European countries could be used to offset the increase or the stabilization of emissions in other member states. The protocol provides a menu of indicative measures that parties that have undertaken commitments under the protocol should consider for meeting their goals: enhancement of energy efficiency,[171] the protection and enhancement of sinks and reservoirs,[172] the increase in the use of renewable forms of energy and carbon sequestration technologies[173] and the reduction of market imperfections (such as subsidies, fiscal exemptions in all greenhouse gas emitting sectors).[174] States must take measures to reduce the emissions of greenhouse gases from aviation and marine bunker fuels by working with the Civil Aviation Organization and the International Maritime Organization.[175] Discussions on emissions trading were heated because many countries rushed to capture the surplus of emission credits of the Eastern European countries and, especially, Russia. Japan and the European Union states wanted to make sure that emissions trading was competitive so as to prevent the United States from acquiring all of Russia's

---

[165] Arts. 3(5) and (6), *id.*
[166] Art. 3(13), *id.*
[167] Art. 4, *id.*
[168] Art. 4(1), *id.*
[169] Art. 4(3), *id.*
[170] Art. 4(4), *id.*
[171] Art. 2(1)(a)(i), *id.*
[172] Art. 2(1)(a)(ii), *id.*
[173] Art. 2(1)(a)(iv), *id.*
[174] Art. 2(1)(a)(v), *id.*
[175] Art. 2(2), *id.*

emissions credits.[176] Eventually, the provision that was included was quite brief; it left the decision about the procedures of emissions trading to the COP that must provide the guidelines for the verification, reporting, and accountability of emissions trading. It is provided that any emissions trading should be supplemental to efforts undertaken domestically to achieve the reduction of emissions.[177]

Joint implementation among developed countries[178] was further elaborated under the Kyoto Protocol with more specific and detailed provisions. For the purposes of meeting their commitments under article 3, Annex I parties may transfer to or acquire from other parties emission reduction units (ERUs) resulting from projects aimed to reduce emissions by sources or removals by sinks. The acquisition of emission reduction units does not mean that parties must forfeit their obligation to take domestic action.[179] Parties that do not fulfil their reporting requirements cannot participate in any ERUs schemes.[180] The COP must establish guidelines for the effectuation of joint implementation and, especially, guidelines on reporting and verification.[181]

The protocol assigns emission targets to countries with economies in transition well below their current emissions. These countries could, thus, get a windfall of credits for reductions achieved because of their economic decline. Countries with economies in transition could trade their credits with countries that have increased their emissions. This could lead to what some have called "hot air trading" dampening incentives for countries to introduce emission reduction controls. As anticipated, after the protocol was adopted, Japan announced a series of joint implementation projects with Russia.[182]

The negotiations on the Clean Development Mechanism (CDM) were even more controversial. CDM is an elaborate name for joint implementation projects between developed and developing countries. The CDM is an attempt to achieve simultaneously environmental protection and local economic development through private financing. The protocol provides explicitly for a Clean Development *Mechanism* and not a Clean Development *Fund* (though the possibility of a fund was discussed). Developing countries were in support of a mechanism that would essentially "green" private investment as a supplement to Official Development Assistance (ODA) that they saw declining. Because developing countries have not undertaken express commitments under the protocol, the concern was to ensure that projects that qualify for joint implementation are projects conceived to advance the goals of the protocol and not projects that would have been undertaken anyway.

The mandate of the CDM is twofold: to help developing countries achieve sustainable development, and to assist developed countries in meeting their commitments by providing the latter with certified emissions reductions (CERs).[183] Such CERS are granted for greenhouse abatement projects developed countries

---

[176] Grubb, *supra* note 111, at 129.

[177] Art. 17, Kyoto Protocol, *supra* note 158.

[178] See art. 6, *id.*

[179] Art. 6(1)(d), *id.*

[180] Art. 6(1)(c), *id.*

[181] Art. 6(2), *id.*

[182] Grubb, *supra* note 111, at 132.

[183] Art. 12(2), Kyoto Protocol, *supra* note 158.

undertake in developing countries. To ensure that the CDM mechanism functions as designed supervision and monitoring procedures are put in place for the functioning of the mechanism. It is provided that emission reductions resulting from CDM projects must "be certified by operational entities," which are to be designated by the Conference of the Parties.[184] Emission reductions must be granted based on "real, measurable and long-term benefits related to climate change."[185] Emission reductions must be "additional" to any emission reductions that would occur in the absence of the certified activity.[186] This provision of additionality has created some confusion about which projects would qualify as additional.

The CDM is administered by an executive board.[187] The Conference of the Parties, at its first meeting, must elaborate on the procedures to be applied to the CDM so as to ensure transparency, efficiency, and accountability through independent auditing and verification of project activities.[188] The protocol provides that proceeds from certified projects – that are projects that have been certified as appropriate for joint implementation through the CDM – can be used to cover the administrative expenses of the CDM. Such proceeds can be used to assist further vulnerable developing countries to meet the costs of adaptation to climate change.[189]

The CDM mechanism provides for early crediting – that is, for crediting of certified emission reductions achieved through joint implementation projects with developing countries starting from 2000, the beginning of the commitment period, up to 2008.[190] This is because many countries and international funding agencies have been involved already in such projects. Although removal of greenhouse emissions by sinks could be subject to joint implementation projects among developed countries, the use of sinks is still a controversial activity in CDM projects. Developing states are concerned that if sinks are included in the CDM equation, some of their natural resources would fall under international scrutiny.

Other provisions that affect the interests of developing countries include articles 10 and 11. These articles do not contain substantive obligations but encourage the transfer of technologies, the development of national and regional programs, and the development of systematic observation systems and data archives.

Monitoring is based on self-reporting. Emissions by sources and removals by sinks must be reported "in a transparent and verifiable manner."[191] Methods to calculate emissions and removals must be based on the methods accepted by the Intergovernmental Panel on Climate Change (IPCC) and the COP.[192] Before the commitment period begins, each state must establish "a national system" for estimating emissions and removals based exactly on the methodologies designated by the IPCC and the COP.[193] National inventories of emissions and removals must be submitted to the COP.[194] The information submitted by the parties must be reviewed by

[184] Art. 12(5), *id.*
[185] Art. 12(5)(b), *id.*
[186] Art. 12(5)(c), *id.*
[187] Art. 12(9), *id.*
[188] Art. 12(7), *id.*
[189] Art. 12(8), *id.*
[190] Art. 12(10), *id.*
[191] Art. 3(3), *id.*
[192] Art. 5(3), *id.*
[193] Art. 5(1) and (2), *id.*
[194] Art. 7, *id.*

"expert review teams" as decided by the COP.[195] These expert review teams are not comprised only of government representatives, as is the norm in other conventions. Instead, these review teams could be composed of experts selected from a number of experts proposed by the parties and from the staff of intergovernmental organizations under the guidance of the COP.[196]

Emissions trading, the CDM, and joint implementation are the three mechanisms that provide some flexibility in meeting the obligations established under the protocol. Flexibility was welcomed by developing countries because of their realization that private investment could be used to spearhead their economies.

Overall, the protocol has been characterized as a remarkable achievement that brought together in an innovative fashion diverse state interests. The EU and small island states obtained targets and timetables for which they campaigned all through the Climate Change Convention negotiations. The United States, and other countries concerned that they are not able to meet their commitments, have been able to build in the protocol a significant amount of flexibility.[197]

2.2.3. Market-Based Regulation of Greenhouse Gases

Joint implementation, emissions trading, and the CDM were further clarified during the Marrakesh Accords. During the Marrakesh Accords, the parties selected the members of the CDM's executive board, which had its first meeting during the seventh conference of the parties. Other decisions taken had to do with the operating modalities of joint implementation and emissions trading. The Marrakesh Accords further provided that the use of flexible mechanisms must supplement domestic action and that parties – in order to be eligible to participate in the flexible mechanisms – must have ratified the Kyoto Protocol and must be in compliance with their reporting requirements. Flexible mechanisms must be open and transparent and allow for participation by NGOs (under the supervision of their governments).

The Marrakesh Accords clarify the following points with regard to joint implementation:

- *the type of projects* that are eligible for joint implementation. Such projects could involve plant replacement (the replacement of a coal plant with a more efficient combined heat plant) or land reforestation. Projects most often undertaken would be those that involve the cooperation of developed countries with countries with economies in transition because of the cost savings that could be achieved through the improvement of infrastructure in such countries;
- *procedures* to be followed for a project to qualify as a joint implementation project. Two types of procedures – namely, track one and track two – are made available.

  a.   Under a track one approach, a state that would issue the ERU meets all the eligibility requirements (e.g., ratification and regular reporting). In that case, the state can issue the ERU without further complications.

---

[195] Art. 8(1), *id.*
[196] Art. 8(2), *id.*
[197] Grubb, *supra* note 111, at 150–51.

b.   Under a track two approach, the state that grants the ERU does not meet the eligibility requirements. In that case, the ERUs granted must be monitored by the Supervisory Committee established under article 6.[198]

The CDM mechanism allows developed countries to implement projects that reduce emissions in the territory of developing countries. The certified emission reduction units (CERs) generated help Annex I countries meet their emission targets and simultaneously assist developing countries in achieving development. A CDM project might, for instance, involve a rural electrification project using solar panels or the reforestation of land. For a CDM project to be certified as such, it must be approved by the designated national authority of both Annex I and non–Annex I countries.

The executive board of CDM started to operate at the seventh COP. The ten members of the board are drawn from a selection of candidates proposed by all the parties but they act in their personal capacity. The COP has established six steps for the functioning of the CDM, usually known as the CDM project cycle:

- The initial task of the board of the CDM is to accredit the operational entities. The purpose of these entities is to validate proposed CDM projects, on the basis of project design documents, to check the project's baseline, and to establish a monitoring plan.
- After the project is validated by the operational entities, the board will register the project.
- Once the project is up and running, the participants will monitor it.
- A different operational entity, from the one initially designated, will verify the monitored emission reductions and certify the emission reductions as CERs.
- On the basis of recommendation of this latter operational entity, the executive board will issue the CERs and distribute them to project participants as requested.
- The CERs generated under the project are subject to a levy called the "share of proceeds." This levy, which is made up of 2 percent of CERs from each project, is to be paid into an adaptation fund to help particularly vulnerable developing countries to adapt to the adverse effects of climate change. Another percentage, yet to be determined, will cover the costs of administration of CDM.[199]

The Marrakesh Accords clarified the emissions trading provisions. Annex I countries can acquire assigned amount units (AAUs) from other Annex I parties that find it easier to meet their emission targets. This gives the parties an opportunity to reduce emissions in whichever way is less costly, independent of which party strictly meets emission targets. Annex I parties also can trade ERUs (from joint implementation), CERs (from CDM projects), or removal units (RMUs) (from sink activities). The transfer and acquisition of units are recorded in national registries. In order to address concerns that Annex I countries may oversell emission credits and, thus, may not meet their emission targets, each party must hold a minimum level of ERUs, CERs,

---

[198] Decision 16/CP.7, Guidelines for the implementation of Article 6 of the Kyoto Protocol, FCCC/CP/2001/13/Add.2, Section II, 2001.

[199] Decision 17/CP.7, Modalities and Procedures for a Clean Development Mechanism, as Defined in Article 12 of the Kyoto Protocol, FCCC/CP/2001/13/Add.2, Section II, 2001.

AAUs, and RMUs in their national inventories. This is named the "commitment period reserve," and it is calculated as 90 percent of a state's assigned amount as defined in article 3.[200] For trading to take place in an orderly fashion, national registries have to be established. Each party should have a national registry of ERUs, CERs, AAUs, and RMUs. Transfers and acquisitions of ERUs, AAUs, CERs, and RMUs must not happen without their inclusion into the national registries.

In addition to national registries, a CDM registry is established and maintained by the executive board of CDM. This registry contains the CER amounts of nonAnnex I countries participating in the CDM. A transaction log is established to be maintained by the Secretariat of the protocol. The purpose of the transaction log is to verify all transactions of ERUs, CERs, AAUs, and RMUs, including the issuance, transfers, acquisition, cancellation, and retirement of credits. If a transaction seems not to be in order, the Secretariat must prevent its execution. The international registry could assume a role similar to a securities and exchange commission as some have proposed. In that capacity, the international registry would ensure that national registries are in compliance with the set rules and standards through reporting, random inspections, and disqualification in cases of noncompliance.[201]

Land-use, land-use change, and forestry (LULUCF) crediting was further clarified during the Marrakesh Accords. LULUCF activities are eligible for crediting against the AAUs in accordance with article 3(4) of the Kyoto Protocol. For such activities to qualify as credits against emissions, they must be based on sound science and be accounted in a consistent fashion. Some examples of LULUCF activities include forest management, cropland management, grazing, land management, and revegetation.

An important concern, during the Marrakesh Accords, was to ensure that flexible mechanisms were not used to nullify commitments undertaken under the protocol. Parties elaborated on the notion of *additionality*. States examined under what circumstances measures undertaken under the flexible mechanisms are additional to already planned activities or measures. If measures that qualify under the mechanisms are not really "additional" to already planned measures, countries would end up taking credit for their business-as-usual behavior.[202]

Additionality becomes an empty concept without the establishment of national baselines. National baselines would require of developing countries to inventory, project and report their emissions. The problem is that developing countries have neither the technical capability nor the political will to establish such national baselines. It is proposed, therefore, as an alternative, that additionality could be assessed, as much as possible, on a project-by-project basis.[203] Another commentator has proposed that baselines can be sector-specific or technology-specific. But again it would be difficult to prove or disprove additionality based on empirical facts.

The parties to CDM (or other joint implementation projects) have an inherent incentive to inflate the amount of projected reductions. Methodologies of developing

---

[200] Decision 18/CP.7, Modalities, Rules and Guidelines for Emissions Trading under Article 17 of the Kyoto Protocol, FCCC/CP/2001/13/Add.2, Section II, 2001.

[201] Theodore Panayotou, Six Questions of Design and Governance, in Issues & Options: The Clean Development Mechanism 45, 52 (José Goldemberg, ed., 1998) [hereinafter Issues & Options].

[202] Grubb, *supra* note 111, at 192.

[203] Panayotou, *supra* note 201, at 50.

baselines must be consistent, thus, among countries, sectors, and technologies. Also, because no right or wrong baselines exist *per se*, the process of auditing and verification of baselines could be a challenge.[204] Several methodological approaches have been proposed for the construction of baselines such as the development of credible quantitative baselines (e.g., in the power sector the average utilization ratio of power plants in the host country or in the investing country); or the isolation of a narrow category of projects that would be considered additional by definition (e.g., renewable energy projects), thus making redundant the need for quantitative baselines.[205]

The simpler approach to defining additionality is to establish a narrow category of projects that would be *a priori* eligible for funding. Projects that do not fall within this category would have to be further evaluated based on other methodological approaches.

Other safeguards against overusing or abusing the flexibility provided for in the protocol involve the inherent competition among the mechanisms eligible for funding. For instance, too much trading with countries with economies in transition – what has been called "hot air" trading – will reduce the value of other legitimate trading. A wide interpretation of the CDM would reduce the value of joint implementation among Annex I countries. The introduction of too many sinks to meet the targets of the protocol will reduce the funding for the energy sector and would delay the updating of obsolete infrastructure. It is hoped that the competition created among the three joint implementation devices would generate some checks and balances in the interpretation of the protocol.[206]

A question that has been raised is whether the CDM should function on the basis of bilateral/project-by-project agreements or whether it should work on a multilateral basis as a portfolio investment mechanism. The portfolio concept would involve projects designed by developing countries requiring the financial support of developed countries. The idea behind the multilateral/portfolio approach is to "shield" developing countries from selling CERs directly to potential investors. Investors would have to buy CERs from the CDM. The CDM would, in turn, channel the investment money to host countries that have submitted bundles of projects to CDM for certification.[207] This multilateral approach is more or less reminiscent of the functioning of the GEF. Proponents of this approach expounded on the following advantages: CDM projects screened for their compatibility with the priorities of developing countries; risk diversification between projects and countries; and elevated prices for CERs, as the CDM would be a monopolistic credit supplier.[208]

Under the bilateral approach, the CDM functions more or less as a facilitator of bilateral agreements between interested investors and developing countries.[209] This approach – one that requires a minimal use of the CDM institutions – proposes a CDM as a clearinghouse mechanism that puts investors in contact with interested countries minimizing, thus, transaction costs and supporting the credibility of the

[204] Farhana Yamin, Operational and Institutional Challenges, in Issues & Options 53, 55, *id.*
[205] *Id.* at 62.
[206] Grubb, *supra* note 111, at 193.
[207] Yamin, *supra* note 204, at 55.
[208] *Id.*
[209] Raúl A. Estrada-Oyuela, First Approaches and Unanswered Questions, in Issues & Options 23, 26, *id.*

system.[210] The bilateral approach could be conceived as advantageous because it resists the temptation of creating yet another international bureaucracy. The bilateral approach is supported by proponents of market mechanisms who trust more the instincts of investors and countries involved rather than central institutional mechanisms.[211]

The nature of the projects eligible for funding may dictate the structure of the CDM. For instance, the Northeast Asian natural gas pipeline project could be conceived as a project that qualifies for funding under the CDM. It would involve many companies and countries and it would replace large amounts of coal-based power production in China. Approaching such a large undertaking on a project-by-project/bilateral basis would be extremely time-consuming. By contrast, a bid of a local utility to convert to renewable energy may be appropriately addressed on a bilateral basis.[212]

Whether it functions on a bilateral or a multilateral basis, all commentators agree that it is important for the CDM to reduce red tape, simplify approval procedures, and keep administrative costs to a minimum. For the CDM to present itself as a viable competitive alternative to joint implementation and emissions trading, it must establish criteria for auditing, verification, and crediting that are comparable and consistent with emissions trading and joint implementation.[213]

Issues of equity have emerged with regard to the type of developing country most likely to benefit from CDM. The CDM would become an engine for the support of projects in emerging economies probably in Asian countries. African countries have expressed concerns that only one in seventy-five pilot projects supported by the CMD is taking place in Africa.[214] To address these equity concerns, it has been proposed to set up regional quotas to ensure that poor regions would receive a share of capital flows and technology transfers.[215]

2.3. Conclusion

The viability of the Kyoto Protocol and the whole Climate Change regime boils down to ratification. For the protocol to enter into force, it must be ratified by parties – including Annex I parties – that accounted for at least 55 percent of the total CO_2 emissions in 1990. This means that if both Russia and the United States refuse to ratify the protocol, the protocol will not enter into force. The United States is not willing to ratify the protocol.

Until 2004, the countries that had ratified the Kyoto Protocol represented 44.07 percent of the emissions targeted. The ratification of the protocol by Russia was, therefore, a precondition for the protocol to enter into force (given the reluctance of the United States to control its greenhouse gases). Statements of Russian officials had placed under doubt the ratification of the protocol. The general speculation, however, was that Russia's doubts regarding ratification had more to do with the

---

[210] Yamin, *supra* note 204, at 55.
[211] *Id.* at 56.
[212] Grubb, *supra* note 111, at 235–36.
[213] Panayotou, *supra* note 201, at 51.
[214] Grubb, *supra* note 111, at 239.
[215] Panayotou, *supra* note 201 at 50.

expected economic windfalls rather than with substantial disagreements with the purpose of the protocol. Because the United States was not eager to participate in the protocol, Russia was unlikely to receive the economic benefits it was hoping to get from selling its extra credits. Under the Kyoto Protocol, Russia's allowances were based on the Soviet era emissions. But the economic decline, that followed the collapse of the Soviet Union, led to the demise of many polluting industries giving Russia emission credits to sell.[216] Eventually, Russia ratified the protocol, and the protocol entered into force in early 2005.

Environmental NGOs were involved in the negotiations of the Kyoto Protocol, but it is unlikely that they would be central in its monitoring and enforcement. The Kyoto Protocol, as some commentators have aptly put it, is a "major economic agreement," and some environmental organizations may encounter difficulties in closely monitoring it.[217]

In 2004, the first projects under the CDM took effect. Some pilot projects have already taken place with mixed results.[218] The European Union is in the process of implementing its emissions trading scheme.[219] And there are many national and corporate emission trading schemes, such as the Chicago Climate Exchange in the United States, which provide experimental avenues for the broader implementation of emissions trading.[220]

3. TRANSFRONTIER AIR POLLUTION

The first attempts to deal with air pollution were rudimentary. Tall smokestacks were used in the 1950s to disperse pollution in the winds. This widely held practice transformed a localized problem into an international issue. One of the consequences was the transfer of pollution from Britain and Germany to downwind states, such as Sweden. Downwind states, which started to experience significant problems

---

[216] Is Kyoto Dead? The Economist, Dec. 6, 2003.

[217] Grubb, *supra* note 111, at 260.

[218] See Miriam Miranda et al., The Social Impacts of Carbon Markets in Costa Rica, International Institute for Environment and Development (IIED), Environmental Economics Programme, July 2004. The authors claim that for countries to take advantage of carbon markets they must have some experience in marketing their environmental management capacities. Costa Rica is an expert in doing that.

Carbon markets can have distributive effects because large reforestation projects may involve exclusions of people from land. Shifting the incentives of rural people from run-of-mill agriculture to forestry – which presents more long-term profits – is the real challenge. Today, reforestation and afforestation are the only activities eligible to participate in global carbon markets. The expectations of countries are high because they are hoping to use the revenues from these markets to better the lives of rural people. But because expectations are high, the results could be disappointing. Many farmers in Costa Rica have been disillusioned with afforestation projects because of the long production cycle and have underestimated contingencies, such as restricted access to other public funds, and high transaction costs.

See also Peter H. May et al., Local Sustainable Development Effects of Forest Carbon Projects in Brazil and Bolivia: A View from the Field, IIED, Environmental Economics Programme, January 2004.

[219] See Directive 2003/87/EC of the European Parliament and Council of 13 October 2003 establishing a scheme for greenhouse gas emission allowance trading within the Community and amending Council Directive 96/61/EC, OJ L 275, 25.10.2003. The European carbon markets are already up and are functioning, see Carbon Trading: Revving up, Economist, July 9, 2005.

[220] Joke Waller-Hunter, Climate Change: The Challenge Continues, OECD Observer, April 6, 2004.

including acidification of their waters, pushed for the adoption of a Convention on Long-Range Transboundary Air Pollution (CLRTAP).[221]

There are various air pollutants that can affect human health and environment. The international efforts to control air pollution have achieved to diminish significantly many such pollutants. Other pollutants are more difficult to regulate, such as Suspended Particulate Matter (SPM) and Persistent Organic Pollutants (POPs).

The main contributor to nitrogen oxide (NO_x) is motor vehicles, thus explaining the high levels of nitrogen oxide in urban surroundings with high road traffic and combustion plants.

The main contributor to sulphur (SO_2) is the burning of oil and coal. Different fuels contain different amounts of sulphur.[222] Oil refineries and power stations account for the majority of sulphur emissions.[223]

Suspended particulate matter (SPM) is another source of air pollution that is much more difficult to control. Particles can be of various kinds and the smaller they are the higher their potential to cause harm by penetrating deep into the lungs.[224] The elusive character of particles makes their regulation difficult because one must be able to identify them and map their movement. The European Environment Agency has declared that exposure to particulate matter is "the largest threat to human health" in many European cities and that member states are likely to face difficulties in complying with future standards.[225] High concentrations of particulate matter contribute to elevated concentrations of ground-level ozone during the summer months.[226] Ozone is an oxidant that causes irritations of the eye and irritations of the airways and can reduce lung capacity.[227]

Other substances that contribute to ozone formation include Volatile Organic Compounds (VOCs). VOCs involve pollutants, such as benzene, ethene, and various other nitrated polyaromatic hydrocarbons. Some of these pollutants are present in diesel motor vehicles and small-scale combustion, such as wood and coal burning.

The main source of carbon dioxide (CO_2) is the burning of fossil fuels. Carbon dioxide exists naturally in the atmosphere. But its rapid increase as a result of industrialization is considered the main contributor to climate change. Carbon monoxide

---

[221] Convention on Long-range Transboundary Air Pollution, Nov. 13, 1979, reprinted in 18 ILM 1442 (1979), available online at http://www.unece.org/env/lrtap/lrtap_h1.htm.

[222] For instance, crude oil contains 3 percent of sulfur while high sulfur coal contains 10 percent of sulfur.

[223] European Environment Agency, Europe's Environment: The Third Assessment – Summary 35 (2003) [hereinafter Third Assessment].

[224] Particles are usually measured as PM10, where PM stands for particulate matter and 10 for the maximum diameter of the particle in micrometers. Recent evidence suggests that particles with even smaller diameter can cause more damage to human health. Particles are produced during combustion and may consist of dust, pollen, and small soot flakes. Particles are formed mainly in the air from sulphur dioxide and nitrogen oxides. Particle formation can occur away from the source presenting a transboundary problem responsible for ground-level ozone and eutrophication. See, generally, Communication from the Commission, The Clean Air for Europe (CAFE) Programme: Towards a Thematic Strategy for Air Quality 2–3, COM (2001) 245 final.

[225] Third Assessment, *supra* note 223, at 35.

[226] See Report to the Commission by the European Environment Agency, Air Pollution by Ozone in the European Union: Overview of the 1999 Summer Session (prepared by Rob Sluyter & Annemarieke Camu, Oct. 1999).

[227] Third Assessment, *supra* note 223, at 35.

(CO) is produced mainly from the incomplete burning of fossil fuels, and it can adversely affect human health.

Heavy metals that contribute to air pollution include mercury, lead, and cadmium. Heavy metals are discharged into the air and water by various industries. The phasing out of leaded petrol and other mandatory reductions of metals have abated to some extent some of these pollutants.

3.1. Legislative Instruments

3.1.1. Convention on Transboundary Air Pollution

The Convention on Long-Range Transboundary Air Pollution (CLRTAP)[228] was signed under the auspices of the UN/ECE in 1979 and entered into force in 1983. Because of the objections of Germany and Britain, the convention did not include binding provisions but just imposed a general obligation on states to reduce long-range transboundary air pollution. A number of protocols that offer concrete standards for the abatement of pollution supplement the convention.

The convention is based on a number of principles, including the preventive principle,[229] and calls for the cooperation between states that are mostly affected by pollution and states from which pollutants originate.[230] The air quality management approach endorsed in the convention is based on the recognition that a total elimination of air pollution may not be feasible and that "air quality management" should be given priority.[231] The parties to the convention undertake to develop the best policies and strategies including air quality management systems by applying the best available technology that is also economically feasible, and by using low- and nonwaste technology.

The convention provides for tasks that states must undertake including research on new technologies; new monitoring techniques; models for understanding the transmission of pollutants and effects of pollutants; economic, social, and environmental assessment of alternative measures; and training.[232]

The convention is administered by an executive body and a Secretariat. The executive body is comprised of representatives of all state parties, and its purpose is to review and to improve the implementation of the convention.[233] The Secretariat's function – fulfilled by the Executive Secretary of the Economic Commission for Europe – is to assist the executive body in its duties.[234]

Today, the convention is administered by a more complex administrative structure. Many specialized working groups have been established that are assisted by task forces.[235]

---

[228] See *supra* note 221.

[229] Art. 2, *id.*

[230] Art. 5, *id.* Article 1(b) defines "long-range transboundary air pollution" as pollution whose physical origin occurs within a national jurisdiction. This pollution, though, has adverse effects on areas under another state's jurisdiction at such a distance that it is usually not possible to distinguish between pollution from domestic sources and pollution from foreign sources. See *id.*

[231] Art. 6, *id.*

[232] Art. 7, *id.*

[233] Art. 10, *id.*

[234] Art. 11, *id.*

[235] The detailed administrative structure of the convention is available online at http://www.unece.org/env/lrtap/conv/lrtap_o.htm.

The monitoring of the convention is undertaken by the "Cooperative Programme for Monitoring and Evaluation of the Long-Range Transmission of Air Pollutants in Europe" (EMEP).[236] The EMEP is an instrument for the review and assessment of air pollution in Europe. At this point, the EMEP collects data on all pollutants regulated under the convention, measures air quality, and develops models on the pattern of pollution dispersion. The EMEP-related data are collected in monitoring stations located in various areas in Europe. Monitoring data demonstrate that the CLRTAP regime commands high levels of compliance.[237]

3.1.2. Regulation of Air Pollutants

The Sulphur Protocols

The first protocol was adopted in 1985 and dealt with the reduction of sulphur emissions, as sulphur pollution was the primary reason for the adoption of the convention.[238] The protocol calls for a 30 percent reduction in sulphur emissions by 1993 in all state parties uniformly.[239] The protocol has been successful. Sulphur emissions in 1993 were reduced by 50 percent taking into account all state parties as a group. State parties have achieved their targets also individually. Eleven out of twenty-one state parties have exceeded actually their targets by achieving reductions close to 60 percent.[240]

The 1994 Sulphur Protocol called for further reductions of sulphur emissions.[241] The protocol – which was adopted after the 1992 Rio Conference[242] – includes many of the relatively new concepts of international environmental law, such as the precautionary approach.[243] The protocol introduced the critical level and critical loads concept. The protocol provides for the specific critical loads of sulphur that must not be exceeded.[244]

A first step to the achievement of the critical loads objective involves the attainment of national emission ceilings within specific deadlines.[245] The introduction of national emission ceilings that must be achieved within specific deadlines (2000, 2005, 2010) broke the long-established tradition of uniform emission standards in Europe. Contrary to the 1985 protocol, which mandated a reduction of pollution by 30 percent all across state parties, the 1994 protocol specifies the levels of reduction per state. The advantage of such an approach is that it takes into account the level of

---

[236] Protocol on Long-Term Financing of the Cooperative Programme for Monitoring and Evaluation of the Long-range Transmission of Air Pollutants in Europe, Sept. 28, 1984, reprinted in 24 ILM 484 (1985), available online at http://www.unece.org/env/lrtap/emep_h1.htm.

[237] See Convention on Long-Range Transboundary Air Pollution: Implementation available online at http://www.unece.org/env/lrtap/conv/conclusi.htm [hereinafter Implementation].

[238] Protocol on the Reduction of Sulphur Emissions or their Transboundary Fluxes by at least 30 percent, July 8, 1985, reprinted in 27 ILM 707 (1988), available online at http://www.unece.org/env/lrtap/sulf h1.htm.

[239] Art. 6, id.

[240] Implementation, supra note 237.

[241] Protocol on Further Reduction of Sulphur Emissions, June 14, 1994, reprinted in 33 ILM 1540 (1994), available online at http://www.unece.org/env/lrtap/sulf_h1.htm.

[242] The 1992 Rio Conference contributed to the reconfiguration of many concepts of international environmental law. See, e.g., Rio Declaration on Environment and Development, Chapter 1.

[243] See Preamble, Protocol on Further Reduction of Sulphur Emissions, supra note 241.

[244] Art. 2(1) and Annex I, id.

[245] Art. 2(2) and Annex II, id.

development of different states. For instance, the percentage reduction required for
Greece between 1990 and 2000 is zero. Greece is even allowed more emissions for
2005 and 2010 given its current emissions and its current state of development.[246]
By such an individualized approach to air pollution the protocol put national emission ceilings for sulphur into effect, something that would be mimicked by later
protocols and eventually by the European Union's differentiated approach to air
pollution.

In addition to the critical loads concept and national ceilings, the protocol provides
the minimum limit values for sulphur emissions that must be achieved by individual
sources.[247] These limit values are immediately applicable to new stationary sources[248]
and, by 2004, to major existing stationary sources with a thermal input of above 500
MWth.[249]

The protocol encourages parties to adopt the most effective measures for the
reduction of sulphur emissions including measures to increase energy efficiency and
the use of renewable energy.[250] State parties should apply the best available control
technologies not entailing excessive costs.[251] A multipage annex includes a list of
the major sulphur producers and the means that they could take to reduce their
emissions.

To ensure compliance, the protocol establishes, for the first time within the
CLRTAP regime, an implementation committee. The purpose of the implementation committee is to review the compliance of states and provide solutions in cases
of noncompliance.[252] Compliance under the protocol, with regard to achieving the
2000 deadline, was high because fifteen out of twenty-one parties seem to be in compliance with the emissions ceilings mandated by the protocol. Another four states are
on their way to full compliance. With regard to limit values, eleven countries have
indicated compliance, whereas the rest of the countries are either noncompliant or
have not provided data on their compliance.[253]

The Nitrogen Oxide Protocol

The purpose of the nitrogen oxide protocol[254] is to stabilize the nitrogen oxide
emissions at 1987 levels by 1994.[255] To pursue this goal, state parties are to establish
national emission ceilings for major sources of nitrogen oxides[256] and to initiate
negotiations on steps to be undertaken to further cut the emissions based on the
critical loads concept.[257]

---

[246] Annex II, *id.*
[247] Art. 2(5), *id.*
[248] Art. 2(5)(a), *id.*
[249] Art. 2(5)(b), *id.*
[250] Art. 2(4), *id.*
[251] *Id.*
[252] Art. 7, *id.*
[253] Implementation, *supra* note 237.
[254] Protocol Concerning the Control of Emissions of Nitrogen Oxides or their Transboundary Fluxes,
Oct. 31, 1988, reprinted in 28 ILM 212 (1989), available online at http://www.unece.org/env/lrtap/
nitr_h1.htm.
[255] Art. 2(1), *id.*
[256] Art. 2(2)(a), *id.*
[257] Art. 2(3), *id.*

The protocol encourages states to initiate and to prioritize research that would help establish the critical loads for nitrogen oxide emissions and, thus, to mandate the appropriate emission reductions for nitrogen oxides.[258] The protocol contains a technical annex inclusive of a number of recommendations on how to best reduce the emissions of nitrogen oxides from stationary sources and mobile sources.

States' reports demonstrate that seventeen out of twenty-six parties have complied with the 1994 deadline to stabilize emissions at 1987 levels. Some countries – Bulgaria, the Czech Republic, Ukraine, and Germany – have gone even further by reducing their emissions by 40 percent. Other countries, however, despite their level of development and participation in the EU, have increased their emissions. For instance, France increased its emissions by 103 percent between 1987 and 1996. It remains to be seen whether countries with economies in transition would keep their NOx levels as low as they are today, as these lower emissions have to do more with the economic slow-down in these countries rather than the adoption of techniques of pollution abatement.[259]

The VOCs, Heavy Metals, and POPs Protocols

The *Volatile Organic Compounds (VOCs) Protocol*[260] gives state parties three options for the reduction of VOCs:

- a 30 percent reduction in the emissions of VOCs by 1999 using any year between 1984 and 1990 as a basis;[261]
- a similar reduction within a Tropospheric Ozone Management Area (TOMA) that ensures that the 1999 emissions do not exceed the 1988 levels;[262] or
- the stabilization of emissions in case the 1988 emissions did not exceed certain limits.[263]

In addition, state parties are required to adopt the appropriate emission standards for stationary[264] and mobile sources[265] and to encourage the development of products that are as much as possible VOCs-free.[266] Furthermore, state parties are to give the

---

[258] Art. 6, *id*.

[259] Implementation, *supra* note 237.

[260] Protocol concerning the Control of Emissions of Volatile Organic Compounds or their Transboundary Fluxes, Nov. 8, 1991, reprinted in 31 ILM 573 (1992), available online at http://www.unece.org/env/lrtap/protocol/91voc.htm.

[261] Art. 2(2)(a), *id*.

[262] Art. 2(2)(b), *id*. Designated tropospheric ozone management areas (TOMAs), for the purposes of this protocol, are certain areas of Canada (the Lower Fraser Valley in the Province of British Columbia and the Windsor-Quebec Corridor in the Provinces of Ontario and Quebec) and Norway.

[263] Art. 2(2)(c), *id*.

[264] Stationary sources that contribute to the creation of VOCs are: the use of solvents; the petroleum industry; the organic chemical industry; small-scale combustion sources; the food industry; the iron and steel industry; the handling and treatment of waste and agriculture. Annex II prescribes the best methods for the reduction of VOCs from stationary sources. See *id*.

[265] It has been estimated that road traffic is the major source of anthropogenic VOCs emissions and that it contributes between 30 and 40 percent of the total man-made VOCs emissions in the ECE as a whole. See Annex III, *id*.

[266] Art. 2(3)(a)(iii), *id*. Labeling is one of the methods to increase consumer awareness.

highest priority to the reduction of most harmful VOCs – that is, VOCs with the highest Photochemical Ozone Creation Potential (POCP).[267]

State parties as a group have achieved the goals set by the protocol. Individually, however, only seven states appear to be in compliance, whereas another four are in the course of being fully compliant. Countries such as France and the Netherlands have yet to provide information to indicate progress and in Norway emissions have increased by more than 50 percent against a stabilization target taking 1988 as the base year.[268]

The Protocol on Heavy Metals[269] concentrates on three metals that are proven to be quite harmful to human health and to the environment, namely, cadmium, lead, and mercury. State parties have to reduce emissions of these harmful metals below their 1990 levels or they can pick an alternative year between 1985 and 1995 as a base year.[270]

The protocol provides for strict limit values for major stationary sources, the use of the best available technology, such as scrubbers and filters, and the initiation of mercury-free processes.[271] The limit values must be achieved within specific deadlines. New stationary sources have to comply with limit values two years after the entry into force of the protocol. Existing stationary sources have to comply with limit values eight years after the entry into force of the protocol.[272]

The protocol requires the parties to phase out leaded petrol[273] and mandates measures to reduce the heavy metal content of different products. Significant exemptions are provided for state parties that cannot achieve the limit values established under the protocol.[274] Parties are required to keep inventories of emissions of heavy metals that would be available for EMEP monitoring purposes.[275]

The Protocol on Persistent Organic Pollutants (POPs)[276] addresses the elimination of pollution caused by pesticides, such as DDT, and other dangerous substances, such as PCBs. Annex I includes the POPs whose production and/or use must be eliminated.[277] Annex II includes the POPs whose use must be restricted.[278] And Annex III includes the POPs whose emissions must be reduced taking as a base a

---

[267] See Annex IV, *id.*

[268] Implementation, *supra* note 237.

[269] Protocol on Heavy Metals, June 24, 1998, available online at http://www.unece.org/env/lrtap/protocol/98hm.htm. The protocol is not yet in force. The European Community has adopted the Protocol. See Heavy Metals Protocol to the 1979 Convention on Long-range Transboundary Air Pollution, OJ L 134/41, 17.05.2001.

[270] Art. 3, *id.* See also Annex I, *id.*

[271] Annex V, *id.*

[272] Annex IV provides the timescales. See *id.*

[273] Annex VI, *id.*

[274] Art. 3(6) and (7), *id.*

[275] Art. 3(5), *id.*

[276] Protocol on Persistent Organic Pollutants, June 24, 1998, reprinted in 37 ILM 513 (1998) available online at http://www.unece.org/env/lrtap/protocol/98pop.htm.

[277] Art. 3(1)(a), *id.* Such substances include: aldrin, chlordane, chlordecone, DDT (only production, use with exceptions) dieldrin, endrin, heptachlor, hexabromobiphenyl, hexachlorobenzene, mirex, PCBs (with exceptions), and toxaphene.

[278] Art. 3(1)(c), *id.* This Annex includes substances the use of which has been prohibited in Annex I with exceptions (such as DDT and PCBs) as well as HCH.

specific year and according to specific timescales.[279] Annex III includes POPs for which specific limit values are prescribed.[280] But when prescribed limit values cannot be met, exemptions are allowed.[281] Other exemptions are possible for research, public health emergency issues, or minor applications.[282] Exemptions, however, are not granted easily. A state requesting an exemption must provide the Secretariat with detailed information about: the name of the substance exempted, the purpose of the exemption, the conditions under which the exemption is granted, and the length of time it applies and to which organization it applies.[283]

State parties are required to keep inventories of emissions of substances included in Annex III and an inventory on the production and use of Annex I and Annex II substances.[284] Efforts to increase public awareness with regard to the use of pesticides, including labeling and other informative activities, also are recommended.[285]

Toward Integrated Protocols

The Protocol to Abate Acidification, Eutrophication and Ground-Level Ozone addresses a number of pollutants in an integrated fashion.[286] The protocol sets emission ceilings for four pollutants – sulphur, nitrogen oxide, VOCs, and ammonia. The protocol sets also specific limit values for major emission sources and requires the use of the best available techniques for pollution abatement. The purpose of national emission ceilings and limit values is to achieve the main objective of the protocol – the reduction of emissions below critical loads.[287]

Most of the substantive provisions of the protocol are included in the Annexes.[288] Annex II specifies all emission ceilings for sulphur, nitrogen oxide, ammonia and VOCs. Annexes IV through VI prescribe the limit values for stationary sources. And Annex VIII prescribes the emission limit values for mobile sources. Annex IX provides for measures that must be taken for the control of ammonia emissions from agricultural sources.

It is estimated that when the protocol is fully implemented it would cut sulphur emissions in Europe by 63 percent, NO_x emissions by 41 percent, VOCs emissions by 40 percent and ammonia emissions by 17 percent compared with the 1990 levels of pollution. It also is estimated that areas with excessive levels of acidification will be reduced from 93 million hectares in 1990 to 15 million hectares. And that excessive

---

[279] See art. 3(5)(a), *id*. Such substances include polycyclic aromatic hydrocarbons (PAHs), dioxins, and furans (PCDD/F), as well as hexachlorobenzene (prohibited in Annex I but allowed for specific production and use in countries with economies in transition).

[280] Art. 3(5)(b)(ii), *id*.

[281] Art. 3(7), *id*.

[282] Art. 4, *id*.

[283] Art. 4(3), *id*.

[284] Art. 3(8), *id*.

[285] Art. 6, *id*.

[286] Protocol to Abate Acidification, Eutrophication and Ground-level Ozone, Nov. 30, 1999, available online at http://www.unece.org/env/lrtap/multi_h1.htm [hereinafter Protocol]. The protocol has been adopted by the European Community, see Protocol to the 1979 Convention on Long-Range Transboundary Air Pollution to abate acidification, eutrophication and ground-level ozone, OJ L 179/3, 17.07.2003.

[287] See art. 2, *id*. For the critical loads of each pollutant, see Annex I, *id*.

[288] See art. 3, *id*.

levels of eutrophication will fall significantly. The life-years lost as a result of exposure to ozone will be about 2,300,000 lower in 2010 than in 1990 and there will be 47,500 fewer premature deaths from exposure to ozone.[289]

3.2. Conclusion

The LRTAP regime has been considered successful in reducing air pollution in Europe. The regime started with a basic framework convention and increased in complexity as the nature and persistence of polluting substances were further evaluated. The regime focused initially on the regulation of each and every polluting substance but increased in sophistication as an integrated approach to pollution management has been eventually adopted. Unlike other international regimes, the institutional structure that has been developed for the implementation of the regime is solid, as the EMEP monitoring system has aptly demonstrated. Overall, the enclosure of the global commons in terms of the control of air quality affected by transboundary air pollution could be characterized as effective.

---

[289] See Protocol, *supra* note 286.

9

Trade and Environment

1. WORLD TRADE INSTITUTIONS

The free movement of goods and services among states has been the exception rather than the norm in international trade. Countries have regulated international trade through a number of tariff and nontariff barriers. Every country has enacted its share of tariff and nontariff rules that put restrictions on foreign imports, thereby making foreign products more expensive than domestic products. These rules have acted as a barrier to international trade and have limited the choices available to the ultimate consumer.

Ideas of liberalism that free trade should be pursued for the benefit of the ultimate consumer, through the gradual elimination of tariff and nontariff barriers, launched the negotiations in 1946 for the development of an International Trade Organization. Eventually, countries agreed to adopt a milder version of a General Agreement on Tariffs and Trade (GATT). GATT acted as a legal agreement/quasi-legal institution for the regulation of international trade with the ultimate goal of bringing down the barriers to trade.

Since its inception in 1946, GATT has gone through several rounds of tariff reductions. In 1994, after seven years of negotiations, the World Trade Organization (WTO)[1] emerged. The WTO manages a legal apparatus that includes the provisions of GATT[2] as well as a General Agreement on Trade in Services (GATS),[3] an Agreement on Trade-Related Aspects of Intellectual Property Rights (TRIPs),[4] an Agreement on Sanitary and Phytosanitary Measures (SPS),[5] and an Understanding

---

[1] Marrakesh Agreement Establishing the World Trade Organization, April 15, 1994, reprinted in 1867 UNTS 154, 33 ILM 1144 (1994) [hereinafter WTO Agreement].

[2] General Agreement on Tariffs and Trade 1994, April 15, 1994, Marrakesh Agreement Establishing the World Trade Organization, Annex 1A, reprinted in 1867 UNTS 187, 33 ILM 1153 (1994) [hereinafter GATT].

[3] General Agreement on Trade in Services, April 15, 1994, Marrakesh Agreement Establishing the World Trade Organization, Annex 1B, reprinted in 33 ILM 1168 (1994) [hereinafter GATS].

[4] Agreement on Trade-Related Aspects of Intellectual Property Rights, April 15, 1994, Marrakesh Agreement Establishing the World Trade Organization, Annex 1C, reprinted in 1869 UNTS 299, 33 ILM 1197 (1994) [hereinafter TRIPs].

[5] Agreement on the Application of Sanitary and Phytosanitary Measures, April 15, 1994, Marrakesh Agreement Establishing the World Trade Organization, Annex 1A, reprinted in 1867 UNTS 493, 33 ILM 1125 (1994) [hereinafter SPS].

on Rules and Procedures Governing the Settlement of Disputes (DSU).[6] These agreements were opened for signature at Marrakesh in 1994 and entered into force in 1995.

The WTO has become the institution through which all important trade matters are discussed, including conflicts between national policies and trade. As an international institution, the WTO presents a much-needed institutional framework alongside the International Monetary Fund (IMF) and the World Bank. The WTO has had already the opportunity to examine many matters that were previously reserved for national policy making. Such is the intrusion of the WTO into national and international policy making that some argue that the WTO is becoming a central lawmaking and adjudicative institution in international affairs.

This chapter examines the dispute resolution mechanism of the WTO with special emphasis on the Sanitary and Phytosanitary Measures (SPS) Agreement and the interpretation of GATT. The role of Trade-Related Intellectual Property Rights (TRIPs) Agreement as it affects intellectual property rights over pharmaceutical inventions and biotechnology is examined in detail.

2. THE TREATIES

From its beginnings, GATT included provisions that were designed to reduce tariff and nontariff barriers. What has been called the "national treatment rule" included in article III of GATT provides that once goods have been imported from another member country they must be treated, by the laws of the importing country, no less favorably than goods produced domestically. Another rule that has been invoked frequently in international transactions is the "most favored nation" rule that provides that member states of the GATT must treat equally their trading partners by providing the same conditions to all of them for imports and exports of "like goods."[7]

Article XX constitutes one of the most discussed articles of GATT because it provides general exceptions to the rules of GATT. Article XX allows for exceptions to free trade for the protection of natural resources and the environment. Article XX provides that:

> Subject to the requirement that such measures are not applied in a manner which would constitute a means of arbitrary or unjustifiable discrimination between countries where the same conditions prevail, or disguised restriction on international trade nothing in this Agreement shall be construed to prevent the adoption or enforcement by any contracting party of measures:
>
> ... (b) necessary to protect human, animal or plant life or health;
>
> ... (g) relating to the conservation of exhaustible natural resources if such measures are made effective in conjunction with restrictions on domestic production or consumption.[8]

---

[6] Understanding on Rules and Procedures Governing the Settlement of Disputes, Marrakesh Agreement Establishing the World Trade Organization, Annex 2, reprinted in 1869 UNTS 401, 33 ILM 1226 (1994) [hereinafter DSU].

[7] Art. I, GATT, *supra* note 2.

[8] For the interpretation of the article, see *infra* Section 3.1.

GATS[9] contains a general exceptions clause in article XIV, which is similar to that included in article XX of GATT. One of the purposes of the new Committee on Trade and Environment (CTE), created under the auspices of WTO, is to examine the interconnection among trade, services, and the environment to determine whether article XIV requires any modification.

Another WTO agreement that goes to the heart of consumer protection involves the Sanitary and Phytosanitary Measures (SPS) Agreement.[10] The SPS agreement provides that member states may adopt sanitary and phytosanitary measures for the purposes of food safety, human, animal, and plant health and safety.[11] But it provides simultaneously that SPS measures must be based on science, should not create unnecessary obstacles to trade, should not arbitrarily discriminate between countries where the same conditions apply. Furthermore, SPS measures must be based on a risk assessment and must be transparent.[12]

The TRIPs agreement[13] provides that countries can recognize patents on most products and processes including pharmaceuticals, modified microorganisms, and microbiological processes (namely, biotechnology devices). Countries can protect plant varieties under patents or other *sui generis* systems, for instance, various versions of plant breeders' rights. The agreement gives countries some sort of discretion in deciding whether patents can be granted to "essentially biological processes for the production of plants and animals" (art. 27.3(b)). There also are exceptions to the provision of intellectual property rights if the refusal to grant such rights is done to protect public order, morality, human, animal, and plant life or health or to avoid adverse environmental effects (art. 27.2).[14] However, the refusal to grant a patent cannot be based on an explanation that the national laws and regulations of a country have yet to approve the product or process. Thus, although this exception could be used occasionally to avert the assertion of intellectual property rights for environmental reasons, it is likely to be strictly interpreted and unlikely to be used lightly for granting derogations from the spirit of the agreement.[15]

3. DISPUTE SETTLEMENT

The 1994 WTO agreement includes an Annex on "Understanding on Rules and Procedures Governing the Settlement of Disputes" (DSU).[16] The DSU establishes the Dispute Settlement Body (DSB), *ad hoc* panels and the Appellate Body. The purpose of the DSB is to administer the dispute settlement proceedings. It is comprised of all members of the WTO and it is a political rather than a judicial body.

[9] See *supra* note 3.

[10] SPS Agreement, *supra* note 5.

[11] Annex A provides what sanitary and phytosanitary measures may include: measures to prevent the introduction of pests, diseases, disease carrying organisms, or disease causing organisms; measures to reduce the risks from food additives, contaminants, toxins, *id.*

[12] For the interpretation of the SPS Agreement, see *infra* Section 3.2.

[13] See *supra* note 4.

[14] See also *infra* Section 4.3.

[15] For an extensive analysis of the TRIPs Agreement, see *infra* Section 4.

[16] See *supra* note 6.

If members of the WTO face a dispute, they may refer the dispute to the DSB, which, in turn, would try to mediate the issue. If mediation or conciliation fails, the parties may ask the DSB to convene a panel. Unlike the recommendations of GATT panels, the recommendations of the WTO panels become binding when they are adopted by the DSB, an adoption that is deemed automatic within sixty days, unless a consensus is formed in the DSB against a panel's recommendation. Furthermore, unlike GATT proceedings, panel decisions can be appealed before the Appellate Body on legal grounds. Again, the report of the Appellate Body is deemed to be automatically adopted by the DSB unless there is a consensus against its adoption.

The DSU has increased the power of panels significantly. The decisions of the panels are not anymore vulnerable to the capriciousness of a member state. This dispute settlement procedure makes possible, for the first time, in the GATT/WTO system third-party adjudication. The general discontent with GATT dispute settlement[17] arrangement, which led to the adoption of the DSU, is indicative of the quest in the international system for effective dispute resolution mechanisms.[18]

Traditional public international law acts as a sort of constitutional law that provides a set of basic norms, and guidelines for their interpretation. The lack of a dispute resolution tribunal with mandatory jurisdiction in international law sets the DSU of the WTO as an enviable exception.

3.1. General Agreement on Tariffs and Trade

The *Tuna/Dolphin* cases were brought before the GATT panels to challenge the extraterritorial application of the environmental legislation of the United States. The GATT panels ruled against the United States in these cases under the rationale that prohibitions of imports of tuna caught in a manner that harms dolphins constituted a quantitative restriction to trade. According to the GATT panels, countries cannot ban the importation of products simply because the process of another country is not compatible with the process preferred by the importing country.[19]

Other cases have been brought against the United States after the establishment of the WTO for the extraterritorial application of its environmental laws and violation of the GATT provisions, namely: the *U.S. Standards for Gasoline* case in 1996 (complaints brought by Venezuela and Brazil) and the *Shrimp-Turtle* case (1998, 2001) (complaints brought by India, Malaysia, Pakistan, Thailand and the Philippines).

In 2000, the *Asbestos* case, regarding the safety of products containing asbestos, was brought by Canada against a French law affecting asbestos and asbestos containing products.

---

[17] However, the record of dispute resolution under GATT was not unimpressive. For instance, between 1948 and 1994 over four hundred complaints were launched and most were settled without the assistance of an adopted report, see Marc L. Busch & Eric Reinhardt, Testing International Trade Law: Empirical Studies of GATT/WTO Dispute Settlement, in The Political Economy of International Trade Law: Essays in Honor of Robert Hudec 457 (D.M. Kennedy & D. Southwick, eds., 2002).

[18] Michael K. Young, Dispute Resolution in the Uruguay Round: Lawyers Triumph over Diplomats, 29 International Law 389 (1995).

[19] Tuna/Dolphin I, reprinted in 30 ILM 1594 (1991); Tuna/Dolphin II, reprinted in 33 ILM 839 (1994).

Other cases of interest involve violations of the SPS agreement. Such cases include the *Hormones* case and the *Australian Salmon* case. These cases are examined later in this chapter.

Gasoline Case

The *U.S. Standards for Gasoline* case[20] was the first case that established a systematic way of looking at article XX of GATT. The case involved the U.S. Clean Air Act, which established standards for the sale of gasoline and gasoline programs in order to ensure that emissions from gasoline combustion did not exceed the 1990 emissions baselines. One of the programs concerned the nonattainment areas. These included nine large metropolitan areas that experienced the worst summertime ozone pollution. All gasoline sold to consumers in these areas was to be reformulated. The sale of conventional gasoline in these nonattainment areas was prohibited. Conventional gasoline, however, could be supplied to consumers in the rest of the United States.

To prevent the dumping of pollutants from reformulated gasoline on conventional gasoline, the Clean Air Act requires that gasoline, sold by domestic refiners, blenders, and importers in the United States, remains as clean as mandated by the 1990 baseline levels. Compliance is measured by comparing emissions from conventional gasoline, sold by domestic refiners, blenders, and importers against emissions calculated based on the 1990 baseline. Regarding both the reformulated gasoline and the conventional gasoline, the 1990 baselines are an integral part of the gasoline rule enforcement. Baselines can be either individual (established by a private entity) or statutory as established by the United States Environmental Protection Agency (EPA).

From an international trade perspective, the problem was that although significant discretion was given to domestic refiners for the establishment of the 1990 individual baselines, the same discretion was not provided to foreign importers. The United States did not make available individual baselines to foreign refiners in the same way as it made possible individual baselines for domestic refiners. In explaining why individual baselines have not been made available for foreign refiners, the United States stressed the difficulties faced by the EPA in monitoring and enforcing such individual baselines. The United States based its argument "on the impracticability of verification and enforcement of the foreign refiner baselines."[21] Venezuela and Brazil, two countries affected by the United States legislation, brought the case before the WTO panel.

The panel, although acknowledging that the difficulties of verification and enforcement are higher for foreign refiners than for domestic refiners, held that these difficulties were insufficient to deny foreign refiners the possibility of establishing individual baselines allowed for domestic refiners.[22]

The United States appealed the decision of the panel. The Appellate Body concurred with the panel's decision.[23] The Appellate Body held that techniques for checking, verification, and assessment of foreign imports are available and are

---

[20] Report of the Panel, United States–Standards for Reformulated and Conventional Gasoline, WT/DS2/R, Jan. 29, 1996.

[21] Para. 6.35, *id.*

[22] Para. 6.28, *id.*

[23] Report of the Appellate Body, United States–Standards for Reformulated and Conventional Gasoline, WT/DS2/AB/R, April 29, 1996.

adequate to permit free trade among countries. The Appellate Body held that the EPA's argument that, in the absence of foreign government cooperation, the quality of refiners could not be reviewed through onsite visits was not tenable. According to the Appellate Body, the United States had not pursued the possibility of entering into cooperative arrangements with the governments of Venezuela or Brazil to conclude that these governments would not cooperate. The United States failed to enter into "appropriate procedures in cooperation" with the governments of Venezuela and Brazil "to mitigate the administrative problems pleaded by the United States."[24]

The Appellate Body relied on the arguments of the United States for affording individual baselines to domestic refiners. The United States had claimed that the imposition of a statutory baseline would have been

> *physically and financially impossible because of the magnitude of the changes required in almost all US refineries; this would have caused a sustained delay in the program* [emphasis in the original].[25]

Given that the United States deemed it infeasible to require its domestic refiners to incur the physical and financial costs of compliance with a statutory baseline, the same amount of consideration should have been granted to foreign refiners. The Appellate Body concluded that the U.S. omission to cooperate with the governments of Venezuela and Brazil and to take into account the costs imposed on foreign refiners by its gasoline programs amounted to an unjustifiable discrimination and a disguised restriction to trade in violation of the chapeau of article XX.[26]

Before concluding that the U.S. legislation violated the chapeau of article XX, the Appellate Body initiated a structured analysis of the article. The Appellate Body followed strictly the language of article XX in applying a two-part test:

1. The first part of the test was whether the U.S. measures were related to the conservation of natural exhaustible resources and whether such measures were made effective in conjunction with restrictions on domestic production or consumption (article XX(g)).
2. If the above conditions were satisfied, the Appellate Body would have to determine whether the U.S. measures constitute an "arbitrary or unjustifiable discrimination" or a "disguised restriction on international trade," according to the chapeau of article XX.[27]

The Appellate Body held that the measures employed by the United States had to do with the conservation of exhaustible natural resources, as clean air should be deemed an exhaustible natural resource. The even-handedness requirement of article XX(g) – that is, the comparable treatment of domestic production and foreign imports – also was satisfied. The Appellate Body, however, eventually struck down the U.S. import restrictions as incompatible with the chapeau of article XX.

---

[24] *Id.* at 19.
[25] *Id.*
[26] *Id.*
[27] *Id.* 10–15.

In reaching its conclusion, the Appellate Body stated the importance and relevance of international law in its decisions. The Appellate Body emphasized that trade rules must not be read in isolation from the general rules of public international law.[28]

1998 Shrimp-Turtle Case

The *Shrimp-Turtle* case[29] involved the extraterritorial application of the U.S. endangered species legislation.[30] According to this legislation, the United States required those who capture shrimp to use approved Turtle Excluder Devices (TEDs) at all times and in all areas (with certain exceptions) where there was the likelihood that shrimp harvesting would affect sea turtles.

Section 609(a) of the Act[31] required the Secretary of Commerce to initiate bilateral or multilateral agreements with foreign governments with regard to the adoption of similar conservation measures by other countries. Section 609(b)(1) imposed an import ban on shrimp harvested with technology that would adversely affect turtles. For shrimp to be imported, they would have to be certified. There are two types of certification that are required annually. The first certification would be issued to countries that have a fishing environment that does not pose a threat to the taking of turtles in the course of shrimp harvesting.[32] The second certification would be granted to countries that provide documentation that they maintain a regulatory program similar to that of the United States. In addition, these countries would have to prove that the incidental taking of sea turtles is comparable to that of the United States. The program put in place by a foreign government had to be comparable to the U.S. program in terms of effectiveness and had to provide for credible enforcement.[33] Countries in the Caribbean/western Atlantic region were exempted from certification for three years, during which time they had to phase in a regulatory program.

The WTO Dispute Settlement panel, to which Thailand, India, Pakistan, and Malaysia brought the case, ruled against the United States using the chapeau of article XX and claiming that the U.S. regulations posed a threat to the multilateral trading system.[34] The Appellate Body upheld the panel's decision but improved on the panel's rationale. The Appellate Body engaged in a structured analysis of article XX, as it had done in the *Gasoline* case. The Appellate Body insisted, as it had done in the *Gasoline* case, that article XX is not so much concerned with a measure applied but with the manner by which a measure is applied – something the panel had not specifically examined.[35] The Appellate Body claimed that the panel, instead of looking at whether the U.S. measure was "*applied in such a manner* as to constitute *abuse or misuse of a given kind of exception* [emphasis in the original]," looked

---

[28] *Id.* at 17 (GATT "is not to be read in clinical isolation from public international law").

[29] Report of the Appellate Body, United-States – Import Prohibition of Certain Shrimp and Shrimp Products, WT/DS58/AB/R, Oct. 12, 1998 [hereinafter Shrimp–Turtle case].

[30] 16 U.S.C. §1531, et seq.

[31] *Id.*

[32] Paras. 2–5, Shrimp–Turtle case, *supra* note 29.

[33] Para. 4, *id.*

[34] Para. 7.61, Report of the Panel, United States – Import Prohibition of certain Shrimp and Shrimp Products, WT/DS58/R, May 15, 1998.

[35] Para. 115, Shrimp–Turtle case, *supra* note 29.

at the general purpose of GATT and the WTO.[36] The Appellate Body repeated that the appropriate method of applying article XX is the one that it prescribed in the *Gasoline* case, which put into effect a two-tiered analysis of article XX.

First, one needs to examine whether a measure adopted falls within the ambit of article XX(g). If the measure is in conformity with article XX(g), it must be examined whether it violates the chapeau of article XX.[37] With regard to the chapeau of article XX, one has to examine, specifically, whether the measure constitutes an arbitrary or an unjustifiable or a disguised restriction to trade.

The Appellate Body proceeded to examine whether the U.S. regulations complied with the two-tiered test it prescribed. According to article XX(g), in order to be valid, the U.S. regulations must relate "to the conservation of exhaustible natural resources."[38] The Appellate Body ruled that living resources "are just as "finite" as petroleum, iron ore and other nonliving resources."[39] The term "exhaustible natural resources," the Appellate Body noted, must be read in conjunction with the "contemporary concerns of the community of nations about the protection and conservation of the environment."[40] The term "natural resources," as mentioned in article XX(g), is not "static" in its content but by definition evolutionary.[41] The Appellate Body referred specifically to the Preamble of the 1994 WTO agreement, which explicitly mentions the "objective of sustainable development."[42] The Appellate Body concluded that turtles constitute exhaustible resources because seven of their species are listed in Appendix I of the CITES.[43] The U.S. regulations are, thus, measures "relating to" the conservation of an exhaustible natural resource.[44]

For article XX(g) to apply, another condition had to be fulfilled: the U.S. regulations must have been made effective "in conjunction with restrictions on domestic production and consumption." The question here was, therefore, whether the restrictions that applied to foreign imports of shrimp into the United States applied also to domestic production.[45] Regarding this matter, the Appellate Body concluded, without hesitation, that the same restrictions that applied to imported shrimp applied similarly to domestic production.

---

[36] Para. 116, *id.*

[37] Para. 118, *id.*

[38] Para. 127, *id.*

[39] Para. 128, *id.*

[40] Para. 129, *id.*

[41] Para. 130, *id.* The Appellate Body cited the Legal Consequences for States of the Continued Presence of South Africa in Namibia (Advisory Opinion), June 21, 1971, (1971) ICJ Reports 12, at 31 and the Aegean Sea Continental Shelf Case, Dec. 19, 1978, (1978) ICJ Reports 1, at 3. The Appellate Body also cited a number of international scholars including Oppenheim's International Law, Ninth Edition (1992). It must be noted that the concept of evolutionary interpretation of terminology used in treaties is applied here for the interpretation of the term "natural resources" included in GATT in order to conclude that both living and nonliving resources are covered by the provision. As GATT was adopted in 1946 and the case was decided in 1998, an actualization of the concept of natural resources was, indeed, necessary.

[42] Para. 129, 1998 Shrimp-Turtle case, *supra* note 29.

[43] Para. 132, *id.* See also CITES Convention (Convention on International Trade in Endangered Species), Mar. 6, 1973, reprinted in 12 ILM 1085 (1973).

[44] Para. 142, 1998 Shrimp-Turtle case, *supra* note 29.

[45] Paras. 143–44, *id.*

Because the United States regulations were in accord with article XX(g), the question was whether they fulfilled the requirements of the chapeau of article XX. Legitimate measures adopted in accordance with article XX(g) must not be used

> in a manner which would constitute a means of arbitrary or unjustifiable discrimination between countries where the same conditions prevail, or a disguised restriction on international trade.

The Appellate Body elaborated further on the level of review required by the chapeau of article XX.

- the measures adopted must not constitute *arbitrary* discrimination between countries where the same conditions prevail;
- the measures adopted must not constitute *unjustifiable* discrimination between countries where the same conditions prevail;
- the measures adopted must not constitute a *disguised* restriction on international trade.[46]

According to the Appellate Body, the chapeau of article XX is an expression of the principle of good faith. The principle of good faith is a principle of general law and an international rule and it controls the exercise of rights of states.[47]

The Appellate Body concluded that the U.S. measures were an "unjustifiable discrimination" because they imposed on an exporting WTO member the adoption of identical regulatory requirements to those applied by the United States.[48] The Appellate Body claimed, thus, that the United States established "a rigid and unbending standard."[49] The U.S. measures failed to take into account "different conditions" that may occur in the territory of other state members of WTO.[50] The failure of the United States to use diplomacy, before engaging in the imposition of unilateral measures, and the failure to enter into negotiations with the affected states constituted the basis of discriminatory behavior.[51] The Appellate Body mentioned the decision taken by the Ministers at Marrakesh to establish a Permanent Committee on Trade and Environment (CTE). In that decision, the ministers referred to the Rio Declaration and Agenda 21[52] that established the terms of reference of the CTE. The Appellate Body also referred to a number of international instruments and the importance of reaching consensus on the adoption of measures that deal with the global environment[53] (e.g., article 5 of the Biodiversity Convention[54] and the Convention on the Conservation of Migratory Species of Wild Animals).[55]

---

[46] Para. 150, *id.*

[47] Para. 158, *id.*

[48] Para. 161, *id.*

[49] Para. 163, *id.*

[50] Para. 164, *id.*

[51] Paras. 166–67, *id.*

[52] Agenda 21, June 5, 1992, available online at the Division for Sustainable Development, United Nations Department of Economic & Social Affairs Web site, http://www.un.org/esa/sustdev/documents/agenda21.

[53] Para. 168, 1998 *Shrimp-Turtle* Case, *supra* note 29.

[54] Convention on Biological Diversity, June 5, 1992, reprinted in 31 ILM 826 (1992).

[55] See Chapter 7, Section 5.1.

In 1996, the United States had concluded a multilateral agreement for the protection of sea turtles with several South American countries (Brazil, Costa Rica, Mexico, Nicaragua, and Venezuela).[56] This Inter–American Convention – as the agreement is called – provided for the Appellate Body the example of what the preferable collaborative course of action for the United States should have been with regard to the protection of sea turtles. The Appellate Body pointed out that the United States was willing to enter into negotiations with some members of the WTO but not with others, which was plainly discriminatory and unjustifiable.[57] The negotiated measures between the United States and other American states allowed for a phase-in period – something that was not accorded to other states – which was another plainly discriminatory fact.[58] As a final evidence of discriminatory behavior, the Appellate Body considered the undertaking by the United States to transfer TED technology to other American states. The United States had not engaged in similar efforts with regard to the transfer of technology to the appellees or other states with which it trades.[59] Because of these factors, the Appellate Body decided that the U.S. measures constituted an unjustifiable discrimination between countries in which the same conditions prevail.

With regard to the standard of arbitrary discrimination, the Appellate Body referred again to the fact that the U.S. measures constitute a "single, rigid and unbending requirement."[60] The U.S. measures impose on countries essentially the same regulatory program that the United States has in place regardless of their differentiating conditions. But these countries, the Appellate Body held, are not accorded an opportunity to be heard or to respond to arguments made against them in the course of certification. Countries that are denied certification are not appraised of the reasons of denial and are not given an opportunity to appeal.[61] Thus, due process requirements are violated and the United States measures – contrary to the letter and the spirit of article X(3) of 1994 GATT – fail to establish certain minimum standards for transparency and procedural fairness in the administration of trade regulations.

Because the Appellate Body therefore found that the U.S. regulations constituted an arbitrary and unjustifiable discrimination, it did not proceed further to examine the third standard provided for by the chapeau of article XX – that of "disguised restriction on international trade."

In making this final determination, the Appellate Body took pains to emphasize that its decision does not constitute an intrusion into the public policy matters of states:

We have *not* decided that the protection and preservation of the environment is of no significance to the Members of the WTO. Clearly, it is. We have *not* decided that the sovereign nations that are Members of the WTO cannot adopt effective measures to protect endangered species, such as sea turtles. Clearly they can and should. And we have *not* decided that sovereign states should not act together bilaterally, plurilaterally

---

[56] Para. 169, 1998 *Shrimp-Turtle* case, *supra* note 29.
[57] Para. 172, *id.*
[58] Para. 173, *id.*
[59] Para. 175, *id.*
[60] Para. 177, *id.*
[61] Para. 180, *id.*

or multilaterally, either within the WTO or in other international fora, to protect endangered species or to otherwise protect the environment. Clearly, they should and do [emphasis in the original].[62]

2001 Shrimp-Turtle Case

After the conclusion of the 1998 *Shrimp-Turtle* case, the United States modified its regulations. According to the new regulations, a country may apply for certification even if it does not use TEDs. In such a case, the country has to prove that it is implementing and enforcing a "comparably effective" regulatory program. The United States also entered into multilateral negotiations with the states concerned, including Malaysia, so as to proceed with a multilateral agreement for protection of sea turtles in the course of shrimp harvesting. The negotiations were not fruitful; as a result, the United States resolved to ban the imports of shrimp from Malaysia. Malaysia claimed that the United States had an obligation, according to the 1998 decision of the Appellate Body, not only to enter into negotiations but also to conclude an agreement.

The panel viewed the obligation of the United States, as imposed by the 1998 *Shrimp-Turtle* decision, as an obligation to negotiate in good faith an international agreement rather than as an obligation to conclude an agreement, and ruled against Malaysia.[63]

The Appellate Body agreed with the panel.[64] The Appellate Body argued additionally that requiring the United States to conclude an agreement with Malaysia – in order to avoid a characterization of the turtle protective measure as arbitrary or discriminatory – would amount to giving Malaysia in effect a veto power over whether the United States can fulfill its obligations under the WTO.[65] The Appellate Body concurred with the panel that the efforts of the United States regarding the negotiation of an agreement with Malaysia were serious and good faith efforts on the basis of "active participation and financial support to the negotiations."[66] Thus, the Appellate Body concluded that a commitment to an, in principle, multilateral method would give ground to unilateral action when the multilateral approach fails to produce desirable results.

Asbestos Case

Another article of the GATT that has come under scrutiny is Article III(4), which includes the national treatment requirement. Article III(4) states:

> The products of the territory of any Member imported into the territory of any other Member shall be accorded treatment no less favorable than that accorded to *like products* of national origin in respect of all laws, regulations and requirements affecting their internal sale, offering for sale, purchase, transportation, distribution or use . . . [emphasis added].

---

[62] Para. 185, *id.*

[63] Para. 5.1, Report of the Panel, United States – Import Prohibition of Certain Shrimp and Shrimp Products, Recourse to Article 21.5 of the DSU by Malaysia, WT/DS58/RW, June 15, 2001.

[64] Report of the Appellate Body, United States – Import Prohibition of Certain Shrimp and Shrimp Products, Recourse to Article 21.5 of the DSU by Malaysia, WT/DS58/AB/RW, Oct. 22, 2001.

[65] Para. 123, *id.*

[66] Para. 132, *id.*

The question that came before the panel was whether Canadian imports into France, such as asbestos fibers, are like certain other kinds of fibers. According to the French authorities, supported by the EU, asbestos fibers were not "like" other fibers because of the health risks associated with asbestos. Canada, by contrast, argued that health risks should not be taken into account when deciding on the likeness of products. The panel agreed with Canada by applying four criteria that had been applied unfailingly in prior cases when deciding the "likeness as below" of products:

1. the properties, nature, and quality of products;
2. the end-uses of products;
3. consumer's tastes and habits; and
4. the tariff classification of products.[67]

The EU sought to reverse the panel's decision, claiming, *inter alia*, that the panel erred in its application of the concept of like products because it excluded from its consideration the health risks associated with asbestos fibers. The Appellate Body[68] agreed with the EU and specified that the inquiry into the first criterion of physical properties of a product should include an analysis of the risks posed by the product on human health. The Appellate Body ruled that the carcinogenicity and toxicity of asbestos fibers are an aspect of their physical properties that separates them from other fibers.[69] The Appellate Body ruled that the panel erred when it failed to take into account evidence relating to the consumers' tastes and habits in relation to asbestos fibers and other fibers.[70]

3.2. Sanitary and Phytosanitary Measures

Hormones Case

The *Hormones* case[71] involved a dispute regarding an import ban imposed by the EU on all meat products produced with hormones. The ban affected countries such as the United States and Canada. The substantive articles of the SPS agreement that came under the review of the panel were articles 3.1 and 3.3, and articles 5.1 and 5.5. These articles mandate that national SPS measures must be based on international standards and that, if a state adopts higher standards than those mandated by international law, these higher national standards must be scientifically justified. Such scientific justification should involve the performance of a risk assessment.

According to article 3.1 of the SPS agreement:

> To harmonize sanitary and phytosanitary measures on as wide a basis as possible, Members shall *base their sanitary or phytosanitary measures on international standards*, guidelines or recommendations, where they exist, except as otherwise provided for in this Agreement, and in particular in paragraph 3 [emphasis added].

---

[67] Paras. 8.130 & 8.132, Report of the Panel, European Communities – Measures Affecting Asbestos and Asbestos-Containing Products, WT/DS135/R, Sept. 18, 2000.

[68] Report of the Appellate Body, European Communities – Measures Affecting Asbestos and Asbestos-Containing Products, WT/DS135/AB/R, Mar. 12, 2001.

[69] Para. 114, *id.* ("This carcinogenicity, or toxicity, constitutes, as we see it, a defining aspect of the physical properties of chrysotile asbestos fibres").

[70] Paras. 121–22, *id.*

[71] Report of the Appellate Body, EC Measures Concerning Meat and Meat Products (Hormones), WT/DS48/AB/R, Jan. 16, 1998 [hereinafter *Hormones* case].

According to article 3.3 of the SPS agreement:

Members may introduce or maintain sanitary or phytosanitary measures which result in a higher level of sanitary or phytosanitary protection than would be achieved by measures based on the relevant international standards, guidelines or recommendations, if there is a *scientific justification* or as a consequence of the level of sanitary or phytosanitary protection a Member determines to be appropriate in accordance with the relevant provisions of paragraphs *1 through 8 of Article 5*. Notwithstanding the above, all measures which result in a level of sanitary or phytosanitary protection different from that which would be achieved by measures based on international standards, guidelines or recommendations *shall not be inconsistent with any other provision of this Agreement* [emphasis added].

The term "scientific justification" is further elucidated in a footnote to article 3.3, in which it is mentioned that scientific justification exists if a member determines, in conformity with the provisions of the SPS agreement, that the relevant international standards, guidelines or recommendations are not sufficient to achieve the appropriate level of sanitary or phytosanitary protection.

Article 3.3 also refers to article 5.1. According to article 5.1:

Members shall ensure that their sanitary or phytosanitary measures are based on an assessment, as appropriate to the circumstances, of the risks to human, animal or plant life or health, taking into account risk assessment techniques developed by the relevant international organizations.

Furthermore, the WTO panels have read article 5.1 in conjunction with article 2.2 of the SPS agreement, which reads as follows:

Members shall ensure that any sanitary or phytosanitary measure is applied only to the extent necessary to protect human, animal or plant life or health, is based on scientific principles and is not maintained without sufficient scientific evidence.

Article 5.5 of the SPS agreement has to do with the application of the standards of consistency in the implementation of SPS measures so that they do not constitute discrimination or disguised restriction on international trade:

With the objective of achieving consistency in the application of the concept of appropriate level of sanitary and phytosanitary protection against risks to human life or health, or to animal and plant life or health, each Member shall avoid arbitrary or unjustifiable distinctions in the levels it considers to be appropriate in different situations, if such distinctions result in discrimination or a disguised restriction on international trade.

Furthermore, article 5.5 is read in conjunction with article 2.3 of the SPS agreement, which provides that:

Members shall ensure that their sanitary and phytosanitary measures do not arbitrarily or unjustifiably discriminate between Members where identical or similar conditions prevail, including between their own territory and that of other Members. Sanitary and phytosanitary measures shall not be applied in a manner which would constitute a disguised restriction on international trade.

The *Hormones* case involved the use of hormones in the production of meat products. The European Union banned the import of such products because of the potential adverse effects of use of hormones on the final consumer. The case had to do with whether such a ban was correctly based on a risk assessment on the use of these hormones and their effect on consumers.

In the *Hormones* case, the panel read article 3.1 expansively.[72] According to the panel, domestic standards based on international standards, as enunciated in article 3.1, means domestic measures that are in conformity with international standards. For domestic measures to be in conformity with international standards, they have to be inclusive of some if not all of the elements of international standards.[73]

The Appellate Body disagreed with this interpretation of article 3.1 by the panel.[74] However, it concurred with the panel that higher standards of protection applied domestically must be based on scientific justification and the risk assessment procedure established in article 5.1. The Appellate Body concurred with the panel that article 5.1 must be read together with article 2.2 and that higher standards must be based on "scientific principles" and should not be maintained "without scientific evidence."[75]

The Appellate Body examined Paragraph 4 of Annex A of the SPS agreement, which provides the definition of risk assessment as "the evaluation of the potential for adverse effects on human or animal health"[76] arising from contaminants, toxins, and disease-causing organisms in foodstuff. The Appellate Body also took into account article 5.2 of the SPS agreement, which provides an indicative list of factors that must be taken into account in conducting risk assessment.[77]

The Appellate Body concluded that the EU had not conducted an appropriate risk assessment with regard to the use of hormones for growth promotion purposes.[78] The Appellate Body stated that the

> monographs and the articles and opinions of individual scientists have not evaluated the carcinogenic potential of those hormones when used specifically *for growth promotion purposes* [emphasis in the original].

On the contrary, according to the Appellate Body,

> the scientific studies referred to by the European Communities in respect to the five hormones involved . . . concluded that their use for growth promotion purposes is "safe," if the hormones are administered in accordance with the requirements of good veterinary practice.[79]

The Appellate Body concluded, therefore, that the EU failed to provide a risk assessment in accordance with articles 5.1 and 5.2 of the SPS agreement. Domestic measures that provide a higher level of protection of human and animal health

---

[72] Report of the Panel, Complaint by the United States – EC Measures Concerning Meat and Meat Products (Hormones), WT/DS26/R/USA, Aug. 18, 1997.

[73] Paras. 157–68, *id.*

[74] See Hormones case, *supra* note 71.

[75] Paras. 178–81, *id.*

[76] Paras. 182–85, *id.*

[77] Para. 187. According to article 5.2: "In the assessment of risks, Members shall take into account available scientific evidence; relevant processes and production methods; relevant inspection, sampling and testing methods; prevalence of specific diseases or pests; existence of pest- or disease-free areas; relevant ecological and environmental conditions; and quarantine or other treatment."

[78] Para. 199, *id.*

[79] Para. 206, *id.*

(article 3.3) must be based on risk assessment. This means that article 3.3 should be read in conjunction with articles 5.1, and 5.2. Failure to comply with article 5.1 cannot be validated based on article 3.3.[80]

The Appellate Body, however, disagreed with the panel that the EU measures constituted discrimination or disguised restriction on international trade in contravention of article 5.5 of the SPS agreement and article 2.3 of the SPS agreement.[81] The Appellate Body stated that there is nothing in the architecture of the EC Directives or in the claims of Canada and the United States to indicate that the EC acted inconsistently with article 5.5 of the SPS agreement.[82]

The Appellate Body examined the relevance of the precautionary principle[83] in the interpretation of the SPS agreement. The Appellate Body stated that the precautionary principle is a controversial principle. Some commentators accept the principle as customary international law, whereas others are more skeptical of the validity of the principle as a principle of international law.[84] The Appellate Body eventually concluded that the precautionary principle cannot override the specific provisions of articles 5.1 and 5.2 of the SPS agreement.[85]

Australian Salmon Case

The *Australian Salmon* case[86] involved the import prohibition into Australia of (fresh, chilled or frozen) uncooked salmon imported from Canada. The panel found that Australia acted in violation of articles 5.1, 5.5, and 5.6 of the SPS agreement and, consequently, was also in violation of articles 2.2 and 2.3 of the SPS agreement.[87] The panel concluded that Australia was in violation of article 5.1 of the SPS agreement because its requirement that salmon should be heat-treated before it is imported was not based on a risk assessment as mandated by article 5.1.[88]

The Appellate Body disagreed with the panel. The Appellate Body argued that the panel should have examined not whether the heat treatment requirement was based on a risk assessment but rather whether the prohibition of import of fresh, chilled, or frozen salmon was based on a risk assessment.[89] The Appellate Body then proceeded to identify whether the salmon import prohibition was based on a risk assessment.

---

[80] Paras. 208–09, *id.*

[81] Paras. 210–12, *id.*

[82] Para. 246, *id.*

[83] The precautionary principle is based on the assumption that action on environmental matters must be taken despite the lack of scientific certainty often reversing the burden of proof and placing it on those who claim that an activity is not damaging. The precautionary principle is included in many environmental instruments, see David Freestone, The Precautionary Principle, in International Law and Global Change 21, 31 (Robin Churchill & David Freestone, eds., 1991). See also Chapter 1, Section 6.3.

[84] Para. 123, *Hormones* case, *supra* note 71.

[85] Para. 125, *id.*

[86] Report of the Appellate Body, Australia–Measures Affecting the Importation of Salmon, WT/DS18/AB/R, Oct. 20, 1998 [hereinafter Salmon case].

[87] Para. 9.1., Report of the Panel, Australia – Measures Affecting the Importation of Salmon, WT/DS18/R, June 12, 1998.

[88] Paras. 8.59, 8.60, *id.*

[89] Para. 115, *Salmon* case, *supra* note 86.

The Appellate Body examined paragraph 4 of Annex 4 of the SPSagreement that identify risk assessment as:

> The evaluation of the likelihood of entry, establishment or spread of a pest or disease within the territory of an importing Member according to the sanitary or phytosanitary measures which might be applied, and of the associated potential biological and economic consequences.[90]

Therefore, the point of a risk assessment under article 5.1 is:

1. identification of diseases, the occurrence of which a state may want to prevent;
2. evaluation of the likelihood of entry, establishment, and spread of diseases;
3. evaluation of likelihood of entry, establishment, or spread of diseases in accordance with the SPS measures that might be applied.[91]

In formulating a risk assessment, Australia had met the first requirement of article 5.1, namely, the identification of diseases the entry and spreading of which must be prevented.[92] Regarding the second requirement, the Appellate Body clarified that the evaluation of "likelihood" must not be associated with the mere "possibility" of spreading a disease but, rather, with the "probability" of disease spreading.[93] In its evaluation of the second requirement, the Appellate Body agreed with the panel that "general and vague statements of mere possibility of adverse effects occurring [that is] statements which constitute neither a quantitative nor a qualitative assessment of probability" do not constitute an appropriate risk assessment.[94] The Appellate Body therefore concluded that Australia's report did not meet the second requirement for a risk assessment as mandated under article 5.1.

The Appellate Body then proceeded to examine the third requirement – namely, whether the SPS measure that Australia proposed to apply could avert the likelihood of entry, spreading, and establishing of a disease. The Appellate Body concluded that the risk assessment conducted by Australia did not evaluate, in terms of effectiveness, the SPS measure.[95]

The Appellate Body concluded that the Australian measure of import prohibition was in violation of articles 5.1 and 2.2 of the SPS agreement.

The Appellate Body examined further whether the Australian import prohibition constituted a disguised restriction of international trade in violation of article 5.5 of the SPS agreement. The Appellate Body followed the three-part examination of article 5.5, which was performed by the panel in the *Hormones* case:

1. whether a state adopts different levels of sanitary protection in "different situations";
2. whether the levels of protection demonstrate differences that are "arbitrary or unjustifiable";

---

[90] Para. 120, *id.*
[91] Para. 121, *id.*
[92] Para. 126, *id.*
[93] Para. 123, *id.*
[94] Para. 129, *id.*
[95] Paras. 133–35, *id.*

3. whether the measure that includes differences in the levels of protection results in "discrimination or a disguised restriction on international trade."[96]

The Appellate Body concluded that Australia was in violation of the first element of article 5.5. The Appellate Body stated that the import prohibition on fresh, chilled, or frozen salmon for human consumption and the admission of imports of other uncooked fish are different situations that can be compared under article 5.5 of the SPS agreement.[97] Overall, the risk of biological and economic consequences is the same for the imports of other fish as for the imports of salmon.[98] Australia had not demonstrated that salmon presents a higher risk than other fish. The different treatment of salmon from other fish, thus, was arbitrary and unjustifiable.[99] The Australian prohibition constituted discrimination and a disguised restriction on trade. To reach this decision, the Appellate Body took into consideration a number of factors:

- the rather substantial difference in the levels of protection between the import prohibition on ocean-caught Pacific salmon as opposed to the tolerance of imports of herring;[100]
- the inconsistency of the SPS measures with articles 5.1 and 2.2 of the SPS agreement;[101]
- the inconsistency between the Australian scientific report that recommended the importation of salmon under certain conditions and the Australian final report of import prohibition;[102] and
- the absence of controls on the internal movement of salmon products within Australia compared with the prohibition on importation of salmon from abroad.[103]

4. INTELLECTUAL PROPERTY RIGHTS AND TRADE

Intellectual property rights are not new. They have existed since ancient times. Monopoly rights were granted to inventors as early as 200 BC. Intellectual property rights regimes have a dual purpose: to motivate inventors by recognizing ownership over the fruits of their intellectual endeavors and to benefit the public by requiring the licensing of inventions. The rationale for the protection of intellectual property goes like this: if inventors generate profits from their inventions they are more willing to innovate.

This rationale lies behind plant breeders' rights, copyrights, trademarks, patents, and other types of intellectual property rights. Successful intellectual property rights systems presuppose the striking of a right balance between the public interest that mandates access to inventions and the private interest that secures the property rights

---

[96] Para. 140, *id.*
[97] Para. 144, *id.*
[98] Para. 147, *id.*
[99] Para. 155, *id.*
[100] Para. 163, *id.*
[101] Para. 165, *id.*
[102] Para. 170, *id.*
[103] Para. 174, *id.*

of inventors through the exclusion of others. Most developed countries offer strict protection of intellectual property rights. The same is not true of developing countries. For many years, India denied intellectual property rights for pharmaceutical and agricultural products based on the rationale that such products are essential for the public welfare. Brazil and Argentina encourage the production of cheap drugs for their population.[104]

To receive protection under an intellectual property rights regime, an inventor has to prove novelty, an inventive step, and nonobviousness. This is the difference between a discovery and an invention. A discovery is not protected under the law because it is an abstract idea, an intangible concept, for example, the discovery of a natural force or a mathematical formula. The application of an idea to create something useful constitutes the core of an invention.[105] It is sometimes difficult to draw the line between discoveries and inventions, especially, in defining what constitutes commercial application. Because of these difficulties, which are even more acute in the field of biotechnology, there are many challenges to biotechnology inventions. As the line of demarcation between invention and discovery fades away in newer applications, the intellectual property rights regime has been challenged by those who claim that knowledge should belong, in principle, to the public domain.

The issue of protection of intellectual property with regard to biotechnology, development of software, and databases has fueled the conflict between the support of intellectual property rights and the provision of what have been called "global public goods," such as health protection, nutrition, and knowledge. Many commentators have protested what they view as the surrender of "public knowledge" to "protected knowledge." The expansion of the protection of intellectual property rights to include upstream inventions has troubled observers who view that it is important to maintain a "public domain" in which knowledge and the exchange of information can be pursued in accordance with scientific norms.[106] In the past, applied research and science were considered two different fields and scientists had little involvement in industry. These firm boundaries do not exist anymore and technology has become science-intensive. The issue is more obvious in biotechnology, in which inventions have immediate commercial applications and, thus, can qualify for patent protection despite the fact that there are advantages to maintain them as open-access knowledge for the future advancement of biomedical research.[107] Examples include genetically engineered micro-organisms, which are now deemed patentable, and mathematical algorithms that produce concrete results. Some commentators have suggested that the increased protection of intellectual property rights

---

[104] Kristin Dawkins, The TRIPs Agreement: Who Owns and Controls Knowledge and Resources?, Institute for Agriculture and Tade Policy (IATP, WTO Cancun Series Paper No. 5, 2003).

[105] See generally Stephen A. Bent et al., Intellectual Property Rights in Biotechnology Worldwide 106 (1987); See also 35 U.S.C. §103 (1988); Convention on European Patents, Oct. 5, 1973, reprinted in 13 ILM 268 (1974).

[106] See Graeme B. Dinwoodie & Rochelle Cooper Dreyfuss, WTO Dispute Settlement and the Preservation of the Public Domain of Science under International Law, in International Public Goods and the Transfer of Technology under a Globalized Intellectual Property Regime 861 (Keith E. Maskus & Jerome H. Reichman, eds., 2005).

[107] Id.

in the United States has stalled innovation and that such protection is an obstacle to the production of new knowledge.[108] Accordingly, intellectual property rights have been labeled as the "second enclosure movement"[109] and doubts have been raised on whether such an enclosure would really spur innovation.[110] This suspicion that surrounds the intellectual property rights regime is apparent in international arenas in the enunciation and implementation of the TRIPs agreement over pharmaceutical products and genetic resources. The debates are demonstrative of the clashes the protection of intellectual property has spurred in international fora.

4.1. Intellectual Property Rights Institutions and Trade

The World Intellectual Property Rights Organization (WIPO) was established in the early 1970s to administer a number of intellectual property rights conventions. The Paris Convention for the Protection of Industrial Property[111] was adopted in 1883 and the Berne Convention for the Protection of Literary and Artistic Works was adopted in 1886.[112] Since then, the organization has grown and it manages 23 treaties and 180 state parties. The fundamental core of the WIPO activities is the protection of intellectual property rights through the creation of international norms and standards. Some of the treaties that the organization administers set out global standards and states that adopt the treaties are bound to apply these standards in their territory. The Paris and the Berne Conventions are examples of such treaties. Recent examples involve the WIPO Copyright Treaty (WCT)[113] and the WIPO Performances and Phonograms Treaty (WPPT).[114] These treaties update intellectual property rights protection given the proliferation of new types of inventions. The Trademark Treaty adopted in 1994[115] and the Patent Law Treaty adopted in 2000[116] have as a purpose to harmonize national standards by simplifying patent and trademark registration.

Other WIPO treaties attempt to establish a global system of intellectual property protection. For instance, the Patent Cooperation Treaty[117] establishes a single international patent application, which has legal effect in all the countries that have adopted the convention. Once a patent is filed, the applicant receives valuable

---

[108] *Id.*

[109] The first enclosure movement involved the process of privatization of communal lands in order to avoid what Garrett Hardin had called "the tragedy of commons." See Garrett Hardin, The Tragedy of Commons, Science 1243, Dec. 12, 1968.

[110] James Boyle, The Second Enclosure Movement and the Construction of the Public Domain, 66 Law and Contemporary Problems 33, 34 (2003).

[111] Paris Convention for the Protection of Industrial Property, Mar. 20, 1883, as latest revised on Sept. 28, 1979, available online at http://www.wipo.int/treaties.

[112] Berne Convention for the Protection of Literary and Artistic Works, Sept. 9, 1886, available online at http://www.wipo.int/treaties.

[113] WIPO Copyright Treaty, Dec. 20, 1996, available online at http://www.wipo.int/treaties.

[114] Convention for the Protection of Producers of Phonograms against Unauthorized Duplication of their Phonograms, Oct. 29, 1971, available online at http://www.wipo.int/treaties.

[115] Trademark Law Treaty, Oct. 27, 1994, available online at http://www.wipo.int/treaties.

[116] Patent Law Treaty, June 1, 2000, available online at http://www.wipo.int/treaties.

[117] Patent Cooperation Treaty, June 19, 1970, as last amended Oct. 3, 2001, available online at http://www.wipo.int/treaties.

information from all the countries under the Patent Cooperation Treaty on the patentability of his/her invention and has information to decide in which of the countries he/she should continue with his/her application. Other agreements that seek to provide a global trademark registration system include the Madrid Agreement Concerning the International Registration of Marks[118] and the Budapest Treaty on the International Recognition of the Deposit of Microorganisms for the Purposes of Patent Procedure.[119]

Furthermore, the WIPO administers a number of treaties that could be characterized as classification treaties. The purpose of these treaties is to create databases on patents, trademarks, and industrial designs that would make easy the retrieval of information. The classification systems that these treaties offer are essential for potential applicants of patents or for those registering a trademark or design. These potential applicants need to search large amounts of information to determine whether their inventions, trademarks, or industrial designs are new. Such classification treaties include the Strasbourg Agreement Concerning the International Patent Classification,[120] the Nice Agreement Concerning the International Classification of Goods and Services for the Purposes of Registration of Marks,[121] and the Locarno Agreement Establishing an International Classification for Industrial Designs.[122] To understand the breadth and extent of patent protection under the WIPO system, suffice it to say that the International Patent Classification system has defined some seventy thousand technology categories. Currently, the WIPO is attempting to establish a WIPOnet – a global intellectual property information network. The purpose of the WIPOnet is to facilitate the digital exchange of intellectual property information between intellectual property offices of member states.

Other functions of the WIPO are to provide technical assistance to developing countries, especially, to least–developed countries. The WIPO has established the Intergovernmental Committee on Intellectual Property and Genetic Resources, Traditional Knowledge and Folklore. The purpose of the committee is to examine access to genetic resources and benefit sharing and the protection of traditional knowledge associated with the exploitation of genetic resources.

Intellectual property rights have now also the backing of the World Trade Organization under the Trade-Related Intellectual Property Rights (TRIPs) Agreement.[123] Before the adoption of the TRIPs agreement, intellectual property rights were not protected under the multilaral trading system established by the GATT. The purpose

[118] Madrid Agreement Concerning the International Registration of Marks, April 14, 1891, as latest amended Sept. 28, 1979, available online at http://www.wipo.int/treaties.

[119] Budapest Treaty on the International Recognition of the Deposit of Microorganisms for the Purposes of Patent Procedure, April 28, 1977, as last amended Sept. 26, 1980, available online at http://www.wipo.int/treaties.

[120] Strasbourg Agreement Concerning the International Patent Classification, March 24, 1971, as amended Sept. 28, 1979, available online at http://www.wipo.int/treaties.

[121] Nice Agreement Concerning the International Classification of Goods and Services for the Purposes of the Registration of Marks, June 15, 1957, as last amended on Sept. 28, 1979, available online at http://www.wipo.int/treaties.

[122] Locarno Agreement Establishing an International Classification for Industrial Designs, Oct. 8, 1968, as last amended Sept. 28, 1979, available online at http://www.wipo.int/treaties.

[123] TRIPs Agreement, Annex IC of the Marrakesh Agreement Establishing the World Trade Organization, April 15, 1994, *supra* note 4.

of the TRIPs agreement is not to replace the intellectual property rights instruments adopted under the umbrella of the WIPO. The purpose of the TRIPs is to ensure, instead, that the high level of protection available to intellectual property holders, through international conventions and domestic systems, is preserved in international trade transactions.[124] As a result, a "conglomerate intellectual property regime" has been developed whereby the two organizations, the WTO and the WIPO, share responsibilities in their respective areas of expertise. Although in the WTO the emphasis is placed on enforcement and dispute settlement, the purpose of the WIPO is to propose new forms of intellectual property protection, to ensure the execution of current intellectual property agreements, and to provide technical assistance to developing countries.[125] It seems that this two-track intellectual property protection system has benefited the WIPO, as it has helped to generate a new spurt of intellectual activity in the organization.[126]

The TRIPs agreement was adopted as part of the package deal during the negotiations that led to the establishment of the WTO. The idea of the TRIPs agreement, which would be attached to WTO package, was initiated by the United States, supported by the European Union, and resisted by developing countries. The United States, which was under pressure from knowledge-based industries – the pharmaceutical, seed, and software industries – proposed the TRIPs agreement to induce developing countries to a system of intellectual property controls. Developing countries have resisted intellectual property rights because of their lack of institutional capacity to enforce such rights.

Furthermore, developing countries are apprehensive of the impacts of intellectual property protection on their nascent economic development. Many developing countries are fully aware that, without what is called "piracy" in the developed world, many products, such as life-saving pharmaceuticals or software and improved seed varieties would be economically prohibitive for their citizens.

As a rule, developed nations have generated most inventions. Therefore, developed countries attempt to protect inventors under various intellectual property right systems. Developing nations are not that much involved in the creation of new technology and, thus, have weak or nonexistent intellectual property rights systems. Developing countries have actually profited from technology developed and patented elsewhere that is not subjected to protection within their territories.

Thus, one could claim that the North-South divide in the area of intellectual property rights has to do with divergent interests with the regard to the protection of such rights. What in the developed world has been considered "piracy," copying of inventions without paying royalties to patent holders, in the developing world is a legal (or illegal) but frequently a legitimate practice tolerated for the purposes of development of national economy. Without "piracy" most developing countries could not afford the newest technologies. By contrast, leaders in the production of

---

[124] A related agreement has been signed between the WIPO and the WTO that entered into force in 1996. See Agreement Between the World Intellectual Property Organization and the World Trade Organization, Dec. 22, 1995, reprinted in 35 ILM 754 (1996).

[125] Laurence R. Helfer, Regime Shifting: The TRIPs Agreement and New Dynamics of International Intellectual Property Lawmaking 22, 29 Yale Journal of International Law (2004), available online at Social Science Research Network Web site, http://ssrn.com/abstract=459740 [hereinafter Helfer 2004].

[126] Id. at 22–23.

new technology, such as the United States, have always considered the trumping of intellectual property rights as an unfair trade practice and have threatened retaliatory sanctions.

Despite their disapproval of intellectual property rights, developing countries eventually acquiesced to the adoption of the TRIPs agreement. This is because the TRIPs agreement was a component of the package deal in which they were able to secure concessions in textiles and agriculture.[127] The more advanced of developing countries also were lured by propositions that a stable intellectual property rights regime would increase foreign companies' interest in direct investment in their territories.[128] Developing countries were granted further transition periods until 2000 to adjust their national systems to the protection of intellectual property rights. Least-developed countries were given even longer transition periods until 2006.[129] Furthermore, certain TRIPs provisions were to be reviewed within four years, after the entry into force of the agreement, to ensure their relevance.[130] Developing countries determined that it was better to adopt a multilateral agreement with harmonized rules than to have to succumb to unilateral trade sanctions. The United States had been able in the past to obtain intellectual property protection concessions for its industries in a number of bilateral agreements with developing countries. Some developing countries figured, therefore, that multilateralism was better than *ad hoc* bilateralism.

At first blush, the transfer of intellectual property issues from the WIPO to the WTO seems unwarranted. The WIPO has been the forum that traditionally has dealt with intellectual property rights and could undertake, states willing, the function of ensuring that such rights are taken seriously in international trade. However, from the perspective of developed countries that wished to enforce intellectual property protection, the WIPO was a weak organization lacking enforcement and dispute settlement procedures. Like other UN organizations, the WIPO was viewed as an organization captured by developing countries' interests[131] and unable to take action. Some commentators have called the transition of intellectual property issues from the WIPO to the WTO as regime shifting[132] or regime/forum shopping.[133] Because developed countries could not have their interests served by the WIPO, they transferred intellectual property under the WTO, an institution that

---

[127] Laurence R. Helfer, Intellectual Property Rights in Plant Varieties: An Overview with Options for National Governments 19, FAO Legal Papers Online #31, July 2002 [hereinafter Helfer 2002].

[128] For an extensive analysis of the reasons why developing countries signed the TRIPs Agreement, see A.O. Adede, The Political Economy of the TRIPs Agreement: Origins and History of Negotiations, paper prepared for the Multi-Stakeholders Dialogue at the Aberdare Country Club in Kenya, July 30–31, 2002 sponsored by the Center for Trade and Sustainable Development (ICTSD), the African Centre for Technology Studies (ACTS) in collaboration with the Quaker United Nations Office (QUNO).

[129] For the transition periods for different countries, see arts. 65–66, TRIPs Agreement, *supra* note 4.

[130] See art. 27(3)(b), *id.*

[131] In the 1970s developing countries were increasingly critical of the patent system. These countries raised their concerns at the WIPO diplomatic conference held between 1980 and 1984 and they demanded a change of the patent rules of the Paris Convention for the Protection of Industrial Property to grant them preferential treatment. The United States strongly opposed the amendment of the convention and the conference reached a standstill. See Helfer 2004, *supra* note 125, at 17.

[132] *Id.*

[133] See Kal Raustiala & David G. Victor, Regime Complex for Plant Genetic Resources, International Organization, Spring 2004, available online at http://ssrn.com/abstract=441463.

they have more control over and in which they could extract more concessions from developing countries based on the "package deal" approach that characterizes most WTO arrangements. The WTO presented more opportunities for compromise and enforcement unavailable in the WIPO regime. The dispute settlement arrangement under the WTO is one of the most effective dispute resolution procedures offered by international law.[134]

The TRIPs agreement is a flexible agreement. Because of its flexibility, the agreement could be interpreted as an effort to enforce a strong version of intellectual property rights in international trade transactions. And this is how developed countries have interpreted the agreement. Another possible interpretation is to view the agreement as a classic free trade agreement whose attempt is not to propose a strong protection of intellectual property rights but to protect free trade from an abuse of such rights. The "safeguard" clauses included in the agreement certainly favor such an interpretation and such an interpretation is preferred by developing countries.

The TRIPs agreement allows for minimum levels of protection of intellectual property rights. Member states can set higher standards in excess of the minimum standards provided for in the agreement.[135] Patent protection in the TRIPs agreement is provided for in articles 27–34. Patents are available for inventions – products or processes – that are new, involve an inventive step, and are capable of industrial application.[136] The inclusion of processes in the patent protection system was in the interest of a pharmaceutical industry that wished to secure not only the final product but also the process through which such product is made. The TRIPs agreement provides that a patent holder must be awarded exclusive rights of making, using, offering for sale, selling, or importing a patented product or process. A patent holder can assign or transfer a patent through licensing.[137] The patent protection must last, at least, twenty years from the date of filing of a patent application.[138] Article 27 provides for what has been called "nondiscrimination" in granting patents to inventors – with regard to the place of invention, the field of technology, and whether products are imported or locally produced.[139]

Developing nations and countries with economies in transition are granted the possibility of postponing the application of patent provisions for four years after the entry into force of the agreement – that is, until January 1, 2000.[140] Least-developed countries had until January 2006 to comply with most of the TRIPs patent provisions.[141] Developing countries that do not provide patent protection for a particular technological area are granted an additional period of five years, until January 1, 2005, to put in place the institutional mechanisms for intellectual property rights in that area.[142]

---

[134] Helfer 2002, *supra* note 127, at 21.
[135] Art. 1(1), TRIPs, *supra* note 4.
[136] Art. 27(1), *id.*
[137] Art. 28, *id.*
[138] Art. 33, *id.*
[139] Art. 27(1), *id.*
[140] Art. 65(2)–(3), *id.*
[141] Art. 66(1), *id.*
[142] Art. 65(4), *id.*

Special treatment for least-developed countries is provided also in article 66(2). Developed countries undertake to provide incentives to enterprises and institutions in their territories for the purposes of promoting and encouraging technology transfer to least-developed country members "in order to enable them to create a sound and viable technological base."

The special needs of developing countries are emphasized again in article 67. Article 67 provides that "developed country Members shall provide, on request and on mutually agreed terms and conditions, technical and financial cooperation in favor of developing and least-developed country Members."

Article 27(2) provides for exceptions to patent protection. Member states may exclude from patentability inventions when this is necessary to protect *ordre public* or morality, including the protection of human, animal, or plant life or health, or to avoid serious prejudice to the environment. The reasons for exclusion must not be based on the fact that commercial exploitation of an excluded invention is merely prohibited by domestic law.

Another possibility for exceptions is provided for in article 30. Article 30 states that members may "provide limited exceptions to the exclusive rights conferred by a patent." Such exceptions must not, however,

> unreasonably conflict with the normal exploitation of the patent and ... unreasonably prejudice the legitimate interests of the patent owner, taking into account of the legitimate interests of third parties.

The question that emerged in interpreting article 30 is whether exceptions allowed by it may violate the nondiscrimination clause provided for in article 27(1). As mentioned earlier, article 27(1) provides that states must not discriminate in granting patents with regard to the type of technology involved, the place of invention and whether the products are locally produced or imported. Thus, if a state grants exceptions with regard to a technological field (for instance biotechnology) it could be claimed that the exception constitutes a violation of the nondiscrimination clause.

Article 31 widens even further the possibility for exceptions by providing for what has been called "compulsory licensing." At the heart of compulsory licensing is the possibility for a state to use a patent without the authorization of the right holder. Because the laws of many states provide for compulsory licensing, the purpose of article 31 is to constrain the circumstances under which a compulsory license may be granted. It is provided, therefore, that compulsory licensing must be considered based on the individual merits of each situation.[143] Before granting compulsory licensing, states must have made efforts to obtain authorization from the right holder "on reasonable commercial terms" without success "within a reasonable period of time."[144] The requirement of an attempt to obtain the authorization of the patent holder can be waived, however, under a national emergency situation or in other circumstances of extreme urgency – but, even under these circumstances, the patent holder must be notified "as soon as reasonably practicable."[145] Other limitations on compulsory licensing are that such licensing must be "authorized

[143] Art. 31(a), *id.*
[144] Art. 31(b), *id.*
[145] Art. 31(b), *id.*

predominantly for the supply of the domestic market"[146] and that the right holder must be "paid adequate remuneration...taking into account the economic value of the authorization."[147] The decision relating to remuneration must be subject to judicial review.[148]

Despite the attempt to put a lid on the possibilities of granting compulsory licenses, article 31 leaves open many questions that could be subject to creative interpretation. One such question has to do with the length of negotiations that a state has to hold with a patent holder before taking the drastic step of compulsory licensing. Another question has to do with the determination of adequate remuneration under circumstances of compulsory licensing. Furthermore, what constitutes national emergency or other circumstances of extreme urgency is left to state discretion.

Another way to circumvent the rights of patent holders is through what has been called "exhaustion." Article 6 of the TRIPs provides that "nothing [in TRIPs] shall be used to address the issue of exhaustion of intellectual property rights." The question, therefore, is whether the patent holder retains any rights after he/she has introduced a product to the market or whether the initial sale of the product "exhausts" the rights of patent holder. If the conclusion is made that the patent holder exhausts his/her rights after the initial sale in a country, then the patent holder is deprived of the possibility to price discriminate and offer the same product in a second country at a higher price. This is because the second country can import the product from the initial country at a lower price, instead of paying the patent holder the higher price he/she requested. Such imports have been called "parallel imports" because the second country has a choice to import a product from the patent holder or to use the initial country of sale. Solving the exhaustion issue would require an answer to the question of whether a patent holder can prevent parallel imports. The issue of parallel imports has been quite acute in the area of patented pharmaceuticals.

Further latitude is provided to TRIPs members through the objectives and principles articles included in the agreement. According to the Vienna Convention on the Law of Treaties,[149] the objectives of an agreement are important in the interpretation of the agreement.[150] The objectives and principles clauses and the exceptions to the TRIPs agreement, analyzed earlier, have been considered "safeguard," "savings" clauses that would allow interpretitve flexibility to developing countries in their implementation of the TRIPs agreement.

In the objectives article,[151] it is mentioned that the protection and enforcement of intellectual property rights should contribute to the transfer and dissemination of technology to the mutual advantage of producers and users in a manner conductive to social and economic welfare. Using this provision, countries could claim

---

[146] Art. 31(f), *id.*

[147] Art. 31(h), *id.*

[148] Art. 31(j), *id.*

[149] Vienna Convention on the Law of Treaties, May 23, 1969, reprinted in 8 ILM 679 (1969).

[150] According to article 30 of the Vienna Convention on the Law of Treaties: "A treaty shall be interpreted in good faith in accordance with the ordinary meaning to be given to the terms of the treaty in their context and in the light of its object and purpose." *Id.*

[151] Art. 7, TRIPs, *supra* note 4.

that a strict interpretation of intellectual property rights, which grants the inventor unqualified exclusive rights, is contrary to the objectives of the agreement because such objectives call for the dissemination of technology and the contribution to social welfare.

The principles article[152] provides in a circular manner that states can take measures to protect public health and nutrition and promote public interest in sectors vital to socioeconomic and technological development. But such measures, it is provided, must be consistent with the TRIPs agreement.[153] Article 8 provides for the need to prevent the abuse of intellectual property rights by right holders who may resort to practices that "unreasonably restrain trade or adversely affect the international transfer of technology."[154] Developing countries could, therefore, claim potentially an abuse of rights by patent holders under the broad provisions of the TRIPs agreement. But such a tendency for broad interpretation is likely to be curbed by the willingness of developed states to enforce a version of the agreement that is, indeed, protective of intellectual property rights.

The enforcement articles of the TRIPs agreement give further latitude to state parties. It is provided, for instance, in article 41, that member states must make sure that appropriate provisions are available under their law to prevent infringement of intellectual property rights. The enforcement of the TRIPs agreement must not take place, however, in such a manner that would create barriers to legitimate trade and safeguards must be provided against the abuse of intellectual property rights.[155] Article 40 is devoted to the control of anticompetitive practices of contractual licensing of products or processes protected by intellectual property rights. The TRIPs agreement provides that countries can in their legislation specify licensing practices that may, in particular cases, constitute an abuse of intellectual property rights having an adverse effect on competition in the relevant market.[156] Furthermore, in article 40(1), it is acknowledged that some licensing practices or provisions that have to do with intellectual property rights may have adverse effects on trade and may impede the transfer and dissemination of technology.

In addition to the specific articles of the agreement, the preamble sets the tone for the implementation and interpretation of the agreement. For instance, paragraph 5 of the preamble mentions that state parties to the agreement recognize "the underlying public policy objectives of national systems for the protection of intellectual property, including development and technological objectives." Paragraph 6 of the preamble emphasizes "the special needs of the least-developed country Members in respect of maximum flexibility in the domestic implementation of laws and regulations in order to enable them to create a sound and viable technological base." From these two paragraphs, one could gauge that the purpose of the TRIPs agreement is to establish intellectual property rights for the purposes of development. Under a developing country view, the TRIPs agreement protects the public domain by

---

[152] Art. 8, *id.*
[153] Art. 8(1), *id.*
[154] Art. 8(2), *id.*
[155] Art. 41(1), *id.*
[156] Art. 40(2), *id.*

providing temporary and restricted rights, the purpose of which is to assist in the materialization of free trade.[157]

The TRIPs agreement is, thus, a flexible agreement. The question is whether developing countries would be able to take advantage of that flexibility to promote an intellectual property rights regime more suitable to their needs. The disputes that arise out of the TRIPs agreement would have to be resolved by the WTO panels or the WTO Appellate Body. At this point, both the United States and the European Union have dominated the dispute settlement system of the GATT/WTO. From 1948 to 2000, the United States was either the complainant or the defendant in 340 GATT/WTO disputes constituting 52 percent of the total number of 654 disputes. The European Union was party to 238 disputes, or 36 percent of all cases. When the United States and the European Union are not complainants or defendants, they are usually third parties to a dispute.[158] Participation in dispute settlement proceedings could be expensive for developing countries. The content of dispute settlement proceedings is based on legalities and expertise in WTO legal matters is needed. Many developing countries do not have that expertise endogenously and cannot also purchase it because it is very expensive (e.g., hiring U.S. and European law firms).[159] Therefore, they refrain from participating in dispute settlement panels and, thus, they do not acquire the expertise needed to defend their interests. Commentators have concluded that because of lack of means and economies of scale – as some developing countries do not have as many disputes to bring to WTO panels as the United States and Europe – developing countries do not get the opportunity to expand their expertise in WTO matters and procedures. This lack of expertise is detrimental to their interests.[160]

4.2. Intellectual Property Rights and Pharmaceuticals

The TRIPs agreement has created an atmosphere of discontent in the developing world with regard to the intellectual property protection of pharmaceutical products. As analyzed in Chapter 1, the WSSD Conference alluded explicitly to the need to prioritize cure for the diseases that afflict developing countries.

The pharmaceuticals debate is examined for two reasons. Pharmaceuticals are important for the fight against certain diseases in the developing world, such as malaria, that are caused by certain environmental conditions. The WSSD Conference, an environmental conference, put in the forefront of the agenda the importance of addressing the various diseases ailing the developing world.

The pharmaceuticals debate is an indicative expression of the battle, at the value level, that characterizes the intellectual property rights regime. The value of rewarding the innovation of an inventor by granting monopoly rights and the value of public domain knowledge that can be accomplished by curbing such monopoly

---

[157] For such a view of copyright law, see L. Ray Patterson & Stanley W. Lindberg, The Nature of Copyright: A Law of Users' Rights (1991).

[158] Gregory Shaffer, Recognizing Public Goods in WTO Dispute Settlement: Who Participates? Who Decides? 7(2) Journal of International Economic Law 459, 470–71 (2004).

[159] Id. at 473.

[160] Id. at 474.

rights. Some actually view the pharmaceuticals issue, under the WTO, as a con-flict among three competing public goods: the generation of new knowledge, the provision of public health, and the development of rules that foster free trade and competition.[161]

The discontent with regard to drug patenting has been brewing since the adoption of the TRIPs agreement. Developing countries have used the World Health Orga-nization (WHO) as an alternative forum to shift their frustration with the TRIPs agreement. WHO, in general, is perceived as an organization more receptive to the needs of developing countries than the WTO.[162] WHO has encouraged developing countries to use the flexible, safeguard clauses of the TRIPs agreement and to avoid the imposition of stringent intellectual property rights on pharmaceuticals. As men-tioned earlier, the TRIPs agreement includes several safeguard clauses that mandate the balancing of intellectual property protection and public health objectives. Such safeguard clauses include the extension of transition periods, the parallel importation of drugs from countries where they are sold more cheaply, compulsory licensing, and exceptions to exclusive rights.[163]

The uproar against the high prices of HIV/AIDS drugs sorely needed for the battle of the AIDS epidemic in Africa galvanized the international community in the early 2000s. A number of pharmaceutical companies sued South Africa for the unauthorized use of HIV/AIDS drugs. The lawsuit created unfavorable publicity for the companies involved and they had to drop their lawsuit in 2001. Furthermore, developed countries, after the adoption of the TRIPs agreement, have engaged in efforts to enforce more stringent intellectual rights protection in developing coun-tries through bilateral agreements that have been called "TRIPs plus" bilateral agree-ments. Such efforts have concentrated on the strict interpretation of the exceptions and flexible arrangements provided for in the TRIPs agreement. The UN High Commissioner for Human Rights and the WHO have criticized such "TRIPs plus" agreements as being in violation of human rights.[164]

Drug patenting became so controversial that a consensus developed that a new instrument was, indeed, needed to appease a general climate of animosity toward drug patent protection. The Doha Declaration was adopted in 2001 to act as the mechanism that would reduce this animosity.[165] The Doha Declaration is based on the recognition of "the gravity of the public health problems afflicting many developing countries and least-developed countries, especially those resulting from HIV/AIDS, tuberculosis, malaria and other epidemics."[166] The declaration acknowledges the importance of intellectual property protection for the develop-ment of new medicines but, at the same time, expresses concerns that such protection could affect drug pricing.[167] The declaration proposes that the TRIPs agreement

---

[161] *Id.* at 459.

[162] See Helfer 2004, *supra* note 125.

[163] *Id.* at 39.

[164] Laurence R. Helfer, Human Rights and Intellectual Property: Conflict or Co-existence?, 5 Minnesota Intellectual Property Review 47, 59 (2003) [hereinafter Helfer Human Rights].

[165] World Trade Organization, Doha Ministerial Declaration on the TRIPS Agreement and Public Health, Ministerial Conference, Fourth Session, Doha, WT/MIN(01)/DEC/2, Nov. 14, 2001.

[166] Para. 1, *id.*

[167] Para. 3, *id.*

"should be interpreted and implemented in a manner supportive of WTO Members' *right to protect public health* and, in particular, to promote access to medicines for all" [emphasis added].[168] Thus, the rhetoric of rights to a public good, namely, health, is used to counterbalance property rights over medicines. The declaration provides that the TRIPs agreement should be interpreted based on its principles and objectives.[169] Such principles and objectives, as mentioned earlier, refer to the transfer and dissemination of technology to the mutual advantage of producers and users and in a manner conductive to social and economic welfare.[170] In order to execute their obligations under the TRIPs agreement, states must adopt measures necessary to protect public health and nutrition and to promote public interest in sectors of importance for the socioeconomic and technological development in a manner that is consistent with the TRIPs agreement.[171] These circular articulations of the objectives and principles sections of the TRIPs agreement are proposed to be used to curb the stringent application of intellectual property rights over pharmaceuticals.

The Doha Declaration further confirms that each member state of the WHO has the right to grant compulsory licenses and the freedom to determine the grounds on which such licenses should be granted.[172] The declaration recognizes that some countries would not be able to implement compulsory licensing because they lack manufacturing capacity and instructs the TRIPs Council to find a solution to the problem.[173] Each member has the right to determine what constitutes a national emergency that would trigger the procedure of compulsory licensing.[174] The Doha Declaration goes on to assert that HIV/AIDs, tuberculosis, malaria, and other epidemics can present a national emergency.[175] The declaration further expands the transition periods with regard to pharmaceuticals, for least-developed countries, until January 1, 2016, and gives the freedom to these countries to seek additional extensions of transition periods.[176] Regarding issues of exhaustion, the declaration leaves it up to member states to determine their own system on exhaustion and, thus, the decision of whether or not to authorize parallel imports.[177]

The Doha Ministerial Declaration has been hailed by developing countries as a victory. A declaration at the ministerial level was considered the most expeditious way of modifying the TRIPs agreement to the benefit of developing countries in

---

[168] Para. 4, *id.*

[169] Para. 5(a), *id.*

[170] Art. 7, TRIPs Agreement, *supra* note 4.

[171] Art. 8, *id.*

[172] Para. 5(b), Doha Declaration, *supra* note 165.

[173] Para. 6, *id.* Developing countries sought to include a provision in the Doha Declaration that would have empowered them to grant compulsory licenses to foreign suppliers to provide medicines for their domestic markets. Developing countries sought also a provision to grant compulsory licenses to domestic producers in order for them to supply medicines to foreign markets. However, these provisions were not eventually included in the Doha Declaration due to developed countries' resistance. See Alan O'Neil Sykes, TRIPs, Pharmaceuticals, Developing Countries, and the Doha 'Solution', University of Chicago Law School, Olin Working Paper No. 140, Feb. 2002, available online at http://ssrn.com/abstract=300834.

[174] Para. 5(b), Doha Declaration, *supra* note 165.

[175] Para. 5(c), *id.*

[176] Para. 7, *id.*

[177] Para. 5(d), *id.*

the face of a public health emergency.[178] The amendment procedure provided for in the agreement is much more cumbersome and time consuming because it requires ratification by national legislative bodies to enter into force.[179] The declaration, being a soft law instrument, cannot formally amend the TRIPs agreement. However, given that it is a declaration adopted at the highest level of the TRIPs apparatus, the ministerial conference, it is likely to be viewed as a persuasive instrument in the interpretation of TRIPs by the WTO Dispute Settlement Body. In the *Shrimp-Turtle* case,[180] the Appellate Body of the WTO relied on a ministerial decision[181] and the Preamble of the WTO agreement to evaluate environmental measures that inhibit free trade. It is hoped, thus, that the Appellate Body would do the same in the case of pharmaceuticals.

Although developing countries and human rights NGOs viewed the declaration as a victory, others viewed it as the beginning of erosion of intellectual property protection that was hard fought for by developed countries and their industries. It has been speculated that the erosion of intellectual property rights protection in the developing world is likely to discourage pharmaceutical companies to engage in drug development useful for the ailments facing developing countries.[182]

4.3. Intellectual Property Rights and Genetic Resources

4.3.1. Letter of TRIPs

The debate on whether intellectual property rights can be granted for the modification of living organisms and biotechnology inventions has yet to subside. Patent rights on biotechnology inventions are granted for innovations that involve the isolation, purification, modification, or manipulation of the natural properties of a substance for future commercial application. The United States was one of the first countries to enact patent rights for biotechnology inventions.[183] In order to receive protection for biotechnology devices, an inventor has to prove novelty, an inventive step, and nonobviousness.[184] More or less similar requirements are followed in the European regulation of patents.[185] By contrast, developing countries have been more reluctant to grant intellectual property rights over living organisms. Some of their objections have been based on moral grounds, but it is not coincidental that most of these objections come from countries that are recipients rather than creators of technological innovation.

---

[178] Frederick M. Abbott, The TRIPS Agreement, Access to Medicines and the WTO Doha Ministerial Conference, FSU College of Law, Public Law Working Paper No. 3, Oct. 2001, available online at http://ssrn.com/abstract=285934.

[179] See art. X, WTO Agreement, *supra* note 1.

[180] See *Shrimp-Turtle* case, *supra* note 29.

[181] Decision of Ministers at Marrakesh to Establish a Permanent Committee on Trade and Environment (CTE). See *Shrimp-Turtle* case, *supra* note 52. See also Abbott, *supra* note 178, at 33.

[182] Sykes, *supra* note 173.

[183] The first court decision that established intellectual property rights over biotechnology in the United States is *Diamond v. Chakrabarty*, 447 U.S. 303 (1980).

[184] See 35 U.S.C. §103 (1988); Convention on European Patents, Oct. 5, 1973, reprinted in 13 ILM 268 (1974).

[185] Directive 98/44/EC of the European Parliament and of the Council of July 6, 1998 on the legal protection of biotechnological innovation, OJ L 213/13, 30.7.98.

Article 27 of the TRIPs agreement provides the basic requirements for patent protection. Article 27 states:

1. Subject to the provisions of paragraphs 2 and 3 [of article 27], patents shall be available for any inventions, whether products or processes, in all fields of technology, provided that they are new, involve an inventive step and are capable of industrial application. [Subject to certain exceptions] patents shall be available and patent rights enjoyable without discrimination as to the place of invention, the field of technology and whether products are imported or locally produced.

2. Members can exclude from patentability inventions, the prevention within their territory of the commercial exploitation of which is necessary to protect *ordre public* or morality, including to protect human, animal or plant life or health or to avoid serious prejudice to the environment, provided that such exclusion is not made merely because the exploitation is prohibited by their law.

3. Members may also exclude from patentability:

(a) diagnostic, therapeutic and surgical methods for the treatment of humans and animals; (b) plants and animals other than micro-organisms, and essentially biological processes for the production of plants and animals other than non-biological and microbiological processes. However, Members shall provide for the protection of plant varieties either by patents or by an effective *sui generis* system or by any combination thereof. The provisions of this subparagraph shall be reviewed four years after the date of entry into force of the WTO Agreement.

Thus, according to article 27(3)(b) plant varieties can be protected under patents or other *sui generis* systems or a combination of both. The same article endorses patent protection for micro-organisms and nonbiological and microbiological processes, thereby providing protection for biotechnology devices. Member states, however, can exclude plants and animals and essentially biological processes for the production of plants and animals from patentability. Developing countries have attempted to interpret article 27(3)(b) strictly as providing protection for micro-organisms but not for cells of plants and animals. There is even a debate over the patentability of micro-organisms and microbiological processes, despite the clear endorsement of their patentability under the TRIPs agreement.

Furthermore, according to article 27(2), countries may refuse to grant patents when this is necessary to protect public order or morality, human, animal, and plant life or health or to avoid adverse environmental effects. But the refusal cannot be based on the fact that the national health and safety regulations of the country have yet to approve the product or process.

4.3.2. State Practice

Plant breeders' rights were the first intellectual property rights to be asserted over living resources. Many countries today have established extensive rights for their breeders and biotechnology inventors with provisions similar to those encountered in patent protection. In the 1920s and 1930s, countries had started to expand intellectual property protection to include plant breeders' rights.[186] The United States introduced the Plant Patent Protection Act,[187] which permits patent rights on asexually

---

[186] Calestous Juma, The Gene Hunters: Biotechnology and the Scramble for Genes 154 (1989).
[187] 35 U.S.C. §161 (1988).

produced plants, and the Plant Variety Protection Act, which provides protection for sexually produced plants.[188] European countries also introduced plant breeders' rights.[189]

Plant breeders' rights are exclusive rights granted to breeders to prevent the unauthorized use of the varieties they concoct. The International Union for the Protection of New Varieties of Plants, known by its French acronym as the UPOV Convention,[190] has unequivocally established plant breeders' rights on plant varieties that are novel, uniform, distinctive, and stable.[191] The 1991 amendments of the convention strengthened breeders' rights by removing the farmers' exception and leaving it up to individual countries to decide whether such an exception is appropriate for their domestic legislation. According to the earlier version of the convention, farmers could save seeds protected under breeders' rights for the following year. Under the 1991 amendments, the ability of farmers to save seeds is to be decided by national legislation.[192] The convention has made it more difficult to use breeders' varieties for experimental purposes. In general, the amendments are an attempt to place breeders' rights on an equal footing with patent rights.

Patent rights are granted for biotechnology inventions and provide stronger protection for those inventions than the protection provided for traditional breeding. In the late 1970s and 1980s, with the development of biotechnology, pressures accumulated for the adoption of stronger intellectual property rights over bioengineered germplasm that would provide more protection for the innovator. Many countries started to introduce patent rights for biotechnological innovations, whereas a parallel system remained for the protection of traditional breeding. The U.S. and EU efforts to establish intellectual property rights over biotechnology were the first such efforts.

Breeders' rights and intellectual property rights over biotechnology give breeders and biotechnology enterprises incentives to produce more varieties by allowing them to reap off sizeable profits from their innovations. As a result, a powerful seed industry has been developed that is becoming increasingly concentrated.

4.3.3. Seed Wars

Although improved germplasm has been protected – either through breeders' rights or patents – and is becoming prohibitively expensive in the developing world,

---

[188] Plant Variety Protection Act (PVPA) of 1970, 7 U.S.C §§ 2321–2583 (1988). The protection provided by a plant patent is not as extensive as the protection granted by a utility patent. Also the standards of novelty, utility and nonobviousness are less strict for plant varieties than utility patents.

[189] See, e.g., Convention for the Establishment of the European and Mediterranean Plant Protection Organization, April 18, 1957, UKTS 44.

[190] The UPOV Convention was adopted in 1961 and was amended in 1978 and in 1991, reprinted in 815 UNTS 89. Forty countries have laws that cover plant breeders' rights. See Commission on Genetic Resources for Food and Agriculture, Second Extraordinary Session, Report on the State of World's Plant Genetic Resources, at 37, CGRFA-EX2/96/2, April 22–27, 1996.

[191] Art. 5, UPOV Convention, id.

[192] See art. 14(1), id. However, national legislation can restrict breeders' rights and allow for the farmers' exception. See art. 15(2), id. See also Adelaida Harris, Why Change the UPOV Convention?, Information Meeting on the Protection of New Varieties of Plants under the UPOV Convention, UPOV/IM/96/3.

unimproved germplasm that has been cultivated and protected for years by people of the developing world has remained, until recently, a free-access resource. In the meantime, the power of the seed industry has increased. The top ten seed companies control a sizeable piece of the total seed market and 90 percent of the agrochemical market.[193]

The power of the seed industry and its ability to set prices for the advanced varieties it produces[194] set off the seed wars of the 1980s. The disputes focused on the open-access policies for unmodified germplasm implemented by gene banks and the IARCs.[195] Developing countries argued that international gene banks benefit essentially multinational seed corporations. The IARCs used to allow, until recently, free access to unimproved germplasm in their collections, but the high-yielding varieties produced by seed companies, by using that germplasm, are quite expensive to acquire because they are protected by patents or breeders' rights. Developing countries argue that it is unfair to have to pay for these varieties, which would have not been developed, without the free-access policies to unmodified germplasm located in international gene banks, and, initially, discovered within their territory.

The seed wars demonstrated the unwillingness of developing countries to keep sharing their germplasm resources with multinational corporations and triggered the adoption of a number of instruments that asserted national sovereignty over germplasm resources. The Biodiversity Convention adopted in 1992 is one of these instruments.[196] The Biodiversity Convention mandates the equitable sharing of benefits derived from the use and exploitation of biodiversity resources.[197] The convention does not define what equitable sharing entails. But equitable sharing has generally been interpreted to mean the sharing by developing countries in the royalty system established by intellectual property rights over modified genetic resources. These are modified resources that were initially found or cultivated by indigenous peoples and farmers in the developing world. Because the Biodiversity Convention could be interpreted to include rules that mandate the sharing of royalties, the U.S. biotechnology industry has urged the U.S. government not to ratify the convention.

However, the adoption of the convention has not been without consequences. Seed and pharmaceutical industries, which, up to the late 1980s, were able to obtain germplasm from developing countries without monetary compensation, must now request permission for access and pay a fee for the use and commercialization of plant resources. The CBD encourages a sort of bilateralism by which corporations and nonprofit organizations must sign agreements with developing countries governments in order to obtain germplasm. These agreements, called Material Transfer Agreements (MTAs), have been used for the transfer of germplasm from developing

---

[193] The seed market and agro-chemical market are valued respectively at US $23 billion and US $31 billion. See Dawkins, *supra* note 104.

[194] *Id.*

[195] The International Agricultural Research Centers (IARCs) were established in the early 1970s and they have been the repository of many crops and plants. They contain today some of the major gene banks of the world. See Chapter 7, Section 2.1.2.3.

[196] See CBD, Chapter 7, Section 2.1.

[197] See art. 16(1) & (3), *id.*

countries to institutions and companies of the developed world that wish to experiment with raw germplasm.

Attempts by corporations to obtain seeds, to isolate their properties, and to claim intellectual property rights over them without acknowledging and compensating the contributions of indigenous peoples and farmers have been called biopiracy.[198] Incidents involving alleged misappropriation of germplasm, and the knowledge associated with it, have acquired international dimensions entangling states, nongovernmental institutions, indigenous farmers, and corporations. Some of these incidents have implicated the IARCs. It has been claimed, for instance, that seed companies frequently acquire germplasm from the centers and, by performing minor modifications, seek to privatize germplasm resources through the intellectual property rights system. Such incidents put in the forefront the debate of whether the isolation and purification of genetic material from its natural state could possibly qualify as an invention entitled to patent protection. The climate of distrust has been reflected in the international instruments that have been adopted that embody the transition from a common heritage system over germplasm to a property rights system.

In addition to the CBD, which essentially does away with perceptions that germplasm could be free-access resource, the evolution of another instrument indicates the gradual transition from a common heritage regime to a property regime.

The International Undertaking on Plant Genetic Resources was one of the first instruments to deal with germplasm resources for food and agriculture. In the 1983 version of the Undertaking, it is mentioned that plant genetic resources are a heritage of mankind and should be available without restriction.[199] The Undertaking was modified in 1989 to clarify that "free access does not mean free of charge."[200] It was modified further in 1991 to clarify that the principle that genetic resources are the heritage of mankind is subject to the "sovereignty of states over plant genetic resources."[201]

4.3.4. TRIPs and Traditional Knowledge

As mentioned earlier, the CBD repeatedly provides for the equitable sharing of benefits, coming from the exploitation of germplasm resources, with the country of origin of those resources. Although the convention does not specifically describe the parameters of equitable sharing, one could gauge that such sharing would not involve the monopolization of rights by a patent holder. Thus, the content of the convention is clearly distributive.[202] The collision between the TRIPs agreement and the Biodiversity Convention (CBD)[203] is a result of the fact that the TRIPs agreement does not provide anything about the equitable sharing of benefits – coming out of innovations using germplasm resources – with the country of origin of such resources. The TRIPs agreement has to do with the protection of intellectual

---

[198] See The Captain Hook Awards for Outstanding Achievements in Biopiracy, News Releases, Rural Advancement Foundation International (RAFI), May 17, 2000.

[199] Art. 1, Resolution 8/83, Twenty-Second Session, FAO Conference, Nov. 5–23, 1983.

[200] Resolution 4/89, Twenty-Fifth Session, FAO Conference, Nov. 11–29, 1989.

[201] Resolution 3/91, Twenty-Sixth Session, FAO Conference, Nov. 9–27, 1991.

[202] See also Raustiala, *supra* note 133, at 25.

[203] Art. 16(1) and (3), CBD, *supra* note 196.

property rights and the potential abuse of such rights. But no article in the TRIPs agreement supports the redistribution of benefits connected with such rights. The TRIPs agreement does not recognize collective property rights for indigenous peoples' innovations in plant resources or farmers' rights.

The discontent with the TRIPs approach to intellectual property rights over genetic resources is evident in the Doha Ministerial Declaration. The Doha Ministerial Declaration instructs the TRIPs council to examine the relationship among the TRIPs agreement, the CBD, and the protection of traditional knowledge and folklore and other relevant developments presented by member states.[204] The TRIPs council is directed to receive guidance from the objectives and principles articles of the TRIPs agreement and to take into account fully the development dimension.[205]

Given the protection of intellectual property rights over bioengineered living organisms, developing countries have claimed that in both biodiversity and biotechnology, the final product of legal protection is a living organism. If developed countries can grant intellectual property rights over genes, developing countries should be able to grant property rights over resources that would have disappeared without the input of indigenous peoples and farmers. From the perspective of the formal intellectual property regime (e.g., the TRIPs agreement), much of indigenous peoples' and farmers' knowledge has been viewed as public domain knowledge and, thus, freely accessible to everyone. Treating indigenous peoples' knowledge as public domain knowledge legitimized the exploitation of such knowledge by outsiders. These outsiders used the knowledge "as an upstream input for later downstream innovations" that they then privatized through intellectual property rights.[206] In this respect, the CBD provides that the knowledge, innovations, and practices of indigenous and local communities can be used only with the approval of those communities and the benefits from use must be equitably shared.[207]

Because intellectual property rights over natural genetic resources are difficult to establish and enforce, it has been proposed that a system of *sui generis* rights must be established. Such *sui generis* rights, under the name "traditional resource rights," it is proposed, would constitute a framework into which the claims of indigenous groups could be integrated.[208] Such rights could be established for all resources *in situ* and *ex situ* that have been experimented with and have been singled out for use by indigenous peoples.

Intellectual property protection for indigenous peoples' traditional knowledge is being explored by the human rights regime since the beginning of the 1990s. The Draft UN Declaration on the Rights of Indigenous Peoples includes an article that provides for the right of indigenous peoples to the full ownership, control, and protection of their cultural and intellectual property.[209] Such property, according to

---

[204] World Trade Organization, Doha Ministerial Declaration, Ministerial Conference, Fourth Session, Doha, WT/MIN(01)/DEC/1, Nov. 14, 2001.

[205] Para. 19, *id.*

[206] Helfer Human Rights, *supra* note 164, at 52.

[207] See Chapter 7, Section 2.1.2.2.

[208] Darrell A. Posey, Intellectual Property Rights and Just Compensation for Indigenous Peoples, 6 Anthropology Today 13 (1990).

[209] Art. 29, Commission on Human Rights, Draft of the United Nations Declaration on the Rights of Indigenous Peoples, UN Doc. E/CN.4/Sub.2/1994/2/Add.1 [hereinafter Draft Declaration].

the declaration, must be subject to restitution if it has been taken without the free
and informed consent of indigenous peoples and in violation of their laws, traditions
and customs.[210]

The Draft Principles and Guidelines for the Protection of the Heritage of Indigenous Peoples[211] define heritage, *inter alia*, as cultural property of all kinds – scientific,
agricultural, medicinal, biodiversity-related, and ecological knowledge, including
innovations based on that knowledge.[212] National laws, for the protection of indigenous peoples' heritage, should guarantee that indigenous peoples obtain full restitution and just compensation for the acquisition, documentation, or use of their
heritage without proper authorization by them.[213] By the same token, third parties are denied the ability to obtain patent, copyright, or other legal protection for
any component of indigenous peoples' heritage unless they can document the free
and informed consent of traditional owners to an arrangement for the sharing of
ownership, control and benefits.[214]

Thus, the Guidelines and the Draft Declaration attempt to ensure that indigenous
knowledge is not free-access knowledge. These provisions are in conformity with
the TRIPs agreement because they provide restrictions for access to traditional
knowledge appreciating, thus, such knowledge as proprietary knowledge. At the
same time, however, the protection of traditional knowledge in these instruments
is schematic because no specific legal entities are designated that would benefit
from legal protection. The absence of enforceable provisions for the protection of
indigenous peoples' knowledge is the weak element of human rights instruments.

The first real confrontation between the human rights regime and the TRIPs
agreement took place in the Sub–commission on the Promotion and Protection of
Human Rights. The sub–commission adopted a resolution in 2000,[215] in which
it challenged the TRIPs agreement as antithetical to the realization of economic,
cultural, and social rights. The resolution noted that actual and potential conflicts
exist between the implementation of the TRIPs agreement and the realization of
economic, social, and cultural rights. The resolution emphasized the obstacles to the
transfers of technology to developing countries and the impacts of TRIPs on the
right to food through the patenting of plant varieties. It alluded to the phenomenon
of biopiracy and the reduction of communities' control over their own genetic
resources and cultural values. The impacts of restrictions on access to pharmaceuticals
and on the right to health also were underlined.

The resolution gave the impetus for the adoption of a number of other soft law
instruments underlining the incompatibility between the human rights regime and

---

[210] Art. 12, *id*.
[211] Sub–commission on the Promotion and Protection of Human Rights, Draft Principles and Guidelines
for the Protection of the Heritage of Indigenous Peoples, Decision 2000/07 [hereinafter Guidelines].
See also Report of the Seminar on the Draft Principles and Guidelines for the Protection of the Heritage
of Indigenous People, Subcommission on the Promotion and Protection of Human Rights, Fifty-second
session, Item 7 of the provisional agenda, UN Doc. E/CN.4./Sub.2/2000/26, June 19, 2000.
[212] Guideline 13, Guidelines, *id*.
[213] Guideline 23(b), *id*.
[214] Guideline 23(c), *id*.
[215] Sub–commission on the Promotion and Protection of Human Rights, Resolution 2000/7 on Intellectual
Property Rights and Human Rights, Aug. 17, 2000.

the TRIPs Agreement.[216] The subcommission itself issued another resolution in 2001 in which it requested the UN Commissioner for Human Rights to seek an observer status in the ongoing review of the TRIPs agreement. The 2001 resolution asked the commissioner to investigate into whether the patent, as a legal instrument, was compatible with the protection of human rights and to conduct an analysis of the impact of the TRIPs agreement on the rights of indigenous peoples. The 2001 resolution encouraged all the special raporteurs on the right to food, education, and adequate housing to include in their reports a review of the implications of the TRIPs agreement for rights that fall under their mandate.[217]

It remains to be seen how the evolution of the debate within the human rights regime will impact the evolution of the TRIPs agreement.

Developing countries have adopted laws that establish collective rights for the knowledge of indigenous peoples. For instance, the Organization of African Unity (OAU) has drafted legislation that provides comprehensive *sui generis* rights, as an alternative to patents, to compensate local communities for developing plant varieties. Ecuador's constitution recognizes collective intellectual property rights. The Andean nations – Bolivia, Columbia, Ecuador, Peru, and Venezuela – have enacted regional intellectual property laws that conform with the TRIPs. Other countries, such as Brazil and Costa Rica, have established rights for indigenous communities to protect their knowledge and resources.[218]

4.3.5. TRIPs and Farmers' Rights

Farmers' rights have been recognized by various international instruments. The 1989 Undertaking on Plant Genetic Resources recognizes, in both Annexes I and II, farmers' rights[219] that are "vested in the international community, as a trustee for present and future generations of farmers," so as to ensure full benefits to farmers and support for their contributions.[220] The recently adopted International Treaty on Plant Genetic Resources also clearly recognizes the rights of farmers[221] but leaves it up to national law to determine the breadth of those rights.[222]

Overall, however, the modern approach to intellectual property rights cannot be well fitted to protect farmers' rights. Intellectual property is fashioned as a discrete innovation, at a moment in time, by identifiable persons. Farmers' rights involve

---

[216] See Commission on Human Rights, Resolution 2001/33 on access to medication in the context of pandemics such as HIV/AIDS, April 20, 2001; Progress Report submitted by Mr. J. Oloka-Onyango and Ms. D. Udagama on globalization and its impact on the full enjoyment of human rights, UN Doc. E/CN.4/Sub.2/2001/10; Report of High Commissioner for Human Rights on the impact of TRIPS Agreement on Human Rights, UN Doc. E/CN.4/Sub.2/2001/13.

[217] Sub–commission on the Promotion and Protection of Human Rights, Resolution 2001/21 on Intellectual Property Rights and Human Rights, Aug. 16, 2001.

[218] Dawkins, *supra* note 104.

[219] See Undertaking on Plant Genetic Resources, *supra* note 200, which recognizes the contributions of farmers to the improvement of plant genetic resources.

[220] *Id.*

[221] International Treaty on Plant Genetic Resources for Food and Agriculture, Nov. 3, 2001, available online at http://www.fao.org/ag/cgrfa/itpgr.htm. Article 9.1 provides that "Contracting Parties recognize the enormous contributions that the local and indigenous communities and farmers of all regions of the world . . . have made and will continue to make for the conservation and development of plant genetic resources which constitute the basis of food and agriculture production throughout the world."

[222] Art. 9.2, *id.*

the protection of innovation that happens through the slow aggregation of novel approaches by many "unknown" members of a community.[223]

A variety of mechanisms have been proposed for the protection of farmers' rights ranging from an international fund to market mechanisms or a mixture of mechanisms.[224]

The implementation of such mechanisms, however, could encounter problems, for example:[225]

- Varieties cultivated by farmers present more diversity in their gene pool than breeder varieties that are uniform and stable. Genetic techniques to identify landraces eligible for intellectual property protection could be costly and inconclusive.
- It would be difficult to identify the farmers to be compensated. There is no global institutional mechanism that represents the interests of farmers. Therefore, either an international association of farmers must be established or states could represent the interests of farmers. But again which farmers of which states must be compensated will become an issue.
- The basis for the contributions to a fund that will compensate farmers could create significant conflict.[226]

As mentioned in Chapter 7, a mechanism to compensate farmers has been adopted under the Treaty on Plant Genetic Resources for Food and Agriculture[227] according to which companies must make payments to a trust account every time a patent removes germplasm from the public domain. This provision imposes, for the first time, a tax on companies that use and experiment with germplasm when such experimentation is fruitful. Many issues, however, remain unresolved, such as the level, form, and manner of payment. The governing body established under the treaty will eventually decide how the payments will be structured and may resolve to impose different levels of payment for different categories of recipients.

5. CONCLUSION

Although one would expect a WTO dispute settlement procedure to always strike the balance in favor of trade liberalization, this has not been the case. The dispute settlement process has progressed cautiously since the first *Tuna-Dolphin* case to include more environmental considerations into the WTO decision-making process. It is remarkable, for instance, that the Appellate Body makes reference to concepts, such as sustainable development. In the 2001 *Shrimp-Turtle* decision, the Appellate

---

[223] Raustiala, *supra* note 133, at 42.

[224] Commission on Plant Genetic Resources, Sixth Session, Item 8 of the Provisional Agenda, Revision of the International Undertaking on Plant Genetic Resources, Analysis of Some Technical, Economic and Legal Aspects for Consideration in Stage II: Access to Plant Genetic Resources and Farmers' Rights, CPGR-6/95/8 Supp. (CPGR-EX1/94/5 SUPP.), June 19–30, 1995.

[225] *Id.*

[226] It has been proposed that contributions could be based on the sales of improved varieties, the value added in agriculture, the gross domestic product, or the scale of a country's contributions to the FAO or the UN. *Id.* at 54.

[227] See *supra* note 221.

Body upheld a unilateral ban on trade based on environmental considerations after evidence was presented that the United States had engaged in sincere efforts to solve the issue multilaterally with no success.

The WTO frequently points out that it has consistently upheld international standards that usually reflect the best practices of developed countries. Such standards, for instance, are included in the SPS agreement that embodies the food standards established by Codex Alimentarius – a joint body of two UN specialized agencies, the WHO, and the FAO. Furthermore, the WTO allows for higher domestic standards, than the established international standards, if a state can prove, by conducting a valid risk assessment, that such standards are justified. The interpretation of the SPS agreement demonstrates that risk assessment based on sound scientific evidence could play a significant role in the future WTO decisions. A state that adopts measures prohibitory of free trade needs to engage in a credible risk assessment that would demonstrate, with some valid probability, that consumer protection is at stake, rather than the protection of a domestic industry.

WTO emphasizes multilateral measures in resolving trade matters as they come into conflict with other legitimate state policies. But WTO has been viewing with suspicion a general resort to unilateralism for the support of national policies even when the national goal to be achieved seems legitimate. Nondiscriminatory unilateralism has been supported only when a country has engaged in good faith efforts to conclude a multilateral treaty that eventually failed.

The TRIPs agreement is a curious development in the history of the WTO, as it does not address the liberalization of trade *per se* but the protection of intellectual property rights. The TRIPs agreement has encountered its first significant challenge with regard to patents granted for pharmaceuticals. Countries have used the exceptions to the agreement and the principles and objectives clauses to support an interpretation of the agreement that facilitates an understanding of property rights as vehicles for the pursuit of a public good – here, public health.

In the case of property rights over biotechnology inventions, countries have challenged the legitimacy (and morality) of declaring property rights over living organisms. In a self-contradictory manner, however, countries have asked for intellectual rights protection on germplasm resources found in nature that have been propagated by indigenous peoples and farmers so as to safeguard the knowledge of those groups and to certify that such knowledge is not free-access knowledge.

Various stakeholders have sought to shift intellectual property rights protection to other international organizations, such as the WIPO, the WHO, the Human Rights Commission, and the FAO. Whether such efforts would lead to the dissipation of theTRIPs agreement or its further expansion and amplification is hard to gauge at this time. Another possibility is that such forum shifting acts just as a temporary tension relief mechanism.

The cases that the DSB has attempted to resolve and the challenges to the TRIPs agreement have given the WTO the opportunity to engage in introspection, so to speak. The WTO gauges the circumstances under which national policies, the pursuit of public good (in terms of environmental standards, SPS measures), and property rights justify a turn away from the pursuit of trade liberalization. The WTO seems to be struggling between two roles. One role has to do with execution of the responsibility of an international trade institution with the goal to support free trade. The other role has do to with an assumption of a role of an arbitrator on issues that are trade-related but also touch the core of public policy making of the nation-state.

There is no doubt that the WTO is involved in some important issues of international policymaking. Some argue that the WTO is not the institution to deal with the articulation of public policy because it is not a democratically elected institution and lacks overall legitimacy and transparency.[228] Lately, and to its credit, the WTO is becoming more open, transparent, and participatory. Public access to the WTO documentation has improved and many of the WTO decisions are available on the WTO Web site. NGOs can attend the plenary meetings of WTO and some 750 such organizations attended the plenary meeting of the WTO in Seattle. A procedure that could enhance transparency in the WTO is the recognition of amicus standing in the dispute settlement procedure. The enhancement of the NGO participation in the dispute settlement process, however, has been resisted by the new members of the WTO, largely developing countries.[229]

Undoubtedly, the WTO today is one of the most authoritative international bodies. The WTO has intruded into many areas of national economic action. Because of its active participation in a variety of international matters, it has been suggested that the Appellate Body of the WTO could become the supreme constitutional/international adjudicative body. Such a transformation could be modeled after the transformation of the European Court of Justice (ECJ). The ECJ (which started basically as a trade court) has become the supreme constitutional body of the European Union. Because of the effectiveness of the WTO, commentators have argued for extension of its jurisdictional reach to other issues including human rights. Despite this optimism, there are fundamental differences between the Appellate Body of the WTO and the ECJ, including the lack of direct effects (that is, decisions binding on nationals of states not only on states) and the teleological approach to interpretation of legislative provisions. As the EU matures, it would become even harder to fairly compare EU developments with international developments.

In a recent study, commissioned by a consultative board put together by the WTO, the role of the WTO as an "international economic regulatory level of government"[230] has been proposed. It has been claimed that the support of the WTO by governments would help them regain the loss of sovereignty that they experience because of globalization. Sovereignty means that governments have meaningful control over their borders, have internal authority, policy autonomy, and are subject to nonintervention. State autonomy and independence are being challenged, however, in the age of globalization in which there are a significant number of market failures, externalities, competition problems, and asymmetries of information.[231] If countries are losing their capacity to regulate in a meaningful fashion at the domestic level, they

---

[228] Robert Keohane & Joseph Nye, The Club Model of Multilateral Cooperation and the WTO: Problems of Democratic Legitimacy, Paper Presented at the Center for Business and Government at Harvard University (June 2000).

[229] The Future of the WTO: Addressing Institutional Challenges in the New Millennium (2005) (This report on the future of the WTO was commissioned by an independent consultative board put together by the Director-General of the WTO).

[230] *Id.* at 34.

[231] *Id.* at 33.

can reclaim that possibility by putting together their resources at the multilateral level. Thus, the loss of control, which is becoming evident at the national or local level, is regained through multilateral efforts.[232] An encouraging trend in this direction is provided by the dispute settlement procedure of the WTO, which has been evaluated as a positive development in the establishment of "rules-based international trade diplomacy." The WTO dispute settlement procedures enhance the "security and predictability" of the international trade system[233] and, as a consequence, of the whole international order.

[232] *Id.* at 34.
[233] *Id.* at 49.

10 Hazardous and Radioactive Wastes

1. STATE OF INTERNATIONAL WASTE TRADE

Waste generation could be conceived a domestic problem that acquired global dimensions as countries started to export their wastes to other countries, especially developing countries. The exports of wastes from developed countries to developing countries that did not have waste regulations and infrastructure caused uproar in international circles, in the beginning of 1980s, and led to the adoption of instruments that have imposed regulatory controls or even have banned waste movements.

Waste transfers to other countries and, especially, to developing countries, were motivated by the high costs of waste disposal in developed countries. Such high costs were due to the Not-In-My Backyard (NIMBY) attitude that inhibited the construction of new waste disposal facilities in many developed countries.

Current trends show that waste generation is on the increase.[1] The biggest waste generators continue to be the United States and member states of the EU. The amount of wastes traded internationally is increasing steadily.[2] The main factor that has contributed to this increase in trade is the growth of transboundary waste movements destined for recovery among the EU countries.[3] Movements of wastes involving developing countries show large fluctuations over time.[4]

The databases available, however, are still incomplete in terms of the data on waste generated and on waste traded. This is because not the same countries report annually on the amounts of wastes they generate and trade. Furthermore, there are still many differences in the national classifications of hazardous wastes.[5] The bulk of the data provided is based on legal, reported waste transfers. Illegal waste transfers are not included in the data unless an illegal waste shipment is apprehended.

---

[1] Global Trends in Generation and Transboundary Movements of Hazardous Wastes and other Wastes 1, Basel Convention Series/SBC No. 02/14, Nov. 2002.

[2] *Id.* at 2.

[3] *Id.*

[4] *Id.*

[5] *Id.* at 1.

2. STATE OF WASTE MANAGEMENT

2.1. Landfill/Geologic Disposal

Today, most hazardous wastes are landfilled. The unsound landfill practices of the past have left numerous abandoned waste disposal sites that require urgent cleanup in many countries. Landfill disposal, however, is still used because it is less expensive than recycling and waste minimization. Technological and other standards preventing contaminants from reaching the groundwater have been developed. These technological standards have made landfill disposal a sounder waste management method. Before constructing a landfill site, the evaluation of the site, including the impact of the site on human health, environment, and life of the neighboring communities, is necessary. Because natural conditions are rarely ideal, landfills frequently are isolated with engineered barriers, such as liners and leak collection systems that control contamination of the surrounding environment and groundwater. Wastes must be securely isolated from the groundwater; the groundwater, as well as the surface water, must be monitored continuously.[6] Landfill infrastructure is important. Waste disposers must additionally have plans for the closure and the postclosure period, especially, regarding the prevention of future groundwater contamination.[7]

Waste isolation from the surrounding environment and aquifers is at the core of radioactive waste management. The IAEA and most countries have espoused geologic disposal as a way to isolate wastes permanently from the surrounding environment. Geologic disposal is based on the multiple barrier concept, which mandates that the long-term safety of radioactive wastes depends on the performance of the components of the whole disposal system, which includes the site, the repository, and the waste package.[8]

In order to select the appropriate radioactive waste site, the geology, hydrology, climate, and topography must be examined and evaluated. The socioeconomic conditions of the communities living around the site must be taken into account, and postoperational surveillance for low-level nuclear wastes is necessary. Monitoring of high-level radioactive wastes may last for one hundred years after disposal in order to allow for retrieval in case of malfunctions. But the long-term safety of the disposal system must not depend on such monitoring. High-level radioactive wastes must be isolated permanently so that future generations will not have to maintain the integrity of the disposal system.

The IAEA has executed many studies on the disposal of radioactive wastes. In 1995, the IAEA promulgated a series of principles that underlined that radioactive waste management must be undertaken in a fashion that would be protective of human health and the environment. Radioactive waste management should not place undue burdens on future generations.[9] Avoiding burdening future generations

---

[6] Elli Louka, Overcoming National Barriers to International Waste Trade: A New Perspective on the Transnational Movements of Hazardous and Radioactive Wastes 78 (1994).

[7] *Id.* at 78 (and accompanying citations).

[8] *Id.* at 79 (and accompanying citations).

[9] The Principles of Radioactive Waste Management (IAEA, Safety Series No. 111-F, 1995).

with radioactive waste management makes long-term waste disposal in secure under-ground facilities necessary. The IAEA has cautioned against the long-term storage of wastes in above-the-ground facilities.[10] This is because of the long periods of time required for radioactive waste to lose radioactivity.[11]

The dumping of low-level radioactive wastes at sea has ceased, whereas the dump-ing of high-level radioactive wastes has been banned by the London Dumping Con-vention since the early 1970s. The prohibitions, however, are not an indication that illegal disposal has not occurred or is not taking place.

2.2. Marine Disposal

The public opposition to landfill/geologic disposal increases the attraction of marine waste disposal. There are no standards for marine disposal in the sense of technological and performance standards that exist for land disposal and incineration. Although it is often stated that some pretreatment of wastes ending up in the sea is desirable, marine disposal relies primarily on the diluting capacity of the oceans.

The effects of toxic and radioactive substances on the marine environment have not yet been sufficiently identified. Although the IAEA has determined that the adverse effects of dumping of low-level radioactive wastes are not high, the dump-ing of low-level radioactive waste in the seas has officially ceased. Countries have engaged in efforts to control the contamination of seas by toxic substances.[12]

2.3. Treatment

Pretreatment has become the precondition for the sound disposal of wastes. Wastes can be treated either at specialized facilities or at the place of waste generation. Haz-ardous waste treatment includes physical, chemical, and biological treatment. Vitri-fication has been frequently used for the treatment of high-level radioactive wastes. Vitrification essentially involves immobilization of liquid wastes by converting them into a monolithic solid. Various treatment methods for low-level radioactive wastes and mixed wastes exist.[13]

2.4. Incineration

The purpose of incineration is the destruction of hazardous wastes. Incineration has been used for the treatment of certain mixed wastes and low-level radioactive wastes.

Despite its obvious advantage – namely, waste minimization – incineration can cause environmental problems. The incineration ash generated during the burning of wastes can be more toxic than the initial waste stream. This ash must be disposed of soundly. Another disadvantage is that incineration causes air pollution. Air pol-lution control equipment (e.g., scrubbers) could be expensive to install and creates

---

[10] Such disposal of wastes is favored in some environmental circles because it allows for the monitoring of wastes. See Louka, *supra* note 6, at 78, n. 26.

[11] IAEA, The Long Term Storage of Radioactive Wastes: Safety and Sustainability: A Position Paper of International Experts (2003).

[12] See Chapter 4, Section 1.

[13] See Louka, *supra* note 6, at 85–86 (and accompanying citations).

the additional problem of having to dispose of scrubber wastes. Because of these problems, incineration is heavily regulated in most developed countries.[14]

The high costs of incineration may make it unattractive for some developing countries. It is doubtful whether the hazardous wastes of a single developing country can justify the economic costs of an incinerator, especially in countries that are not heavily industrialized.[15] Even localities in developed countries have had sometimes trouble feeding their incinerators, and have enacted, for that purpose, flow control laws that prohibit waste exportation.

A case in point involves the arbitration proceedings that were brought under NAFTA[16] regarding an export ban of PCB wastes from Canada to the United States alleging a breach of articles 1102, 1105, 1106, and 1110 of the NAFTA agreement.[17] The U.S. company that initiated the proceedings, SDMI, argued that that its interest in the Canadian PCB wastes was due to the declining global supply of PCB wastes. The SDMI needed the Canadian PCB wastes to maintain its economic viability.[18] Before the filing of the SDMI claim, the Canadian PCB industry had been engaging in extensive lobbying in order to persuade Canada to ban PCB waste exports.

The NAFTA arbitration tribunal concluded that the Canadian export ban was based on the intent to "protect and promote the market share of enterprises that would carry out the destruction of PCBs in Canada and that were owned by Canadian nationals."[19] Because the ban was not based on environmental reasons, but on a protectionist rationale, the tribunal ruled against it. It is interesting to note that the tribunal was not persuaded by Canada's argument that, according to the Basel Convention, countries must become self-sufficient in the management of their wastes.[20]

2.5. Recycling and Reprocessing

Recycling has been promoted as a sounder waste management method than incineration and land disposal. A major obstacle to recycling, however, is the unstable market for recycled products. Ironically, laws encouraging recycling and waste minimization contribute to the instability of international markets by increasing the supply of recyclable materials without simultaneously stimulating demand.[21]

The reprocessing of radioactive wastes is quite controversial. The purpose of reprocessing is to recover the uranium and plutonium of spent nuclear fuel. Reprocessing reduces the volumes of high-level radioactive wastes but creates greater volumes of intermediate- and low-level wastes. Certain countries do not engage in reprocessing because they view it as undesirable for economic and national security reasons.

---

[14] *Id.* at 87.

[15] *Id.*

[16] North American Free Trade Agreement, Dec. 17, 1992, reprinted in 32 ILM 289 (1993).

[17] S. D. Myers, Inc., ("SDMI") v. Government of Canada, Partial Award, Nov. 11, 2000 (NAFTA Arbitration Case).

[18] Para. 92, *id.*

[19] Para. 162, *id.*

[20] Para. 185, *id.*

[21] Louka, *supra* note 6, at 87 (and accompanying citations).

Reprocessing is undesirable because it produces plutonium that can be used in the production of nuclear weapons. It is also unnecessary because uranium supplies seem adequate to satisfy demand.

Other countries such as France, the United Kingdom, Germany, and Japan view reprocessing as an essential part of the fuel cycle or as a way to postpone painful decisions on permanent waste disposal.[22] The insistence of these countries on reprocessing has caused friction in international relationships. The transfers of reprocessed spent fuel from France to Japan, in combination with the latter's decision to modify its nuclear energy production in order to use mixed plutonium and uranium, have caused great anxiety to its neighboring countries. Some of these countries fear that Japan has accumulated more plutonium than it needs for peaceful purposes. The reprocessing facilities of the United Kingdom have been the subject of international arbitration proceedings regarding the right of the public to know the operational details of such facilities.[23]

The collapse of Eastern Europe and the treaties for the destruction of nuclear weapons have introduced an additional dimension to the international politics of nuclear waste. In order to prevent nuclear weapons from falling into the hands of terrorists or undemocratic regimes, the United States agreed with Russia to purchase the weapons destined for destruction, and to use them as fuel in its nuclear power plants.

It is debatable whether material destined for reprocessing should be treated as waste or as material. During the adoption of the Convention on the Safety of Spent Fuel Management and on the Safety of Radioactive Waste, there was significant debate about whether spent fuel, held at reprocessing facilities, should be covered under the scope of the convention. India objected to the convention's coverage of reprocessing. But, notably, countries such as France, Japan, and the United Kingdom, all of which have reprocessing facilities, seemed more willing to include reprocessing under the auspices of the convention. Eventually, reporting on reprocessing was left at the discretion of state parties.[24] It would have been desirable if the convention had covered expressly reprocessing adding, thus, safeguards preventing the unauthorized use of nuclear material.

3. INTERNATIONAL INSTRUMENTS

3.1. Hazardous Wastes

The Basel Convention
The Basel Convention[25] is the global instrument regulating cross-border waste movements.

---

[22] *Id.* at 89, n. 120.

[23] See *OSPAR* case, Chapter 3, Section 4.2.

[24] For the debates during the negotiations of the convention, see Summary Record of the Fourth Plenary Meeting of the Diplomatic Conference Convened to Adopt a Joint Convention on the Safety of Spent Fuel Management and on the Safety of Radioactive Waste Management, RWSC/DC/SR.4, Sept. 5, 1997.

[25] Basel Convention on the Control of Transboundary Movements of Hazardous Wastes and their Disposal, March 22, 1989, reprinted in 28 ILM 649 (1989).

The convention attempts to regulate waste movements by imposing restrictions because, as emphasized in the preamble, restrictions reduce transfrontier movements and provide incentives for sound waste management. The convention adopts the proximity and self-sufficiency principles.[26] Each country must become self-sufficient in waste management and wastes are to be disposed of as close as possible to the place of generation. However, there are qualifications to the adoption of proximity and self-sufficiency principles. The convention stipulates that state parties must ensure the availability of "adequate" waste facilities located "to the extent possible" within their jurisdiction.[27] It also provides that waste shipments must be reduced to the minimum consistent with environmentally sound and efficient management.[28] The proximity and self-sufficiency principles, thus, are not articulated in a way that would discourage a broader interpretation of the principles.

The convention provides that states must ensure that waste movements are allowed only if the exporting state does not have the capacity to deal with its own wastes[29] or if the exported wastes are to be recycled or recovered in the state of destination.[30] Any other waste movements may still be allowed as long as they do not conflict with the goals of the convention.[31] This reference to the convention's goals is circular and does not provide any further clarification on what appropriate waste management may involve.

The convention further establishes the prior notification and informed consent procedure. State parties must prohibit waste exports, unless they receive the prior written consent of the importing state.[32] More specifically, the exporting state or the generator must notify in writing the importing country and the other concerned states.[33] The importing state must respond in writing and consent to, refuse, or require additional information for the waste transfer.[34] The exporting state must not allow a waste export until the notifier has received a written consent of the importing state, and confirmation from that state of a contractual relationship between the exporter and the disposer specifying that the wastes will be managed soundly.[35] Transit states also must consent to the waste movement, but they may waive their right to consent.[36] Every waste movement must be covered by insurance or other financial guarantee as required by the importing or transit states.[37] The disposer must, on receipt of the wastes, notify the exporter and the exporting state about the completion of disposal. If the exporting state does not receive this information in due course, it must notify the importing state.[38] States can bypass the excessive bureaucracy embedded in the system of prior notification by agreeing to adopt a general notification procedure when wastes possessing the same physical and chemical

[26] Art. 4(2)(b) and (d), *id.*
[27] Art. 4(2)(b), *id.*
[28] *Id.*
[29] Art. 4(9)(a), *id.*
[30] Art. 4(9)(b), *id.*
[31] Art. 4(9)(c), *id.*
[32] Art. 4(1)(c), *id.*
[33] Art. 6(1), *id.*
[34] Art. 6(2), *id.*
[35] Art. 6(3), *id.*
[36] Art. 6(4), *id.*
[37] Art. 6(11), *id.*
[38] Art. 6(9), *id.*

characteristics are transported to the same destination, and through the same customs offices in the exporting, importing, and transit states.[39] The general notification procedure may last for one year.

Exporting states must take back wastes that cannot be disposed of as agreed even if the importing state has given its consent for the transfer.[40] The exporting state must repatriate wastes transferred illegally because of the conduct of the exporter.[41] If it is the importer that engages in illegal trafficking, the importing state must undertake the environmentally sound management of wastes.[42] If neither the exporter nor the importer can be held responsible, the states concerned must cooperate in order to ensure that the wastes will be disposed of soundly as soon as possible.[43] Illegal waste trafficking, according to the convention, involves waste movements without notification or consent, or with consent obtained through falsification, misrepresentation, or fraud.[44] It is also illegal to dispose of wastes by violating the convention or the general principles of international law.[45]

Developing countries succeeded in inserting in the convention provisions on information exchange, technology transfers and financial assistance.[46] The convention provides that states must establish regional or subregional centers, funded voluntarily, for training and technology transfers.[47] States must consider the establishment of a fund that will assist them in cases of emergency resulting from transportation and disposal accidents.[48] They may conclude pertinent bilateral, multilateral, or regional arrangements.[49]

Liability and noncompliance provisions included in the negotiated drafts have not been incorporated in the final version. Liability issues were left to be decided later in a protocol that was eventually adopted in 1999.[50] A proposed noncompliance provision was weakened and adopted as just a verification procedure.[51]

The purpose of the Basel Convention is to establish procedural controls on the transfers of hazardous wastes. In order to accomplish this goal, the convention establishes rules — the requirement of prior notification and informed consent — under the assumption that such rules would facilitate the monitoring of waste movements. As mentioned earlier, the convention does not specify what constitutes sound waste management and, therefore, it could be interpreted to condone free waste transfers provided that prior notification and informed consent requirements are satisfied. Further amendments to the convention, however, have undermined such an interpretation.

---

[39] Art. 6(8), *id.*
[40] Art. 8, *id.*
[41] Art. 9(2), *id.*
[42] Art. 9(3), *id.*
[43] Art. 9(4), *id.*
[44] Art. 9(1)(a)–(d), *id.*
[45] Art. 9(1)(e), *id.*
[46] Art. 10, *id.*
[47] Art. 14(1), *id.*
[48] Art. 14(2), *id.*
[49] Art. 11, *id.*
[50] Art. 12, *id.*
[51] Art. 19, *id.*

Regional Instruments

The Bamako Convention adopted by the OAU[52] incorporates radioactive wastes in the definition of hazardous wastes.[53] It also includes in the hazardous waste definition hazardous substances banned in the state of manufacture.[54] Apart from the expansive hazardous waste definition, the convention follows in the steps of the Basel Convention and imposes even more stringent restrictions on transfrontier waste movements.

The convention bans all waste imports into the African region, and, thus, is in harmony with the Lomé Treaty with which the European Community banned waste exports to sixty-eight African, Caribbean, and Pacific (ACP) countries.[55] Waste imports into the African region, according to the Bamako Convention, are illegal and a criminal act.[56] The waste import prohibitions are not accompanied with enforcement and monitoring mechanisms.[57] The convention does not prescribe a liability regime. It merely provides that state parties must adopt domestic legislation imposing strict, unlimited and joint and several liability on waste generators.[58] The Bamako Convention Secretariat has not been granted more extensive authority than the Basel Secretariat to oversee and enforce the ban.[59]

Waste exports from the African region to third countries are not prohibited. A proposal to ban waste exports from the African region to other developing countries was not fruitful during the negotiations of the convention. The Bamako Convention prohibits sea dumping and sea incineration.[60]

With respect to waste movements within the African region, the Bamako Convention requires prior notification and informed consent but dispenses with the general notification procedure provided for in the Basel Convention.[61] It stresses that waste disposal in the state of origin should be preferred,[62] and that waste movements should be reduced to a minimum. The convention puts further emphasis on the precautionary principle[63] and on clean production methods that exclude "end-of-pipe" pollution controls of any kind.[64]

The provisions on waste transfers between African countries emphasize unduly the proximity and self-sufficiency principles. A loyal implementation of these principles will artificially isolate African countries, which could benefit from regional

---

[52] See Bamako Convention on the Ban of Import into Africa and the Control of Transboundary Movement and Management of Hazardous Wastes within Africa, Jan. 29, 1991, reprinted in 30 ILM 775 (1991). The OAU declared in Resolution 1199 that the Basel Convention was insufficient to protect African countries. It specified that a prohibition of waste shipments into Africa was more appropriate than regulation, and that African countries should agree on a common position to improve the Basel Convention. See OAU Council of Ministers Res. CM/Res. 1199 (XLIX) (June 12, 1989).

[53] Art. 2(2), Bamako Convention, id.

[54] Art. 2(1)(d), id.

[55] Fourth ACP-EEC Lomé Convention, Dec. 15, 1989, reprinted in 29 ILM 809 (1990).

[56] Art. 4(1), Bamako Convention, supra note 52.

[57] Art. 12, id.

[58] Art. 4(3)(b), id.

[59] Art. 16, id.

[60] Art. 4(2), id.

[61] Art. 6(6), id.

[62] Art. 4(3)(d), id.

[63] Art. 4(3)(f), id.

[64] Art. 4(3)(g)–(h), id.

facilities built to receive the aggregate amount of small waste volumes of individual countries. African countries also could engage in waste trade and exchanges with each other, and, generally, foster bilateral and multilateral relationships to solve their waste management problems.

Other regional agreements that are based on prohibitions and restrictions of waste movements include the Waigani Convention[65] and the Protocol on the Prevention of Pollution in the Mediterranean by Transboundary Waste Movements.[66]

Despite the international prohibitory climate, some countries have entered into agreements for the cooperative management of their wastes.[67]

Basel Amendments and the OECD Decisions

Eventually, even under the framework of the Basel Convention, it was decided that the principle of prior notification and informed consent could not curb waste movements and that a system that bans waste transfers to developing countries was necessary. In 1995, with a new article 4A – the export ban amendment – the parties to the Basel Convention decided to prohibit the exports of hazardous wastes for final disposal.[68] State parties decided also to phase out and prohibit, by December 31, 1997, any exports of wastes destined for recovery operations from Annex VII countries to all other countries.[69] Annex VII includes all OECD countries, the European Union, and Liechtenstein. This decision of the parties to the Basel Convention has been incorporated into EU legislation.[70] The Basel Export Ban Amendment, however, has yet to enter into force.

The Basel Convention was further amended in 1998 with the adoption of detailed lists of wastes in Annexes VIII and IX. Annex VIII contains wastes that are subject to the controls of the convention.[71] Annex IX contains wastes that are not considered hazardous – probably destined for recycling operations – and therefore, not subject

---

[65] The Convention to Ban the Importation into the Forum Island Countries of Hazardous and Radioactive Wastes and to Control the Transboundary Movement and Management of Hazardous Wastes within the South Pacific Region, Sept. 16, 1995. The Convention entered into force in October 2001. As of December 2002, the following parties had ratified the convention: Australia, the Cook Islands, the Federated States of Micronesia, Kiribati, Papua New Guinea, Samoa, the Solomon Islands, and Tuvalu.

[66] Protocol on the Prevention of Pollution of the Mediterranean Sea by Transboundary Movements of Hazardous Wastes and their Disposal, Oct. 1, 1996.

[67] See Agreement of Cooperation between the United States of America and the United Mexican States Regarding the Transboundary Shipments of Hazardous Wastes and Hazardous Substances, Nov. 12, 1986. See also Waste Shipment Agreement between Germany and Zimbabwe, May 31, 1994.

[68] See Katarina Kummer, The Basel Convention: Ten Years On, 7 Review of the European Community & International Environmental Law 227 (1998).

[69] The ban amendment to the Basel Convention had not entered into force as of May 2006.

[70] See Council Decision 97/640/EC of 22 September 1997 on approval, on behalf of the Community, of the Amendment to the Convention on the Control of Transboundary Movements of Hazardous Wastes and Their Disposal (Basle Convention), as laid down in Decision III/1 of the Conference of the Parties, OJ L 272/45, 04.10.1997.

[71] Annex VIII (list A) wastes are subject to the controls of the convention but their designation as hazardous should not prevent the use of Annex III to demonstrate that they are nonhazardous. Annex III provides a list of characteristics of hazardous wastes (e.g., toxicity, flammability etc), see Guide to the Basel Convention Control System for Hazardous Waste adopted by the Fourth Meeting of the Conference of the Parties, Feb. 1998 available online http://www.basel.int/pub/instruct.html.

to the requirements of convention.[72] This list of wastes that are innocuous, unless proven otherwise, should help revitalize the recycling industry and should be viewed as a welcomed addition to the regime of the convention.

The concern of unnecessarily suffocating the recycling industry by a too pro-hibitive regime propelled the OECD member countries to adopt more flexible requirements for waste transfers destined for recycling operations. A 1992 OECD Decision[73] classified wastes under three lists:[74]

1. the green list – wastes can be transferred like any other good;
2. the amber list – wastes are subject to notification and consent but consent may be implied;
3. and the red list – waste transfers require always the written consent of the importing country.[75]

Given the 1998 amendments to the Basel Convention, the OECD decided to adopt the lists of wastes established under the Basel Convention and to get rid of the red list transfer procedure. According to the new Decision,[76] wastes are classified under two control systems: the green list control system and the amber list control system. Wastes on the green list (which coincides with Annex XI of the Basel Convention) can be exported without particular restrictions except for those applied to the usual transfers of commercial goods. Wastes on the amber list (Annex II and Annex VIII of the Basel Convention) can be transferred only after the written or tacit consent of the importing country. An abbreviated procedure is provided for wastes destined for preconsented facilities (these are facilities prespecified to receive recyclable wastes and are known as such to both importing and exporting parties).[77]

The OECD's dispensing of the red list procedure means that *written* consent is no longer a requirement even for potentially quite hazardous wastes, such as PCBs, PCTs, and asbestos that were previously controlled under the red list procedure. It is not surprising that the simplification of the OECD procedures has created consternation in some circles that deplore the 2001 OECD Decision as an attempt to dampen the requirements of the Basel Convention.[78] The jurisdictional coverage of OECD decisions, however, does not expand to the politically charged waste

---

[72] Annex XI (list B) wastes are not considered hazardous unless they contain Annex I material causing them to exhibit the characteristics listed in Annex III. Wastes that contain material listed under Annex I are considered hazardous wastes and are strictly regulated under the convention. *Id.*

[73] OECD Decision C(92)39/Final on the Control of the Transboundary Movements of Wastes Destined for Recovery Operations, April 6, 1992.

[74] The Decision was based on a system of classification of wastes known as the International Waste Iden-tification Code (IWIC). The system was abandoned in the 2001 Decision, see *infra* note 77, in favor of the classification system adopted under the Basel Convention.

[75] For more details on this decision, see Louka, *supra* note 6, at 58.

[76] Decision of the Council Concerning the Revision of Decision C(92)39/Final on the Control of Trans-boundary Movements of Wastes Destined for Recovery Operations, C(2001)107/Final, May 21, 2002.

[77] For the repercussions of the 2001 Decision, see OECD Working Group on Waste Prevention and Recycling Guidance, Manual for the Implementation of the OECD Decision C(2001)107/Final, ENV/EPOC/WGWPR(2001)6/FINAL, Oct. 17, 2002.

[78] Basel Action Network (BAN) & European Environmental Bureau (EEB), Comments on the Review and Revision of the European Union Waste Shipment Regulation, Nov. 2001.

transfers, that is, waste transfers to developing counties. OECD decisions apply only to wastes transferred from OECD countries to other OECD countries.

3.2. Radioactive Wastes

In 1990, the IAEA adopted guidelines for the transfers of nuclear wastes "for which no use is foreseen" – not for spent fuel, which is destined for reprocessing for the purposes of further usage. These guidelines require the notification and informed consent of the importing and transit countries before a nuclear waste transfer.[79] The IAEA guidelines, however, do not include the proximity and self-sufficiency principles, principles obviously unsound for the management of radioactive wastes because they would involve the multiplication of radioactive repository sites.

In the area of radioactive waste management, the most significant regulatory development since the early 1990s is the adoption of the Convention on the Safety of Spent Fuel Management and on the Safety of Radioactive Waste Management adopted in 1997.[80] The convention entered into force in 2001.

The convention deals with all the steps involved in nuclear waste management that have to do with the safety of spent fuel[81] and the safety of radioactive waste.[82] The convention includes general provisions regarding the importance of building the appropriate legislative and regulatory framework and the creation of a regulatory body that would deal with waste management.[83]

The convention clearly specifies that the "prime responsibility for the safety of spent fuel or radioactive waste management rests with the holder of the relevant license." If such licensee is not available, the state, within the jurisdiction of which spent fuel or radioactive waste management takes place, must be responsible.[84]

Article 27 of the convention deals with the transboundary movement of radioactive wastes. Although this article provides that the state that imports radioactive waste must be notified and must give its consent, notification, and consent are not required of the states of transit. Transboundary movements through states of transit must be subject to the obligations that apply to the particular mode of transport utilized.[85] The prior notification and informed consent of states of transit were subject to heated discussions during the negotiations of the convention. Although prior notification and consent of transit countries are required for the movement

---

[79] IAEA, General Conference Resolution on Code of Practice on International Transboundary Movement of Radioactive Waste, Sept. 21, 1990, reprinted in 30 ILM 556 (1991).

[80] Joint Convention on the Safety of Spent Fuel Management and on the Safety of Radioactive Waste Management, GOV/INF/821-GC(41)/INF/12, Sept. 5, 1997, available online at http://www.ieae.org/Publications/Documents/Conventions [hereinafter Joint Convention].

[81] Chapter 2 (regarding existing facilities, proposed facilities, design and construction of facilities, assessment of safety, and operation of facilities), *id.*

[82] Chapter 3 (including the design, construction, and operation of facilities and the assessment of their safety as well as institutional measures after closure), *id.*

[83] Arts. 18, 19 & 20, *id.*

[84] Art. 21, *id.*

[85] Art. 27(1)(ii), *id.*

of hazardous wastes, the same rule does not apply for radioactive waste transfers. Some countries have considered the different treatment of hazardous wastes and radioactive wastes, in terms of the prior consent of the countries of transit, as a *non sequitur*.[86]

Regarding the specific details of radioactive waste transfers, a resolution was adopted during the negotiations of the convention. The resolution refers to the 1990 IAEA guidelines, the International Maritime Dangerous Goods Code (IMDG), and the IAEA-specific regulations with regard to the transfers of radioactive material.[87] The purpose of these IAEA regulations is to protect the public from radiation exposure during the transfers of radioactive material. The regulations do so by providing specific technological standards that would achieve, *inter alia*, the effective confinement of radioactive material, emergency response, quality assurance, and compliance assurance.[88]

Another provision that caused heated debate is that the convention does not cover spent fuel destined for reprocessing.[89] According to article 3(1) of the convention,

> Spent fuel held at reprocessing facilities as a part of a reprocessing activity is not covered in the scope of this Convention unless the Contracting Party declares reprocessing to be part of spent fuel management.

Thus, waste destined for reprocessing is not covered under the convention unless a state party voluntarily decides to include reprocessing under the auspices of the convention.

The convention is to be monitored through a peer review process. According to article 30, a review meeting is to be held in which parties are to examine reports submitted by fellow state parties. The reports submitted by state parties must include, according to article 32, their spent fuel management policy/practices, radioactive waste policy/practices, and criteria used to define and to categorize radioactive waste. State parties must include in their reports a list of their spent fuel and nuclear waste management facilities, an inventory of spent fuel and nuclear wastes regulated under the convention, and a list of facilities in the process of being decommissioned.[90]

The matters discussed during the review meetings of parties must be available to the public in summary reports.[91] Because the management of spent fuel and radioactive waste is a national security concern – especially regarding the possibility

---

[86] Summary Record of the Fifth Plenary Meeting of the Diplomatic Conference Convened to Adopt a Joint Convention on the Safety of Spent Fuel Management and on the Safety of Radioactive Waste Management, RWSC/DC/SR.5, Sept. 5, 1997.

[87] IAEA Regulations for the Safe Transport of Radioactive Material (IAEA Safety Standards Series, No. TS-R-1l, 1996).

[88] *Id.* at 1–17.

[89] Summary Record of the Fourth Plenary Meeting of the Diplomatic Conference Convened to Adopt a Joint Convention on the Safety of Spent Fuel Management and on the Safety of Radioactive Waste Management, RWSC/DC/SR.4, Sept. 5, 1997.

[90] Art. 32(2), Joint Convention, *supra* note 80.

[91] Art. 34, *id.*

of nuclear wastes falling in the hands of terrorists – the convention has provided for the confidentiality of the information given by state parties.[92]

Another convention that does not specifically deal with radioactive waste management but regulates nuclear safety overall is the Convention on Nuclear Safety.[93] This convention was the result of a series of expert meetings that took place between 1992 and 1994. The purpose of the convention is to commit state parties that operate nuclear power plants to maintain a high level of safety. Implementation is based on persuasion that is to take place during the peer review meetings for which state parties are to provide reports. The first peer review meeting took place in 1999. The peer review process has been valuable because of the insights exchanged among the parties and the opportunity for self-assessment it provides.[94]

Another convention that could be invoked within the context of radioactive waste management and transfers but also applies generally to enhance overall nuclear safety is the Convention on Early Notification of a Nuclear Accident.[95] This convention was adopted in 1986, following the Chernobyl nuclear plant accident, and establishes a notification system for nuclear accidents that may have transboundary effects. The treaty requires state parties to report on an accident's location, time, radiation releases, and other effects. The convention entered into force in 1986. The convention was invoked by Turkey in 1999 in relation to suspicions regarding a missing nuclear source.[96]

The illicit trafficking of radioactive material has been a source of concern.[97] In this context, the Convention on the Physical Protection of Nuclear Material commits parties to ensure the protection of nuclear material under their jurisdiction (e.g., within their territory or on their ships and aircraft).[98] The issue of cooperation in the protection, recovery, and return of stolen nuclear material is under discussion within the framework of the convention.

Other developments in the field of nuclear energy involve:the establishment of Western European Nuclear Regulators' Association (WENRA) which is made up of the heads of nuclear regulatory authorities of the nine states of the European Union that have nuclear power plants – namely Belgium, Finland, France, Germany, Italy, the Netherlands, Spain, Sweden and the UK – and Switzerland. The group was established in 1999. Another organization involved in nuclear waste management is the Nuclear Energy Agency of the Organization for Economic Co-operation and Development (NEA/OECD) as well as the International Commission on Radiological Protection. The World Association of Nuclear Operators (WANO) plays an important role in radioactive waste management.

---

[92] Art. 36, *id.*

[93] Convention on Nuclear Safety, June 17, 1994, reprinted in 33 ILM 1514 (1994), available online at http://www.iaea.org/Publications/Documents/Conventions.

[94] IAEA General Conference, Measures to Strengthen International Co-operation in Nuclear, Radiation and Waste Safety, Forty-fourth regular session, Subitem 14(b) of the provisional agenda, at 1, GC(44)/INF/, Aug. 17, 2000 [hereinafter IAEA General Conference].

[95] Convention on Early Notification of a Nuclear Accident, Sept. 26, 1986, reprinted in 25 ILM 1370 (1986), available online at http://www.iaea.org/Publications/Documents/Conventions.

[96] IAEA General Conference, *supra* note 94, at 2.

[97] *Id.* at 3.

[98] Convention on the Physical Protection of Nuclear Material, Oct. 26, 1979, available online at http://www.iaea.org/Publications/Documents/Conventions.

4. NATIONAL REGULATORY DILEMMAS

4.1. The United States

4.1.1. Management of Hazardous Wastes

The management of hazardous waste in the United States is regulated by the Resource Conservation and Recovery Act (RCRA).[99] The RCRA regulates hazardous wastes but not abandoned waste sites. The cleanup and liability rules for abandoned waste sites are provided for in the Comprehensive Environmental Response, Compensation and Liability Act (CERCLA).[100]

The RCRA outlines the goals of U.S. waste management policy and sets waste minimization as the primary goal. Wastes that cannot be minimized must be treated, stored, or disposed of so as to reduce the current and future threats to human health and the environment.[101]

For hazardous waste facilities to operate, they must obtain permits.[102] Before granting permits for the operation of hazardous wastes facilities, the U.S. Environmental Protection Agency (EPA) must inform the public through hearings and notify local governments.[103] The RCRA contains specific requirements for design and operation of disposal facilities. New landfills must meet some minimum technological requirements, such as double liners, leachate collection systems, and groundwater monitoring.[104] The regulations give flexibility to facility operators not to comply with the minimum requirements if they can prove that the location of disposal facility and alternative designs and operating practices can provide the same level of effectiveness as the technological requirements.[105]

The enforcement mechanisms at the disposal of the EPA range from administrative orders to civil and criminal penalties.[106] The RCRA provides for compulsory insurance of owners and operators of hazardous waste facilities[107] during the time of operation and for thirty years after the closure of the facility.

Although the RCRA sets the standards for waste disposal, the CERCLA[108] prescribes strict, unlimited, and retroactive liability for actors involved in waste management and creates a fund, the Hazardous Substances Superfund, to clean up hazardous waste disposal sites.[109] The Superfund is financed by taxes on chemical and oil importing companies and by taxes on general revenues. It is frequently replenished because each time the EPA cleans up a hazardous waste site it recovers the costs from

---

[99] 42 U.S.C. §6901 et seq. The RCRA was adopted in 1978 and amended in 1984.
[100] The CERCLA was fist enacted in 1980. It was amended by the Superfund Amendment and Reauthorization Act in 1986 (SARA). Both these acts are referred to as "CERCLA" or as "CERCLA as amended by SARA." See 31 U.S.C. §§9601–9675 (1986).
[101] 42 U.S.C. § 6902(b).
[102] 42 U.S.C.§6925.
[103] 42 U.S.C.§6974(b).
[104] 42 U.S.C.§6924(o).
[105] 42 U.S.C.§6924(o)(2).
[106] 42 U.S.C. §6928.
[107] 42 U.S.C. §6924(a).
[108] CERCLA, *supra* note 100.
[109] 42 U.S.C. § 9611(a).

the private responsible parties.[110] Often the discovery and apportionment of liability among responsible parties entail time-consuming and very expensive settlement[111] and litigation procedures, which involve hundreds of parties.[112]

Under the CERCLA, four persons are strictly liable for releases or threatened releases of hazardous wastes from a disposal facility: the current owner of a disposal facility, the owner or operator of a facility at the time of disposal,[113] the generators of hazardous wastes disposed of at a facility, and the transporters of hazardous wastes.[114] Their liability includes all costs of removal or remedial action at hazardous waste sites[115] incurred by the federal or state government and all other necessary response costs incurred by any other person. Liability under the CERCLA covers damages to property and to the environment but does not include personal injuries. Liability under the CERCLA can be characterized as virtually absolute because the defenses provided are limited.

4.1.2. Management of Radioactive Wastes

High-Level Radioactive Wastes

The management of high-level radioactive wastes and spent fuel in the United States is regulated by the Nuclear Waste Policy Act (NWPA).[116] High-level nuclear waste could be generated by civilian nuclear reactors or by energy defense facilities. The purpose of the NWPA is to resolve the impasse of finding the final nuclear waste repository.

Until the construction of permanent facilities, owners and operators of nuclear power plants must provide interim storage onsite.[117] The expansion of such interim storage, if needed, must be licensed by the Nuclear Regulatory Commission. If temporary storage is exhausted, the federal government assumes automatically responsibility for the wastes.

The quest for the location of an appropriate repository for nuclear wastes has been quite challenging. This is because of the relentless public opposition to the construction of any nuclear waste repository.[118] None of the communities that have been chosen for radioactive waste disposal wishes to receive radioactive wastes in its backyard. At this point, plans are proceeding regarding the establishment of a permanent repository in Yucca Mountain, Nevada. The current schedule provides for construction to begin in 2006 and for full operation to take place by 2010. In 1999, the Department of Energy (DOE) issued a Draft Environmental Impact Assessment for the proposed repository in Yucca Mountain.

---

[110] 42 U.S.C. § 9604.

[111] 42 U.S.C. § 9622.

[112] United States Office of Technology Assessment (OTA), Coming Clean: Superfund Problems Can Be Solved 28–29 (1989).

[113] See 42 U.S.C. §9601(20)(A).

[114] 42 U.S.C. §9607(a)(1)–(4).

[115] See 42 U.S.C. §9601(D)(23)–(24).

[116] 42 U.S.C. §10101 et seq. The act was adopted in 1982 and amended in 1987.

[117] 42 U.S.C. §10151(a)(1).

[118] For the history of the process of finding and nominating suitable sites, see Louka, *supra* note 6, at 142–46.

The Waste Isolation Pilot Plant (WIPP) in New Mexico is going forward regarding the disposal of transuranic defense waste.[119] The first shipment of transuranic waste was delivered to the WIPP in March 1999, making it the world's first operational geologic repository for long-lived radioactive waste.[120]

Low-Level Radioactive Wastes

The management of low-level radioactive waste has been entrusted to the Low-Level Radioactive Waste Act (LLRWA).[121] Low-level radioactive waste is defined simply as waste that is not high-level waste or spent nuclear fuel. The LLRWA is designed on the premise that low-level radioactive wastes can be managed more effectively on a regional scale. For this reason, states are required to enter into "compacts," that is, association agreements with each other. The purpose of these compacts is to establish regional disposal facilities. State compacts can enter into agreements with other compacts for the disposal of low-level radioactive wastes. When the act was about to be adopted, low-level radioactive waste was disposed of at Barnwell, South Carolina; Richland, Washington; and Beatty, Nevada. These facilities, however, were running out of space.

After the act was adopted, multiple compacts[122] have been formed and certain states have remained unaffiliated.[123] Some compacts seem to have functioned reasonably well. This is so because they are located close to disposal facilities that have remained open to them. Other states have encountered difficulties in locating a disposal facility, with notable examples being Texas and California.[124]

---

[119] OECD/NEA, Nuclear Waste Bulletin, Update on Waste Management Policies and Programmes 97–100, No. 13, Dec. 1998.

[120] IAEA General Conference, *supra* note 94, at 9.

[121] 42 U.S.C. §2021b *et seq.*

[122] The Northwest Compact (Alaska, Hawaii, Idaho, Montana, Oregon, Utah, Washington, and Wyoming). Washington is the designated disposal state.

The Southwestern Compact (Arizona, North Dakota, California, and South Dakota). California is the designated disposal state but has had many difficulties in finding a disposal site.

The Rocky Mountain Compact (Colorado, New Mexico, and Nevada).

The Midwest Compact (Indiana, Iowa, Minnesota, Ohio, Missouri, and Wisconsin).

The Central Compact (Arkansas, Kansas, Louisiana, Nebraska, and Oklahoma). Nebraska is the designated disposal state.

The Texas Compact (Texas, Vermont, and Maine).

The Appalachian Compact (Delaware, Maryland, Pennsylvania, and West Virginia). Pennsylvania is the designated disposal state.

The Northeast Compact (Connecticut, New Jersey, and South Carolina). Connecticut and New Jersey are the designated disposal states.

The Southeast Compact (Alabama, Florida, Mississippi, Tennessee, Georgia, and Virginia).

There are a number of unaffiliated states, including New York, Puerto Rico, Michigan, Rhode Island, North Carolina, and New Hampshire, as well as the District of Columbia. It is worth noting that Michigan was part of the Midwest compact, but it was expelled because of its inability to find a disposal facility. For updates on compact action, see the Web site of the U.S. Nuclear Regulatory Commission, http://www. nrc.gov/waste/llw-disposal/compacts.html.

[123] Louka, *supra* note 6, at 150–52.

[124] In Texas, attempts to locate a site in West Texas have generated opposition and environmental justice concerns as a large percentage of population in the region is of Hispanic origin and poor. Opponents also claim that a waste repository will pollute the Rio Grande River and affect relationships with Mexico. Two Mexican states at the border of Rio Grande have stated their opposition to the development of

The problems associated with finding appropriate disposal sites have not had substantial influence on the volumes of low-level radioactive waste generated. In 1998, approximately 1,419 thousand cubic feet of low-level radioactive waste was disposed of amounting to a fourfold increase over the preceding year.[125]

Overall, the compact scheme, as implemented today, has been criticized as wasteful and inefficient. When Congress passed the LLRWA, it never contemplated that states would form so many compacts and even would choose to go alone. Studies have demonstrated that incorporating existing compacts into four compacts and minimizing the number of potentially constructed sites to four could result in savings of approximately $3 billion.

Under the compact scheme, states usually undertake the obligation to build a disposal facility under the understanding that in a few years some other state would build such a facility. This unnecessarily increases the number of disposal facilities.[126] Recently, several states and many compacts have questioned the necessity of building disposal facilities. In 1997, the Midwest compact decided to stop progress toward the development of a facility. North Carolina did the same in 1997. New Jersey postponed plans to build such a facility in 1998. Connecticut, Massachusetts, Michigan, and New York have ceased their siting process for an indefinite period. Forecasts for diminishing waste volumes and the existence of facilities that seem able to handle the wastes have been factored into these decisions of states to postpone looking for repositories.[127] Today, despite the existence of three disposal facilities,[128] most of the waste is handled by one facility, the Envirocare facility in Utah, which accepts close to 76 percent of all low-level radioactive waste generated.

4.1.3. Management of Waste Trade

The EPA regulates hazardous waste transfers with the manifest system. The manifest system is supposed to provide "cradle-to-grave" monitoring of hazardous wastes.[129] The manifest contains the name of the disposal facility to which wastes are to be transported and consists of four copies: one copy is for the generator to keep, one for the transporter, and one for the disposer. The disposer, after receiving the wastes, has to send a copy of the manifest back to the generator. In this fashion, the generator verifies the actual receipt of the wastes by the disposer. If a generator does not receive a copy of the manifest within thirty-five days of handing the wastes over to the

---

a site. In California, the Ward Valley location has created concerns about possible leakage from the potential site and environmental justice concerns as the Native Americans in the region have expressed opposition to the site.

[125] For the volumes of waste generated, see the Web site of the U.S. Nuclear Regulatory Commission, http://www.nrc.gov/waste/llw-disposal/statistics.htm.

[126] Louka, *supra* note 6, at 154.

[127] Report of the National Conference of State Legislatures, Low-Level Radioactive Waste Management: State and Compact Update, State Legislative Report, Vol. 23, No. 9, Mar. 1988.

[128] The Barnwell facility, located in Barnwell (South Carolina), currently accepts all wastes except for those coming from the Northwest compact and from the Rocky Mountain compact. Beginning in 2008, it would accept wastes only from the Atlantic compact states (Connecticut, New Jersey, and South Carolina).

Another facility is the Hanford facility located in Hanford, Washington. It accepts wastes from the Northwest and Rocky Mountain compacts.

The Envirocare facility located in Utah accepts wastes from all the states. See the Web site of the U.S. Nuclear Regulatory Commission, http://www.nrc.gov/waste/llw-disposal/locations.html.

[129] 42 U.S.C. §6922(5).

transporter, he/she must determine the fate of wastes by contacting the transporter and disposer. The generator also must inform the EPA by filing an exception report. Many times, however, manifests have been falsified by hazardous waste transporters who dump the waste illegally and keep the disposal fee.[130] Low-level radioactive waste shipments must be accompanied by a manifest.

Hazardous waste exports to other countries are possible only after the prior notification and informed consent of the receiving country or in accordance with a bilateral treaty between the United States and the importing country.[131] The prior notification and informed consent requirement is in harmony with the Basel Convention. Overall, however, U.S. regulations are less stringent than the Basel Convention requirements.

In the United States, certain states have attempted to ban or otherwise control waste imports into their territories from other states of the federation claiming that such imports are environmentally unsound. The U.S. Supreme Court, however, has struck down such prohibitions and restrictions as incompatible with the commerce clause of the constitution.[132] The U.S. Supreme Court has underlined the notions of economic nationhood, community, and interdependence, and has cautioned against the economic isolationism of states. According to the Court, a state may not "isolate itself from a *problem common to many*[133] by erecting a barrier against the movement of interstate trade,"[134] even if that trade involves wastes.

4.2. European Union

4.2.1. Management of Hazardous Wastes

Wastes are regulated in the European Union by the Waste Framework Directive,[135] which deals with any type of waste. Hazardous wastes are addressed specifically by the Hazardous Waste Directive.[136] The Waste Framework Directive defines, for the first time, "waste" at the Union level. Hazardous wastes are defined more clearly in the Hazardous Waste Directive than in prior regulatory efforts.

The Hazardous Waste Directive regulates the management of hazardous wastes. Every disposal and recycling facility must obtain a permit.[137] Recycling facilities and enterprises that use onsite disposal, however, may be exempted from permit

---

[130] See United States General Accounting Office (GAO), Illegal Disposal of Hazardous Waste: Difficult to Deter or Detect (GAO/RCED-85-2, 1985).

[131] 42 U.S.C. §6938(a).

[132] The commerce clause is called "dormant" because it is not explicitly stated in the constitution. According to the constitution: "The Congress shall have Power . . . To regulate Commerce with foreign Nations, and among the several States, and with Indian Tribes . . ." See U.S. CONST, Art. I, §8, cl. 3. The Supreme Court in Welton v. Missouri, 91 U.S. 275 (1875) held that uniform commercial legislation is essential in order to protect commerce and that the inaction of Congress on this matter should be interpreted to mean that interstate commerce is free and uninhibited.

[133] Emphasis added.

[134] City of Philadelphia v. New Jersey, 437 U.S. 617, 628 (1978). For other decisions of the Court and lower courts on this matter, see Louka, *supra* note 6, at 136–39.

[135] Council Directive 91/156/EEC of 18 March 1991 amending Directive 75/442 on waste, OJ L 78/32, 26.03.1991 [hereinafter Framework Directive].

[136] Council Directive 91/689/EEC of 12 December 1991 on hazardous waste, OJ L 377/20, 31.12.1991 [hereinafter Hazardous Waste Directive].

[137] Art. 9(1), Framework Directive, *supra* note 135.

requirements if states have enacted general rules for the activities[138] undertaken by these enterprises, specifying the types and quantities of wastes handled and the conditions under which the exemptions may apply.[139] Facilities have to register, however, even if exempt.[140] Waste collectors and transporters must register as well.[141]

Recycling is treated favorably in both directives due to the importance attached to its advancement. The Framework Directive explicitly provides that the principal goals of waste management are waste reduction and recycling.[142]

Member states must establish an integrated and adequate network of disposal facilities that incorporates the best available technology not entailing excessive costs (BATNEEC).[143] The purpose of this network is to enable both the EU and individual states to implement the proximity and self-sufficiency principles. These principles are outlined in the directive in a flexible manner. Self-sufficiency must be compatible with "geographical circumstances or the need for specialized installations for certain types of wastes" and the proximate facility must be "appropriate."[144]

The implementation of waste management legislation has encountered many obstacles. In 2002, the European Commission initiated a number of actions against member states for the bad application of the framework directive. It is difficult to apply the directive in many of the existing installations of member states. There are, consequently, many complaints about illegal dumps, groundwater contamination, insufficient environmental impact assessments, and inadequate waste planning.[145] The Commission has taken action against member states for failure to transpose the Hazardous Waste Directive and failure to communicate information about their disposal and recovery facilities to the Commission.[146]

Incineration and Landfill Legislation

A single legal framework for the incineration of all waste was necessary to improve legal clarity and enforceability of incineration standards. This framework was adopted in 2002.[147] The directive provides multiple requirements for the operation of

---

[138] Art. 4, *id.*

[139] Art. 11(1), *id.*

[140] Art. 11(2), *id.*

[141] Art. 12, *id.*

[142] Art. 3, *id.*

[143] Art. 5, *id.* Art. 6(1), Hazardous Waste Directive, *supra* note 136.

[144] According to the proximity principle, wastes must be disposed of in "one of the nearest appropriate installations, by means of most appropriate methods and technologies..." See art. 5, Framework Directive, *supra* note 135.

   See also A Communication from the Commission, Community Strategy for Waste Management, reprinted in European Community Environmental Legislation 162 (EEC, 1992). The communication was endorsed by the Council in a resolution of May 7, 1990 on waste policy, see Council Resolution of 7 May 1990 on waste policy, OJ C 122/2, 18.05.1990 ("Here 'the nearest' [facility] does not necessarily, in every case, mean close-by. To achieve the best possible distribution of installations, account must be taken of requirements and capacities for treatment. The distribution of plants for reception of domestic refuse, for example, cannot be the same as for installations for disposing of halogenic chemical waste.").

[145] Commission of the European Communities, Fourth Annual Survey on the Implementation and Enforcement of Community Environmental Law 2002, at 16, SEC (2003) 804, July 7, 2003 [hereinafter Survey on Enforcement].

[146] *Id.* at 17.

[147] Directive 2000/76/EC of the European Parliament and of the Council of 4 December 2000 on the incineration of waste, OJ L 332/91, 28.12.2000 [hereinafter Incineration Directive].

incinerators.[148] The purpose of the directive is to prevent or limit the negative effects on humans and the environment resulting from the emissions and discharges of incinerators into the air, water, groundwater, and soil. This is to be accomplished by setting "stringent operational conditions" and establishing limit values for the emissions of incineration plants.[149] The detailed emission limit values and discharges are set in the annexes to the directive.[150]

The Directive for Landfill Disposal[151] provides certain basic standards for sound landfill management. The purpose of the directive is to harmonize the technical standards for landfill disposal among states so that disparities do not exist that cause the transfer of wastes to technically inferior and, thus, cheaper facilities.[152] The directive attempts to accomplish this through the establishment of a standard procedure for the acceptance of wastes in landfills and a standard classification of wastes that are to be accepted in landfills.[153] The objective of the directive is to achieve the goals of sound waste management by establishing "stringent operational and technical requirements" for landfill operation.[154]

No landfill operation can function without a permit. The directive prescribes waste acceptance procedures,[155] control and monitoring procedures during the operational phase,[156] and measures that must be taken during closure and after closure.[157] The directive incorporates actively the polluter pays principle because it provides that all costs of caring for a landfill, including the costs of closure, must be included in the price the operator charges for waste disposal.

4.2.2. Management of Radioactive Wastes

The EU established the first action plan for the management of radioactive wastes in 1980. This 1980–1992 plan included provisions for a continuous analysis of the situation with regard to the management of radioactive wastes, consultation on the practices of sound radioactive waste management, and research and development.

The plan, which covers the period between 1992 and 1999, encourages states to cooperate in developing a common approach towards the harmonization of waste management strategies and practices. It encourages cooperation with countries outside the EU that produce radioactive waste, especially countries of Central and Eastern Europe. Cooperation includes the provision of lists of storage installations that states intend to construct and put into service, and a list of management practices and strategies. A 1992 resolution provides a preliminary system for radioactive waste classification.[158]

---

[148] Art. 4, *id.*

[149] Art. 1, *id.*

[150] See arts. 7 & 8, *id.* See also Annex V and Annex IV, *id.*

[151] Council Directive 1999/31/EC of 26 April 1999 on the landfill of waste, OJ L 182/1, 16.07.1999.

[152] Preamble (10), *id.*

[153] Preamble (20), *id.*

[154] Art. 1(1), *id.*

[155] See art. 11, *id.*

[156] Art. 12, *id.*

[157] Art. 13, *id.*

[158] Council Resolution of 15 June 1992 on the renewal of the Community Plan of Action in the field of radioactive waste, OJ C 158/3, 25.06.1992. According to this system, wastes are classified as: transition radioactive waste (mainly of medical origin), low- and intermediate-level waste and high-level radioactive waste.

All states produce some amounts of radioactive waste, but the quantities produced in certain states do not warrant the development of specialized radioactive disposal facilities. Countries without nuclear power production have abandoned plans to seek permanent disposal for their radioactive waste, whereas countries that produce nuclear power (for instance, the Netherlands, Italy, and the United Kingdom) have postponed their plans to develop a radioactive waste facility for the foreseeable future. The Commission has recommended that countries should continue their efforts to find suitable permanent repositories for radioactive waste and that common rules should be set for the decontamination of radioactive material. The Commission has proposed that the EU must strive for self-sufficiency in radioactive waste management but that transfer of wastes outside the EU should not be excluded.[159] The EU has adopted, therefore, a more relaxed approach to the transfer of radioactive waste than to the transfer of hazardous waste. This is because of the difficulties involved in finding appropriate radioactive waste disposal sites.

The accession of Eastern European countries – most of which have nuclear facilities that need to be decommissioned – brings to the fore the issue of nuclear waste management with a new urgency. In 2003, the Commission tried to address the issue of radioactive waste management by proposing two new directives: a Directive on the Safety of Nuclear Installations[160] and a Directive on the Management of Spent Fuel and Radioactive Waste.[161] Emphasis is placed on "sharing facilities and services wherever possible" for the disposal of nuclear waste[162] and on the desirability of regional repositories.[163] Unfortunately, regional repositories are ruled out constantly because of the politics of the NIMBY syndrome, which is still quite powerful in many European countries.

The search for a permanent radioactive waste repository has been a challenge for many countries. Belgium is in search for a permanent geological site for vitrified, high-level waste.[164] The same is true with the Czech Republic, which is elaborating the conceptual design of an underground disposal site.[165] France already has near surface facilities for low- and intermediate-level waste, whereas the search for a high-level waste repository continues.[166] Germany has shipped its wastes to France and the United Kingdom for reprocessing but, as many large containers of reprocessed wastes return to Germany, a place is needed for their disposal. At this point, two disposal sites for low- and intermediate-level wastes are available, but the German government has abandoned plans to open a third.[167]

---

[159] Communication and fourth report from the Commission of 11 January 1999 on the present situation and prospects for radioactive waste management in the European Union, COM (98) 799 Final.

[160] Proposal for a Council (Euratom) Directive setting out basic obligations and general principles on the safety of nuclear installations, COM (2003) 32 final, Jan. 30, 2003.

[161] Proposal for a Council (Euratom) Directive on the management of spent nuclear fuel and radioactive waste, COM (2003) 32 final, Jan. 30, 2003.

[162] Id.

[163] From a strictly environmental viewpoint, a small number of repositories facilitate monitoring and are likely to contain the environmental impact.

[164] OECD/NEA, Nuclear Waste Bulletin: Update on Waste Management Policies and Programmes, No. 13, at 55, Dec. 1998.

[165] Id. at 64.

[166] Id. at 65–66.

[167] Id. at 68.

4.2.3. Management of Waste Trade

In 1984, the EU adopted a Directive[168] that established the prior notification and informed consent procedure before a waste transfer to another member state or a third country. This Directive has been replaced by a much more detailed Waste Transfer Regulation.[169] The regulation affirms the importance of proximity and self-sufficiency principles for waste transfers among European Union countries, the Union's exports, and the Union's imports. The regulation prescribes a considerably more specific notification procedure and allows for prohibitions and restrictions on waste movements. For example, it bans waste exports from the EU to African, Caribbean, and Pacific (ACP) countries, regardless of the waste management method used.[170] The regulation places controls on the transfers even of what could be characterized as recyclable materials to the consternation of the recycling industry and some developing countries that are in need of such material.

The purpose of the regulation is to impose a series of procedural obstacles on waste transfers in the hope that those willing to transfer wastes will be deterred from doing so. The need to simplify the nature of the regulation is expressed in EU strategy documents.[171] Notification and informed consent requirements also are imposed for the transfers for radioactive waste, but they are not as stringent as those imposed for the transfers of hazardous wastes.[172]

The European Court of Justice (ECJ) had the opportunity to adjudicate on the regulatory controls of waste trade among member states of the EU.[173] The *Wallonia* case,[174] regarding Wallonia's waste import prohibition from other member states and regions of Belgium, is an example. The import prohibition affected both solid and hazardous wastes. The ECJ held that member states could not impose total bans on hazardous waste shipments because the 1984/86 Directive, which regulated waste movements at that time, established a procedure – prior notification and informed consent – that governs hazardous waste movements.[175]

---

[168] Council Directive 84/631/EEC of 6 December 1984 on the supervision and control within the European Community of the transfrontier movement of hazardous waste, OJ L 326/31, 13.12.1984. The directive was amended by a 1986 directive. See Council Directive 86/279/EEC of 12 June 1986 amending Directive 84/631/EEC on the supervision and control within the European Community of the transfrontier shipment of hazardous waste, OJ L 181/13, 04.07.1986.

[169] Council Regulation (EEC) No 259/93 of 1 Feb. 1993 on the supervision and control of shipments of waste within, into and out of the European Community, OJ L 30/1, 06.02.1993.

[170] Art. 18, *id.*

[171] See Council Resolution of 24 February 1997 on a Community strategy for waste management, OJ C 76/1, 11.03.1997, which invites the Commission to examine the possibility of simplifying the administrative procedures of Regulation (EEC) No 259/33.

[172] Council Directive 92/3/Euratom of 3 February 1992 on the supervision and control of shipments of radioactive waste between Member States and into and out of the Community, OJ L 35/24, 12.02.1992.

[173] Commission of the European Communities v. Kingdom of Belgium (*Wallonia* Case), Case C-20/90, 1992 E.C.R. I-4431. But the Court seems to have limited the scope of the decision to waste destined for disposal, see Chemische Afvafstoffen Dusseldorp BV and Others v. Minister van Volkshuisvesting, Riumtelijke Ordening en Milieubeheer (Dusseldorp Case), Case C-203/96, June 25, 1998.

[174] *Wallonia* case, *id.*

[175] *Id.*

With respect to solid wastes, the Court admitted that wastes are goods and that article 28,[176] which prohibits quantitative restrictions on the imports of goods, also must apply to waste imports. However, the Court conceded that wastes are commodities of atypical nature, because of their effects on the environment. The Court took into account the massive influx of wastes into Wallonia and concluded that such an influx constitutes a real danger to the environment because of the limited capacities of Wallonia.

The Court rejected the Commission's argument that other states' wastes were not more harmful than Wallonia's own waste and that, consequently, the Belgian legislation had discriminated against out-of-Belgium waste. The Court relied on article 174 of the EU treaty that provides that EU environmental action must be based on the principle that environmental damage should, as a priority, be corrected at the source.[177] The Court argued that this provision implied that wastes should be eliminated as close as possible to the place of their production. In support of this argument, the Court cited the Basel Convention signed by the EU and upheld the Belgian import prohibition of solid waste imports.

5. CONCLUSION

Stringent national regulatory standards on the disposal and treatment of wastes led to waste exports to countries with less strict legislation but also with the lack of infrastructure for dealing with wastes. An environmental externality was, thus, transferred to other states and regions.

Waste transfers to other states, especially developing countries, have been perceived as unfair. This perception of unfairness is supported by general notions of environmental law that the polluter (the generator or the state in which waste is generated) must pay. In the case of waste transfers to developing countries, the polluter usually paid very little in comparison what he/she would have paid had he/she disposed of the wastes in the place of generation. Hazardous waste was simply dumped in developing countries and essentially left in the hands of states that did not have the know-how to manage it safely.

The first instinct against mismanaged waste transfers is to ban such transfers. In fact, many countries did so and prohibited waste imports into their territory. Such prohibitions are based on the principle that each state must become self-sufficient in waste management. Other countries have adopted a more cooperative attitude and have allowed waste imports as long they are notified about such imports and give their consent. The procedure of prior notification and informed consent has been the regulatory instrument of choice in the international arena for the transfers of hazardous and radioactive wastes.

Prohibitions and the regulation of waste transfers through procedural safeguards are not likely to prevent always waste mismanagement. Because wastes are perceived as materials of no use, unless a trail of paperwork is created through which generators are checking on disposers and disposers are checking on transporters, illegal disposal is likely to ensue. Constant cross-checking and record creation are likely to diminish

[176] *Id.*
[177] *Id.*

the likelihood of collusion among these three responsible parties to illegally dispose of wastes. However, because written documents can always be falsified, especially in the absence of a strong monitoring apparatus, some illegal disposal of wastes is always likely to happen.

Forcing generators and countries to own their wastes in what could be characterized as a forced enclosure of an externality could generate beneficial outcomes if wastes have had some value for those who produce them. As long as wastes are perceived as valueless materials, waste generators would always be tempted to find ways to dispose of them as cheaply as possible but not always as effectively as possible.

With regard to waste transfers among countries with similar economic development, it is unclear why regulatory notification and stringent consent requirements are necessary for each waste shipment. This is especially so for countries that attempt to create a Union and among states of a federation such as the United States. The U.S. Supreme Court struck down state prohibitions on the imports of other states' wastes based on the notion of nationhood. The ECJ, by contrast, supported restrictions and prohibitions based on environmental considerations. It may be that the divergent court prescriptions have to do with the different maturity levels of the federations involved, as the EU is still emerging and is still a contested federation.

11

Liability and State Responsibility

Liability and state responsibility rules determine whether the polluter pays principle is a principle of consequence in international environmental law or if it is just a principle that hardly applies in practice. From the regimes examined in this chapter, one gets a mixed picture. Most international liability regimes channel liability to the person who is in control of an environmentally damaging activity. In the case of oil pollution and the sea transfer of hazardous substances, the person in control is the shipowner. In the case of nuclear pollution, it is the operator of a nuclear power plant. In the case of carriage of dangerous goods, it is the carrier of dangerous goods. In the case of waste exports, the person who gives notification to the country of destination that a waste transfer is to take place is the person who is liable until the disposer takes control of the waste. From that point on, the disposer is considered liable. The Lugano Convention similarly holds the operator liable for incidents that result from a dangerous activity.

The channeling of liability to the person in control of a dangerous activity is necessary in order to reduce the transaction costs of finding the responsible person. A presumption, therefore, is made that the person in control of the activity should be the liable person. Liability is strict because a fault liability regime would have created further costs of finding whether the person in control was actually at fault. A further presumption, thus, is made that most activities, especially those that involve ultrahazardous substances, are likely to create some environmental externalities no matter the amount of precaution taken.[1] The person in control of the activity should bear the costs of these externalities.

At the same time, however, most international regimes apply a broader version of polluter pays principle that views society, which benefits from industrialization and the engagement in dangerous activities that such industrialization entails, as accountable. Thus, most regimes provide for additional compensatory mechanisms supported by entities, which cannot have control over the specific incidents that give rise to liability but are responsible in a broader sense as receivers of benefits from the dangerous activity. In the oil pollution regime, for instance, a fund is created through which oil-receiving industries contribute money to supplement compensation provided by the shipowner. In case the shipowner is at default, the

---

[1] See also Charles Perrow, Complex Organizations: A Critical Essay (1972).

fund covers the compensation that should have been provided by the shipowner. In other words, it is the "customers" who initiate the transfer of oil who are considered partly responsible for the externalities generated from oil transport.

In the nuclear liability regime, the operator is primarily responsible. But it is provided that the nuclear installation state, from which the liable operator conducts its business, and all other states that have subscribed to the nuclear liability regime have to contribute to supplement the compensation provided by the nuclear operator. The contributions are determined by a formula based on the GNP (or the UN rate of assessment) and the nuclear power of sponsoring states. Thus, in the nuclear liability regime, one could claim that states that have nuclear power share an implicit understanding that a nuclear accident could happen in any country that has nuclear power. The conviction that a nuclear accident could happen in any state gives rise to a sense of solidarity that resists an automatic response to assign responsibility to the state where a nuclear accident happens to occur. It is worth noting, in this context, that none of the countries that were affected by the Chernobyl accident brought charges against the then Soviet Union based on some doctrine of state responsibility, as they could have done. Some commentators have viewed this lack of action against the Soviet Union as recognition among states that pointing a figure at the responsible state may backfire in the future, especially as accidents and leaks cannot be totally avoided, no matter what the level of precaution taken.[2]

A broad definition of the polluter pays principle, to implicate a society that benefits from dangerous activities, is at odds with an understanding of the historical origins of the principle. The purpose of the polluter pays principle, as initially envisioned, is to make industries absorb the negative externalities they create. If one views not industry but society, in general, as the beneficiary from dangerous activities, then the responsibility for the occurrence of environmental accidents should shift to the society at large. The international system, at this point, attempts to forge a balance between a *stricto sensu* version of the polluter pays principle and a broader version that takes into account collective choices that societies make to undertake dangerous activities and, thus, the benefits and costs emanating from such activities.

Furthermore, for a *stricto sensu* version of the polluter pays principle to work, industry must not be able to pass on the costs that come from its activities to consumers. The ability of the industry to pass on the costs to consumers depends on the elasticity of demand and options available to consumers to switch to less dangerous substitutes. If such substitutes are not available or are available but not as affordable as the products they are to replace, then the polluter pays principle is unlikely to affect the competitiveness of a polluting industry. The oil industry enjoys, to some degree, a quasi-monopoly, given the overall dependence of the world on oil. For that reason, governments subsidize the nuclear energy industry as an alternative source of energy. One could conceptualize both the Brussels Convention and the Convention on Supplementary Compensation for Nuclear Damage (CSC) elaborated in Section 3 of this chapter, which provide state-sponsored compensation in case of a nuclear accident, as a form of subsidy to the nuclear industry. States are aware that a nuclear accident could wipe out the economic basis of nuclear industry. And, therefore, states are ready to step in to protect the industry.

[2] *Id.*

Some liability instruments have yet to function in a satisfactory manner. These include the CRTD Convention (Convention on Civil Liability for Damage Caused During Carriage of Dangerous Goods by Road, Rail and Inland Navigation Vessels), the HNS Convention (International Convention on Liability and Compensation for Damage in Connection with the Carriage of Hazardous and Noxious Substances by Sea), the Basel Protocol, and the Lugano Convention. All of these instruments involve dangerous substances. The CRTD Convention involves the carriage of dangerous substances by land. The HNS Convention involves the carriage of dangerous substances by sea. The Basel Protocol involves the international transfers of hazardous waste. The Lugano Convention attempts to establish a comprehensive liability regime for the impact of dangerous activities on the environment. One of the reasons that these regimes have yet to acquire a wide acceptance is the lack of a robust insurance market willing to provide coverage for such activities. In the case of oil pollution, the development of insurance markets in the form of P&I Clubs (Protection & Indemnity Clubs) preceded the development of the oil pollution regime. In the case of nuclear accidents, states have been willing to shoulder some costs (although major nuclear powers have yet to ratify some of the conventions). For dangerous activities, neither a ready international insurance market exists, willing to provide back up for the functioning of an international liability regime, nor do states seem willing to directly subsidize such activities.

Another factor, which undermines the insurability of dangerous activities at the transnational level and the development of international insurance markets, is the diffuse character of these activities. It is hard to think of an industrial activity that does not involve some sort of a dangerous substance. Even agriculture and forestry involve often dangerous chemicals and pesticides. Pollution from dangerous activities comes from many and diffuse sources. This is the reason why it is difficult to encourage the development of international insurance markets for such activities or to develop supplementary compensation mechanisms, such as a fund modeled on the Oil Pollution Funds. The question that needs to be answered before the establishment of such a fund is which industries would contribute to the fund. If the answer is that most industries entangled in dangerous activities would be required to contribute, then the logistics of developing such a fund would bar its establishment. If the answer excludes certain industries, questions of equity would undermine the development of a fund. The HNS Convention attempted to establish a fund as a second tier for compensation by singling out certain industries to contribute to the fund. But the logistics of contributions to the fund are more complex than those of the oil regime. This lack of simplicity may undermine the adoption and smooth functioning of the HNS Convention.

Furthermore, certain instruments, such as the Lugano Convention, are too ambitious in their attempt to establish a liability regime for all dangerous activities that have an impact on the environment. The problem with such a general liability regime is that, in principle, pollution is a legal activity authorized by states. Most states today do not ban pollution. Instead, they attempt to regulate it. Because tolerance for pollution and, thus, regulations vary from state to state, it is difficult to establish a general liability regime for the impact of dangerous activities on the environment. As long as the parameters between legal and illegal pollution remain indeterminate under international law, so, too, would the liability system established and the willingness of states to support such a liability system.

1. OIL POLLUTION

The oil pollution regime vividly illustrates the preoccupation of the oil industry with limited liability as the type of liability that does not jeopardize insurance availability. The first conventions dealing with oil pollution were conventions on limitations of liability. The idea of limiting liability for oil pollution damage preceded the idea of creating a comprehensive regime for oil pollution.[3]

The evolution of the oil pollution regime could be characterized as reactive rather than anticipatory. The regime evolved as a reaction to a number of oil spills, which provided a constant proof of its inadequacy. The regime was initially formulated as a response to the 1969 *Torrey Canyon* incident. The *Amoco Cadiz* disaster of 1978 and the *Exxon Valdez* oil spill in Alaska in 1989 exposed some of the inadequacies of the regime, especially with regard to the level of compensation available to injured parties. As a result of these incidents, the regime was amended in 1992. But further oil pollution incidents, such as *Erika* (1999) and *Prestige* (2002), made necessary further amendments.[4]

The oil pollution regime is comprised of the 1969 Convention on Civil Liability for Oil Pollution Damage[5] and the 1971 Fund Convention.[6] These conventions have been amended by the 1992 Convention on Civil Liability for Oil Pollution Damage[7] and the 1992 Fund Convention.[8] To be a party to a fund convention, a state must be party to the respective liability convention.

---

[3] See, e.g., International Convention for the Unification of Certain Rules Relating to the Limitation of Liability of Owners of Sea-going Vessels, Aug. 25, 1924, reprinted in International Maritime Conventions 1383 (Ignacio Arroyo, ed., 1991); International Convention Relating to the Limitation of Liability of Owners of Sea-going Ships, Oct. 10, 1957, reprinted in International Maritime Conventions 1389.

[4] Måns Jacobsson, The International Compensation Regime 25 Years on, in IOPC Funds' 25 Years of Compensating Victims of Oil Pollution Incidents 13, 13–14 (IOPC Funds, 2003) [hereinafter 25 Years].

[5] Convention on Civil Liability for Oil Pollution Damage, Nov. 29, 1969, reprinted in 973 UNTS 3, 9 ILM 45 (1970). See also Protocol to the 1969 International Convention on Civil Liability for Oil Pollution Damage, Nov. 19, 1976, reprinted in 16 ILM 617 (1977). As of August 24, 2004, there were still forty-four state parties to the 1969 Convention.

[6] Convention on the Establishment of an International Fund for Compensation for Oil Pollution Damage, Dec. 18, 1971. See also Protocol to Amend the 1971 International Convention of the Establishment of an International Fund for Compensation for Oil Pollution Damage, Nov. 19, 1976, reprinted in 16 ILM 621 (1977). Because of denunciations, the 1971 fund convention ceased to be in force in May 24, 2002.

[7] Protocol of 1992 to Amend the International Convention on Civil Liability for Oil Pollution Damage, Nov. 27, 1992, available online at http://www.imo.org/Conventions/contents. A 1984 Protocol that was drafted was never ratified. The liability limits in the 1992 liability convention were further increased by a 2000 amendment to the convention; see 2000 Amendments to Civil Liability Convention, Oct. 18, 2000. The amendments entered into force on Nov. 1, 2003 [hereinafter Convention].

[8] Protocol of 1992 to Amend the International Convention on the Establishment of an International Fund for Compensation for Oil Pollution Damage, Nov. 27, 1992, available online at htttp://www.iopcFund. org. A 1984 protocol that was adopted was never ratified. The 1992 fund protocol was amended in 2000 to increase the contributions to the fund; see 2000 Amendments to Fund Convention, Oct. 18, 2000. The amendments entered into force on Nov. 1, 2003 [hereinafter Fund].

The oil and tanker industry, anxious to avoid liability under international conventions, accordingly devised voluntary compensation schemes. One such scheme, the Tanker Owners Voluntary Agreement Concerning Liability for Oil Pollution (TOVALOP), provided for strict and limited liability of shipowners in the same manner as the Conventions on Civil Liability. Another scheme, the Contract Regarding an Interim Supplement to Tanker Liability for Oil Pollution (CRISTAL), consisted of a fund similar to the funds prescribed by the fund conventions.[9] By adopting voluntary compensation schemes, the oil industry had hoped to demonstrate to governments that international treaties were unnecessary or, at least, to influence the emerging international norms for oil pollution. The TOVALOP and the CRISTAL funds, however, ceased to operate in 1997 because the industry started to appreciate the benefits of international liability rule-making.

The 1992 Liability Convention imposes on shipowners strict and limited liability for oil pollution damage, and joint and several liability when two or more ships are involved and the pollution damage is not reasonably separable.[10] Although the convention channels liability to the shipowner, other people that perform services for the ship – such as the manager, charterer, or operator of a ship – can be held liable if the damage resulted from their intentional act or omission, or through their recklessness, and they knew that such damage would probably result.[11] The convention does not hold liable the builder or the repairer of a ship.

Shipowners can limit their liability by creating a limitation fund. The amount that a shipowner needs to contribute to his/her limitation fund has increased significantly since 1969, with the latest amendment in 2003.[12] But shipowners are not entitled to limit their liability if the pollution damage was the outcome of an intentional act or omission, or if it was the outcome of reckless behavior with knowledge that such damage would probably result.[13] The limitation fund established by the owner is distributed among the claimants in proportion to the amount of their claims. The distribution of claims is a smooth procedure when the total amount claimed does not exceed the limitation fund established by the owner; otherwise, it may be delayed.[14]

A plaintiff can bring an action for compensation, under the convention, only in the courts of a state party where the damage occurred.[15] Nevertheless, a plaintiff is still able under the rules of private international law to bring an action in the courts

---

[9] For more details concerning TOVALOP and CRISTAL, see C. Hill, Maritime Law 311–16 (1989).

[10] Art. IV, Convention *supra* note 7.

[11] Art. III(4), *id*.

[12] According to article V(1) as amended in 2000, see *supra* note 7, shipowners can limit their liability to an amount of: 4,510,000 SDR (U.S.$6.6 million) for a ship not exceeding five thousand units of gross tonnage; 4,510,000 SDR (U.S.$6.6 million) plus 631 SDR (U.S.$992) for each additional unit of tonnage for a ship with tonnage between 5,000 and 140,000 unites of tonnage; and 89,770,000 SDR (U.S.$131 million) for a ship of 140,000 units of tonnage or over. The unit of conversion applied as of August 2, 2004, is 1 SDR = U.S.$1.460880. See also Explanatory Note Prepared by the 1992 Fund Secretariat, International Oil Pollution Compensation Fund, Aug. 2004.

[13] Art. V(2), Convention, *supra* note 7.

[14] See Günther Doeker & Thomas Gehring, Liability for Environmental Damage 30 (Research Paper No. 32, UNCED, 1992).

[15] Art. IX, Convention, *supra* note 7. Article VIII also provides that the plaintiff has a right to compensation only if he/she brings an action within three years from the date when the damage occurred. No action can be brought "after six years from the date of the incident which caused the damage."

of another state if the person responsible for pollution damage is domiciled within that state.[16]

The convention provides for compulsory insurance of shipowners who carry more than two thousand tons of oil in bulk.[17] One of the advantages of compulsory insurance is that it drives businesses with insufficient assets to cover pollution damage out of the market. But this effect is tempered because only shipowners carrying more than two thousand tons of oil are compelled to maintain insurance.[18] Enforcement is left to national governments, which have to make sure that ships that they register maintain insurance and carry an insurance certificate on board.[19] Ships registered in state parties with no insurance certificate are not allowed to engage in the business of carrying oil.[20] Ships registered in nonstate parties also are required to hold such a certificate whenever they enter or leave ports or offshore terminals of state parties[21] so that they do not acquire a competitive advantage over ships of state parties.[22] State parties should mutually recognize certificates they issue and a ship registered in a nonstate party can obtain such a certificate from the authorities of any state party.[23]

The liability convention applies exclusively to pollution damage caused within the territory or the territorial sea or the EEZ.[24] The 1992 convention has improved on the 1969 convention's definition of oil pollution damage. Compensation covers not only personal injuries but also property damages and loss of profit.[25] Claims for compensation for impairment of the environment are limited to the cost of reasonable measures actually undertaken or to be undertaken to reinstate the environment.[26] But the convention does not provide details on causation or guidance on the quantification of damages, such as loss of future earnings. The convention leaves this task to national courts.

Another innovation of the 1992 convention is that it establishes liability not only for actual pollution damage but also for "a grave and imminent threat of causing such damage."[27] Thus, plaintiffs can now be compensated not only for preventive measures after pollution has occurred but also for measures taken to avert threats of pollution.

The fund convention supplements the liability convention. Its main purpose is to compensate pollution victims in case the protection afforded by the liability convention is inadequate.[28] The 1971 version of the fund convention included a provision

---

[16] D. W. Abecassis & R. J. Jarashow, Oil Pollution from Ships: International, U.K., and U.S. Law and Practice 220–21 (1985). See also Hill, *supra* note 9, at 288. See also Tullio Scovazzi, Industrial Accidents and the Veil of Transnational Corporations, in International Liability for Environmental Harm 395, 413–21 (Francesco Francioni & Tullio Scovazzi, eds., 1991).

[17] Art. VII(1), Convention *supra* note 7. That means that tankers that carry less than two thousand tons do not have to take out insurance.

[18] Abecassis, *supra* note 16, at 223.

[19] Art. VII(2) and (4), Convention, *supra* note 7.

[20] Art. VII(10), *id.*

[21] Art. VII(11), *id.*

[22] Abecassis, *supra* note 16, at 225.

[23] Art. VII(7), Convention, *supra* note 7.

[24] Art. II (ii), *id.* The EEZ was added with the 1992 Protocol.

[25] Art. I(6), *id.*

[26] *Id.*

[27] Art. I(8), *id.*

[28] Art. 2(1)(a), Fund, *supra* note 8.

of indemnification of shipowners.[29] The issue of indemnification of shipowners was debated at great length during the drafting of the 1971 fund convention because of the conflict of interests between states with shipping industries and oil-receiving states that finance the fund.[30] In the end, the provision was abolished in the 1992 fund convention.

The 1992 fund provides compensation for pollution damage[31] only if a claimant is unable to obtain full and adequate compensation under the liability convention.[32] Additionally, it provides for recovery of preventive costs as defined in the liability convention.[33]

The limits of the fund have increased steadily since the 1971 inception of the fund. According to the 1992 version of the fund, the amount paid could not exceed 135 million SDR (U.S.$197 million), including the sum paid by the shipowner or his/her insurer under the 1992 liability convention. This limit was increased by about 50 percent in 2003 to 203 million SDR (U.S.$297 million). This increased amount applies to incidents that occur after the date of adoption of the 2003 amendment to the fund – that is, after November 1, 2003.[34] The 1992 fund convention has clarified the provisions for the distribution of compensation to claimants. Claims against the fund are to be distributed *pro rata* regardless of the extent to which they have been satisfied by the limitation fund of the liability convention.[35] According to fund practice, the claims covered are restoration of the environment, loss of livelihood, loss of income, and environmental damage.

The fund's settlement procedure is remarkable. The fund has developed a claims manual that includes a simple procedure for claim settlement.[36] The fund has a good working relationship with the Protection and Indemnity (P&I) Clubs of shipowners, and claimants can bring their claims just once to either of these two bodies.[37] Subsequently, the club and the fund divide among themselves the amount paid to the claimant. P&I Clubs are composed of shipowners who are organized together to mutually indemnify each other against lawsuits in cases of damage to cargo or injuries to third parties. The clubs started to operate in the nineteenth century when underwriters at Lloyd's would cover only three-quarters of hull damage.[38] Today,

---

[29] Art. 2(1)(b), 1971 Fund, *supra* note 6.

[30] Abecassis, *supra* note 16, at 261.

[31] See art. 1(2), Fund, *supra* note 8.

[32] Art. 4(1), *id.* According to this article, the claimant cannot obtain full and adequate compensation in three cases: when no liability for damage arises under the Liability Convention; when the owner liable under the Liability Convention is financially incapable of meeting his/her obligations; or when the damage exceeds the owner's limitation fund.

[33] Art. 1(2), Fund, *supra* note 8. See art. I(8), Convention, *supra* note 7.

[34] Art. 4(4), Fund, *id.*

[35] Art. 4(5), *id.*

[36] Abecassis, *supra* note 16, at 272.

[37] *Id.* at 272–73. The P&I Clubs and the oil pollution fund use the same technical experts and surveyors who are instructed jointly and report directly to their respective parties. The costs of experts used are shared between the P&I Clubs and the oil pollution fund in proportion to their liabilities. If there is a conflict of interest, the oil pollution fund uses different experts. It is not uncommon for the P&I Clubs and the fund to establish a joint claims office. See Jacobsson, *supra* note 4, at 17–19.

[38] B. Farthing, International Shipping 49 (1987).

P&I Clubs cover 90 percent of the world shipping. They provide unlimited coverage in most cases except for oil pollution and nuclear incidents.[39]

The fund allows prepayment of damages if the shipowner is entitled to limited liability under the liability convention, and undue financial hardship is demonstrated.[40] The fund also makes available credit facilities to state parties "in imminent danger of substantial pollution damage."

The fund is financed by enterprises of oil importing states that receive in the relevant calendar year more than 150,000 metric tons of oil.[41] This means that the costs of paying for the fund are shouldered by the "customers" of the oil-producing industry.[42] A state with modest oil imports or a major exporter can become party to the fund convention and enjoy full protection without having to impose on its industry to contribute to the fund.[43] Enforcement is left to states that must ensure that the industry's financial obligations to the fund are fulfilled and must impose sanctions when necessary.[44] The 1992 fund convention, furthermore, prescribes that states can be held liable, if their failure to police contributors causes financial loss to the fund.[45]

The oil pollution regime could be a model regime for environmental accidents with international implications. The regime does apply a broader version of the polluter pays principle in which it is not only the person in control of a dangerous activity that is held liable – the individual shipowner (representing the shipping industry) – but also the customer (the oil receiving industry). Some commentators have characterized the oil pollution fund – that is, financed basically by oil-importing states that receive more than a specified amount of oil – as an expression of solidarity among states in case of major tanker spills.[46]

Overall, the 1992 liability convention and the fund convention have clarified many of the provisions of the conventions they amended. They prescribe explicitly compensation for economic loss and recovery of expenditures for restoration of the environment. They provide for compensation even when the shipowner has not established a limitation fund. The only shortcoming of the regime has been limited liability, which always was viewed as insufficient to cover losses resulting from environmental disasters. The inadequacy of liability limits is evidenced by the repeated increases of these limits after environmental disasters.[47] After the *Amoco Cadiz* disaster, France, a state party to the 1974 convention, refused to collect the money deposited in the limitation fund because of limited liability constraints. Instead,

---

[39] *Id.*

[40] Abecassis, *supra* note 16, at 273.

[41] Art. 10(1), Fund, *supra* note 8.

[42] Exporting states do not contribute to the fund. The Japanese industry is currently one of major contributors to the fund. The Japanese industry contributed 20 percent of the 1992 fund's budget. See Klaus Töpfer, Beyond the Marketplace: IOPC Funds and the Environment, in 25 Years 37, *supra* note 4, at 39.

[43] Abecassis, *supra* note 16, at 279.

[44] Art. 13(2), Fund, *supra* note 8.

[45] Art. 15(4), id.

[46] Hans Corell, The Law of the Sea and the IOPC Funds, in 25 Years 33, *supra* note 4, at 36.

[47] Doeker, *supra* note 14, at 37–38.

France brought an action in the United States, the domicile of the ship's builder and operator.[48]

The inadequacy of liability limits seems to have been rectified, however, after the 2003 amendments to the 1992 regime. The oil pollution funds have provided compensation in 125 oil pollution incidents and have paid out U.S.$660 million to victims of oil pollution. Most of the claims have been settled out of court.[49]

The oil pollution regime has been supplemented by the International Convention on Civil Liability for Bunker Oil Pollution Damage, adopted in 2001.[50] The development of a Bunkers' Oil Pollution Damage Convention was under the radar of the IMO from 1996, when it was estimated that half of the total number of pollution claims arose from incidents involving ships not carrying oil cargo. Even for larger oil spills, it was confirmed that the number of nontanker vessel spills was significantly greater than the number of tanker spills.

The Bunkers' Liability Convention is modeled on the 1992 Oil Pollution Convention. Article 1(5) defines bunker oil as any hydrocarbon mineral oil, including lubricating oil, used or intended to be used for the operation and propulsion of a ship, and any residues of such oil. This convention, as with the 1992 liability convention, provides for strict liability of shipowner.[51] The liability is limited.[52] An owner of a ship of over one thousand gross tonnage must maintain insurance or financial security in the amount that is not exceeding the amount calculated in accordance with the Convention on Limitation of Liability for Maritime Claims.[53] The convention will enter into force after eighteen states, including five states with ships of combined gross tonnage of one million, have ratified it.[54]

2. HAZARDOUS MATERIALS TRADE

2.1. CRTD Convention

The Convention on Civil Liability for Damage Caused during Carriage of Dangerous Goods by Road, Rail and Inland Navigation Vessels (CRTD)[55] was prepared by the UN Economic Commission for Europe (ECE), but other countries can become signatories.[56] The convention imposes strict and limited liability on operators of

---

[48] In re Oil Spill by the Amoco Cadiz off the Coast of France on March 16, 1978, 954 F. 2d 1279 (7th Cir. 1992).

[49] Jacobsson, *supra* note 4, at 17.

[50] International Convention on Civil Liability for Bunker Oil Pollution Damage, Mar. 23, 2001, available online at http://www.imo.org/Conventions [hereinafter Bunker Liability Convention].

[51] Art. 3, *id.*

[52] Art. 6, *id.*

[53] Art. 7, Convention on Limitation of Liability for Maritime Claims, Nov. 19, 1976, reprinted in 16 ILM 606 (1976). Protocol of 1996 to amend the Convention on Limitation of Liability for Maritime Claims, May 9, 1996, reprinted in 35 ILM 1433 (1996).

[54] Art. 14, Bunker Liability Convention, *supra* note 50.

[55] Economic Commission for Europe, Convention on Civil Liability for Damage Caused During Carriage of Dangerous Goods by Road, Rail and Inland Navigation Vessels (CRTD), Oct. 10, 1989, U.N. Doc. ECE/TRANS/84 (1990), U.N. Sales No.E.II.E.39 (including Explanatory Report) [hereinafter CRTD Convention]. The convention has not yet come into force.

[56] Art. 22, *id.*

railway lines, persons in control of vehicles carrying dangerous goods, and persons in control of inland navigation vessels.[57]

In order to facilitate the identification of the liable person, it is presumed that the person in whose name the vehicle is registered is liable. When such registration does not exist, the owner is held liable, unless he/she can prove that another person was in control of the vehicle with or without his/her consent.[58]

The primary concerns of the drafters of the treaty – to protect potential victims and to minimize insurance costs – are recurrent throughout the convention.[59] The possibility of channeling liability to the owner of goods was not pursued because ownership may change many times during transportation making identification of the owner burdensome.[60] Channeling responsibility to the producer of goods also was excluded because producers have no control over carriage. Moreover, carriage may take place many years after production. It would be unfair, therefore, to require the producer to maintain insurance just in case of some future transportation accident. Moreover, dangerous goods are often transported together, and it is difficult to distinguish which producer's goods have caused the damage.[61] Imposing liability on the shipper similarly was viewed as impractical. The shipper would have to take out insurance for each and every consignment, and it would be difficult, at the time of an accident, to figure out which shipper's substance had caused the damage.[62]

Placing liability on the carrier seemed the most practical solution because the carrier has control over the movement of goods, can be identified easily by the victims, and can take out insurance on an annual basis. Carriers, however, opposed this solution. They claimed that accidents occur because of the inherent danger of goods carried, and that imposing liability on the carrier would increase insurance costs, distort competition, and drive many carriers out of business. The carriers proposed joint responsibility of carriers and shippers. Joint responsibility, however, was not a workable solution because it was considered impractical to place responsibility on the shipper, and because most governments considered joint and several liability too complex. However, recognizing the inequities of placing responsibility on carriers, when other persons are also responsible, the convention renders the consignor or consignee liable for accidents caused during loading or unloading without the carrier's participation. In addition, joint liability is established when both the carrier and another person are involved in loading and unloading.[63] But, for the reasons mentioned earlier, persons other than the carrier do not have to take out insurance.[64]

The issue of whether liability should be limited or unlimited was a source of controversy during the drafting of the treaty. Some governments argued for unlimited

---

[57] Art. 1(8), *id*. According to article 1(8)(a), when the vehicle carrying dangerous goods is carried on another vehicle the operator of that other vehicle will be considered the carrier. According to article 8, when an incident involving two or more vehicles has caused inseparable damage, both carriers will be held jointly and severally liable.

[58] Art. 1(8), *id*.

[59] Explanatory Report, *id*. at 6.

[60] *Id*.

[61] *Id*.

[62] *Id*. at 7.

[63] Art. 6, CRTD Convention, *id*.

[64] Art. 6(2)(a), *id*.

liability, contending that the domestic application of unlimited liability has not affected the availability of compulsory insurance.[65] As a compromise, limited liability was adopted;[66] thus, carriers must establish a limitation fund with the court where the lawsuit is brought.[67] It was made clear, however, that individual governments may adopt higher limits or unlimited liability.[68] Carriers are not entitled to limited liability when the damage was caused by their intentional or reckless act or omission, or by an intentional or reckless act of their servants and agents.[69]

Carriers are not to be held liable in cases of *force majeure*, and if the consignors or other persons failed to inform them about the dangerous nature of goods. The carriers also must prove that they did not know, or were not required to know, that the goods carried were dangerous.[70] Carriers are exonerated from liability if the damage resulted from an intentional or negligent act or omission of the victim.[71] When a carrier is not liable other persons may be held liable, but many important provisions of the convention will not apply to those other persons.[72]

Following in the steps of the oil pollution convention regime, the CRTD Convention provides for compulsory insurance.[73] The insurance covers not only the carrier mentioned in the insurance policy; it also covers any other person in control of the vehicle at the time of an accident.[74] States concluded that insurance companies are capable of insuring carriers, and believed that, because of the limited liability, even small carriers would be able to obtain insurance. The insurance companies were in favor of such scheme. They claimed that, although strict liability might initially increase premiums, such an increase would be reassessed subsequently depending on the number and severity of claims.[75] The monitoring of implementation of insurance provisions is left to state parties. Each state party must designate competent authorities that will issue or approve certificates verifying that carriers have obtained insurance.[76]

In order to speed up the settlement of disputes, claims for compensation may be brought directly against the insurer. The action against the carrier or its insurer must be brought within three years from the date the victim knew or should have known of the damage and the identity of carrier, or within ten years from the date of the incident.[77] Actions may be brought in the state party where the damage occurred, where the incident took place, or where preventive measures were taken. In addition, an action may be brought in the habitual residence of a carrier, for example, in the state of registration of the vehicle of the carrier.[78]

---

[65] Explanatory Report, *id.* at 9.
[66] Art. 9, CRTD Convention, *id.*
[67] Art. 11, *id.*
[68] Art. 24, *id.*
[69] Art. 10, *id.*
[70] Art. 5(7), *id.*
[71] Art. 5(5), *id.*
[72] Art. 7, *id.*
[73] Art. 13, *id.*
[74] Art. 13(2), id
[75] Explanatory Report, *id.* at 9.
[76] Art. 14, CRTD Convention, *id.*
[77] Art. 18, *id.*
[78] Art. 19, *id.*

Some states proposed a fund in case compensation exceeds the liability limits, but the proposal did not gain the support of the majority of governments. It was recognized that the oil importers sponsoring the oil pollution fund were more readily identifiable than industries dealing with dangerous substances.[79]

The definition of dangerous goods is inclusive.[80] The convention refers to the ADR,[81] which contains extensive lists of dangerous substances that are frequently updated. This ensures that carriers will be knowledgeable about the substances that may trigger liability under the convention.

The damages covered under the convention involve loss of life or personal injury and loss of or damage to property.[82] Recovery for pure economic loss is not explicitly covered by the convention. During the drafting of the convention, many states resisted the explicit exclusion of pure economic loss in the convention, and maintained that, because national laws were still evolving, such issues should be addressed by domestic legislation.[83] Loss or damage caused by pollution of the environment is also recoverable, although such damage, other than loss of profit, is restricted "to costs of reasonable measures of reinstatement actually undertaken or to be undertaken."[84] The costs of preventive measures and loss or damage caused by preventive measures also may be recovered.[85] Preventive measures are defined as measures taken after the occurrence of the polluting incident.[86] The polluting incident is identified as an occurrence or occurrences having the same origin that cause damage or create a grave and imminent threat of causing damage.[87]

The CRTD Convention was opened for signature in 1990 but up to the time of writing only two countries have signed it: Germany and Morocco. The lack of interest in the convention is a result of the lack of fully developed insurance markets for the carriage of dangerous goods. The Inland Transport Committee for the Economic Commission for Europe is considering modifications to the convention with regard to the limit to liability and insurance requirements that would ease the ratification process.

2.2. HNS Convention

Initially, attempts to impose liability on shippers for the carriage of hazardous and noxious substances by sea[88] was met with strong resistance from the chemical industry. The chemical industry claimed that liability should not lie with the shippers of

[79] Explanatory Report, id. at 10.

[80] Art. 1(9), CRTD Convention, id.

[81] European Agreement concerning the International Carriage of Dangerous Goods by Road (ADR), UN Doc. ECE/TRANS/80 (Volume I and II).

[82] Art. 1(9), CRTD Convention, supra note 55.

[83] Explanatory Report, id. at 17–18.

[84] Art. 1(9)(c), CRTD Convention, id.

[85] Art. 1(9)(d), id.

[86] Art. 1(11), id.

[87] Art. 1(12), id.

[88] 1991 Draft Convention on Liability and Compensation in Connection with the Carriage of Hazardous and Noxious Substances by Sea, IMO Doc. LEG 64/4, Jan. 25, 1991. See also 1993 Draft International Convention on Liability and Compensation for Damage in Connection with the Carriage of Hazardous and Noxious Substances by Sea, IMO Doc. LEG 68/4, Jan. 5, 1993.

hazardous substances but with shipowners under the traditional rules of maritime law. The diversity and number of chemical industries, it was argued, made it difficult to create an international liability system.

The HNS Convention eventually was adopted in 1996.[89] The convention is divided into three chapters: Chapter I includes the general provisions; Chapter II provides for shipowner's liability; and Chapter III for the establishment of a fund. The convention is structured on the model of the oil pollution and fund conventions. The convention provides for a strict liability regime for shipowners,[90] a list of defenses to liability,[91] rules of joint and several liability for damage that is not reasonably separable,[92] and compulsory shipowner insurance.[93] Article 9 provides for limits to liability that must not in any case exceed 100 million SDR (US$128 million).[94] The liability is not limited if the shipowner acted recklessly with knowledge that damage would occur.[95] States may decide not to apply the convention for ships of gross tonnage of two hundred and below, which carry HNS only in packaged form and are engaged in voyages between the ports of the same state.[96] Two neighboring states can agree to apply similar conditions on ships that operate between their ports.[97]

Under Chapter III, the convention establishes a HNS fund that, like the 1992 oil pollution fund, would compensate any person who suffers damage under the convention. Damage under the HSN fund is provided for victims of pollution who cannot obtain compensation because the shipowner is not liable, or the shipowner is unable to meet his/her obligations, or the damages exceed the shipowner's liability limits.[98] Contributions made to the fund are assigned to four accounts, a general account[99] and three separate accounts – one for oil, one for liquefied natural gas (LNG), and one for liquefied petroleum gas (LPG).[100] Contributions to the fund are made by entities that receive a certain minimum quantity of HSN cargo during the preceding calendar year.[101] The amount of compensation payable by the fund must not exceed 250 SDR (U.S.$320 million), including an amount of 100 SDR (U.S.$128 million), which could be claimed from the shipowner.[102]

The convention will enter into force after twelve states have adopted it, four of which must have more than two million units of gross tonnage in HNS shipping.

The convention has been ratified by four states including the Russian Federation. The EU states are to ratify the convention by 2006 and the convention is expected to enter into force by 2008. Issues that need to be resolved, after the convention

[89] International Convention on Liability and Compensation for Damage in Connection with the Carriage of Hazardous and Noxious Substances by Sea, May 3, 1996, reprinted in 35 ILM 1406 (1996).

[90] Art. 7(1), *id.*

[91] Art. 7(2)–(3), *id.*

[92] Art. 8, *id.*

[93] Art. 12, *id.*

[94] Art. 9(1), *id.*

[95] Art. 9(2), *id.*

[96] Art. 5(1), *id.*

[97] Art. 5(2), *id.*

[98] Arts. 13(1) and 14(1), *id.*

[99] Art. 16(1), *id.* See also arts. 18(1) and 1(5)(vii), *id.*

[100] Art. 16 (2), *id.*

[101] Art. 19, *id.*

[102] Art. 14(5)(a) and (b), *id.*

enters into force, are whether the fund component of the convention would function jointly with the oil pollution funds, which would reduce overall administrative costs, or whether it would function separately. Economies of scale support the collaboration among the funds. The HSN fund could build on the expertise of the oil pollution fund.

2.3. Liability for Waste Trade

The purpose of a Liability Protocol to the Basel Convention is to provide a comprehensive regime of adequate compensation.[103] The Basel Convention is the international convention that regulates the transfrontier movements of wastes based on the prior notification and informed consent of the importing country before a waste transfer to that country.

Damage under the protocol includes:loss of life or personal injury, loss or damage to property, loss of income deriving from an economic interest in the environment, costs of measures of reinstatement of the impaired environment limited to costs of measures actually taken or to be undertaken and costs of preventive measures.[104] According to the protocol, measures of reinstatement mean any reasonable measures aiming to assess, reinstate or restore damaged or destroyed components of the environment.[105]

The protocol applies to damage caused during the transboundary movement of hazardous wastes and their disposal, including illegal traffic, from the point that wastes are loaded for transport in the state of export.[106] But certain exceptions are provided for in the protocol.[107]

The protocol provides for strict liability. The rule of liability established under the protocol is that the notifier of waste transfer is strictly liable until the disposer takes possession of wastes. When the wastes enter the control of the disposer, the disposer is liable.[108] Fault liability is established also for any person who causes or contributes to damage by his/her lack of compliance with the provisions of the Basel Convention or by his/her wrongful intentional, reckless, or negligent acts or omissions.[109]

When strict liability applies, it is limited.[110] For fault liability, no limits apply.[111] Persons who could be liable under the protocol must maintain insurance or other financial guarantees up to the amounts of limited liability established in Annex B.[112] Courts that are competent to hear complaints are the municipal courts of the state where damage was suffered, or where the incident occurred, or where the defendant

---

[103] Protocol on Liability and Compensation for Damage Resulting from Transboundary Movements of Hazardous Wastes and their Disposal, Dec. 10, 1999.

[104] Art. 2(2)(c), *id.*

[105] Art. 2(2)(d), *id.*

[106] Art. 3(1), *id.*

[107] Art. 3(2), *id.*

[108] Art. 4(1), *id.*

[109] Art. 5, *id.*

[110] Art. 12(1) and Annex B, *id.*

[111] Art. 12(2), *id.*

[112] Art. 4(1), *id.*

maintains its habitual residence or its place of business.[113] The protocol provides for the mutual recognition of enforcement of municipal courts' judgements.[114] Claims under the protocol can be brought within ten years from the date of the incident or within five years from the date the claimant knew or ought reasonably to have known of the damage.[115]

For the protocol to enter into force, it needs twenty ratifications. At the time of writing, seventeen countries have signed the protocol, of which only Denmark, France, Finland, Sweden, and Switzerland could be considered significant hazardous waste producers. The EU and the United States have not signed the protocol. Only three states have ratified the protocol.

3. NUCLEAR ENERGY

The IAEA-OECD nuclear liability regime is comprised of three conventions: the OECD-sponsored Paris Convention (amended in 2004);[116] the Brussels Convention that supplements the Paris Convention (amended in 2004);[117] and the IAEA-sponsored Vienna Convention as amended in 1997.[118] Because state parties to the Paris Convention are not parties to the Vienna Convention and vice versa, a joint protocol relating to the application of the Vienna and Paris Conventions[119] has been adopted. The joint protocol provides that a state party to either the Vienna Convention or Paris Convention, when it is a party to the joint protocol, can recover damages from a nuclear plant operator located in any state that is party to either convention.[120]

---

[113] Art. 17, *id.*

[114] Art. 21, *id.*

[115] Art. 13, *id.*

[116] Paris Convention on Third Party Liability in the Field of Nuclear Energy, July 29, 1960, reprinted in 1041 UNTS 358. The convention was further amended in 1964, 1982, and 2004. See 2004 Protocol to Amend Convention on Third Party Liability in the Field of Nuclear Energy of 29th July 1960, as amended by the Additional Protocol of 28th January 1964 and by the Protocol of the 16th November 1982, February 12, 2004, available online at http://www.nea.fr/html/law/legal-documents.html (OECD/NEA Web site) [hereinafter Paris Convention].

[117] Brussels Convention Supplementary to the 1960 Convention on Third Party Liability in the Field of Nuclear Energy, Jan. 31, 1963, reprinted in 956 UNTS 264. The Brussels Convention was amended in 1964, 1982, and 2004. See 2004 Protocol to Amend the Convention of 31 January 1963 Supplementary to the Paris Convention of 29 July 1960 on Third Party Liability in the Field of Nuclear Energy, as amended by the Additional Protocol of 28 January 1964 and by the Protocol of 16 November 1982, Feb. 12, 2004, available online at http://www.nea.fr/html/law/legal-documents.html (OECD/NEA Web site) [hereinafter Brussels Convention]. The 1982 version of the Brussels Convention has entered into force.

[118] Vienna Convention on Civil Liability for Nuclear Damage, May 21, 1963, reprinted in 1063 UNTS 265. The convention was amended in 1997. See Protocol to Amend the Vienna Convention on Civil Liability for Nuclear Damage, Sept. 12, 1997, reprinted in 36 ILM 1454 (1997) [hereinafter Vienna Convention].

[119] Joint Protocol Relating to the Application of the Vienna Convention and the Paris Convention, Sept. 21, 1988, reprinted in 42 Nuclear Law 56 (NEA, 1988).

[120] All of these conventions deal with the peaceful uses of nuclear power. The only convention that touches on the military uses of nuclear power has not entered into force because of the sensitivity of national security issues. See Convention on the Liability of Operators of Nuclear Ships, May 25, 1962. The convention provides for strict and limited liability of operators of nuclear ships (arts. 2–3). No other person except for the operator can be held liable (art. 2). Operators of warships are also held liable (art. 1(11)).

In addition to this combined IAEA-OECD led regime, in 1997, the IAEA adopted a new Convention on Supplementary Compensation for Nuclear Damage (CSC).[121] Despite its name – which is somewhat misleading – the convention does not supplement any existing conventions. It is, instead, an instrument that states can adopt independent of whether they have subscribed to any of the components of the IAEA-OECD led regime.

The CSC Convention defines nuclear damage as:loss of life or personal injury; loss of or damage to property; economic loss; costs of measures of reinstatement of the impaired environment if such measures are taken or are to be taken; and loss of income deriving from an economic interest in any use or enjoyment of the environment.

The convention provides for sources of compensation – based on the installed nuclear capacity of state parties and a UN rate of assessment – a total of 300 SDR per unit of installed nuclear capacity (U.S.$400 million).[122] The convention was adopted under the pressure of the United States, which viewed that a system of sharing liability among nuclear power states made more sense in case of a catastrophic nuclear accident than that of channeling liability exclusively to the operator. For the convention to enter into force, it needs to be ratified by at least five states with a minimum of four hundred thousand units of installed nuclear capacity. After its entry into force, any state can accede to the convention.[123] The United States and Ukraine, states with significant nuclear power, have signed the convention but have yet to ratify it.

The first version of the IAEA-OECD led regime was adopted in the 1960s. The regime was amended in the 1980s but still considered grossly inadequate in terms of providing compensation for nuclear accidents. The negotiations for the update of the IAEA-OECD regime were contentious. Controversies included the potential inclusion of military installations under the liability system, the extent of increase of operator's liability, the inclusion of damage to the environment under the definition of nuclear damage, and the establishment of an international claims tribunal to handle claims arising from nuclear accidents.

The 2004 updated version of the IAEA-OECD regime retains the basic characteristics of the regime it amended. It imposes strict[124] and limited liability on the operator of a nuclear installation,[125] and joint and several liability when two or more operators are liable and the damage is not reasonably separable.[126] Channeling liability exclusively to the operator avoided the excessive administrative costs of identifying the liability of other actors, such as suppliers and transporters. The conventions also impose compulsory insurance on the operators of nuclear facilities. But the specification of the amount, type, and terms of such insurance is left to each state party.[127]

---

[121] Convention on Supplementary Compensation for Nuclear Damage, Sept. 12, 1997, reprinted in 36 ILM 1473 (1997) [hereinafter CSC Convention].

[122] Art. IV, *id.*

[123] Art. XX, *id.*

[124] According to article 9 of the Paris Convention, *supra* note 116, and article IV(1)–(3) of the Vienna Convention, *supra* note 118, operators are not held liable in cases of *force majeure* (including armed conflict, hostilities, civil war, and insurrection).

[125] Arts. 3, 6, and 7, Paris Convention, *id.*; Art. V, Vienna Convention, *id.*

[126] Art. 5, Paris Convention, *id.*; Art. II(2)(a), Vienna Convention, *id.*

[127] Art. 10, Paris Convention, *id.*; Art. VII, Vienna Convention, *id.*

The conventions prescribe liability for damages caused by radioactive waste transportation and disposal.[128] The definition of nuclear damage has been expanded under the IAEA-OECD led regime. Under the 1982 version of the regime, nuclear damage was defined as loss of life or property or damage to people or property. The 2004 version of the regime defines nuclear damage as: loss of life, personal injury; damage to property; economic loss; costs of measures of reinstatement of the impaired environment; loss of income deriving from an economic interest in any use or enjoyment of the environment incurred as a result of a significant impairment of that environment; and costs of preventive measures.[129] The nature, form, and extent of compensation are left to be arranged by the competent national court.[130]

The 2004 Brussels Convention prescribes an interesting compensation scheme: a portion of the compensation is paid by the operator's insurance, another by the installation state, and the remaining balance by state parties, according to a special formula based on the GNP and the nuclear power of those parties.[131] Victims can bring claims under the conventions principally in the courts of the state where the nuclear incident occurred.[132] Under the general rules of private international law, however, any state suffering damages has jurisdiction over such claims and plaintiffs can engage in forum shopping.

The updated IAEA-OECD conventions and the CSC Convention have improved the nuclear liability regime considerably. Liability limits have increased significantly since the 1960s but still may be conceived as inadequate in light of a disaster such as Chernobyl. The overall liability amounts that can be recovered under the Paris Convention are €700 million.[133] But this amount is supplemented by the Brussels Convention, which provides for €1,500 million per nuclear incident. Out this amount of €1,500 million, €700 million is provided by the insurance of nuclear operator in accordance with the Paris Convention; €500 million is provided by the state in whose territory the nuclear installation of the liable operator is located; and the final €300 million is provided by the contracting parties according to a formula based on their GNP and nuclear power.[134] This is a significant increase in compensation in comparison with the compensation offered by prior versions of the regime. Further compensation could be made available under the CSC Convention, provided that a state party to the IAEA-OECD regime has ratified the CSC Convention.

The liability limits established under the Vienna Convention are 300 million SDR (US$400 million). A state also may decide to limit the liability of the operator to 150 million SDR, provided that the rest of the amount – up to 300 million SDR – is made available by public funds of that state.[135] In addition to this 300 million SDR – and

[128] Art. 1(a)(ii), (iv), and (v) and art. 8, Paris Convention, *id.*; see also Art. I(g),(h), and (j), Vienna Convention, *id.*

[129] Art. 1(a)(vii), Paris Convention, *id.*; Art. I(k), Vienna Convention, *id.*

[130] Art. 11, Paris Convention, *id.*; Art. VIII, Vienna Convention, *id.*

[131] Art. 3, Brussels Convention, *supra* note 117. See also art. 12, Brussels Convention, *id.* Thirty-five percent of the contribution is based on the GNP of state parties and 65 percent of the contribution is based on their nuclear power.

[132] Art. 13, Paris Convention, *supra* note 116. Art. XI, Vienna Convention, *supra* note 118.

[133] Art. 7, Paris Convention, *id.*

[134] Art. 3, Brussels Convention, *supra* note 117.

[135] Art. V, Vienna Convention, *supra* note 118.

provided that a state has ratified the CSC Convention – more compensation can be provided under that convention.

States that have not ratified any component of the IAEA-OECD led regime but have adopted the CSC Convention are entitled to compensation under that convention.

Other innovations of the IAEA-OCED updated regime is the extension of the geographical application of the conventions to include the EEZ[136] and extension of the periods within which claims can be brought that are now more in sync with the realities of nuclear accidents.[137]

Overall, the nuclear liability regime, as it has been updated, could provide significant amount of compensation in case of a nuclear accident. Given the extent of a catastrophe that a nuclear accident could create, however, no compensation limit seems sufficient to cover all possible damages. States had to strike a reasonable balance, therefore, between the real costs of restitution in case of a nuclear accident and what could be provided reasonably in such circumstances by the insurance industry. As long as insurance for nuclear accidents is limited, increasing the liability limits will not do much to address effectively the problem of compensation in case of a nuclear accident.

In addition to the increased amounts of compensation, both the updated IAEA-OECD regime and the CSC Convention are more comprehensive and consistent. The definition of nuclear damage, for instance, is more or less consistent in all the treaties that make up the regime and the same is true for the amount of time given to bring claims. One could claim that a thirty-year period (from the date of a nuclear incident) for bringing claims is still not sufficient, given the long latency periods of nuclear substances. During the drafting of the instruments, a balance had to be struck between the need to establish certainty – that is, an important goal in law – and the need to pursue justice for victims of nuclear accidents. Extending the expiration period to more than thirty years was viewed as increasing uncertainty to the point of affecting the insurability of nuclear operators.

The nuclear liability regime is a clear demonstration of the mixed feelings that states hold about the polluter pays principle. Liability is initially channeled to the operator. But then states are to pick up costs based on their nuclear power, their GNP, or the UN rate of assessment. It could be said that the CSC Convention is based on the principle of solidarity rather than a polluter pays principle as states are to share the costs of a nuclear accident based on a UN rate of assessment and their nuclear capacity.

Overall, an international regime can be deemed successful if, at a minimum, countries that are relevant for the success of the regime adopt it (that is ratify the related treaties) and then make some attempts to implement it. The nuclear liability regime has yet to be ratified. The United States and the Russian Federation –[138] major nuclear powers, relevant to the success of the regimes – have not ratified

[136] Art. 2(a), Brussels Convention, *supra* note 117; Art. 2(a), Paris Convention, *supra* note 116; Art. IA, Vienna Convention, *supra* note 118.

[137] Art. VI, Vienna Convention, id; Art. 8, Paris Convention, id; Article 6, Brussels Convention, *id*.

[138] The Russian Federation signed the 1982 version of the Vienna Convention in 1996 but has not ratified it.

any of international conventions. The Paris Convention has entered into forced and has been ratified by France, the United Kingdom, and Germany, countries with significant nuclear operations in Europe. The 1982 Vienna Convention also has entered into force. It has been ratified by countries that have or are surrounded by nuclear plants and nuclear operations. Such countries include the breakup republics of the Soviet Union, the Czech Republic, Slovakia, and Poland. The 1997 version of the Vienna Convention has entered into force but none of the parties that ratified the convention is a major nuclear power.[139]

It remains to be seen how the 2004 IAEA-OECD regime would be received and whether states would decide to employ means to further simplify the nuclear liability regime that is currently addressed in two fora under separate but yet related instruments. It would be interesting to find out whether the CSC Convention, which has the support of the United States, could acquire wider acceptance. The nuclear liability regime could be characterized as a conglomerate regime based on a number of rules that cross over each other. The United States, for instance, which was unhappy with the IAEA-OECD regime, decided to create an alternative/additional regime based on the CSC Convention. The OECD regime and the IAEA regime, respectively, adopted in a regional and an international forum have been joined together by a protocol that creates a more comprehensive regime. The success of these regimes would depend on the deep pockets of the countries that decide to ratify them.

4. LIABILITY FOR DAMAGE TO THE ENVIRONMENT

The 1993 Convention on Liability for Damage Resulting from Activities Dangerous to the Environment adopted by the Council of Europe[140] aims to provide adequate compensation for damage resulting from activities dangerous to the environment and to provide for prevention of damage and restitution.[141] The convention holds the operator[142] of a dangerous activity liable for incidents that cause damage and does not provide for specific limitations on liability.[143] An incident under the convention is defined as any sudden occurrence, or continuous occurrence, or any series of occurrences having the same origin that cause damage or create a grave and imminent threat of causing damage.[144]

The convention requires each party to ensure that operators are covered by insurance up to a certain limit by taking into account the risks of the activity.[145] Damages covered under the convention include loss of life or personal injury, loss or damage to property, costs of preventive measures, and any loss or damage caused by

---

[139] Countries that have ratified the convention as of 2004 include: Argentina, Belarus, Latvia, Morocco, and Romania. Romania has one nuclear power reactor that generates 10 percent of its electricity. Nuclear power covers some of Argentina's energy needs. The convention entered into force on October 4, 2003, with five ratifications.

[140] Convention on Civil Liability for Damage Resulting from Activities Dangerous to the Environment, June 21, 1993, reprinted in 32 ILM 480 (1993).

[141] Art. 1, *id.*

[142] An operator is defined as the person who exercises control over a dangerous activity. See art. 2(5), *id.*

[143] See, e.g., arts. 5 and 6, *id.*

[144] Art. 2(11), *id.*

[145] Art. 12, *id.*

preventive measures.[146] The convention applies to environmental damage that is loss or damage by impairment of the environment, but compensation in this case is limited to the costs of reasonable measures of reinstatement actually undertaken or to be undertaken.[147] The convention defines "measures of reinstatement" as any reasonable measures aiming to reinstate or to restore damaged or destroyed components of the environment, or to introduce, when reasonable, an equivalent of these components.[148]

The convention does not apply to tolerable levels of pollution under local relevant circumstances.[149] Furthermore, the convention does not apply if the operator can prove that damage was caused by war or a natural phenomenon of an exceptional, inevitable, and irresistible character;[150] by the intent of a third party;[151] as a result of compliance with an order or compulsory measure of a public authority;[152] or by a dangerous activity lawfully undertaken in the interests of persons who suffered the damage.[153] Contributory fault of the person suffering the damage could result in the reduction of or no compensation.[154]

Action under the convention can be brought within three years after the claimant knew or ought to have reasonably known of the damage and the identity of the operator.[155] And no action can be brought thirty years after the date of the incident that caused the damage.[156] The convention provides examples of situations in which court action can be taken.[157]

The convention covers requests by public interest organizations, whose purpose is the protection of environment, that comply with the internal requirements of the law of the state where the request is submitted. Such requests may involve the cessation of a dangerous activity and can be made only before the courts of the place where the dangerous activity occurs.[158] The convention includes additionally extensive provisions for access to information.[159]

The convention has yet to be ratified. This has to do with the lack of express liability limits, the grand range of dangerous activities covered,[160] the provisions for access to information, and the prominent role given to NGOs under the convention. Given the absence of express limits to liability, obtaining insurance under the convention would not be easy. Another issue that the convention has not clarified is the distinction between tolerable levels of pollution and actionable polluting incidents.

---

[146] Art. 2(7)(a)–(c), *id.*
[147] Art. 2(7)(c), *id.*
[148] Art. 2(8), *id.*
[149] Art. 8(d), *id.*
[150] Art. 8(a), *id.*
[151] Art. 8(b), *id.*
[152] Art. 8(c), *id.*
[153] Art. 8(e), *id.*
[154] Art. 9, *id.*
[155] Art. 17(1), *id.*
[156] Art. 17(2), *id.*
[157] Art. 19(1), *id.*
[158] Arts. 19(3) and 18(1)(a), *id.*
[159] See arts. 13–16, *id.*
[160] The convention covers dangerous activities defined broadly provided that they are performed professionally including the activities conducted by public authorities. See art. 2(1), *id.* The convention also covers genetically modified organisms and micro-organisms and dangerous substances. See art. 2(2)–(3), *id.*

Because of this, it is difficult for the convention to acquire wider acceptance. The ratification requirements of the convention, however, are low. The convention will enter into force after the date on which three states, including at least two member states of the Council of Europe, have ratified it.[161]

5. STATE RESPONSIBILITY

The International Law Commission (ILC)[162] has dealt with the issue of state responsibility for thirty years and eventually adopted draft rules in 2001.[163] Although these rules do not have binding force, as they have not been adopted formally by states, they provide, nevertheless, guidance for the development of international law. The ILC has defined state responsibility as the commission of a wrongful act by a state. According to the commission:

> Every internationally wrongful act of a State entails the international responsibility of that State.[164]

The commission clarifies what a wrongful act entails. According to the commission:

> There is an internationally wrongful act of a State when conduct consisting of an action or omission: (a) Is attributable to the State under international law; and (b) Constitutes a breach of an international obligation of the State.[165]

The breach of an international treaty obligation, for instance, would be a wrongful act and a state would be responsible, in principle, unless some defenses apply.[166] The same is true with the violation of a peremptory norm of international law (e.g., the prohibition against slavery). Apart from these specific circumstances, however, and in the case of pollution in general, a state will not necessarily be held responsible. For a state to be held responsible for pollution, such pollution must be wrongful under international law. If such pollution is legal, then the state cannot be held responsible.

Because the concept of state responsibility applies to wrongful acts of states and because most pollution does not constitute a wrongful act, states have tried to concoct a concept of "International Liability for Injurious Consequences Arising out of Acts *not* Prohibited by International Law." The idea behind a concept of international liability is to make possible strict liability for states for ultrahazardous activities taking place within their borders. The progression of the concept of international liability in international environmental law will be discussed later in this chapter.

State responsibility for wrongful activities is not encountered frequently in the international environmental arena. This is because most treaties do not contain specific environmental standards the breach of which could be considered a wrongful

---

[161] Art. 32(3), *id.*

[162] The ILC is a group of legal experts established by the UN General Assembly whose purpose is the codification and development of international law. As seen in Chapter 5, the ILC has proposed rules that have been quite influential in the development of watercourse law.

[163] See Draft Articles on Responsibility of States for Internationally Wrongful Acts, adopted by the International Law Commission at this Fifty-third session (2001), Official Records of the General Assembly, Fifty-sixth session, Supplement No. 10 (A/56/10, chp.IV.E.1), Nov. 2001.

[164] Art. 1, *id.*

[165] Art. 2, *id.*

[166] See art. 20 et seq., *id.*

act. On the contrary, many environmental agreements are quite broad in their articulation and provide for many exceptions and derogations. It would be difficult for
a claimant state to establish international responsibility unless it can point to a specific violation of an international rule that has binding effects on the defendant state.

Sometimes states, even hegemonic states, accept responsibility. One such case
includes the admission of responsibility by the United States for its nuclear testing in
the Marshall Islands. According to the 1983 Compact of Free Association between
the United States and the Marshall Islands:

> The Government of the United States accepts the responsibility for compensation
> owing to citizens of the Marshall Islands or the Federated States of Micronesia for
> loss or damage to property and person of the citizens [of the Marshall Islands and
> Federated States of Micronesia] resulting from the nuclear testing program which the
> Government of the United States conducted in the Northern Marshall Islands between
> June 30, 1946, and August 18, 1958.[167]

In 1944, during World War II, the United States captured the Enewetak Atoll
and the Bikini Atoll from the Japanese. In 1947, both the Enewetak people and the
Biniki people were removed from their territory for the purposes of conducting
nuclear testing by the United States. The relocation was to be temporary – not to
exceed a period of three to five years.

During the period between June 1946 and August 1958, the United States conducted sixty-seven nuclear atmospheric tests in the Marshall Islands – of which
forty-three were conducted at Enewetak Atoll and twenty-three at the Bikini Atoll.
The most potent of those tests was the so-called Bravo test, a fifteen-megaton device
detonated on March 1954 at the Bikini atoll. The test by itself was equivalent to one
thousand Hiroshima bombs.

In the early 1970s, following a limited cleanup of the Bikini Atoll, some of the
Bikini community returned to the atoll to live there.[168] But in 1978, following a
medical examination of Bikinians, it was concluded that people living there had
ingested high amounts of radioactive cesium-137 and needed to be removed again
immediately.[169]

The United States and the Marshall Islands entered into an agreement to implement Section 177 of the 1983 compact.[170] In that agreement, the United States
recognized the contributions and sacrifices made by the people of Marshall Islands

---

[167] Section 177(a), Compact of Free Association of the United States of America, and the Governments
of the Marshall Islands and the Federated States of Micronesia, signed by the United States and by the
Federated States of Micronesia and the Republic of the Marshall Islands on October 1, 1982 and June
25, 1983, respectively. See also Compact of Free Association Act of 1985 [P.L. 99–239], Jan. 14, 1986
[hereinafter Compact of Free Association].

[168] Before the Nuclear Claims Tribunal of Republic of the Marshall Islands, Memorandum of Decision and
Order, In the Matter of the People of Enewetak, et al., Claimants for Compensation, NCT No. 23–0902,
April 13, 2000, available online at http://www.nuclearclaimstribunal.com [hereinafter *Enewetak* case].

[169] Before the Nuclear Claims Tribunal of Republic of the Marshall Islands, Memorandum of Decision and
Order, In the Matter of the People of Bikini, et al., Claimants for Compensation, NTC No. 23–04134,
March 5, 2001, available online at http://www.nuclearclaimstribunal.com [hereinafter *Bikini* case].

[170] Agreement between the Government of the United States and the Government of Marshall Islands
for the implementation of Section 177 of the Compact of Free Association, June 25, 1983 [hereinafter
Section 177 Agreement].

with regard to the nuclear testing program.[171] The implementing agreement sets out the details of compensation. Under the agreement, the United States provided the Marshall Islands with the sum of US$150 million as a financial settlement of damages for the purpose of creating a fund.[172] The fund is to be invested with a performance goal of achieving at least $18 million per year in distributions.[173] The fund must be able to generate about US$270 million for distribution over a period of fifteen years.[174] The agreement also calls for the establishment of a claims tribunal, which would have jurisdiction to render judgments on all claims past, present, and future of the citizens and nationals of the Marshall Islands.

The tribunal was established, recognized claims, and awarded damages for:

- loss of use of property (e.g., the fact that people have been denied the use of their property for years);
- future denied use;
- restoration of land based on the IAEA principle that policies for radiation protection of populations outside national borders from releases of radioactive substances should at least be as stringent as those for the population within the country of release, which meant the application of the more stringent United States standards; and
- hardship, which encompasses the uprooting of people from their homes, changes in their ways of life, loss of control over their lives, and the undermining of traditional authority.

As a matter of procedure, with regard to the award of damages, it is interesting to note that the tribunal established thirty-six medical conditions that were irrefutably presumed to be the result of the nuclear testing program.[175] The suffering that was caused because of the involuntary relocations has been described in the proceedings of the tribunal.[176]

The tribunal awarded the people of Bikini a total amount of US$563,315,500.[177] The total amount the tribunal awarded in the case of Enewetak was US$341,049,311.[178]

Issues of state responsibility also are implicated in the *Nauru* case. The exploitation of Nauru started in 1908, when the Germans were in control of the Nauru

---

171 Preamble, *id.*
172 Art. I, Section I, *id.*
173 Art. I, Section 2(a), *id.*
174 Art. II, *id.*
175 Diseases, for which compensation was provided, are available online at http://www.nuclearclaimstribunal. com.
176 In the *Enewetak* case, it is mentioned that the "once self-sufficient people [of Enewetak] has been transformed into dependent wards of the United States." With the relocation "the structure of men's lives had been radically altered, and the time previously spent on canoes was replaced with boredom and meaningless activity." See *Enewetak* case, *supra* note 168.
177 This includes $278,000,000 for past and future loss of use of the Bikini Atoll; $251,500,000 to restore Bikini to a safe and productive state; and $33,815,500 for suffering by the people of Bikini as a result of their relocation.
178 This includes $199,154,811 for the past and future loss of the use of Enewetak Atoll; $107,810,000 to restore the atoll to safe and productive use; and $34,084,500 for the hardships suffered by people as a result of their relocation to Ujelang.

territory and began to mine large deposits of phosphate located there. The island fell into the hands of Australia in the early months of World War I. The League of Nations subsequently set up a mandate system for the island that was administered by Australia, New Zealand, and the United Kingdom. After World War II, Australia became the principal administrator of the island under a United Nations trusteeship agreement. The independence of the island was eventually granted in 1968. Nauru has large quantities of phosphate, the majority of which it exports to Australia as fertilizer for its poor agricultural soils. Because of the extensive mining of the island, 80 percent of the island is now barren.

The dependence on phosphate exports has affected the lifestyle of people. Because most of the land has been used for mining, Nauruans import most of their food. Since independence in 1968, the Nauru government has earned AU$100–AU$120 million per year from phosphate exports.

Nauru filed a claim before the ICJ against Australia in 1989. The goal of Nauru was to obtain compensation from Australia for phosphate mining that took place before its independence. Nauru claimed that Australia was responsible for breaching its international obligations, which included:

- obligations emanating from its role as the administrator of the trusteeship agreement;
- the basic responsibility of an administrator of a territory not to bring changes in the condition of that territory that cause irreparable damage to or substantially prejudice the existing or contingent legal interest of another state with respect to that territory; and
- compliance with the principle of self-determination and the sovereignty of states over their natural resources.[179]

Australia disputed the jurisdiction of the ICJ, claiming that the Nauru government had mismanaged the phosphate export funds. Australia also claimed that the agreements it signed with Nauru at the time of independence nullified future claims. The ICJ:

- was not receptive of the argument that the issue of phosphate exploitation had been settled by the very fact of the termination of the trusteeship agreement because Nauru and Australia had not entered into proceedings relating to the rehabilitation of the phosphate lands;
- concluded that the local authorities of Nauru had not waived in any way their claim relating to the rehabilitation of the phosphate lands;
- did not accept the Australian argument that the General Assembly resolution that terminated the trusteeship agreement terminated also the rights of the Nauru people with regard to the rehabilitation of their land; and
- concluded that the claim of Nauru was admissible because it was submitted within a reasonable time.[180]

---

[179] Paras. 1–6, Case Concerning Certain Phosphate Lands in Nauru, (Nauru v. Australia), (Preliminary Objections), June 26, 1992, (1992) ICJ Reports 240.

[180] Paras. 8–38, *id.*

Australia and Nauru eventually reached a settlement agreement in 1993. According to the agreement, Australia was to award Nauru AU\$107 million in compensation for environmental damage. Nauru waived any further claims regarding the phosphate mining or the administration of the island during the trusteeship era.[181]

Despite the settlement, the future of the islanders does not seem very hopeful. A possible scenario would involve the rehabilitation of land after the cessation of mining and the development of infrastructure – namely, a hospital, schools, and government buildings. The cost of rebuilding the ecosystem of the island in terms of importing topsoil, nutrients, and engaging in other rehabilitative measures could cost about AU\$200 million and could take up to thirty years. Another scenario involves the evacuation of the Naurans from the island.[182]

A further rehabilitation and development agreement was signed between Nauru and Australia in 1994.[183] The agreement identifies possible sectors and activities that should be assigned priority in the rehabilitation of Nauru, such as forestry, education, industrial development, and public administration. Assistance provided for in the agreement includes the provision of materials, goods, and equipment for the purposes of development; the granting of scholarships to Nauru nationals; and the assignment of Australian experts and advisers to the island.[184] The agreement is to remain in force for twenty years but must be reviewed frequently within that period of time.[185]

The *Rainbow Warrior Affair* has elucidated further issues of state responsibility, especially, with regard to the length that states are willing to go in order to avoid bearing the consequences of their wrongful actions.

In July 1985, a team of French agents sabotaged and sank the *Rainbow Warrior,* a vessel belonging to Greenpeace International, an NGO vocal in the pursuit of environmental objectives. At the time of the sabotage, the *Rainbow Warrior* was located in a New Zealand harbor. As a result of the sabotage, one of the members of the crew was killed. The two agents responsible for the sabotage were arrested in New Zealand. They pleaded guilty to charges of manslaughter and criminal damage and were sentenced by a New Zealand court to ten years of imprisonment.

France demanded the release of the agents and threatened New Zealand with trade sanctions. New Zealand claimed that trade sanctions were illegitimate in this case and asked for compensation for the damage it incurred from the incident.

The parties agreed for the Secretary-General of the United Nations to mediate the dispute and agreed to accept the ruling of the Secretary-General independent of whether it was favorable to their interests. The Secretary-General awarded New Zealand damages and requested that France refrain from taking measures that would inhibit trade between New Zealand and the EU. New Zealand, according the ruling,

---

[181] Agreement between Australia and the Republic of Nauru for the Settlement of the Case in the International Court of Justice Concerning Certain Phosphate Lands in Nauru, Aug. 10, 1993, (1993) Australian Treaty Series No. 26.

[182] Michael E. Pukrop, Phosphate Mining in Nauru, TED Case Studies, Case Number 412, May 1997, available online at http://www.american.edu/projects/mandala/TED/Nauru.htm.

[183] Rehabilitation and Development Co-operation Agreement between the Government of Australia and the Government of the Republic of Nauru, May 5, 1994, (1994) Australian Treaty Series No. 15.

[184] Art. 2, *id.*

[185] Art. 22, *id.*

had to release the French agents to France and the agents were to spend the next three years on an isolated French military base in the Pacific.[186]

The transfer of agents occurred in July 1986, after the signing of an agreement between the parties that included the clauses agreed during the UN mediation. In December 1987, France claimed that one of the agents had to be transferred to France because of an "urgent, health related" matter. New Zealand's request to examine the agent before the transfer was denied. After receiving medical treatment in France, medical experts from New Zealand examined the agent to conclude that, despite the health problem alleged, urgent transfer was not necessary. New Zealand's medical experts concluded that the French agent, after receiving treatment, could be transferred back to isolation in the Pacific. But France refused to transfer the agent back to isolation and the agent remained in France.

The second agent was repatriated in 1988 when France notified New Zealand accordingly about the agent's condition that made necessary repatriation and asked New Zealand's consent for such repatriation. As New Zealand's medical team was about to arrive to the island, France – citing urgent circumstances – precipitated the agent's evacuation. The agent was repatriated and never returned to seclusion.

New Zealand initiated the arbitration proceedings provided for in the 1986 agreement.[187] France argued that it was not able to fulfill its obligations under the agreement because of *force majeure* circumstances.

The arbitration tribunal cited factors of state responsibility, as formulated by the International Law Commission, which preclude wrongfulness even if an unlawful act is committed. Such factors include *force majeure*, necessity, and distress. The tribunal noted that *force majeure* implies the existence of circumstances that would make the compliance of a state with an international obligation impossible – not merely burdensome. Distress involves the existence of circumstances that have to do with the serious threat to life or physical integrity of a state organ or of persons entrusted to its care. Necessity has to do with circumstances that involve the vital interests of a state.

The tribunal concluded that *force majeure* was not an applicable defense for France. This is because France's compliance was not impossible but merely burdensome.

The tribunal explained that for distress to apply, three conditions had to be satisfied:

- the existence of exceptional medical or other circumstances of extreme urgency, provided that a prompt recognition of these circumstances was obtained from or demonstrated by the other party;
- the reestablishment of the original situation of compliance once the circumstances of emergency no longer applied; and
- a good faith attempt to obtain New Zealand's consent under the 1986 agreement.

The tribunal maintained that in the case of the first agent who required medical treatment, France acted in accordance with its obligations. France evacuated the

---

[186] Conciliation Proceedings (New Zealand v. France): Ruling of the UN Secretary General Perez de Cuellar, New York, July 5, 1986, reprinted in 26 ILM 1346 (1987).

[187] New Zealand v. France, April 30, 1990.

agent without the consent of New Zealand because of its urgent medical condition that required treatment not available in the military base in the Pacific. The
tribunal concluded, however, that France violated its obligations under the 1986
agreement when it refused to turn back the agent to isolation after the medical treatment was completed. France was also in breach of its obligations, under the 1986
agreement, because of its repatriation of the second agent without the consent of
New Zealand.

Despite France's breach of its obligations, the tribunal did not require the return of
the agents to isolation. At the time of the tribunal's proceedings, France's obligations
had expired. The agreement that was signed in 1986 between France and New
Zealand required for the agents to remain in isolation for three years. In 1989, when
the tribunal rendered its rulings, that obligation had expired.

The tribunal ordered France to establish a fund to promote the close and friendly
relationships between the two countries. France had to make the initial contribution
to the fund in the amount of U.S.$2 million as a form of compensation owed to
New Zealand.

Another state activity that provoked claims of state responsibility is nuclear testing.
France's nuclear testing over the Pacific involved issues of state responsibility because
of the fallout of radioactive material on Australia's and New Zealand's territory.
Australia and New Zealand claimed that France had committed a wrongful act by
conducting nuclear atmospheric tests that caused nuclear fallout. More specifically,
Australia claimed that the tests violated its right to be free from atmospheric weapons
testing by any country. Australia claimed that radioactive fallout on its territory and
its dispersion in Australia's airspace, without its consent, violated its sovereignty
over its territory. Australia argued that the radioactive fallout interfered with ships
and aircraft in the high seas and airspace and caused pollution in the high seas.[188]
Furthermore, Australia alleged that:

- the radioactive fallout on its territory had given rise to measurable concentrations of radio-nuclides in foodstuffs and in people and had resulted in additional
  radiation doses to the persons who lived in the hemisphere and in Australia in
  particular;
- any radioactive fall out was potentially dangerous to Australia and its people and
  any injury caused would be irreparable;
- the conduct of French nuclear tests in the atmosphere created anxiety and concerns among Australian people;
- the effects of nuclear tests on the environment could not be undone and would
  be irremediable by any payment of damages; and
- infringement on the freedom of movement of the people of Australia in the high
  seas and the airspace was irremediable.[189]

---

[188] Para. 22, Nuclear Tests Case, (Australia v. France), (Interim Measures), June 22, 1973, (1973) ICJ Reports
99. For a similar case that was brought by New Zealand against France, see Nuclear Tests Case, (New
Zealand v. France), (Interim Measures), June 22, 1973, (1973) ICJ Reports 135.

[189] Para. 27, Nuclear Tests Case, (Australia v. France), id. For similar claims made by New Zealand, see para.
23, Nuclear Tests Case, (New Zealand v. France), id.

The response that France gave to the claims of Australia goes to the heart of the problem of state responsibility regarding environmental matters. France:

> expressed its conviction that in the absence of *ascertained damage* attributable to its nuclear experiments, they did not violate any rule of international law, and that, if the infraction of the law was alleged to consist in a violation of a legal norm concerning *the threshold of atomic pollution* which should not be crossed, it was hard to see what was the precise rule on which Australia relied [emphasis added].[190]

With this response, France pointed out two issues that are basic for the articulation of state responsibility in matters of transboundary pollution:

- the difficulty of proving damages, especially in incidents that involve hazardous and radioactive substances whose effect on human health and the environment is cumulative and may not appear immediately; and
- the issue of the absence of international standards that set thresholds of pollution. In the absence of international standards that set thresholds of pollution, it would be hard to prove that a state that pollutes violates an international rule.

The ICJ did not get to decide on the issue of state responsibility. France challenged the jurisdiction of the ICJ. When the ICJ was about to decide the question of jurisdiction,[191] France, in a number of public statements, declared its intention to stop atmospheric testing "under normal conditions" and to shift its operations underground. Despite objections from New Zealand and Australia that the qualification "under normal conditions"[192] for the cessation of atmospheric testing did not offer sufficient assurance that nuclear testing would cease, the Court concluded that:

- the unilateral declaration of France to stop nuclear testing involved an undertaking of an *erga omnes* obligation to stop such testing;[193]
- the dispute no longer existed; and[194]
- proceeding with the case would have no meaning.[195]

Thus, the ICJ did not eventually decide whether nuclear atmospheric testing was consistent with the applicable rules of international law.

6. INTERNATIONAL LIABILITY

One of the first articulations of the concept of international liability for acts not prohibited by international law but that could have, nevertheless, injurious

---

[190] Para. 28, *Nuclear Tests* Case, (Australia v. France), *id*.

[191] *Nuclear Tests* Case, (New Zealand v. France), (Judgment), Dec. 20, 1974, (1974) ICJ Reports 457. See also *Nuclear Tests* Case, (Australia v. France), (Judgment), Dec. 20, 1974, 1974 ICJ Reports 253 [hereinafter Australia case].

[192] According to one of the statements made by French authorities: "Thus the atmospheric tests which are soon to be carried out will, in the normal course of events, be the last of this type." See para. 35, Australia case, *id*.

[193] Para. 50, *id*.

[194] Para. 55, *id*.

[195] Para. 56, *id*.

consequences is encountered in the Space Liability Treaty.[196] The treaty provides
that a state that launches a space object

> shall be absolutely liable to pay compensation for damage caused by its space object
> on the surface of the earth or to aircraft flight.[197]

Thus, although launching space objects is a legal activity, states are to bear the
costs of such an activity by undertaking to pay compensation for the injurious
consequences of space launching on other states. Damage is defined as: loss of life,
personal injury or impairment of health, loss of or damage to property of states or
of persons, or loss of or damage to property of intergovernmental organizations.[198]
In some cases, liability could be joint and several.[199]

The treaty was empirically tested shortly after its adoption. Canada used the
treaty to file a claim against the Soviet Union for compensation for damage caused
by the intrusion into Canadian airspace of the Soviet satellite, *Cosmos 954,* and the
deposition on the Canadian territory of highly hazardous radioactive debris. The
satellite entered the Canadian airspace in the morning hours of January 24, 1978.
The Soviet Union failed to notify Canada regarding the intrusion. A notification
would have prompted Canada to adopt appropriate measures more swiftly. Canada
demanded about C$6 million in compensation based on the absolute liability prin-
ciple included in the Space Liability Convention. Canada based its claim on article
XII of the Space Liability Treaty. Article XII provides:

> The compensation which the launching State shall be liable to pay for damage under
> this Convention shall be determined in accordance with international law and the
> principles of *justice and equity*, in order to provide such reparation in respect of the
> damage as will restore the person, natural or juridical, State or international organiza-
> tion on whose behalf the claim is *presented to the condition which would have existed if the
> damage had not occurred* [emphasis added].

Canada claimed, *inter alia*, that the Soviet Union failed to give Canada prior
notification of the imminent entry of the nuclear-powered satellite and failed to
provide timely and complete answer to the Canadian questions of January 24, 1978,
concerning the satellite. Canada claimed that the Soviet Union failed, thus, to reduce
the "deleterious results" of the intrusion of satellite into the airspace of Canada.
Eventually Canada and the USSR settled the claim for C$3 million.[200]

The notion of international liability can be traced in some of the early cases
decided by international tribunals, such as the *Corfu Channel* case and the *Trial
Smelter* case. In the *Corfu Channel* case, the ICJ stated that it is every state's obligation

---

[196] Convention on International Liability for Damage Caused by Space Objects, March 29, 1972, reprinted
in 961 UNTS 187. As of February 2001, eighty-one states including the United States and the Russian
Federation had ratified the treaty. Negotiations for the adoption of the convention lasted from 1963 to
1972.

[197] Art. II, *id.*

[198] Art. I, *id.*

[199] Arts. IV and V, *id.*

[200] Settlement of Claim between Canada and the Union of Soviet Socialist Republic for Damage Caused
by "Cosmos 954", Released on April 2, 1981.

not to knowingly allow its territory to be used for acts contrary to the rights of other states.[201]

In the *Trial Smelter* case, the arbitration tribunal concluded that, under the principles of international law, no state has the right to use or permit the use of its territory in a manner as to cause injury by fumes to the territory of another state when the polluting acts are of serious consequence and the injury is established by clear and convincing evidence.[202]

Thus, the *Trial Smelter* case, by launching a definition of state liability for pollution, introduced a problematic about the circumstances in which such liability applies. According to the tribunal, the polluting acts must be "of serious consequence" and the injury must be established with clear and convincing evidence. An issue that a decision maker has to resolve, therefore, is the amount of pollution that is considered of serious consequence. Raising the evidentiary bar so that the injury is further demonstrated clearly and convincingly is bound to be prohibitive for the articulation of many environmental claims. This is because the effects of pollution on humans and nature are often inconclusive and the amount of scientific certainty surrounding the causal connection between pollution and injury is generally low.

Because of the difficulties of establishing with clarity a concept of state liability, the ILC undertook the task to define the parameters of the concept. The undertaking was fraught with difficulties from the beginning, especially, as the commission tried to distinguish between the concept of state responsibility for wrongful acts committed under international law and international liability for acts that – although not prohibited under international law – have harmful consequences on other states.

The concept of international liability, as initially articulated by the various rapporteurs of the commission, did not include only the requirement for payment of damages, because of an act's injurious consequences, but also the primary obligation to prevent, inform, and negotiate.[203] Thus, international liability becomes a unique liability concept in that it includes both the primary obligation to prevent, inform, and negotiate and the obligation to make reparations. By including in the concept of international liability primary obligations, international liability was presented in a manner foreign to a legal understanding of liability. The term "liability" in legal discourse denotes the breach of an obligation.[204]

Other objections to the concept of international liability come from the difficulties of translating the concept in other languages. Although both the terms "liability" and "responsibility" exist in English, the same is not true for Spanish and French, in which the term "responsibility" is used to describe both liability and responsibility.

---

[201] See Chapter 1, Section 4.5.

[202] *Id.*

[203] For a discussion of the concept of international liability in its initial stages, see Elli Louka, The Transnational Management of Hazardous and Radioactive Wastes 26–29 (and accompanying citations) (Orville H. Schell Center for International Human Rights, Yale Law School, Occasional Paper 1992).

[204] See Alan E. Boyle, State Responsibility and International Liability for Injurious Consequences of Acts not Prohibited by International Law: A Necessary Distinction? 39 International & Comparative Law Quarterly 1 (1990); Günther Handl, Liability as an Obligation Established by a Primary Rule of International Law, XVI Netherlands Yearbook of International Law 49 (1985).

Because the terms "liability" and "responsibility" are used to describe two distinct legal concepts, the absence of equivalent distinctive words in other languages creates significant problems.[205]

Eventually, the ILC published its first draft articles on international liability in 2001, twenty-three years after the initial undertaking of the topic. It is interesting to note that the commission tried to distinguish between the primary obligation and the breach of the obligation. The first set of draft articles that were adopted in 2001 have to do with the "prevention of transboundary harm from hazardous activities."[206]

The second set of articles that the commission is still working on have to do with "international liability for injurious consequences arising out of acts not prohibited by international law" or what also may be called – referring directly to the newly articulated set of primary rules – "international liability in case of loss from transboundary harm arising out of hazardous activities."[207] The notion of international liability, as elaborated now, has to do with the allocation of damages in case of a transboundary harm arising out of hazardous activities.

With regard to the first set of draft articles adopted in 2001 that deal with the primary obligation, a number of provisions are noteworthy. For a state of origin to authorize a hazardous activity, it must perform a risk assessment. In this risk assessment, it must gauge the transboundary harm caused by the contemplated activity.[208] If, by performing a risk assessment, the state of origin concludes that the activity is likely to cause "significant transboundary harm" on another state, it must provide timely notification to the affected state. Such notification must contain a risk assessment of the activity and other relevant information.[209] No authorization of an activity is to take place before the elapse of six months pending the receipt of a response of the state likely to be affected.[210]

Article 9 further provides that states shall enter into consultations, at the request of any of them, with the goal to adopt "acceptable solutions" so that measures can be taken to avoid significant transboundary harm or the risk of such harm.[211] To avoid perceptions that consultations could become a delaying tactic, it is provided that states must agree, in the beginning of consultations, for a reasonable time frame for their conclusion.[212] States are urged to seek solutions based on an "equitable balance of interests" analyzed in detail in article 10.[213] If the consultation process fails to produce mutually agreed solutions, the state of origin is requested to take

---

[205] Louka, *supra* note 203, at 27.

[206] Draft articles on Prevention of Transboundary Harm from Hazardous Activities adopted by the International Law Commission at its Fifty-third session, Official Records of the General Assembly, Fifty-sixth session, Supplement No. 10 (A/56/10, chp V.E.1), 2001 [hereinafter Draft Articles].

[207] See Second Report on the Legal Regime for the Allocation of Loss in Case of Transboundary Harm Arising out of Hazardous Activities by Pemmaraju Sreenivasa Rao, Special Rapporteur, International Law Commission, Fifty-sixth Session, May 3–June 4 & July 5–Aug. 6, 2004, UN Doc. A/CN.4/540 (2004) [hereinafter Allocation Articles].

[208] Art. 7, Draft Articles, *supra* note 206.

[209] Art. 8(1), *id.*

[210] Art. 8(2), *id.*

[211] Art. 9(1), *id.*

[212] *Id.*

[213] Art. 9(2), *id.*

into account the interests of states likely to be affected if it decides to go ahead and authorize the hazardous activity.[214]

Article 10 provides a nonexhaustive list of factors that must be taken into account in balancing the interests of states, including:

- the degree of risk of significant transboundary harm and the availability of means of preventing, minimizing, or repairing such harm;
- the importance of the activity to the state of origin (including social, economic, and technical advantages) in relation to the potential harm of the state affected;
- the risk of significant harm to the environment and the availability of means of preventing such harm, minimizing the risk of harm or restoring the environment;
- the degree to which the state of origin and, as appropriate, the state affected are prepared to contribute to the costs of prevention;
- the economic viability of the activity in relation to the costs of prevention, the possibility of carrying out the activity somewhere else, or replacing it with an alternative activity;
- the standard of prevention which a state likely to be affected applies to the same or comparable activities and the standards applied in comparable regional and international practice.

This list is quite wide-ranging. What is interesting, in this context, is the lack of reference to the concept of strict liability for specific hazardous activities. Instead, the commission seems to have adopted a relativist view of undesirable hazardous activities affected by the interests of parties and by the economics of the specific situation. Overall, the view adopted seems to point to the direction that it is not the nature of the activity *per se* that would banish the activity but the interests served and the costs and benefits associated with the pursuit of these interests.[215]

The draft articles do not include many references to the polluter pays principle.[216] Actually, it is mentioned that one of the factors to be taken into account in performing the equitable balancing of interests is the degree to which the state of origin

> and, as appropriate, the State likely to be affected are prepared to contribute to the costs of prevention.

The idea that a state likely to be affected by a hazardous activity would be prepared to contribute to the costs of prevention is, in principle, antithetical to a *sticto sensu* understanding of the polluter pays principle.

The prominence of a balance of interests approach in the configuration of the primary obligation of prevention of harm demonstrates an inclination of international environmental lawmaking toward a notion of common responsibility. This notion of common responsibility is based on an understanding that all states engage in some kind of hazardous activity and, thus, are likely to suffer and impose on other states undesirable externalities.

---

[214] Art. 9(3), *id.*

[215] See also Ronald H. Coase, The Problem of Social Cost, 3 Journal of Law & Economics 1 (1960).

[216] The ILC has expressed explicitly doubts about whether the polluter pays principle could be considered as a widely accepted principle in international law. See International Law Commission Report, Chapter VII, 188–194 (2004), available online at http://www.un.org/law/ilc/reports/2004.

This notion of the equitable balancing of interests is found actually in many fields of international law, such as the law on watercourses,[217] high seas fisheries,[218] and maritime boundary delimitation.[219] It is found also in specific treaties such as the Rhine Protocol on Chlorides[220] and the Agreement on the Definitive Solution of the Salinity of the Colorado River.[221] The question is whether issues regarding transboundary harm are addressed better under an equitable balancing of interests approach or under a more predictable approach (e.g., under a strict liability regime).[222] At this stage, the ILC has opted for flexibility instead of predictability. Maybe it has opted wisely.

The second set of rules that the commission is still debating has to do with the allocation of loss arising out of hazardous activities.[223] Some states have noted correctly that the principle of allocation of loss deviates from the polluter pays principle.[224] Other states have noted that placing liability on states in whose territory a hazardous activity occurs is unfair. States have noted that, in most cases, hazardous activities benefit the operator and that state liability, as provided for in international conventions, is in principle supplementary.[225] States have claimed that even if liability were primarily channeled to them, they would have to devise ways to allocate the costs of liability internally to different domestic actors.[226]

The commission has examined the international private liability regimes (e.g., the oil pollution regime, the Lugano Convention, and the Basel Protocol). From the proposed allocation articles, the ILC seems to have concluded that current rules of international liability channel liability primarily to the operator. States retain the role of providing residual, supplementary compensation to victims. Overall, however, the commission remains torn between establishing a primary state liability rule or proposing supplementary state liability. For instance, a version of article 4 of the debated articles on state liability places responsibility directly on the state of origin for providing compensation:

> The State of origin shall take necessary measures to ensure that prompt and adequate compensation is available for persons in another State suffering transboundary damage caused by a hazardous activity located within its territory or in places under its jurisdiction or control.[227]

The alternative version of article 4 shifts from the notion of state liability to a regime of private liability:

> The operator of a hazardous activity located within the territory or in places within the jurisdiction and control of a State shall be liable for the transboundary damage caused

---

[217] See Chapter 5.

[218] See Chapter 6.

[219] See Chapter 1, Section 6.6.

[220] See Chapter 5, Section 5.4.2.

[221] See Chapter 5, Section 5.5.2.

[222] For a very interesting discussion on this topic, see Alan E. Boyle, Codification of International Environmental Law and the International Law Commission, in International Law and Sustainable Development: Past Achievements and Future Challenges 61, 80, 81 (Alan Boyle & David Freestone, eds., 2001).

[223] Allocation Articles, *supra* note 207.

[224] *Id.* at 4.

[225] *Id.* at 9.

[226] *Id.* at 10.

[227] *Id.* at 24.

by that activity to persons or environment or natural resources within the territory or in places under the jurisdiction and control of any other State or to environment . . . "[228]

Article 5 also provides that state liability must be supplementary:

The States concerned shall take the necessary measures to establish supplementary funding mechanisms to compensate victims of transboundary damage who are unable to obtain prompt and adequate compensation from the operator of a [legally] established claim for such damage under the present principles.[229]

The debates that are shaping the regime of allocation of costs in the case of transboundary harm resulting from hazardous activities demonstrate the lack of willingness of states to subscribe to an international liability regime that would hold them primarily responsible for transboundary harm. It is not surprising, therefore, that questions about state liability revert eventually to discussions about private liability. For activities that states cannot effectively control, the argument goes, private liability is more sensible. For activities that they are willing to tolerate, the question goes back to the balance of interests between the state that is willing to tolerate and other adversely affected states.

7. CONCLUSION

Strict liability is the applicable rule in most international regimes that deal with environmental pollution. Strict liability is justified in international environmental law. The nature of harm that results from hazardous activities is such that it is difficult to establish, in a credible fashion, causation between the polluting incident and the harm that occurred.

Even if liability is strict, however, it is usually limited both in terms of securing defenses and in terms of caps that are placed on the amounts of compensation that can be requested. When the first private liability regimes were established, the potential lack of insurance for polluting industries was of paramount concern. Insurance markets are now available for some international private liability regimes, whereas others are still struggling because of feeble insurance markets.

Furthermore, none of the regimes negates the polluter pays principle but, at the same time, they propose a broader perspective on the identity of polluter. Most regimes hold the operator of a hazardous activity primarily responsible but provide supplementary compensation mechanisms either in the form of industry contributions or in the form of state subsidization. The international liability regime, as it is progressing in the work of the ILC, is more preoccupied with the equitable allocation of costs resulting from polluting activities rather than with assigning responsibility to a state in which a polluting activity originates.

---

[228] *Id.* at 25.
[229] *Id.* at 28.

International Treaties and Other Instruments

Additional Protocol to the Convention on the Protection of the Rhine Against Pollution by Chlorides, Sept. 25, 1991, 1840 UNTS 372

Adjustments and Amendments to the 1987 Montreal Protocol (Copenhagen Adjustments and Amendments), Nov. 25, 1992, 32 ILM 874 (1993)

Adjustments and Amendments to the 1987 Montreal Protocol (London Adjustments and Amendments), June 29, 1990, 30 ILM 537 (1991)

African Charter on Human and Peoples' Rights (Banjul Charter), June 27, 1981, 21 ILM 58 (1982)

African Convention on the Conservation of Nature and Natural Resources, Sept. 15, 1968, 1001 UNTS 3

African Convention on the Conservation of Nature and Natural Resources, July 11, 2003

Agreement between Kazakhstan, Kyrgyz Republic, Tajikistan, Turkmenistan and Uzbekistan on the Status of the International Aral Sea Fund and its Organizations, April 9, 1999

Agreement between South Africa, Swaziland and Mozambique Relative to the Establishment of a Tripartite Permanent Technical Committee, Feb. 17, 1983

Agreement between the Federal Republic of Nigeria and the Republic of Niger Concerning the Equitable Sharing in the Development, Conservation and Use of their Common Water Resources, July 18, 1990

Agreement between the Government of the People's Republic of Bangladesh and the Government of the Republic of India on Sharing of the Ganges waters at Farakka and on Augmenting its Flows (Ganges Agreement), Nov. 5, 1977, 17 ILM 103 (1978)

Agreement between the Government of the United Kingdom of Great Britain and Northern Ireland and the Government of Egypt Regarding the Construction of the Owen Falls Dam, Uganda, May 30/May 31, 1949

Agreement between the Government of the United Kingdom of Great Britain and Northern Ireland and the Government of Egypt Regarding the Construction of the Owen Falls Dam in Uganda, July 16, 1952

Agreement between the Government of the United States and the Government of Marshall Islands for the Implementation of Section 177 of the Compact of Free Association, June 25, 1983

Agreement between the Government of United Arab Republic and the Republic of Sudan for the Full Utilization of the Nile Waters, Nov. 8, 1959, 453 UNTS 51

Agreement between the Governments of the Republic of Kazakhstan, the Kyrgyz Republic and the Republic of Uzbekistan on Cooperation in the Area of Environment and Rational Nature Use, Mar. 17, 1998

Agreement between the Governments of the Republic of Kazakhstan, the Kyrgyz Republic, and the Republic of Uzbekistan on the Use of Water and Energy Resources of the Syr Darya Basin, Mar. 17, 1998

Agreement between the Republic of Kazakhstan, Kyrgyz Republic, Republic of Tajikistan, Turkmenistan and Republic of Uzbekistan on Joint Activities in Addressing the Aral Sea and the Zone around the Sea Crisis, Improving the Environment, and Ensuring the Social and Economic Development of the Aral Sea Region, Mar. 26, 1993

Agreement between the Republic of Zimbabwe and the Republic of Zambia Concerning the Utilization of the Zambezi River, July 28, 1987

Agreement between the United States and Canada Concerning the Water Quality of the Great Lakes, April 15, 1972, 11 ILM 694 (1972)

Agreement between the United States and Canada on the Water Quality of the Great Lakes, Nov. 22, 1978, 30 UST 1383

Agreement Concerning the Creation of a Marine Mammal Sanctuary in the Mediterranean (France, Italy, Monaco), Nov. 25, 1999

Agreement Concerning the Niger River Commission and the Navigation and Transport on the River Niger, Nov. 25, 1964, 587 UNTS 21

Agreement Establishing the South Pacific Regional Environmental Programme, June 16, 1993

Agreement for the Establishment of a General Fisheries Commission for the Mediterranean, Nov. 6, 1997

Agreement for the Establishment of a General Fisheries Council for the Mediterranean, Sept. 24, 1949

Agreement for the Establishment of the Indian Ocean Tuna Commission, Nov. 25, 1993

Agreement for the Implementation of the Provisions of the United Nations Convention on the Law of the Sea of 10 December 1982 Relating to the Conservation and Management of Straddling Fish Stocks and Highly Migratory Fish Stocks, Dec. 4, 1995, 34 ILM 1542 (1995)

Agreement of Cooperation between the United States of America and the United Mexican States Regarding the Transboundary Shipments of Hazardous Wastes and Hazardous Substances, Nov. 12, 1986

Agreement on Co-operation for the Sustainable Development of the Mekong River Basin, April 5, 1995, 34 ILM 864 (1995)

Agreement on Co-operation in the Field of Joint Management and Conservation of Interstate Water Resources (Aral Sea Region), Almaty, Feb. 18, 1992

Agreement on Cooperation in Research, Conservation and Management of Marine Mammals in the North Atlantic, April 9, 1992

Agreement on Regional Co-operation in Combating Pollution of the South East Pacific by Hydrocarbons or other Harmful Substances in Cases of Emergency (Lima Agreement), Nov. 12, 1981

Agreement on the Action Plan for the Environmentally Sound Management of the Common Zambezi River System, May 28, 1987, 27 ILM 1109 (1988)

Agreement on the Application of Sanitary and Phytosanitary Measures, April 15, 1994, Marrakesh Agreement Establishing the World Trade Organization, Annex 1A, 1867 UNTS 493, 33 ILM 1125 (1994)

Agreement on the Conservation of African Eurasian Migratory Waterbirds, June 16, 1995

Agreement on the Conservation of Bats in Europe, Dec. 4, 1991

Agreement on the Conservation of Cetaceans of the Mediterranean and the Black Seas, Nov. 24, 1996

Agreement on the Conservation of Nature and Natural Resources adopted by the Association of South East Asian Nations (ASEAN Agreement), July 9, 1985

Agreement on the Conservation of Seals in the Wadden Sea, Oct. 16, 1990

Agreement on the Conservation of Small Cetaceans of the Baltic and North Seas, Sept. 13, 1991

Agreement on the International Commission for the Protection of the Rhine against Pollution, April 29, 1963

Agreement on the International Dolphin Conservation Program, May 15, 1998

Agreement on the Protection of Rhine against Chemical Pollution, Dec. 3, 1976, 16 ILM 242 (1976)

Agreement on Trade-Related Aspects of Intellectual Property Rights (TRIPs), April 15, 1994, Marrakesh Agreement Establishing the World Trade Organization, Annex 1C, 1869 UNTS 299, 33 ILM 1197 (1994)

Agreement Relating to the Implementation of Part XI of the United Nations Convention on the Law of the Sea of Dec. 1982 (Sea-bed Agreement), July 28, 1994

Agreement to Initiate a Program to Strengthen Regional Coordination in Management of Resources of Lake Victoria (African Region), Aug. 5, 1994

Arrangement on the Protection, Utilization, and Recharge of the Franco-Swiss Genevese Aquifer, June 9, 1977

ASEAN Agreement on Transboundary Haze Pollution, June 10, 2002

Bamako Convention on the Ban of Import into Africa and the Control of Transboundary Movement and Management of Hazardous Wastes within Africa, Jan. 29, 1991, 30 ILM 775 (1991)

Bangkok Declaration on Human Rights, April 2, 1993

Basel Convention on the Control of Transboundary Movements of Hazardous Wastes and their Disposal, Mar. 22, 1989, 28 ILM 649 (1989)

Berne Convention for the Protection of Literary and Artistic Works, Sept. 9, 1886

Brussels Convention Supplementary to the 1960 Convention on Third Party Liability in the Field of Nuclear Energy, Jan. 31, 1963, 956 UNTS 264

Budapest Treaty on the International Recognition of the Deposit of Microorganisms for the Purposes of Patent Procedure, April 28, 1977

Cartagena Protocol on Biosafety to the Convention on Biological Diversity, Jan. 29, 2000, 39 ILM 1027 (2000)

Convention between Mexico and the United States for the Distribution of Waters of Rio Grande, May 21, 1906

Convention Concerning Indigenous and Tribal Peoples in Independent Countries, June 27, 1989, 28 ILM 1382 (1989)

Convention Establishing the Eastern Pacific Tuna Organization, July 31, 1989

Convention for Co-operation in the Protection and Development of the Marine Environment of the West and Central African Region (Abidjan Convention), Mar. 23, 1981, 20 ILM 746 (1981)

Convention for Co-operation in the Protection and Sustainable Development of the Marine Environment of the North East Pacific, Feb. 18, 2002

Convention for the Conservation and Management of the Vicuna, Dec. 20, 1979

Convention for the Conservation of Southern Bluefin Tuna, May 10, 1993, 1819 UNTS 360

Convention for the Conservation of the Red Sea and Gulf of Aden Environment (Jeddah Convention), Feb. 14,1982

Convention for the Establishment of an Inter-American Tropical Tuna Commission, May 31, 1949, 80 UNTS 3

Convention for the Establishment of the European and Mediterranean Plant Protection Organization, April 18, 1957, UKTS 44

Convention for the Establishment of the Lake Victoria Fisheries Organization (African Region), June 30, 1994, 36 ILM 667 (1997)

Convention for the Prohibition of Fishing with Long Driftnets in the South Pacific (Wellington Convention), Nov. 29, 1989, 29 ILM 1454 (1990)

Convention for the Protection and Development of the Marine Environment of the Wider Caribbean Region (1983 Cartagena Convention), Mar. 24, 1983, 22 ILM 221 (1983)

Convention for the Protection, Management and Development of the Marine and Coastal Environment of the Eastern African Region (Nairobi Convention), June 21, 1985

Convention for the Protection of Natural Resources and Environment of the South Pacific Region, Nov. 25, 1986

Convention for the Protection of Producers of Phonograms against Unauthorized Duplication of their Phonograms, Oct. 29, 1971

Convention for the Protection of the Marine Environment and Coastal Areas of the South East Pacific (Lima Convention), Nov. 12, 1981

Convention for the Protection of the Marine Environment and the Coastal Region of the Mediterranean (1995 Barcelona Convention), June 10, 1995, OJ L 322/34, 14.12.1999

Convention for the Protection of the Marine Environment of the North East Atlantic (OSPAR Convention), Sept. 22, 1992, 32 ILM 1069 (1993)

Convention for the Protection of the Mediterranean Sea against Pollution (Barcelona Convention), Feb. 16, 1976, 15 ILM 290 (1976)

Convention for the Protection of the Natural Resources and Environment of the South Pacific Region (Noumea Convention), Nov. 25,1986, 16 ILM 38 (1987)

Convention for the Protection of the Ozone Layer (Vienna Convention), Mar. 22, 1985, 26 ILM 1529 (1985)

Convention on Access to Information, Public Participation in Decision-making and Access to Justice in Environmental Matters (Aarhus Convention), June 25, 1998, 38 ILM 517 (1999)

Convention on Biological Diversity, June 5, 1982, 31 ILM 822 (1992)

Convention on Civil Liability for Damage Caused During Carriage of Dangerous Goods by Road, Rail and Inland Navigation Vessels, Oct. 10, 1989

Convention on Civil Liability for Damage Resulting from Activities Dangerous to the Environment, June 21, 1993, 32 ILM 480 (1993)

Convention on Civil Liability for Oil Pollution Damage, Nov. 29, 1969, 973 UNTS 3, 9 ILM 45 (1970)

Convention on Civil Liability for Oil Pollution Damage, Nov. 27, 1992

Convention on Conservation of Nature in the South Pacific (Apia Convention), June 12, 1976, (1990) Australian Treaty Series, No. 41

Convention on Cooperation for the Protection and Sustainable Use of the Danube River, June 29, 1994, OJ L 342/19, 12.12.1997

Convention on Early Notification of a Nuclear Accident, Sept. 26, 1986, 25 ILM 1370 (1986)

Convention on Environmental Impact Assessment in a Transboundary Context, Feb. 25, 1991, 30 ILM 800 (1991)

Convention on European Patents, Oct. 5, 1973, 13 ILM 268 (1974)

Convention on Future Multilateral Co-operation in North East Atlantic Fisheries, Nov. 18, 1980

Convention on Future Multilateral Cooperation in the Northwest Atlantic Fisheries, Oct. 24, 1978

Convention on International Civil Aviation, Dec. 7, 1944, 15 UNTS 295

Convention on International Liability for Damage Caused by Space Objects, Mar. 29, 1972, 961 UNTS 187

Convention on International Trade in Endangered Species of Wild Flora and Fauna, Mar. 6, 1973, 12 ILM 1085 (1973)

Convention on Limitation of Liability for Maritime Claims, Nov. 19, 1976, 16 ILM 606 (1976)

Convention on Long-range Transboundary Air Pollution (CLRTAP), Nov. 13, 1979, 18 ILM 1442 (1979)

Convention on Nature Protection and Wildlife Preservation in the Western Hemisphere, Oct. 12, 1940, 161 UNTS 193

Convention on Nuclear Safety, June 17, 1994, 33 ILM 1514 (1994)

Convention on Oil Pollution Preparedness, Response and Co-operation, Nov. 30, 1990, 30 ILM 735 (1991)

Convention on Persistent Organic Pollutants, May 22, 2001, 40 ILM 532 (2000)

Convention on Supplementary Compensation for Nuclear Damage (CSC Convention), Sept. 12, 1997, 36 ILM 1473 (1997)

Convention on the Conservation and Management of Fishery Resources in the South East Atlantic Ocean (SEAFO), April 20, 2001

Convention on the Conservation and Management of Highly Migratory Fish Stocks in the Western and Central Pacific Ocean, Sept. 5, 2000

Convention on the Conservation of Antarctic Marine Living Resources (CCAMLR), May 20, 1980

Convention on the Conservation of European Wildlife and Natural Habitats (Bern Convention), Sept. 19, 1979, European Treaty Series No. 104

Convention on the Conservation of Migratory Species of Wild Animals (Bonn Convention), June 23, 1979, 19 ILM 15 (1980)

Convention on the Establishment of an International Fund for Compensation for Oil Pollution Damage, Dec. 18, 1971

Convention on the High Seas, April 29, 1958, 450 UNTS 82

Convention on the Law of Non-Navigational Uses of International Watercourses, May 21, 1997, 36 ILM 700 (1997)

Convention on the Liability of Operators of Nuclear Ships, May 25, 1962

Convention on the Physical Protection of Nuclear Material, Oct. 26, 1979

Convention on the Prevention of Marine Pollution by Dumping of Wastes and Other Matter (London Dumping Convention), Dec. 29, 1972, 1046 UNTS 120

Convention on the Prohibition of Fishing with Long Driftnets in the South Pacific, Nov. 23, 1989, 29 ILM 1454 (1990)

Convention on the Protection and Use of Transboundary Watercourses and International Lakes, Mar. 17, 1992, 31 ILM 1312 (1992)

Convention on the Protection of the Black Sea against Pollution, April 21, 1992, 32 ILM 1101 (1993)

Convention on the Protection of the Marine Environment of the Baltic Sea (1992 HELCOM Convention), April 9, 1992

Convention on the Protection of the Rhine, April 12, 1999, OJ L 289/31, 16.11.2000

Convention on the Protection of the Rhine against Pollution by Chlorides, Dec. 3, 1976, 16 ILM 265 (1977)

Convention on Wetlands of International Importance (Ramsar Convention), Feb. 2, 1971, 996 UNTS 245

Convention Relative to the Preservation of Fauna and Flora in their Natural State (African Region), Nov. 8, 1933

Convention Respecting Measures for the Preservation and Protection of the Fur Seals in the North Pacific Ocean, July 7, 1911

Convention to Ban the Importation into the Forum Island Countries of Hazardous and Radioactive Wastes and to Control the Transboundary Movement and Management of Hazardous Wastes within the South Pacific Region, Sept. 16, 1995

Cooperative Agreement for the Conservation of Sea Turtles of the Caribbean Coast of Costa Rica, Nicaragua and Panama, May 8, 1998

European Landscape Convention, July 19, 2000, European Treaties Series (ETS) no. 176

Exchange of Notes between His Majesty's Government in the United Kingdom and the Egyptian Government in regard to the Use of the Waters of the River Nile for Irrigation Purposes, Note by Mohamed Mahmound Pasha to Lord Lloyd, May 7, 1929

Framework for General Co-operation between the Arab Republic of Egypt and Ethiopia, July 1, 1993

General Agreement on Tariffs and Trade, April 15, 1994, Marrakesh Agreement Establishing the World Trade Organization, Annex 1A, 1867 UNTS 187, 33 ILM 1153 (1994)

General Agreement on Trade in Services, April 15, 1994, Marrakesh Agreement Establishing the World Trade Organization, Annex 1B, 33 ILM 1168 (1994)

Helsinki Convention on the Protection of Marine Environment of the Baltic Sea Area, Mar. 22, 1974, 13 ILM 546 (1974)

Inter-American Convention for the Protection and Conservation of Sea Turtles, Dec. 1, 1996

Interim Convention on the Conservation of North Pacific Fur Seals, Feb. 9, 1957

International Convention for the Conservation of Atlantic Tunas (ICCAT), May 14, 1966, 637 UNTS 63

International Convention for the Prevention of Pollution from Ships, Nov. 2, 1973, 12 ILM 1319 (1973)

International Convention for the Regulation of Whaling, Dec. 2, 1946, 161 UNTS 72

International Convention for the Safety of Life at Sea, Nov. 1, 1974, 1184 UNTS 3

International Convention for the Unification of Certain Rules Relating to the Limitation of Liability of Owners of Sea-going Vessels, Aug. 25, 1924

International Convention on Civil Liability for Bunker Oil Pollution Damage, Mar. 23, 2001

International Convention on Liability and Compensation for Damage in Connection with the Carriage of Hazardous and Noxious Substances by Sea, May 3, 1996, 35 ILM 1406 (1996)

International Convention on Oil Pollution Preparedness, Response and Co-operation, Nov. 30, 1990, 30 ILM 735 (1991)

International Convention Relating to Intervention on the High Seas in Cases of Oil Pollution Casualties, Nov. 29, 1969, 9 ILM 25 (1970)

International Convention Relating to the Limitation of Liability of Owners of Sea-going Ships, Oct. 10, 1957

International Covenant on Civil and Political Rights, Dec. 16, 1966, 999 UNTS 171

International Covenant on Economic, Social and Cultural Rights, Dec. 16, 1966, 993 UNTS 3

International Treaty on Plant Genetic Resources for Food and Agriculture, Nov. 3, 2001

International Tropical Timber Agreement (ITTA), Jan. 26, 1994, 33 ILM 1014 (1994)

Israeli-Palestinian Interim Agreement on the West Bank and the Gaza Strip, Sept. 28, 1995, 36 ILM 551 (1997)

Joint Convention on the Safety of Spent Fuel Management and on the Safety of Radioactive Waste Management, Sept. 5, 1997

Locarno Agreement Establishing an International Classification for Industrial Designs, Oct. 8, 1968

Lusaka Agreement on Co-operative Enforcement Operations Directed at Illegal Trade in Wild Fauna and Flora, Sept. 9, 1994

Madrid Agreement Concerning the International Registration of Marks, April 14,1891

Marrakesh Agreement Establishing the World Trade Organization (WTO Agreement), April 15, 1994, 1867 UNTS 154, 33 ILM 1144 (1994)

Nairobi Convention for the Protection, Management and Development of the Marine and Coastal Environment of the Eastern African Region, June 21, 1985

Nauru Agreement Concerning Cooperation in the Management of Fisheries Resources of Common Interest (Western and Central Pacific Ocean Region), Feb. 11, 1982

Nice Agreement Concerning the International Classification of Goods and Services for the Purposes of the Registration of Marks, June 15, 1957

North American Free Trade Agreement, Dec. 17, 1992

Oslo Convention for the Prevention of Marine Pollution by Dumping from Ships and Aircraft, Feb. 15, 1972, 932 UNTS 3

Paris Convention for the Prevention of Marine Pollution from Land-Based Sources, June 4, 1974, 13 ILM 352 (1974)

Paris Convention for the Protection of Industrial Property, Mar. 20, 1883

Paris Convention on Third Party Liability in the Field of Nuclear Energy, July 29, 1960,1041 UNTS 358

Patent Cooperation Treaty, June 19, 1970

Patent Law Treaty, June 1, 2000

Polar Bear Agreement, Nov. 15, 1973, 13 ILM 13 (1973)

Protocol Amending the Interim Convention on Conservation of North Pacific Fur Seals, Oct. 12, 1984

Protocol Amending the Interim Convention on Conservation of North Pacific Fur Seals, Oct. 14, 1980

Protocol Concerning Co-operation in Combating Oil Spills (Cartagena Oil Spills Protocol), Mar. 24, 1983, 22 ILM 240 (1983)

Protocol Concerning Co-operation in Combating Pollution Emergencies (South Pacific Region), Nov. 25, 1986

Protocol Concerning Co-operation in Combating Pollution in Cases of Emergency (Western and Central African Region), Mar. 23, 1981, 20 ILM 756 (1981)

Protocol Concerning Co-operation in Preventing Pollution from Ships and, in cases of Emergency, Combating Pollution of the Mediterranean Sea, Jan. 25, 2002

Protocol Concerning Cooperation in Combating Marine Pollution in Cases of Emergency (Eastern African Region), June 21, 1985

Protocol Concerning Cooperation in Combating Pollution by Oil and other Harmful Substances in Cases of Emergency, (Arabian Gulf Region), July 1, 1979,17 ILM 526 (1978)

Protocol Concerning Marine Pollution Resulting from the Exploration and Exploitation of the Continental Shelf (Arabian Gulf Region), Mar. 29, 1989

Protocol Concerning Pollution from Land-based Sources (Arabian Gulf Region) Feb. 21, 1990

Protocol Concerning Protected Areas of Wild Fauna and Flora in the Eastern African Region, June 21, 1995

Protocol Concerning Regional Cooperation in Combating Pollution by Oil and other Harmful Substances in Cases of Emergency (Red Sea and Gulf of Aden Region), Feb. 14, 1982

Protocol Concerning Specially Protected Areas and Wildlife to the Convention for the Protection and Development of the Marine Environment of the Wider Caribbean Region (Kingston Protocol), Jan. 18, 1990

Protocol Concerning the Control of Emissions of Nitrogen Oxides or their Transboundary Fluxes (Protocol to the CLRTAP), Oct. 31, 1988, 28 ILM 212 (1989)

Protocol Concerning the Control of Emissions of Volatile Organic Compounds or their Transboundary Fluxes (Protocol to the CLRTAP), Nov. 8, 1991, 31 ILM 573 (1992)

Protocol Concerning the Protection of the Mediterranean Sea Against Pollution Resulting from Exploration and Exploitation of the Continental Shelf and the Seabed and its Subsoil (1994 Madrid Offshore Protocol), Oct. 14, 1994

Protocol for the Conservation and Management of Protected Marine and Coastal Areas of the South East Pacific, Sept. 21, 1989

Protocol for the Prevention of Pollution of the Mediterranean Sea by Dumping from Ships and Aircraft or Incineration at Sea, June 10, 1995

Protocol for the Prevention of Pollution of the South Pacific Region by Dumping, Nov. 25, 1986

Protocol for the Protection of the Mediterranean Sea against Pollution from Land-based Sources and Activities, Mar. 7, 1996

Protocol for the Protection of the South East Pacific against Pollution from Land-based Sources (Quito Protocol to the Lima Convention), July 22, 1983

Protocol of 1992 to Amend the International Convention on Civil Liability for Oil Pollution Damage, Nov. 27, 1992

Protocol of 1992 to Amend the International Convention on the Establishment of an International Fund for Compensation for Oil Pollution Damage, Nov. 27, 1992

Protocol of 1996 to Amend the Convention on Limitation of Liability for Maritime Claims, May 9, 1996, 35 ILM 1433 (1996)

Protocol on Environmental Protection to the Antarctic Treaty, Oct. 4, 1991, 30 ILM 1461 (1991)

Protocol on Further Reduction of Sulphur Emissions (Protocol to the CLRTAP), June 14, 1994, 33 ILM 1540 (1994)

Protocol on Heavy Metals (Protocol to the CLRTAP), June 24, 1998

Protocol on Inserting Amendments and Addenda in the Agreement between the Governments of the Republic of Kazakhstan, the Kyrgyz Republic, and the Republic of Uzbekistan on the Use of Water and Energy Resources of the Syr Darya Basin, May 7, 1999

Protocol on Intervention on the High Seas in Cases of Marine Pollution by Substances other than Oil, Nov. 2, 1973, 1313 UNTS 3 (1983)

Protocol on Liability and Compensation for Damage Resulting from Transboundary Movements of Hazardous Wastes and their Disposal, Dec. 10, 1999

Protocol on Long-Term Financing of the Cooperative Programme for Monitoring and Evaluation of the Long-range Transmission of Air Pollutants in Europe (Protocol to the CLRTAP), Sept. 28, 1984, 24 ILM 484 (1985)

Protocol on Persistent Organic Pollutants (Protocol to the CLRTAP), June 24, 1998, 37 ILM 513 (1998)

Protocol on Pollutant Release and Transfer Registers (Kiev Protocol to the Aarhus Convention), May 21, 2003

Protocol on Preparedness, Response and Co-operation to Pollution Incidents by Hazardous and Noxious Substances, Mar. 14, 2000

Protocol on Shared Watercourse Systems in the Southern African Development Community (SADC) (1995 SADC Protocol), Aug. 28, 1995, 34 ILM 854 (1995)

Protocol on Shared Watercourses in the Southern African Development Community, Aug. 7, 2000

Protocol on Strategic Environmental Assessment to the UN/ECE Convention on Environmental Impact Assessment in a Transboundary Context (SEA Convention), May 21, 2003

Protocol on Substances that Deplete the Ozone Layer (Montreal Protocol), Sept. 16, 1987, 26 ILM 154 (1987)

Protocol on the Control of Marine Transboundary Movements and Disposal of Hazardous Wastes (Arabian Gulf Region), Mar. 17, 1998

Protocol on the Prevention of Pollution of the Mediterranean Sea by Transboundary Movements of Hazardous Wastes and their Disposal, Oct. 1, 1996

Protocol on the Prevention, Reduction and Control of Land-Based Sources and Activities to the Convention for the Protection and Development of the Marine Environment of the Wider Caribbean Region, Oct. 6, 1999

Protocol on the Reduction of Sulphur Emissions or their Transboundary Fluxes by at Least 30 Percent (Protocol to the CLRTAP), July 8, 1985, 27 ILM 707 (1988)

Protocol on Water and Health to the 1992 Convention on the Protection and Use of Transboundary Watercourses and International Lakes, June 17, 1999, 38 ILM 1708 (1999)

Protocol Relating to the 1973 International Convention for the Prevention of Pollution from Ships, Feb. 17, 1978, 17 ILM 546 (1978)

Protocol to Abate Acidification, Eutrophication and Ground-level Ozone (Protocol to the CLRTAP), Nov. 30, 1999

Protocol to Amend the Brussels Supplementary Convention to the Paris Convention, Feb. 12, 2004

Protocol to Amend the 1971 International Convention of the Establishment of an International Fund for Compensation for Oil Pollution Damage, Nov. 19, 1976, 16 ILM 621 (1977)

Protocol to Amend the Paris Convention on Third Party Liabililty in the Field of Nuclear Energy, Feb. 12, 2004

Protocol to Amend the Vienna Convention on Civil Liability for Nuclear Damage, Sept. 12, 1997, 36 ILM 1454 (1997)

Protocol to the 1969 International Convention on Civil Liability for Oil Pollution Damage, Nov. 19, 1976, 16 ILM 617 (1977)

Protocol to the 1981 Convention for the Protection of the Marine Environment and Coastal Areas of the South East Pacific against Radioactive Pollution, Sept. 21, 1989

Protocol to the Convention on the Prevention of Marine Pollution by Dumping of Wastes and Other Matter (London Convention), Nov. 7, 1996, 36 ILM 1 (1997)

Protocol to the United Nations Framework Convention on Climate Change (Kyoto Protocol), Dec. 11, 1997, 37 ILM 22 (1998)

Regional Convention for Co-operation on Protection of the Marine Environment from Pollution (1978 Kuwait Convention), April 24, 1978, 1140 UNTS 133

Rehabilitation and Development Co-operation Agreement between the Government of Australia and the Government of the Republic of Nauru, May 5, 1994

Revised Protocol on Shared Watercourses in the Southern African Development Community (SADC), Aug. 7, 2000, 40 ILM 321 (2001)

Rotterdam Convention on the Prior Informed Consent (PIC) Procedure for Certain Hazardous Chemicals and Pesticides in International Trade, Sept. 10, 1998, 38 ILM 1 (1999)

Trademark Law Treaty, Oct. 27, 1994

Treaties between Great Britain and Ethiopia, relative to the frontiers between Anglo-Egyptian Soudan, Ethiopia, and Erythroea, May, 15, 1902

Treaty between Egypt and Sudan for the Full Utilization of the Nile Waters, Nov. 8, 1959, 453 UNTS 51 (1959)

Treaty between his Majesty's Government of Nepal and the Government of India Concerning the Integrated Development of the Mahakali River including Sarada Barrage, Tanakpur Barrage and Pancheshwar Project (Mahakali Treaty), Feb 12, 1996, 36 ILM 531 (1997)

Treaty between the Government of the Republic of India and the Government of the People's Republic of Bangladesh on Sharing of the Ganga/Ganges Waters at Farakka, Dec. 12, 1996, 36 ILM 519 (1997)

Treaty between the United States and Mexico Relating to the Waters of the Colorado and Tijuana Rivers and of the Rio Grande (Rio Bravo) from Fort Quitman, Texas to the Gulf of Mexico, Feb. 3, 1944, 3 UNTS 314

Treaty Establishing the European Economic Community (EEC Treaty or Treaty of Rome), Mar. 25, 1957, 298 UNTS 3

Treaty for Amazonian Cooperation, July 3, 1978, 17 ILM 1045 (1978)

Treaty of Peace between the State of Israel and the Heshemite Kingdom of Jordan, done at Arava/Araba crossing point (Israel/ Jordan Peace Treaty), Oct. 26, 1994, 34 ILM 43 (1995)

Treaty on Cooperation in Fisheries Surveillance and Law Enforcement in the South Pacific Region (Niue Treaty), July 9, 1992

Treaty on Fisheries between the Government of Certain Pacific Islands and the Government of the United States of America, (1988) Australian Treaty Series, No. 42, April 2, 1987

Treaty on the Establishment and Functioning of the Joint Water Commission between the Government of the Republic of South Africa and the Government of the Kingdom of Swaziland, Mar. 13, 1992

Treaty on the Non-Proliferation of Nuclear Weapons, July 1, 1968, 729 UNTS 161

Treaty Relating to Cooperative Development of the Water Resources of the Columbia River Basin, Jan. 17, 1961, and exchange of notes Jan. 22, 1964 and Sept. 16, 1964, 542 UNTS 244

Treaty Relating to the Boundary Waters and Questions Arising along the Boundary between the United States and Canada, Jan. 11, 1909

Tripartite Interim Agreement between the Republic of Mozambique and the Republic of South Africa and the Kingdom of Swaziland for Co-operation on the Protection and Sustainable Utilisation of the Water Resources of the Incomati and Maputo Watercourses, Aug. 29, 2002

Understanding on Rules and Procedures Governing the Settlement of Disputes (DSU), Marrakesh Agreement Establishing the World Trade Organization, Annex 2, 1869 UNTS 401, 33 ILM 1226 (1994)

UNESCO Convention for the Protection of the World Cultural and Natural Heritage, Nov. 16, 1972, 11 ILM 1358 (1972)

United Nations Framework Convention on Climate Change, May 9, 1992, 31 ILM 849 (1992)

United Nations Convention on the Law of the Sea (UNCLOS), Dec. 10, 1982, 21 ILM 1261 (1982)

U.S.-Mexico Agreement on the Permanent and Definitive Solution to the Salinity of the Colorado River Basin, TIAS No. 7708, 12 ILM 1105 (1973)

Vienna Convention on Civil Liability for Nuclear Damage, May 21, 1963, 1063 UNTS 265

Vienna Convention on the Law of the Treaties, May 23, 1969, 8 ILM 679 (1969)

Western Indian Ocean Tuna Organization Convention, June 19, 1991

WIPO Copyright Treaty (WCT), Dec. 20, 1996

Cases

Index